INFORMATION RESOURCE MANAGEMENT

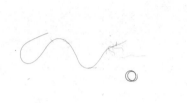

The Irwin Series in Information and Decision Sciences

Consulting Editors   Robert B. Fetter   Claude McMillan
                         Yale University   *University of Colorado*

Another Richard D. Irwin, Inc. text, by Donna Hussain and K. M. Hussain

Information Processing Systems for Management,

provides management students with an understanding of how computers work and how they can be applied to the operations of a firm. The primary focus is on the development and administration of information systems, and on computer applications across the entire spectrum of business use.

INFORMATION RESOURCE MANAGEMENT

Donna Hussain

K. M. Hussain

New Mexico State University

1984 RICHARD D. IRWIN, INC. Homewood, Illinois 60430

ISBN 0-256-02990-3

Library of Congress Catalog Card No. 83–81770

Printed in the United States of America

1 2 3 4 5 6 7 8 9 0 K 10 9 8 7 6 5 4

PREFACE

Computers today are used for operations, control, and planning, and to improve office efficiency. Indeed, few businesses have been left untouched by the computer revolution. Though computers facilitate corporate decision making and management of operations, they do add to the work of managers since computer resources must be managed. This book explains how to acquire, organize, monitor, and control computer resources and discusses management problems unique to computer environments. It is addressed primarily to business managers responsible for computer resources (or students of management), but should also be of interest to data processing professionals.

This textbook does not require a course prerequisite. It is a stand-alone text written for the upper division undergraduate or the masters student. The introductory material on hardware, software, peripherals, data, development of information systems, control, security, and distributed processing is also found in a companion volume, *Information Processing Systems For Management*, but the focus of that volume is on how computers assist managers in their jobs, rather than on computer resource management. Between the two books, the DPMA model curriculum recommendation CIS15 is covered, as are most of the curricula suggestions provided by the Association for Computing Machinery in courses IS8 and IS9. Neither text discusses the internal workings of a computer, how to program, nor the history of computing.

The authors wish to thank colleagues and reviewers for their helpful comments and corrections to the manuscript. These include Robert Brennan, Don Cartlidge, Dan Costley, Joseph Denk, William Daugherty, John Eoff, Keith Hennigh, James Mensching, and Emery Peterson. Also Robert B. Fetter, Claude McMillan, Eric K. Clemons, John M.

Nicholas, Marvin Rothstein, Robert B. DesJardins, Daniel Robey, and O. Maurice Joy, for their reviews and critiques of the developing manuscript. Any errors that still remain are the responsibility of the authors. We are also indebted to Roy Hasseldine for administrative assistance during our year in New Zealand, and to Tahira Hussain and Susan Greenwood for their secretarial help.

Donna Hussain

K. M. Hussain

CONTENTS

PART SIX

ORGANIZATION OF RESOURCES   403

PART SEVEN

THE COMPUTER PROCESSING ENVIRONMENT   519

INFORMATION RESOURCE MANAGEMENT

PART ONE

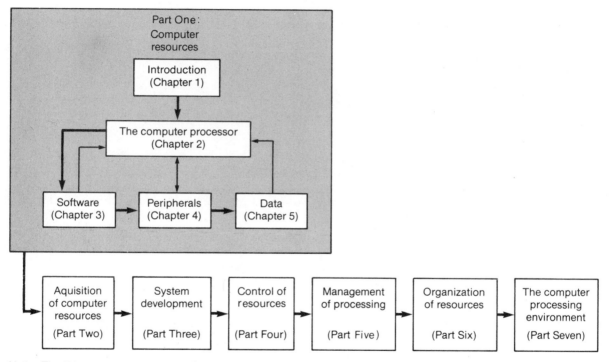

Part One:
Computer
resources

Introduction
(Chapter 1)

The computer processor
(Chapter 2)

Software
(Chapter 3)

Peripherals
(Chapter 4)

Data
(Chapter 5)

Aquisition
of computer
resources

(Part Two)

System
development

(Part Three)

Control of
resources

(Part Four)

Management
of processing

(Part Five)

Organization
of resources

(Part Six)

The computer
processing
environment

(Part Seven)

Note: The thin arrows represent the flow of data and information.
The thick arrows show the sequential flow of the parts of the book.

COMPUTER RESOURCES

*The corporations which will excel
in the 1980s will be those that
manage information as a major
resource*

John Diebold

***Introduction to
Part One***

A book on how to manage computer resources must first describe the resources to be managed. The purpose of Part One is to introduce the reader to the technical components of computerized information systems: the central processor, software, peripherals, and data. This part serves as background for readers with no computer experience. Readers who have worked with computers or taken introductory courses in computer science may choose to skip Part One and begin their study of the text with Part Two, although they may find the chapters a useful review of basic computer concepts and terminology.

Chapter 1 is an introductory chapter to the text. It describes how businesses benefit from computer technology. It also describes how technology has added to the responsibility of corporate managers who must now manage computer resources. An outline of the book is included in the chapter as well.

Chapter 2 tells what processors do and compares modes of processing. A section is also devoted to the contribution of microtechnology to processing.

Software is the subject of Chapter 3. The emphasis is on how data is processed and how programming languages work rather than on how to program. The chapter classifies software, with operating systems software and applications software described.

Peripherals, including equipment for input, storage, output, and teleprocessing, are examined in Chapter 4.

Finally, data technology and the management of data technology are considered in Chapter 5.

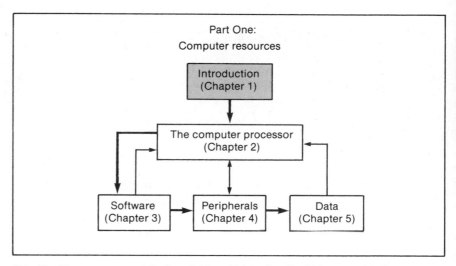

Note: The thin arrows represent the flow of data and information. The thick arrows show the sequential flow of the parts of the book.

CHAPTER 1

Introduction

*The old world was characterized
by a need to manage things. The new
world is characterized by a need
to manage complexity.*

Stafford Beer

Whatever criterion one uses to measure the growth of computing, whether it be numbers of computers, spending on resources for computer processing, or expansion of computer applications, it is clear that our society is becoming increasingly reliant on computers. Experts predict that by the mid–1980s, some 7 million computers will be installed in the United States—seven times the number in use when the decade began, as shown in Figure 1.1. Spending on data processing will increase from 2.1 percent of the GNP and $101 per capita in 1970 to a projected 8.3 percent and $670 in 1985.[1] Data processing personnel have increased from 835,000 in 1974 to an estimated 1,104,000 in 1985[2] and the number of end users is doubling every one to two years.[3] Other growth statistics are seen in Figures 1.2 and 1.3. We are an information-based society with nearly half of our work force engaged in information industries. No wonder the development of computers with the ability to process and manipulate information on a large scale has had a revolutionary effect on the way Americans do business.

Modern information machines emerged during World War II. The

---

[1] AFIPS study quoted in *Datamation* 24, no. 2 (February 1978), p. 101.

[2] *Datamation*, February 1978, p. 104.

[3] Gideon Gartner, "IBM: The Next $20 Billion," *Datamation* 25, no. 1 (June 1979), p. 80.

Figure 1.1   **Estimated number of computers**

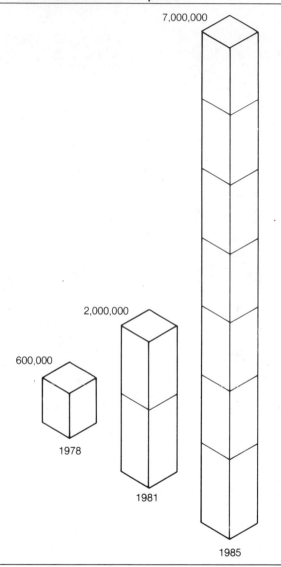

Source: IBM, *Information Processing: Dollars to Cents*, G320–6852–0 1–82.

emphasis at that time was on data processing—the development of machines to reduce clerical costs and the volume of paperwork. Early computers processed business transactions primarily for financial applications—their use economically justified since they increased the productivity of clerks.

As performance improved with advances in technology and as

Figure 1.2   **Estimated number of terminals per 100 professionals in the United States**

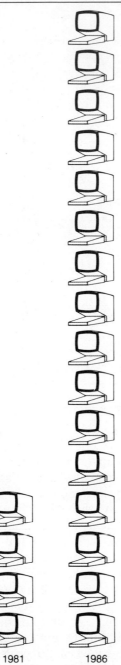

1981   1986

Source: IBM, *Information Processing: Dollars to Cents*, G320–6852–0 1–82.

Figure 1.3   **Projected computer performance**

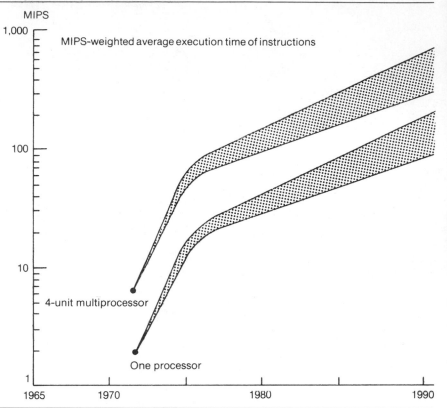

Source: Adapted from Rein Turn, *Computers in the 1980s* (New York: Columbia University Press, 1974), p. 91.

equipment became cheaper, more robust, and portable, applications expanded. With this expansion came a shift in focus away from systems that would simply save money to computers that would improve methods of operation. At the same time, the types of organizations using computers broadened. By the mid-1960s, when computers with miniaturized solid logic technology and integrated circuits reached the market, change in the computer industry was increasing exponentially, and the computer revolution was well launched.

Computers today deliver nearly 1,700 times the performance of computers in the early 1950s (see Table 1.1). Processing that cost $1 in 1952 cost $.0076 in 1981. A modern computer logic chip which fits in the eye of a needle contains the processing power of about 4,000 two-inch-high vacuum tubes of 30 years ago.[4] Processing speed is

---

[4]IBM, *Information Processing: Dollars to Cents*, G320-6852-0 1-82.

Table 1.1	Example of relative improvement in computer performance (IBM computers)	
	1952	1
	1956	20
	1965	105
	1973	405
	1978	838
	1981	1,689

Source: IBM, *Information Processing: Dollars to Cents*, G320–6852–0 1–82.

measured in picoseconds (one trillionth of a second). Further minia-turization, faster speeds, greater reliability, and lower costs are pre-dicted for the future. Though transactional processing is still the prev-alent use of computers in business, new dimensions have been added to conventional data processing: word and text processing which have led to electronic offices; process monitoring on factory floors; and the use of information systems in planning, control, and operational man-agement. It is suggested that on the scale of human evolution, our modern ability to process and manipulate information by computers has a significance equivalent to the development of written language or the invention of the printed book.

The modern corporate manager has two roles in relation to com-puter systems: as user and as manager of information resources. As users, managers have greater access than formerly to information needed for planning, organizing, staffing, directing, and controlling the operations of an organization, and they benefit from the speed of information processing. Computers facilitate their role as decision makers and operational managers.

But computer technology has also placed a burden on corporate managers because information resources have to be organized and managed. Computer equipment must be selected and purchased. Staff must be hired and trained, and the computer department integrated in the firm's organizational hierarchy. Development of new systems and operations need to be budgeted, monitored, and evaluated. In ad-dition, policies and programs must be implemented that will facilitate change and promote within the firm a receptive environment to com-puterization.

In many firms, the corporate manager assigned responsibility for information services will pass the major share of the burden of infor-mation resource management to a computer department director. However, with microtechnology, advances in telecommunications, the establishment of computer networks, improved user interface, the widespread use of personal computers in small businesses, and the expansion of applications, the burden of resource management is today shifting to user management. It is increasingly common for users to choose equipment, design and develop new systems, and control their own computer operations. The increasing popularity of distributed processing suggests that more and more users will manage information resources in the future.

Fortunately, effective management of information resources does not require technical training in electronics or programming skills. However, background knowledge regarding data, hardware, and software is required. Problems unique to computer environments and system development must be understood. System managers also need to know the precise bounds of their responsibility. How much control over information system development is needed? What responsibilities should be delegated to EDP technicians? What are the legal implications of computer data processing? What alternatives exist for organizing information resources?

The purpose of this book is to answer such questions—to provide the reader with background knowledge essential for management of information resources. Computing power is getting cheaper as labor costs rise (see Figure 1.4), providing impetus to computerization. As more and more money is spent on computerized systems, the importance of efficient and effective management of information resources will grow. It is hoped that this text will prepare readers for responsibilities that a computerized society is thrusting upon managers.

Figure 1.4   **Labor and computing costs***

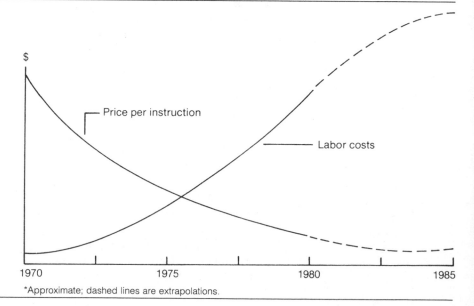

$

Price per instruction

Labor costs

1970   1975   1980   1985

*Approximate; dashed lines are extrapolations.

BOOK OUTLINE

This textbook is divided into seven parts, as shown in Figure 1.5.

Part One, "Computer Resources," includes chapters on the computer processor, software, peripherals, and data. It compresses an introduction to computer terminology and basic computing concepts into just four chapters, making the chapters somewhat encyclopedic in nature. The information included is background to the main focus of the text, the management of these resources. With the coverage in Part One the book is a stand-alone text for those with no background in computing, and will serve as a review for readers who have had computing experience.

Part Two, "Acquisition of Computer Resources," describes how to solicit bids for computer equipment and software, how to select a vendor, how to arrange financing, and how to negotiate vendor contracts.

Ways to mobilize information resources so that the business needs are met is the subject of Part Three, "System Development." Planning for an information system is first described. Stages of development are next explained. Finally, control of information resources during development (project management) is examined.

Information resources of operational systems must also be managed. Part Four, "Control of Resources," describes how to evaluate systems to ensure that resources are being fully utilized, how to monitor processing to minimize machine and human error, how to protect the privacy of data, and how to secure resources from misuse or abuse. The role of auditing in a computer environment is also discussed. All of the mechanisms of control described in this part must be incorporated in the system's development.

Part Five, "Management of Processing," discusses day-to-day concerns of managers responsible for information resources. Scheduling, budgeting, standards, and management of resistance to change are subjects of the chapters in this part.

"Organization of Resources" is the focus of Part Six. The structure of computer departments is described, as is the organization of distributed processing. Oversight mechanisms, staffing, and services available to users and computer departments are also examined.

Finally, Part Seven, "The Computer Processing Environment," discusses issues of concern to managers of information resources. An overview of the computer industry is first presented. Chapters follow on the impact of information systems on management, and on computers and the law. The book closes with a review of why some information systems succeed and others fail.

A list of key words and a set of discussion questions follow each chapter, as does a selected annotated bibliography recommending

Figure 1.5   **Organization of book**

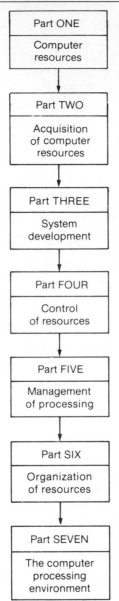

supplementary reading. Case studies also supplement many of the chapters. Some chapters also have exercises.

Two glossaries appear in the appendix. The "Glossary in Prose" is a narrative that presents an overview of the book's contents while introducing computer terminology. Readers may find it helpful to peruse this glossary before beginning study of the text as well as during review. A detailed outline of the contents of this book can be obtained by reading in a series the part introductions, and by reading the summaries that appear at the end of each chapter.

A standard glossary, with operational definitions of computer terms, is also located in the appendix, as is a list of the abbreviations and acronyms found in the text.

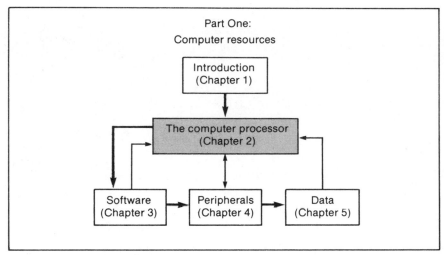

Note: The thin arrows represent the flow of data and information.
The thick arrows show the sequential flow of the parts of the book.

CHAPTER 2

The computer processor

We are reaching the stage where the problems that we must solve are going to become insoluble without computers. I do not fear computers. I fear the lack of them.

Isaac Asimov

A computerized information system has four main components: data, output, computer programs, and the processor. The relationship between these parts is shown in Figure 2.1. The processor is the machine, the computer itself, the device which solves problems and manipulates data. This chapter tells, in brief, what a processor does and how it operates. Modes of processing are also introduced. In addition, the contribution of microelectronics to processing will be examined and forecasts made regarding processors of the future. The remaining components of computerized information systems will be discussed in Chapters 3 and 4 which follow.

Figure 2.1   **Main components of an information system**

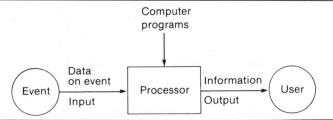

WHAT DO PROCESSORS DO?

Every transaction in business generates data and this data must be handled according to predetermined business procedures. For example, for each order received by a warehouse, shipping invoices must be prepared, inventory records adjusted, bills sent, and payments credited. This order data can be processed manually by office staff. However, when data sets are large in volume and complex in nature, manual processing can be costly, slow, subject to error, and monotonous. As one might expect, machines have been designed to process data, improving both the accuracy and speed of data handling.

Though office machines, such as typewriters, adding machines, and cash registers have been in existence for some time, Herman Hollerith is credited with the first data processing machine. It was designed to process the 1890 census data and did so with greater accuracy and in one third the time required for previous manual census processing. Hollerith developed a card on which data could be represented by coded holes, a card (the **Hollerith card**) which has since been produced in such massive quantities by IBM that it is commonly called the **IBM card.** The cards were fed into Hollerith's machine which tabulated the coded data.

Early data processing machines were electrical and primarily performed accounting operations, which explains why they were called **electrical accounting machines** or **EAM** equipment. Punched cards passed, one at a time, between photo cells carrying electric current. Wherever the holes appeared, current passed through the card. The characters represented by the holes were then read by machine in the form of electrical impulses and interpreted as the characters the holes represented, be they data or instructions on how to process the data. Since the cards usually contained data for one record, such as all sales data for one transaction, such processing was known as **unit record processing.**

As technology advanced and the amount of data to be processed increased, electronic computers replaced the earlier machines, and data processing acquired a new name, **electronic data processing** or **EDP.** Today, computers process words as well as data so that the term **information processing,** meaning data plus word processing, is more appropriate. Nevertheless, *EDP* continues to be a commonly used term by computer personnel. For most speakers it is no longer a strict acronym but a term synonymous with information processing. This expanded definition of EDP is used in this text.

Digital computers[1] operate on the principle that all digital data can

---

[1]Digital computers process discrete data, analog computers process continuous data (for monitoring temperature, pressure, and flow of liquids in manufacturing, for example), while hybrid computers handle both discrete and continuous data. Since digital data are most commonly used for business decision making, this chapter limits itself to a discussion of the digital computer.

be represented by unique arrangements of the digits 0 and 1. These **binary digits,** called **bits,** can be represented by two states (on and off in a switch, different states of electrons in a vacuum tube, or high and low voltage in a transistor). The answers to true-false statements, for example, can be coded in binary digits: that is, off = false, on = true. The British mathematician George Boole designed algebra (Boolean algebra) using the true-false concept for a logical analysis that is electronically represented in gates. A **gate** controls the flow of information by providing an output signal only when the input signals are in prescribed states. Combinations of gates enable computations to be made such as addition, subtraction, multiplication, division, or comparisons.

UNIVAC was the first computer to become commercially available for data processing. Since its introduction in 1951, processors have made advances in speed, accuracy, capacity, and scope of data processing. Changes have come in large jumps of performance (called computer **generations**) instead of slowly and gradually as might be expected. In the first computer generation, vacuum tubes were used; in the second, transistors; in the third, integrated circuits. Some authors identify a fourth generation, large-scale integration.

The technology of computers is beyond the scope of this text. However, we will describe what computers can do and briefly outline how computers contribute to decision making. But the main focus of the book is to explain how computing resources should be managed.

COMPARISON OF MANUAL PROCESSING, EAM, AND COMPUTER PROCESSING

A mix of manual processing, EAM, and computer processing is found in the business world today. Although both EAM and computer processing require an initial investment for costly equipment, large volume processing reaches a break-even point where the use of equipment is economically justified. Savings in processing occur for added volume beyond this point.

Figure 2.2 illustrates this concept. In this figure, variable costs are shown by the slope of the total cost lines. (Total cost is the sum of variable and fixed costs.) It will be noted that the slope of AB for manual processing is steeper than CD, the slope for machine processing. (CD includes EAM and other office machines such as bookkeeping equipment.) That means that the variable cost per unit processed is higher in manual processing, though its fixed cost OA (desk, pencil, paper) is lower. The break-even point P, representing processing volume OE, is the point beyond which machine processing is warranted. For less volume, manual processing remains more economical, the shaded area showing the savings that would accrue if manual instead of machine processing were used.

Figure 2.2   **Break-even points for machine and computer processing**

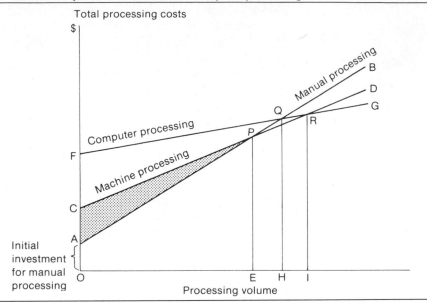

The slope of computer processing is even flatter, though initial costs are higher. The break-even point compared to manual processing (*AB*) is *Q*, for volume *OH*. The break-even point where computer processing costs match machine processing costs, *R*, requires an even larger volume of data processing (*OI*). That is, manual data processing is most economical for low volume (*OE*), machine processing is recommended for medium-volume processing, and computer processing is most economical after volume *OI* is reached.

This figure is merely a model. In an actual case, the starting point on the X axis and the slopes of the lines will depend on the equipment used and the wage scale. But the general concept that this figure illustrates would still apply. As the volume of data processing increases, the switchover from manual to machine to computer processing becomes economically justified. For large volume processing, beyond *OI* in Figure 2.2, computer processing is the cheapest way to generate information. (Computer processing has other advantages as well, such as greater accuracy and speed.)

COMPONENTS OF A COMPUTER PROCESSOR

The **central processor (CPU)** of a digital computer has three parts as shown in Figure 2.3: an **arithmetic and logic unit,** a **memory and storage unit,** and a **control unit.**

Figure 2.3   **The organization of a digital computer system**

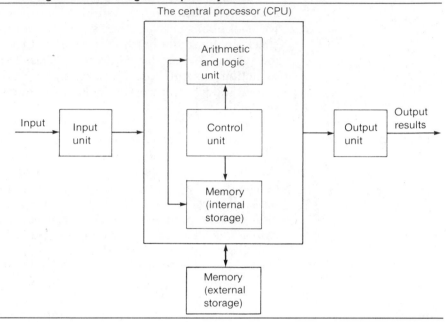

Input data are stored in internal memory until ready to be processed. Also stored are instructions concerning computations to be performed. These calculations, such as addition and multiplication, are carried out by the arithmetic-logic unit which also performs logical operations, such as comparisons. The control unit coordinates the sequence of instructions and flow of data between units.

Intermediate calculations and other information related to the transformation of input are also stored. If the volume of data to be stored is too large for the **internal memory,** or **main memory** of the CPU, it can be stored in the **external memory,** or **secondary storage,** on devices such as magnetic tapes or disks.

MODES OF PROCESSING

Computers can process data in a variety of modes. These modes are described below.

Batch processing   The first computers used **batch processing.** Many digital computers still handle batch processing though faster processing methods have been developed. Batch processing is the technique used by those of us who collect our bills for once a month payment. Instead of locating checkbook, pen, stamps, and envelopes each time a bill arrives, we write all of our checks at one sitting upon receipt of our monthly paycheck. In computer batch processing, either the computer operator or the system itself collects jobs in batches. This results in a significant reduction in setup costs since repetitive handling of each job is eliminated, though a processing delay of minutes, hours, or days may result.

Remote processing

When the source of data is distant from the computer, the delay in batch processing is compounded. The use of telecommunication lines (e.g., telephone), instead of a messenger or mail, to speed the transfer of data directly to the CPU is called **remote processing.** If the processing is not processed in batch, but processed directly by the CPU, the term **on-line remote processing** is used. This processing mode requires special control programs for receiving, checking, scheduling, and observing priorities for data processing services. **Remote job entry** is common among businesses having multiple sources of data generation.

Time sharing

The fast processing speed of computers means a single CPU can serve many terminals. **Time sharing** is a mode of operations in which several users share a computer facility. When time sharing was first initiated, fair-use rules had to be developed because first-come first-served had the disadvantage that users with small jobs often had to wait until users with long jobs were serviced. Priorities were set by management to guide scheduling. Today, computers have nanosecond processing speeds, so **round-robin service,** giving all users a small slice of computing time in turn, is common. Service is so fast that it appears as if all users are handled simultaneously. Most time-sharing users are unaware that they are sharing the CPU with others.

Time sharing has proved particularly valuable to small businesses unable to afford computers and software equipment of their own, for they can now have access to large computer systems by sharing overhead costs with others. Even some large computing centers use time sharing in order to meet their computing needs during peak hours or to provide access to data bases, computer software, or a larger memory capacity than available in-house. A summary of the characteristics, advantages, and disadvantages of time sharing appears in Table 2.1.

Online real time

Real-time computer processing is used for instantaneous processing and continuous updating of the data base. This is needed in airline reservations, for example, because ticket agents need updated information on available seats—information that takes into account sales that might have occurred minutes before in other cities. Real time requires **online terminals** (terminals physically connected to the

Table 2.1	Time sharing
	Characteristics
	Central computer accessible to multiple users for input and output. Telephonic connections between computer and user at remote sites.
	Advantages
	Enables small user to have access to a large computer system, sharing overhead costs with other users. Reduces overhead cost even for large user. Provides access to data bases and generalized applications programs. Faster response than batch. Enables interactive and conversational use of computer. No geographic restriction except for cost of transmission. Convenience of use.
	Disadvantages
	When system is down, all users sharing the system are affected. Higher cost than batch processing. Loss of security. Data is subject to violation either due to accident or design. Response time can drop with increase in number of users, especially those with large scientific problems to process. Possible loss of priority when large competitive demands are placed on system.

computer or in direct communication through telecommunications to the CPU). Therefore, such systems are called **online real-time systems (OLRT).**

Distributed processing

Distributed data processing is giving computing capability to branch offices or field locations of a firm. The computers at each site are linked through telecommunications so that a company-wide processing **network** is established. The network configuration varies from one organization to another as does the degree of autonomy of the distributed processing sites. This mode of operations, made practical by advances in teleprocessing and microelectronics, is currently gaining in popularity. Chapter 20 discusses at length the effect of this mode on operations and management.

Combining processing modes

It is possible to combine some of the modes of processing described above. For example, time sharing may be online real time, and remote processing is used by many distributed processing centers.

CONTRIBUTION OF MICROELECTRONICS TO PROCESSING

The central processing unit of computers has been radically altered by advances in solid state physics and integrated circuitry. Vacuum tubes and transistors have been replaced by **large-scale integration** of circuitry on chips. Microelectronics has reduced computers in size, speed, and price, and lowered relative failure rates per gate. Microprocessors, microcomputers, and minicomputers, in widespread use to-day, incorporate this improved technology. The use of microtechnology in processing is described below.

Microprocessors

Microelectronics means that an entire CPU can now be placed on a single chip. A **microprocessor** is a miniaturized CPU designed to perform specific functions in products and to make needed adjustments necessary for changed conditions. Through sensors, input on performance is collected. The microprocessor evaluates this data against preset standards, and through an actuator, makes control adjustments. For example, in cars, a microprocessor can optimize consumption of fuel by sensing the air environment (temperature, velocity, density) and adjusting the mixture of air and fuel accordingly.

Table 2.2 is a list of products where microprocessors are commonly used. In many of these products, more than one micro might be used. In cars, for example, micros might be incorporated as part of skid con-

Table 2.2

Uses of microprocessors

Industrial products	*Consumer products*
Aircraft subsystems	Automobile subsystems
Blood analyzers	Blenders
Cash registers	Burglar alarms
Communication devices	Calculators
Copying machines	Cameras
Dictating machines	Clocks
Gasoline pumps	Clothes dryers
Lab equipment control	Dishwashers
Machine control	Electric slicing knives
Measuring instruments	Fire alarms
Medical diagnostics	Food blenders
Pacemakers	Hair dryers
Robots	Heating systems
Scales	Microwave ovens
Scanners	Monitoring of home utilities
Taxi meters	Fuel/heat/water/light
Telephone switching	Ovens
Testing instruments	Pinball machines
Toasters	Radios
Traffic lights	Refrigerators
TV camera	Slow cookers
Vending machines	Stereo systems
etc.	Telephones
	Television sets
	Washing machines
	Watches
	etc.

trol, theft deterrent control, braking control, and speed control—to name just a few applications.

Microcomputers

A **microcomputer** is a complete small computer system, the main processing parts of which are semiconductor integrated circuits. A microcomputer can be constructed on a chip or chips, and be much smaller than a fingertip, as illustrated in Figure 2.4. Microcomputers are designed for specific applications. They are found in video game machines, point-of-sale terminals, microwave ovens, gas station pumps, and pollution monitoring devices, to name just a few examples.

Minicomputers

When **minicomputers** were first developed, they were the labeled mini because they were smaller in speed, size, and capacity than other computers on the market. The term continues to be used even though minis today are very fast in computation and no longer always small in size.[2] For example, the first PDP-11, though called a mini, stood 6 feet high and occupied 14 by 18 inches of floor space without printer.

Minis are general-purpose computers characterized by higher performance than microcomputers, more powerful instruction sets, and a wider selection of available programming languages and operating systems. At least originally that was the distinction. Today, with ex-

Figure 2.4   **A microcomputer on a chip placed against a fingertip**

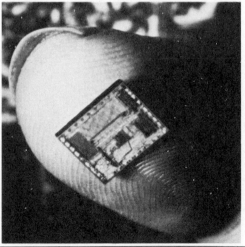

Courtesy Intel Corporation

---

[2]Myles E. Walsh, "Where Have All the Minis Gone." *Infosystems* 25, no. 7 (July 1978), pp. 62–73.

panded microcomputer capabilities, the tendency is to speak of minis and microcomputers as if there were little difference between the two.

In comparison to medium and large-scale computers, minis cost less, have lower processing speeds, a relatively small memory, and less software support. The low speed is a result of an architectural characteristic: small **word** size which restricts the number of instructions in the computer's repertoire. Nevertheless, as technology has advanced, minis have added to their computing capacity so that today minis are comparable to what were former medium-scale computers, blurring the lines of division between the two.[3]

Over a third of the production of minis is bought by companies called **original equipment manufacturers (OEM)** who resell the minis with their own software as a **package** for applications in accounting, sales, control of manufacture, and other specialized business functions. Such packages enable small businesses with low budgets and nontechnical personnel to purchase and use a computer.

Some of the uses of minicomputers are listed in Table 2.3. The sale of desk-top minis to businesspersons and homeowners as personal computers is one potentially explosive market. Software is being developed for entertainment and computing applications such as check-

Table 2.3	**Uses of minicomputers**
Current	*Future*
Bank terminals	Badge and credit-card checking
Blood analyzer	Bartenders
CAI (computer-assisted instruction)	Elevator control
Cash register	Gas pump control
Communication	Medical diagnosis
Storing and forwarding messages	Online calculations in hotels
Monitoring telephone lines	Hotel bill
Education	Restaurant
Input validation on terminals	Tip
Instrumentation	Passenger movement control
Mixers (e.g., paint and other substances)	Physician control of information on patients
Numerical control	Plant schedule control
Personal computer	Process control
Printing	Security and access control
Editing	Shopping scales
Typesetting	Simulation
Page layout	Stock and commodity applications
Process control	Typewriters
Stand-alone computer for small businesses	Vending machines
Text editing	

---

[3]Frederick W. Miller, "The Impending Merger of Minis and Main Frames," *Infosystems* 25, no. 4 (April 1978), pp. 45–6.

book balancing, keeping a calendar of events, calculating income taxes, monitoring investments, updating address lists, and typing letters.

COMPUTER PROCESSORS IN THE FUTURE

The 1980s will see many new applications for micros and minis. In addition, computers will grow more powerful. Users will be able to choose from a wide array of processors: minis and micros at one end, supercomputers at the other, with various configurations of processing modules in between differing in capability and speed. Physical size will not necessarily be indicative of computing power. For example, teleprocessing networks will enable the small terminal user to have access to large data bases and processing capabilities which formerly only large equipment configurations could provide.

One technological development that shows promise is IBM's **Josephson computer,** named after the Englishman who theorized that electrical flow becomes faster at low temperatures because of lack of resistance. The Josephson processor will operate at $-269°$ C, its circuits, referred to as cryogenic devices, sitting in liquid helium at 4° C. On/off switching will be in 7 billionths of a second, enabling 70 million instructions per second. This computer is roughly 14 times faster than the most powerful IBM computer of the l970s. It only awaits engineering to fit into a three-pound package, a package projected for the mid-1980s.

Another development, also at IBM, is the introduction of a totally new family of circuits called **current injection logic** which utilize a thousand times less energy than transistor circuits and operate at about 13 picoseconds,[4] twice or thrice as fast as Josephson circuits. Still another promising line of research is being conducted at the Herrit-Watt University in Edinburgh on electronic lasers to make an optical switch turn on and off in a trillionth of a second. Such speed, combined with the Josephson computer, makes computers with 250 million instructions per second a distinct possibility in the 1990s.

TCM (thermal conduction modules) is under development at IBM as is HEMT (high electron mobility transistor technology) at Fujitsu in Japan. A **distributed array processor,** using thousands of microprocessors in parallel, is also being developed. It is projected that chips will be available that are one hundredth the width of human hair, containing lines half a micron in size. A single chip in the future might contain entire systems for a radar network, a library, or a factory.

---

[4]As an analogy, a picosecond is to a second what a second is to 31,710 years.

The Japanese government and Japanese computer industry have announced that they are joining forces to produce a fifth generation computer by the 1990s, a supercomputer with 10 times the speed of computers now under development. Fearful that the United States will lose its dominance in computing to the Japanese, Microelectronics and Computer Technology Corporation (MCT) has been founded—a research operation jointly funded by 10 top American computer companies. MCT will concentrate in four research areas: integrated-circuit packaging, computer architecture, software technology, and computer-aided design and manufacturing systems.

It should be recognized, however, that what is technically feasible may not be implemented in the immediate future. MCT, for example, is for research only. Marketing of products will be left to individual member companies. It takes time to design new products to incorporate computing advances, time to develop secondary technologies needed for such products, and time to gain the confidence of consumers.

SUMMARY AND CONCLUSIONS

This chapter has discussed the evolution of computers. Minicomputers have more computing capacity than the first electronic computer, (ENIAC), are 30 times faster, have a larger memory, are thousands of times more reliable, consume the power of a light bulb rather than that of a locomotive, and occupy 1/30,000 the volume. They also cost less that 1/10,000 as much.[5]

Minis and micros can be purchased by mail order or at local department stores. The trend is continuing toward further miniaturization, faster speeds, greater reliability, and lower costs. Past improvements were due to technological changes in the basic components of the CPU, which evolved from the vacuum tube to transistors, and from small-scale integration to large-scale integration, then to very large-scale integration and chip technology. Technological advances have resulted in increased concentration of circuitry (gate density) by a factor of 100, or two magnitudes $(10;^2)$. Another two orders of magnitude are predicted for the 1980s. Yet another order of magnitude is necessary to approach the gate density of the human brain.

Micros are being incorporated in home products to make them "smart." That is, they are able to evaluate the environment and the desires of the user and activate correcting adjustments where necessary. In the future they will commonly appear in clocks, thermostats,

---

[5]"All That Is Electronic Does Not Glitter," *The Economist* 274, no. 7122 (March 1–7, 1980), pp. 53–54.

light switches, radios, toasters, vacuum cleaners, and so forth. Micros and minis will also appear in industrial products, in the factory, and in communications.

Micros, minis, and **maxis** (large computers) and even supercomputers can only do what they are programmed to do. Their intelligence is based on instructions that tell the CPU how to process data. This subject, programming, is examined in Chapter 3.

KEY WORDS

Arithmetic and logic unit

Batch processing

Binary digits

Bits

Central processor (CPU)

Control unit

Current injection logic

Digital computers

Distributed array processor

Distributed data processing

Electrical accounting machines (EAM)

Electronic data processing (EDP)

External memory

Gate

Generation

Hollerith card

IBM card

Information processing

Internal memory

Josephson computer

Large-scale integration

Main memory

Maxi

Memory and storage unit

Microcomputer

Microprocessor

Minicomputer

Network

Online real-time systems (OLRT)

Online remote processing

Online terminals

Original equipment manufacturers (OEM)

Package

Real time

Remote job entry

Remote processing

Round-robin service

Secondary storage

Time sharing

Unit record processing

Word

DISCUSSION QUESTIONS

1. What are the economic considerations and conditions that can justify the use of computers?

2. Distinguish between manual, machine, and computer processing in terms of:
   a. Equipment used.
   b. Economic justification.
3. Distinguish between batch processing, time sharing, online real-time systems, and distributed processing. Give an example of each mode of processing in business.
4. What is the effect of an increase in the following on the break-even point between computer processing and other means of processing?
   a. Volume of processing.
   b. Fixed cost.
   c. Variable cost.
5. Distinguish between:
   a. General-purpose and special purpose computer.
   b. Microcomputer and microprocessor.
   c. Microcomputer and minicomputer.
6. What is meant by the microelectronic revolution? Has this revolution affected you? How? Will it affect businesses? How?
7. What unique hardware features are required for a system operating in an OLRT environment as opposed to a batch environment?
8. What is meant by computer generations? How have computer generations affected the user in business?
9. Is the advance of computer technology too fast paced for society to adapt and adjust to the new technology? If so, how should the pace be slowed, if that is possible? What can be done to help society absorb and exploit computing advances in an orderly fashion?
10. What mode(s) of processing would you recommend for the following applications and situations?
    a. Payroll.
    b. Warehouse storing furniture.
    c. Warehouse storing vegetables and fruit.
    d. Office needing computers for scientific computations.
    e. Top manager needing a data base 1,000 miles away.
    f. Analyst needing a compiler not available in state.
    g. Profit and loss statement.
    h. Typing letters daily.
    i. Preparing monthly statements on sales.
    j. Performing weekly inventory control.
    k. Making car rental reservations.
    l. Controlling a refinery.
11. Has microtechnology democratized the computer by bringing it within the reach of the average citizen? How will this enrich society? Or will it result in cultural shock?
12. Is our social, legal, and political structure capable of handling and coping with the rapid changes brought about by microtechnology?
13. Can microtechnology improve productivity and thereby improve the standard of living in the poorer countries of the world?

14. "Computer technology has advanced faster than our ability to use it fully. What we need now is not more innovation and faster computers but time to assimilate the power and versatility of computers and effort to apply them more fully." Comment.

SELECTED ANNOTATED BIBLIOGRAPHY

On modes of processing

Awad, Elias M. *Introduction to Computers in Business.* Englewood Cliffs, N.J.: Prentice-Hall, 1977. Chaps. 4 and 6.
Chapter 4 is a discussion of the general and specific purposes of analog, digital, and hybrid computers. Also discussed are minis, micros, and computers of different sizes from portable to large-scale computers.

House, William C., ed. *Data Base Management.* New York: Petrocelli Books, 1974. Part V, pp. 330–97.
Included are five chapters on processing methods: batch, remote access, dedicated, time sharing, and real time. An excellent coverage of the subject.

Mader, Chris, and Hagin, Robert. *Information Systems: Technology, Economics and Applications.* Chicago: Science Research Associates, 1974. Pp. 291–309.
This text has an excellent chapter (13) on time sharing and interactive computing. The emphasis is on the economics and applications to business.

Sackman, Harold. *Mass Information Utilities and Social Excellence.* Princeton, N.J.: Auerbach Publishers, 1971. 254 pp.
The author has had many years of experience working with time sharing, especially at Rand, using large systems for defense. He discusses the implications of mass time sharing on home managers, businesspersons, and society. He subscribes to the philosophy that every individual possesses the right of free access to knowledge and that "information power ultimately resides in the public." Sackman also discusses the issue of individual and collective human intelligence being affected by computers.

On microelectronics

Firebaugh, Morris, et al. "A Feast of Microcomputers." *Personal Computing* 2, no. 11 (November 1978), pp. 60–81.
This article reviews the use of microcomputers for education, home, and business. It discusses 15 computers in terms of their hardware, software, prices, and capabilities. The systems are each evaluated and rated. This article will, of course, soon be outdated, but such articles appear periodically in many journals such as *Datamation* and *Personal Computing*.

Forester, Tom. *The Microelectronics Revolutions.* Cambridge, Mass.: MIT Press, 1980. 581 pages.
This is an excellent selection of some 40 articles organized into eight chapters, each chapter ending with a guide to further reading. The selections are well balanced between optimists, such as Herbert Simon, and critics, like Weisenbaum. Microelectronics is such a fast moving field that

everything written soon becomes obsolete. This book, however, is worth having as a reference volume.

Roland, John. "The Microelectronic Revolution." *The Futurist* 13, no. 2 (April 1979), pp. 81–90.

A futurist view and a very optimistic one. Roland discusses the applications of microcomputers in business and everyday life, applications in which security and privacy of information are protected. A provocative look at micros and their effect on society.

Scientific American. *Microelectronics*. San Francisco: W. H. Freeman, 1977. 145 pp.

This softcover book is a reprint of the September 1977 special issue of *Scientific American* on microelectronics. It has 11 articles written on the entire range of microelectronics, including the technical aspects of circuitry and production. But throughout, the text is successfully addressed to the layman in nontechnical language. There are numerous stand-alone diagrams, including many that are multicolor, contributing to an easier understanding of the material.

The subjects covered include the concepts and manufacturing of microelectronic circuits and chips, both CPU and storage chips, personal computers, and the application of computers to instrumentation, process control, communication, and data processing. In most cases, the state of the art is reviewed and future trends identified. A superb and understandable discussion of a very technical subject.

Additional references on advances and innovation in computers can be found in the footnotes and bibliography of Chapter 24 on the computer industry.

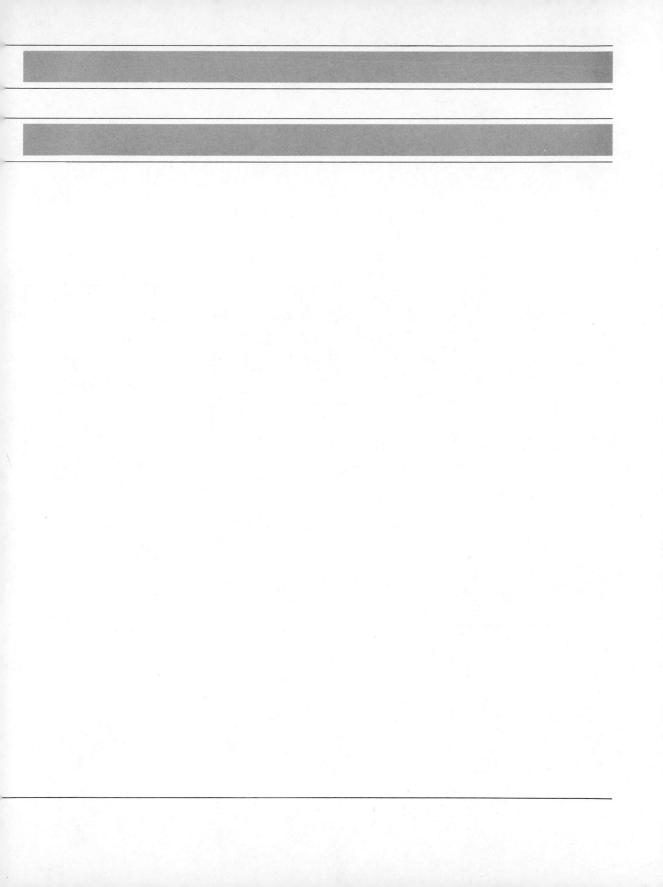

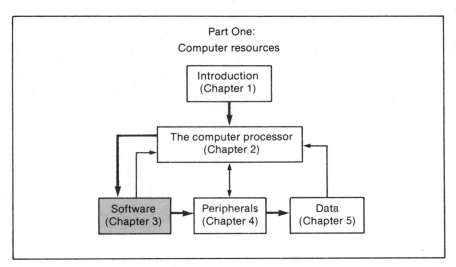

Note: The thin arrows represent the flow of data and information. The thick arrows show the sequential flow of the parts of the book.

CHAPTER 3

Software

Computer programming as a practical human activity is some 25 years old, a short time for intellectual development. Yet computer programming has already posed the greatest intellectual challenge that mankind has faced in pure logic and complexity.

Harlan D. Mills

Computer equipment, called **hardware,** is circuitry and metal. **Programs** give life to this hardware, enabling computers to perform calculations and process information. They are sets of instructions and decision rules for processing. Unlike hardware that is physical, something that can be touched, programs represent decision logic, the intellectual process for solving problems. Being the antithesis of hardware, programs are called **software.**

This chapter describes the processing operations that computer software can perform. It compares programming languages and also discusses programs for operating systems and applications.

PROCESSING OF DATA

A computer does computations by using arithmetic **operators** (add, subtract, multiply, etc.). But what operators should be used, which data have to be processed, and the sequence of operations to be performed must all be specified by programs. The composition of data and how data are processed are factors that determine how programs will be written and what programming languages are most appropriate. But in order to explain this further, the structure of data first needs to be discussed.

Variables that users need to record, such as name, date, and price, are called **data elements,** the values of which are expressed by a combination of **characters.** These characters may be numeric (0–9), alphabetic (A–Z), special symbols (i.e., /, $, %), or operators (+, −, ×). For example, alphabetic characters are used to represent the data element "name," and a combination of numeric characters and alpha characters would represent the data element "invoice number" (e.g., AC325).

In computer processing, each character is represented by a unique set of binary digits (**bits**). Numbers in the base 10 number system will be rewritten in binary, since only binary configurations are recognized by the computer's circuits in the CPU, as explained in the preceding chapter. For example, 9 in base 10 is 1001 in binary; 153 is 10011001. Binary codes also represent alpha characters, symbols, and operators. Therefore, all data elements can be translated into bits which can be processed electronically by computer.

In data processing, related data elements constitute a **record.** An accounts payable record might consist of a vendor's name, identification number, and amount of sale. All accounts payable records for all vendors would constitute a **file,** an accounts payable file. Businesses generally have many functional files, including a payroll file, a production file, an accounts payable file, and so forth.

A function that includes transactions—events such as goods delivered or received, or accounts paid or received—has a **transaction file** in which transactional data of a temporary nature are recorded. Permanent data on the function are kept in a **master file** which is periodically updated from the transaction file, the latter being destroyed or kept as backup once updating takes place. The updated master is used in processing.

Updating requires processing of two files, transferring relevant information from the transaction file to the master. If data on both files were at random, merging the two would be a complex task. As an analogy, imagine placing a thousand letters, each addressed to a specific customer, in preaddressed envelopes which are in no special order. This manual task would be simplified by sorting and stacking both letters and envelopes in alphabetical order by last name of customer, then matching and merging the two piles while stuffing the envelopes. In computer batch processing, records on both the transaction and master file must be sorted before data on the two files can be merged. Updating requires a **key data element** (a data element common to two or more files) in order to match or merge sorted files.

Table 3.1 shows data in a master file before and after sorting by vendor number. This sorting is done by a computer program. Data on the transaction file have also been sorted by a computer program by

Table 3.1   **Updating a master file**

Unsorted records on master file
	3000510	Hall, A. E.	$120.20
	3285000	Adams, J. M.	210.00
	2003250	Jackson, K. M.	150.00

(Each record has ID number of vendor, name of vendor, and amount payable, in that order.)

Master file
(Sorted by vendor number in ascending sequence)
	2003250	Jackson, K. M.	$150.00
	3000510	Hall, A. E.	120.00
	3285000	Adams, J. M.	210.00

Transactional file
(Sorted by vendor number listing amounts paid)
| | 2003250 | | $100.00 |
| | 3285000 | | 110.00 |

Master file after updating
	2003250	Jackson, K. M.	$ 50,000
	3000510	Hall, A. E.	120.00
	3285000	Adams, J. M.	100.00

Updated master file resorted into alphabetic sequence
(output)
	Adams, J. M.	3285000	$100.00
	Hall, A. E.	3000510	120.00
	Jackson, K. M.	2003250	50.00

vendor number. An applications program then instructs the computer to deduct the amounts paid listed on the transaction file from the corresponding record of amounts due on the master file. This is done one record at a time in sequence.

The master file, when updated, is then ready for additional processing. In Table 3.1, processing concluded with a printout made of the updated master resorted alphabetically for convenient access. Other processing might be matching, merging, comparing, or performing computations with master file figures such as calculating totals, balances, or averages. The results might then be classified into categories, summarized, and reported for use by different levels of management. These operations, summarized in Figure 3.1, are common business applications done by computers according to programmed instructions. These instructions, prepared in a form a computer can understand, are written in a **programming language.** That is, a program (a set of instructions) written by a **programmer** in a programming language tells the computer what operations to perform. How these languages work will now be explained.

Figure 3.1   **Basic business operations by the CPU**

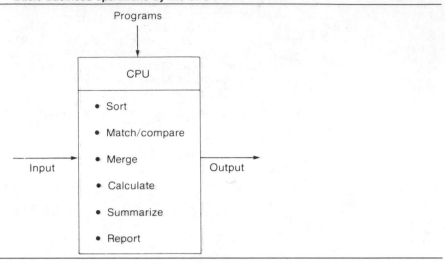

PROGRAMMING LANGUAGES

The first programming language developed and the most elemental is **machine language.** Instructions in machine language are a series of base 10 numbers which are converted internally by the computer into binary digits recognized by the CPU. Figure 3.2 shows a machine language instruction for an early computer, the IBM 1620. The instruction has three parts. The first two digits represent the operation code (add, subtract, move data, etc.). In this example, code 21 represents add. The data will, therefore, be channeled through circuitry that will perform addition. (Other circuitry exists for other arithmetic operations.) The second and third parts are **operands** where data are stored, called a **storage location** or **address.** In this case, the datum in storage location 14000 is 120; the datum in storage location 12002 is 30. The machine instruction 211400012002 means: add the datum stored in operand 1 to datum stored in operand 2, and then store the result in operand 1. That is, take the datum 120 (which in this case is regular weekly pay in dollars), add it to datum 30 (overtime pay), and store the result (150) in location 14000.

Writing programs in machine language has many drawbacks.

1.   It is necessary to keep track of storage locations and their contents, for contents keep changing, as in the example above where datum in location 14000 switched from regular daily pay to total weekly pay.

2.   It is necessary to remember operation codes.

Figure 3.2   **An example of machine language instruction**

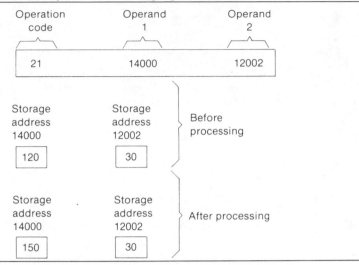

3. There are many instructions to write, one for each machine command.

4. The language is machine dependent. Each CPU has a unique circuitry design so that the form and structure of instructions used may vary from one manufacturer to another, and possibly from one model to another as well. That means the program is not **portable** from one computer to another.

To overcome some of these problems, the first **assembly language** was developed in the 1950s. An instruction in this language, also for the IBM 1620, with the same meaning as the previous example, 211400012002 is: A RGP OTP. Here, the numeric operation code 21 is replaced by the alphabetic code A, and the addresses have been replaced by variable names RGP (regular pay) and OTP (overtime pay). The computer has an internal program, called an **assembler,** to convert alphabetic letters (and symbols) into binary digits. The assembler also converts storage location names when new variables are stored there so that RGP becomes TP (total pay). In other words, the assembler converts the assembly language program, called the **source program,** into its machine language equivalent, an **object program.** This process is shown in Figure 3.3.

Assembly programs are less difficult to write than programs in machine language because the need to remember storage locations and contents is eliminated. Also, alphabetic operation codes are easier to remember than numeric codes, especially when the abbreviations are meaningful. But criticisms 3 and 4 of machine languages still remain:

Figure 3.3   **Assembly language translation process**

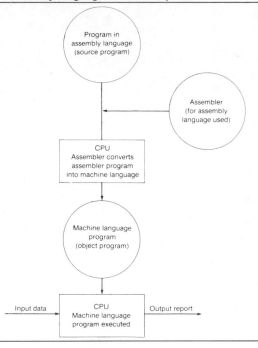

a large number of instructions must be written, and the language is nonportable.

As a result, high level programming languages have been developed, languages closer to English. Instructions in COBOL, a language commonly used for business applications, look like this:

ADD REGULAR-PAY, OVERTIME-PAY GIVING TOTAL-PAY
or PAY = REGPAY + OVTPAY
or PAY = RGP + OTP

As with assembly languages, a translation of these instructions is done internally before the program is executed. But for **high level languages,** the translation is done by a **compiler,** not an assembler.

High level languages overcome all of the drawbacks of machine languages. The compiler keeps track of storage locations and contents. Operation codes are familiar symbols. A major gain over machine or assembly languages is that few instructions are necessary. In 1957 when FORTRAN was developed, a set of 47 FORTRAN instructions equaled approximately 1000 machine language commands.[1] Furthermore, high level languages are portable, provided the other computer

---

[1]Richard A. McLaughlin, "The IBM 704: 36 Bit Floating-Point Money Maker," *Datamation* 21, no. 8 (August 1975), p. 45.

has an appropriate compiler. In addition, because instructions resemble English, high level languages are easy to learn, quick and less tedious to write and modify, and easy to check for errors. Many such languages are also self-documenting.

There has been a proliferation of high level languages in recent years, as shown in the cartoon in Figure 3.4. Many of these languages are for special types of problem solving. COBOL, for example, was designed specifically for business data processing applications. FORTRAN, effective in complex matrix calculations, APL, BASIC, PASCAL, PL/1, and RPG are other general purpose languages commonly favored by businesspersons.

A number of query languages have been developed in recent years

Figure 3.4 **The Tower of Babel of programming languages**

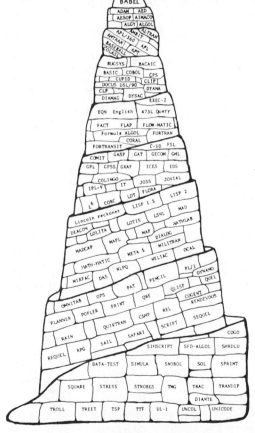

And the Lord said, . . . let us go down, and there confound
their language, that they may not understand
one another's speech (Genesis, 11: 6-7)

Source: Adapted from Jean E. Sammet, *Programming Languages: History and Fundamentals* (Englewood Cliffs, N.J.: Prentice-Hall Inc., © 1969, front cover. Reprinted by permission.

that are English-like. That is, the computer recognizes a limited English vocabulary, but the instructions must be in a prescribed format. Table 3.2 shows how a user would request in four different query languages (SEQUEL, SQUARE, QUERY BY EXAMPLE, and IQF) a list from a computer's data base of employees who work for Smith and make under $20,000. It is often assumed that, ideally, computers should be programmed in natural languages such as English or French. It has been postulated, however, that too many ambiguities exist in natural languages for them to be efficient programming vehicles. Empirical studies show that formal query languages are better able to help users identify their needs and formulate problems so that computers can be of assistance.[2]

Some languages are designed to extract data from a file or a data base and format it into a desired report. Such a language is called a **report program generator (RPG).** Some RPGs are independent of data base or query facilities, while others are an extension of data base query languages.

Report generators may have arithmetic and logic capabilities, but

Table 3.2   **Examples of query languages**

a.   English:
     Find employees working for Smith who make under
     $20,000.

b.   SEQUEL: SELECT NAME
               FROM PERSONNEL
               WHERE MANAGER = 'SMITH'
               AND SALARY <20000

c.   SQUARE: EMP   ('SMITH',<'20000')
                 NAME   MANAGER,SALARY

d.   QUERY BY EXAMPLE:

PERSONNEL	NAME	MANAGER	SALARY
	P*	Smith	<20000

e.   IQF: (1)   FROM PERSONNEL FILE
            (2)   FOR SMITH MANAGER
            (3)   AND FOR SALARY <20000
            (4)   LIST NAME

*P stands for print, identifying desired output.

_____
[2]See D. W. Small and L. J. Weldon, "The Efficiency of Retrieving Information from Computers Using Natural and Structured Query Languages," Rep. SA1-78-655-WA (Arlington, Va.: Science Applications, 1977) and Ben Schneidermann, "Improving the Human Factors Aspect of Database Interactions," *ACM Transactions on Database Systems* 3, no. 4 (December 1978), pp. 433–37.

instructions have to be written for implementing these capabilities. This is avoided in **application generators** which call modules to perform the functions of an application. The input specifies which arithmetic and logical operations are to be performed, what data to use, and the output to be generated. This greatly speeds up application development. When an application requires operations which the application generator cannot create, the generator is still useful providing that it allows the inclusion of routines written in a program language.

The growing use of terminals for data entry by clerks and for information retrieval by management has led to the development of **terminal interactive languages.** These languages have a special capability: computer-directed or computer-prompted queries assist in data collection and retrieval. For example, should a user want a list of Houston suppliers, a **menu** might appear on the terminal screen asking:

Do you want:

1.   Names of suppliers located in Houston?
2.   Names of companies supplying Houston projects?
3.   Names of suppliers associated with Houston in some other way?

If the second response is correct, the user types the number 2 on the keyboard. Should further clarification be needed by the system, a new menu may appear. Or the user may be asked to fill in blanks or make yes/no choices. The advantage of such programming is obvious: only a little knowledge of computers is required in order for users to retrieve data from the system.

Special languages are also being developed to facilitate the display and manipulation of data on graphic terminals. Some **graphic languages** are interactive, enabling users to ask for data and to specify how they want it displayed. Like report generators, some graphic packages have arithmetic and logic capabilities.

At the present time, much language research is being conducted to make languages easier to write. Already **fourth generation languages (4GLs)** are being introduced, languages such as FOCUS, NOMAD, RAMIS, and MANTIS that are nonprocedural in nature. Instead of giving the computer commands that tell how to process information (as in FORTRAN, COBOL, and ALGOL), these new languages employ a small set of powerful commands that tell the computer what to do. Not only is programming productivity increased, but end users with no prior programming experience can do their own programming, enter their own data, and run their own reports without relying on data processing personnel. (It is estimated that 75 percent of all 4GL programming can be done by users with only two days of training.) Specialist programmers, however, are still needed to handle complex applications and to fine tune the main nonprocedural code.

In spite of the advantages of 4GLs, a negative reaction is exhibited by many computer processing departments to these languages. This is due, in part, to fear of the unknown and to resistance to change. Managers of computing who have gained their seniority by the old methods don't like to see their power bases eroded, their budgets reduced, or their control over standards diminished—all of which occurs when programming is transferred to end users. It is the enthusiasm of users that is promoting 4GLs, and the fact that 4GLs are helping to wipe out applications backlogs. With further language research, we may even reach a point in time when programming becomes automated, eliminating many programmers and programming languages.

CLASSIFICATION OF SOFTWARE

There are two main types of software: **operating systems software** and **applications software.** Figure 3.5 shows the types of software found in each category. The sections which follow will discuss these programs.

Operating systems software

Every computer requires programs for the operation of the CPU and peripheral equipment though most users are unaware of their existence. These programs are generally provided by the manufacturer

Figure 3.5   **Types of software**

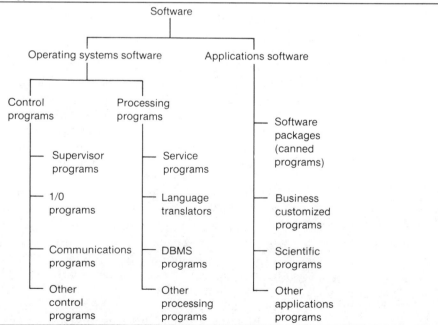

and are unique to the model. Data processing personnel are vitally concerned with **operating programs** for their objective is to maximize the efficiency of operations, minimize human intervention, and facilitate the task of the user in accessing data and/or peripheral equipment. To achieve these objectives, two main sets of programs exist: **control programs** and **processing programs.**

Control programs. The **supervisor,** also called the **executive, monitor,** or **controller,** is the most important control program. It coordinates all the hardware of the computer system and handles job scheduling, queuing, and storage allocation. It also keeps logs and does job accounting for each job processed. Finally, the supervisor communicates with the human operator through the console regarding the status of computer system operations.

I/O control programs are a collection of subroutines for the input of data and output of information dealing with the actual physical location and format of data and with its logical organization into data elements, records, and files. These programs handle input/output scheduling, error corrections, and various functions necessary to create and maintain files. For business applications, I/O control programs may constitute between 30 and 45 percent of all programmed instructions.

Communications programs perform message switching and remote inquiry. Other control subroutines exist for specialized functions. But, in essence, control programs manage data (input, output, storage, and retrieval), execute processing programs, and govern job preparation and scheduling.

Processing programs. **Service programs** are a major subclassification of processing software, performing calculations and other repetitive routines, such as sorting and merging which are frequently needed in business applications. Other service programs include automatic program testing and debugging software. Many service programs are unique to a machine, manufacturer, or environment, so they will not be specifically mentioned due to the lack of generality in their use.

Assemblers, compilers, and interpreters (translation programs to convert application program languages into machine language) are also classified as processing programs. In addition there are **housekeeping** or **utility programs.** These consist of programs needed for standard and frequent operations, such as listing data in storage, called **dumping,** or converting data from one storage medium to another.

Another set of processing programs is needed for the task of administering large data bases serving a large number of users. Existing operating systems have proved inadequate with the growth of common data bases, an increase in users, and the establishment of computer networks. Software to provide greater integration of data, complex file structures, online access, and additional facilities for data base reorganization, data privacy, breakdown recovery, and independence of applications programs has had to be developed. Software to perform these functions is called a **data base management system (DBMS).**

In brief, access to large and complex data bases is facilitated in DBMSs by software (a **data definition language (DDL)** and a **data manipulation language (DML)**)[3] which converts instructions in programs written in high level languages, such as FORTRAN or COBOL, into information that the operating system requires. Additional software, called the **data base manager,** guides the operating system in retrieving the needed data by keeping track of the logical and physical organization of all data in the base.

Not all computer systems require a DBMS, but some experts have predicted that by the mid 80s, 75 percent of data processing organizations will be DBMS users.[4] At present, much research is being conducted on DBMS topics, including research on query languages, graphic interfaces, data base definitions, data base restructuring, data and applications migration, and distributed data bases.[5] The spread of DBMS will also depend on the emergence of DBMS standards, the abatement of debate on data models, and the production of data base machines.

Applications software

Applications software is the second principal category of software. These programs are purchased or developed in-house to enable users to generate information or solve problems.

In the past a clear distinction existed between the applications software for scientific purposes and that for business purposes. Formerly, users in the natural sciences needed to solve complex formulas involving numerous computations but with relatively small input and output. In contrast, business applications generally required the handling of large volumes of input and output, but the actual computations were relatively simple and repetitive. As a result, computer hardware and software were designed either for scientific applications or for business applications.

This distinction has faded. Many computers are now designed to meet both scientific and business needs, and many programming languages available today claim capability over the entire range of prob-

---

[3]The word *language* in this context is confusing because DDL and DML are interface software, not languages in the strict sense.

[4]For a survey and comparison of data models for a DBMS, see *ACM Computing Surveys* 8, no. 1 (March 1976).

[5]For a report on ongoing research with 415 references, see C. Mohan, "An Overview of Recent Data Base Research," *Data Base* 10, no. 2 (Fall 1978), pp. 1–24.

lems.[6] Furthermore, many business applications, as in the area of planning and control, have scientific characteristics. For example, planning is often computation-intensive, involving statistics and regressive equations as complex as computations in scientific programs, though still a large volume of input and output must be processed as in other business applications.

Nevertheless, a distinction between scientific and business applications can still be made. The two utilize different hardware configurations, languages are designed to specialize in one of the two areas, and many programmers focus on only one type of application.

Since many firms have similar information requirements, programs using common decision rules (to perform statistical computations, sorting, merging, and standard applications, such as payroll and inventory control) can serve many organizations. Businesses needing such programs can save development costs and time by purchasing predeveloped **software packages** with self-supporting documentation for their needs. These programs may require modification, but generally they are ready for immediate use, a convenience that parallels that of canned food. Hence they are called **canned programs.**

Software packages are available for both scientific and business applications. Many vendors provide such packages free as a service to their customers. Other packages can be leased or purchased from **software houses,** companies that develop software.

SUMMARY AND CONCLUSIONS

Business data processing includes sorting, merging, calculations, summarizing, and reporting. To perform such processing, software is needed: applications software, which specifies decision rules and sequencing necessary for processing; and operations software, necessary for translating applications programs into machine language and for operating computer hardware.

A programming language is needed to implement a program. The most efficient language to run in terms of computer time is machine language, but this language is complex and difficult to learn. Languages closer to natural languages take more computer running time but are easier to learn and faster to write. Because skilled programmers are an expensive scarce resource while computer time is becoming cheaper, machine language is used infrequently in business today. Even operating systems are no longer always written in machine language.

---

[6]In the early days of computers, 25 percent of applications (or 90° of a pie) were scientific applications and 75 percent (270°) were business oriented. IBM's first computer claiming to serve 100 percent of users' needs (or 360° of the pie) was called the IBM 360.

Figure 3.6   **High and low language spectrum**

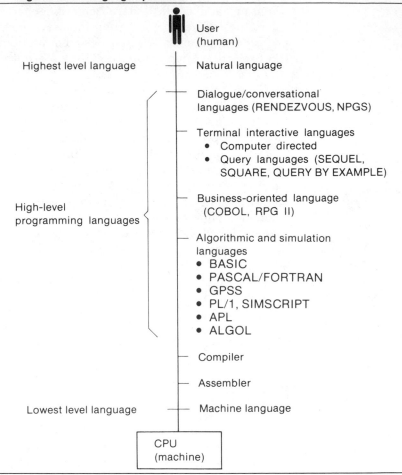

How one ranks computer languages in the high level category is subjective, depending on need and background. Languages commonly used for business applications are ranked according to the authors' point of view in Figure 3.6.

As for the future, software will become increasingly sophisticated, more user-friendly, and the number of applications programs will expand. Software costs will rise, becoming a larger share of the total system cost and approaching 90 percent for large systems. More special-purpose packages will appear in the 80s (many packages being sold off-the-shelf), and there will be more automation of the programming process. Users will benefit from greater discipline in software design and improved techniques in programming, such as structured techniques. Software in a language close to English, which enables a manager to enter input and generate output from a terminal in a conversational and interactive mode, is the trend of the future.

a

KEY WORDS

Address	Key data element
Application generator	Machine language
Applications software	Master file
Assembler	Menu
Assembly language	Monitor
Bits	Object program
Canned program	Operands
Characters	Operating program
Communications programs	Operating systems software
Compiler	Operators
Control programs	Portable
Controller	Processing program
Data base management system (DBMS)	Program
	Programmer
Data base manager	Programming language
Data definition language (DDL)	Record
Data elements	Report program generator (RPG)
Data manipulation language (DML)	Service program
	Software
Dumping	Software houses
Executive	Software package
File	Source program
Fourth generation language (4GL)	Storage location
Graphic language	Supervisor programs
Hardware	Terminal interactive language
High level language	Transaction file
Housekeeping program	Updating
Interpreter	Utility program
I/O control program	

DISCUSSION QUESTIONS

1. What is an operating system?

2. What is the difference between a natural language, such as English, and a formal programming language? Under what circumstances would it be desirable for programming languages to approach natural languages?

3. What factors must be considered when selecting a programming language for a given business problem?

4. What is a utility program? Are such programs useful in business processing? Give three examples. Where would you obtain a utility program?

5. What is a software package? Give three examples. How are packages used and where can they be obtained?

6. Would software packages be more appropriate for small rather than large businesses? Why? What are the limitations of packages? What are some advantages?

7. What are the limitations of all translator languages, including compilers?

8. What are the advantages and disadvantages of machine languages? When are machine languages used for business applications?

9. What knowledge of programming is essential for a middle or top business manager? If a language must be learned, what language(s) would you recommend for each level of management?

10. Distinguish between:
    a. Source and object program.
    b. Low and high level languages.
    c. Applications and systems programs.

11. Comment on this statement: Computers are neutral and unbiased, doing only what they are instructed to do. Who then is responsible for computer error?

SELECTED ANNOTATED BIBLIOGRAPHY

Calingert, Peter. *Operating System Elements: A User Perspective.* Englewood Cliffs, N.J.: Prentice-Hall, 1982. 240 p.
This book describes the assumptions underlying operating system design, the goals for which an operating system exists, and the techniques used to achieve these goals. The book is written for persons studying programming systems for the first time.

Edwards, Perry, and Broadwell, Bruce. *Data Processing.* Belmont, Calif: Wadsworth, 1979, pp. 174–292.
This is a module on programming languages including a sample business-

type problem solved in BASIC, FORTRAN IV, COBOL 1974, RPG II, PL/1, and APL and an evaluation of these languages. Well written with enough detail to appreciate the special characteristics of each language.

Everest, Gordon C. "Database Management Systems—A Tutorial." In *Readings in Management Information Systems,* ed. G. B. Davis and G. C. Everest. New York: McGraw-Hill, 1976.

An excellent tutorial written by a member of the CODASYL Systems Committee which authored the *Feature Analysis of Generalized Data Base Management Systems.* Discusses the concepts and functions of a DBMS.

Heidom, G. E. "Automatic Programming through Natural Language Dialogue: A Survey." *IBM Journal of Research and Development* 20, no. 4 (July 1976), pp. 302–13.

An excellent survey of the use of natural languages for programming. Applications for queuing, accounting, and customized business are discussed. Numerous examples of output are displayed. The article also includes a discussion of research issues.

O'Brien, James A. *Computers in Business Management: An Introduction.* Homewood, Ill.: Richard D. Irwin, 1982, pp. 146–72.

An excellent treatment of software. Nothing on languages but a survey of all programs needed to run a computer system.

Pratt, Terrence W. *Programming Languages: Design and Implementation.* Englewood Cliffs, N.J.: Prentice-Hall, 1975, 530 p.

This is a text for computer science courses on programming languages. However, it is neither technical nor mathematical. It describes seven languages (FORTRAN, ALGOL 60, COBOL, PL/1, LISP 1.5, SNOBOL 4, and APL) and evaluates them in terms of structure, simplicity, clarity and unity of language concept, ease of extension, external support, and efficiency.

Sammet, Jean E. "The Use of English as a Programming Language." *Communications of the ACM* 9, no. 3 (March 1966), pp. 228–30.

This 1966 article has a high ratio of still pertinent and provocative problems raised per page.

Schlussel, George. "When Not to Use a Data Base," *Datamation* 21, no. 11 (November 1975), pp. 82, 91, and 98.

A short article cautioning users against joining the bandwagon of DBMS.

Wegner, Peter. "Programming Languages: The First 25 Years." *IEEE Transactions on Computers* C-25, no. 12 (December 1976), pp. 1207–25.

The author discusses 30 milestones in the history of programming. Thirteen milestones concern development. Evaluated are assemblers, FORTRAN, ALGOL 60, COBOL 61, ALGOL 68, SIMULA 67, and LISP. Ten milestones are programming concepts and theories, and the remaining seven concern software engineering technology. The article is descriptive with the technical portion separated so it can be easily skipped. The author captures the sense of excitement and the enormous variety of activity that was characteristic of the first 25 years of programming.

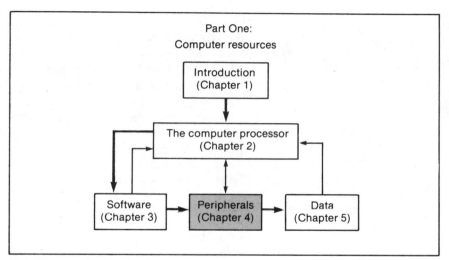

Note: The thin arrows represent the flow of data and information. The thick arrows show the sequential flow of the parts of the book.

CHAPTER 4

Peripherals

If computers are so fast, why do we spend so much time waiting around the computer center?

Computer graffiti

Peripherals are units of equipment distinct from the central processing unit which provide the system with outside communication. Included are input/output devices, auxiliary storage units, and communications equipment. Formerly such equipment was under the jurisdiction of data processing personnel. But with distributed data processing and the trend toward easy-to-operate, less expensive peripherals, managers today may select peripherals and supervise their use.

This chapter will examine the characteristics, capabilities, and limitations of peripherals. Peripherals represent a major share of hardware costs, as high as 90 percent in some operations.

INPUT EQUIPMENT

Humans collect data to be processed by the computer. Units that are used to get the data into the CPU from the human user are called **input devices.** Input devices may be **offline,** not directly under control of the CPU, or **online,** in which case the device communicates directly with the CPU.

Of all peripherals, input equipment is the most troublesome from management's point of view because input is human-intensive, prone to error. Users, not skilled EDP operators, prepare input and operate input equipment, often at remote sites where technical assistance is

51

unavailable. Minimizing errors and seeing that the equipment is maintained and efficiently operated is management's responsibility.

Furthermore, input equipment is the greatest bottleneck in computing operations. CPU speed is measured in nanoseconds, input speed in seconds when input is initiated by humans. **Input-bound systems** result when data waiting to be processed by high speed computers backlogs due to the slowness of input equipment. Correcting this situation through purchase of new devices or revised approaches to input preparation is also a problem for management.

Cards are still used for input, though they are becoming outdated. Keypunch equipment is needed to convert the input data onto the cards (a machine-readable medium), a verifier checks the accuracy of the keypunching, and a card reader then transfers the data from the cards to the computer.

Figure 4.1 shows examples of **conversion equipment** and input devices for input which is noncard at the time of input. The top path, in which a document is encoded on magnetic tape, is an example of offline input. But this same document read by a scanner is converted online (bottom path) when the scanner transmits directly to the CPU.

Figure 4.1   **Noncard input to a computerized information system**

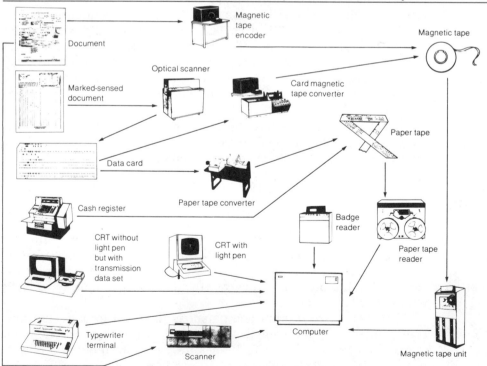

Online input is reducing in price, becoming increasingly competitive with offline equipment, such as card and paper tape readers and mark-sense scanning offline devices. Also, online conversion reduces the opportunities for human error. Types of online input terminals commonly used in business are described below.

Online terminals

Terminals connected to the CPU can be used exclusively for input, or for both input and output. Figure 4.2 shows the variety of terminals available. An **intelligent terminal** is one that is programmable. It might incorporate a minicomputer capable of performing computing tasks without using the mainframe CPU (such as editing and validating data at the point of entry, a feature that helps reduce operator errors). Such intelligent terminals are useful in banking, reservations, insurance, and accounting applications where data entry volume is large. A **dumb terminal** enters data and programs, and solves problems online, with the CPU doing all the processing.

Terminal input may be keyed, scanned, or collected by voice recognition equipment. Each of these input methods will be described below.

Keyed input. Many terminals have a keyboard like a typewriter, with added push buttons for calling upon programs from the central computer facility to solve problems. A **teletype terminal** (one example) can have both input and output capabilities. Slowness is the major problem with this device because input is limited by the operator's typing ability, and output by teletype speed.

Figure 4.2   **Classification of terminals**

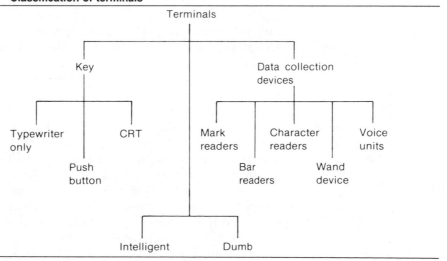

CRTs (cathode ray tube terminals) also key input which is displayed on a screen resembling that of a TV. Information may appear character by character or page by page. In either case each character can be addressed (accessed) for making changes. The screen is a grid with characters at intersections of two coordinates. An operator moves a **cursor,** a symbol such as a dash, to locations on this grid by pressing the cursor key. Wherever the cursor is stationed, a character may be entered to fill the space or replace an existing character. Some systems use a symbol operated by a control lever called a **joystick** (instead of a cursor), or a physical device called a **mouse,** but the principle is the same.

The page image will fade unless it is **refreshed** (continually redisplayed), a process which requires added hardware capability, increasing the price of the CRT unit. There is the additional cost of an add-on printer if a hard copy of the screen image is desired. Ordering merchandise, recording inventory levels, and accounting are examples of business applications for which the CRT is particularly well suited.

Some CRTs also have **graphic capabilities.** Lines and curves can be drawn on the tube so that vectors rather than characters are displayed. These are generated by a computer program which locates points on the screen matrix and joins them in the desired pattern. Graphic CRTs have different features which vary in cost and sophistication. Some have a data tablet that digitizes the coordinates of points on a hand-drawn sketch. Others have blinking characters (for emphasis), brightness and color choice, zooming and scaling (enlargement and reduction), character reversal, protected formats, partial screen transmission, or the ability to overstrike a character—to mention just a few of the features available.

The use of graphic CRTs for production design is an application that has been used extensively in the automotive and electronics industries. Visual display is also appropriate for computer-assisted instruction, drafting and mapping, chart preparation, blueprints, and layouts.

Some CRT terminals use a **light pen** instead of (or in addition to) a cursor to indicate position on the face of the CRT. The usual light pen is a hand-held pencil-like device, attached to the CRT by an electrical cable, with a photosensitive element hardly larger than a pin head at one end. This element is held touching the CRT screen and it generates an electrical pulse when the position to which it is pointing is swept by the writing beam within the CRT. The associated circuitry and software relates the timing of these impulses to the position of the pen. The light pen can be used to draw lines and figures on the screen, to indicate and move portions of drawings around the screen, and to make a choice between menu items. The pen itself is not expensive, but the software that must accompany it is.

Heat- and touch-sensitive CRT screens are also being developed to supplement keyed input. Since input peripherals are the focus of much research at the present time, one can expect that input technology will advance at a fast pace in coming years, especially in the area of scanning equipment.[1]

Data scanning terminals. Some terminals scan documents such as inventory tags, plastic credit cards, or badges, converting the data on these into computer-readable form and storing the information for later processing. The data needs to be prerecorded on the object to be scanned in the form of special marks, bars, or characters. Such online input terminals eliminate the labor and error of operator data conversion and reduce the time required for data entry. However, documents in poor condition (smudges, creases, tears, or dirt) can be misread.

One scanning device commonly found in retail stores is a portable wand which resembles a plastic pistol. The **wand,** connected by cable to the data collection terminal, captures data through a sensor at its tip when waved past a bar tag or encoded data, such as the Universal Product Code (UPC) on grocery labels.

Voice recognition equipment. **Voice recognition equipment** is another type of pattern recognition device used for input. Such equipment is conceptually similar to optical scanners in that patterns are traced and represented by a set of bits (0 and 1 bits). However, converting speech, an airborne signal, into digital data is a far more complex process than reading marks or bars, for voice patterns include variables in sound, pitch, tone, and loudness. Pronunciation also varies from individual to individual, and a person's mood, circumstance, or health can affect speech characteristics. Furthermore, telephone lines distort voice signals. A voiced command given by more than one speaker will not sound exactly alike even when identical words are used, nor will an exact match of voice patterns occur with the same speaker over time.

One method of overcoming some of the problems listed above is to store voice profiles of individual users. In a get-acquainted session, the computer flashes vocabulary words on a screen which the user repeatedly vocalizes, creating a voice profile which the computer stores. Another approach is to store a set of standard voices for a limited vocabulary, a vocabulary chosen according to the client's use of voice recognition equipment. Such an approach would permit travelers to request timetable or gate number information at railway stations or airports, for example.

---

[1]For more on this subject, see Tom Logsdon, *Computers and Social Controversy* (Potomac, Maryland: Computer Press, 1980), pp. 281–306.

At present, voice recognition is effective only for limited applications. Each word pronounced by the client must be surrounded by an overlay of silence extending $\frac{1}{10}$ to $\frac{1}{4}$ of a second. A string of words in a sentence or words spoken quickly require a storage capacity and processing time far too expensive for practical use. In the future, however, advances in technology of voice reproduction and reduction in memory costs will undoubtedly make voice recognition units for even large vocabularies cost-effective.

Voice recognition devices are currently in use in factories where the hands of an employee are busy so that data entry by typewriter or optical scanner would break hand motion, reducing throughput. Instead, the worker voices input through a headset, continuing prescribed hand tasks. This adds one more dimension and source of input and increases productivity. Voice recognition can also be used for identification purposes in restricted areas of factories, or as security in banking or cash dispensing.

STORAGE

The characteristics of peripheral **storage devices** are summarized in Table 4.1. The **cassette** and **floppy disk** are products of recent technology. Both are compact, cheap, and very simple to operate, though of the two the floppy disk (or **diskette**) is the more useful because it allows random access. It is also popular because it can be handled, even transported in a notebook or attaché case, without being damaged. Floppies come in different sizes (5 to 8 inches in diameter), store data on one or two sides, and have a capacity of bytes measured in millions. They are replacing cards, cartridges, and even cassettes for cheap medium-size storage, complementing other new storage technology for large memories, such as bubble memory, charged coupled devices, and random access memory using metal-oxide semiconductor technology.

OUTPUT PERIPHERALS

Figure 4.3 illustrates common **output devices** and media. Note that terminals and CRTs discussed earlier in this chapter as input devices can serve for output as well. A printer is an example of equipment used solely for output. The characteristics of major output equipment are summarized in Table 4.2.

COM (computer output on **microfilm** or **microfiche**) reduces the volume of printed paper in a business, saving space and storage costs, but a large capital investment is needed for the special equipment

Table 4.1   Characteristics of external storage equipment

Equipment	Media	Primary functions	Typical I/O speed range	Typical storage capacity	Major advantages and/or disadvantages
Magnetic tape drive	Magnetic tape	Secondary storage (sequential access) and input/output	15,000–340,000 bps (bytes per second)	Up to 160 million characters per tape reel	Inexpensive, with a fast transfer rate, but only sequential access
Magnetic tape cassette	Magnetic tape cassette	Secondary storage and input/output	3,000–5,000 cps (characters per second)	1–2 million characters/unit	Small, inexpensive, and convenient, but only sequential access
Magnetic strip storage unit	Magnetic strip cartridge	Mass secondary storage	Data transfer: 25,000–55,000 cps Access time: up to several seconds	Up to 500 billion bytes per unit	Relatively inexpensive, large capacity, but slow access time
Magnetic disk drive	Magnetic disk	Secondary storage (direct access) and input/output	Data transfer: 100,000–1,000,000 bps Access time: 20–200 ms (microseconds)	Up to 100 million characters per disk pack	Large capacity, fast direct access storage device (DASD), but expensive
Floppy disk drive	Magnetic diskette	Input/output and secondary storage	10,000 cps	250,000 to 1,500,000 characters/disk	Small, inexpensive, and convenient, but slower and smaller capacity than other DASDs
Magnetic drum unit	Magnetic drum	Secondary storage and input/output	Data transfer: 230,000–1,500,000 bps Access time: 10–100 ms	Up to 200 million characters	Fast access time and large capacity, but expensive

Source: James A. O'Brien, *Computers in Business Management* (Homewood, Ill.: Richard D. Irwin, 1975), p. 85

Figure 4.3   **Output devices and media**

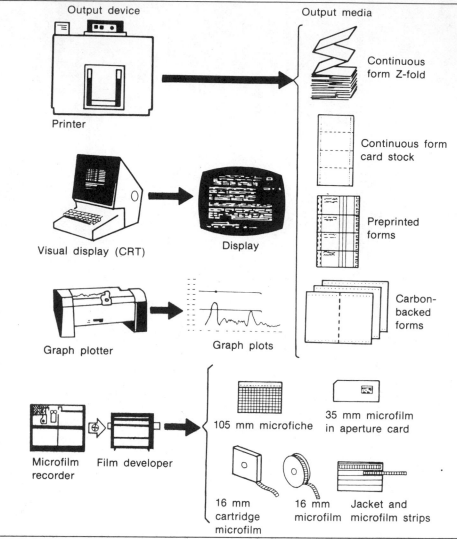

required to read and to print hard copies of film or fiche. Updating is also expensive and time-consuming, so this media is not appropriate for operational data. At the present time COM is cost-effective only when output volume is large and the frequency of retrieval small.

Voice output reverses the process of voice recognition discussed earlier. Digitized data of the human voice for a given vocabulary is

Table 4.2   **Characteristics of major output equipment**

Equipment	Media	Primary functions	I/O Speed range	Major advantages and/or disadvantages
Line printer	Paper (hard copy)	Printed output of paper reports and documents	200–11,000 lpm (lines per minute) 10–400 cps (characters per second)	Fast and low-cost hard copy, but inconvenient and bulky
CRT terminal	"Soft" display	Keyboard input and output	250–50,000 cps output	Convenient and inexpensive, but limited display capacity and no hard copy
Plotter	Paper	Output	Resolution of up to 200 points per inch of output	Important when graphic output is needed; expensive, especially the table model that can plot back and forth
Computer output, on microfilm, (COM)	Microfilm spool/ strips/ cartridge Microfiche Aperture card	Output that has archival significance	1,000–30,000 lpm	Reduces paper volume drastically, faster to retrieve than paper but requires special equipment to read and print hard copy. Expensive to update.

stored in the computer memory. To verbalize a message, a microprocessor selects the desired words, strings them together, draws the digitized data for these words from the memory, and converts the data to an analog signal through filters and amplifiers. Speech synthesis has improved in recent years. Computers today can speak with variable pitch and loudness, can phrase sentences with appropriate pauses, and even reproduce regional and local accents.

Voice output has numerous applications. It can supplement visual display in computer-assisted instruction, and aid in teaching and translating foreign languages. In data processing, validation of input by audio feedback improves efficiency. Errors often pass undetected when operators check input documents against input entry on a CRT screen with eyes shifting from document to screen. Errors are caught more easily during audio validation when the eyes of the operator focus solely on the input document. However, voice output raises noise levels, a good example of how the solution to one problem creates another.

TELEPROCESSING EQUIPMENT

Though processing by a CPU is measured in nanoseconds, users do not benefit from this speed if the time required to move data to and from the computer is slow. Cards and paper printouts create delays simply because of their bulk. Even with the use of compact tapes, diskettes, or cassettes, transfer of input from dispersed locations, such as sales offices, branch offices, or plants, to a centralized computer may be time-consuming, as the process of delivering output may be.

Teleprocessing to instantly transmit input and output is one method of speeding operations. The term *teleprocessing* is often used as a synonym for *telecommunications*, and may mean both the communication of data and its related processing. Teleprocessing equipment transfers data and information between computers and users at remote points by telephone, satellite, or some other communication channel. Two types of specialized equipment are needed: data transmission media, and equipment to transmit and receive the data from the communication line.

Data transmission

Data transmitted through telecommunication channels may be moved only a few feet within a single office building or thousands of miles. Regardless of distance, three variables exist in data transmission: types of channels, speed of transmission, and mode of transmission.

Types of channels.   A communication line or channel can be simplex, half duplex, or full duplex. These channels are compared in Figure 4.4. The **simplex channel** enables communication of information in only one direction, from source to computer or from computer to user. No interchange is possible. There is no indication of readiness to accept transmission nor any acknowledgment of transmission received. A **half-duplex system** allows sequential transmission of data in both directions, but this involves a delay when the direction is reversed. The ability to transmit simultaneously in both directions requires a **duplex** or **full duplex system.** Though more costly, this system decreases processing time because it enables output to be displayed on a terminal while input is still being sent.

Speed of transmission.   Transmission of data is measured in **baud.** In most communication lines, a baud is one bit per second. The capacity of the channel is a data rate called **bandwidths** or **bands.** This gives a measure of the amount of data which can be transmitted in a unit of time.

By combining speeds, bandwidths, and types of channels, one has a spectrum of capabilities, the cheapest and most limited being a simplex telegraphic grade channel, the most versatile and expensive being a full duplex broadband system.

Figure 4.4

Types of channels in telecommunications

Type	Transmission direction	Graphic representation	Example
Simplex	One direction only	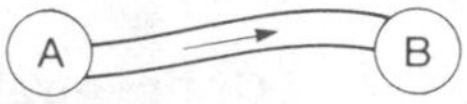 A → B	• Radio • Television
Half duplex	One direction only at any one time. Can be in both directions in sequence	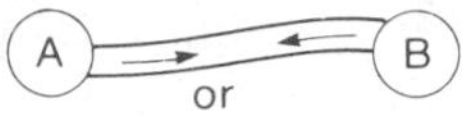 A ⇄ B or	• Walkie-talkie • Intercom
Duplex or Full duplex	In both directions simultaneously	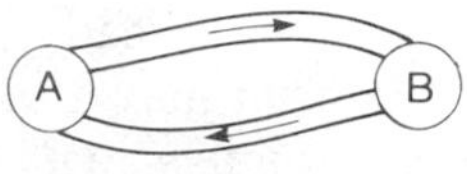 A ⇄ B	• Picture-telephone • Dedicated separate transmission lines (such as a presidential "hot line")

Modes of communication services. There are over 2,000 telecommunication carriers in the United States. AT&T for telephone and Western Union for wire and microwave radio communications are two of the better-known large companies. In addition, there are specialized common carriers, such as MCI and Datron, which provide point-to-point or switched services in heavy traffic areas. These services send data over public lines passing through exchanges and switching facilities called **switched lines.** In contrast, users have full access to the line on **private** or **leased lines.** Some companies with private lines connecting branches and plants refer to their private lines as **tie lines.**

Carriers in the United States are licensed by the FCC (Federal Communications Commission), which regulates services and transmission by wire, radio, satellite, telephone, television, telegraph, facsimile (documents) and telephoto.

Equipment at the users' end

A user needs a terminal, a multiplexer or concentrator, and a modem when transmitting and receiving data to and from a computer over a communication line.

Terminals. **Terminals** have been described earlier in this chapter. They may be intelligent or nonintelligent keyboard terminals, video display units, Touch-Tone phones, input readers such as card, tape or OCRs, or voice recognition devices.

Multiplexer. A **multiplexer** improves transmission efficiency by combining multiple lines from terminals of slow transmission speeds into one fast broadbeam transmission line. Multiplexer functions at the terminal end in both receiving and transmitting data are illustrated in Figure 4.5.

Concentrator.   A multiplexer assumes that all terminals need equal priority of access and have equal density of use. When some terminals operate less frequently than others, resulting in underutilization of transmission lines, slow terminal lines can be concentrated into a few faster channels for transmission. This is done by a device called a **concentrator.**

A concentrator serving many terminals will poll each terminal. If one is ready to transmit or needs to receive data, it is then engaged. A user may also initiate a request for service. If all channels are engaged, the user will get a busy signal and must wait in turn. Terminals share a channel, unlike multiplexing where each terminal has its own channel. The optimal number of channels and terminals per concentrator depends on the frequency of terminal use, the average time spent per usage, the cost of equipment, and cost of waiting by a user.

Also unlike a multiplexer, the concentrator performs intelligent functions such as routing messages and checking for codes and errors. Some of these functions are performed by minicomputers which also control part of the communications network.

Modem.   Data from a terminal or a computer are in digital signals, while the transmission is in analog signals (except for recent transmission modes such as satellites). A digital-analog converter, called a **modulator,** is used for sending data and an analog-digital converter, called a **demodulator,** is used for receipt of data. The modulator/demodulator is commonly called a **modem.** An illustration of the digital

Figure 4.5   **Multiplexer**

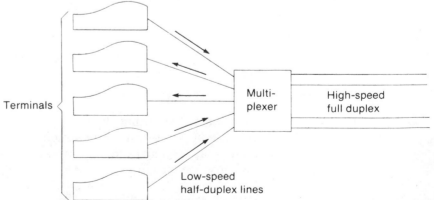

Figure 4.6   **Digital and analog signals**

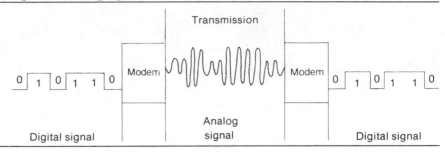

and analog signals and their conversion by a modem is shown in Figure 4.6.

Equipment at the computer end

Computer systems utilize interface equipment between data transmission and the CPU for the following functions:

1. To compensate for the relatively slow speed of transmission compared to the speed of the computer.
2. To check security authorization.
3. To translate transmission codes.
4. To exchange recognition signals with the terminal, referred to as **handshaking.**
5. To detect errors and take corrective action where necessary.
6. To edit and preprocess data.
7. To route messages according to priority of messages.
8. To buffer and store information before routing, if necessary.
9. To keep communication teleprocessing statistics.

Some general purpose computers equipped for remote communications have internal capabilities to handle some or most of the above functions. But when the number of terminals serviced is large and the data processed voluminous, channels become clogged and the **buffer** (a storage device) swamped with messages for the CPU. Consequently, the efficiency and effectiveness of the computing system drops below acceptable levels.

To alleviate this problem, equipment called a **front-end processor** can be programmed to relieve the CPU or host computer of teleprocessing responsibilities. The front-end programmable processor is cheaper and more easily maintained, programmed, and modified than the host computer because of its more limited and specialized functions, and because of its detachment from the CPU.

Figure 4.7 shows a sample configuration for a front-end processor with many **ports** or connection points for transmission lines and many terminal devices. Companies differ in system configuration and

Figure 4.7   **One configuration of a front-end processor**

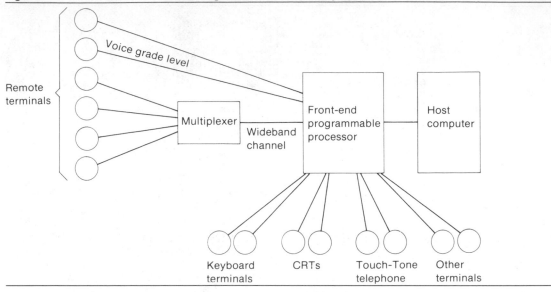

have front-end processors with different capabilities. Some front-end processors are capable of:

1. Message switching between terminals.
2. Performing stand-alone data processing when the teleprocessing load is low or absent.
3. Accepting messages from local lines with mixed communication modes of transmission.
4. Performing the function of multiplexers and concentrators.
5. Providing access to external storage and other peripherals.
6. Facilitating time sharing.
7. Supporting network processing.

SUMMARY AND CONCLUSIONS

Peripherals are needed for input, output and storage of data. They are also needed to transmit data to and from the CPU when the user is remote from the computer. Some peripherals are acquired and maintained by EDP personnel though shared by all users in an organization. For example, printers, plotters, large storage devices, and front-end processors would fall into this category. Other equipment, such as optical character readers and COM devices, though technical, may be under the user's jurisdiction. User responsibility is generally for equipment that is compact, easy to operate, and inexpensive—

equipment that can be employed in conjunction with minis and micros in a distributive processing environment such as point-of-sale terminals, data entry terminals, floppy diskettes and diskette drives, and scanners.

Figure 4.8 summarizes common input, output, and storage media

Figure 4.8   **Summary of input, output, and storage media and peripherals**

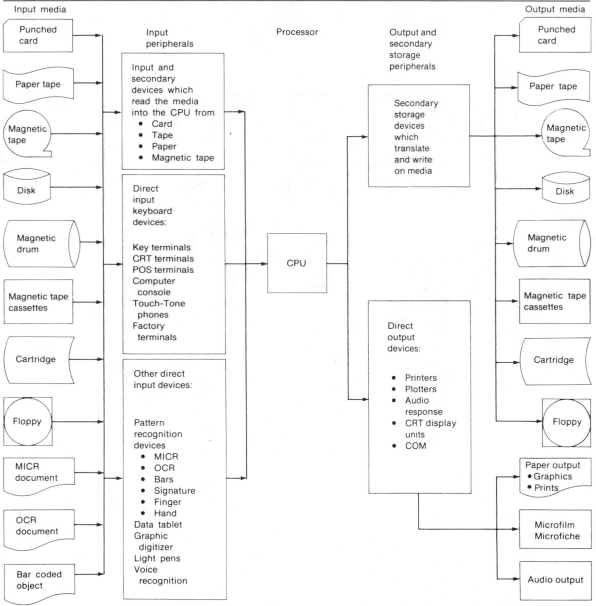

and equipment. Figure 4.9 shows peripheral devices used in telecommunications. The peripheral market is extremely volatile, with new companies and equipment continually entering into competition; therefore no attempt has been made in this chapter to identify actual equipment models, manufacturers, or prices or to mention all devices available. Technological advances mean that the performance of all peripherals is improving while prices are dropping. Whenever peripherals are needed, a cost-benefit study should be made of available equipment to determine which models are cost-effective in view of an individual firm's requirements.

Figure 4.9   **Examples of transmission modes and input/output devices**

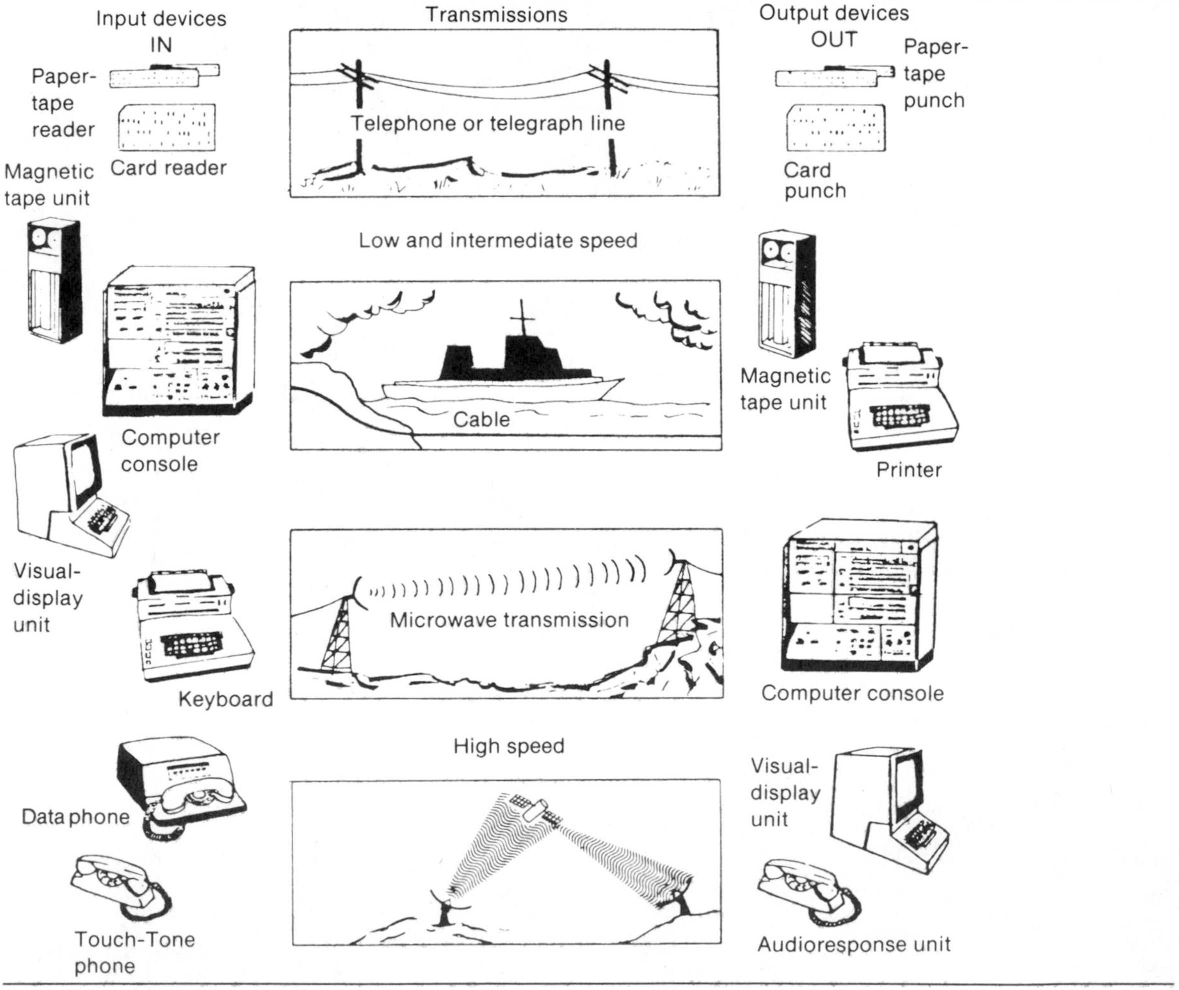

Source: Andrew Vazsonyi, *Introduction to Data Processing,* 3rd ed. (Homewood, Ill.: Richard D. Irwin, 1980), p. 223.

KEY WORDS

Bands

Bandwidths

Baud

Buffer

Cathode ray tube (CRT)

COM

Concentrator

Conversion equipment

Cursor

Demodulator

Diskette

Dumb terminal

Duplex system

Floppy disk

Front-end processor

Full duplex system

Graphic capabilities

Half-duplex system

Handshaking

Input-bound systems

Input device

Intelligent terminal

Joystick

Leased line

Light pen

Microfiche

Microfilm

Modem

Modulator

Mouse

Multiplexer

Offline

Online

Output device

Peripherals

Port

Private line

Refreshed

Simplex channel

Storage device

Switched line

Teleprocessing

Teletype terminal

Terminal

Tie line

Voice recognition equipment

Wand

DISCUSSION QUESTIONS

1. What is the difference between online and offline devices? Give three examples of each. What circumstances favor each?

2. Compare printers, CRTs, and COMs as computer output devices. Cite business examples where each has the comparative advantage.

3. When would voice input and output be appropriate? Why is voice recognition equipment limited in use at the present time?

4. What is a light pen? Explain its uses.

5. Are peripherals essential to the operation of a computer? How do they contribute to the performance of a computer?

6. Compare the advantages and disadvantages of:

     a. Remote and console terminals.
     b. Badge and audio terminals.
     c. Tape and disk storage.
     d. Intelligent and dumb terminals.
     e. Simplex and duplex transmission channels.
     f. Multiplexers and concentrators.

7. Why are telecommunications important to computer processing?

8. What are the main components of a telecommunication system? Draw a diagram showing these components. Describe the interrelationships which exist between the components.

9. What functions are performed by a front-end processor? Under what circumstances is a front-end processor necessary or desirable? Give examples.

10. Discuss the factors which a firm must consider in choosing teleprocessing equipment.

SELECTED ANNOTATED BIBLIOGRAPHY

Axner, David H., and Fonnie H. Regan. "Alphanumeric Display Terminal Survey." *Datamation* 24, no. 6 (June 1978), pp. 183–219.

170 products from 76 vendors are evaluated in this article in terms of model highlights, display features, communication facilities, keyboard, and peripheral pricing.

This survey will undoubtedly be outdated by the time this review is read. That is the nature of the computer industry, particularly with regard to peripherals. The purpose of this citation is to draw attention to surveys and evaluation articles that appear periodically in the literature, in publications such as *Datamation, Mini-Micro Systems, Infosystems, Datapro,* and *Data World.*

Datapro Research Corporation. *Datapro '70.*

This is a looseleaf reference service in three volumes on computer equipment, software, media, and supplies. New products are described and evaluated. For peripherals, see volume 3. In addition to product briefs, there is a periodic update section called "All about . . ." Some of the topics covered are display terminals, printers, disk drives, disk packs, data entry devices, key entry and data collection equipment, COM, optical readers, and plotters. In each case, the state of the art is reviewed, the advantages and limitations discussed, vendors' names and addresses listed, and most important of all, models on the market are evaluated in detail.

Datapro is a consumer's guide written in nontechnical language. In a competitive and innovative industry, this is a valuable reference for anyone planning to acquire computer equipment. *Data World* is a similar reference service.

FitzGerald, Jerry, and Tom S. Eason. *Fundamentals of Data Communications.* New York: John Wiley & Sons, 1978.

An excellent text, covering communication concepts, hardware, software, and errors, as well as networks and common carriers.

IBM Systems Journal 18, no. 2 (1979), pp. 186–350.
This is a special issue on telecommunications, including IBM's own use of telecommunications, one of the most advanced telecommunications systems in existence, with 8,200 devices, applications, and its communication architecture, the SNA. Also discussed are emerging international telecommunications standards and three excellent nontechnical articles by Halsey et al. on public networks, their evolution, interfaces, and status; an article by Frazer on the future of telecommunications; and a tutorial on network architecture and protocols by Greer.

Kimbleton, Stephen R., and Michael G. Schneider. "Computer Communication Networks: Approaches, Objectives and Performance Considerations." *Computing Surveys* 7, no. 3 (September 1975), pp. 129–73.
This comprehensive survey is addressed to the nonspecialist. It describes network functional components and their interaction. It advances the hypothesis that the packet-switched networks provide the most appropriate technology for supporting multimodel traffic between hosts. The functional components of the packet switch are examined. The paper concludes with a description of three networking examples and identification of areas for future research. The article has a detailed bibliography of 191 references.

Martin, James. *Future Developments in Telecommunications*, 2d ed. Englewood Cliffs, N.J.: Prentice-Hall, 1977.
This is the fourth book written by the author on teleprocessing. It discusses the use of teleprocessing, its synthesis and technology. Like other Martin books, this one is very well organized and illustrated.

Mayo, John S. "The Role of Microelectronics in Communication." *Scientific American* 237, no. 3 (September 1977), pp. 192–208.
A well-illustrated nontechnical discussion of a technical subject. This issue is a special one on microelectronics as it relates to computing. It is also available in a separately bound volume as a *Scientific American Book*. Highly recommended as a tutorial for a layman on microelectronics, microprocessors, and microcomputers.

Rothfeder, Jeffrey. "Networking the Workplace." *Personal Computing* 7, no. 7 (June 1983), pp. 79–87.
An excellent discussion of LANs (local area networks) that claims increased efficiency, better informed managers, and less downtime on peripherals.

Sanders, Ray W. "Comparing Network Technology." *Datamation* 24, no. 7 (July 1978), pp. 88–93.
This article discusses digital switching and includes a detailed survey of 10 years of packet switching.

White, Wade, and Morris Holmes. "The Future of Commercial Satellite Telecommunication." *Datamation* 24, No. 7 (July 1978), pp. 94–102.
An excellent, well-illustrated article on a little-documented subject. Has details on one system: TDMA (Time-Division Multiple Access).

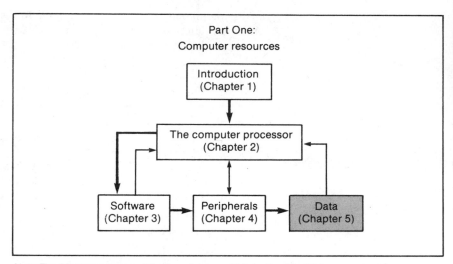

Note: The thin arrows represent the flow of data and information. The thick arrows show the sequential flow of the parts of the book.

CHAPTER 5

Data

If you want to converse with me, define your terms.
Voltaire

The input of computer processing is data prepared in machine-readable form according to prescribed conventions, the **data** being a representation of facts, concepts, or instructions necessary for decision making or operations. Data may be collected and stored for each processing activity, but, more commonly, data records are consolidated in a **data base.** A **common data base** consists of an integrated data base shared by organizational units within an enterprise.

The value of an information system is directly related to the quality of the data base. Garbage in–garbage out is an apropos data processing cliché. To ensure that output is meaningful, that an information system does, in fact, provide useful information for decision making, management must be involved in the creation and maintenance of data bases. Indeed, data management is an integral part of computer resource management. The purpose of this chapter is to introduce data technology and data management to readers, to describe how data is created, organized, prepared, stored, accessed, maintained, and controlled.

DATA ELEMENTS

Recorded facts or observations are one type of data. 3258 is data, but abstract data. 3258 could be an invoice number, an account number, a machine part number, or an employee number. The data needs to be related or associated with a specific entity in order to be meaningful.

Let us assume that 3258 is the employee number of Mr. Jones. Other attributes about Mr. Jones might also be collected, such as age, marital status, or address. An attribute for which data is collected is called a **data element.** The data element "employee number" for Jones has the value 3258. The data element "name," in this case, has the value JONES. The value of the data element "sex" is MALE for Jones, or a code representation meaning male, such as 2. These data elements form a logical grouping yielding the information: Jones, employee number 3258, is male. By collecting other data on Jones, such as academic record, date hired, or weekly pay, a **logical record** of employee Jones can be created.

There are many kinds of data elements. A summary list of data elements commonly used in information systems, classified by function, appears in Table 5.1. When a data base is designed, managers and analysts decide what functional data elements need to be collected to produce desired system output. The process of determining what data elements are needed is described in the next section of this chapter.

Another method of classifying data elements is by source. Facts and observations are examples of **primitive data,** also called **raw data.** Assigned codes belong to this category as well.

In addition to raw data, data may be **derived.** That is, data can be determined by manipulating or processing data elements. For example, the data element "average number of hours worked per employee" is calculated by dividing the data element "total number of hours worked" by the data element "number of employees." Another example would be values for the data element "age of employee." The value of this data element could be derived from the employee's date of birth and the current date.

Though the actual computation is done by computer program, management is responsible for specifying derivation rules. In the above examples, the rules are obvious, but in many instances alternative ways of deriving data exist. For example, firms differ in procedures

Table 5.1   **Classification of data elements by function**

Data elements by function	Person with prime responsibility
Transaction Reference	Manager
Planning Linking Control Security	Manager and analyst
Identification Checking Other data elements	Analyst

for calculating markups and discounts. When derived data is included in the data base, the formula or algorithm used must be defined and documented.

Still another type of data, classified by source, is **estimated data.** The value of the data element "future cost of production" is an example. Estimated data elements are commonly used in planning.

SELECTING DATA ELEMENTS FOR COLLECTION

Data elements are often used for generating more than one report. When a common data base already exists, data elements needed for new reports may already be in the system. To identify these existing data elements, an **input/output table (I/O table)** can be used.

An example of an I/O table is shown in Table 5.2. The table has a horizontal axis listing output reports and files. The vertical axis lists data elements necessary for these reports. When new reports are added to the system, new columns are added to the table. Data elements already existing in the system required for these reports are checked off. If the new report requires data not in the common data base, a new row to the I/O table will be necessary and additional data must be collected.

Sometimes needed data can be derived from existing data in the system. For example, if the company represented in Table 5.2 were to require the age of each employee for a new report (Report 3), this information could be calculated from the date of birth already in the data base in File 1. Note that Report 3 is from a different file from that in which date of birth is stored. In such cases, a linking data element

Table 5.2   **Partial I/O table**

Files / Reports Data elements (inputs)	File 1		File 2
	Report 1	Report 2	Report 3
1. Employee ID (identification no.)	X	X	X
2. Name	X	X	
3. Address	X	X	
4. Date of birth	X	X	
5. Sex		X	
6. Academic qualifications			X
7. Field of specialization			X
8. Years of experience			X
9. Year of first employment		X	

is needed to connect the two files in processing in order to derive the needed data. (Linking is described later in this chapter.)

Data elements excluded from an I/O table include the report heading names or column headings that appear on output. Also excluded are data elements written into the applications programs such as norms for checking value weights and control-related data. Page numbers and subtotals of totals (derived data) would also be created by programs. In addition, the computer generates data such as time and date, which appear on printouts at the time of processing. None of these data elements need be included in the I/O table since they are of a technical nature, the responsibility of EDP personnel.

The identification of data elements that need to be collected when a report or file is designed is deduced after studying the information needs of management and the output required. For example, if a personnel report is expected to list the number of female professional employees with masters degrees as output, the input for such a report must include data on the academic qualifications and sex of each employee. Similarly, if a report on accounts receivable is to show the distribution of aging of accounts (that is, the distribution of the time the accounts are outstanding), the input for the report must include the invoice dates so that aging can be calculated. If a report is expected to compare dollar values of sales with quotas for each sales representative, then both quotas and sales would have to be entered as input. In other words, corporate goals and information needs of management at all levels must studied and from these needs the data elements required for reports ascertained.

An illustration of this process is shown in Figure 5.1. Here the information needs of a production distribution company are analyzed.[1] A chart has been prepared listing company goals: decreased administrative overhead, improved inventory control, shortened accounts receivable cycle, and increased sales activity. For simplicity's sake, only one of the goals is subdivided in Figure 5.1, that of shortening the cycle of accounts receivable, and only one of these subgoals, filling orders quickly, is further traced to the report level. From the reports identified in the chart, an I/O table, Table 5.3, has been prepared. This I/O table would be merged to an I/O table previously compiled for data elements in the firm's data base (if a data base already exists). By studying the table, analysts can learn which data elements need collection for the new reports and which already exist in the data base.

Data elements for future requirements should also be included in a data base. Adding data elements after a common data base has been

---

[1]For details, see Thomas R. Finneran and J. Shirley Henry, "Structured Analysis for Data Base Design," *Datamation* 23, no. 11 (November 1977), pp. 99–113.

Figure 5.1   **Analysis of information needs**

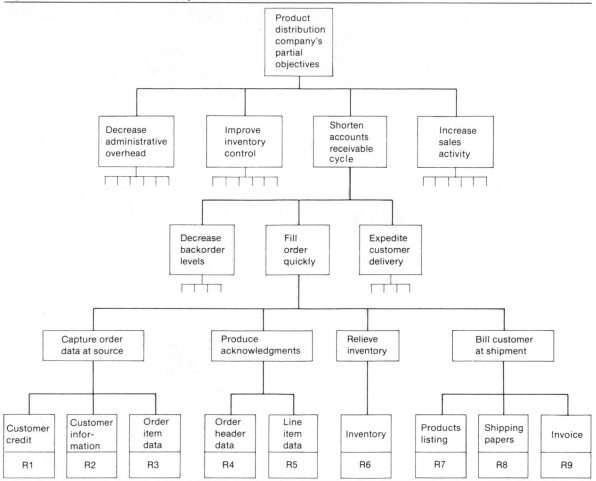

organized can be a costly and disruptive process, analogous to adding
plumbing and electrical connections to a house after the walls have
been painted. So data elements for future use should be anticipated
and incorporated in the base when the base is designed. However,
predicting needed elements is a far more difficult task than studying
an I/O chart and deducing what data elements need collection for current reports. It is management's responsibility to make such predictions—to chart the company's future data needs. Data element needs
should be anticipated for the estimated life of the information system.

Managers and analysts designing the data base must be cognizant

Table 5.3 **I/O table for a distribution company**

Data elements / Reports	R1	R2	R3	R4	R5	R6	R7	R8	R9
Each customer									
ID	x	x	x	x				x	x
Name	x			x				x	x
Credit rating	x								
Credit unit	x								
Sold-to address		x		x				x	x
Ship-to address		x		x				x	x
Shipping instructions		x		x				x	x
Product number		x		x				x	x
Sales tax rate		x		x					x
Territory code		x							
Each item record									
ID			x		x	x	x	x	x
Description			x		x	x	x	x	x
Order quantity			x		x	x	x	x	x
Price/unit			x		x				x
Ship from warehouse			x						
Warehouse location						x	x		
Discount					x				
Each shipment record									
ID							x	x	x
Ship date							x		
Bill location							x		
Ship warehouse location							x		
Ship quantity								x	x
Weight								x	
Freight class							x		
Net amount									x
Sales tax									x

that future changes in management may occur or that shifts in the style of current decision makers may take place. The data base must be flexible in content and format to allow for such changes. For example, today's manager may want an analysis of sales in dollars per sales representative. In the future, the same manager or a later replacement may demand dollar sales per product. Such shifts in the need for information must be possible within the framework of the data base.

Figure 5.2   **Flow of data between levels of management**

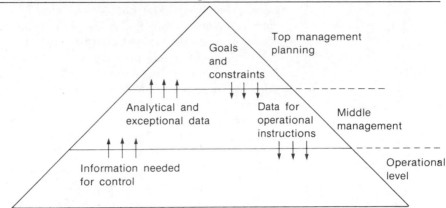

DATA ELEMENT DICTIONARY

Data for operations, control, and planning may be shared by several levels of management (Figure 5.2) or sharing may occur along organizational lines (Figure 5.3). Though the same data is used, the use to which the data is put will undoubtedly vary from level to level.

For example, the value of the data element "dollar sales" by sales representative Smith is used at the control level to evaluate the performance of Smith, and over a period of time this data may determine whether a bonus is given or Smith is released. Smith's data reclassified in terms of products sold, when combined with sales data from

Figure 5.3   **Flow of data along organizational lines**

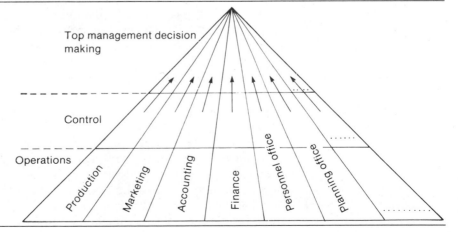

other sales representatives, can be used at the planning level for future sales projections. The data could also be used to generate derived data, such as average sales by sales representatives per month per product. Sales data might also be used at regional, national, or international headquarters of the company for planning advertising campaigns or revising product lines. Thus, the value of Smith's dollar sales is data that could be used at all levels of decision making.

Smith's data are meaningful only if data elements are carefully defined so that all users know what the data represents and interpret it in the same manner. This need for definitions arises whenever people wish to communicate with one another and have a large or complex vocabulary. Dictionaries are a reference for word definitions in natural languages, such as English and French. Data elements are also defined in dictionaries so that all data users know their exact meaning. A **data element dictionary (DED)** has to be designed for each information system using data elements.

Data elements are described in the DED by characteristics and attributes called **descriptors.** Not all DEDs use the same descriptors because every information system has unique requirements. DEDs are prepared with the specialized needs of a given system in mind. The relative importance of descriptors, logical groupings of descriptors, and constraints of space will all influence DED design.

The following basic descriptors of interest to managers are included in most DEDs: name, definition, derivation algorithm, unit of measure, format, width of field, validity rules, identification, and status. Technical descriptors of interest to analysts and programmers also appear in the DED. A manager may not use these descriptors but they are included since the dictionary is designed for all users of the information system.

A sample page from a DED is shown in Figure 5.4. A DED is simply a collection of pages of such data element definitions. Small systems may use preprinted DED pages, filling in the blanks by typing in information on each data element. In larger systems, the DED will be in machine-readable form, stored in the computer and accessed by programs for screen display, or printed as output (page printouts corresponding to the sample). Computer programs can also use the information in the DED to generate reports and tables for analysis when the DED is in machine-readable form.

Unlike single-volume French or English dictionaries, data element dictionaries are often in many volumes, corresponding to functions—such as personnel or production. Each level of decision making in an organization may have a dictionary set that differs in content from sets at other levels, for only data elements needed at that level will be included. The set of functional DEDs needed at the division level will therefore differ in content from the DEDs required by the corporate

Figure 5.4   **Sample page of a DED**

ABC COMPANY
DATA ELEMENT DICTIONARY

Name of Data Element	Marital status
Variable Name	MARISTATUS
Definition	Indicates whether or not a person is legally and currently married
Classification & Coding	1. Unmarried 2. Married 3. Other
Uses	For calculation of tax, deductions, and personnel profile
Derivation Rules (if any)	Source is Personnel Form 201A to be completed by person concerned.
Units (if any)	None

Format	Numeric	Justification	N.A.

Width of Field	One digit

Validity Rules	Required [X] Definite Error	Range 1-3	Content	Other
	Optional [ ] Possible Error			

PERSON PROCESSING FORM	Diana Sandalian
Date Issued	02/10/81
Status	Already implemented
Comments	The "other category" is expected to be less than 5%. If more, or another category is needed such as divorced, further coding subclassification is advisable.

headquarters, though there will be many data elements common to both sets. Definitions must be consistent at all levels in the functional DEDs. This consistency gives data upward compatibility and lets data collected at the operational level of the organization be uniformly interpreted when used at higher levels of the organization.

ORGANIZATION OF DATA

Once data needs are identified and data elements are defined in DEDs, data must be organized so later processing and retrieval will be fast and efficient. There are two types of organization: logical and physical.

Logical organization is the grouping of data elements in the data base to facilitate data base use. For example, all data elements relating to payroll might be grouped together for user convenience. This logical organization of data is the responsibility of management.

Physical organization, on the other hand, is planning the physical storage of data elements in the data base. Technicians, not management, are responsible for determining the storage medium location of data and for providing access to that data for retrieval and processing.

Logical organization

There are many steps to the logical organization of data. First, data elements required to produce a specified output must be determined. Then a **record** is formed by grouping related data elements with one another. An employee record would consist of related data elements such as name of employee, address, date of birth, department, and salary code, as mentioned earlier when describing the record of Mr. Jones. An invoice logical record might include customer identification, customer address, item(s) bought, purchase date(s), and price(s). Related logical records constitute a **file.** An employee personnel file, for example, would be a collection of all employee records. A business may have an advertising file, a payroll file, a marketing file, a production file, and so forth. A **data base** consists of a collection of integrated data files.

A graphic representation of data organization from data element to the data base is shown in Figure 5.5. Theoretically, there is no limit to the number of data elements in a record, the number of records in a file, or files in a data base. In practice, however, the values of k, m, and n in Figure 5.5 are constrained by factors such as storage space on a tape and disk. Efficiency poses additional restraints. A file used primarily for accounts payable is more efficient when limited to data elements relevant to that application. Interdepartmental rivalry in many businesses also tends to limit file size. A unit which has created a file for a specific purpose may resist the enlargement of that file by

Figure 5.5   **Data organization from data element to data base**

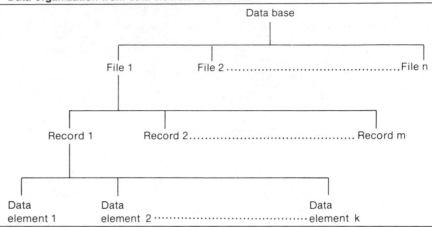

other departments, fearing that the expansion will result in loss of control over that file.

A manager is concerned with the hierarchy of data which begins with data elements, but data elements are themselves composed of **character sets.** The characters may be alphabetic (a–z), numeric (0–9), or special symbols such as / * % $. Since a computer cannot store characters per se, a still lower level of data organization is required. A character is represented by a set of **bytes,** each byte consisting of **bits,** generally eight bits to a byte. In most machines, bytes are aggregated further into **words** for efficient access on storage devices. The input which is collected and arranged in logical order by a manager and the output which crosses the manager's desk will be in characters. Bits, bytes, and words are the concern of computer technicians.

Physical organization

Some logical records are long, requiring many physical units of storage, such as cards, tape, or disks. Physical records are grouped into physical files, just as logical records are grouped into logical files.

A computer needs an aid to locate data belonging to a logical file stored on one or more physical files. Data is located by an **address** which "points" to the data's location. The space allocated a data element on a physical record is called a **field.**

In the early days of computing, cards were the physical records used in data processing. The physical space on cards is measured in columns. In planning, the physical number of columns, called **width of field,** and column assignments were specified on a **data layout sheet.** Figure 5.6 shows how the personnel file of John Doe, a logical record, would be assigned space on a card. In this case, two cards (two physical records) are required for this single logical record.

The use of cards becomes cumbersome and is too slow when a log-

Figure 5.6   **Card form layout**

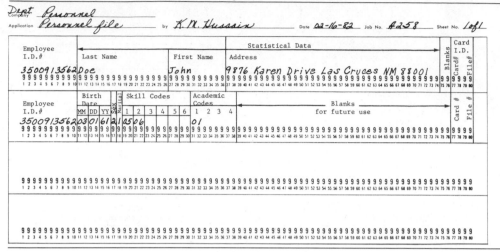

ical record requires many physical cards (10 cards per record are not uncommon); when a large number of logical records need processing (payroll for a firm of 20,000 employees, for example); and when processing is frequent. In such cases, logical records on tape are preferable.

Figure 5.7 shows the transference to tape of a logical record stored on cards. Note that the employee number appears only once on tape, whereas it must be restated on each card of the logical record. Instead of a data ID, a header label is used at the beginning of each tape to identify the logical records on the tape. The logical records themselves are separated by an **inter-record gap (IRG)** which identifies the end of one logical record and signals the start of another. In planning the location of data on tape, a data layout is used to identify each data element and its sequencing. Data is located in processing by searching the entire tape.

The use of magnetic tape is appropriate for sequential processing when all logical records in a logical file need processing: for example, the reconciliation of bank accounts or payroll processing. But tape is inappropriate for handling individual logical records. An analogy can be made to taped music. For listening to a series of songs, tapes are excellent. But tapes do not let the listener hear a single song over and over, nor can the song order be changed. When data of a single logical record is frequently needed, then a computer **disk,** a **random storage device,** is used instead of tape.

A representation of a logical record on magnetic disk is shown in Figure 5.8. The data is stored on tracks on the disk wherever there is

Figure 5.7   **Illustration of the transformation of two physical cards for one employee record into one logical tape record**

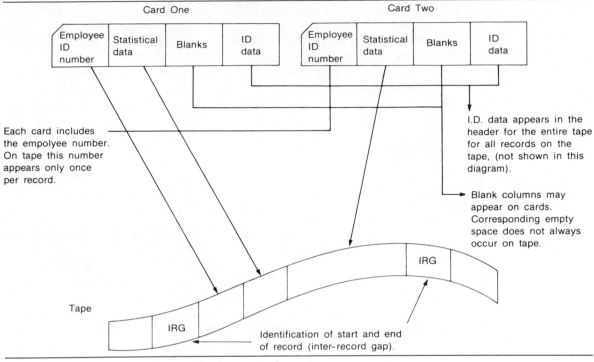

Card One

Card Two

| Employee ID number | Statistical data | Blanks | ID data |

| Employee ID number | Statistical data | Blanks | ID data |

Each card includes the empolyee number. On tape this number appears only once per record.

I.D. data appears in the header for the entire tape for all records on the tape, (not shown in this diagram).

Blank columns may appear on cards. Corresponding empty space does not always occur on tape.

IRG

Tape

IRG

Identification of start and end of record (inter–record gap).

Figure 5.8   **A logical record stored on random storage disk**

Data elements belonging to one logical record are shown on a disk system. Data elements are stored where space is available and the next data element in the chain is identified by its address (referred to as a **pointer** and indicated as an arrow).

space, so the logical record may appear in several discontinuous parts. The space for storing the logical record is not prescribed. Space availability and the time of data collection will determine the location of the data on the disk. However, the entire logical record can be retrieved, for each segment ends with a pointer indicating the address where the data is continued on the disk.

Decisions regarding physical storage equipment for data are made when a data base is designed. The choice of storage media affects processing costs. Disks enable random processing, a processing mode essential when data must be retrieved quickly. However, this shortened response time costs more than time-consuming sequential processing of tapes.

COMMON DATA BASE

A **common data base** consists of integrated files (so data elements in more than one file can be accessed when processing reports) that are shared by users. The files must be linked by a **key data element,** a data element common to two or more files. Table 5.4 helps illustrate the concept of **linkage.** Key data elements appear in bold print. The data element "item number," which appears in both the order line item file and the inventory file, is one example of a key data element. Given an item number, a computer program can locate the invoice

Table 5.4	Data elements in each record in each file

Customer file	*Invoice header file*
Data elements for each customer	Data elements for each invoice
ID (customer)	**ID (customer)**
Name	**Invoice no.**
Address	Ship-to address
Credit rating	Shipping instructions
Credit limit	Purchase order number
Territory code	**Warehouse code**
Sales tax code	

Order line item file	*Inventory file*
Data elements for each item	Data elements for each item
Invoice no.	**Warehouse code**
Item number	**Item number**
Order quantity	Item description
	Item price
	Discount rate

number and order the quantity from the order line item file, and can list the item description and the price and discount rate from information which is stored in the inventory file. The use of a common data element in both files permits such file integration.

A business may have more than one data base. It may also keep some of its data out of a common pool; for example, specialized data used by only one group or department.

Determining what data to include in a common data base is often an arduous process. Users do not always agree on what is and what should be common data. They fear that security and privacy of data are endangered in a common pool. Managers who have built up an empire of data resist losing control over that data. They may not want others to know such data exists or to share in its use. There may be genuine problems in reaching agreement on data element definitions, and difficulties in coordinating the timing of data creation. Standardization is necessary in a common data base. This means users may have to change practices in collecting and handling data.

In deciding what constitutes a common data base, all potential contributors to that base should participate. When consensus is not possible, conflicts must be resolved or arbitrated by management at a higher level. Unfortunately, interorganizational politics too often determine what data is placed in the common data base when, instead, the decisions should be based on technological and economic factors.

Though user resistance may slow formation of common data bases, their evolution should be systematic and progressive for the advantages of common pools of data are many. Data required by many users is collected only once, data redundancy is eliminated, and a single operation will update the data for all users. When procedures are standardized for gathering and recording data for a common pool, the data itself becomes more reliable. And finally, communication improves because a common terminology defined in the DED is used by both analysts and managers.

DATA PREPARATION

Once the data base is designed, the data itself must be collected, coded, converted into machine-readable form, and validated before it can be used. These procedures, shown diagrammatically in Figure 5.9, are called **data preparation.** Management and analysts must provide guidelines for data preparation to ensure that data is complete and coded for maximum processing efficiency and validity.

Surprisingly, much data collected for a data base is derived from documents. This data must be converted into machine-readable form such as cards, disks, or tape before being entered into the data base.

Figure 5.9   **Overview of data preparation**

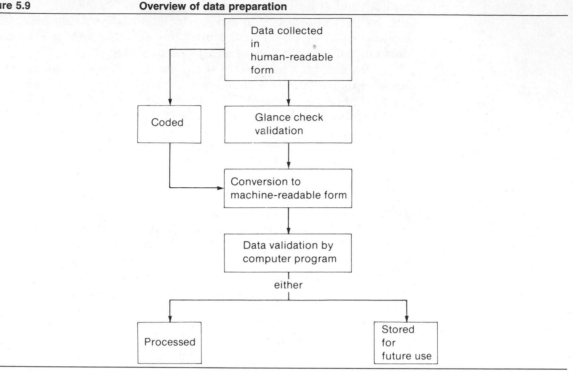

The equipment required for this conversion was discussed in Chapter 4. An overview of online and offline input collection devices was also discussed in that chapter.

DATA BASE ADMINISTRATION

As data grows in volume within a business, a system is required to keep track of data elements in data bases. Management needs to know what organizational units create data, and which programs and files use particular data elements. Should collection of a specific data element be discontinued, for example, a manager would need to know which reports would be affected. Users sometimes need assistance in locating data elements when the exact title or spelling of the element name has been forgotten. In such cases, a **KWIC (Key Word in Context)** or **KWOC (Key Word out of Context)** index is helpful. (See sample extract in Table 5.5.) Lists and tables containing such reference information on the data base can be generated by a set of programs drawing on all available knowledge about the elements in the firm's data base. These lists or tables form **directories.**

Table 5.5   **KWIC extracts**

	Data element number
EMPLOYEE-HISTORY-DATA	1.1.10
EMPLOYEE-JOB-STARTDATE	1.3.18
EMPLOYEE-JOB-STATUS	1.3.19
EMPLOYEE-JOB-TITLE	1.3.20
EMPLOYEE-NAME	1.2.02
EMPLOYEE-NUMBER	1.2.03
PAST-EMPLOYEE-NUMBER	1.2.13
•	
•	
•	
•	
•	
INVOICE-CREDIT	3.2.02
INVOICE-DATE	3.2.04
INVOICE-NUMBER	3.2.04
JOB-NUMBER	1.3.02
EMPLOYEE-JOB-STARTDATE	1.3.18
EMPLOYEE-JOB-STATUS	1.3.19
EMPLOYEE-JOB-TITLE	1.3.30
JOB-WAGE-RATE	1.3.24
•	
•	
•	

Because data element dictionaries and directories both provide organizational information about data elements, the two are closely related and often developed together, forming a **data element dictionary/data directory system (DED/DD system).** (This acronym is sometimes shortened to **DD/D** for data dictionary/directory.) Together, dictionaries and directories serve as a repository of information for data processing personnel and users and as an information source for systems and applications programs. An example of the latter would be a directory of validation rules, or one showing the form of data elements, such as mode of data representation, format, and compaction. Information on the physical location of data or code files are additional examples of directories that can be used in processing.

A DED/DD system requires considerable organization and control. In many firms a **DED/DD committee** is responsible for the content of the DED and directories, decides what equipment and software are required for developing and maintaining a DED/DD system, and decides what procedures and mechanisms are needed for control of data resources.

A sample DED/DD control mechanism is diagrammed in Figure 5.10. Although the ultimate authority to authorize change in a DED/DD system may rest with a DED/DD committee, as shown in this fig-

Figure 5.10   **Mechanism for controlling the DED/DD**

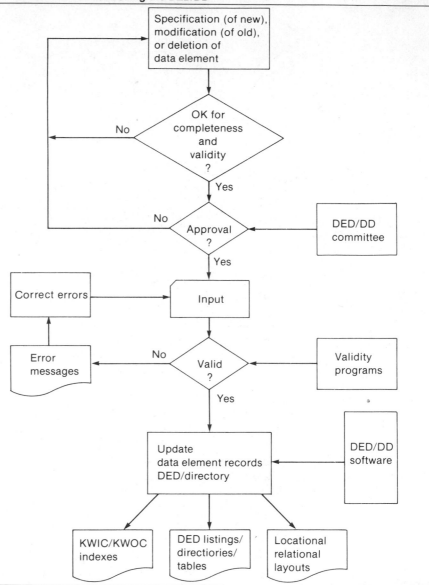

ure, in reality change commonly involves a sequence of approval
steps in which users, programmers, analysts, and data processing
management play a role. The exact personnel involved will depend
on the organization's procedures in the past, the system's complexity,
and personalities. For example, when a report is requested by man-

agement for which a new program is to be written, the programmer may find that data elements not in the data base are needed. This need may be brought to the attention of a data processing manager who will then request approval of the DED/DD committee for the additions. Some firms may skip this intermediate step, however, authorizing programmers to approach the committee directly.

Not shown in Figure 5.8 is the duty of the committee to periodically review the existing DED for redundancies and duplications and another important committee role—that of recognizing the need for revision of the DED due to changes in organizational needs, structure, and personnel.

Many DED/DD committees delegate responsibility for DED/DD systems to a **data base administrator (DBA).** This DBA usually administers the total DED/DD system according to committee guidelines. Table 5.6 summarizes the main duties commonly delegated to DBAs. Data base design, operations, and monitoring the common data base are primary tasks. Authorized changes to the data base must be made to dictionaries and directories under the data base administrator's supervision. Such changes may require moving data from one storage medium to another, a move which entails careful logging and tagging if data is to be quickly and effectively accessed. Maintenance also includes checking for continuity and completeness of data. Continuity is especially important for planning data with longitudinal integration (integration over time). The modification of historical files is required when definitions of data elements and classifications change. Continuity is threatened by breakdowns in processing, particularly those of online systems where loss of data may result. Procedures for backup, recovery, and restart for all possible types of breakdowns, including natural disasters, must be planned.

A DBA is also delegated responsibility for the quality (accurateness and reliability) of the data base. Logging and auditing procedures need to be established and performance (cost and response-time) monitored. Screening procedures to identify authorized users at minimal cost and inconvenience should be devised to protect the data from misuse. Security of access can be achieved through passwords (or passkeys), and reference to directories listing data to be accessed, the time of permissible access, and terminal.

Both legislative and executive powers are needed by data base administrators. They must not only make rules but be able to enforce these rules for all users at all levels of the organizational hierarchy.

Special equipment, such as cryptographic equipment, and special software are used to administer a data base. The terminal in the data base administrator's office may be the only terminal with authority to makes changes to the DED, for example. In security-sensitive systems, the data base administrator's terminal may list all changes to the sys-

Table 5.6   **Functions of a data administrator**

Data base design	Retrieval
Content	Search strategies
Creation	Statistics
Reconciling differences	Access
Dictionary/Directory	Frequency of processing
Create	Space use
Maintain	User utilization
Data compression	Response time
Data classification/coding	Design operational
Data integrity	procedures
Backup	Access to data base
Restart/recovery	Access for testing
	Interfaces
Data base operation	Testing system
DED custodian/authority	
Maintain	*Monitoring*
Add	Quality of data
Purge	validity
Data base maintenance	Performance
Integrity	Efficiency
Detect losses	Cost
Repair losses	Use/utilization
Recovery	Security/privacy
Access for testing	Audit
Dumping	Compliance
Software for DED/DD	Standards
Utility programs	Procedures
Tables/indexes, etc., for	
end user	*Other functions*
Storage	Liaison/communications with:
Physical record structure	End users
Logical-physical mapping	Analysts/programmers
Physical storage device	Training on data base
assignments	Consultant on file design
Security/access	Design operational
Assign passwords	procedures
Assign lock/key	Access to data base
Modifying passwords/keys	Access for testing
Logging	Interfaces
Cryptography	
Modification	

tem that need to be monitored. Some systems will alert the DBA when a user tries many access codes from the same terminal in a short period of time, for this may indicate an attempt to break a code. A timely response by the administrator may prevent breach of the system's security.

Software is also needed to generate reports related to use, operation, and monitoring the data base. A sample list of reports and programs which commonly support a DED/DD system appears in Table 5.7.

Table 5.7	Reports and programs to support the DED/DD system
	Listings of DED
	KWIC/KWOC indexes
	Listings of directories
	Testing data generator
	Data division generator
	JCL generator
	Implementing hardware and software changes
	Data validator
	Access controller
	Data definition controller
	Data structure converter
	Data storage assigner
	Statistical reports on utilization
	Comparison routine
	Utility routines
	Logging
	Editing
	Dumping
	Garbage collector

SUMMARY

An important resource of computerized information systems is data. Data elements needed for business applications must be determined, the data collected and organized both logically and physically, and the data base monitored and controlled.

One method of determining which data elements are required for applications is to trace the input needed for every data element in the output. To see if the data base contains the needed data, an input/output table is used. Data elements needed for processing, such as those required for linking, identification of data, security, and control, are determined by analysts.

Data elements are defined in DEDs, data element dictionaries. Data directories are extensions to the DED, providing reference information regarding data relationships of data elements defined in the DED. Special DED/DD software can be used to generate tables and lists regarding data which are needed to administer the data base, such as indexes of data elements names and locations, or matrices to identify users or collectors of data elements.

Once the data elements for an application are identified, they must be conceptually organized into a logical entity. Related data elements constitute a record, related records constitute a file, and related files are a data base. The data is then collected and stored on a physical medium, such as card, tape, or disk.

Whatever the form of storage, files must be linked by a common data element if they are to be related and the data shared. This common sharing in a common data base reduces redundancy, storage space, processing time, data preparation, time, and effort, and it improves security while promoting standardization. This sharing of a common data base also enables the data of different organizational divisions to be correlated for preparation of computerized reports. But it does cause organizational problems because users do not always want to pool data, and are often unwilling to submit to the standardization and discipline required for such sharing.

In many firms, a DED/DD committee is responsible for creating, maintaining, and monitoring the company's data resources. Because of the complex and technical nature of data management, however, the committee may delegate this responsibility to a data base administrator. Special DED/DD software assists the DBA in monitoring and controlling data bases. Large and complex data systems require a DBMS, described briefly in Chapter 3.

KEY WORDS

Address

Bit

Byte

Character set

Common data base

Data

Data base

Data base administrator (DBA)

Data element

Data element dictionary (DED)

Data element dictionary/data directory system (DED/DD system or DD/D)

Data layout sheet

Data preparation

DED/DD committee

Derived data

Descriptor

Directory

Disk

Estimated data

Field

File

Input/output table (I/O table)

Inter-record gap (IRG)

Key data element

KWIC (Key Word in Context)

KWOC (Key Word out of Context)

Linkage

Logical organization

Logical record

Physical organization

Primitive data

Random storage device

Raw data

Record

Width of field

Word

DISCUSSION QUESTIONS

1. Distinguish between data and information.
2. What is a data element?
3. What is the difference between raw and derived data? Give examples in your area of specialization.
4. How do analysts determine which data elements need to be collected for a given report? What problems arise?
5. What is a common data base? What are its characteristics? Why is a common data base desirable?
6. Conflicts arise when establishing common data bases. What are they? How can they be reduced or eliminated?
7. What is the difference between the physical and logical structure of data? Give an example using the same set of data elements.
8. What are fixed and variable costs in designing a file? Give examples.
9. Why should the cost of maintaining files be evaluated carefully? How do maintenance costs depend on the content of the file? Give examples. How can maintenance costs be reduced?
10. What power accrues to the person responsible for a common data base? How can this power be misused? Can misuse be avoided? How?
11. What are the differences between a DED, a DD, and a DED/DD system?
12. What software is required (if any) to operate a DED, DD, or DED/DD system? Should such software be developed internally in each firm or be purchased from a vendor or software house?
13. What tables in a data directory might be useful for:
    a. A user-manager.
    b. A programmer.
    c. Programs.
    d. A DBA.
14. A DBA needs staff assistance to manage a large and complex common data base. If only three staff members were assigned to a DBA, what assignments would you recommend each be given?

EXERCISES

1. Design cards for a personnel file for the following data elements. (Assume two cards per person.):
   Name
   Home address
   Date of birth (correct to the day)
   Sex
   Marital status
   University major
   Fixed monthly salary
   Commission rate

2.   Trace one character used in a personnel data base (specify one if you do not have access to a personnel data base) through all levels of the hierarchy of data. Draw a diagram showing your hierarchy of data.

3.   In the table below, check the data elements that should be included in a bank deposit file, production inventory file, and accounts payable file.

Data element	Bank deposit file	Production inventory file	Accounts payable file
Name of part			
Name of depositor			
Account number			
Address of vendor			
Address of deposit			
Part description			
Name of vendor			
Discount code			
Unit price			
Amount deposited			
Vendor account number			
Quantity ordered			
Quantity of goods			
Amount withdrawn ($)			
Safety check			
Price			
Invoice number			
Current stock on hand			
Balance ($)			
Invoice date			
Quantity sold			

4.   Prepare a sheet for a DED for the data element "date of birth." If you feel you do not have sufficient information to do this exercise, then make a reasonable assumption, state it, and justify your assumption. How can this information in the DED be used by a data directory?

SELECTED ANNOTATED BIBLIOGRAPHY

Bridges, Terry. "Database Machines—What and Why." *Data Management* 20, no. 11 (November 1982), pp. 14–16.
 Bridges argues that database machines can relieve systems of using up computing resources to handle conventional DBMSs.

Canning, Richard G. "The Cautious Path to a Data Base." *EDP Analyzer* 11, no. 6 (June 1973), pp. 1–12.

This issue discusses data base problems. The advice offered is: develop long-range plans; have a series of short projects; have compatibility, maintainability, and convertability; get in-depth user involvement; and obtain management involvement where it counts.

Clifton, H. D. *Business Data Systems*. Englewood Cliffs, N. J.: Prentice-Hall, 1978, pp. 229–35.
A good systematic discussion of coding classification and design.

Curtice, Robert M. and Jones, Paul E., Jr. *Logical Data Base Design*. New York: Van Nostrand Reinhold, 1982. 272 pp.
A wealth of practical guidelines developed over 14 years of experience gained while consulting for Arthur D. Little, Inc.

Flanagan, Patrick. "Need Information? You Name It, Data Bases Supply It." *Office Administration and Automation* 64, no. 3 (April 1983), pp. 42–48.
An excellent survey of the many data bases that can be accessed by a terminal and a telephone line. The article discusses General Electric Information, the Dow Jones News/Retrieval, and Wall Street Journal Transcript Service.

House, William C., ed. *Interactive Decision-Oriented Data Base Systems*. New York: Mason/Charter, 1977, 470 p.
This is an old book, yet it does cover well the basic concepts of physical and logical organization of a data base. It also has five examples of data base design in business: banking; order entry sales and inventory; cost accounting; manufacturing; and report dissemination.

Lyon, John K. *The Data Base Administrator*. New York: John Wiley & Sons, 1976, 170 p.
The author discusses the responsiblities of a data base administrator and tools used on the job. This book is written by a practicing computer scientist at Honeywell who has written extensively on the subject of data bases.

Martin, James. *An End-User's Guide to Data Bases*. Englewood Cliffs, N.J.: Prentice-Hall, 1981. 144 pp.
Any data base installation which does not model its data in a logical form before doing the physical design is throwing money down the drain, according to Martin. Advice on how this modeling should be done is given in this book. Excellent chapters on ownership of data and considerations that affect machine performance are also included.

Uhrowczki, P. P. "Data Dictionary/Directories." *IBM Systems Journal* 12, no. 4 (1973), pp. 332–50.
One of the earliest and still authoritative articles on the subject. It has a good discussion and diagrams on physical organization, logical organization, and reports generated by DED/DD systems. A good appendix on definitions of data base terms is included.

Walsh, Miles E. "Update on Data Dictionaries," *Journal of Systems Management* 20, no. 8 (August 1978), pp. 28–39.
This article discusses the concept, implementation, and use of data dictionaries and DED/DD systems. It has many samples of dictionary reports.

PART TWO

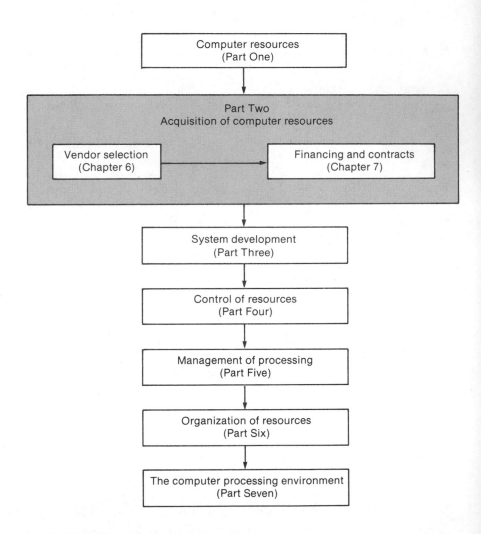

ACQUISITION OF COMPUTER RESOURCES

Introduction to Part Two

A computerized information system requires the resources introduced in Part One. Part Two describes the acquisition of these resources: how to request bids, evaluate proposals, and select a vendor (Chapter 6). Alternative methods of financing are also reviewed and contract negotiations discussed (Chapter 7).

It would be mistaken to assume that the procedures recommended in this part apply only to the acquisition of hardware. Software should be selected with equal care. Indeed, today's complex software, such as data base management systems, requires a major capital outlay and costly support services in terms of maintenance, personnel, and training programs. The selection principles outlined are as valid in reaching a cost-effective acquisition decision for software as for hardware. The principles also apply to both large and small acquisitions, though analysis of options may be less formal and less rigorous in the latter case.

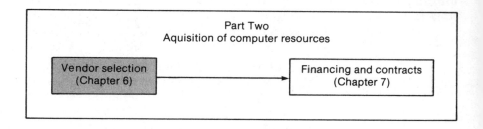

CHAPTER 6

Acquisition of computer resources:

Vendor selection

An investment in knowledge always pays the best interest.

Benjamin Franklin

During the design phase of the development of an information system, a list of equipment and software for the new system is prepared. Some of these resources may already be available in-house. For example, the firm may have a computer center with many of the required peripherals. But should the firm lack necessary software or should mandated equipment be fully committed to other projects, acquisition of resources will be necessary.

This chapter will describe the preliminary steps in the acquisition process. Included are sections on how to translate needs into vendor proposals, how to evaluate alternative proposals and vendor claims, and criteria for selection of a vendor. The subject of computer resource acquisition is continued in Chapter 7 with a discussion of methods of finance, contract negotiations, and liaison with vendors during implementation. Figure 6.1 outlines the sequence of the acquisition process in graphic form, showing which steps are considered in each chapter. Two chapters have been devoted to acquisitions because of the complexity of the process and the importance of procurement decisions. Indeed, the ultimate performance of an information system may depend on quality of acquisitions, and large capital investments can be at stake.

In large business corporations, procurement procedures may be formal, involving a full-time staff. In smaller firms, acquisition decisions

Figure 6.1   **Procurement process for computer resources**

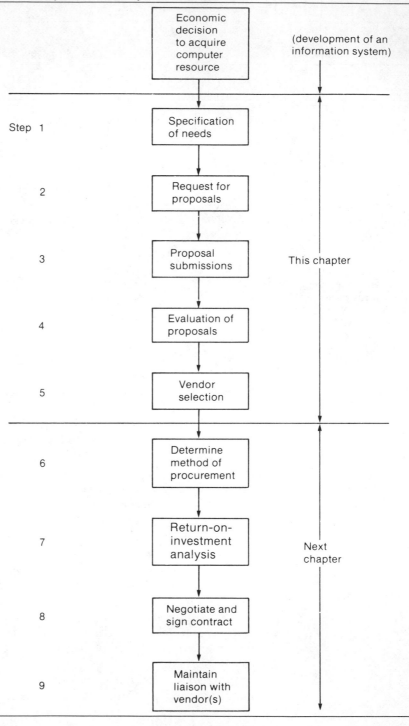

are often made informally, even secretly, by one individual. But in both cases, the steps in the procurement process described in the next two chapters apply, for the principles involved are not related to corporate size or degree of formality in decision making.

REQUEST FOR PROPOSALS: NEED SPECIFICATIONS

The first step in procuring computer resources is the preparation of a document to be presented to vendors, outlining exact specification of needs, whether the need be equipment or software. This document, called a **Request for Proposals (RFP),** is similar to, and an extension of, user specifications drawn up in the development cycle of an information system. Since the vendor who responds will have a particular product to push for sale, it is important that the buyer's statement of need include operational details in clear, unambiguous terms so that the buyer, not the vendor, sets product specifications.

Who decides what specifications are to be included in the RFP? That will depend on the resource to be procured and the size and structure of the firm. If only a small peripheral for exclusive use by one department is needed, the department head alone may write the specifications. At the other extreme, specifications for a major acquisition affecting many users and requiring a large capital outlay (a DBMS, for example) would probably be made by a team including user representatives, technical personnel, a financial officer, and someone from the upper levels of corporate management. Often outside consultants are included as well.

When specifying needs in the RFP, the buyer must indicate mandatory features (for example, minimum capability in a computer) which must be included in the bid. In establishing these requirements, care must be taken lest they be too restrictive so that no vendor has a product that qualifies, or too lax so that a large number of vendors respond. Processing proposals is a time-consuming task: three to six submitted proposals is optimal.

It is often helpful to consult with vendors when drawing up mandatory requirements. Vendors can help evaluate the legitimacy and validity of requirements, though firms should be cautious of vendor bias. Vendors can also indicate whether their companies would be in a position to submit a bid. This, in effect, acts as a preselection process, reducing the number of RFPs that need to be sent.

Canvassing vendors can be done informally, on the telephone, for example, or by a document called **Request for Information (RFI).** On the basis of the information collected, a matrix, such as that in Table 6.1, can be compiled, showing which vendors have the capability of meeting requirements requested. If, upon examination of the matrix, it is noted that most vendors fail to qualify, requirements can be re-

Table 6.1   **Vendors' ability to meet mandatory requirements**

Vendor	1	2	3	4	. . . .	15	16
Capability to meet current needs in one shift and 5-year future needs in three shifts	X	X	X	X		X	X
Real-time response of 35 seconds for 95 percent of the time	X	X	X	X		X	
Communication facilities	X		X	X		X	X
COBOL and FORTRAN IV compiler	X	X		X		X	X

laxed. If too many qualify for ease in processing proposals, additional mandatory features can be added.

Once mandatory requirements are set, noncritical but "nice-to-have" features should be determined. For example, many users want terminal screens to have a color capability. Some features have a functional value: others may be wanted "to keep up with the Jones." Buyers should distinguish between these two categories when evaluating proposals with optional features.

Sometimes requirements show a bias toward one supplier, which other vendors consider unfair. Complaints may be strong enough to force buyers to reevaluate mandatory requirements. To avoid the ill will engendered by such situations, it is advisable that the RFP state minimum acceptable values for parameters which more than one vendor can meet, rather than high values which eliminate all competitors but the vendor favored.

OTHER COMPONENTS OF RFP

Although a major portion of the RFP is delegated to need specification, information should be given on procedures, schedules, and the user environment, and required documentation should be explained. Table 6.2 is a sample list of contents showing what items a RFP should include.

General information on the buyer (item 8) is needed to help vendors understand the environment in which the product under consideration will operate. This should consist of:

Résumé of firm and product.

Projected rates of growth.
  Data volumes—maximum, minimum, and average.
  File characteristics.
  Input/output characteristics.
  Response time—maximum, minimum and average.
  Constraints.

Table 6.2	Sample contents of a RFP
	1. Need specification
	2. Mandatory features
	3. Desired features
	4. Performance data wanted
	5. Cost data needed
	6. Information needed on vendor
	7. Documentation required from vendor
	8. General information on buyer
	9. Request for vendor demonstration or presentation
	10. Procedural details: How to handle questions / Liaison
	11. Schedule: Bidder's conference / Proposal due date / Award date
	12. General comments

Table 6.3 is a further elaboration of item 6 of the RFP sample contents, listing the data the vendor should supply to help the buyer evaluate whether the vendor is reliable and has the necessary expertise and support facilities to back up a bid proffered.

PROPOSAL SUBMISSION

Vendors, upon receipt of a RFP, will prepare their bids. During this preparation period, it is useful for the buyer to keep in close contact, answering questions and clarifying the RFP, if necessary. Sometimes the RFP will be altered during this period as a result of vendor comments or objections. If so, all vendors receiving the RFP should be so informed.

This liaison and dialog with vendors can be very educational for the acquisition committee. It can teach them about advances in the computer industry and help them identify and weigh the importance of various features. Such knowledge will prove of value when proposals are later evaluated.

Table 6.3	Information to be supplied by vendor

1. Experience of firm with computer resources
   Recent mainframe and micro technology
   Inquiry and response capabilities
   Communication capabilities
   Graphics
2. System development expertise
   Experience
     Design
     Implementation
     Human engineering
3. Technical assistance available
   Systems support
   Engineering support
     Nature
     Experience
     Response time
     Maintenance
4. Training to be provided
   Facilities
   Courses
   Materials
   Instructors available
   Media used
5. Research and technical programs of firm
   Human engineering
   Education and training
6. Names and addresses of recent customers

VALIDATION OF PROPOSALS

When the acquisition is a minor piece of equipment, validation of proposals can easily be done by technicians in the user department. But when a computer or computer system is to be purchased, checking proposals and validating vendor claims may take an acquisition team many months. There are two basic approaches to validation: a literature search and a study of vendor justifications. When performance is crucial, hand timing, benchmarks, and simulation are also useful tests. Each of these validation techniques will now be considered.

Literature search

With reference to validation of proposals, a **literature search** does not mean a book survey, for the time lag in book production means books cannot keep current with computer advances. Rather publications, such as *DataWorld*, published by Auerbach, or *DataPro*, by McGraw-Hill, should be studied. Journals provide up-to-date evaluations of computer resources, especially peripherals and packaged software, a service similar to that of consumer bulletins.

Literature searches are time-consuming. One needs to find relevant articles, be able to interpret the information correctly, and then find a common basis for comparing equipment (or software) evaluated by different sources. Another limitation is that such checks can only be done after the product has been on the market for some time. Should the acquisitions committee be considering recently developed computer resources, enough time may not have elapsed for evaluation of these resources to reach print. (Risks in acquiring new technology should not be underestimated. Hardware may still have bugs, delivery may fall behind schedule, software prove unavailable, etc.)

One can supplement a literature search by asking other customers of the vendor how they evaluate the vendor's products and services. This is the reason a list of customer names is requested in the RFP. Usually, only the names of satisfied customers will be supplied, but those customers may refer the buyer to dissatisfied firms, which should be consulted as well.

Vendor justifications

In this approach, the vendor is asked to justify the proposal submitted. Care must be taken that vendor selection is based on the merits of the product, not on a slick sales promotion. Many managers are **"satisficers,"** preferring to deal with vendors who have proved reliable, helpful, and satisfactory in the past. Such managers are particularly receptive to this sales approach to proposal validation. **"Optimizers,"** or those who attempt optimization, usually choose the more time-consuming literature search and validation (which requires more technical expertise as well).

Hand timing

In **hand timing,** one multiplies the engineering time to perform each set of operations by the number of these sets in each application program to determine run time. This calculation is matched with the vendor's time claims, to verify the performance capability stated in the vendor's proposal. Hand timing is feasible in simple processing, but is beyond present capabilities for complex processing configurations, such as parallel processing or multiprocessing.

Benchmarks

A **benchmark** test measures computer equipment performance under typical conditions of use. The problem is defining "typical conditions of use" because the benchmark will be a small set of programs selected to represent the work stream. In a bank the number of transactions processed on a single mid-week day might be a fairly accurate sample of transactions throughout the year, but in a manufacturing plant the workload may vary from day to day, or week to week. The choice of a representative workload must, therefore, be made with care, and the set of programs selected for the benchmark should include all important functions of processing, such as sorting, matching, updating, and queries.

Table 6.4	**Factors to be considered when preparing a benchmark**

Representative workload
  Current
    Normal
    Peak
  Future
    Normal
    Peak
Representative time requirements
  Compile
  Execute
  Input/output
Representative equipment requirements
  Memory
    Internal (core)
    External
  Input/output channels
  Communication equipment
  Peripherals
Representative processing
  Files
  Functions and types of processing
    Sort/merge
    Update
    Computing
      Matrix
      Simulation

Table 6.4 lists some of the factors to be included in a benchmark. Note that not only time, equipment, and processing must be representative, but that current workload and future projections should be considered. One can allow for growth by multiplying test-run time by a multiplier called an **extension factor,** which varies according to each class of programs.[1]

Benchmark testing may mean running the test programs on several different computers for the purpose of comparing execution speed, throughput, etc. Since the buyer doesn't have the equipment, this means arranging with others for the testing. Even when neighboring firms are willing to lend use of their equipment for testing, the buyer will have difficulty finding the exact combination of CPU features, peripherals, and software needed for the testing.

Another problem may be that the application programs in the benchmark (programs in current use) are in a different language than the system to be evaluated. For example, the benchmark programs

---

[1]For details on extension factors, see Martin L. Rubin, *Data Processing Administration* 6 (Princeton, N.J.: Auerbach Publishers, 1971), pp. 235–40.

may be in COBOL, whereas APL will be the language of the new system. In such cases, new programs must be written for test purposes. Though preparing special benchmark programs has a high learning value, the effort is not always trivial. The time spent on programming can be quite costly.

Vendors often assist buyers in locating equipment for benchmark tests. They may contact clients on the buyer's behalf, or allow use of their own equipment for testing, as does IBM at its regional centers.

Simulation

An alternative to benchmark testing is to lease or purchase a special **simulation program,** such as SCERT, CASE, or SAM,[2] which can be run on equipment already available in-house to simulate workload processing on equipment configurations under consideration. Or a computer service organization can be contacted to run the simulation.

A simplified representation of the flow of a SCERT simulation can be seen in Figure 6.2. This figure does not show all the stages within each phase, nor does it show all phases necessary for complex modes of operation, such a multiprogramming or real-time processing. However, the basic logic of the simulation is illustrated.

The first phase of simulation is to develop a mathematical model of the desired information system (Box 2, Figure 6.2) based on data that define the environment, system, and files (Box 1). In parallel, a mathematical model of the hardware and software system under consideration is developed (Box 5) based on the configuration to be tested (Box 4) and on information on resource capabilities stored in SCERT's factor library (Box 3). The simulation is then run (Box 6). The output (Box 7) will include not only information on utilization of each main hardware component but information on core requirements, software performance, and costs as well. When output proves unsatisfactory, changes can be made to the resources in the configuration (Box 4) and the simulation rerun (Box 6).

By definition, simulation will not give an optimal solution. It only provides information on different alternatives. The committee must exercise judgment on which configurations to test, for simulation runs are expensive. In making a choice from alternatives tested by simulation, the committee must be sure no constraints are violated. For example, a desirable solution may cost more than can be allocated to the system. The most satisfactory solution may turn out to be one vendor's CPU combined with another vendor's peripherals.

Simulation is a useful aid in validating a vendor's claims, but it

[2]For CASE and SAM, see F. Warren McFarlan and Richard L. Nolan, *The Information Systems Handbook* (Homewood, Ill.: Dow Jones-Irwin, 1975), pp. 410–12. For details on SCERT logic and samples of output, *see* Warren F. McFarlan, Richard L. Nolan, and David P. Norton, *Information Systems Administration* (New York: Holt, Rinehart & Winston, 1973), pp. 208–32.

Figure 6.2   **Simplified flow of SCERT**

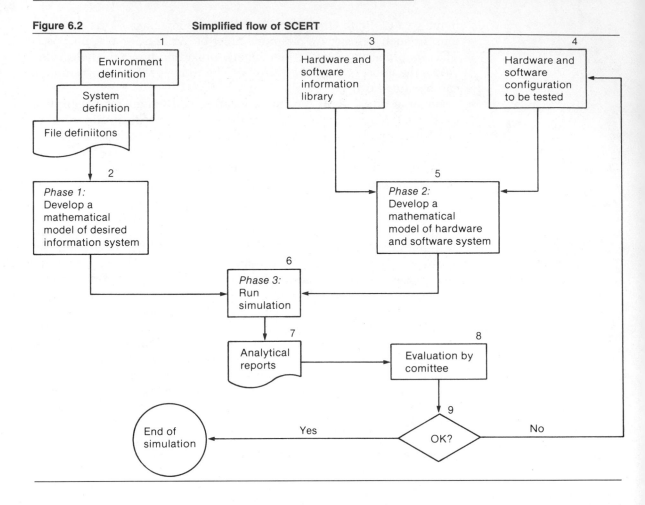

should be realized that there is generally significant difference between predicted and actual levels of performance. To minimize error in predicted performance levels, updated, correct, and complete information on equipment and software capabilities must be included in the simulation run.

Comparison of   Confidence in hand timing, benchmarks, and simulation as meth-
validation techniques   ods of validating time claims of vendors differs according to the application under consideration. Figure 6.3 is a confidence chart for processing-limited applications and input/output applications, prepared by Edward Joslin. Note that hand timing is least favored, whereas benchmarks are given almost a 100 percent confidence rating for both types of applications.

Figure 6.3   **Confidence in the timing approaches of hand timing, simulation, and benchmarks**

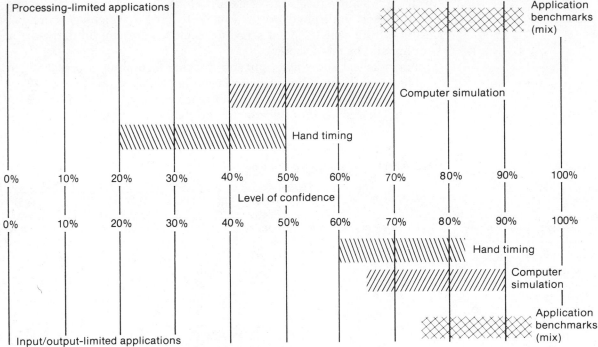

Source: Edward O. Joslin, *Computer Selection* (New York: Addison-Wesley Publishing, 1968), p. 105.

SELECTION OF VENDOR

In the acquisition of simple equipment, a quick review of proposals may suffice when choosing a vendor. Even when purchasing complex equipment, many buyers are tempted to avoid a long formal selection process. They opt instead to stick with vendors with whom they have had satisfactory dealings in the past as long as their proposals meet objectives. A formal review of proposals, however, should lead to the "best" choice, resulting in a system with high efficiency and effectiveness. A formal evaluation of proposals may be the policy of the firm or may be required by law, as is the case with governmental acquisitions.

The weighted-score method and cash-value method are two techniques that can assist an acquisitions team in vendor selection. These will be discussed below.

Weighted-score method

The **weighted-score technique** is used to evaluate vendors who all meet mandatory requirements. In this system, desired features are weighted and each vendor scored on a scale of 1–10 according to how well each feature meets buyer expectations. A vendor's score per feature is then multiplied by its weight to give a weighted score per feature, from which a total score for each vendor can be derived (by adding all weighted scores).

A worksheet showing application of this technique is presented in Table 6.5. Column 1 lists decision criteria. Weights are shown in Column 2, reflecting the relative importance of each criterion as evaluated by the acquisitions team. In this table, for example, ability of

Table 6.5   **Worksheet for the weighted-score method**

(1)	(2)	Vendor A		Vendor B		Vendor C	
		(3)	(4)	(5)	(6)	(7)	(8)
			Wtd.		Wtd.		Wtd.
Decision criterion	*Weight*	*Score*	*score*	*Score*	*score*	*Score*	*score*
Hardware							
Meet needs of growth	3	7	21	7	21	5	15
Throughput/$	5	8	40	6	30	5	25
Communications	2	4	8	8	16	6	12
Real-time capability	1	1	1	5	5	3	3
Storage	2	8	16	6	12	7	14
I/O interface	2	6	12	6	12	6	12
Site restrictions	1	4	4	6	6	8	8
Reliability	3	9	27	6	18	8	24
Ease of use	1	6	6	8	8	6	6
Total for hardware . . .			135		128		119
Software							
Monitors	5	8	40	9	45	4	20
Compilers	4	7	28	9	36	3	12
Multiprogramming	1	8	8	8	8	6	6
Query capability	1	7	7	6	6	5	5
Data management	3	7	21	9	27	4	12
Reliability	3	8	24	9	27	6	18
Packaged software	2	8	16	9	18	5	10
Utility software	2	8	16	9	18	6	12
Documentation	4	7	28	7	28	8	32
Total for software			188		213		127
Other							
Cost	40	4.5	180	3	120	9	360
Engineering support	3	9	27	7	21	3	9
Systems support	4	9	36	6	24	1	4
Education	5	7	35	7	35	5	25
Reputation and stability	2	10	20	7	14	5	10
Delivery date	1	6	6	5	5	9	9
Total for other items . .			304		219		417
Total for each vendor .			627		560		663

hardware to meet growth needs is ranked three times higher than a real-time capability.[3]

Assignment of weights is subjective and may cause disagreements among team members who are given the responsibility for calculating the table. Should top management intervene when a stalemate is reached? Have veto power? To reach consensus, long and heated discussions may sometimes take place with arm-twisting and power politics playing a role.

The next step is scoring vendors. For example, according to Table 6.5, Vendor A's hardware rates an 8 for storage capacity whereas Vendor B's system is only given a 6. Scoring is also a subjective activity, sometimes even more difficult than assigning weights. Often an individual or group with expertise on a given feature will be given responsibility for scoring that feature. When newly developed systems are being evaluated, fair scoring may require considerable effort, involving literature searches, calculations, and customer satisfaction checks.

The weighted score of each criterion is calculated by multiplying each vendor's scores by the values in column 2. A vendor's total can be calculated by summing its weight scores. This calculation is done for each vendor. The vendor whose proposal gets the most points is chosen. According to Table 6.5, this would be Vendor C.

There are weaknesses to the weighted-score method that should be recognized, in addition to the problem of subjectivity already mentioned in assigning weights and scores. One problem is that each criterion is given a separate value and assumed to be independent. But many features have a greater value when linked than the sum of their values when separate. This is like the classic example used in economics regarding beehives and fields of clover. The higher yields due to synergism when bees and clover are brought into proximity can be compared to the higher production of computers when features, such as telecommunications and minicomputers, are connected. The weighted-score method may not take this causality into account, though there is no reason why telecommunications and minicomputers cannot be listed as required features.

Another major weakness is that the assignment of weights does not include cost considerations, such as those listed in Table 6.6. The vendor receiving the highest weighted score may not have the best proposal when cost/benefit ratios are analyzed. A lower weighted score may, in fact, give more value per dollar. One solution is to use the weighted-score method only when evaluating proposals with the

---

[3]In verifying growth needs, estimates need to be made for future workloads. For a probabilistic approach to this problem, see E. M. Timmerick, "Computer Selection Methodology," *Computer Surveys* 5, no. 4 (December 1973), p. 213.

Table 6.6	Cost elements of proposals

One-time costs
   Cost of computer resources to be acquired
   Cost of auxiliary resources to be acquired
   Site
      Site preparation
         Electricity
         Facilities, e.g., false floor
         Security facilities
   Transportation
      Freight
      Insurance
   Installation
   Conversion
      Programs
      File
      Personnel
      Documentation
Recurring costs
   Personnel
   Program development
   Operations
   Maintenance
   Supplies
   Communication
   Insurance
   Backup

same total costs. In practice, however, proposals identical in cost are rarely submitted. Those that vary slightly in price seldom include exactly the same features.

Cost-value method

The **cost-value method** attempts to equalize bids of features so that costs can be compared. Costs of desired features not included in proposals are added to each vendor's bid. The cost of each feature is based on the lowest cost estimate of acceptable alternatives available when making the calculations. A dollar value should also be calculated for operating the system without the desired feature, and this figure used if it is less than the cost of the feature itself. Total costs are then compared, selection being based on the bid with the least cost.

For example, suppose a proposal is submitted that does not include a software feature the buyer wishes to have. This software can either be developed in-house or purchased. To this initial expenditure, the cost of maintaining the software for the life of the system is added. In Table 6.7, a value template showing figures for this hypothetical soft-

Table 6.7   **Value template for the desired software (for one vendor only)**

Developing the software in-house	$12,000
Maintenance for life of system	4,000
	$16,000
Development of software by software company	15,000
Maintenance for life of system	4,000
	$19,000
Cost of doing without the software, i.e.,	
degraded system and decreased efficiency	$12,000

ware omission, the cost of developing the software in-house plus maintenance would be $16,000; the cost of software purchased and maintained, $19,000. The buyer estimates $12,000 as the cost of degraded service without the desired software. Of the three figures, the $12,000 is lowest, so this figure is the amount to be added to the basic price of the vendor's bid when alternative bids are compared during the selection process.

Sometimes a value can be subtracted when a requirement is over-fulfilled. If June 1987 is the specified delivery date, a vendor who promises delivery in March, three months early, is given credit. A vendor who can't deliver until September '87 is penalized. In the value template in Table 6.8, the buyer estimates that the March delivery will result in $2,000 in savings to the company. This value is then subtracted from Vendor C's proposal cost. Late delivery, September 1987, is assessed as costing the company $4,000, a figure added to Vendor B's bid.

Table 6.9 shows the cost-value method applied to an actual case: acquisition of a DBMS. This case has been chosen because it demonstrates that the cost-value method, usually applied to hardware acquisition, is equally valid for software. It also lists the features many companies seek when choosing a DBMS.[4]

The costs are genuine, though the table has been simplified. (Thirty-six features have been consolidated into 10 and only 2 vendors instead of the original 4 are compared.) Note that Vendor A's

Table 6.8   **Value template for delivery dates**

	Vendor A	Vendor B	Vendor C
Date of delivery	June 87	Sept. 87	March 87
Value	0	+$4,000	−$2,000

---

[4]For more on software buying, see the special issues of *Datamation* 26, no. 12 (December 1980) and 27, no. 9 (August 1981).

Table 6.9	Cost calculations for selection of a DBMS		
	Cost items	Vendor A ($000)	Vendor B ($000)
	Cost of vendor proposal	$208	$102
	Interface to a higher level language; i.e., BASIC	42	18
	Natural language query facility including communications interface	20	50
	Equipment interdependence (52k/machine)	51	104
	Data element dictionary	—	57
	Supporting equipment necessary . .	—	20
	Inverted file	—	70
	Recovery procedures	—	55
	Security	55.5	5
	Conversion of data base	34	95
	Total	$410.5	$596

proposal price was twice that of Vendor B, but that when the value of omitted features is added, the total cost of A's system is lower than B's system. Also notice the high cost of conversion listed in the table. Conversion costs must be considered when acquiring new hardware, for existing application programs may have to be altered to run on the new equipment. The most efficient hardware may turn out to be unacceptable because of such conversion costs.

The cost-value method does away with weighted value judgments and scores. It takes into consideration costs and feature interactions. But the problem of subjectivity still remains when estimating the life of a system, the cost of degraded service due to lack of features, or the benefits to be gained from overfulfilled requirements. Nevertheless, fewer subjective judgments are required than for the weighted-score method.

A major disadvantage with the cost-value approach to vendor selection is that it requires much time and effort to complete the evaluation. The DBMS selection effort cited in Table 6.9 took three and a half man-years of effort for a team of seven (head of information systems, consultant, three systems programmers, two applications programmers). Note that no representative of corporate management was on the team. In this case, management delegated selection responsibility because the choice of a DBMS requires considerable technical expertise. Other firms commonly include a management representative in the selection process regardless of the technical nature of the acquisition decision.

SUMMARY

In 1978, a survey of data processing users showed that 8.4 percent of the firms made major equipment changes every year, 11.31 percent every two years, 16.7 percent every three years, 13.8 percent every four years, and 13.1 percent every five years.[5] Since technology in the computer industry is advancing rapidly (making current equipment quickly obsolescent or cost-ineffective), since new computer applications are continually being developed, and since the dropping cost of computers is bringing them into budget range for a growing number of firms, this pace of major equipment change will most likely continue, if not accelerate. Choosing what computer resources to acquire is becoming a management decision that recurs frequently. When considering acquisition options, managers must answer questions such as:

Should we implement a real-time system, replacing the batch mode?

Should we replace current hardware with the latest model on the market or wait for new models being developed?

Should we use minis in a network and distributed processing mode?

Should we implement a DBMS or wait for the debate on data models to settle?

Acquisition decisions are often made by a team appointed by corporate management, which determines need specifications, sends out RFPs, evaluates returns, and selects vendors. The network diagram in Figure 6.4 traces this process. This diagram is consistent with Figure 6.1, but has greater detail.

Validation of proposals may include a literature search and vendor justification. Hand timing, benchmark tests, and simulation are techniques for verifying performance claims. Two procedures have been explained in this chapter for evaluating proposals: the weighted-score method and the cost-value approach. Once a decision is reached, all vendors submitting proposals should be notified of the choice.

At all stages in the acquisition process, judgemental decisions are made and they are subject to error. One cannot state future computer needs with certainty, nor predict a company's growth with accuracy. Assigning values to development costs or desired features is difficult at best. However, the procedures outlined in this chapter should help

---

[5]"Cash or carry?" *Computer Decisions* 10, no. 5 (May 1978), p. 22.

Figure 6.4   **Critical path diagram of the acquisition process**

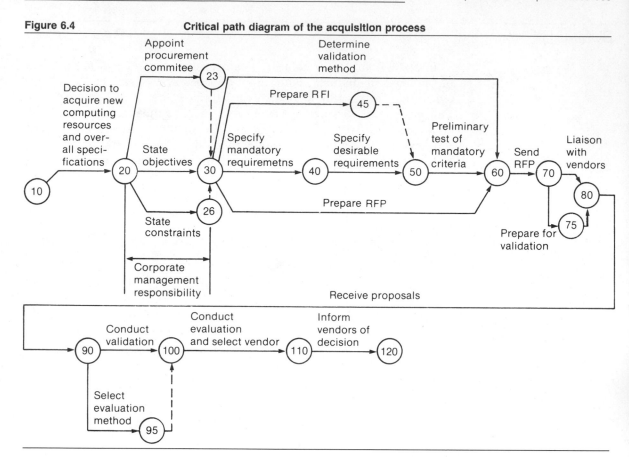

reduce the risk in acquisitions and help firms reach cost-effective procurement decisions.

Vendor selection is a time-consuming activity requiring technical expertise. Constantly changing technology and the large number of possible configurations available complicates the problem of choosing the best vendor proposal. The acquisition process does not end with vendor selection, for there are financial decisions to be made and contracts to be negotiated. Chapter 7 continues the discussion on acquisitions, dealing with these latter topics.

CASE STUDY: ACQUISITION OF RESOURCES, GOVERNMENT OF AUSTRALIA

This case study, the acquisition of resources for the Government of Australia, has been chosen because it illustrates the process of vendor selection and the magnitude of decision making when a large system is planned and bids evaluated.

An on-line national computer center in Canberra is being developed by the Australian government for its Social Security Department. Planned for 1986 or 1987, the center will be connected with on-line regional files, and will have the ability to access and update files from 7,266 work stations with color capability.

The Australian government currently uses IBM equipment. The RFP for the proposed center demanded IBM-compatible mainframes, IBM operations software, IBM communications protocol, and IBM's SNA-compatible office systems. This IBM slant to the RFP locked out the BUNCH companies (Burroughs, Univac, NCR, CDC, and Honeywell). Much publicity was given to IBM-Australia's contract bid. It appeared that IBM would win the contract without contest.

240 consultants helped evaluate bids and 100 man-years of effort went into the vendor selection process. The award announcement came as a surprise. Instead of IBM, IBM-compatible vendors were selected. Amdahl won a contract worth $28 million for mainframes, Storage Tech a $17 million contract for disk drives, and Wang a $73 million contract for office systems and communications gear. When maintenance, training, and support are added, another 50 per cent will be added to these figures, especially for Wang's part of the project.

As part of their contracts, all three U.S. firms had to agree to produce an Australian-based facility. In the case of Wang, this will be a million-dollar plant in Canberra employing over 300 people to produce color display units. With this plant, Wang will not only displace the traditional domination of the British company ICL in Australia, but give Wang a manufacturing beachhead in the South Pacific and Asia.

Other related contracts went to the Computer Corporation of America for 204 data base management systems and to IBM-Australia for some operating systems, some hardware, and some supporting software packages.

KEY WORDS

Benchmark	Request for information (RFI)
Cost-value method	Request for proposals (RFP)
Extension factor	Satisficers
Hand timing	Simulation program
Literature search	Weighted-score technique
Optimizers	

DISCUSSION QUESTIONS

1. Under what circumstances would you use the weighted-score method as opposed to the cost value approach? Under what circumstances would you use neither? Explain.

2. Taking the multiplication product of two subjectively ranked values in the weighted score method means the results are worthless. Comment. Can the problem be eliminated or minimized? How?

3. Why is it difficult to determine weights and score vendors in the weighted score method? How can these difficulties be eliminated or at least reduced?

4. The cost-value approach is sound in its concept and in its implementation. Do you agree with this statement? If so, why?

5. If the weighted-score method were to be used in selecting computer resources, who should do the:
    a. Scoring?
    b. Weighting?

6. Should the composition of the groups performing the scoring and weighting depend on:
    a. Size of institution?
    b. Complexity of resource to be selected?
    c. Cost of resources?
    d. Other factors?

7. Should the selection of vendors vary according to the type of computer resources being chosen? What selection process would you recommend for:
    a. Hardware selection, such as a CPU?
    b. Application software?
    c. Peripherals?
    d. DBMS?

8. In the selection process of a medium-size computer, who should be responsible for:
    a. The acquisition decision?
    b. Preparation of the RFP?
    c. Preparation of specs for a CPU?
    d. Liaison with vendor?

9. Would your answers differ in Question 8 for selection of:
    a. Software packages?
    b. Terminals?
    c. A DBMS?
    d. A hardware-software system?
        Explain.

10. When and why is the selection process important to an organization?

11. What are some of the difficulties and frustrations faced in the selection process by the:
    a. Selection committee?

      b. User?
      c. Technical personnel?

12. List and rank sources that you would trust when collecting data for the selection process.

13. What are special problems in selecting computer resources that are:
    a. Being developed and not yet commercially available?
    b. Only recently commercially available?

14. What are difficulties in determining criteria for selection?

15. What main activities precede or follow selection of computer resources in the development process? Could selection be a bottleneck delaying the entire project?

16. Should the selection process be treated as a project and be subject to project planning and project control?

17. How can one best validate and evaluate a vendor's claims?

18. Is the selection process getting more difficult with more advanced computer technology? Explain.

19. Why must compatibility be considered when making selections?

20. Why and how can SCERT or other simulation programs help in the acquisition process?

SELECTED ANNOTATED BIBLIOGRAPHY

Cohen, Jules A., and Catherine Scott McKinney. *How To Computerize Your Small Business.* Englewood Cliffs, N.J.: Prentice-Hall, 1980, 171 p.
This is actually a guide to computer selection. More than half the book is an acquisition case study. Many completed forms and details on financial and economic criteria are included. The book is well written and not too technical.

Joslin, E. O. *Computer Selection.* Reading, Mass.: Addison-Wesley Publishing, 1968, 216 p.
Joslin has many years experience in computer selection with the U.S. Navy. Later writings elaborate and refine the techniques described in this book, but this original text, a classic in the field, is definitely worth reading.

McQuaker, R. J. *Computer Choice: A Manual for the* Practitioner. Amsterdam, Netherlands: North-Holland Publishing Company, 1978, 177 p.
This is a case study in computer selection from the late 1970s for one of the world's largest online real-time banking systems. The book is difficult to read because it is typewritten, not typeset, and the text is very detailed, but it is a good case study including many useful appendices.

Pooch, Uldo W., and Rahul Chattergy. *Minicomputers: Hardware, Software, and Selection.* St. Paul, Minn.: West Publishing, 1980, pp. 271–320.
Chapter 8 is an informative chapter on the acquisition of minicomputers.

Wooldridge, Susan. *Software Selection*. Philadelphia, Penn.: Auerbach Publishers, 1973, 183 p.

This excellent book on software selection is written for managers and nontechnical readers. It claims to be a guide to more than 600 organizations selling software. Included are chapters on evaluation (containing a cost–benefit analysis) and acquisitions.

Yearsley, Ronald, and Roger Graham (eds.) *Handbook* of Computer Management. Epping, Essex, England: Gower Press, 1973, 328 p.

The selection of equipment is a subject to be found in most handbooks. This book, published in England, has a viewpoint which is different and refreshing.

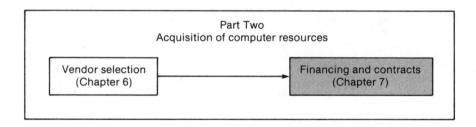

Part Two
Acquisition of computer resources

Vendor selection
(Chapter 6)

Financing and contracts
(Chapter 7)

Acquisition of computer resources:

Financing and contracts

Better one safe way than a hundred on which you cannot reckon.

Aesop

This chapter continues the discussion on acquisitions begun in Chapter 6. Once resource needs are specified, requests for proposals sent out, submissions evaluated, and a vendor selected (Chapter 6), financing must be arranged and a contract signed. This chapter considers the pros and cons of rental, purchase, and lease alternatives, concluding with sections on contract negotiations and contract preparation. The emphasis is on hardware financing and contracts, though software examples are given.

APPROACHES TO FINANCING

How should acquisitions be financed? Rental, purchase, or lease? A decision on financing computer resources differs from conventional acquisition decisions because unique pricing patterns have evolved in the computer industry over the years. The industry was monopolistic at the beginning, with **rental** the only option. This changed in the 1950s following antitrust litigation. At that time the Justice Department set price guidelines and prodded IBM to offer users a **purchase** choice. (More on the role of litigation in shaping the computer industry is found in Chapter 26.) But users continued to favor rentals due to the continual improvement in performance and decrease in price

123

of new models reaching the market. In effect, the high technology of the industry discouraged users from investing in the purchase of equipment that would quickly become obsolete.

Leasing also became an alternative in the 1950s when the government, through a consent decree with IBM, required the company to lease as well as sell equipment. IBM's response was to lease at a high price. Recognizing a business opportunity, entrepreneurs stepped in and formed leasing companies in competition with IBM. These leasing companies first purchased equipment from computer manufacturers, then leased it to users at a lower cost than rentals. They competed by depreciating equipment over a longer lifetime than manufacturer rentals, relying on the premise that equipment could be kept in service far longer than manufacturers allowed and could be leased to a series of users. The favorable investment climate of the early 1970s also fostered growth of leasing companies. Today, leasing firms are thriving, though their market is volatile. The introduction of each new family of IBM computers, for example, tends to disrupt the market, at least temporarily, as users wait for new equipment instead of leasing the old.

In the next sections of this chapter, the advantages and limitations of rental, purchase and lease options will be discussed. Numerical examples will illustrate the computations to be made when considering each alternative.

RENTALS

When computing was limited to unit record punched card equipment, rental was the only user option. This changed in 1956 with the **IBM Consent Decree,** an out-of-court settlement of an antitrust suit against IBM filed by the government because of IBM's alleged monopolistic control over much of the existing data processing equipment. In the decree, IBM agreed to allow customers to purchase computing equipment, and a reasonable ratio between rentals and purchase price was established. Though ratio obligations have since expired, they have been maintained by IBM under the watchful eye of the Justice Department.

Computer rentals today are desirable when equipment is needed only for short periods and user demand is unstable or uncertain. A major advantage is that the user does not have to worry about maintenance. The price of rental, however, is high so that renting for more than two or three years will cost more than the purchase price. Another drawback is that there is usually a charge for overtime use beyond a specific number of hours a month, which may be as much as 40 percent higher than the regular rental fee.

PURCHASE

Many users hesitate to purchase computer equipment because of fears of **obsolescence.** This fear is justified because computers have made quantum jumps in service and performance in recent years: from unit record equipment to batch processing, to online real-time systems and teleprocessing, to distributed processing and word processing. Competitive pressures often require firms to have the latest equipment available. In the airline industry, for example, once American Airlines went online with reservations, all major airlines had to follow suit to retain their customers.

The continual drop in price of computers also makes users hesitant to buy. In 1979, for example, the IBM 4331 could be purchased for $65,000, replacing an earlier equivalent machine, a mid-range model of the IBM 370, which cost $350,000. No wonder users are unwilling to commit themselves to a major capital outlay when they know that the capability they need will cost considerably less in the future. Storage costs have dropped equally dramatically. The IBM 4300 series costs $15,000 per megabyte of storage. In an earlier series, the cost was $75,000 per megabyte for equivalent storage.

The **price-performance ratio** has also improved over time, as shown in Figure 7.1. A rule of thumb in the industry states that prices drop arithmetically while performance increases geometrically. Cost-performance improvements are cyclical, coming every five or six years as new families of computers are introduced, with sales peaking halfway between. Note the delivery curves for the IBM 360 and 370, as shown in Figure 7.2. The down slopes indicate that businesspersons are leery about acquiring equipment when a new model is expected. Though it is not in the interest of computer manufacturers to shorten the time period between models (a new model may take away sales of equipment recently put on the market before development costs and expected profit can be realized), competition within the industry and from foreign manufacturers, especially Japanese firms, is forcing companies to place new models on the market at an ever faster pace. The speed with which IBM is introducing its 4000 series supports this thesis.

Purchase has advantages, however, that counterbalance, in part, the liability of obsolescence. There are tax benefits in purchasing computer resources that should be considered. The IRS permits **depreciation** of hardware and software of an information system over 5–6 years. In addition, **investment tax credits** are available when systems are purchased or leased. Credits are more powerful than expense deductions because they reduce tax by one dollar for every dollar of credit. However, the amount and type of equipment for which credits are allowed varies according to the business climate and the prevail-

Figure 7.1   **Price-performance comparison over limited range**

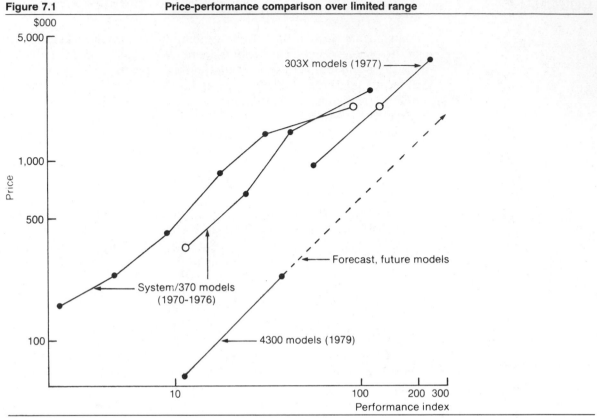

Source: Adapted form *Fortune* 100, no. 2 (July 30, 1979) p. 58.

ing tax laws passed in Washington. Computers also have a **salvage value,** sometimes as high as 40 percent of purchase price, though not all equipment will find buyers, as owners of RCA, Memorex, General Electric, or XDS systems can testify. But some computer equipment has a **useful life** of up to 10 years in the United States and even longer abroad. (Useful life can be operationally defined as the time period during which the required workload can be economically processed by the equipment in question.) The IBM 1400 series is still functional and popular in developing countries 20 years after being unveiled in the United States. In 1980, for example, one out of four computers in India was from this series.

At first glance, purchase is also very much cheaper than rental. A $1,600,000 computer would cost $533,344 in rent per year, making three years' rental more than the purchase price. This comparison is simplistic, however, for it does not allow for investment credit and maintenance depreciation which benefit the purchaser, nor does it

Figure 7.2   **Delivery cycles of IBM 360 and 370**

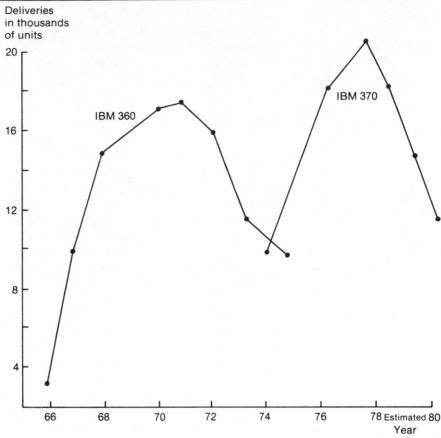

Source: *Dun's Review* 110, no. 10 (July 1977), p. 83.

discount for the **present value (PV)** of cash flows for each of the years of useful life. (The discounted rate used for calculating present value is the average rate of return on investment.)

Other factors which have a bearing when comparing the advantages of purchase versus rental are:

Life expectancy of computer resource.

Time expected until next generation.

Reliability of resource (tried and proven?).

Expected hours of usage.

Stability of applications and usage.

Likelihood of modification or updating of resource.

Borrowing rate.

Discount rate.

Depreciation method.

Depreciation rate.

Property tax rate.

Corporate tax rate.

Investment tax credit rate.

A firm must also consider the availability of capital for a purchase. When financial resources are limited, competing projects may be given funding priority. Many firms, especially nonprofit organizations and governmental departments, find the bureaucratic procedures required for purchases and the time lag in getting bids and evaluating proposals not worth the effort: thus these organizations frequently prefer rentals.

Calculations for rental and purchase of a medium-to large-size computer that take into consideration some of the variables cited above are shown in Table 7.1. Data on which the calculations are based appear in the first section of the table. Calculations for purchase and rental are then shown. In these two sections each column represents one year of transactions. A positive number indicates outflow or cost; a negative number (in parenthesis) indicates inflows or savings. The total net outflow equals the sum of costs less inflows.

To represent future costs as a present value so they can be compared with the present purchase price, the totals must be multiplied by a present value factor, as shown in Table 7.1. The present value of purchase and the present value of all other related costs after income tax are then totaled. The $687,082 represents the PV of purchase outflows. This figure should then be compared with cash outflows for rentals over the same time period, discounted to their present value. In Table 7.1, rental equals $1,126,184. Purchase, therefore, costs $439,102 less than rental in present value.

According to this table, the **cut-over point** is about three years. That is, if the useful life of the system is near three years or longer it would be cheaper to buy than rent.

This is merely an example. For some manufacturers, the cutover point could be 2–3 years. Variables will differ from one situation to another, although purchase is always less than rental over a period of five years, even when maintenance costs are included. Many of the variables affecting the calculations are exogenous (external), that is, beyond a firm's control. Borrowing rates, tax rates, or investment tax credit rates would fall in this category. Other variables, though internal, are not always easy to estimate or manage. For example, demand for application and debugging programs may mean more run time is spent than anticipated, raising rental costs because of overtime fees. Were this to occur, the cutover period would be affected.

Table 7.1   Purchase versus rent calculations

Data on which purchase calculations are based

1. Purchase basic price $1,600,000
2. Estimated useful life . . . . 5 years
3. Maintenance contract $3,040/month
4. Property tax 12,960/year
5. Investment tax credit (ITC) . . . . . . 10 percent
6. Depreciation (ACRS)* . . . . Taken over 5 years with rates 15, 22, 21, 21, and 21 percent for each year
7. Discount rate . . . . 10 percent
8. Tax rate (state and federal) . . . . . 50 percent
9. Salvage value at end of 5th year . . . $500,000

Maintenance/year $36,480
Tax savings/year @ 50 percent 18,240
Net cost on maintenance $18,240/year

Calculations for purchase (inflows shown in parenthesis);

	Year 1	Year 2	Year 3	Year 4	Year 5
Original purchase price	$1,600,000				
Maintenance	0	$ 0	$ 0	$ 0	$ 0
Property tax (net)	0	18,240	18,240	18,240	18,240
Cash savings from		6,480	6,480	6,480	6,480
depreciation	0	(120,000)	(176,000)	(160,000)	(160,000)	(160,000)
Investment tax credit	0	(106,000)	0	0	0
Salvage value	0	0	0	0	(500,000)
Cash outflow	$1,600,000	($201,280)	($151,289)	($143,280)	($143,280)	($643,280)
Present value (PV) factor	1.0	.9091	.8264	.7513	.6830	.6209
PV of cash outflow	$1,600,000	($182,983)	($125,017)	($107,646)	($ 97,860)	($399,412)
Total PV of cash outflow for five years						$687,082

Calculations for rental

	Year 1	Year 2	Year 3	Year 4	Year 5
Rental	$593,244	$593,244	$593,244	$593,244	$593,244
Tax savings from rental (50 percent rental)	(296,622)	(296,622)	(296,622)	(296,622)	(296,622)
Total outflow	$296,622	$296,622	$296,622	$296,622	$296,622
Present value (PV) factor	.9091	.8284	.7513	.6830	.6209
PV of cash outflow	$269,659	$245,128	$224,632	$202,593	$184,172
PV of cash outflow for five years						$1,126,184

*ACRS = Accelerated cost recovery system.

Usually a stable demand for a computer resource over its calculated payback period is needed before purchase (instead of rental) can be economically justified. There is obviously no point in buying unneeded equipment or software. Sometimes firms are able to rectify purchase errors by passing inappropriate or redundant resources to other departments or subsidiaries or, in certain families of equipment, modifying or updating the resource to fit their needs.

Purchase and rental are not the only options. Leasing should also be considered.

LEASING

Leasing is usually the best alternative when computer resources are needed for a three- to four-year period. Leasing rates cannot compete with rentals for short periods of time (one to two years). Purchase is generally the best option when the useful life of the resource will be five or more years.

The popularity of leasing is based on fears of obsolescence should a purchase be made, and experience that the advantages of rentals often prove illusory. Many firms that choose rental (because they want the latest resources and hope to switch models whenever new equipment is introduced) find it takes more than two years to develop an information system and learn to use effectively the computer they have rented. If they switch models after two years, they face the trauma of conversion before being experienced with equipment at hand. If they keep the rental, the cost is uneconomical compared with leasing. Computer personnel favor three to four years to develop a system before a change in equipment is made. Leasing provides this stability while avoiding dangers of obsolescence. Other advantages of leasing include the fact that equipment can usually be obtained without a long wait, and, unlike rentals, a computer can often be used 24 hours a day without penalty.

Leasing companies may also offer leases with the option to purchase. Firms without necessary funds to buy, or firms uncertain of the demand for the resource under consideration, often choose this option. They make monthly lease payments for a specified period or up to a given amount, then take title. Normally this approach costs little more than a straight lease. Sometimes it costs even less. No wonder 22.9 percent of the users in a 1977 survey exercised this option.[1]

A decision to lease or lease with the option to buy should be based on a **discounted cash-flow analysis.** Calculations showing costs for

---

[1]This survey is reported in "Cash or Carry," *Computer Decisions* 10, no. 5 (May 1978), pp. 19–24.

Table 7.2   **Calculation for lease**

Data on lease environment

1. Lease payment $600,000/year
2. Period of lease . . . .   5 years
3. Maintenance $24,000/yr
4. Property tax . . . .   Lessee pays
5. Investment credit . . . .   Tax benefit to lessor
6. Depreciation . . . .   Tax benefit to lessor
7. Discount rate . . . .   10 percent
8. Marginal tax rate . . . .   50 percent

Lease payments	$600,000/year
Tax savings (50 percent)	300,000
Net lease cost	$300,000/year

Maintenance	$24,000/year
Tax savings (50 percent)	12,000
Net cost on maintenance . . .	$12,000/year

After-tax cash outflow	*Year 1*	*Year 2*	*Year 3*	*Year 4*	*Year 5*
Lease	$300,000	$300,000	$300,000	$300,000	$300,000
Maintenance	12,000	12,000	12,000	12,000	12,000
Property tax	5,265	5,265	5,265	5,265	5,265
Total	$317,265	$317,265	$317,265	$317,265	$317,265
PV factor	$\frac{1}{(1.10)^1}$	$\frac{1}{(1.10)^2}$	$\frac{1}{(1.10)^3}$	$\frac{1}{(1.10)^4}$	$\frac{1}{(1.10)^5}$
Present value (PV) factor	.9091	.8264	.7513	.6830	.6206
PV of total after-tax cash outflow	$288,426	$262,188	$238,361	$216,692	$196,895
Total PV of cash outflow for five years $1,202,562					

straight lease for a period of five years appear in Table 7.2. A lease-purchase decision, that is, purchase after a one-year lease, is figured in Table 7.3. The calculations are similar to those made earlier when comparing rental and purchase, though more variables are involved in leasing (see Table 7.4). Again, each column in the tables represents a year of transactions, with costs discounted to present value. Straight lease has a PV of $1,202,562 (from discount annuity tables) compared to the lease-purchase alternative costing $947,770. According to these calculations, given the assumptions of the problem, lease-purchase is the better alternative, saving $254,792.[2]

Some of the variables used in these two sets of calculations differ from Table 7.1, which compares rental and purchase. For example,

---

[2]Present value calculations may lead to erroneous conclusions when comparing different kinds of equipment with different useful lives. In such cases, the total cost of equipment alternatives should be converted to annuities over the lives of the respective alternatives and a comparison then made of these annuities.

Table 7.3   **Calculations for lease/purchase**

Data on environment

Lease payments	$600,000/year
Period of lease	1 year
Maintenance	$24,000/year (Note the difference from purchase case)
Property tax	$10,530/year after purchase
Investment credit	10 percent claimed on purchase
Depreciation	Straight line on five years after acquisition
Discount rate	10 percent
Tax rate	50 percent
Useful life	5 years
Portion of rentals deducted from purchase price . . .	($320,000)
Purchase price	$1,600,000 − 320,000 = $1,280,000
Resale value at end of 5 years	$300,000

Cash outflows	Year 1	Year 2	Year 3	Year 4	Year 5
Lease	$600,000	$ 0	$ 0	$ 0	$ 0
Purchase price	0	1,280,000	0	0	0
Maintenance	12,000	12,000	12,000	12,000	12,000
Property tax	0	5,265	5,265	5,265	5,265
Tax savings from depreciation	0	(160,000)	(160,000)	(160,000)	(160,000)
Investment tax credit	0	(85,000)	0	0	0
Resale value	0	0	0	0	(300,000)
Total outflow	$612,000	$1,052,265	($142,735)	($142,735)	($442,735)
Present value (PV) factor . . .	.9091	.8264	.7413	.6830	.6209
PV of cash outflow	$556,369	$ 869,592	($105,809)	($ 97,488)	(274,894)

Total PV of cash outflow for five years $947,770

Table 7.4   **Variables in leasing**

Lease payments
Leasing period
Maintenance cost
Discount rate
Tax rate
Costs for installation
Costs for shipping
Costs for system checking and integration
Conditions for upgrading and updating
Conditions for renewal
Depreciation rate
Investment tax credit rate
Recipient of investment tax credit (either lessor or lessee)

the depreciation rate has been altered. This is to show the reader that calculations are not always made on the basis of the same variables. Indeed, in an actual case, few of the variables or values of the variables listed may be applicable since a change in government in Washington can affect tax laws, discount rates, and useful life allowances. Also, the length of the lease period will affect calculations. The longer the term of lease, the lower the monthly payment. In the 1977 survey cited earlier, three years was the most common term of lease (20.6 percent), though some seven-year leases did exist (2.5 percent).

In addition, leasing vendors differ in their charges. Rates will be higher if a vendor has both developed and manufactured the equipment to be leased because it will be necessary to recover R&D costs. Rates are also affected by the payback period and how often lease equipment is updated. The lowest rates are charged by **third-party leasing firms** which purchase equipment directly from a manufacturer. They set a low rate structure (made possible, in part, by the tax benefits they derive from the purchase) and operate at a low profit margin. Rates are usually based on a computer life from 8 to 12 years and the expectation that equipment will be leased to three or more consecutive users.

The third-party lessor gambles on the firm's marketing ability to find users for older models, in addition to users for up-to-date equipment. Many mundane jobs do not require the latest technology. And the lessor knows that the pool of potential customers is expanding, due to a growing public awareness of the value of computers coupled with the dramatic drop in computer price. Also, firms are allocating an increasing share of revenues to computer processing. Large corporations, for example, spent 3 percent of revenues on data processing in 1975, 6 percent in 1978, with 8 percent predicted in 1982.[3] In addition, new equipment is becoming increasingly modular, flexible, reliable, and upwardly compatible, lessening risk to the lessor.

Nevertheless, lessors are cautious. If uncertain about the market for re-leasing equipment after their first customer, they may simply choose not to buy a given model to lease. In 1979, for example, the only leasing company to offer IBM's 303K series (introduced in 1978) was Itel and then for a minimum of seven years, reflecting lessor uncertainty about the residual value of the series. Lessors want innovations in computer technology but models that have demonstrated their market value. The lessor's perception of the market and degree of

---

[3]Bro Uttal, "How The 4300 Fits IBM's New Strategy," *Fortune* 100, no. 2 (July 30, 1979), p. 62. Another study reported in *Datamation* 102, no. 5 (May 1981), p. 5, states that 1 percent of total corporate resources are spent on data processing departments. Exact figures vary from source to source and depend on the type of corporation under consideration.

aversion to risk will determine what equipment is bought and placed on lease.

OBJECTIVES OF CONTRACT NEGOTIATIONS

Once computer resources are selected and the decision reached on whether to rent, purchase, or lease, **contract negotiations** with the vendor begin. During negotiations, both parties will try to improve their economic position. A vendor trying to break into the market may have to accept less favorable terms than a well established vendor, and may come out the loser in a zero sum game (buyer gains at the expense of the vendor.) But it is possible for both negotiating parties to settle on a contract to their mutual advantage. For example, a firm may express interest in particular equipment to a leasing company which the leasing company then purchases, taking advantage of investment tax credits. The vendor can then pass this advantage, in part, to the firm in favorable lease terms, such as lower payments, lower maintenance fees, or added services.

Misunderstandings sometimes exist in vendor–client relationships because the two parties have dissimilar backgrounds and use different terminologies. A primary objective of negotiations is to specify in legally binding unambiguous terms the rights and obligations of both vendor and client. Detailed specifications will help produce a workable, enforceable document and help avoid disagreement that can lead to ill will, or litigation.[4]

CONTRACT CONTENTS

Contracts will vary according to the nature of the product (hardware or software), the complexity of the system, and the personalities and past experiences of the negotiators. The basic contents of an acquisition contract should include the following:

Requirement specifications.
Critical commitments implied in demonstration and presentations.
Acceptance criterion.
Remedies for vendor non-performance.
Penalties.
Arbitration.

---

[4]For a discussion on this subject, see Robert A. Bucci, "Avoiding Hassles with Vendors," *Datamation* 20, no. 7 (July 1974), pp. 68–72.

Warranties.

Guarantees.

Performance bonds.

Services.

   Training.

   Documentation.

   Systems and engineering help.

Financial arrangements on acquisition.

Patents/proprietary rights.

Limitations and disclaimers.

One cannot generalize on the level of detail or specificity required. Even definition of terms may be subject to misinterpretation. Contracts ultimately depend on good will of both sides, but skilled negotiators and legal advice, either in-house lawyers or consultants experienced in computer acquisition contracts, are recommended. It is also useful to have computer technicians and financial personnel on the negotiating team. Many buyers take the initiative and prepare a contract well in advance to be used as a basis of discussion during the negotiations, recognizing that vendors are experienced adversaries who may not include all the clauses the buyer considers mandatory in contracts they propose. At best, negotiations are a bargaining dialog. Confrontation is in the interest of neither party.

A major problem with computer contracts is that few laws specifically regulate computer transactions. Equipment sales do fall under Article 2 of the Uniform Commercial Code adopted by most states, but few specific legal guidelines govern the sale of separate software systems. This is unfortunate since software companies have less stability and maturity than hardware firms and need a legal framework. For the buyer this means that a software firm's reputation is very important in vendor selection.

CONTRACT IMPLEMENTATION

Once a contract is signed, its execution requires close **liaison** between buyer and vendor. When multiple vendors contribute to a computing system, liaison increases in complexity. Though a one-vendor proposition is favored for simplifying the acquisition process and ease in detecting/correcting malfunctions, the system generally costs more than when components are supplied from a number of competing firms. Indeed, the 1969 unbundling decision by IBM has resulted in the establishment of many companies offering components and peripherals at a lower price, with better performance and more features, than many giant corporations offer. As a result, it is quite common today for buyers to contract with several vendors even though interconnecting resources can add considerable time and effort to problems of conversion and add stress to the buyer–vendor relationship. Indeed, the end user often gets caught in the crossfire between vendors when there are system failures during installation and testing.[5]

Fortunately, the computer industry is moving toward **plug-compatible machines,** especially for IBM equipment. This means that a **plug-compatible manufacturer,** such as Amdahl, is able to replace an IBM computer with one of their machines without affecting systems software, applications, or peripherals. Though a few bugs may develop, in principle the change should be transparent to the user, reducing considerably the liaison headaches that formerly plagued buyers of multivendor computer resources.

SUMMARY AND CONCLUSIONS

In this chapter the advantages and limitations of rent, purchase, and lease alternatives have been discussed. Possible alternatives are shown in Figure 7.3. Modifications of these basic choices are also offered by many firms: e.g., IBM offers a fixed term plan, an extended term plan, and a term-lease plan.

The decision of whether to rent, purchase, or lease is complex because of the many factors to be considered, and what is best for one

Figure 7.3   **Rent, lease, and purchase alternatives**

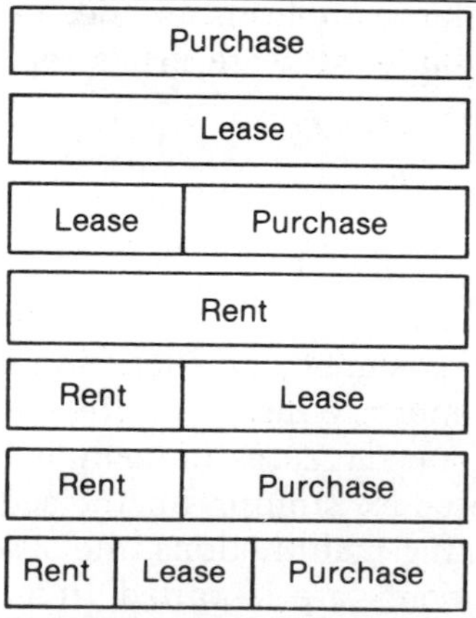

| Purchase |
| Lease |
| Lease | Purchase |
| Rent |
Rent	Lease
Rent	Purchase
Rent	Lease	Purchase

---

[5]For one of many such cases, read Ronald S. Lemos, "A Diary of a Multi-Vendor Purchaser," *Datamation* 26, no. 5 (May 1980), pp. 177–80.

Figure 7.4

Comparison of equipment cost and upgrading flexibility for purchase, lease, and rent

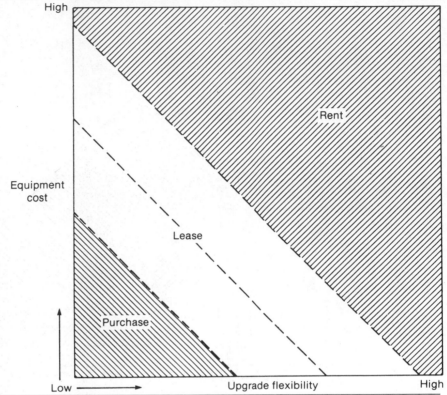

Source: F. Warren McFarlan and Richard L. Nolan, *The Information Systems Handbook* (Homewood, Ill.: Dow Jones-Irwin, 1975), p. 473.

firm will not necessarily be appropriate for another. Figure 7.4 displays the trade-offs that must be compared. This figure shows that the low equipment cost of purchasing gives the buyer less upgrading flexibility than rental or lease, whereas rental costs are high but equipment more easily upgraded. Another set of criteria is shown in Figure 7.5: administrative costs and acquisition complexity. A decision based on these criteria alone would favor purchase.

In making an acquisition choice, each firm, after studying its environment, should base its choice on:

1. The financial climate. This includes availability of funds, both internal (opportunity costs) and external (banks and lending institutions); governmental policies on depreciation; and property taxes on purchases.
2. Anticipation of technological advances. Will more reliable, com-

Figure 7.5   **Acquisition complexity and administration costs for purchase, rent, and lease**

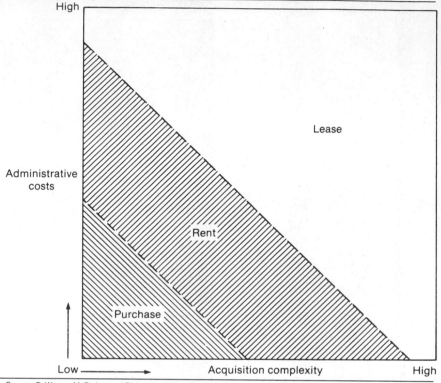

Source: F. Warren McFarlan and Richard L. Nolan, *The Information Systems Hardbook* (Homewood, Ill.: Dow Jones-Irwin, 1975), p. 474.

patible, and cheaper computer resources soon be released? Will new innovative systems have a longer useful life, increasing their residual value to lessor?

3.   User demand projections. Current and future user demand projections, as well as predictions on the secondhand usefulness of the resources to other units in the organization when the original user updates.[6]

4.   Ability to maintain equipment. If lacking maintenance knowledge and experience, rental or lease options may be advisable.

5.   Decision-making structure. Rentals or leasing may be expedient (though not necessarily economically sound) if firms have cumbersome procedures for letting bids and making acquisition decisions.

---

[6]For more on this subject, read Bro Uttal, "Fortune-Tellers in the Computer Base," *Fortune* 102, no. 11 (December 1, 1980), pp. 134–40.

Table 7.5   **Comparison of purchase, lease, or rent**

	Rent	Purchase	Straight lease
Separate maintenance contract necessary?	No	Yes	No
Investment tax credit possible?	No	Yes, but subject to change by government policy	No
Depreciation possible?	No	Yes	No
Rent/lease payments tax deductible as expense? . . .	Yes	Not applicable	Yes
Useful life	1–2 years	More than 5–6 years	6 months to 6 years
Capital outlay needed?	No	Yes	No
Total cost for period of 5–6 years or more	Highest	Lowest	Higher than purchase

Table 7.5 is a summary comparison of rent, purchase, and lease alternatives.

Leasing as an option began in 1961. By 1970, over a hundred leasing firms existed. The future of leasing will depend on rental pricing policies of manufacturers, governmental policies regarding investments, and the speed with which new generations of computer resources are introduced to the market. The survival of individual leasing firms depends on how well they read industry trends, how finely they time purchases, and how successful they are in finding sequential users for leased resources.

Negotiation of acquisition contracts requires technical and legal expertise. When implementing contracts, close liaison with vendors may reduce the stress of conversion. Fortunately, interfacing equipment is becoming less of a problem with the introduction of plug-compatible machines.

CASE STUDY: FEDERAL MISMANAGEMENT OF A SOFTWARE DEVELOPMENT CONTRACT*

Close to $1 million was spent by a federal agency on a software development contract that produced no usable software, according to a General Accounting Office (GAO) report in 1979. A number of reasons were cited for the boondoggle, including failure of the agency to fully complete specification of systems requirements before issuing a request for proposals and the length of time the agency took to review software submitted by the contractor for approval. However, a poorly

*Source: "GAO Tells a $970,000 Horror Story," *Computerworld* 13, no. 48 (December 3, 1979), p. 12.

written contract was the major problem.

The agency wanted an integrated personnel/payroll system and signed a fixed-price contract for phased software development to be completed in 15 months for $445,158. But the contract did not state systems requirements, omitted specification of acceptance testing procedures, did not identify quality criteria for documentation, and failed to require agency approval of completed phases. Both parties admitted that contract terminology was vague. Delivery dates, scope of work, and costs were revised many times. Indeed, amendments were added to the contract 13 times, increasing the cost of the contract to $1,037,448.

Eventually the agency canceled the contract after rejecting the general system design proposed and deciding the contractor còuld never deliver an acceptable system within time and cost constraints. The agency tried to withhold payment for poor performance, but finally agreed upon a negotiated settlement price of $970,000. None of the software prepared by the contractor was ever used.

KEY WORDS

Contract negotiations	Plug-compatible machines
Cutover point	Plug-compatible manufacturer
Depreciation	Present value (PV)
Discounted cash-flow analysis	Price–performance ratio
IBM Consent Decree	Purchase
Investment tax credits	Rental
Lease	Salvage value
Liaison	Third-party leasing firm
Obsolescence	Useful life

DISCUSSION QUESTIONS

1. Who should make the decision on purchase or lease? What factors determine the choice? When should a direct lease be favored over a third party lease?

2. Is knowledge of the law necessary when selecting computing resources? Why? Who should provide this knowledge?

3. On what factors will the answer to Question 2 depend?

4. Compare the advantages and limitations of purchase, rent, and lease of computer resources.

5. In the selection process under what circumstances would you hire a:
   a. Consultant?
   b. Lawyer?
   What qualities and qualifications would you look for?

6. In acquiring which of the following resources would you employ a lawyer?
   a. Hardware.
   b. Software—applications.
   c. Hardware-software system.
   d. Turnkey system.
   e. Software, such as a DBMS.

7. Why is the preparation of a contract for computer resources different
   from the preparation for a contract for construction of a building, or for
   equipment, such as a lathe?

8. Do problems of acquisition vary depending on the source of the resource,
   i.e., hardware vendor, a software house, or consulting company? Explain.

9. Is planning necessary for the acquisition process? If so, why? Who
   should do it? At what stage of the development process should it be
   done?

10. How does the acquisition of computer resources vary conceptually and
    in implementation due to the:
    a. Size of the organization acquiring the resource (i.e., small or large
        business)?
    b. Value involved?
    c. Range of services to be offered by resource being acquired?
    d. Number of subcontractors involved?
        What special precautions and steps should be taken?

11. Time is an important element in the acquisition process. Comment.

12. What are the problems of vendor liaison after an acquisition is made?
    How can these problems be minimized?

SELECTED ANNOTATED BIBLIOGRAPHY

Brandon, Dick H., and Sydney Segelstein. *Data Processing Contracts Structure, Contract and* Negotiations. Cincinnati, Ohio: Van Nostrand Reinhold, 1976, 465 p.
   This book treats many topics on acquisitions omitted from the Hussain
   text, while covering the subtopics of Chapter 7 in greater detail. One new
   topic, for example, is a discussion of risk and exposure anlysis of contracts. Cases are used to illustrate each topic. The authors premise is that
   the buyer should take the initiative in all contract negotiations.

Computer Negotiations Report is a journal devoted to the negotiation process
   for computer resource acquisitions. As an example, see vol. 4, issue 1
   (1980) for a detailed account on how to achieve and maintain control over
   the negotiation process.

Freed, Roy N. "The Tax Advantages of Leasing." *Computer Decision* 11, no.
   10 (October 1979), pp. 22–76.
   This article may well be outdated by the time you read it but it illustrates
   the type of information that one must have before making an acquisition
   decision.

Goldberg, Alan L. "Financing Alternatives for Hardware and Software." *Small Systems World* 10 (December 1982), pp. 30–34.
Rental, operating lease, financial lease, and purchase are compared. An example of the acquisition of $70,000 of equipment is used to illustrate cash value flow analysis for the four alternatives.

Joslin, Edward O. *Computer Selection*. Fairfax Station, Va.: Technology Press,1977, 215 p.
The 1977 edition is an augmented version of Joslin's classic book on selection of computers using the cost-value approach, a book that first appeared in 1968. Material added to the original text includes financing of computer acquisitions, the selection of small computers, and a discussion of the workload and the role of management in the task of computer acquisition.

Oliver, R. J. "Third Party Leasing." In *Handbook of Computer Management*, ed. R. D. Yearsley and G. M. R. Graham. Epping, England: Gower Press, 1973, pp. 107–15.
This essay takes a historical view of third party leasing, discussing the motivation of lessor and lessee, and evaluating the future outlook of third-party leasing. A very informative and highly readable article.

Rubin, Martin L., ed. Handbook of Data Processing, vol. 6. *Data Processing Administration*. Princeton, N.J.: Auerbach Publishers, 1971, 600 p.
This is an old but still very relevant source. Rubin's discussions on the computer selection process (Chapter 7), proposed evaluation (Chapter 8), and purchase, lease, or rent decisions (Chapter 9) supplement sections on acquisition in the Hussain text. Good numerical examples show the reader what calculations are useful when making acquisition choices.

Watson, Hugh J., and Archie B. Carroll. *Computers for Business: A Managerial Emphasis*. Plano, Tex.: Business Publications 1980. 530 p.
Chapter 11 of this textbook discusses both the selection and acquisition of computer resources. It integrates these topics backward with planning and forward with installation, appraisal, follow-up, and the review process. However, this integration is achieved at the expense of brevity and there is a loss of detail in so broad a coverage. Assignments, a case study, and good references follow the chapter.

Watson, Richard. "You and Your Computer Contract." *Small Systems World* 6 (June 1979), pp. 38–40.
A useful article on an important subject. Note that the source is not one of the major journals in the field. Useful articles, written for specialized readerships, appear in the most unexpected journals.

Weidler, Gregory. "Purchase or Lease?" *Journal of Systems Management* 27, no. 6 (June 1976), pp. 28–35.
This is a very thorough analysis of purchase and lease choices, with numerical examples of the calculations on cash flow and checklists for the prospective buyer. This article was used extensively to check the contents of the Hussain text Chapter 7.

PART THREE

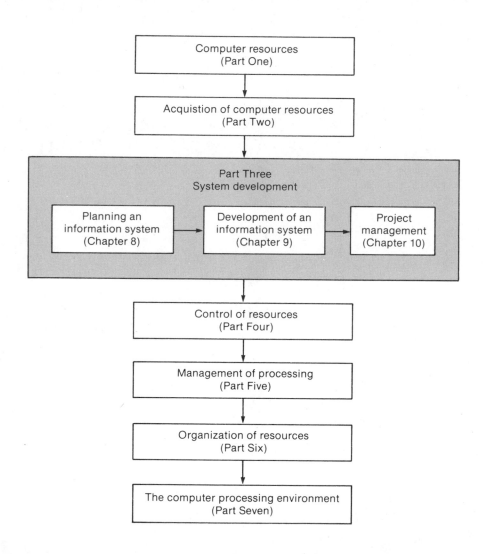

SYSTEM DEVELOPMENT

Part Three tells how to mobilize computer resources to provide the information needs of a business. The three chapters describe how to plan for an information system, develop the system, and control resources during development.

Chapter 8 is the planning chapter. It discusses the necessity of establishing planning goals, outlines approaches to planning, and lists common planning errors.

The development cycle is the subject of Chapter 9. Development begins with ascertaining the output needed in decision making. Then a feasibility study is conducted to determine whether or not a system can be designed to produce the desired output, given the firm's objectives and constraints. System specifications must next be defined in operational terms. Computer programs have to be written, forms for collecting data designed, and operational procedures established. Once the system is tested and results are satisfactory, conversion takes place. All of these steps are discussed in the chapter.

The final chapter in this part, Chapter 10, concerns management of systems development. The chapter outlines the responsibilities of a project manager for systems development, examines project organization, and reviews techniques, such as PERT and GERT, for project control.

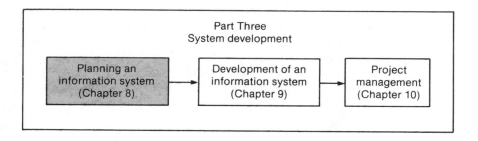

Part Three
System development

Planning an
information system
(Chapter 8)

Development of an
information system
(Chapter 9)

Project
management
(Chapter 10)

CHAPTER 8

Planning an information system

When you fail to plan, you are planning to fail.

Dr. Robert Schuller

No business can introduce a new product line or penetrate a competitor's market without careful **planning.** Indeed, planning the distribution of a firm's personnel, equipment, and financial resources is a prime responsibility of management. With the widespread use of computers today, information has been added to this list of corporate resources. Only through planning can the necessary information be obtained for managing and controlling daily operations and for charting a firm's future.

Another reason information planning is of importance is that information systems are costly. Indeed, total expenditures for data processing are on the rise. Throughout the country, as the range of computer applications has expanded, the demand for information has multiplied, requiring firms to allocate larger and larger slices of their budgets to information processing. The development of an information system is also time-consuming, and a long lead time is often needed for equipment acquisition; these are additional reasons planning is required.

Furthermore, planning is technologically important. Though a firm may be able to implement only a subsystem in a functional area at the start, due to financial constraints, a future integrated system should be envisioned from the beginning and the system designed to permit growth. In building construction, a house cannot add a second story unless the foundation, when poured, allows for this addition. Information systems, likewise, require careful planning for future expansion. Failure to lay the groundwork for growth—to establish linking elements and a plan for integration—may require costly reconstruction of existing systems and considerable dislocation when growth of the information system takes place.

Planning is a framework for orderly development of information systems. In this chapter, the nature of the planning will be examined. Steps in the planning process will be described, planning goals and guidelines recommended, and common planning errors listed. Finally, the formulation of tactical strategies for implementation of an overall information system will be discussed.

ESTABLISHING GOALS FOR THE PLANNING PROCESS

Before beginning to specify long-range and short-range plans for the development of an information system, MIS (management information system) planners should establish **goals** for the planning process itself. These goals might be technical, such as an aim to formulate plans that would reduce operation costs to a given level, or might be more general, such as the following set of objectives proposed by Sherman Blumenthal.[1]

1. To avoid overlapping development of major systems elements.
2. To help ensure a uniform basis for determining sequence of development in terms of payoff potential, natural precedence and probability of success.
3. To minimize the cost of integrating related systems with each other.
4. To reduce the total number of small, isolated systems to be developed, maintained, and operated.
5. To provide adaptability of systems to business change and growth without periodic major overhaul.
6. To provide a foundation for coordinated development of consistent, comprehensive, corporate-wide and inter-organizational information systems.
7. To provide guidelines for and direction to continuing systems-development studies and projects.

All plans which emerge from planning committees should meet the planning goals. (Planning committees are described later in the chapter.) The goals can also be used in implementation control, as standards for measuring EDP performance.

There is no formula to ensure good planning. But flexibility—a re-

---

[1]Sherman C. Blumenthal, *Managerial Information Systems: A Framework for Planning and Development* (Englewood Cliffs: N.J.: Prentice-Hall, 1969), p. 13.

sponsiveness on the part of committee members to changing technology and business conditions—is a must. And periodic revision and updating should be an integral part of planning when developing information systems.

APPROACHES TO SYSTEMS PLANNING

What sets the planning process in motion? Where does the impetus for a new or expanded information system begin? Systems planning is **top-down** when upper management initiates planning. This may be in response to altered market conditions, technological advances, or any number of circumstances that alert management to the need for change. This approach is also used when EDP is first introduced into a firm, for the new EDP department will be structured according to management directives.

Sometimes, however, the process is reversed, with planning being **bottom-up,** that is, with users or EDP technicians signaling the need for change. Top management will still accept, modify, or reject recommendations from a planning committee regarding systems development, but in this case proposals for new policies or system development will be initiated by the EDP department or operational management.

Differences in the style of planners were apparent to Ephraim McLean and John Soden at a conference on long-range planning.

> Participants (planners) saw two quite different roles for themselves—the "reactive" service role and the "proactive" change-agent role. . . . The reactive participants took a largely defensive posture, justifying their lack of regard for the strategy of the overall enterprise by stressing the importance of being responsive to users' immediate requirements. Their major problem ironically was a lack of credibility and confidence on the part of their respective user communities. On the other hand, the proactive group sought ways of actively interacting with the strategic planning effort of the host organization.[2]

Proactive planners also tend to be more concerned with **coalescence planning** than **reactive planners.** Coalescence planning in this context refers to integrating computer applications: for example, combining office automation with text processing, record management with information retrieval, or making one group responsible for all telecommunications and electronic mail.

---

[2]Ephraim R. McLean and John V. Soden, *Strategic Planning for MIS* (New York: John Wiley & Sons, 1977), p. 65.

PLANNING GUIDELINES

Though differences in procedures and approaches to planning exist, general **guidelines** for all planning committees can be stated. Plans should fit within the framework of corporate goals and policies specified by top management during initial stages of planning. How changes, such as new technology, a relaxation of constraints, or the firm's growth, might affect long-range plans should be explained and alternative courses of action proposed. Sometimes a simulation model is helpful. The effect of plan modifications should also be examined. For example, the committee might calculate how a 10 percent reduction or increase in funding would affect system operation.

Responsibility for collecting data should be assigned to specific individuals on the planning committee or staff. Special assignments should also be made for needed research. The staff assisting the committee should be rotated. This will lead to job enlargement and may be a factor easing the throes of later conversion, for involvement in planning usually stimulates interest, and interest usually dissipates resistance to change. When a clash exists between management priorities and technical decisions, the planning committee should resolve the conflict.

The **planning document** itself should include a statement of objectives and should outline how MIS technology will serve user needs as they are projected for the future. Projects and desired output should be described with requirements detailed for personnel, equipment, facilities, expenditures, reorganization, and education of employees. Overall time schedules for implementation should be drawn up, and a control mechanism established to ensure plans are carried out.

In addition, procedures for evaluating the plan during the course of implementation should be set up. The entire planning process should also be reviewed as part of the planning document, listing mistakes and weighing strengths and weaknesses of the planning team. This will alert future planning committees to problems that may arise and serve as a guide for developing improved procedures and approaches to planning.

Figure 8.1 shows the data flow for planning information systems. Given goals, policies, and constraints, the chart traces how planners determine hardware, software, and personnel needs for the projected **information system (IS),** and how these needs add to existing corporate requirements. For example, a change in services demanded will make it necessary to recalculate resource needs. So will the development of a new IS. Time projections and cost estimates should be made simultaneously for they are interrelated. The amount of time programmers will spend developing software or time needed to train technicians to operate a new IS, for example, are cost factors.

Figure 8.1   **Data flow for planning information systems**

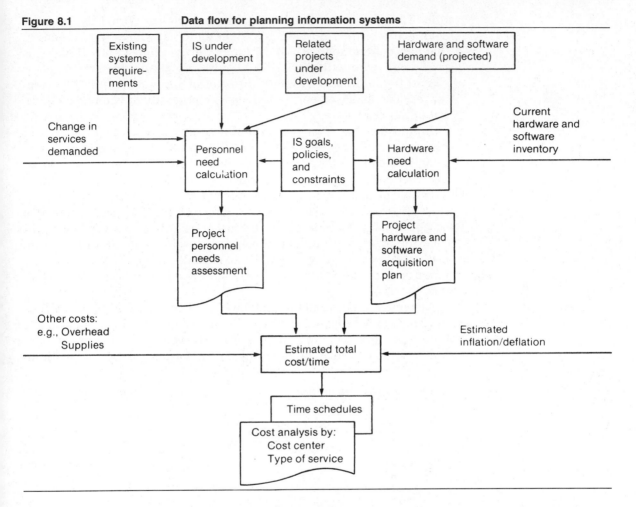

This flowchart is applicable whatever the time horizon of plans, although it should be recognized that cost estimates will be less accurate for long-range than for short-term planning, due to the difficulty of forecasting inflation rates and changes in market conditions.

THE PLANNING PROCESS

A plan or set of plans for the development of an information system is generally made by corporate management or a special committee assigned to the task, the planning committee being called the **MIS Committee,** the **Information Systems Planning Committee,** the **Steering Committee** (which will have other roles as well), or some similar title. The size of an organization, its experience with EDP, and the complexity of the information system under consideration are factors that will determine the composition of the committee. Functional vice presidents who will be users should be committee members, as should the information systems director or computer center representatives. Top management should also be represented when a large capital outlay is at stake.

Inputs that this planning committee must consider are shown in Figure 8.2. Users' needs, both unfulfilled and projected needs, must be specified. The competitive environment should be analyzed. (What information and facilities would be competitively advantageous?) Technological trends should be evaluated and political realities assessed. (Are there legal and regulatory restraints? What will people accept? What is feasible, given the corporate power structure?) In addition, the firm's goals, resources, and constraints should be reviewed. EDP management may analyze these inputs for the committee and propose recommendations, or the committee may independently evaluate them.

Generally, a **hierarchy of plans** with different time horizons will be formulated. A **long-range plan** will project four to five years in the future (the fast pace of technological advance in the computer field limits the usefulness of planning much farther ahead); a **medium-**

Figure 8.2   **Inputs to the planning process**

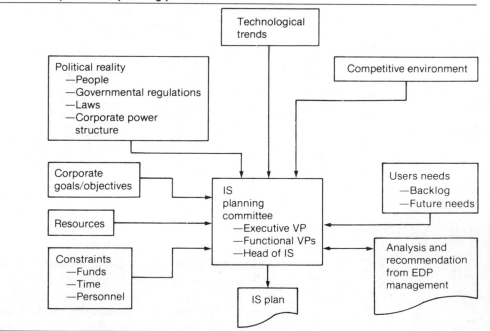

Figure 8.3  **Planning progression**

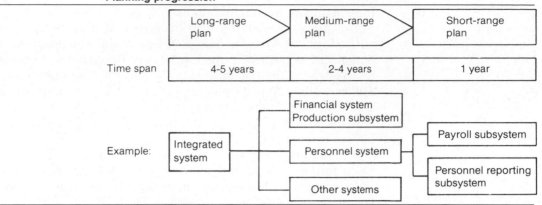

range plan is for two to four years; and a **short-term plan** will cover a one-year period.

The relationship of long-, medium-, and short-term plans is shown in Figure 8.3. Here, a total integrated system is the long-range goal. This requires the implementation of many subsystems, such as production and personnel, which are medium-term objectives. The personnel file is further subdivided into units such as personnel reporting and payroll, which become immediate concerns. Only when short-range objectives have been fully implemented can medium-range goals be achieved. Likewise, the integrated MIS requires satisfactory fulfillment of medium-range plans.

Short-term plans should be specific, indicating time schedules, budget, and allocation of resources such as equipment, software, and personnel. Funding and resource needs must also be projected for medium- and long-range goals, but this is far more difficult. Too often committees do not foresee technological advances or the expansion of computer applications which will affect their capacity, and consequently do not allow sufficient resources for future needs. **Capacity planning** is particularly difficult in telecommunications and word processing, new fields where technology is changing rapidly.[3] The same is true for interactive and distributive processing. Some firms poll specialists, asking them to assess what computer capabilities are in the offing. Others regularly monitor current operations, comparing them with past predictions in an effort to improve forecasting ability. It is recommended that planning committees constantly monitor the

[3]For an excellent discussion of capacity planning and capacity management, see Lawrence H. Cooke, Jr., "Planning for Growth," *Datamation* 25, no. 14 (December 1979), pp. 181–86. A number of good articles on the subject can also be found in *IBM Systems Journal* 19, no. 1 (1980).

state of technology and be willing to modify plans midstream to ensure adequate capacity planning.

The plans received by EDP management from the planning committee form the basis for daily EDP operations and establish the direction of EDP activities for the future. A policy statement should also be received from the committee, outlining, for instance, what mode of EDP operations is to be adopted (centralized, decentralized, or distributed), where EDP fits into the organizational structure of the firm, and how the EDP department is to operate (as a service or cost center). If EDP is to be a cost center. then pricing rules should be established. EDP management, in turn, makes recommendations to the committee about future projects and services, based on the state of technology and an assessment of departmental capabilities. The planning process is therefore cyclical, as illustrated in Figure 8.4.

Figure 8.4   **Planning: a cyclical process**

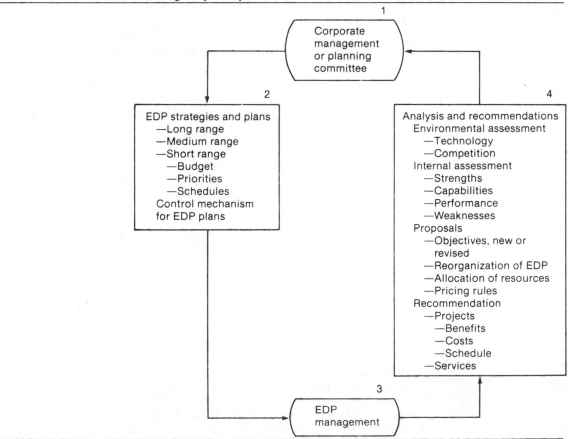

PRIORITY SETTING

In establishing long-, medium-, and short-range plans, the planning committee must consider priorities. When an integrated MIS is the long-range goal, for example, which projects should be implemented first? Should this decision be made in committee or left to the appointed project manager? The exact role of MIS committees with regard to **priority setting** varies from one organization to another. The alternatives include:

1. Committee sets project priorities.
2. Projects are classified into priority groups by the committee, based on corporate objectives and financial criteria, but the project manager sets priorities within each group on the basis of technological criteria.
3. Priority guidelines are set by the committee but actual project priorities are left to the project manager. For example, the committee may establish goals, such as to implement the distributed computing concept, or to speed response time in a specific functional area. The project manager decides the order of projects to meet these goals.
4. A mix of the above. That is, the committee proposes priorities, which are passed to project personnel for comment. Management reviews all recommendations, then makes a final determination of priorities.

Regardless of who makes priority decisions, the criteria listed in Table 8.1 should be the basis for priority setting. Remember, all projects considered have already been reviewed in the feasibility study and have been approved after economic, financial, organizational, and technological feasibility analysis. The purpose of Table 8.1 is to list factors that should be taken into consideration in setting the order in which approved projects will be developed.

Notice that contribution to profitability and growth rate are economic and financial criteria of importance. What happens when one project contributes to profitability but has little impact on growth rate, while a competing project has the reverse effect? Assuming the projects are matched in other economic respects, which would be given higher priority when resources are limited? The choice would be the manager's, based on noneconomic and nonfinancial considerations. For example, federal, state, or local regulations may have to be met, a competitor may offer a service that must be matched, or the dictates of public relations require highly visible projects be given priority. A delayed delivery date of needed equipment or the unavailability of programmers and analysts might affect priority scheduling.

Table 8.1   **Criteria for setting priorities among EDP projects**

Economic and financial criteria
Benefit/cost ratio
Rate of return
Contribution to profitability
Growth rate
Payback period
Risk factors

Organizational/institutional criteria
Contribution to organizational goals/objectives
Internal political decisions
    (e.g., personal preference of decision maker)
Public relations effect
    (e.g., improve corporate image)

Environmental criteria
Required by regulations
    Federal
    State
Impact on competition
    (e.g., response time must equal or better competitors'
Lawsuit requires information

Technical criteria
Isolated, simple, and modular project
High visibility of project
User understanding, cooperation, and commitment to project
Management support and commitment
Basic subsystem to system
Basic module for operations
    (e.g., data base system)
Availability of skilled personnel
    User/operator
    Technical personnel for development and maintenance
Availability of needed technology
    Current
    Future

Managerial considerations
Contribution to quality of decision making
    Better information
    Faster availability
    Information easy to assimilate
Human factors
    (e.g., employee resistance)

Or a lawsuit to which the firm is a party may mean resources have to be delegated to projects related to the suit.

When EDP personnel evaluate priorities, they prefer projects where user cooperation, support, and enthusiasm are assured. Analysts like projects that are simple and modular, especially when the development team has been newly constituted and is yet untried. They also prefer projects with quick and conspicuous results.

Risk is also a major factor to be considered: risk in schedule slippage, risk of degraded quality of product, risk of cost overruns, and risk of failure. During development, risk assessment may change. If risk increases beyond a certain threshold, management must consider abandoning the project entirely to cut losses.

What causes some projects to be more risky than others? F. Warren McFarlan suggests three factors: size, stability of structure, and technology.[4] Size risk includes the number of work hours required for the project, the estimated project time, and number of user projects involved. Structure risk includes factors such as the attitude of the user, degree of commitment of top level users, and degree and number of changes required. Technical risk involves the degree of user unfamiliarity with hardware, the degree of project team unfamiliarity with software, and degree of knowledge of both user and team of the proposed new application.

But how does one measure these variables? McFarlan gives no quantitative or cardinal rules of measure. He also does not explain how to evaluate risk when some variables increase risk while others decrease it. In the latter instance, one might prepare a table of variables, such as Table 8.2. This table considers eight alternative risk mixtures. For simplicity, only two states of each variable are allowed. Projects have been ranked in the right-hand column, but the exercise is highly subjective. The reader might choose a different order of priority. This is a good example of the problems of priority setting because no formulas exist for establishing numerical weights to risk factors.

Thus far, risk has been considered among competing alternatives within a single long-range project. But when assessing risk, the overall position of the firm should be evaluated, for a firm should not become encumbered with too many high risk projects at one time. Also, a balance between short-term and long-term projects should be sought.

Table 8.2   **Factors considered in risk assessment**

Project	Size	Structure	Technology	Priority assignment
A	Small	Stable	Old	1
B	Small	Stable	New	2
C	Small	Unstable	Old	3
D	Small	Unstable	New	4
E	Large	Stable	Old	5
F	Large	Stable	New	6
G	Large	Unstable	Old	7
H	Large	Unstable	New	8

[4]F. Warren McFarlan, "Portfolio Approach to Information Systems," *Harvard Business Review* 59, no. 5 (September-October, 1981), pp. 142–50.

And in addition, balance is needed between service-oriented projects and those which improve the infrastructure of the firm.

Priority setting is complex due to the many variables involved. The fact that priority decisions are basically subjective makes the planning committee's role even more difficult, for large sums of money may be involved and the success of a development project may well depend on astute priority decision making.

PROBLEMS IN PLANNING

At the McKinsey-UCLA conference on MIS planning reported by Ephraim McLean and John Soden (1974), the conferees identified the following as major pitfalls encountered in launching a planning effort. The list is in order of importance according to the executives surveyed, the first problem common to 60 percent of the planners, the last experienced by approximately one third of the planners.[5]

1. Lack of free communication and commitment to change.
2. Planner overoptimism.
3. Absence of corporate plan.
4. Top-down analysis not performed.
5. Lack of formal planning procedures.
6. Lack of credibility with users.
7. Lack of time.
8. Ignoring political side of planning.
9. Lack of top management support.
10. Action plans not developed from long-range plan.
11. Alternative MIS strategies not defined and/or evaluated.
12. Not enough data secured to make results credible.
13. Long-range plan draft not reviewed with user management.

Overoptimism, lack of top-down analysis, ignoring corporate politics, and failure to define or evaluate alternative MIS strategies were cited as the major problems when developing plans. Failure to plan implementation step by step was an error that plagued the conferees when using long-range plans.

PREPARATION FOR IMPLEMENTATION

Once corporate management approves the plan for a new IS, tactical plans are formulated for **implementation**.[6] Figure 8.5 shows imple-

[5]McLean and Soden, *Strategic Planning*, pp. 75–76.

[6]For a good discussion of tactical plans, see D. E. Hussey, *Corporate Planning: Theory and Practice* (Oxford: Pergamon Press, 1974), pp. 224–46.

Figure 8.5 **Implemention of plans**

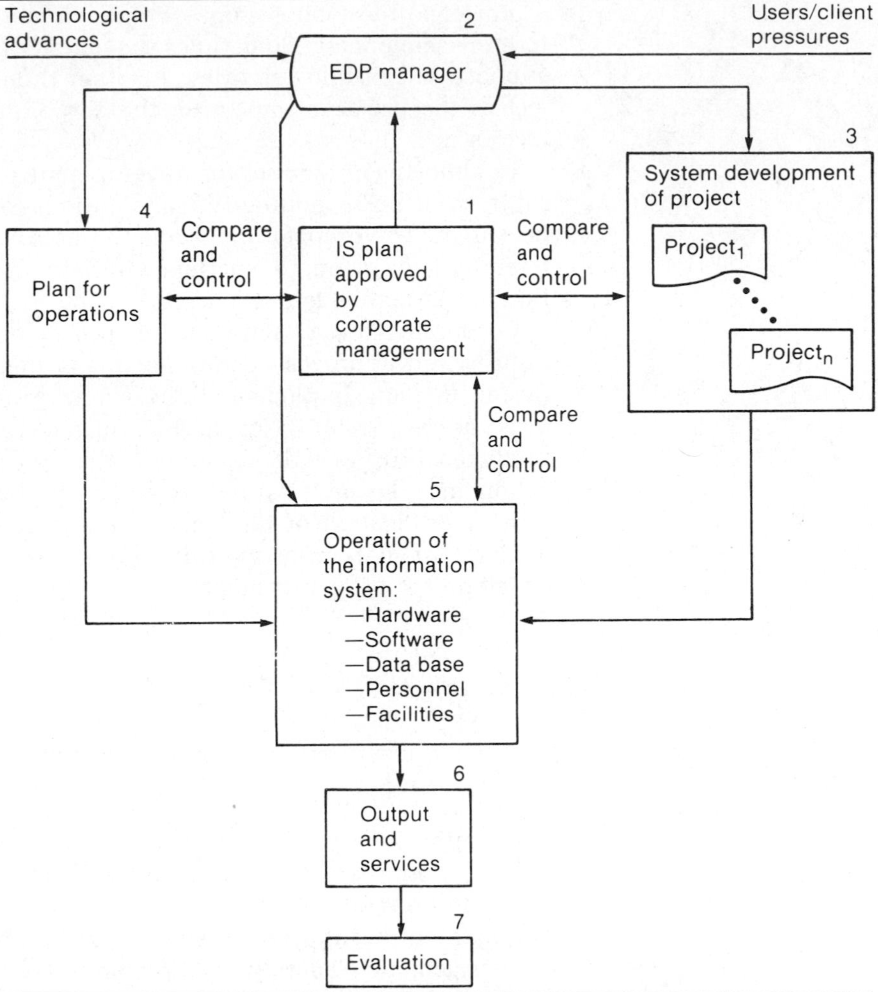

Technological advances

Users/client pressures

mentation steps. The EDP manager (Box 2) plans for operations (Box 4) based on the IS plan (Box 1) and supports system development (Box 3).

System development is organized into projects, each consisting of a discrete set of activities which are targeted for completion on given dates. Usually the overall IS plan will set the priorities for systems projects, based primarily on financial and economic criteria. However, when guidelines are general, EDP management may determine priorities, applying technical criteria or weighing projects from a system analyst's point of view. The complexity of projects, the importance of a project to the total system, or the availability of resources may determine sequencing. Sometimes the extent of operational management support will decide priorities. At other times high visibility of a project or the project's impact on the corporate image may be decisive factors.

In choosing personnel for development projects, individuals skillful in envisioning nontraditional solutions to unique problems should be sought. The preparation of operational plans (Box 4) requires a different type of planner: experience in daily operations, such as production or marketing, is needed.

Corporate management monitors project development through committees and approves operational plans that are consistent with the overall IS plan. Implementation of new systems and operations (Box 5) is the responsibility of the EDP manager. The output and services produced (Box 6) will be periodically evaluated (Box 7). Corrective action may be necessary to remedy problems identified. This may mean modification of the original plan, new strategies or schedules for implementation, or the initiation of a new planning cycle for the development of new systems.

SUMMARY

Planning is of prime importance in managing a firm's assets such as equipment, personnel, and good will. The computer revolution has added information to this list of valued resources, and planning the development of information systems has become a new responsibility of management. Generally, a MIS committee is appointed to formulate both long- and short-range plans based on corporate goals, balancing user needs against constraints, as illustrated in Figure 8.1. The planning process itself is cyclical, for the EDP department implements MIS plans yet it also alerts top management to the need for change and proposes new systems to the planning committee.

MIS committees vary in planning strategies. Top-down, bottom-up, proactive, and reactive planning styles are common. But there are rules of thumb, planning guidelines that should be followed by all committees, and there are common errors in planning that should be avoided. The overall IS plan becomes the basis for tactical implementation plans, leading to operations and evaluation, as illustrated in Figure 8.5.

CASE STUDY: CAPACITY PLANNING AT AMERICAN EXPRESS COMPANY*

American Express is a large diversified company with assets of over $14 billion and almost 38,000 employees. In 1979, data processing management in the traveler's cheque division thought that their IBM 370/168 was operating close to capacity. The division's computer workload had doubled in the preceding year due to the steady growth in volume of traveler's cheque transactions and the transfer to the division of processing for two other company services: money orders and travel. Before ordering another computer, however, management decided to use the software physics approach to capacity planning developed by the Institute of Software Engineering (ISE) to find out how close to maximum capacity they were operating.

The first step was to define workload in units of software work. This meant computing the software work for data transfers to and from disk and tape, and computing units performed by the CPU for each application. The latter calculations were based on CPU power figures for the 370/168 provided by ISE multiplied by the amount of CPU execution time for each application. Practical maximum power was also calculated from the power figures when power equals work performed by the CPU per second. Then the workload by hour of the day for anticipated average and peak days in the coming six months was plotted against the practical maximum capacity.

This plotting showed that during peak hours the workload would exceed the practical maximum, a condition that would occur with increasing frequency as the months passed despite fine tuning of the system. Service and response times would be affected. Management was convinced that an additional computer was needed. As a result of this capacity analysis, an IBM 3032 was ordered.

KEY WORDS

Bottom-up	**Goals**
Capacity planning	**Guidelines**
Coalescence planning	**Hierarchy of plans**

*Source: Richard G. Canning, ed., "Quantitative Methods for Capacity Planning," *EDP Analyzer* 18, no. 7 (July 1980), pp. 3–4. Pages 9–11 of the same issue contain details on software physics; pages 11–13 give other methods of capacity planning, such as BEST/1.

Implementation	Planning document
Information system (IS)	Priority setting
Information Systems Planning Committee	Proactive planner
	Reactive planner
Long-range plan	Risk
Medium-range plan	Short-term plan
MIS Committee	Steering Committee
Planning	Top-down

DISCUSSION QUESTIONS

1. Is planning necessary for all computer projects? Why? What are the environmental prerequisites that make it:
    a. Essential?
    b. Desirable?
    c. Unnecessary?

2. Is planning for computer projects more difficult and complex than for noncomputer projects? Explain.

3. Consider the planning of a project for the implementation of a large computerized information system. Compared to a noncomputer system for the same purpose, would the computer system:
    a. Require a different planning process?
    b. Be more complex?
    c. Require different planning techniques and skills?
        Explain.

4. Is the planning for a software project different from a:
    a. Hardware (CPU equipment) project?
    b. Teleprocessing-oriented project?
    c. Distributed processing project?
    d. Turnkey system?
    e. Hardware and software project?

5. What should be the role of an outside independent consultant or consulting company in the planning process?

6. Should top management be concerned with the planning of a functional information system? Explain.

7. Should the EDP manager be involved in corporate planning? To what degree? Under what conditions?

8. Is planning of computer systems best accomplished by an individual or a committee? If the latter, how should it be constituted?

9. In the planning of an information system, what are the unique problems in assessing and estimating:
    a. Risk?
    b. Time of completion?
    c. Cost of completion?
    d. Personnel resources needed?

10. Should planning be top-down or bottom-up? Explain both approaches and compare their advantages, limitations, and dangers.

11. What criteria would you use in ranking computer projects in the planning stage?

12. What levels of management (corporate and EDP) should be concerned with each of the following levels of computer planning?
    a. Strategic.
    b. Tactical.
    c. Operational.

13. Should there be standards for computer planning? If so, suggest them.

14. In planning of a computer information system, what are some of the main variables in each of the following:
    a. External environment?
    b. Technological environment?
    c. Political environment?
    d. Social environment?
    e. Crisis-prone environment?

SELECTED ANNOTATED BIBLIOGRAPHY

Bush, Robert L, and K. Eric Knutsen. "Integration of Corporate and MIS Planning: The Impact of Productivity." *Data Base* 9, no. 163 (Winter 1978), pp. 4–7.
This is good discussion of the roles and responsibilities of the different "players" in MIS planning. Excellent exhibits on planning calendars and manpower forecasting are included.

IBM. *Business Systems Planning/Information Systems Planning Guide,* GE-20-05271, 96 p.
This IBM manual is written in a matter-of-fact style. It has good diagrams and examples culled from the experience of planners of both large and small systems.

McLean, Ephraim R., and John V. Soden. *Strategic Planning for MIS.* New York: John Wiley & Sons, l977, 489 p.
This book includes a good chapter on the theory of planning. Planning guidelines are also recommended based on the planning experiences of 20 MIS executives surveyed. In addition, 16 planning case studies are described, the companies representing both the private and public sectors. IBM, TRW, Hughes Aircraft, Xerox, and TWA are among the firms studied. The appendix has examples of content pages of plans as well as samples of forms and instruments used in planning.

Rush, Robert L. "MIS Planning on Distributed Data Processing Systems." *Journal of Systems Management* 9, no.3 (August 1979), pp. 17–25.
Though the title suggests otherwise, this article includes a discussion of MIS planning in both distributive and nondistributive data processing environments. Sample schedules, charts, and forms are also presented.

Soden, John V. "Pragmatic Guidelines for EDP Long-Range Planning." *Data Management* 13, no. 9 (September 1975), pp. 8–13.
This is a good article on planning for an MIS including contents of a plan, approaches to planning (reactive versus proactive), hierarchy of plans, and guidelines for planning. Excellent diagrams support the text.

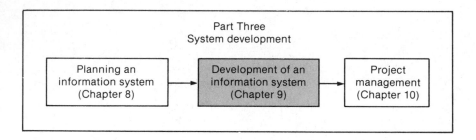

Part Three
System development

| Planning an information system (Chapter 8) | → | Development of an information system (Chapter 9) | → | Project management (Chapter 10) |

Development of an information system

We build systems like the Wright brothers
built the airplane—build the whole thing, push it
off a cliff, let it crash, and start all over
again.

R. M. Graham

A computing time of a few seconds is all that is required for many reports produced by an information system. But to generate these same reports may take months or years of development. This is because the planning, design, and implementation of every computer output requires a set of time-consuming activities that must be performed in a predetermined sequence.

The cycle of development of an information system, shown in Figure 9.1, is the subject of this chapter. System development consists of a feasibility study, determination of systems requirements, design, implementation, testing, conversion, and development evaluation. Each of these activities will be discussed in sections which follow. Although Figure 9.1 does not show the recycling process that may take place at each stage of development, the figure should serve as a useful frame of reference for the reader.

FEASIBILITY STUDY

Once the need for a new information system is perceived, a **feasibility study** determines whether or not an information system can be

Figure 9.1   **Flowchart for system development**

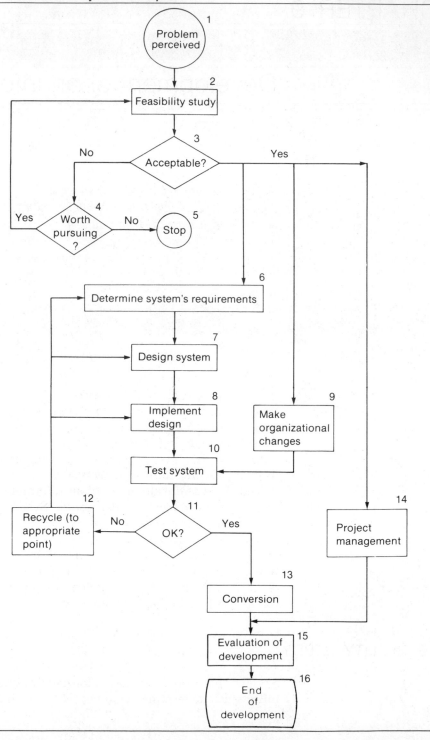

developed to meet desired objectives within expected constraints. The study will also estimate the cost of the proposed information system (monetary and organizational) and outline what benefits to expect from the system. On the basis of the feasibility study, corporate management will decide whether to initiate development of the proposed system or discontinue its consideration.

Feasibility studies are not required for each new report, but they are recommended when proposed systems require a large investment of the firm's resources or involve major change. Some experts suggest that unless a firm is breaking new ground or wants to be on the leading edge of technology, it is wiser to adopt a system already developed by another firm, vendor, or software house than to use company resources for in-house system development. It may be necessary to conduct a preliminary study in order to choose between these alternatives. After surveying external solutions and giving the company's objectives, resources, and constraints a cursory review, the team will have to decide whether to recommend development of a unique system. A decision to proceed with development of a customized major information system should lead to a full-fledged feasibility study of development alternatives.

Though a feasibility study postulates a new system, it does not guarantee success. The system may still fail in the testing phase. However, a thorough feasibility study should identify problems which will face the development team and establish whether solutions are feasible, thereby minimizing risk of development failure.

Figure 9.2 is a flowchart showing the steps of a feasibility study. The work can be divided into four phases:

1. Organizing for the feasibility study.
2. Search for a solution.
3. Feasibility analysis.
4. Choice of a solution.

Organizing for a feasibility study

The first phase of any feasibility study is organizing for the study itself. Once the need for change has been recognized (Box 2, Figure 9.2), the problem must be defined and formulated by management (Box 3). Then personnel must be appointed to the feasibility study team (Box 4). Members should be knowledgeable regarding computer systems, able to work with people, and informed about the firm's structure, philosophy, objectives, policies, and operations. Representatives from management should be included on the team to give it the status and authority necessary to elicit cooperation from all organizational levels of the company. It may be necessary to add consultants to the team when company personnel lack experience in the type of project under consideration.

Team size generally varies from two to eight. There is greater divi-

Figure 9.2   **Flowchart for feasibility study**

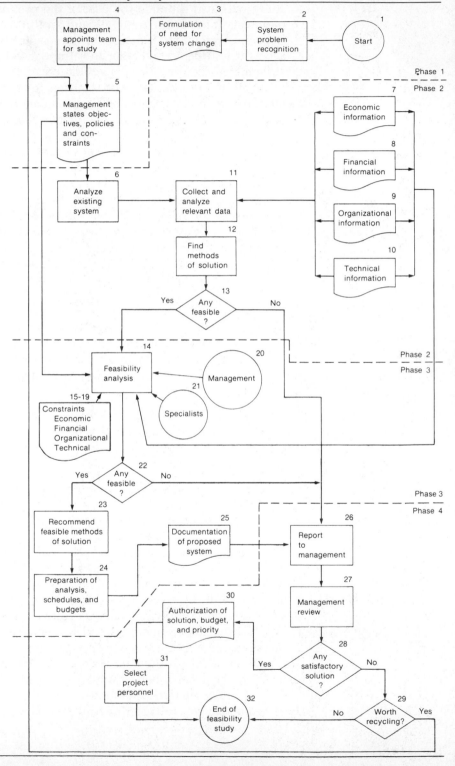

sion of labor on large teams and more flexibility in staffing, making it easier to ensure team expertise. But personality conflicts may emerge in large teams which hinder the team's functioning. When complex systems are under consideration, teams are generally more successful when the chair is drawn from the upper levels of management.

After the feasibility team has been appointed, management must state the objectives of the study, and specify policies and constraints that will affect development of the system proposed (Box 5). This step is delayed until the feasibility study group has been assembled because a team-management dialogue is helpful during this organizational phase. The team's questions about variables, and demands for clarification and elaboration, assist management in defining the study objectives in operational terms. Without this interaction, objectives are often stated in ambiguous, generalized terms. Teams demand specifics, ensuring that resource constraints for the project and the limits of acceptable organizational change are carefully defined.

Authorization to cross departmental boundaries for collecting information should be given the study team during this organizational phase. When complex system development is proposed, this authority must come from top management.

Search for solutions

The search for solutions (Phase 2) usually begins with a study of current operations, the collection of all relevant information on the environment so that the performance of existing systems can be evaluated and a determination made of changes needed (Box 6, Figure 9.2). A broad survey-type analysis should then be made of possible solutions (Box 12) based on data that has been collected regarding economic, financial, organizational, and technical information (Boxes 7–10), and a decision reached whether any glaring reasons for declaring the project unfeasible exist (Symbol 13). For example, if management has allocated only $100,000 for the operation of a terminal system and the team discovers that the minimum equipment cost of such a system is in the range of $150,000, the team should submit its findings to management and the study be terminated. If proposed solutions pass this initial scrutiny, they should be subject to a detailed feasibility analysis, which occurs in Phase Three which follows.

Feasibility analysis

Feasibility analysis is the formal testing of alternative solutions formulated in the preceding phase (Box 14, Figure 9.2). The development team, with the help of management (Box 20) and specialists (Box 21), tests solutions against economic, financial, organizational, and technological constraints (Box 15–19).

Economic feasibility is testing to see whether expected benefits will equal or exceed expected costs. This is easier said than done, for it is difficult to assign a precise monetary value to benefits since most benefits of information systems cannot easily be measured in dollars. For example, how can one measure the value of accurate, timely information on sales or production which the new system will deliver, information that the firm has had no experience using? Stating costs accurately is a problem as well. User requirements are frequently underestimated during the initial stages of a project and escalate as the project develops. Because of such problems, many teams make range estimates of expected benefits and costs, with probability assessments for values within the range.

A proposed system with a good benefits/cost ratio may be rejected, nevertheless, because lack of money prevents implementation. Though study teams often consider economic and financial constraints jointly, **financial feasibility** (checking costs against available funding) is a separate decision. Whereas computer analysts determine costs, users, in consultation with financial advisors, determine whether borrowed money will be available for the project, whether internal financing will suffice, or whether a combination of external and internal financing can be arranged. Other projects may be in competition for the company's limited financial resources. The time value of money, the accounting rate of return on investment, and the profitability index are examples of calculations that will be made during a study of financial feasibility, calculations that may be decisive in recommending a proposed system's implementation or rejection.

Organizational feasibility is testing proposed solutions against organizational constraints. Is there support at operational and middle management levels? Are qualified systems personnel available? Will employee resistance to change undermine the effectiveness of utilizing computer technology in decision making? Decision tables, such as the one in Table 9.1, are often used by teams in the determination of organizational feasibility when evaluating alternative solutions.

Finally, technological constraints may also rule out proposed solutions. Lack of equipment to perform certain types of operations, such as machine reading of handwriting, is one example. In many unstructured decision-making situations, no mathematical or statistical techniques exist at the present time for determining optimal problem solutions. An information system is not **technologically feasible** for such problems.

When a number of solutions prove feasible (Exit Yes, Symbol 22, Figure 9.2), the study team must develop priorities for ranking solutions. The team should then recommend the top-ranked solution to management, though alternatives in order of preference should also be presented (Box 23). A report should accompany the recommendation listing anticipated benefits and consequences of the solution, dollar resources required for implementation, problems that might be encountered by the development team, and a time schedule (Box 24). All proposals should be documented (Box 25).

Table 9.1   **Decision table for testing organizational feasibility**

	Rule 1	Rule 2	Rule 3	Rule 4	Rule 5	Rule 6	Rule 7	Rule 8
Top manager support	N	N	N	N	Y	Y	Y	Y
Operational and middle management support	Y	Y	N	N	Y	Y	N	N
Experienced analysts available	Y	N	Y	N	Y	N	Y	N
Discontinue study		X	X	X				
Hire consultants (assume available)						X		X
Train analysts						X		X
Continue study with caution	X						X	X
Continue with enthusiasm					X			

Key: Y = Yes.
      N = No.
      X = Action to be taken.

Choice of a solution

The fourth and last phase of the feasibility study is initiated when the study team presents its report to management (Box 26, Figure 9.2). The findings in the report should then be carefully reviewed by corporate management (Box 27). Though management representatives should have participated in the team's deliberations when costs and benefits were weighted, when values to intangible variables were imputed, when effects of conflicting factors were estimated and trade-offs evaluated, a reassessment of these value judgments after the study is complete is advisable. Estimates should be recalculated and a check made to ensure all relevant variables are specified.

Should management decide that proposed solutions are unacceptable (Exit No, Symbol 28), recycling of development activities may be initiated (Symbol 29). Constraints might be relaxed or objectives scaled down in order to find an acceptable feasible solution. Acceptance of a solution from the alternatives proposed by the study team (Exit Yes, Symbol 28) is followed by decisions necessary for implementation, such as authorization of a budget, the establishment of a time schedule for design and implementation, and the formulation of development priorities (Box 30). Management must appoint a project manager, a knowledgeable person experienced in managing systems change, and assign a development team (Box 31). The team determines the requirements of the new system, designs it, and oversees implementation and conversion. The feasibility study is terminated at this point and the feasibility study team disbanded.

Feasibility studies are costly and time-consuming but they are of value. If properly conducted, they reduce the risk of spending the company's resources on development projects that fail. When the team recommends a solution that later proves unfeasible, the cause can usually be attributed to one or more of the following errors:

1. The team used a crash approach which did not provide sufficient time for all of the phases of the study.
2. A nonintegrated approach was used, the team failing to consider the role of change in the long-range plans of the firm.
3. There was poor leadership and poor staffing of the feasibility team.
4. Objectives and constraints were not adequately specified.
5. The feasibility study lacked organizational support.
6. Incorrect estimations were made by the team. These generally result from underestimating the difficulty of the problem to be solved, incorrectly stating resource requirements, failure to recognize the organizational impact of the project, or errors in estimating organizational resistance to change.
7. User management in the application area did not review objectives of the project or participate in development.

DETERMINING SYSTEM REQUIREMENTS

Figure 9.3 shows the steps in the next stage of an information system's development: **determination of system requirements.** At this point, users' needs and system specifications that were stated in general terms in the feasibility study are restated in greater detail to provide the operational framework for the system's design.

The key to determining users' requirements is data collection, because only by gathering facts and opinions about operating procedures and changes needed can the development team draw up a list of system specifications. The data collected during the feasibility study is used, but additional information is needed at this stage. A literature search (Box 2, Figure 9.3), statements (Box 3), meetings (Boxes 4, 6, and 7), and the use of data collection instruments (such as the Study

Figure 9.3 **Determining system specifications**

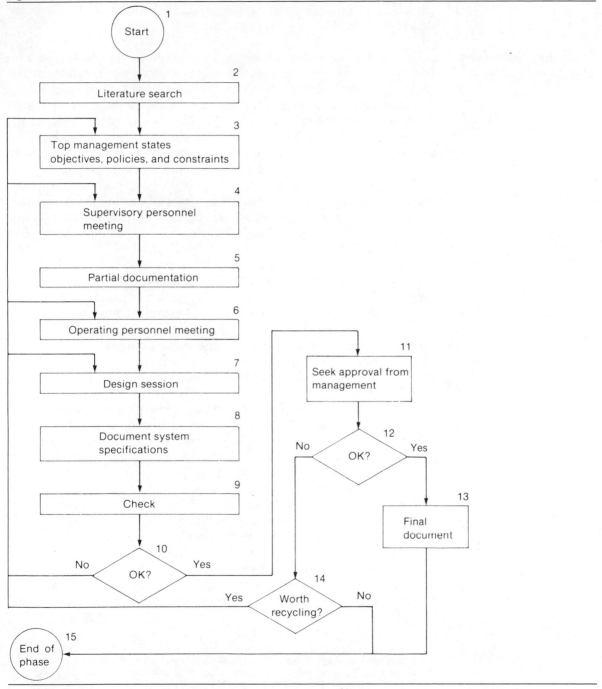

Organization Plan or the Accurately Defined System) are methods of gathering data to assist users and analysts in defining needs. These are described below.

Tools and techniques of data collection

One technique of data collection is a **literature search.** Analysts on the development team can learn about the firm's organization, operations, products, internal structure, and stated objectives by studying the firm's annual reports, catalogs, and publicity material. A search might also be made of monographs, periodicals, professional journals, house organs, books, and promotional literature from manufacturers to learn about systems used by other firms, and to review and update knowledge about data processing equipment and capabilities.

Interviews of management and users by the development team help the team assess user priorities. The views of management, systems personnel, and specialists, including consultants, can also be solicited at **meetings.** The design sessions themselves are often a forum for data collection.

The **Study Organization Plan (SOP),** a method developed by IBM for collecting information and designing a new system, consists of a number of forms to be completed by development teams. Included are a Resource Usage Sheet, which helps identify the resources (personnel, equipment, and materials) utilized by each organizational unit; an Activity Sheet, which identifies the inputs, outputs, and file usage of each activity; the Operation Sheet, which helps developers determine the volumes and lapse times for each operation; the File Sheet, which aids collection of data on each file's characteristics; the Message Sheet, which identifies recorded or unrecorded communications entering or leaving an operation; the Input-Output Sheet, which lists input-output specifications when completed; the Required Operation Sheet, which records details of operational elements within flowchart diagrams; and Resource Sheets, which help determine quantity and cost data on each resource used.[1]

Accurately Defined System (ADS), a method for data collection similar to SOP, was designed by National Cash Register Corp. (NCR). It also uses forms for collecting information on outputs, inputs, data files, computations, and system logic. Both SOP and ADS are time-consuming and costly, but they are systematic and thorough methods of collecting data needed to analyze bottleneck areas and identify where change can bring added efficiency and effectiveness to data

---

[1]For a discussion of the SOP method, Phase 1 and 2, see *IBM Study Organization Plan, The Method Phase I,* No. 7-20-8136-0, and *The Method Phase II,* No. F 20-8137-0, pp. 38 and 27, respectively. For more recent IBM methodology, see IBM, *Business Systems Planning—Information Systems Planning Guide,* No. GE 20-0527-3, 3d ed., July 1981.

processing. Both provide the development team with data on which to base the design of a new system.

There are numerous other approaches to data collection for system specification[2], such as normative analysis, decision analysis, and the critical success factors method. This latter methodology elicits factors that are critical to the success in performing user functions and making decisions related to the new system.

Process charts, flowcharts, data flow diagrams, and decision tables are additional instruments of data collection. An example of a **process chart** used to analyze an accounts receivable procedure is shown in Table 9.2. Each step is traced, the time taken is recorded, and the volume handled noted. An analysis of the chart will identify redundant steps and problems, helping the team focus on areas in data processing where improvements need to be made.

Table 9.2   **An example of a process chart**

PROCESS CHART WORK SHEET

Please read instructions on other side before completing this form.

Job: Accounts Receivables   Page 1 of 1

Charted by: J. Williams   Date: 02-05-80

Procedure ___ Method

Number	Details of Step	Delay / Operation / Transportation / Storage / Check/Control	Time	Required	Number	Comment
1	Wait for daily receipts and log them		2-3-4 h			
2	Wait for batch		2-3-4 d			
3	Glance verification		50-90-120 m			
4	Corrections made		2-4-7 h			
5	Sent for keypunching		1-2-4 h			
6	Key punching		2-3-4 h			
7	Sent to Computing Center		10-20-60 m			Recycled 2
8	Run edit program		1-2-8 h			times at an
9	Return diagnostics to A/R		1-2-4 h			average
10	Errors await correction		1-4-16 h			
11	Correct errors		40-60-120 m			
12	When no errors, logged		5-10-12 m			
13	Records stored		5-8-10 m			
14	Payment sent to bank		4-8-10 m			
15	Enroute to bank		4-4-8 hrs			
16						

Abbreviations used   d = days   h = hours   m = minutes

---

[2]For an excellent survey, see G. B. Davis, "Strategies for Information Requirements Determination," *IBM Systems Journal* 21, no. 1 (1982), pp. 4–30.

Identifying users'
objectives, policies,
and constraints

On the basis of collected data using the tools discussed in the preceding section, users' requirements must be identified at each organizational level. As mentioned earlier, meetings will be held with top management (Box 3, Figure 9.3), supervisors (Box 4), and operational personnel (Box 6) to define **objectives** for the new system (what the user wishes to accomplish), **policies** (guidelines that determine the course of action for accomplishing the objectives), and **constraints.**

Theoretically, a study of stated policies should help clarify objectives. However, policy manuals are often outdated, and frequently it is the unstated preferences, priority rankings, biases, and prejudices that determine the success or failure of systems. The development team must be sensitive to the environment and recognize political[3] and human factors as well as economic, financial, organizational, and technological constraints.

Determining
performance
specifications

The next step is defining users' requirements in operational terms (Box 7, Figure 9.3). That is, performance specifications must be listed in detail. These include:

Output: Content, format, quantity, availability, response time, frequency, distribution list, retention.

Processing: Decision rules, accuracy, significance of results, current and future capacity.

Input source: media, procedures, validity checks.

Security: Input (organization, maintenance, decision rules), output (nature of access, list of those allowed access, control of access, identification), hardware, software, audit (general or specific, internal or external).

Backup system: Items needing backup, nature of backup procedures, and maintenance.

Documentation of these specifications (Box 8) should be completed soon after the specification sessions take place while memories of events are still fresh. This should include a record of discussions (verified by participants) and a listing of definitions used and assumptions made.

Approval procedures

When the system requirements statement has been completed and documented, the statement should be checked for factual and statistical accuracy (Box 9, Figure 9.3). A check should also be made to ensure that the proposed system meets stated objectives. Then a series of approval decisions must be made. If users and systems personnel who participated in the project are satisfied (Exit Yes, Symbol 10),

---

[3]For an excellent discussion of political factors, see Richard K. Lindren, "Politics and System Justification," *Computerworld* 17, no. 2 (January 1983), "In Depth," pp. 1–8.

management approval is sought (Box 11). If dissatisfaction exists, re-cycling may be initiated (Exit Yes, Symbol 14 to Boxes 3, 4, 6, and 7) or the project terminated (Exit No, Symbol 14). Termination is not always a reflection on the quality of work of the development team. Environmental conditions may have altered which disallow project completion, such as the unavailability of expected resources or changes in management priorities.

If management decides to implement the project (Exit Yes, Symbol 12), documentation on system specifications will be finalized (Box 13).

DESIGN OF THE SYSTEM

There are two basic strategies that can be used in system design: bottom-up analysis or top-down design. In a **bottom-up approach,** the need for subsystems is identified and the modules designed, tested as independent units, then integrated into a total system.[4] This approach is evolutionary in nature, for operational modules of transaction files can first be designed, with later additions of modules for updating, control, and planning as the need develops.

The **top-down approach,** also called **structured design,**[5] starts by defining goals of the organization, the means to achieve these goals, the actions necessary to implement the means, and finally, the information needed for these actions. This approach is one of elaboration and clarification. The skeletal version of the new system is first de-signed before the system is subdivided into manageable components for development.

A decision on which of these two design approaches to use is made by the developers when the team starts to design the data base, pro-cedures, and program solutions, and blueprints the physical layout required for the system. Figure 9.4 is a network diagram for the design phase of development. Usually a number of design subcommittees are

---

[4]For a discussion of this approach, see Sherman Blumenthal, *Management Informa-tion Systems* (Englewood Cliffs, N.J.: Prentice-Hall, 1969), pp. 20–24. Blumenthal also discusses the approaches of organization chart, data collection, data bank, integrate later, and integrate now.

[5]For a discussion by one of the earliest and strongest proponents of the structured approach, see Edward Yourdon and Larry L. Constantine, *Structured Design* (Engle-wood Cliffs, N.J.: Prentice-Hall, 1979), 473 p. See also Tom D. Marco, *Structured Anal-ysis and System Specification* (New York: Yourdon, 1978), 352 p., and Chris Gane and Trish Sarson, *Structured Systems Analysis: Tools and Techniques* (Englewood Cliffs, N.J.: Prentice-Hall, 1979), 231 p.

For a comparison of the structured approach with other approaches, such as Jackson Methodology, META Stepwise Refinement (MSR), and Higher Order Software (HOS), see Lawrence J. Peters and Leonard L. Tipp, "Compare Software Design Methodolo-gies," *Datamation* 23, no. 11 (November 1977), pp. 89–94.

Figure 9.4   **Network diagram for design stage in system development process**

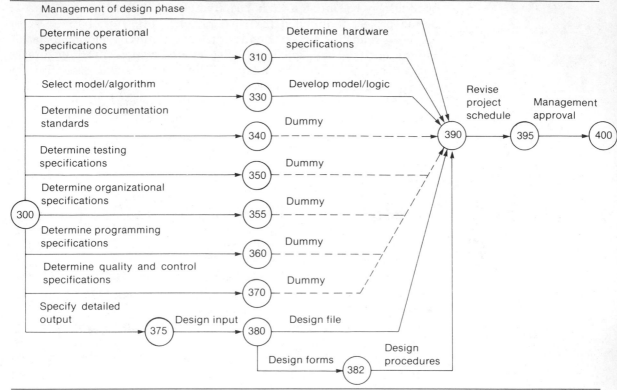

formed so that responsibility is distributed for the **design activities** described below.

Operational and hardware specification design

Though overall operational and hardware specifications are decided when system requirements are determined, technical decisions regarding operational standards and hardware specifications are made at design sessions (activities 300-310-390, Figure 9.4). For example, if scanning equipment for reading input data has been recommended, operational specifications prepared in the design phase might be:

Speed > (more than) 1,600 documents/hour.

Error rate $\leq$ 1/10,000 markings.

Maintenance $\not>$ (no more than) 24 hours at any one time.

Cost $\not>$ (no more than) $4,000/year.

Capability = Read markings on document and convert to cards at least 400 markings per document. Document size should be 8½ inches by 11 inches. Medium darkness of markings will suffice.

The development team generates a document with such detailed specifications for the use of technicians responsible for hardware selection, programming, and testing of the new system.

Model selection and development

The model required for problem solution must be selected and developed (activities 300-330-390, Figure 9.4). In simple applications—such as payroll, accounts payable, or reports—flowcharts and decision tables can be used as long as relationships are stated in detail and all decision rules necessary for computation appear. Computer applications, such as inventory control, queuing, scheduling, and planning, require complex mathematical models that must be developed.

Design of documentation standards

There is both **developmental** and **project control documentation.** The former is a description of the system itself (objectives, characteristics, decision rules) and descriptions of choices and decisions made during the development process. The latter concerns project development organization (personnel, time, materials, money).

The development team must decide what documentation standards to use for both developmental and project control documentation, what documentation manuals need be written and what they should include, how documentation should be tested, who is responsible for documentation preparation, time schedules for documentation completion, and how documentation will be distributed (activity 300-340).

Design of testing specifications

Testing specifications to be determined in the design phase (activity 300-350) include choice of testing approach. Some firms will design and test a pilot study. Others favor a parallel or dry run, testing the new system while the old is still in operation. Modular testing and conversion is still another option.

System designers also decide what to test and how to test. They assign personnel to perform tests, identify control points where testing should take place, decide how to evaluate test results, and establish procedures for recording and distributing test results.

Design of organizational specifications

New systems may require changes in a firm's organizational structure. Personnel may have to be retrained, transferred, hired, or fired. Such changes may result in a broadened (or narrowed) span of control for managers and alter departmental responsibilities. Unfortunately, not all staffing needs are known in the early stages of development.

For example, the number and skills of operational personnel required for a new system will depend on equipment selected. But as soon as organizational requirements are determined (activity 300-355), staffing and reorganization should begin because these activities have a long gestation period.

Design of programming specifications

Programming specifications (activity 300-360) should include information on the capability, logic, and features of the programs to be written. The programming language(s) to be used should also be stated. System designers are responsible for establishing program standards.

Design of quality and control specifications

Quality and control are related because the function of control is to ensure specific levels of quality. System designers must set quality standards for each system component, such as input, output, and processing, then identify control points and methods of control to ensure that the standards are met (activity 300-370). Chapter 12 discusses the subject of quality control at length. Design specifications are sent to the programming group so quality control capabilities can be programmed, and sent to personnel responsible for testing the system prior to conversion.

Design of input and output specifications

In a functional sense, input comes before output. But from a design viewpoint, the order is reversed because input depends on output requirements.

Output. Output specifications (activity 300-375) should ensure that the new system provides all the information users need for current decision making. In addition, output that might be needed for decision making in the future should be projected and included in the specifications since the incremental cost of producing added information is relatively small at the design stage compared to the cost of redesigning the system at a later date. Processing is costly, however, and data overload can impede users from locating and accessing essential information. The development team must, therefore, scrutinize proposed output closely and weigh proposed benefits against costs before determining exactly what output the new system should produce.

The design of output will vary with the user's style of management. The mode of processing (real time versus batch) and the nature of output (printed versus terminal, or print versus graphic) will also influence design. Nevertheless, there are some basic **principles of design** that apply to all output. They are as follows:

1. Legends, headings, and output formats should be standardized whenever possible.

2. Acronyms, abbreviations, and terms used in the output should be defined.

3. Algorithms and assumptions on which calculations are based should be available to users of the output.

4. Output should be hierarchical in presentation so that the user can access data easily at each level required without having to search through all the data.

5. The amount of data, its accuracy, and precision should be governed by how the output is to be used.

6. Exceptional data should be displayed in a manner that facilitates comparison of actual values with expected values, the comparison being in meaningful units.

7. The content of the output should be listed in a menu, especially when output appears on a terminal.

8. Psychological and intellectual limitations of users in absorbing output should be taken into consideration when designing the quantity and format of output data displayed per frame.[6]

9. Users' needs should govern the level of aggregation of output.

Output specifications, once determined, are sent to personnel involved in programming, physical preparation, and testing. The specifications are also needed by team members responsible for input specifications.

Input. In designing input (activity 375-380), the development team must decide what data needs to be collected in order to produce the output users desire. Too much data leads to inefficiency in storage and processing: too little will lead to ineffectiveness because the desired output will not be available.

Once the scope of the data base has been determined, the data must be organized in files and stored so that it can be readily retrieved and used as a shared resource by many managers. This sharing across division and department lines complicates design specifications because not all users have the same needs for reliability, validity, integrity, and security of data. Should files be integrated horizontally, vertically, and longitudinally? What about backup? How will files be updated? These decisions are part of **file design** (activity 380-390).

Another aspect of input development is the design of forms for input data collection (activity 380-382). Procedures for preparing input

---

[6]For designs of display output, see James Martin, *Design of Man-Computer Dialogues* (Englewood Cliffs, N.J.: Prentice-Hall, 1973). For a discussion of human factors in output design, see Henry M. Parsons, "The Scope of Human Factors in Computer-Based Data Processing Systems," *Human Factors* 12, no. 2 (April 1970), pp. 165–75, and Lance A. Miller and John C. Thomas, Jr., "Behavioral Issues in the Use of Interactive Systems," *International Journal of Man-Machine Studies* 9, no. 5 (September 1977), pp. 509–36.

and disseminating output should also be designed and documented in a Procedures Manual for users (activity 382-390).

Revise project schedule

An additional activity in the design phase is revising the project schedule (activity 390-395). Once detailed design specifications have been determined, more accurate time estimates for completing activities can be made. Also, some activities may have been added that were not anticipated when the schedule was first drafted. This revision is the responsibility of the project manager.

Management approval

The revised schedule, the system definition, and design specification documents are presented to management for approval at the conclusion of the design phase (activities 395-400). Although management may have participated in design sessions, a review of the total design package by management is needed at this stage and a formal decision made on implementation. Lack of approval means either termination of development or recycling those activities designated unsatisfactory. Approval is followed by implementation of the design.

IMPLEMENTATION

A major activity in the **implementation** of a computerized information system is programming. The main program(s) must be written (or software packages purchased) so that the system produces the information expected, and programs must be prepared for storing data, checking data, and maintenance. Since a fine line exists between programming design and implementation, it is not always possible to state where the latter begins. Some development teams provide so much detail in the design phase that programmers need only translate each design specification into a computer instruction. Other design teams merely specify logic in general terms, giving programmers responsibility for detailing this logic.

Hardware selection is also an implementation activity. Formerly this activity was delegated to hardware and systems personnel, but today the responsibility for selection of minis, micros, and input-out equipment is being assumed by operational managers. Site preparation, installation of new equipment, and equipment testing follow.

Finally, implementation consists of file preparation (creating new files or restructuring the old), orientation, and training so that employees are familiar with the new system and know how to operate it, and completion of company reorganization if the system alters the span of control of existing departments.

TESTING THE SOLUTION

The testing process involves a comparison of desired performance (as stated in the users' requirements specifications) with actual performance. Problems should be identified and corrections made if tolerances are exceeded.

First, tests must be planned. This means test data must be prepared and staff selected to perform the tests. Testing is usually done at four levels. **Component testing** is checking the parts of the system, such as a piece of equipment, the performance of an individual operator, or the effectiveness of a form, procedure, or program. **Functional testing** is at a higher level of aggregation. It measures the performance of related components in a functional subsystem. **Subsystem testing** checks the interrelationships of functions tested individually in the preceding test. Finally, **system testing** checks overall results. This can be done by pilot tests, parallel runs, or simulation.

The four testing levels are illustrated in Figure 9.5. Perhaps a practical example will help make the concept of testing levels meaningful. A financial system can be subdivided into financial subsystems of accounting, manufacturing, engineering, marketing, and inventory subsystems. Each of these subsystems has many functions. The accounting subsystem includes payroll, accounts payable, accounts receivable, general ledger, costing, assets, liabilities, income, expenses, and tax functions. Each function is further subdivided into components. The payroll function includes wages, social security, W-2 forms, editing, balancing, journal, register, check writing, and payroll statement components. Testing begins at the component level of this hierarchy, continues at higher levels of aggregation, and ends up with the total systems check.

The testing process ends when test results at each level are satisfactory. Unsatisfactory testing at any level requires recycling, as shown

Figure 9.5   **Levels of testing**

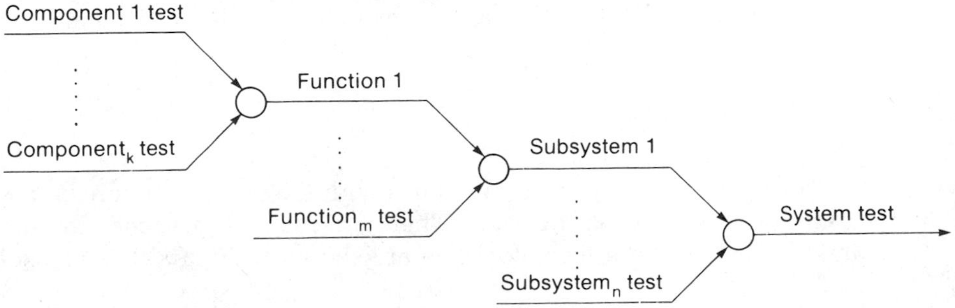

Component 1 test

Function 1

Component$_k$ test

Subsystem 1

Function$_m$ test

System test

Subsystem$_n$ test

Figure 9.6 **Recycling of testing process**

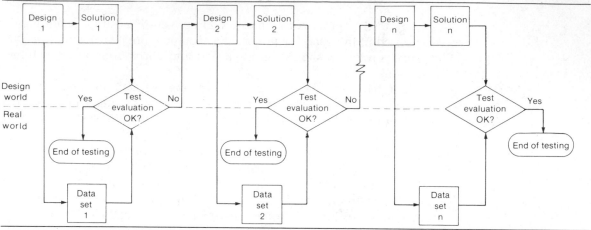

in Figure 9.6.[7] Should Design 1 fail, system developers must search for flaws and correct them, then test the revised system's design. In complex systems, the value of n (the number of revisions) may be 3 or 4. If n is large, responsibility may lie with users who have failed to adequately specify needs, with systems personnel who did a poor design job, or with the development process itself which was not carefully planned and controlled. The value of n is seldom 1, even with capable personnel. Management should recognize that recycling is a part of the development process and be prepared for it. Formal recycling controls should be established, such as procedures for recording the need for change, and documenting the modifications completed. Information about these changes must then be channeled to affected groups.

At the conclusion of favorable testing, the test results should be presented to management for approval. This is management's final check to see that the system satisfies goals and objectives. By formalizing user acceptance, the development team minimizes the possibility that users will complain at a later date that the system fails to satisfy requirements.

CONVERSION

The development process concludes with the cutover or **conversion** from the old system to the new. There are many approaches to conversion. Three of the most common are shown in Figure 9.7. The **se-**

---

[7]For a detailed discussion, see Z. D. T. Bross, *Design for Decisions* (New York: Macmillan, 1953), pp. 171–82.

Figure 9.7   **Approaches to conversion**

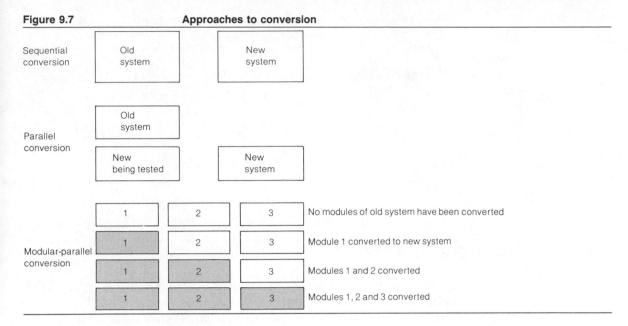

Sequential
conversion

Parallel
conversion

Modular-parallel
conversion

1	2	3	No modules of old system have been converted
1	2	3	Module 1 converted to new system
1	2	3	Modules 1 and 2 converted
1	2	3	Modules 1, 2 and 3 converted

quential approach means that the complete switchover from old to new system is made on a given date. Sometimes old and new systems are run in **parallel** for a period of time. Large and complex systems are generally phased in one **module** or subsystem at a time. This reduces the workload on personnel responsible for conversion and at the same time helps isolate problems of the new system while minimizing the consequences of potential system failure.

EVALUATING THE SYSTEMS DEVELOPMENT PROCESS

Before the development team is dispersed, evaluation of the systems development process should take place. Mistakes should be identified and analyzed to see why they were made and how they could have been avoided. The purpose of such an analysis is not to exchange accusations and recriminations, but to learn from the past so that similar mistakes won't be repeated when future information systems are developed. The efficiency and effectiveness of the new system should be scrutinized and the benefits versus costs assessed. A critical review of the need for recycling during the development process, of liaison and communication problems which arose, and of schedule slippage should lead to improved procedures and approaches for other projects.

Figure 9.8   **Network diagram of the development of an information system**

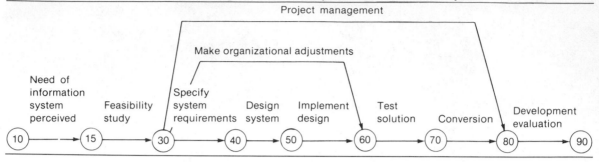

SUMMARY AND CONCLUSIONS

The development of an information system should consist of the following activities: perception of need, the feasibility study, specification of system requirements, design, implementation, testing, conversion, and development evaluation. Figure 9.8 is a network diagram of these activities. Note that organizational adjustments (30–60) are done in parallel to specification, design, and implementation stages. Project management, likewise, parallels development activities—from the feasibility study through conversion—since each activity needs to be scheduled, allocated resources, and controlled to see that requirements are met and the project completed within time constraints. Project management is the subject of the next chapter.

Management has prime responsibility for certain activities of development, as shown in Table 9.3, and delegates other activities to the development team. However, throughout development, management should work in harmony with technicians to ensure that the system

Table 9.3   **Personnel with prime responsibility for development activities**

Activities of development	Person(s) with prime responsibility
Feasibility study	Management
System requirements	Management*
Design system	Development team
Implement system	Development team
Test system	Development team
Acceptance of tests	Management*
Organizational changes	Management
Conversion	Development team
Evaluation of development . . .	Mixed responsibility (management and team)

*Manager of the relevant application area or manager directly involved.

developed meets managerial needs. Because managers and technicians differ in background, training, and perspective, communication
between the two can become strained during system development.
Disagreements may arise over what can be done and what should be
done. The cartoon in Figure 9.9 shows what happens when communication during development is lacking. One of the purposes of this
chapter, indeed of the entire text, is to provide managers and technical personnel with a common vocabulary and basic knowledge on information systems so similar misunderstandings do not arise.

The names given to the development activities described in this
chapter may vary from one organization to another, for there is no
standardization of terms among authors or industries regarding development cycles. This is due to the newness of computerized information systems themselves. Nevertheless, most development schemas
follow the stages of development described in this text though they
may combine several activities, add activities, or use other names.
(Note the activities and names in the SABRE case study, p. 191.) One
development sequencing, expressed in poetry, is as follows:

(Canto the first: Proposal)
"An information system," said the president, J.B.,
"Is what this company sorely needs, or so it seems to me:
An automated, integrated system that embraces
All the proper people, in all the proper places,
So that the proper people, by communications linked,
Can manage by exception, instead of by instinct."

(Canto the second: Feasibility study)
They called in the consultants then, to see what they could see,
And to tell them how to optimize their use of EDP.
The consultants studied hard and long (their fee for this was sizable)
And concluded that an information system was quite feasible.
"Such a system," they repeated, "will not only give you speed,
It will give you whole new kinds of information that you need."

(Canto the third: Installation)
So an information system was developed and installed
And all the proper people were properly enthralled.
They thought of all the many kinds of facts it could transmit.
And predicted higher profits would indeed result from it;
They agreed the information that it would communicate
Would never be too little, and would never be too late.

(Canto the last: Output)
Yet when the system went on line, there was no great hurrah,
For it soon became apparent that it had one fatal flaw:
Though the system functioned perfectly, it couldn't quite atone
For the information it revealed—which was better left unknown.[8]

---

[8]Marilyn Driscoll, "An Information System," *The Arthur Young Journal* (Winter
1968), p. 318.

Figure 9.9   **Lack of communication in project development**

As envisioned by the development team.

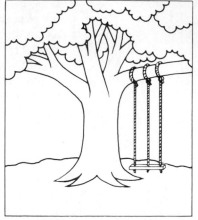

As specified in the product request.

As designed by the senior designer.

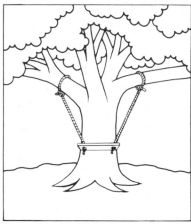

As perceived by the implementor.

As installed.

What the customer wanted.

CASE STUDY: DEVELOPMENT OF THE SABRE SYSTEM

American Airlines recognized the need for a computerized information system in 1954, for the company was finding it increasingly difficult to maintain accurate and timely manual records on passengers. The conventional system of assigning agents quotas for seats was unsatisfactory. When local agents sold out their seat allotments, passengers were often lost to the airline due to delays in locating a vacancy held by an agent in another part of the country. Lost revenues resulted.

It took 10 years of development and more than $30 million to make the desired computerized central reservation system operational, a system that has been under continual modification since. SABRE includes control as well as reservation functions. For example, the system will not accept incorrect data, such as a code for a nonexistent flight, or incomplete input. Reservation information is used to provide caterers with estimates of the number of meals to be prepared, arrival and departure desks receive passenger lists, and flight control is given weight and loading information which also guides management in assigning crew and maintenance personnel. Furthermore, the system keeps accounts of funds receivable for each day, month, flight, and route. SABRE processes all flight information received from dispatch centers, adjusting scheduled flights and stops as well.

The chronology of SABRE's development was as follows:

Preliminary study	1954–1958
Precontractual analysis	1958–1959
Contract	1959
Functional requirements	1960–1962
Program specifications	1960–1962
Program coding	1961–1964
Single path testing	1961 on
Equipment arrival	January 1962
Package testing	1961–1962
Final checkout	Oct.–Dec. 1962
Test city parallel operation	Dec. 1962–Mar. 1963
First firm cutover	April 1963
Several more cities cutover	May 1963
Further cutover delayed pending addition of memory to 7090	June–Nov.1963
Remainder of American cities added to system	Nov. 1963–Dec. 1964

Source: R. W. Parker, "The SABRE System," *Datamation.* 11, no. 9 (September 1965), p. 52.

Note that many of the activities of development are worded differently from activity names in this chapter and one (contract) is new. Note also the period of time it took for system development. The preliminary study itself lasted four years.

SABRE is a museum piece today both literally and figuratively. (A Washington, D.C., museum has a display on SABRE.) The experience gained from this "first" large-scale real-time information system has contributed to the development of the more advanced reservation systems in current use among airlines, hotels, car rentals, theaters, and even national parks for camping spaces.

KEY WORDS

Accurately Defined System (ADS)

Bottom-up approach

Component testing

Constraints

Conversion

Design activities

Developmental control documentation

Documentation

Economic feasibility

Feasibility study

File design

Financial feasibility

Functional testing

Implementation

Interviews

Literature search

Meetings

Modular conversion

Objectives

Organizational feasibility

Parallel conversion

Policies

Principles of design

Process chart

Project control documentation

Sequential conversion

Structured design

Study Organization Plan (SOP)

Subsystem testing

System testing

System requirements

Technological feasibility

Top-down approach

DISCUSSION QUESTIONS

1. Do all information systems go through the same stages of development? Explain.

2. Why is the development of an information system a cycle?

3. Describe how you would organize a development team to design and implement an inventory control system for six warehouses and a $30

million volatile inventory. Would the team composition change if the system were to be OLRT, as opposed to a batch system?

4. Is a feasibility study important in the development of an information system? Why? Is it essential for all information systems?

5. Describe the phases of a feasibility study.

6. Describe the difference between economic, financial, organizational, and technological feasibility.

7. What considerations lead to a "GO" decision following the feasibility study? Who makes that decision?

8. Why do some systems fail even though a feasibility study was successfully completed?

9. What information needs to be gathered and synthesized before users' needs can be specified?

10. Empirical studies have shown that the user specification stage is the most difficult developmental stage. Why do you suppose this is true?

11. Explain the purpose of SOP, ADS or similar information collection techniques.

12. Describe the activities in the design phase of system development.

13. Why is documentation important? What documentation specifications must be designed?

14. List principles of output design. Would these fit all applications, including output for production, marketing, finance, and use of a home personal computer?

15. Why does design of output precede input design?

16. What is the difference between design and implementation in the development of an information system?

17. What role should management play in systems development?

18. Describe the four levels of testing. What are the advantages and disadvantages of testing in this manner?

19. Describe different approaches to conversion.

20. What is the purpose of evaluating the system development process following conversion?

SELECTED ANNOTATED BIBLIOGRAPHY

Benjamin, Robert T. *Control of the Information System Development Cycle.* New York: John Wiley & Sons, 1971, pp. 41–90.
This is a good discussion of the development cycle, including the phases of a feasibility study, systems specification, design, implementation, and alterations. The author's use of numerous charts and tables is helpful.

Burch, John G., Jr., et al. *Information Systems: Theory and Practice,* 2d ed. New York: John Wiley & Sons, 1979.
This textbook has an extensive coverage of the development cycle including phases of specifying users' needs. A case study includes calculations,

flowcharts, memos, and documentation generated. A good nontheoretical presentation.

Couger, J. Daniel; Mel A. Colter; and Robert W. Knapp. *Advanced Systems Development/Feasibility Techniques*. New York: John Wiley & Sons, 1982, 506 p.

This is an excellent set of readings on techniques of analysis, including optimizing techniques for system design and implementation. Specifically included are chapters on structured analysis, BSP, PLEXSYS, and PSL/PSA.

Davis, Gordon B. *Management Information Systems: Conceptual Foundations, Structure, and Development*. New York: McGraw Hill, 1974, pp. 413–39.

A tightly written description of the development cycle with a good discussion of the human factors involved in development.

Kanter, J. *Management-Oriented Management Information Systems*. Englewood Cliffs, N. J.: Prentice-Hall, 1977, chap. 4, pp. 92–133.

This chapter discusses three main sets of activities in the development and implementation cycle: analysis, synthesis, and implementation. Detailed activities are also identified. Unfortunately, the pie diagrams used do not emphasize the sequential and cyclic relationship of the activities. There is, however, an excellent discussion of economic analysis as part of the feasibility study.

Kirk, F. G. *Total System Development for Information Systems*. New York: John Wiley & Sons, 1973.

Chapter 4, pp. 31–40, has an excellent diagram showing the interrelationship of the different phases of development. Each of these phases is subsequently discussed in a full chapter.

Mixon, S. R. *Handbook of Data Processing Administration, Operations and Procedures*. New York: AMACOM, Division of American Management Association, 1976, pp. 127–270.

This text includes chapters on system design: input forms design, output/report design, DED, systems control, data base design, program functions, modular programming, and program specifications design. There is also an excellent chapter on testing.

Rubin, Martin L. *Introduction to the System Life Cycle*, vol. 1. New York: Brandon/Systems, 1970, pp. 61–104.

This is a multivolume handbook with a chapter in volume 1 on system design, including sections on detailed analysis, design decisions, design objectives, and system specifications. There are also three chapters relating to implementation that discuss the subjects of programming, documentation, and system installation.The next two volumes are on documentation forms and standards. All volumes are well written and include numerous illustrations.

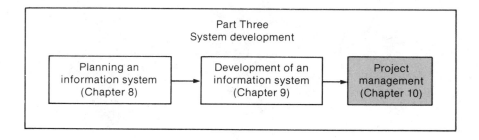

CHAPTER 10

Project management

*The genius of good leadership is to leave
behind a situation which common sense, even
without the grace of genius, can deal with
successfully.*

Walter Lippmann

A **project** is a temporary assemblage of resources (equipment and personnel) to solve a one-shot problem. Planning, organizing, and controlling these resources is called **project management.**

This chapter will present an overview of project management for the development of an information system. Aspects of project management unique to computer processing projects will be stressed. The use of computers for project control will also be discussed.

INITIATING A PROJECT

The steps in initiating a project are shown in Figure 10.1. Organizational goals, policies, and priorities (Box 1), users' needs (Box 2), technological developments and trends (Box 3), processing needs (Box 4), and the overall system plan (Box 5) are evaluated by a steering or planning committee, which proposes new projects (Box 6). In the feasibility study (Box 7), alternative solutions to problems are reviewed. The decision on which project to recommend for implementation should be based on input from both managers and technicians, two groups which differ in selection criteria. Management is concerned with benefit/cost ratios, organizational priorities, and investment trade-offs. Computer personnel will recommend automation of jobs involving a high volume of repetitive work, situations with a high

Figure 10.1   **Planning for a project**

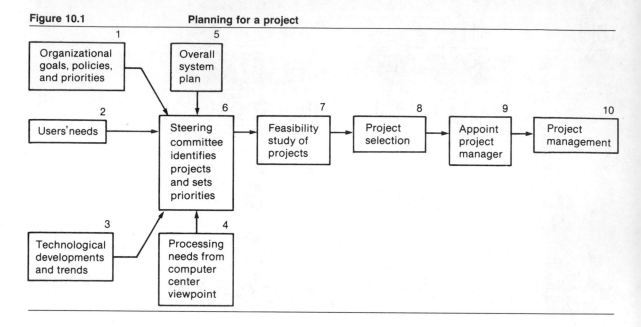

probability of success where conspicuous results can be achieved quickly. They prefer to avoid areas where employees are strongly opposed to change. From an analyst's viewpoint, departments that are the source of basic data for others, or departments so isolated that system failure will not adversely affect the rest of the organization, should be the first departments given information systems.

Once corporate management selects a project (Box 8) based on recommendations from the feasibility committee, a project head is appointed (Box 9) who is in charge of project management (Box 10). This head should be both a leader, directing and motivating a team chosen from different functional departments and status levels within the organization, and a manager, with skill in planning, organizing, and controlling projects. In addition, technical knowledge, or a willingness and ability to learn the technical aspects of the project, is needed. In the past, project director was the common title for this head. Recently the term **project manager** has become popular, a term that will be used in this text.

The project manager will generally report to a special committee appointed by corporate management to oversee the project. This committee may have a variety of names. Project review committee, steering committee, or user and administrative committee are all common names. But all have the same function: to assist the project manager in interpreting the firm's policies, to clarify users' needs, and to monitor the progress of the project.

Figure 10.2   **Project organization**

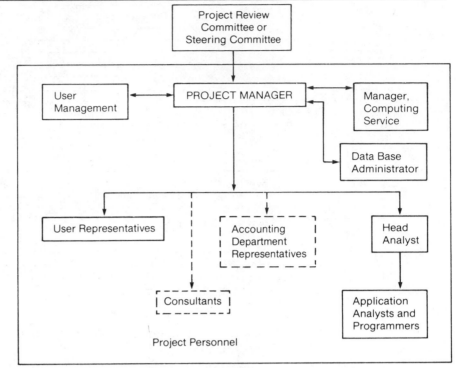

Note: Units enclosed in dotted lines often participate in information system development.

The project manager will also have inputs and support from user management, the data base administrator, and the computer center director in a staff relationship. User representatives and technical personnel will have a line relationship. Consultants and accounting department representatives assigned to the project may also fall in this latter category. Figure 10.2 shows these relationships in graphic form. Typically, 70 percent or more of the total resources needed for a project must be within the project manager's direct control for a successful project.

Figure 10.3 shows the responsibilities of a project manager. The principal functions of a project manager (to plan, schedule, and control) will be described in the sections that follow, for they form the basis of project management.

TEAM STRUCTURE

One of the first acts of a project manager is to structure the project development team. There are several approaches to the organization

Figure 10.3   **Responsibilities of a project manager**

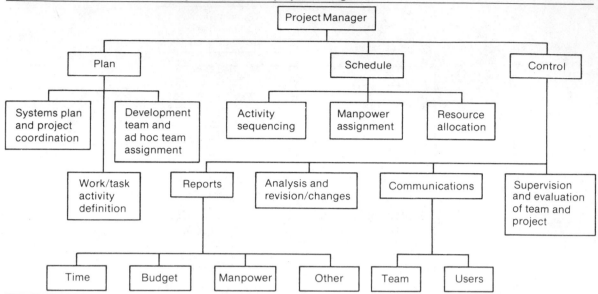

of such teams: **functional organization, project organization,** and **matrix organization.**

In computer projects, small work teams may be assigned specific specialized tasks, such as the development of models or software. Perhaps this explains why many call project personnel a task force and Alvin Toffler labels project management an ad-hocracy in *Future Shock.*

Organization by function generally keeps traditional line-staff relationships with a vertical flow of authority and responsibility. This type of organization, however, proves inappropriate when system projects require cooperation and resources from many line units, which is the case in most information system projects. As M. Stewart states:

> The essence of project management is that it cuts across, and in a sense conflicts with the natural organization structure. . . . Because a project usually requires decisions and actions from a number of functional areas at once, the main inter-dependencies and the main flow of information in a project are not vertical but lateral. . . . Projects are characterized by exceptionally strong lateral working relationships, requiring closely related activity and decisions by many individuals in different functional departments.[1]

[1]M. Stewart, "Making Project Management Work," in *Systems Organizations, Analysis Management: A Book of Readings,* ed. D. I. Cleland and W. R. King. (New York: McGraw-Hill, 1969), pp. 295–96.

Project organization is the creation of a unit with responsibility for all aspects of project development. In this schema, professional, technical, and administrative staff are hired for the duration of the project. But there are serious problems in attracting competent personnel when projects are organized in this manner. Many professionals are unwilling to join projects that offer no job security, and dislike jobs of this nature that have a fluctuating workload.

A **matrix organization** combines functional and project approaches to project management. In a matrix organization, the staff is "borrowed" from functional divisions. In the case of a development team, the team members might be drawn from accounting, marketing, operations research, and IS departments. Which employees are borrowed is negotiated by the project manager with functional department heads, the choice usually being based on the availability of personnel and the qualifications demanded by the project. Sometimes department heads are reluctant to release competent personnel, but the advantage of having a member on the team who can represent the department's interests while gaining experience on the project is recognized by most heads.

One problem with matrix organization is that project members have two bosses. They are responsible to the project manager for work assignments, yet their permanent supervisors retain jurisdiction over personnel matters such as salary and promotions. The two "bosses" may clash in values and objectives, with the project member caught in between. This potentially explosive situation can be defused if ground rules are negotiated between the project manager and functional heads regarding shared authority and responsibility over project members before the team is constituted.

The advantages of matrix organization may be summarized as follows. Matrix organization:

1. Allows a project manager to cut across vertical organizational divisions.
2. Involves functional departments, and is responsive to their needs, because representatives will be on the project staff.
3. Has access to the resources in all functional departments (on a negotiated basis).
4. Provides a "home" for the project personnel after the completion of the project.
5. Does not permanently disrupt organizational subgroupings or the continuity of seniority, fringe benefits, etc.

An example of matrix organization is shown in Table 10.1. This table illustrates the concept that both individuals and departments may be assigned to development teams, and may participate in several projects simultaneously.

Table 10.1   **A sample matrix organization of project teams**

Personnel assigned	Project						
	B19	B20	P5	P7	. . .	S3	. . .
Users: Manufacturing Able	X		X			X	
Zani		X	X				
Marketing		X					
Finance Babb		X	X				
Sutherland	X		X			X	
R&D						X	
Support: Accounting/Finance	X		X	X		X	
Lead Analysts Adams			X				
Brennan	X					X	
Stark				X			
Programmer	X	X	X	X		X	
Other: Consultant		X					

Management style may be one factor in the choice of project organization. A two-dimensional grid relating organization to managerial priorities is shown in Figure 10.4. In this grid, functional organization represents strong concern for people, less for production. Project organization exhibits a greater concern for production than people, whereas matrix organization shows a high concern for both people and production.

Once the overall team structure is established, work teams must be organized. With regard to programming projects, Harlan Mills recommends a team under a chief programmer who is the main designer and architect of the system and who supervises structured walk-throughs and formal reviews of design and coding.[2]

---

[2]H. D. Mills, *Chief Programmer Teams, Techniques and Procedures,* IBM, Internal Report, (January 1970). See also F. T. Baker, "Chief Programmer Team, Management of Production Programming," *IBM Systems Journal* 11, no. 1 (1972), pp. 56–73.

Figure 10.4   **Project organization in the management grid**

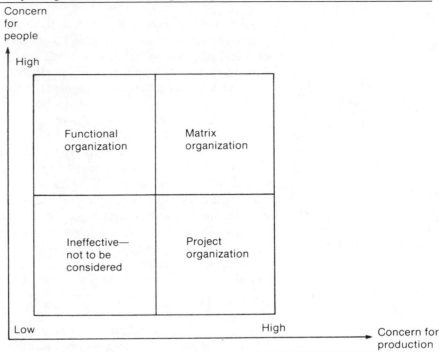

Source: Adapted from Edmund B. Daly, "Organizing for Successful Software Development," *Datamation* 25, no. 14 (December 1979), p. 112.

Such teams, according to Mills, achieve high technical standards and produce programs that are simple, obvious, and transparent; the team effort minimizes problems with egocentric programmers who want to save a millisecond here, an instruction there, to prove their brilliance. Gerald Weinberg proposes a more democratic approach, advocating rotating leadership among programmers according to the problem at hand.[3] Opponents of this system call it "structured anomaly." The exact organization favored in a given project depends on the experience and temperament of the project manager.

There is much anecdotal material on teams but little hard data identifying environmental variables that affect team performance. This section has suggested some factors in team structure that affect development efforts but there is wide disagreement on what makes projects, especially programming projects, successful.

---

[3]Gerald M. Weinberg, *The Psychology of Computer Programming* (New York, Van Nostrand Reinhold, 1971), pp. 56–59.

TEAM SIZE

Once team structure is decided, team members must be appointed. A decision on optimal team size has to be made at this juncture. This problem plagued operations research workers as far back as the 1940s and 50s and still haunts EDP projects. Studies in group dynamics have suggested that an optimal team size is 5–7 members and that as group size increases, job satisfaction drops, with absenteeism and turnover increasing. But some computer development projects are far too complex to have such small teams. The design of software for IBM's system 360, for example, required 5,000 man-years for completion. The team, obviously, needs to be large enough to complete the project within a reasonable time frame.

Regardless of team size, the collective judgment is that teams must be a balance of theoreticians and practitioners, idealists and realists, scientists and humanists, and generalists and specialists. But as teams enlarge to encompass this balance, many agree that Parkinson's third law applies: Expansion means complexity, and complexity, delay. Certainly, as teams grow in size, crosscurrents increase. The formula $K\left(\dfrac{K-1}{2}\right)$ where K = number of persons on the team, can be used to derive potential interchanges between team members as team size increases. Figure 10.5 shows a curve plotted according to this formula.

Figure 10.5   **Interactions as a function of project team size**

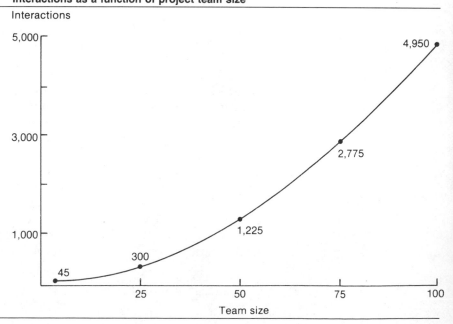

Interactions

5,000 · 4,950

3,000 · 2,775

1,225

1,000 · 300

45 · 25 · 50 · 75 · 100

Team size

One can see from this curve that the number of potential interchanges increases nonlinearly as teams enlarge.

If a large team is divided into small work groups, the problem is not solved, because coordination of these groups requires additional levels of management, thereby increasing the number of superior–subordinate relationships.[4]

Empirical research on the effect of the curve in Fig. 10.5 confirms **Fried's Law,** that there is an inverse relationship between effectiveness (production) and group size in complex technical projects (programming, electronic design, engineering, etc.).[5] Both Fried and Gerald Weinberg[6] have formulas to prove this axiom. Though they differ slightly, both agree that when team size increases beyond a certain point, the percentage of productive time diminishes. According to Fried's formula, when working a 40-hour week, the productivity of a team of 94 is less than that of a team of 20. Productivity peaks with a team size of 70. Figure 10.6 shows this productivity curve, and demonstrates the fallacy in the reasoning that if the life cycle of development is 200 man-years, then 100 persons will take two years, or 200 persons one year.

The problem with small development teams is that they may be unable to achieve team balance. Also, many computer projects have a given period of time during which development must take place in order to complete implementation on schedule. In such projects, a large rather than small team may be needed in order to have sufficient man-days of effort to complete the project on time.

When development tasks depend on completion of one activity before another begins, however, large teams may prove ineffective, for a point is reached where additional workers cannot be used to speed up development. Some project managers attempt crash development when projects fall behind schedule, but this too has severe limitations. As Fred Brooks states in his book, *The Mythical Man-Month*, "Adding people to a late project only makes it later." Crash development teams also have a high cost due to lower productivity, overtime, overcrowding, etc. In addition, problems in coordination arise when teams are large. Figure 10.7 shows the relationship of cost with time of completion according to empirical evidence.

Optimal team size will depend on the nature and complexity of the

---

[4]For the Graicunas formula on these relationships, see L. Gulick and L. Urwick, eds., *Papers in the Science of Administration* (New York: Institute of Public Administration, 1937), pp. 181–87.

[5]Louis Fried, *Practical Data Processing Management* (Reston, Va.: Reston Publishing, 1979), p. 142.

[6]Weinberg, *The Psychology of Computer Programming*, p. 69. Weinberg states that as a rough rule, three programmers organized into a team can do only twice the work of a single programmer of the same ability.

Figure 10.6

Productive hours according to team size

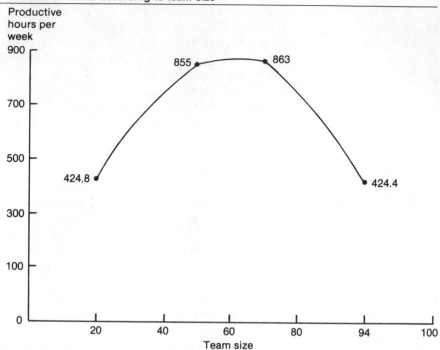

Figure 10.7

Project cost as a function of time for completion

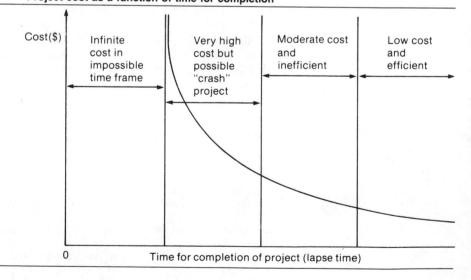

project. Unfortunately, there is no simple formula to assist a project manager in determining this optimal size. But the factors discussed in this section should be taken into consideration when team members are appointed.

PROJECT CONTROL

There are many formal techniques of project planning and control. The simplest is the **Gantt chart,** where every activity is represented by a horizontal bar on a time scale. But if one activity is delayed in a complex set of interrelated activities, there is no way of telling from the chart which other activity or activities will be affected.

A path or network diagram may be used instead. These show interrelationships, clearly establishing which activities must be completed before others can begin. The critical path can also be calculated (that is, the set of activities where delay retards the entire project). This information is needed to determine how long the project will take. If the time for each activity is known with certainty, **CPM (Critical Path Method),** a computerized scheduling technique, can be used. When times can only be estimated, **PERT (Program Evaluation Review Technique)** can be applied. This latter scheduling technique allows for three types of time estimates; optimistic time, most likely time, and pessimistic time. PERT is more appropriate than CPM for project management of information systems because the time needed for development activities is seldom known with certainty.

Another computerized scheduling technique frequently used is **GERT, (Graphic Evaluation Review Technique).**[7] CPM, PERT, and GERT all require that tasks and activities first be identified, then defined. The activities are next put into sequence (or placed in parallel) and this order expressed in graphic form. Then a time is assigned to each task and resources are allotted.

The advantage of GERT is that is allows looping. A loop is exemplified when three activities (A, B, and C) must be completed before another (D) is initiated, but A must be done before B, B before C, and C before A, as depicted in Figure 10.8. Such loops frequently occur in information systems development. GERT also allows alternative paths (either E or F in Figure 10.8), whereas PERT conventions require that all activities be performed in a set sequence. That is, PERT allows "AND" relationships, whereas using GERT, one can specify the prob-

---

[7]For an excellent introductory discussion, see E. R. Clayton and L. J. Moore, "GERT vs. PERT," *Journal of Systems Management* 2, no. 2 (February 1972), pp. 11–19. For a detailed discussion, see the book by L. J. Moore and E. R. Clayton, *GERT Modeling and Simulation* (New York: Petrocelli/Charter, 1976), 227 p.

Figure 10.8   **Illustration of GERT**

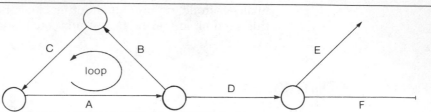

ability of alternative paths in an "OR" relationship, such as *E* or *F*, in addition to the "AND" relationship.

Another advantage of GERT is that the time of project completion is calculated with probability (*p*) associations. For example, the completion time might be 20 weeks with $p = 0.6$, and 26 weeks with $p = 0.8$.

GERT has disadvantages, however. It requires more data than PERT (data on probabilities, which may be expensive to collect), and GERT computer programs are not readily available. Computer programs for PERT, many with refinements, such as optimization (of cost and time) and both personnel and equipment leveling, are more commonly supplied by vendors.[8] As a result, PERT is more often used than GERT for information system development. It is perfectly adequate as long as the user makes allowance for its limitations. For example, when calculating time estimates, the PERT user should include time estimates for possible looping.

In spite of these planning techniques, computer projects are notorious for **time** and **cost overruns.** The overruns listed in Table 10.2, which were cited in a 1978 survey, are fairly typical. Making accurate time estimates appears to be a major stumbling block. The usefulness of CPM, PERT, and GERT as a basis for scheduling is dependent on the reliability of these estimations. Since PERT and GERT utilize three time estimates, these techniques are generally more realistic than CPM, but the problem still arises regarding the objectivity or bias of the person or group making the estimates. Certainly, estimates should be made by those responsible for, and with knowledge and experience in, the activities in question.

Sometimes activities are so innovative that no one with expertise is available in-house to make time estimates. In such cases, an outside expert may be consulted or the estimate may be made on the basis of the time required for similar activities to reach completion. Many

---

[8]For a survey of 43 software packages and a critical discussion of such software, see Perry Peterson, "Project Control Systems," *Datamation* 25, no. 7 (June 1979), pp 147–48, ff.

Table 10.2	Project time and cost performance

Time
On time 6
Over the estimated time 14
Actual time/estimated time
    Mean   210%
    Median   140%
    Range 75–900%

Cost
Within budget 2
Over budget 18
Actual cost/budget
    Mean   195%
    Median   152%
    Range 82–500%

Source: Gary W. Dickson and Richard F. Powers, "MIS Project Management Myths, Opinions, and Reality," in *Information Systems Administration*, ed. F. Warren McFarlan, Richard L. Nolan, and David P. Norton. (New York: Holt, Rinehart & Winston, 1973), p. 406.

times, the estimate will be no more than a guess. When opinions vary, consensus or averaging of time estimates may be necessary.

Software preparation, both systems and applications software, has the worst record for accuracy in time estimates of all project development activities, even though many formulas exist for calculating programming time needed. One such formula, proposed by Lawrence Putnam, is as follows:[9]

$$t_d = S_s / (C_k \, K^{1/3})$$

where

t_d = Development time
S_s = Number of end product-lines of source code delivered
C_k = State of technology constant
K = Life cycle in man-years

Though there is disagreement among experts about the manner of measuring programming time variables and about the relationship between these variables, such formulas do help identify what variables should be considered.

When a record exists of past productivity of employees on development projects, a project manager can use this data in making target schedules. But with the high mobility of analysts and programmers, there will always be new personnel of untested ability assigned to the project, and even known workers will not necessarily have stable pro-

---

[9]Lawrence H. Putnam and Ann Fritzsimmons, "Estimating Software Costs," *Datamation* 25, no. 11 (October 1979), p. 171.

ductivity. Studies have shown that productivity may vary as much as a factor of 10 even among experienced programmers. A few software firms using standardized methodology and having permanent staff have completed up to 88 percent of their projects within 20 percent of their time/cost estimates, but firms not specializing in software are doing very well to come even close to this performance.

In practice, a variety of techniques are used to make time estimates for information system development projects. In a survey of 57 software projects analyzed by John Lehman, the following techniques were used:[10]

Estimates based on a similar project 70%
Formula 38
Cost and schedule dictated 21
Provided by someone who has a knack
  for estimating correctly 14
Crystal ball (or similar means) 11
Bottom-up aggregating 4
Simulation techniques 2
Other 5

At best, a project manager can only approximate the time needed for activity completion. Estimates are generally based on a set of heuristics rather than on elaborate formulas.

SCHEDULING

Once time estimates are made, activities can be scheduled and resources assigned to each activity. Most of **scheduling** is straightforward sequencing. But when parallel activities are scheduled, care must be taken that adequate resources are available. For example, if two software activities are scheduled for simultaneous development, will enough programmers skilled in the right language be available? The schedule should also keep employees working, avoiding lulls with idle personnel. Minimizing peaks and troughs of worker demand is known as manpower leveling. Such leveling does not mean merely juggling numbers—employees in the aggregate—because special skills may be needed for a given task. For example, it is no good assigning a programmer who knows only FORTRAN to a project to be written in COBOL.

Project time completion and total project cost are recalculated once scheduling is completed to see if they fit within the time/cost constraints in the project authorization document. If not, rescheduling is necessary, dropping desired but not essential activities, reshuffling re-

---

[10]John H. Lehman, "How Software Projects Are Really Managed," *Datamation* 25, no. 1 (January 1979), p. 120.

sources, perhaps even cutting quality. In some cases, the constraints themselves may be reviewed and revised.

PROJECT REVIEW

Once scheduled, the activities are implemented. During the project lifetime, the project manager must constantly review procedures, monitor activities, and take corrective actions where necessary, communicating with all concerned what changes have been made. Development must also be periodically measured against project objectives to make sure the project is on track. Of the 57 software firms studied by Lehman, systems requirement review took place in 58 percent of the firms, systems design review in 68 percent, preliminary design review in 83 percent, and critical design review in 81 percent. Only 4 percent of the firms had no formal reviews whatsoever. Informal reviews also occurred with frequency: daily in 12 percent of the firms; weekly in 45 percent; monthly in 10 percent; as required in 45 percent; and not at all, 40 percent.[11]

During development, inaccurate time estimates need to be corrected and, where possible, work assignments adjusted, especially in critical activities, so that the entire project can be completed on schedule. Time estimates may have been based on incorrect assumptions or based on inadequate definition of activities, as suggested earlier in this chapter. But factors such as illness of personnel or late delivery of essential equipment may also affect schedules adversely. The high turnover of personnel in computer projects is also a factor in many project delays. In Lehman's study, turnover was as follows:[12]

Position	Average projects	Late projects
Project manager	68%	90%
Functional analyst	60	97
DP analyst	20	28
Programmer	38	53
Support librarian	32	37
Secretary	63	79
Administration	33	40
User representative	32	39

Finding a competent replacement and then training and orienting the new employee are time-consuming activities which may result in a project falling behind schedule.

Changed user specifications is also a reason many projects need to reschedule during development. In Lehman's survey, the need to re-

---

[11]Ibid., p. 128.

[12]Ibid., p. 121.

write specifications fell into three categories: errors, ambiguities and inconsistencies in specifications in 40 percent of the cases; changed specifications in 35 percent; and a need for better understanding of the project in 25 percent.[13]

In all projects, a point is reached when specification and design are "frozen" and no further modifications can be allowed because they will delay the entire project, cause unjustifiable dislocation, or be excessively costly. The project manager must have authority to overrule users, even users in high levels who otherwise outrank the manager, when project changes are demanded after this stage.

The status of activities, highlighting any rescheduling and assignment adjustments, must be regularly reported to users and personnel working on the project. In computer projects, because of the diversity of technical background, attitude, status, and motivation of persons associated with the project, communication is a major problem.

COMPUTER SOFTWARE FOR PROJECT CONTROL

Reports on the status of activities needed by the project manager for **project control** can be prepared by hand. But when projects are complex and frequent updates on many status entries are needed, special computer software can generate the needed information far more efficiently. Computer service utilities, which have a library of appropriate software, often provide this service to firms without computers. Firms with computers are generally provided the necessary software by their vendors. Standard reports generated for project control include:

Activity status reports, sorted by:
    Organizational units
    Activity
    Overruns
    Time
    Cost
Budget
    Standard
    Exceptional
    Comparisons
    Costing
    Loading
      Manpower
      Equipment

---

[13]Ibid., p. 120.

Work schedules, sorted by:
    Start date
    Finish date
    Float/slack

Software for many other types of reports may also be supplied by the vendor or purchased by the user. Programs for reports may differ in their degree of complexity. For example, one report might calculate the critical path of a project, listing constraints on the network; another might show alternative paths should one or more constraints be relaxed. Some programs optimize manpower loading, or cost. Others produce output in graphic form. "What if?" programs test the effect of changing the sequence of activities or altering time estimates on the ultimate cost of the project and date of completion. Some software makes calculations interactively, showing the consequences for each of many alternatives.

By analyzing the appropriate reports, the project manager can identify potential bottlenecks or problems and use the information provided to determine a solution. Budgetary reports provide a powerful cost control capability, identifying how much has been spent by each person or organizational unit and for what, then comparing these expenditures with the target budget. Many of the reports will be sent to project personnel and users to keep them informed on the status of the project's development.

Once a project is fully implemented, the project should be evaluated. Mistakes should be identified and analyzed as to why they were made and how they could have been avoided. The purpose of such an analysis is to record problems (and solutions) for the benefit of future projects, so similar mistakes won't be repeated. For example, an explanation of the heuristic rules used for making time estimates and then an accounting of personnel completion rates and causes of delays would be useful data for future project planning. Evaluation data can also help establish cause/effect relationships in the development process, helping to identify which techniques and approaches to development suit the firm's unique environment.

The project manager should also evaluate the performance of employees on the project.[14] Such evaluations may be the basis for future raises or promotions and project assignments. The project manager should guard against penalizing persons for not keeping to target schedules, however, for in project development there are many uncertainties over which an individual has no control. If personnel are unjustifiably penalized for delays, morale will suffer and employees will

---

[14]For an elaborate schema for personnel evaluation and appraisal, see Harold Kerzner, "Evaluation Techniques in Project Management," *Journal of Systems Management* 31, no. 2 (February 1980), pp. 10–19.

be unwilling to commit themselves to future development projects. It is advisable that the policy on delays be announced before the start of a project, so that the work atmosphere remains conducive to high productivity when inevitable delays occur.

PHASE-OUT

Following evaluation, project personnel are reassigned to other organizational units in the firm, the budget is reconciled, and a project final report is submitted to corporate management.

SUMMARY AND CONCLUSIONS

To ensure completion of computer system development projects within time and funding constraints, formal project management is advisable for all but the most simple systems. Project management is a sequence of steps which begins with the selection of the project manager and development team. It entails definition of tasks and activities, the making of time estimates for these activities, scheduling, and control through reviews, monitoring, and correcting procedures. Special software can be used to generate reports on the status of the activities for users and project personnel. These reports also serve the project manager in analysis and project control. Figure 10.9 is a network diagram of the steps of project management described in the chapter.

It should be pointed out that some computer scientists downgrade the importance of project management with regard to project success. It is C. R. Hoare's opinion, that:

> Basically all problems are technical. If you know what you want to do and you have the necessary technical background, there is no point in making a great management problem out of it. Obviously a certain amount of resource control and personnel work have to go on, but that's all.[15]

This, however, is a minority opinion. It is the authors' view that project management should be used in developing computer systems. Indeed, most firms engaged in information systems development utilize the project management techniques described in this chapter.

A key resource in successful project management is the project manager. The manager should be a person "of superhuman qualities: a first-class technician, an outstanding manager, tactful, patient, hum-

---

[15]In *Software Engineering Techniques,* ed. J. N. Baxton and B. Randell (Birmingham, England: NATO Science Committee, 1970), p. 53.

Figure 10.9   **Network diagram for project management**

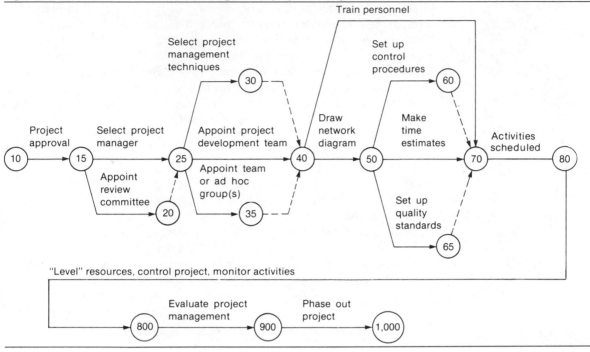

ble, persistent, shrewd, infallible and farseeing."[16] In addition, the project manager must have the confidence of corporate management in order to be given the authority commensurate with development responsibility. (At times, a project manager may have to overrule users at high levels in the corporate structure.)

Mike Sanders characterizes the role of a project manager as a planner and player.[17] Planning entails arrangement of development modules as to time, space, priority, and effort. Playing entails juggling problem pieces to determine cause and outcome, and jiggling project form accordingly. Successful project managers are largely intuitive and are able to blend together numerous uncontrolled, uncertain, and unstructured variables into a more controlled environment.

But even competent project managers with the aid of computer programs for project control cannot guarantee project completion without overruns. There are just too many variables in computer system development. For example, user specifications may change, analysts and

[16]Quoted in Norman Sanders, *A Manager's Guide to Profitable Computers* (London: AMACOM, 1978), p. 106.

[17]Mike Sanders, "Planning and Playing: Project Management Plus," *Computer Data* (March 1977), pp. 19–21. Reviewed in *Data Processing Digest* 23, no. 6 (June 1977), p. 16.

programmers may be unavailable or leave their jobs, or predictions about computer technology and methodology may prove in error. No wonder few computer projects meet their targets. Lehman's study showed that only 54 percent of the projects met deadlines. The remainder had delays ranging from 1–24 months, the average delay being seven months. Cost overruns were even more prevalent than time delays: 58 percent of the projects cost more than estimated, only 4 percent, less.[18] Disheartening as this may be, without project control the time delays and cost overruns would undoubtedly have been far higher.

Which project management techniques to use depends on the project environment. In Table 10.3, F. Warren McFarlan identifies eight project types and the tools needed to ensure project success, the tools being internal integration, external integration, formal planning and formal control. A listing of what each of these tools includes appears in Table 10.4 on the following page.

In summary, project management attempts to bring order and control to project development. As one observer, N. J. Reza, has stated, successful project development is accomplished "not through providential guidance nor through any unique expertise, but rather through the application of time tested methods which are wholly dependent

Table 10.3		Project types and relative contribution of tools to ensuring success			
Project type	Project description	External integration	Internal integration	Formal planning	Formal control
I	High structure, low technology, large	Low	Medium	High	High
II	High structure, low technology, small	Low	Low	Medium	High
III	High structure, high technology, large	Low	High	Medium	Medium
IV	High structure, high technology, small	Low	High	Low	Low
V	Low structure, low technology, large	High	Medium	High	High
VI	Low structure, low technology, small	High	Low	Medium	High
VII	Low structure, high technology, large	High	High	Low+	Low+
VIII	Low structure, high technology, small	High	High	Low	Low

Source: F. Warren McFarlan, "Portfolio Approach to Information Systems," *Harvard Business Review* (September/October 1981), p. 147.

[18]Lehman, "How Software Projects Are Really Managed," p. 128.

on adequate resources, both personnel and financial, and a well developed plan."[19]

Table 10.4 **Tools of project management**

External integration tools	Internal integration tools
Selecton of user as project manager	Selection of experienced DP professional leadership team
Creation of user steering committee	Selection of manager to lead time
Frequency and depth of meetings of this committee	Frequent team meetings
User-managed change control process	Regular preparation and distribution of minutes within team on key design evolution decision
Frequency and detail of distribution of project team minutes to key users	
Selection of users as team members	Regular technical status reviews
Formal user specification approval process	Managed low turnover of team members
Progress reports prepared for corporate steering committee	Selection of high percentage of team members with significant previous work relationships
Users responsible for education and installation of system	Participation of team members in goal setting and deadline establishment
Users manage decision on key action dates	Outside technical assistance
Formal planning tasks	*Formal control tasks*
PERT, critical path, etc., networking	Periodic formal status reports versus plan
Milestone phases selection	Change control disciplines
Systems specification standards	Regular milestone presentation meetings
Feasibility study specifications	Deviations from plan
Project approval processes	
Project postaudit procedures	

Source: F. Warren McFarlan, "Portfolio Approach to Information Systems," *Harvard Business Review* (September–October 1981), p. 149.

[19]N. J. Reza, Jr., "Insuring Successful Systems Implementation," *Data Management* 10, no. 5 (May 1969), p. 24.

CASE STUDY: PROJECT MANAGEMENT AT AIRBORNE FREIGHT CORP.*

Airborne Freight, with offices in 77 locations within the United States and in 10 foreign countries, is the second largest American air freight forwarder. The company has some 2,000 employees, including 16 analysts and programmers. In 1975, a consulting company that was studying Airborne Freight's data processing function recommended the installation of a project control and accounting system. After spending three man-months trying to develop a system in-house, Airborne Freight investigated project management packages on the market.

The corporation chose SDM/70 as fitting its needs. SDM/70 breaks system development into nine phases, starting with user specification and ending with post-implementation review. Each phase identifies tasks, each task having a fully specified end product, checklists, and preformatted forms. Guidelines are also provided for methodologies like HIPO and structured programming, quality review, training, and organization.

When a development project is undertaken, Airborne Freight appoints a development committee, which includes representatives from upper management or staff of user departments, to review documentation and monitor development progress. A steering committee, composed of three vice presidents and the systems manager, meets monthly to review all projects and assign priorities.

The following benefits from project control are recognized by the firm:

a.   Improved communication between systems personnel, user departments, and top management.
b.   False planning starts avoided.
c.   Uniform tasking of projects without loss of flexibility.
d.   Planning and development credibility promoted with users.

KEY WORDS

Cost overruns

CPM (Critical Path Method)

Fried's Law

Functional organization

Gantt chart

GERT (Graphic Evaluation Review Technique)

Matrix organization

*Source: Richard G. Canning, ed., "Progress in Project Control," *EDP Analyzer* 15, no. 12 (December 1977), pp. 3–4.

Organization by function

Project

Project control

Project management

Project manager

Project organization

PERT (Program Evaluation Review Technique)

Scheduling

Time overruns

DISCUSSION QUESTIONS

1. What are the main responsibilities, functions, and activities of project management? Which of these should be assigned to:
   a. Project manager?
   b. Project review committee?
   c. Permanent computer department staff?
   d. Project team?

2. Should a committee be responsible for project control and management? What should the committee's relationship be to the project manager? What should be its functions? What skills should members have? How many should be on the committee? You may wish to qualify your answers by specifying the project environment.

3. To what extent is project management essentially crisis management? Can this be changed? If so, how?

4. What should be the composition of a project team for each of the following development projects?
   a. Application of accounts receivable project.
   b. Integrated application of accounts receivable, purchasing and production.
   c. Implementation of a data base management system.
   d. Automation on the factory floor.
   e. Use of numerical control machines.
   f. Implementation of computer-aided design.
   g. Information retrieval for a company library containing books on technology, patent rights, and industries similar to the company.
   h. Automation of the offices in the division of marketing.
   i. Acquisition and installation of a medium-size computer.
   j. Decentralization and distribution of computing to three distributed sites.
   k. Design and implementation of a system of internal control for EDP.

5. What project control techniques (e.g., CPM, Gantt, etc.) would you use in each part of Question 4?

6. List special problems and dangers in project management in each of the projects in Question 4.

7. What mode of project organization (functional organization, matrix organization, or project organization) would you recommend for each of the projects in Question 4?

8.   What qualities in a project manager would be required in each project in Question 4?

9.   Should project management itself be controlled? If so, why and how?

10. Why is management of computer projects different from noncomputer projects? What special approaches or cautions are required?

11. Computer projects are notorious for cost overruns and time schedule slippages. Why? How can these be minimized without a loss in the quality of the final product?

12. What is the role of top corporate management in relation to project management?

13. What is the role, if any, of outside consultants and consulting houses in project management?

14. When should computer software be used for project management? Explain.

SELECTED ANNOTATED BIBLIOGRAPHY

Brandon, Dick H., and Max Gray. *Project Control Standards*. New York: Auerbach Publishers, 1970, 204 p.
    This book is in the style of a manual. It has detailed checklists and many samples of computer output. Though somewhat outdated, it has a good description of five project control packages: MANAGE, ASTRA, PCS/360, PMS/360, and RMS. A detailed bibliography is also included.

Cleland, David I., and William R. King. *Systems Analysis and Project Management*. New York: McGraw Hill, 1975, 398 p.
    This book discusses the process and principles of project management. The author is not new to the field, having first published this text in 1968.

Gildersleeve, Thomas R. *Data Processing Project Management*. New York: Van Nostrand Reinhold, 1974, 321 p.
    This excellent book is well organized and well structured. The section on costing of projects is especially good. Approximately 100 pages of appendices are included. Highly recommended.

Journal of Systems Management.
    This journal is oriented toward project management. Readers will find updated articles on subjects such as computer programs for project control, and techniques for personnel appraisal and time estimations.

McBurney. N. R. "Domesticating the Project Management Monster." *Data Management* 16, no. 5 (May 1978), pp. 38–44.
    If you like diagrams and samples of computer printouts, you will enjoy this article. It is particularly good on the data and files required for project control.

Sanders, Norman. *A Manager's Guide to Profitable Computers*. London: AMACOM, 1978, 261 p.

Project management is as good an excuse as any to read this delightful book full of analogies and anecdotes. It totally lacks the formalism of usual texts on this subject, having no footnotes or bibliographies, and succeeds in being a pleasant, readable book on a difficult, serious subject. The illustrations by Tony Hart add to the humor.

Weist, Jerome D., and F. K. Levy. *A Management Guide to PERT/CPM*. Englewood Cliffs, N.J.: Prentice-Hall, 1977, 277 p.

This easy-to-read book includes a discussion of PERT, GERT, PDM, DCPM, and other networks. Technical and mathematical explanations are delegated to appendices of the relevant chapters.

PART FOUR:

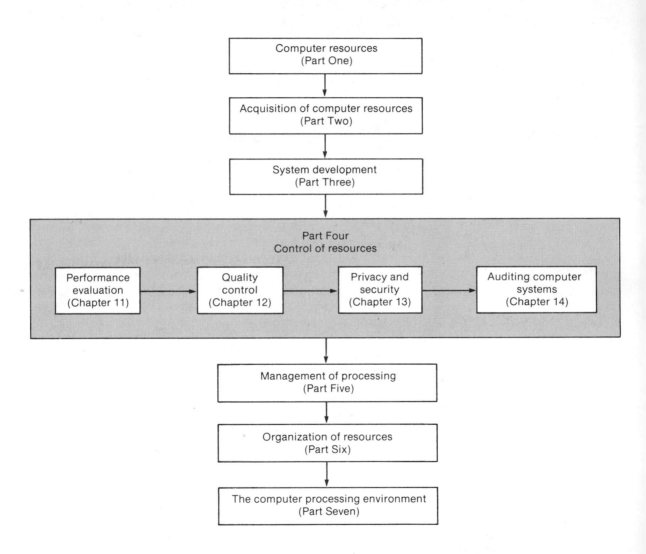

```
          ┌─────────────────────────────┐
          │   Computer resources        │
          │      (Part One)             │
          └─────────────────────────────┘
                        │
                        ▼
          ┌─────────────────────────────┐
          │ Acquisition of computer     │
          │ resources (Part Two)        │
          └─────────────────────────────┘
                        │
                        ▼
          ┌─────────────────────────────┐
          │   System development        │
          │     (Part Three)            │
          └─────────────────────────────┘
                        │
                        ▼
```

Part Four
Control of resources

| Performance evaluation (Chapter 11) | → | Quality control (Chapter 12) | → | Privacy and security (Chapter 13) | → | Auditing computer systems (Chapter 14) |

```
                        │
                        ▼
          ┌─────────────────────────────┐
          │ Management of processing    │
          │      (Part Five)            │
          └─────────────────────────────┘
                        │
                        ▼
          ┌─────────────────────────────┐
          │ Organization of resources   │
          │      (Part Six)             │
          └─────────────────────────────┘
                        │
                        ▼
          ┌─────────────────────────────┐
          │ The computer processing     │
          │ environment (Part Seven)    │
          └─────────────────────────────┘
```

CONTROL OF RESOURCES

Introduction to Part Four

Part Four is closely related to Part Three insofar as all of the mechanisms of control described in Part Four must be incorporated in a system's design during system development. Indeed, evaluation, quality, privacy, security, and control specifications must be included in the systems requirement statement.

The purpose of devoting a separate part of the book to control is to emphasize the importance of preventing errors and of protecting information from unauthorized access or illicit use in the business world today. The need for control and security of business data, of course, predates the use of computers. But the speed of computer transactions and the volume of confidential data processed by computer means that inadequate controls can lead to problems of a much higher magnitude than formerly. Consider, for example, the large sums of money being transferred daily with electronic fund transfer (EFT) and the scope for embezzlement if EFT security can be breached.

Chapter 11 discusses how a computer center evaluates its own performance, outlining evaluation criteria and methods of collecting data on performance. Operations that need evaluation are also identified. Chapter 12 describes control points in processing where systems should be monitored for human and machine error, and suggests solutions to common problems.

Privacy and security issues are the subject of Chapter 13. Layers of protection are recommended, including access restrictions to computer resources, processing controls, physical safeguards, and organizational policies to discourage employee malfeasance. Finally, Chapter 14 describes computer audits by individuals not employed by the computer facility so that a measure of objectivity in evaluating operations can be obtained. The role of auditors in controlling controls is also explained.

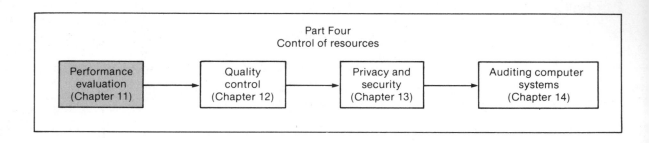

Part Four
Control of resources

| Performance evaluation (Chapter 11) | Quality control (Chapter 12) | Privacy and security (Chapter 13) | Auditing computer systems (Chapter 14) |

CHAPTER 11

Performance evaluation

The perfect computer has been developed. You just feed in your problems—and they never come out again.

Al Goodman

In order to ensure quality computing, the performance of a computer center should be regularly evaluated. This evaluation, called **CPE (computer performance evaluation),**[1] consists of a comparison of actual performance with desired performance in resource utilization, operations, and service, as shown in the model in Figure 11.1. When performance fails to measure up to prescribed standards, corrective action followed by reevaluation is required. A satisfactory performance rating indicates no immediate need for change but is no grounds for complacency. Computing is not a static field. New technology, an altered business climate, increased load, or demand for new applications can suddenly turn contented clients into frustrated users. For this reason, the evaluation cycle should be scheduled at regular intervals so that system weakness can be identified and rectified before it becomes chronic. Evaluation should also be initiated whenever problems arise.

Performance evaluation is, in effect, a mechanism of control. How this mechanism works is the subject of this chapter. First, critical performance variables that need to be evaluated are identified and the criteria for evaluation described. This is followed by a discussion of how performance data is collected, measured, and analyzed. Finally, corrective action and evaluation of the evaluation process itself are considered.

---

[1] Other terms frequently used are *computer performance management* and *computer performance monitoring.*

Figure 11.1   The process of performance evaluation

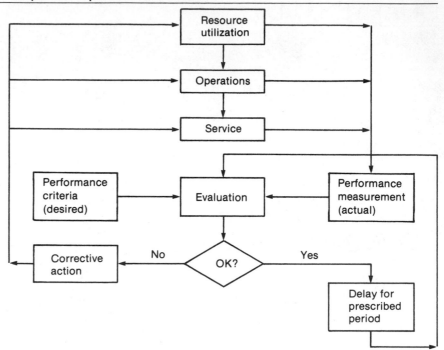

Sections that follow correspond to steps in the evaluation process, detailed in Figure 11.2. Personnel, timing, and evaluation tools and techniques will be discussed at each step, when relevant. It should be noted that this chapter deals with micro evaluation by the computer center staff, the first level of performance control. The role of auditors external to the computer center, who also evaluate performance, will be considered in Chapter 14.

IDENTIFY WHAT IS TO BE EVALUATED

Though the computer center director is responsible for implementing **performance objectives,** the objectives themselves may come from a variety of sources. Corporate management, users, project development teams, steering committees, planning groups, data administrators, and EDP personnel may all have a voice in specifying objectives. Which objectives should have priority and which should be evaluated on a regular basis is usually a management decision, made by the individual or group with authority to supervise computer center operations or by the head of the computer center.

Figure 11.2   **Steps in evaluation**

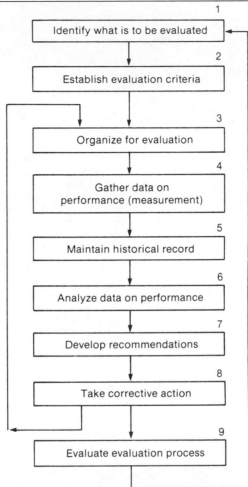

In computing there are three broad categories that need to be evaluated: **resource utilization, operations,** and **service.** Each of these categories is subdivided into evaluation activities, as shown in Figure 11.3. Evaluation of resource utilization, for example, will consist of a review of hardware, software, and personnel performance. The evaluation of daily operations is usually distinct from evaluation of systems development, and many firms consider planning so important that separate evaluations are held for capacity planning, contingency planning, long- and short-term planning, and systems development planning. But the exact breakdown and scope of subcategories in a given firm will depend on the complexity of computing functions performed by the computer center and on managerial choice.

Figure 11.3   **Performance components to be evaluated**

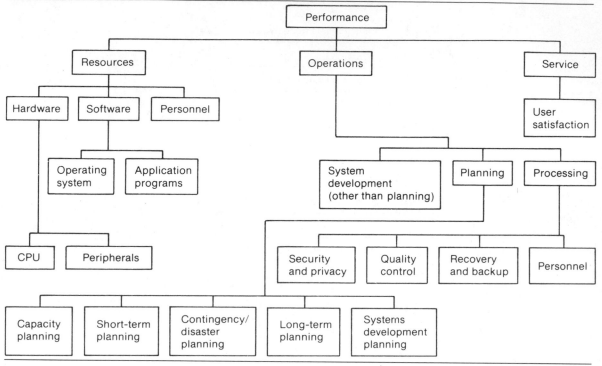

EVALUATION CRITERIA

Efficiency of operations and effectiveness of product are basic **evaluation criteria.** Throughput, productivity, utilization, and cost are measures of efficiency. Availability, quality, timeliness, accuracy, and reliability determine effectiveness. (See Figure 11.4.) In the sections which follow, these terms will be defined and discussed.

Efficiency

Efficiency (η), the ratio of output (O) to input (I), $\eta = O/I$, is an old concept used in production management. But in computing, the benefit of output cannot always be calculated in tangible units. How can one measure the monetary value of a timely report, accuracy, or the absence of fraud? By keeping input constant, however, a change in output can be noted. If output increases, efficiency is increased. If output decreases, efficiency is decreased. That is, if I is constant and O $\uparrow$, then η $\uparrow$. Conversely, if O is constant and I $\downarrow$, then η $\uparrow$. Using this measure, efficiency of use of computer resources (equipment, software, personnel, materials, funds) can be evaluated.

Throughput, productivity, utilization, and cost are all considered

Figure 11.4   **Components of performance**

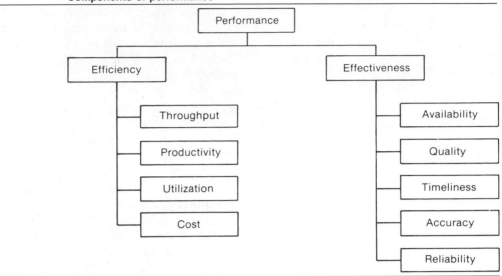

when evaluating efficiency. These criteria of performance are described below.

Throughput. The design of equipment, in part, determines computer **throughput**, the amount of work that can be performed during a given period of time. Throughput is advertised, known to the buyer at the time of purchase. CPU throughput may be measured in KOPS (thousands of operations per second) or MIPS (millions of instructions per second). Unfortunately, these measurements are not as standardized as horsepower or kilowatt hours, so one cannot always compare the throughput of computers sold by different vendors.[2]

CPU throughput, however, is rarely the prime processing constraint. Rather, peripheral devices used in preprocessing (such as keypunching equipment and optical recognition equipment) or postprocessing (such as printers, bursters, decolators, and routing equipment) limit efficiency. Such peripheral devices advertise throughput as a selling feature so competing models can be compared. When sales claims prove unsubstantiated, the vendor can theoretically be held accountable.

Productivity. **Productivity** is the term usually applied to throughput performance of personnel. One can evaluate the efficiency of data

---

[2]See Edward J. Lias, "Tracking the Elusive KOPS," *Datamation* 26, no. 11 (November 1980), pp. 99–105.

entry operators without difficulty, for number of keystrokes per hour can be measured and compared to standard tables. Tables also exist for lines of code (LOC) produced by programmers, but most firms are more concerned with quality than quantity of code, and recognize that a programmer's output is a function of the programming language used, program methodology and design, the complexity of the logic, the program's size, the organization of the programming team, the work environment, and programming experience.

Quality as a measure of productivity is a subjective judgment. This is particularly true in computing where the flaws and errors of programmers and analysts may take a long time to surface, often long after the employee has left the firm's employ. The problem of evaluating productivity is one that requires further discussion. Chapter 22 on staffing deals with this subject.

Utilization.   Another gauge of efficiency is **utilization,** the ratio of what is used to what is available. A high utilization value may indicate that bottlenecks will occur in the future: a low value, possible overcapacity. The information collected when evaluating utilization serves as a basis for capacity planning and scheduling, in addition to providing a measure of efficiency.

Cost.   Efficiency is increased when **cost,** with constant output, drops. One way to evaluate performance is by comparing budgeted with actual expenditures and reviewing trends in cost indexes, such as the following:

$$\text{Material cost index} = \frac{\text{Cost of materials}}{\text{Total cost of computing center}}$$

$$\text{Personnel cost index} = \frac{\text{Cost of personnel}}{\text{Total cost of computing center}}$$

$$\text{Software maintenance index} = \frac{\text{Cost of maintenance (software)}}{\text{Total cost of computing center}}$$

In computing, inefficiency can often be traced to waste of materials (cards, tapes, paper) and run time. Habits of waste frequently develop when user departments do not pay for computing services and computer time is not constrained. By charging for services, costs may be lowered dramatically. This is an example of a budgetary policy that may affect performance efficiency.

Effectiveness

A system may be inefficient yet still be effective. For example, a program may produce the desired output and hence be effective, but take so much computer time to operate that the cost of the output is more than its value.

Computer centers are concerned with both efficiency and effectiveness. **Effectiveness** evaluation is based on objectives of a given system. Criteria of evaluation include availability, quality, timeliness, accuracy, and reliability, which are described below.

Availability. Machine **availability** may be measured as the percent of time equipment is in service. A company with three shifts which has half an hour daily down time (for breakdowns or maintenance) has an availability index of roughly 98 percent. As down time is reduced, system effectiveness will increase. The problem with this index is that if the numerator in the ratio is fixed and the denominator changes, the index changes, though the machine is no less available from the operational point of view. For example, if the half hour down time occurs during operations when the machine is utilized only 12 hours instead of 24, the index changes from 96 percent to 98 percent though no change in machine availability because of down time has taken place. (Restrictions on availability due to priority scheduling or overloading is a separate problem of scheduling and capacity planning.)

One can also evaluate availability in absolute terms. If a job requires 300 minutes setup and run time on a specific date the question arises: is that 300 minutes available when needed?

Quality. Though this term has many connotations, the ratio of jobs that must be rerun to jobs executed is a common measure of **quality.** Other aspects of effectiveness related to quality (timeliness, accuracy, and reliability) are discussed below.

Timeliness. **Response time,** the length of time between an initial request for service and job completion, is another measure of effectiveness. No manager is satisfied if reports are outdated or no longer relevant by the time processing is concluded. **Timeliness** is related to waiting time, length of queue, and backlog, all of which can be measured. Another timeliness indicator is percentage of requests completed on schedule.

Development, as well as operations, should be evaluated for timeliness. A computer center must deliver new systems when promised and process existing applications on time. The project development index that needs to be reviewed is ratio of projects completed on schedule to total projects undertaken.

The number of days a project is delayed should also be scrutinized. It is often better to have four projects that are each delayed one day than to have one project 10 days late.

Accuracy. **Accuracy** can be defined as the absence of error. But what constitutes an error? When a calculated value is 1.962256, one can truncate the number to 1.96 when the unit is dollars and cents, but not when 1.962256 represents millions of dollars. A misspelled name on the mailing list for an advertising circular would be regrettable but not crucial. But suppose the misspelling were the name of the chairman of the board in a firm's annual report?

These examples illustrate that accuracy must be carefully defined when evaluating system effectiveness. The permissible magnitude of error should be established, rate of acceptable error defined (e.g., one in a million calculations), and error limits set in absolute terms (e.g., number of allowable errors per month). Degree of accuracy should be set not only for computer processing, but for peripherals, telecommunications, and data entry as well.

Reliability.   **Reliability** is an illusive concept though many formulas have been published to measure it[3] and even a theory of reliability has been proposed.[4] The problem is that too many variables in reliability calculations cannot be precisely measured.

The probability of failure is a good example.[5] And how does one determine personnel reliability? Sickness, accidents, absenteeism, turnover, training, motivation, and employee honesty are factors that contribute to reliability, but how can one measure or predict the role of these factors when making a reliability assessment? There are also no universal standards for measuring the ease with which a system can be maintained or recover from failure. Should reliability be based on the effort, cost, or time required to keep a system operational?

Software reliability (a function of the complexity of the software, the competence of programmers, and viability of a given development approach) is also difficult to assess. What standards of measurement should be used to estimate probability of software failure, or potential monetary loss in the event the information expected or needed is not produced? The problem of identifying software errors compounds the difficulty of measuring system effectiveness in terms of reliability. The system may appear to function smoothly but be producing inaccurate output due to inherent, undetected software errors.

Conflicts between evaluation criteria

Before concluding this section, a word should be said about the interrelationships that exist between performance criteria. In many cases, a high rating of effectiveness for one criterion precludes a high

---

[3]See George A. Champine, "What Makes a System Reliable?" *Datamation* 24, no. 9 (September 1978), p. 199; C. D. Hurtado, "EDP Effectiveness Evaluation," *Journal of Systems Management* 29, no. 1 (January 1978), pp. 18–21; and Donald E. Peeples, "Measure for Productivity," *Datamation* 24, no. 5 (May 1978), pp. 222–30.

[4]Michael G. Walker, "A Theory on Software Reliability," *Datamation* 24, no. 9 (September 1978), pp. 211–14.

[5]Gilb uses probabilities extensively in his approach to performance evaluation. See T. Gilb, *Software Metrics* (Cambridge, Mass.: Winthrop Publishers, 1977), 282 p.

Figure 11.5 Response time–cost curve

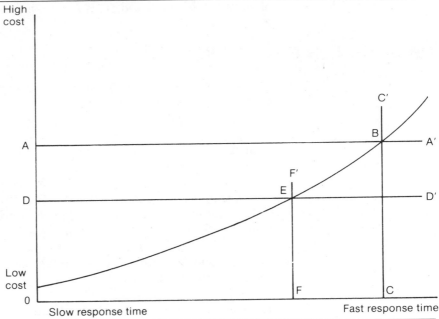

rating for another. For example, lowering response time may raise costs, and vice versa. If the response time–cost curve for a given firm is as illustrated in Figure 11.5, with *OC* an acceptable response time and *OD* an acceptable cost, it is evident that compromise is necessary, for they yield different points on the curve. At point *E*, for example, the cost corresponds to *DD'* but the response time *FF'* is slower than *CC'*. At point *B*, the response time corresponds to *CC'* but the cost *AA'* is higher than *DD'*. One of the two variables has to give, or both may be compromised somewhat to fall within points *E* and *B* on the curve. This means either a slower response time or higher cost than originally desired.

The same type of trade-off may exist between other variables, such as quality and cost, or quality and timeliness, as shown below.

Quality control⟶ quality ↑ ⟶ desirable
costs ↑ ⟶ undesirable } Conflict

Quality control⟶ quality ↑ ⟶ desirable
timeliness ↓⟶ undesirable } Conflict

Indeed, more than two criteria maybe in opposition in a given situation. Management must then search for a satisfactory or acceptable mix of controllable factors, setting acceptable levels so that the effect of conflicts is minimized. This is not an easy task.

ORGANIZE FOR EVALUATION

Who performs the evaluation? Many computer centers appoint a staff member, who is technically competent and knowledgeable regarding organizational policies and procedures, to evaluate the center's performance. Other firms prefer that the evaluation be done by someone who has no role in daily computer operations, preferring the objectivity of an employee from a different department. This evaluator can bring a fresh perspective to performance evaluation. Still other firms hire a consultant, an outsider, to evaluate operations. J. Kanter claims that outside evaluators are used by three out of five large companies, and two out of five small and medium size companies.[6] (Note: the evaluation being discussed is the first level of performance control. The role of auditors, both in-house and external auditors, will be discussed in Chapter 14.)

Performance evaluation should be a regularly scheduled activity. The staff member responsible for evaluation should be appointed, a budget for evaluation activities drawn up, and the purpose and scope of the evaluation publicized. Evaluations should be conducted openly, not secretly, with the evaluator known to workers. Employees can be helpful to evaluators in identifying and diagnosing poor performance, and their cooperation is needed when corrective procedures are initiated.

The frequency of evaluations will vary from one firm to another. Most managers weigh the cost of evaluation in effort, computer time, and organizational disruption, against potential cost due to unidentified inefficiency and ineffectiveness, and schedule evaluations accordingly.

DATA COLLECTION AND MEASUREMENT

Once performance criteria are specified and variables identified, data on the values of variables must be collected for future analysis. This can be done by logging, using monitors, or canvassing users. (A sample questionnaire used in determining system effectiveness appears in Chapter 14.) The many sources of data required for performance evaluation are shown in Figure 11.6.

---

[6]Jerome Kanter, *Management-Oriented Information Systems*, 2d ed. (Englewood Cliffs, N.J.: Prentice-Hall, 1977), p. 166. Kanter does not cite the year of his findings or his source. But the numbers seem plausible.

Figure 11.6   **Sources of data for performance evaluation**

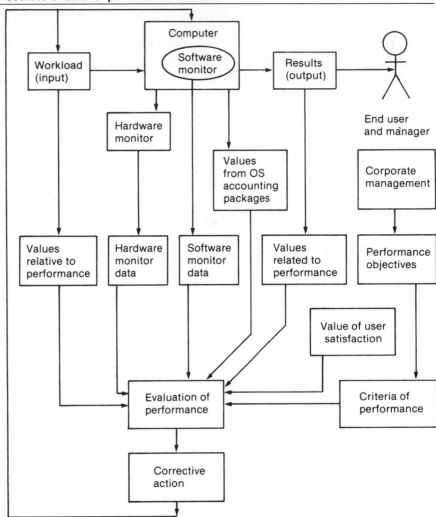

Logging statistics

    An evaluator may collect performance statistics and log the data manually.[7] This might include length of down time for maintenance, or the calculation of performance indices. Hand collection of data is costly because even a simple calculation (such as percent of jobs delivered on schedule) requires someone to search job records for data, and there is always the possibility of error in the calculation itself.

---

[7]See Richard T. Due, "Predicting Results with Statistics," *Datamation* 26, no. 5 (May 1980), pp. 227–30.

Job accounting programs can replace manually collected statistics in some areas, but again, cost is a factor albeit much less so.

Monitors

Data can also be collected by hardware and software monitors, the various types of which are listed in Figure 11.7 and described below.

Hardware monitors are equipment with sensors in input and output channels which record desired data on instrument panels or on tape for later analysis. An **accumulating monitor** is a counter used in simple computational environments. It might be used to count the number of jobs completed in a given time period, for example. A **logical monitor** is essentially a minicomputer used in more complex processing, such as multiprogramming. Both types of hardware monitors are suited for collecting utilization statistics and data on component conflicts—data needed for capacity planning.

A **software monitor** is an application program that is part of the operating system or stored in the computer. It collects data by reading internal tables, status registers, memory maps, operation system control blocks, etc., then uses one or more programs to analyze and report on the data collected. Software monitors can generate utilization figures as hardware monitors do, and can also report on the performance of systems and applications programs.

Software monitors are of two types. An **event-driven monitor (EDM)** interacts with the operating system's interrupt-handling mechanism and can monitor almost every occurrence of the event being studied. A **time-driven monitor (TDM)** is a periodic sampling system, activated at user-specified intervals. TDMs fall into two categories: a system, or configuration, monitor which generates information on system components, and program monitors.

Figure 11.7   **Types of monitors**

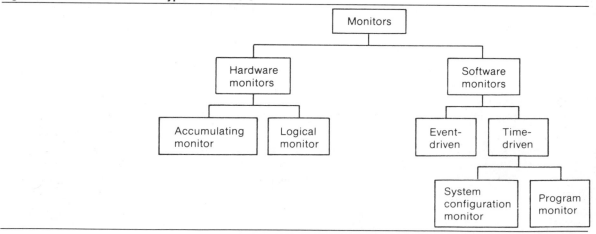

Table 11.1   **Comparison of hardware and software monitors**

Hardware monitors	*Software monitors*
Advantages	Advantages:
Accurate data on short-term activities.	Easy to use.
Measures systems overhead.	Low acquisition costs.
No CPU or storage overhead.	Flexibility in choosing options for data collection.
Well suited for computing utilization.	
Wide variety of counter measures possible.	
Disadvantages:	Disadvantages:
High acquisition cost.	Significant CPU and storage overhead.
Long setup time.	Cannot measure utilization for concurrent events.
Needs skilled operator.	Has low priority for CPU access.
Number of sensor probes is limited.	Must be reprogrammed for changes in operating system.
Probes can be accidentally disconnected, damaged, or incorrectly connected, resulting in false data.	

Table 11.1 compares the advantages and limitations of hardware and software monitors.[8]

Special studies

Data on user satisfaction can be collected from questionnaires and interviews. The problem is designing relevant questions and motivating the respondent to reply candidly. Factors that should be evaluated are listed in Table 11.2.[9]

It is helpful if questionnaires are designed so answers can be mark-sensed or read by optical scanning equipment. A terminal might also be used, with answers collected by one-stroke responses or by touch, using touch-sensitive screens.

MAINTAIN HISTORICAL RECORD

When evaluating performance data, it is useful to compare current performance with records from the past. For this reason, historical records need to be maintained. Performance data stored in a data bank

---

[8]For more discussion of monitors, see William B. Engle, "Making the Most of Performance Monitors," *Computer Decisions* 10, no. 11 (November 1978), pp. 50 ff., and Gary J. Nutt, "Tutorial: Computer Systems Monitors," *Computer* 8, no. 11 (November 1975) pp. 51–60.

[9]For a questionnaire used in evaluating output reports, see S. Neumann and E. Seger, "Evaluate Your Information System," *Journal of Systems Management* 31, no. 3 (March 1980), pp. 36–37.

Table 11.2	**Performance factors to be evaluated**
	1. Timeliness of operations and reports.
	2. Validity and completeness.
	3. Achievement of predetermined acceptable levels of operations.
	4. Frequency of errors.
	5. Response time required to meet users' requests.
	6. Effectiveness of measures to control data and protect both security and privacy of information.
	7. Software performance.
	8. System reliability.
	9. Achievement of long-range goals.
	10. Frequency of unscheduled down time and its percentage of total scheduled time.
	11. Availability and usefulness of documentation.
	12. Degree of incorporation of latest technology.
	13. Quality and turnover of personnel.
	14. Availability and effectiveness of training.
	15. User perception of EDP quality and service.
	16. Openness of communication lines between users and EDP personnel.

Source: Adapted from J. G. Kitzer, "A Model for System Design," *Journal of Systems Management* 23, no. 10 (October 1972), p. 30.

help with longitudinal analysis, setting standards, identifying performance trends, and calculating moving averages.

ANALYZE PERFORMANCE DATA

Without analysis of collected performance data, the collection effort is wasted. Yet too often sheaves of performance data are stacked on an evaluator's desk waiting for analysis that never takes place. Time must be set aside so data are reviewed and interpreted.

Analysis usually starts with a glance check at data to see if the values of variables are reasonable. This may be followed by a trend analysis and a check to see how performance measures up to local, national, and industrial standards.

An analyst would check performance data, such as the sample figures on CPU utilization listed in Figure 11.8. If the 95 percent were for three shifts, excluding preventative maintenance (often 5 percent), the computer would be running near full capacity. Management would then be informed of the need for expansion or acquisition of a larger system.

The 60 percent utilization figure for preprocessing and 20 percent for postprocessing is acceptable, but may hide bottlenecks at specific equipment. For this reason, disaggregated data should be collected; for example, utilization statistics on all channel ports as well as utilization figures for tapes, disks, and other input/output devices. The 49

Figure 11.8   **Data on performance for analysis**

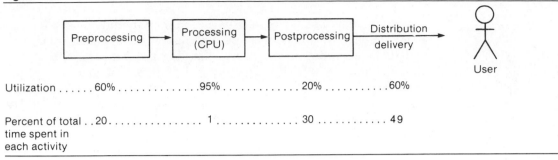

Utilization . . . . . . 60% . . . . .95% . . . . 20% 60%

Percent of total . . 20 . . . . 1 . . . . 30 49
time spent in
each activity

percent figure for distribution activities in this sample is high compared with other computer systems. This may be one area of performance that can be readily upgraded if delivery procedures are changed.

DEVELOP RECOMMENDATIONS

On the basis of data analysis, evaluators must make a set of recommendations to improve performance, supported by reviews and reports. A sample listing of what should be included in these documents appears in Table 11.3.

Table 11.3   **Reviews, reports, and recommendations by performance evaluators**

Reviews
    Service levels
    Priorities
    Workloads
    Forecasts of:
        Resource needs
        Personnel
    Acceptance levels
    Relevance and obsoleteness
    Cost effectiveness
Reports
    Exceptional
    Summary
    Technical
    Financial
Recommendations
    Cost-effective innovations
        Technical
        Organizational
    Corrective actions to improve performance

TAKE CORRECTIVE ACTION

Recommendations for corrective action may include changes in resource usage, new procedures and techniques, revised user interfaces, or perhaps alteration of the firm's planning process. The aim of corrective action should be not merely to bring performance to targeted levels but to raise performance to higher standards. Though the evaluator recommends how to improve performance, the responsibility for implementing the recommendations lies with the computer center head.

EVALUATE EVALUATION PROCESS

The final responsibility of the evaluator is to evaluate the evaluation process itself. That is, problems in planning, organizing, and implementing the evaluation should be identified, changes in the basic premises or philosophy of evaluation suggested (if any are needed), and tools and techniques for future evaluations recommended. Such an evaluation is particularly important following a computer center performance evaluation because firms are still learning how to conduct such evaluations. They simply don't have much experience evaluating computing operations because of the newness of electronic processing. The speed with which technological advances take place in computing also complicates the evaluator's role because new models of equipment and new applications software are continually being introduced.

SUMMARY

Performance objectives are set by corporate management. To make sure that a computer center meets performance objectives, periodic evaluations should be scheduled and they should also be triggered when problems arise.

Evaluation begins by identifying what is to be evaluated and setting evaluation criteria. For example, Texas Instruments has approximately 250 performance indicators that it evaluates regularly. The number and nature of criteria will vary from firm to firm and depend on managerial preference and processing maturity. Once criteria are established, performance data should be gathered and analyzed, and corrective actions recommended. Finally, the evaluation process itself should be evaluated.

Figure 11.9   **Efficiency and effectiveness evaluation**

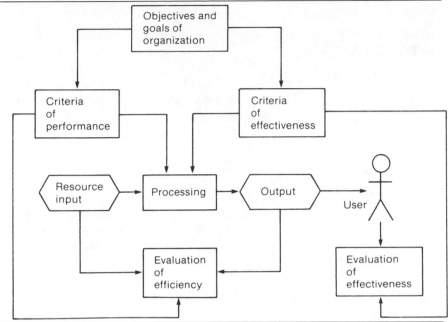

In the evaluation process, criteria of performance are compared with data on input, processing, output, and user satisfaction. The data are gathered by the performance evaluators, by hardware and software monitors, or by operating system accounting packages. Both efficiency and effectiveness are evaluated. Efficiency is a quantitative economic concept, the relationship of output to input, whereas effectiveness is far more subjective, depending on the user's perception of output. The difference in the evaluation of these two criteria is shown in Figure 11.9. Once corrective action is taken, the evaluation process should be repeated regularly.

Evaluation, as described in this chapter, is one level of performance control. A later chapter, Chapter 14, deals with computer center audits.

CASE STUDY: MEASURING PRODUCTIVITY AT GTE
DATA SERVICES*

Data Services at General Telephone & Electronics (GTEDS) manages data centers for 14 telephone companies. These centers range in size from 22 people at an IBM 360/40 shop to a site with three IBM 370/165s employing 300 people.

In 1972, a program to measure GTEDS's productivity was initiated for computer operations and output. Under this program, weights are assigned by management for each aspect of performance (reflecting both effectiveness and efficiency), and points awarded for meeting goals. For example, efficiency measures include the percent of rerun time to total computer time, the job mix on a single computer (multi-programming activity percent), device utilization, percent overtime to regular labor hours, job steps per data control hour, and test turnaround. Effectiveness points are awarded for timeliness, the number of projects completed on time within cost (weighted by size), and responsiveness in correcting errors.

The data center productivity measurement program at GTEDS has been so successful that the concepts have been extended to systems development and maintenance. Almost all functions have shown long-term improvements under the system.

GTEDS uses the Job Accounting Report System from Johnson Systems, Inc., to extract time accounting information from computer resources and summarize it into hardware performance statistics. QUICK-TROL from Quality Data Products, Inc., is the system used to capture systems and programming time against approved customer requests for service. These software packages cost about $6,000 each. The ALERT package from COMTEN, costing around $9,000, is used to measure disk and tape management. (Estimates 1978 prices.)

Each data center spends approximately two man-days a month compiling statistical results and producing final summaries. (Headquarters contributes an additional three man-days a month to this process.) The review and update of operating procedures is the responsibility of one full-time staff member working with data center line management.

---

*Source: Donald E. Peeples, "Measure for Productivity," *Datamation* 24, no. 5 (May 1978), pp. 222–30.

KEY WORDS

Accumulating monitor

Accuracy

Availability

Cost

CPE (Computer performance evaluation)

Effectiveness

Efficiency

Evaluation criteria

Event-driven monitor (EDM)

Hardware monitors

Job accounting programs

Logical monitor

Operations

Performance objectives

Productivity

Quality

Reliability

Resource utilization

Response time

Service

Software monitor

Throughput

Time-driven monitor (TDM)

Timeliness

Utilization

DISCUSSION QUESTIONS

1. Why and how is the performance evaluation of the development process different from the evaluation of:
   a. Computer equipment?
   b. User satisfaction of computing services?
   c. Computer personnel?

2. What is necessary to initiate a program of performance evaluation for a computer center?

3. Comment on the following statement: Mathematical formulas and models are not useful when evaluating performance in a computer center.

4. Performance appraisal of a computing activity is highly subjective. It should be conducted by a psychologist or sociologist rather than a computer scientist. Comment.

5. How is the performance evaluation of computing in a bank different from a similar evaluation in:
   a. A manufacturing business?
   b. A wholesale firm having a large warehouse?
   c. A large office?

6. What is a monitor? What are the functions of monitors?

7. How can components of an information system, such as hardware, software, and procedures, be evaluated separately? Is such evaluation desirable?

8. Describe how an information system is evaluated. When should evaluation take place? Who should be responsible?

9. What is the difference between the efficiency and effectiveness of an information system? How can they be evaluated?

EXERCISES

1. Two programmers, A and B, have each completed programs of equal complexity. Statistics on their performance are given below.

	A	B
Lines of code	3200	2800
Number of output reports	5	4
Time taken (units of time)	6	5
Language used	PASCAL	FORTRAN
Response time	12	13

If you were manager, how would you evaluate each programmer on a scale of 1–5 (1 is lowest)? Explain the reasons for your evaluation.

2. Two CPUs are being operated in your shop. Which has a better performance, X or Y?

	X	Y
Cache memory	256K	512K
CPU cycle time	.3 micro sec.	.2 micro sec.
CPU memory	8 Meg.	10 Meg.
I/O channels	8	12
I/O channels at 3 megabytes	2	1
Manufacturer	A	B

SELECTED ANNOTATED BIBLIOGRAPHY

Gilb, Tom. *Software Metrics*. Cambridge, Mass.: Winthrop Publishers, 1977, 282 p.

Software is defined as nonhardware elements, including procedures, organization, documentation, data ware, and logic ware (programs). Metrics, as defined by the author, simply means "measure." The book is devoted to "all the people who have patiently tried to explain to me why it was 'impossible', 'impractical' or 'uneconomic' to measure software 'quality'." The text looks very formal and mathematical, but all that is required is a knowledge of probabilities and a serious effort.

Herzog, John P. "Systems Evaluation Technique for Users." *Journal of Systems Management* 26, no. 5 (May 1975), pp. 30–35.

This article is specifically addressed to the line manager and describes a scoring system by which a system can be evaluated in terms of problems solved, objectives satisfied, and reliability of input, output, and processing.

King, William R., and Jaime I. Rodriquez. "Evaluating Management Information Systems." *MIS Quarterly* 2, no. 3 (September 1978), pp. 43–52.
This article describes an evaluation model that measures attitudes, value perceptions, information usage, and decision performance. The model is applied to a strategic planning information system.

Mathis, Robert L., and R. H. Seelton. "Performance Appraisal." *Journal of Systems Management* 30, no. 1 (June 1979), pp. 16–18, and 30, no. 2 (July 1979), pp. 9–13.
This series of two parts is a good overview of the subject. It includes a discussion of nine approaches to performance appraisal, including MBO, EDO, user surveys, ROI, budget performance, and post-implementation review.

Norton, David P., and Kenneth G. Raw. *A Guide to EDP Performance Management*. Wellesley, Mass.: QED Information Sciences, 1978, 310 p.
The authors introduce 47 measures within the conceptual framework of performance evaluation. Definition, interpretation of results, interrelationships, evolution of concept, caveats, and audience for each measure are presented. There is also an extensive bibliography with 67 pages of annotations. This is an excellent book on performance management.

Performance Evaluation Review
This is a publication of the ACM (Association for Computing Machinery) special interest group on measurement and evaluation. It includes both mathematical and nonmathematical articles and reports on special workshops and conferences on the subject.

Schaeffer, Howard. *Data Center Operations*. Englewood Cliffs, N.J.: Prentice Hall, 1981, pp. 301–67.
This text has one chapter devoted to computer performance and another to computing center performance evaluation. Both are useful reading for those wanting an introduction to the subject, though the book would also be appropriate for a professional manager of a data center. The text has good illustrations and many samples of forms and reports used in performance evaluation. It also has a comprehensive checklist for data center evaluation. (See appendix 1).

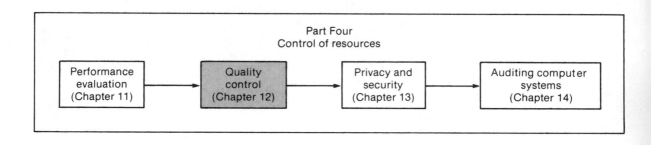

Part Four
Control of resources

Performance evaluation (Chapter 11) → Quality control (Chapter 12) → Privacy and security (Chapter 13) → Auditing computer systems (Chapter 14)

CHAPTER 12

Quality control

Sign on computer center wall:
Mistakes made while you wait.

Never before in history has it been possible to make so many mistakes in so short a period. Because of the rapidity of computer calculations and the repetitious nature of computer operations, undetected errors compound at an alarming rate. Some errors are built into the system by poor design, some result from programming oversight, but many are procedural mistakes or the result of careless machine operation, such as the use of an outdated code, the wrong input tape, or incorrect output distribution.

The determination of technical control measures to ensure accuracy, timeliness, and completeness of data is generally the responsibility of EDP personnel. However, management needs to identify which data need protection, and should specify standards of control after weighing monetary costs to implement control measures against the risk of inadvertent errors and security violations. The cost of delays and inconvenience to employees from controls must also be considered. For example, companies can go too far with controls, causing production to fall off because access to computers is made difficult for bona fide users or because procedures impede performance.

This chapter will describe how information systems should be monitored for human and machine error. Figure 12.1 shows where control points in processing are necessary. Potential threats to data quality and privacy at each point will be discussed, countermeasures to these threats will be suggested, and the personnel responsible for control will be identified. System security and the prevention of unauthorized access or illicit use of information, touched briefly in this chapter, will be discussed in depth in Chapter 13.

Figure 12.1   **Stages of processing and quality control points**

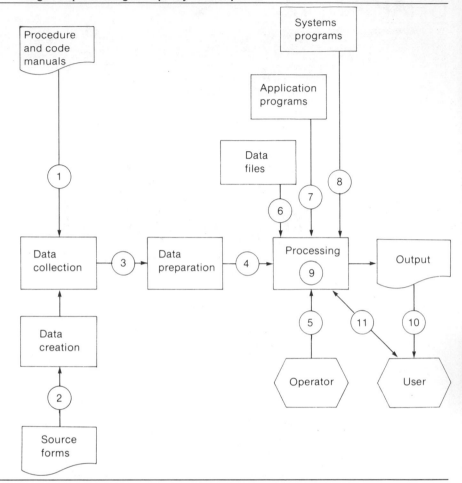

CONTROL POINTS

***Control of procedure
and code manuals
(Circle 1, Figure 12.1)***

Table 12.1 summarizes common sources of error when using procedure and code manuals and suggests control solutions. In many firms, the data base administrator (DBA) or someone on the DBA's staff is responsible for establishing codes at the request of users, and for coordinating assignment of codes so that redundant coding schemes do not occur. Publication, maintenance, and distribution of uniform code manuals is also delegated to this individual. Code users provide feedback to EDP personnel regarding the effectiveness of procedures and codes, and may initiate changes when the manuals prove unsatisfactory. In this way, users contribute to control over procedures and codes.

Table 12.1 **Control of manuals**

Error	Cause	Solution
Wrong procedure or code used	Manual incorrect Manual incomplete	Testing upgraded Improved updating procedures Location control of manuals
	Manual ambiguous Language of manual inappropriate to user	Manual preparation by technical writers Testing of documentation by users User documentation standards
	Manual unavailable when needed	Improved documentation distribution
	Use of unauthorized manual	Policies to control duplicating and copying of manuals
	Carelessness	Documentation of frequency of errors and source Performance checks of manual users

***Form control
(Circle 2)***

A common method of collecting data for an information processing system is through the use of forms. Analysts who design forms and program input validity checks are primarily responsible for controlling errors at this checkpoint. **Turnaround documents** are being increasingly used by businesses to reduce errors. For example, banks provide customers with deposit slips already printed with their name, address, and account number. Only spaces for date and amount need to be filled. By reducing the amount of data the customer must provide, the opportunity for error is minimized. Other examples of turnaround documents are the tear-off sections of utility and credit card bills that must accompany bill payment, and preprinted complaint forms that come with mail order merchandise.

Error-free data collection may be impossible, but errors can be minimized by complying with the following principles of **form design.**

1. Instructions should be easy to understand.
2. Input codes (if used) should be unique and unambiguous.
3. Adequate space, without crowding, should be allowed for completing information.
4. Questions should be sequenced to avoid confusion and should be worded unambiguously.

5. Lines for typed answers should conform to-typewriter spacing.
6. Vertical alignment on forms to be typewritten should enable clerks to use tabs.
7. Larger spaces for handwritten data should be provided than for typewritten data.
8. Only variable values should be requested.
9. No information should be lost when the form is filed or bound.

In addition, the color of forms should be chosen for emphasis and ease of reading (light brown and light green print have been found empirically to be easy on the eye), the forms should be shaded for horizontal reading of lines of data without the drifting of sight, print should be spaced to facilitate reading, and related data should be grouped together. All of these measures facilitate accurate data conversion by operators when the information is readied for the computer.

The importance of careful form design cannot be overemphasized. A firm with an application asking for name, address, birthdate, father's name, and date of high school graduation found that many persons entered their father's date of graduation whereas the information desired was the applicant's own high school graduation date. In this case, poor sequencing of questions and inadequate clarification of the question resulted in misinterpretation. Careful form design should minimize such misunderstandings. Pretesting a form by sample users is one method of detecting such design errors.

The entry of numbers on forms is also a frequent source of errors. For example, handwritten ones and sevens often look alike. The use of boxes on forms for numerical data seems to encourage the user to write numbers legibly. Data processing personnel commonly use the European convention of placing a dash on the stem of a seven (7) to distinguish it from a one. They also place a dash on the Z (Z) so it won't be mistaken for a 2, and a slash through the zero (Ø) to distinguish it from the letter O. (Unfortunately, this latter convention is the opposite of the practice in the military).

Date entries such as 3/1/52 can also cause problems of interpretation since the American convention of month/day is reversed in some European countries.[1] Here again the use of boxes is advisable. By using the box form design the danger of reversing the date order is elim-

MONTH	DAY	YEAR

---

[1]The convention proposed for interchange of data regarding dates is year/month/date. For details, see *Communications of the ACM* 13, no. 1 (January 1970), p. 55.

inated, though there still remains the possibility that Mo, meaning Monday, might be filled in as day of birth instead of the desired date. But well-written instructions for filling out the form, coupled with sample correct and incorrect responses, should eliminate such errors.

Boxes are also used for coding. Some forms have a space reserved on the right-hand column with boxes used by a coder to code information written on the left-hand side of the form. The form is then used as a document for direct data entry.

Another variation is a series of boxes which users check to indicate a condition. One such example is:

Input boxes are also used on forms that can be read by special machines, though the boxes may then have to be marked by a special pencil. This technique, called **mark-sensing,** reduces processing time and inaccuracies in processing since data need not be manually converted into a machine-readable format.

Table 12.2 summarizes frequent causes of errors in filling out forms and possible control solutions.

Table 12.2   **Form control**

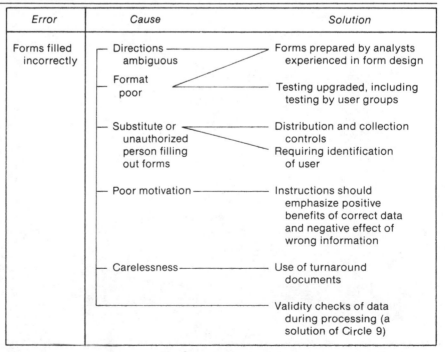

**Data collection
(Circle 3)**

One of the most important control locations is controlling data collection. Data collection is not only the source of many careless errors but is also the focus of much criminal activity.

For example, a Blue Cross/Blue Shield claims examiner mailed forms to relatives who filled them in with real names and policy numbers to defraud the system of $128,000. In another recorded case of fraud, 11 employees of the county Department of Social Services in Los Angeles issued checks to themselves using terminated welfare accounts. Other cases of manipulation of input data include: an IRS clerk who awarded a relative unclaimed tax credits; the theft of $100,000 from a bank account, using the MICR number found on a discarded deposit slip; and a conspiracy between an accounting clerk and a grocer resulting in a theft of more than $120,000 over the years by issuing false invoices for undelivered food.

Inadvertent errors can be equally harmful to an organization. The code of equipment costing $20,000 was erroneously used to code the price of 50 manuals of that equipment. This mistake resulted in an inflated inventory value of one million dollars.

Table 12.3   **Data collection control**

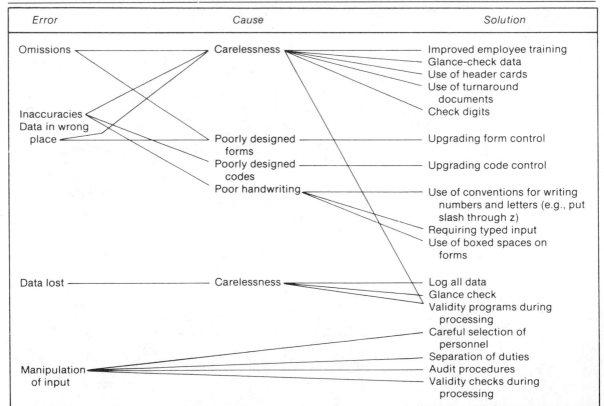

Error	Cause	Solution
Omissions	Carelessness	Improved employee training
		Glance-check data
		Use of header cards
		Use of turnaround documents
Inaccuracies		Check digits
Data in wrong place	Poorly designed forms	Upgrading form control
	Poorly designed codes	Upgrading code control
	Poor handwriting	Use of conventions for writing numbers and letters (e.g., put slash through z)
		Requiring typed input
		Use of boxed spaces on forms
Data lost	Carelessness	Log all data
		Glance check
		Validity programs during processing
		Careful selection of personnel
		Separation of duties
Manipulation of input		Audit procedures
		Validity checks during processing

Table 12.3 summarizes common errors in data collection and suggests possible control solutions.

Data preparation (Circle 4)

Errors in data preparation occur when data is incorrectly converted into machine-readable form. Control is exercised by the department responsible for the data preparation. Recommended control measures are summarized in Table 12.4.

Ways to detect error and procedures to correct mistakes are not all that is needed. The source of the errors should be traced and procedures amended so that the same errors do not recur. By reorganizing the location of data preparation, for example, one firm reduced input errors from 15 percent to 2 percent. Originally clerks had coded information on forms from user transactional records, the forms later being used to keypunch input at the EDP center. By moving keypunchers for EDP to user departments, coding forms were eliminated and input keypunched directly from source documents. The input was then given in batches to the processing center for validation by computer and the computer generated error listings. The input, after correction by the keypunchers, was then submitted as input. This procedural change, with responsibility for data preparation no longer shared (each department blaming the other for errors), helped reduce input errors significantly.

Operations (Circle 5)

Though employees can be trained in emergency procedures should flood, earthquake, fire, or an explosion interrupt operations, a safe-

Table 12.4   **Summary of data preparation errors and solutions**

Error	Cause	Solution
Incorrect data	Poorly written keypunch instructions	Upgraded procedures manual, including visual aids
	Hardware error	Proper maintenance
	Carelessness	Verification of keypunching by a second operator
		Use of check digits
Card handling errors (cards misplaced, put out of order, damaged, or duplicated inadvertently)	Carelessness	Glance check
		Validity programs
		Upgraded employee selection and training
	Poor procedure	Upgraded procedure testing
		Log data

guard for an information system against such disasters is backup data files stored in a secure vault at another location. Also, complete **backup** processing facilities at another computer center tested for restart and recovery may be provided. Backup is also good insurance against intentional errors or willful damage, such as sabotage. Indeed, incidents of sabotage to computer equipment and data files have increased in recent years, particularly in industries engaged in politically sensitive research such as nuclear energy or chemicals that might be used in warfare.

In handling sensitive information, the following basic operating precautions are also recommended. There should always be two operators present. Work schedules should be changed frequently so that no single operator handles the same programs over a long period of time. No employees should be assigned processing tasks when a conflict of interest might arise. (For example, bank employees should not handle programming that will affect their own accounts.) Finally, proof of authorization and sign-in/sign-out controls for handling sensitive files should be initiated, and neither programmers nor analysts should be assigned routine operating tasks.

Though many controls are needed to prevent malicious intrusion during data preparation and operations because information systems are vulnerable during these activities, most breakdowns and errors can be traced to lax procedures and careless operators. And these incidents can be costly indeed. For example, the running of an accounts payable program using an outdated price list cost one firm $100,000. Another expensive mistake: a bank shredder fed a printout of sensitive data on depositors with the line of print parallel to the blades instead of at right angles. As a result, strips of readable confidential data were thrown in the trash where they were spotted, retrieved, and peddled at a local bar by a drifter. The cost to the bank? Reward money for return of the strips and an incalculable loss of customer confidence.

More stringent control procedures could also have prevented the following incident. A Chicago hotel mixed address tapes, sending letters to vendors instead of to past guests explaining recent hotel renovations and urging the guests to return. Instead of goodwill, the hotel received irate calls from vendors whose spouses were citing the letters as evidence of their infidelity.

Failure to test control procedures produced the following fiasco. When a fire broke out in a computer center, employees discovered that narrow doors barred passage of fire extinguishing equipment.

But who was to blame when a corrosive leak in an air-conditioning system destroyed a computer several floors below? It simply isn't practical to devise control methods for all possible threats to an information system. Controls are costly, and too many controls can impede

Table 12.5 **Control of operations**

Error	Cause	Solution
Incorrect operation	Poor instructions	Upgraded personnel selection, training, and procedure testing
	Carelessness	Checking of data file labels
Machine breakdown	Poor maintenance	Upgraded maintenance
		Testing upgraded
		Upgraded personnel selection
	Careless operators	Upgraded training
	Act of nature (flood, storm)	Backup equipment
		Shutdown devices
	Fire	Emergency training
		Heat and smoke alarm
		Fire extinguishers
		Panic switches
Fraudulent operation	Sabotage	Intrusion detectors
		Police patrol
	Desire for personal gain	At least two people on duty
		Steel or steel mesh on windows and doors
		Control physical access
		Control access to files
		Remove conflict of interest
		Vary work schedules
		Strict supervision
		Upgrade personnel selection
		Bond personnel
Data not processed on time	Documents lost or misrouted	Establish documentation procedures (logging, checking record totals, etc.)

operations. The controls summarized in Table 12.5 are those most frequently adopted for operations.

Data files (Circle 6)

If data files are centrally stored, a librarian generally is assigned responsibility for control. Otherwise the owner of the data is responsible. Table 12.6 summarizes the types of control needed to protect data files.

There are numerous cases of errors and fraud relating to data files cited in computer literature. Stolen programs have been held for ransom. Disgruntled employees have maliciously scratched or destroyed tapes. At the Arizona State Finance Center, a backup card file was used for making Christmas decorations. In another organization, an

Table 12.6 **Summary of data file controls**

Error	Cause	Solution
Warped cards, dirty tape or disks	Poor physical storage	Controlled humidity storage "Clean room" conditions Special cabinets Periodic cleaning
	Lack of clearly defined responsibility for data files	Centralized storage under a librarian
Destruction of files	Inadequate procedures	Upgrade storage procedures
	Natural disaster	Special vaults Backup data
	Theft, fraud, or sabotage	Controlled access to files: Data librarian Lock words Control labels

employee moving files to storage wedged the vault open but forgot to remove the wedge after the move was complete. Though the vault was fireproof, a fire swept through the open door and destroyed hundreds of tapes.

In most cases, destruction of data files can be attributed to lax security. Since files are also vulnerable to industrial espionage, the need for data safeguards at this control point is vital.

Programming controls (Circles 7,8)

Many mistakes in computerized systems can be attributed to faulty programming. One bank, for example, lost $300,000 by paying customers interest on 31-day months. A hyphen omitted from a programming card caused a rocket being tested to head for Rio. It had to be destroyed mid-flight, at a loss of $18,500,000. Unintentional errors may result from an incorrect algorithm, erroneous programming logic, or a cause as minor as one out-of-sequence programming statement. Training, care, strict adherence to standard programming procedures, and proper documentation should minimize such problems.

The controls summarized in Table 12.7 should trace inadvertent errors and also help prevent fraud. Control measures should be initiated and enforced by EDP personnel responsible for systems analysis and programming. Unfortunately, programming fraud is difficult to detect and the crimes themselves are often quite ingenious. The first federal prosecution of computer crime in 1966 was against a bank pro-

Table 12.7   **Programming controls**

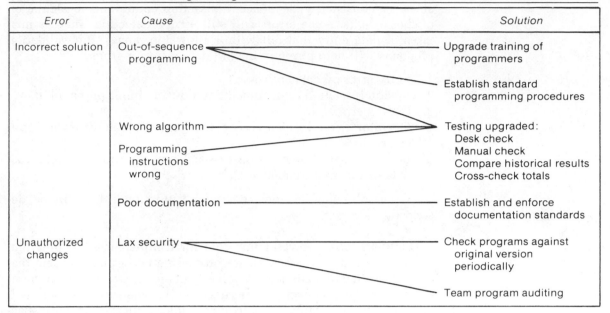

Error	Cause	Solution
Incorrect solution	Out-of-sequence programming	Upgrade training of programmers
		Establish standard programming procedures
	Wrong algorithm	Testing upgraded: Desk check Manual check Compare historical results Cross-check totals
	Programming instructions wrong	
	Poor documentation	Establish and enforce documentation standards
Unauthorized changes	Lax security	Check programs against original version periodically
		Team program auditing

grammer who programmed the system to omit his name from a list generated daily of overdrawn accounts. He withdrew large sums of money before being caught. Control measures, however, did not bring about his downfall. The overdrafts were detected when the computer broke down and the bank had to revert to manual processing.

Another programmer assessed a 10-cent service charge to each customer and put the amounts in a dummy account under the name of Zwicke. By chance, a PR man decided to award a bonus to the first and last name on the firm's alphabetical list of customers. The bogus Zwicke was accordingly discovered.

Nibble theft, stealing small amounts of money over a period of time, is more difficult to detect than **bite-size fraud,** the embezzlement of large sums. The latter can be uncovered by auditing and checking for unreasonable values or control totals. But no matter how well designed the controls, someone will think up a new technique for cheating the system. Constant vigilance is required.

Processing (Circle 9)   At the time of processing, many errors in data preparation which pass control points 2, 3 and 4 can be caught by the computer itself using stored **validation rules.** These rules, determined by users, should be specified with care for underspecification may lead to undetected errors, causing the system to produce unreliable information, whereas overspecification adds unnecessarily to processing costs. Validation tests include checks for completeness, format, range, reason-ableness, consistency, sequence, transaction count, and recalculation of check digits. Some errors will still escape detection, such as mistakes of data entry that fall within allowable ranges. But validation programs will help pinpoint invalid data resulting from:

1. Entry error by data collector.
2. Misinterpretation of documentation during input preparation.
3. Coding errors.
4. Operator errors in data conversion (largest single cause of input error).
5. Errors in data transmission or data handling (for example, lost data or incorrect sequencing).

In the following sections, common validation rules will be described.

Completeness.   A validation rule for **completeness** requires that all characters be expressed before processing takes place in data that has a prescribed length, such as nine digits for a social security number. Completeness checks are necessary only when missing data will affect results so completeness requirements should be carefully specified. For example, it would be necessary to halt processing of an order with a truncated product number or one with quantity blank, whereas the order could probably be filled if the client's middle initial were absent or a digit omitted from the client's phone number.

Format.   Permuted characters can be specified in validation programs, and the data checked against these predetermined rules. For example, a validation program can be written to identify as an error an alphabetic character in a dollar data field, or numeric data in names. The check can divide the **format** into subfields. An address may be assigned numeric fields for house number and zip code, but alphabetic blocks for street and city.

Range.   A check rule may state that data entry is limited to predetermined values, or a range of values. If M and F are used as sex codes, only these two characters would be valid in the sex code field. Any other letter or number would be listed as an error. Similarly, a **range of values** could be specified. If a firm's minimum wage/hour rate were $4 and the maximum $9, the computer could be programmed to identify as invalid any data with values under or over these amounts, errors called definite or **fatal** errors. The computer might also be programmed to identify possible or **suspected errors,** data near the limits of acceptable values. For example, if few employees earn over $8, a listing of employees in the $8–9 range could be provided for recheck. The validation rule would be as follows:

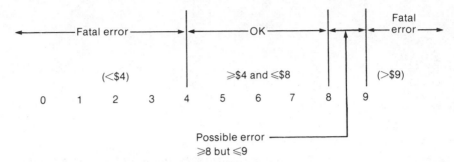

Fatal errors identified by the validation program would have to be traced and corrected. The data would then be reprocessed. Possible errors are checked and corrected, if necessary. An overriding code will permit processing of suspected data that proves valid.

Reasonableness.   In any given situation a number of checks for **reasonableness** could be postulated. Date of employment cannot pre-date a worker's birth, a probationary student cannot graduate with honors, and so forth. The cost of processing such checks must be weighed against losses (monetary and credibility) should errors pass undetected. Such decisions require management's judgment.

Consistency.   Data values can be checked by collecting the same raw data from two or more sources, or generating the values of a data element from input to be matched with the keyed value for that same data element. The latter method is used to check totals, for example. If the information on Table 12.8 were keyed, a computer validity pro-gram could add $53.20, $32.80, and $39.90 in Batch 1 and match the total with the batch total $125.90 entered as input. Or each invoice total could be calculated by computer (price times quantity) and the product compared to the figure listed in the value column. Any dis-crepancy would be identified on an error listing. Most frequently, in-valid data is a mistake in keying the input.

A **hash total** entered as input is also a useful check for **consistency.** All the data in one transaction is totaled even though the units are not the same. The computer then totals the "hash" independently (320 + 16 + 3.20 + 53.20 in the first transaction in Figure 12.8), and com-pares the total with the keyed hash total of 392.40. Since many trans-actions involve 80 to 100 characters, the hash total is an important validity check.

Duplicate processing is another method of checking for consis-

Table 12.8   **Transaction data**

	Invoice number	Quantity (units)	Price $	Value $	Batch total	Hash total
Batch 1	320	16	3.20	53.20		392.40
	321	8	4.10	32.80		365.90
	323	21	1.90	39.90	125.90	511.70
Batch 2	324	25	4.00	100.00		363.00
	325	31	4.20	130.20		490.40
	326	9	5.80	52.20		393.00
	327	5	6.10	30.50	312.90	681.60
				438.80	438.80	

tency. A firm needing to determine a coefficient to two decimal places (from complex calculations for the allocation of over $4 million) used both COBOL and FORTRAN to make the calculations. Because of the large amount of money involved, it was helpful to compare calculations made by the two compilers, which differed in features such as rounding and truncation rules.

Sequence.   In Table 12.8, invoice 322 is missing. A validity test for **sequencing** would identify this situation. The document may have been mislaid or lost, in which case corrective action, such as recollection of the data, would take place. But often an explanation, such as a canceled order, will be found. In processing payrolls, logs are kept of checks damaged, destroyed by the printer, or checks left blank—a record that is searched when a sequence validity test flags an error.

Transaction count.   When a given number of transactions are to be processed, this total is entered as input. The transactions are again counted during processing. An invalid state will be identified if the totals do not match. This will alert operators to a lost document, or records stuck to one another, or possibly even multiple processing of the same transaction.

Self-checking codes.   A code is sometimes used to check for transposition of data or data entry errors, situations that often occur in data elements consisting of a long string of digits. This code, called a **check digit,** is calculated by a prescribed set of rules based on the value of the digits in the number and their locational relationships. The code is then added to the data element number and recalculated every time that data element is processed. If the recalculated value does not coincide with the original check digit, an error is identified.

Modulus 10 is one technique for calculating a check digit. In this technique, the position of digits in a number is significant. Digits in odd positions (such as first, third, fifth, and so forth) are added for a subtotal. Digits in even positions are multiplied by 2 and the digits in the products added together for a second subtotal. The subtotals are then added and divided by ten. The number that must be added to the remainder to make it divisible by 10 is the check digit.

For the number 142796539, the check digit, according to these rules, is 2. To demonstrate the derivation of the check digit, the number will be aligned in two rows, digits in odd positions separated from digits in even positions. The calculations are then performed as follows:

	Multiplied by 2	Subtotal of digits in row
1 2 9 5 9	No	1 + 2 + 9 + 5 + 9 = 26
4 7 6 3	Yes	8 + (1 + 4) + (1 + 2) + 6 = 22
		Total = 48

Remainder when total is divided by 10 = 8
Number to be added to remainder to equal 10 = 2
New check digit = 2

New number = 1427965392

To test the working of the check digit, study the following example in which the value of one digit is changed.

Original number   1 4 2 7 9 6 5 3 9 $\boxed{2}$
New number   4 4 2 7 9 6 5 3 9 $\boxed{2}$
                   └→error in value   └→ original
                                              check digit

	Multiplied by 2	Subtotal of digits in row
4 2 9 5 9	No	4 + 2 + 9 + 5 + 9 = 29
4 7 6 3	Yes	8 + (1 + 4) + (1 + 2) + 3 = 22
		Total = 51

Remainder after dividing total by 10 = 1
Number to be added to remainder to equal 10 = 9
New check digit = 9
Original check digit = 2

New check digit does not equal original check digit. Therefore, an error exists.

In the following example, two adjacent digits are transposed.

Original number   1 4 2 7 9 6 5 3 9 2
New number   (4 1)2 7 9 6 5 3 9 2 ← check digit

└error from single transposition

	Multipled by 2	Subtotal of digits in row
4 2 9 5 9	No	4 + 2 + 9 + 5 + 9 = 29
1 7 6 3	Yes	2 + (1 + 4) + (1 + 2) + 6 = 15
		Total 44

Remainder after dividing total by 10 = 4
Number to be added to remained to equal 10 = 5
New check digit = 6
Original check digit = 2

The new check digit does not equal the original check digit.
Therefore, an error exists.

The problem with Modulus 10 is that double transposition can take place without affecting the check digit (for instance, 5431 transposed as 3154). Modulus 11, another method of calculating a check digit, overcomes this problem. In Modulus 11, each digit in the value of the data element is assigned a separate weight, such as numbers in an ascending or descending scale. Each digit is then multiplied by its corresponding weighted value, and the products are totaled. The number that must be added to this total to make it divisible by 11 is the check digit. All types of transposition (double, triple, and so forth) and data entry errors are caught by this technique.

The use of a check digit has disadvantages. It adds to the length of numbers and increases data preparation effort, the time required for processing, and storage space requirements. The longer number is also harder to remember. But when reliability is important and the number is repeatedly used in processing, detection of errors may be worth the inconvenience and cost. Self-checking codes are commonly the last digit in identification numbers for employees, vendors, customers, accounts, and parts. Their use will identify posting of incorrect transactions.

Other processing controls, the responsibility of EDP personnel, are summarized in Table 12.9.

Output controls
(Circle 10)

Output is the product of all input and processing. If proper control is exercised in each of the steps discussed earlier, the output should be free of error. But most firms add output controls in an information system's design to cross check for errors that may have slipped past earlier controls. Responsibility for these controls is divided between EDP personnel producing output and management using the output. These controls are summarized in Table 12.10.

Table 12.9   **Processing controls**

Error	Cause	Solution
Records lost	Carelessness	Validity checks Upgrade training of personnel Log jobs
Use of incorrect file	Carelessness	Use standard labels for all files Programs to automatically generate updated data
Lack of necessary supplies	Carelessness	Upgrade planning and inventory control

Many output mistakes can be caught by cursory sight checks. For example, a payroll run of paychecks issued without decimal points could be easily spotted by a alert operator, for the amounts would be unreasonable. In addition, many of the validation programs used for input can be run to control output.

Teleprocessing (Circle 11).   Access controls and the use of cryptography protocols (described in Chapter 13) are methods of protecting data during teleprocessing. **Parity checks** facilitate error detection. A bit of data is added to each set of bits representing a character so that the total number of 1 bits is odd (for an odd parity check) or even (even parity check). Upon receipt of the transmission, the bits are

Table 12.10   **Output control**

Error	Cause	Solution
Inaccurate output	Processing errors	Audits Validation programs Interfile comparison Defer large-volume printing until proof data checked Sample check of output with corresponding input
	Operation error	Sight check
Incomplete output	Operation or processing error	Check page counts Check control totals for each process of report

added and compared to the parity rule. When an error is detected, a signal is sent for retransmission of the data.

Checking for the use of a prescribed pattern of ones and zeros to represent characters is another method of tracing errors. Automatic checking of prescribed patterns can make this a self-checking code. This raises costs, however, since additional check bits must be transmitted and processed.

Fortunately, improved technology, such as large-scale integrated circuitry (LSI), is reducing the error rate in communication systems and improving reliability.

SUMMARY AND CONCLUSIONS

This chapter examines controls for documentation, forms, data collection, data preparation, operations, data files, programming, processing, output, and teleprocessing. Deciding how much control is necessary is a management dilemma. Too much control is costly: it can impede work and affect morale. Too little control permits inaccuracies and security infractions, reducing the usefulness of the system.

The importance of carefully designed controls cannot be overstressed. Most readers will have personally experienced the frustration of trying to correct a billing error resulting from inadequate control procedures. Indeed, a major source of public distrust of computers can be traced to such experiences, the feeling of consumers that they are being victimized by computerized systems. In a survey reported by T. D. Sterling,[2] four or more contacts were required by one third of the individuals negotiating clarification or solution of computer errors. Billing mistakes were by far the most common category of error (81 percent), the types of these errors falling into the following categories:

Payment not credited	7.9%
Incorrect amount of payment credited (overcharged)	12.8
Incorrect amount of payment credited (undercharged)	4.3
Billed for already settled account	7.3
Charged for nonexistent expenditure	29.9
Not given credit on returned item	5.5
Charged interest without cause	14.0
Billing error caused by misdirected bill	7.3
Other	10.9
All billing errors	100.0%

[2]T. D. Sterling, "Consumer Difficulties With Computerized Transactions: An Empirical Investigation," *ACM Communications* 22, no. 5 (May 1979), pp. 285–87.

Distribution of error by type of transaction was as follows:

Credit service and special credit card . . .	16.7%
Oil company (heating, gasoline)	9.9
Utility company (gas, phone, electric)	16.7
Department store	22.2
Mail order business	16.0
Insurance	1.9
Bank or savings institution (not including checking)	4.3
Checking account	4.9
Government (municipal)	0.6
Government (federal	2.5
Other	4.3
All errors	100.0%

Since a firm's reputation depends on the quality of its customer service, inadequate controls over computerized information can lead to decrease of clients, a decline of profits, and a loss of goodwill.

Control measures should be planned, implemented, tested, and evaluated during the development of an information system. It is both expensive and disruptive to add controls at a later date. This is especially true of online and real-time systems. This chapter has focused on batch systems, but the need for controls applies to all modes of operation.

Chapter 13, which follows, will discuss system security, a subject closely related to quality control.

CASE STUDY: CHECK DIGIT ON BOOK NUMBERS

When publishers and book distributors began using computers in order processing and inventory control in the late 1960s, it became evident that unique identification numbers were needed for books. Several international conferences addressed the problem and alternative numbering systems were proposed. The system chosen, the International Standard Book Number (ISBN), is a 10-digit number with four parts, consisting of a group identifier (national, geographic or other grouping of publishers), publisher's prefix, title identifier, and check digit.

The check digit is used to detect errors in book numbers when processing orders. A calculation based on the other nine digits of the book number using Modulus 11 is performed almost instantaneously by the computer to check whether numbers have been transposed or miscopied, the source of the majority of ordering errors. Use of the check digit guards against more than 99 percent of these errors.

An example of how the ISBN check digit is calculated for Hussain and Hussain, *Information Processing Systems for Management,* 1981 edition, appears below.

```
ISBN number       0  2  5  6  0  2  4  8 2
ISBN weights     10  9  8  7  6  5  4  3 2
```

Weighted
  values   0 18 40 42 0 10 16 24 4
(ISBN digits multiplied by ISBN weight)

Weighted total: 0 + 18 + 40 + 42 + 0 + 10 + 16 + 24 + 4 = 154
          Number to be added to total to make it divisible by 11 =   0
                                                    Check digit =   0

ISBN number = 0–256–02482–0

If the check digit had been calculated as 10, an X would have been used instead of the number, since only one character is assigned to the check digit. ISBN 0-256-02121-X, for James A. O'Brien's text *Computers in Business Management: An Introduction,* 1979, fits this pattern.

KEY WORDS

Backup	Modulus 11
Bite-size fraud	Nibble theft
Check digit	Parity checks
Completeness	Range of values
Consistency	Reasonableness
Duplicate processing	Self-checking codes
Fatal error	Sequencing
Form design	Suspected errors
Format	Transaction count
Hash total	Turnaround documents
Mark-sensing	Validation rules
Modulus 10	

DISCUSSION QUESTIONS

1. Distinguish between:
   a. External and internal control.
   b. Organizational and administrative control.
   c. Process and operational control.

2. Comment on the statement: A computer system adds to the probability of errors, fraud, and destruction of data and information.

3. Comment on the statement: Computers never make mistakes. People do.

4. What are some of the common causes of errors in computer systems? Classify them in terms of:
   a. Source.
   b. Motivation.
   c. Importance.
   d. Difficulty to trace.
   e. Difficulty to correct.

5. What is the difference between the design and implementation of controls? Where does each start and end? How do design and implementation overlap?

6. Can error-free data be guaranteed? Can error-free results be guaranteed? Explain your answers.

7. Identify control points where measures should be taken to ensure security of data. Explain what measures you would require and why?

8. How can careless errors be reduced?

9. What is the need and significance of editing or validation? At what point in processing must they be performed? What resources are necessary?

10. Can the following errors be caught by validation? In each case state the validation rule.
    a. $93A2.4.
    b. DR. HUSS3IN.
    c. $3 2.64.
    d. WAGE $1686 per hour.
    e. Account number incorrect.
    f. Age incorrect by one year.
    g. Age incorrect by 100 years.

11. When should a file be verified? Must all the contents be verified in each verification run?

12. What is the difference between verification of new data for content errors and editing for format errors? How is each done? Must each be done?

13. Explain six validation rules for data.

14. What are common causes for invalid data?

SELECTED ANNOTATED BIBLIOGRAPHY

Burch, John G., Jr.; Felix R. Strater; and Gary Grudnitski. *Information Systems: Theory and Practice.* New York: John Wiley & Sons, 1979, chap. 14.
An excellent chapter in a popular text. Control points are identified and how control should be designed and implemented for each control point are discussed.

Gustafson, John R. "EDP Internal Auditing," in *The Information Systems Handbook,* ed. F. Warren McFarlan and Richard L. Nolan. Homewood, Ill.: Dow Jones-Irwin, 1975, pp. 192–205.
EDP controls are called different names. In this book, the term *internal auditing* is used. The author, a vice president and auditor of a large insurance company, writes with authority on the control environment, with details relegated to an appendix.

Haden, Douglas H. *Total Business Systems: Computers in Business.* New York: West Publishing, 1978, chap. 9, pp. 186–297.
This book shows the technical and practical background of the author. The chapter is well organized and has numerous thought-provoking exercises at the end.

Mair, W. R., et al. *Computer Control and Audit.* Wellesley, Mass.: Q.E.D. Information Sciences, 1978, chap. 4, pp. 34–43.
An excellent chapter on the concept and objectives of control. The chapter also discusses areas of control, costs and benefits of control, types of control, and preventive, detective, and corrective controls.

Note: Additional references on quality control appear in the annotated bibliographies of Chapter 13 on security and Chapter 14 on auditing.

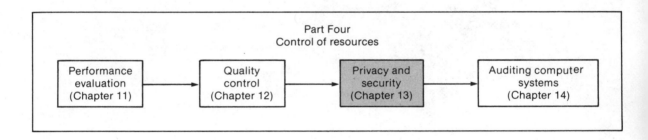

Part Four
Control of resources

| Performance evaluation (Chapter 11) | → | Quality control (Chapter 12) | → | Privacy and security (Chapter 13) | → | Auditing computer systems (Chapter 14) |

CHAPTER 13

Privacy and security

*Advanced technology has created new
opportunities for America as a nation, but it has
also created the possibility for new abuses of the
individual American citizen. Adequate safeguards
must always stand watch so that man remains master
and never the victim of the computer.*

Presidential address to the nation, February 23, 1974

Most commercial, industrial, and financial organizations process and transmit proprietary and sensitive information in the course of their daily activities. Protecting privacy and securing data from criminal access is a major concern. Equipment, software, manuals, forms, and other components of computer systems are also vulnerable to willful damage and theft.

The purpose of this chapter is to examine the issue of privacy, then to outline security measures that help safeguard not only data but all computing resources from intrusion. Recovery following natural disasters is also discussed. Management's responsibility in planning and implementing security is presented and the question, "How much security is essential?" is addressed.

PRIVACY RIGHTS

American society is founded on the primacy of individual rights, with no right more sacrosanct than the right to **privacy.** No wonder that computer technology, which has fostered vast data banks, instantaneous information retrieval, and worldwide data transmission through satellite networks, is viewed by the public with alarm. George Orwell's *1984* is a disquieting specter.

The first legislative act to provide safeguards against privacy abuse by computers was the **1971 Fair Credit Reporting Act.** But publication in 1973 of *Records, Computers and the Rights of Citizens,* also known as the HEW Report,[1] is credited with raising awareness in state and federal legislative assemblies as to the dimensions of the problem. The **Privacy Act of 1974** followed. It stated that the right to privacy is a personal and fundamental right protected by the Constitution of the United States, and it set guidelines for the collection, maintenance, use, and dissemination of personal information by federal agencies.

Rights addressed in the act are:

1. **Right of notification.** Each agency that maintains a system of records is required to publish in the *Federal Register* at least annually a notice of the existence and character of the records. This must include name and location of the information system, categories of records maintained, the uses of the records, and policies regarding access and disposal. When records are disseminated to other agencies under compulsory legal processes, reasonable effort must be made to notify the individuals involved.
2. **Right to accuracy and relevance.** Agencies are charged with collecting and maintaining information that is current and accurate, and may only keep records that are relevant and necessary to accomplish their mandates.
3. **Right to confidentiality.** Agencies must establish administrative, technical, and physical safeguards to protect the security and confidentiality of records.
4. **Right to access.** Knowing the existence of recorded data is not sufficient if access to that data is restricted or the data unintelligible (coded or recorded on magnetic tape, for example). The act recognizes an individual's right to access one's own record and review and copy it.
5. **Right to challenge.** Amendment of records may be requested when an individual believes personal data are not accurate, relevant, timely, or complete.
6. **Right for correction.** The act states that procedures should be established for record amendment.
7. **Right of control.** No records may be made available for another purpose without an individual's consent. Only such information necessary to accomplish the purpose of the agency may be collected. (Exceptions are listed, e.g., records for law enforcement or use by Census Bureau.)

---

[1]See W. H. Ware, ed., *Report of the Secretary's Advisory Committee on Automated Personal Data Systems* (Washington, D.C.: U.S. Government Printing Office, 1973).

8. **Right to redress.** Individuals may bring civil action in district courts against agencies that fail to comply with provisions of the act and be rewarded damages. Officers and employees of agencies are also liable to criminal penalties for willful disclosure of information to any person not entitled to it.

The act also created a **Privacy Protection Study Commission** to determine the extent to which provisions of the act should apply to the public sector, to recommend further standards and procedures to protect information in governmental, regional, and private organizations, and to advise the President and Congress on further courses of action. During 18 months of study and testimony, the commission examined matters such as confidentiality of tax and bank records, the use/misuse of mailing lists, and the role of social security numbers in linking files. Though the commission, in its report to the President, counseled that the Privacy Act not be extended to the public sector, it recommended that its philosophy and principles should be.[2]

The 1974 Privacy Act, though limited to federal agencies, changed the focus of public concern over privacy issues. Before the act, discussion was on how to curb the harm of computer privacy abuse. After passage of the act, public concern broadened, focusing on the right of individuals, groups, and institutions to determine when, how, and to what extent personal information about them is communicated to others. This right to control the circulation of information is today considered essential to personal freedom.[3]

Additional federal legislation is currently being studied to extend the protection of the 1974 act. Most states also have privacy laws that supplement federal legislation to some degree.[4] Some local laws on privacy also exist, as in Berkeley, California.[5] The Council of Europe and the Organization of Economic Cooperation and Development (OECD) are two bodies which are interested in international ramifications of privacy issues,[6] but there are no laws as yet to protect per-

---

[2]The Commission's report to the President, *Personal Privacy in an Information System*, no. 052-003-00395-3 (Washington, D.C.: U.S. Government Printing Office) is available from the Superintendent of Documents, Washington, D.C., 20402.

[3]For more discussion of the issues, see Alan F. Westin, D. Lufkin, and B. J. David, *The Impact of Computer Based Information Systems on Citizens' Liberties in the Advanced Industrial Nations* (Washington, D.C.: Marshall Fund in the United States, 1973) and Arthur Miller, *The Assault on Privacy* (Ann Arbor, Mich.: University of Michigan Press, 1971).

[4]Paul B. Demitriades, "Administrative Security and Data Privacy Legislation," *Journal of Systems Management* 27, no. 10 (October 1976), p. 26. Since state laws are constantly changing, one should check journals, such as *Information Age,* for legislative updates.

[5]Lance Hoffman, "Privacy Law Affecting Design," *Computers and Society* 15, no. 4 (Winter 1974), pp. 6–8.

[6]See OECD, *Transborder Data Flow and the Protection of Privacy* (Paris, France: Organization of Economic Cooperation and Development, 1979), 335 p.

sonal data from transborder data flow. Recently a number of firms have adopted privacy policies, showing their awareness of public concern over privacy issues. IBM, for example, has endorsed four principles of privacy, listed in Table 13.1.

The public has reason for its concern over computer **privacy abuse.** In the United States, some 445 million individual records exist in credit agencies, commercial banks, mailing list data banks, and the Social Security Administration. The federal government itself has an estimated 3.8 billion records.[7] Consider the potential for harm should

Table 13.1   **IBM's policy on privacy**

Four principles
of privacy

For some time now, there has been a growing effort in this country to preserve the individual's right to privacy in the face of expanding requirements for information by business, government and other organizations.

In searching for appropriate guidelines, private and governmental groups have explored many avenues and considered many aspects of the privacy question.

As a company with a vital interest in information and information handling, IBM endorses in their basic purpose four principles of privacy which have emerged from various studies, and which appear to be the cornerstones of sound public policy on this sensitive issue.

1.   Individuals should have access to information about themselves in record-keeping systems. And there should be some procedure for individuals to find out how this information is being used.

2.   There should be some way for an individual to correct or amend an inaccurate record.

3.   An individual should be able to prevent information from being improperly disclosed or used for other than authorized purposes without his or her consent, unless required by law.

4.   The custodian of data files containing sensitive information should take reasonable precautions to be sure that the data are reliable and not misused.

Translating such broad principles into specific and uniform guidelines will, of course, not be easy. They must be thoughtfully interpreted in terms of the widely varying purposes of information systems generally.

In particular, the proper balance must be found between limiting access to information for the protection of privacy on one hand, and allowing freedom of information to fulfill the needs of society on the other.

But solutions must be found. And they will call for the patient understanding and best efforts of everyone concerned. In this search, IBM pledges its full and whole-hearted cooperation.

IBM

Source: Courtesy of International Business Machines Corp.

---

[7]R. W. Davis, "Privacy or Security in Data Systems," *Computers and People* 23, no. 3 (March 1974), p. 240. For more on data banks, see R. Turn, "Privacy Protection in Information Sys tems," *Advances in Computers* 16 (New York: Academic Press, 1977), p. 227.

only 1 percent of these records be in error or misused. In a 1978 survey by Louis Harris & Associates of 1,513 individuals, 54 percent of the respondents felt privacy rights are inadequately protected, and 80 percent felt that computers make it easier to obtain confidential information improperly.[8]

Other responses to the survey indicate that:

> The privacy issue is not solved or fading away. It is going to become more intense in the next decade, as privacy serves as the handle with which a still considerably alienated public seeks to define and install greater measures of individual or social control over an organizational system whose powers have been vastly increased by computer uses in the last 20 years. . . . Most Americans now see privacy as one of the central "quality-of-life" issues of our times.[9]

PRIVACY IMPLEMENTATION

Managers in business firms, although not bound by the 1974 Privacy Act, should be cognizant of and sensitive to privacy issues. The following measures will help ensure that individual rights are respected when personal data is collected, maintained, and used in the course of a firm's daily operations.

1. Store only essential data. Purge irrelevant and outdated information, or data that is unnecessary but "nice to have." This will not only reduce the danger of privacy invasion, but will diminish the information glut which plagues many firms, and lower storage costs as a consequence.
2. Improve the security of data. Periodically review and update physical safeguards and carefully screen personnel. Many computer systems in use today were designed before widespread concern over privacy issues, and hence lack adequate data protection. Future legislation clarifying privacy in the business sector will undoubtedly spur manufacturers to produce security technology that will be sufficiently rugged to resist determined attack and sufficiently economical to encourage use.
3. Identify which data elements are "sensitive" and add data descriptions to these elements so they can be easily extracted from the data stream for control inspections and correction. Require management approval when use of these elements is extended to new applications.
4. State as policy that personal data should be complete, accurate, and timely. This requirement is a good business procedure for

---

[8]Alan F. Westin, "The Impact of Computers on Privacy," *Datamation* 25, no. 24 (December 1979), p. 190 and 193.

[9]Ibid., p. 194.

most data, irrespective of privacy ramifications. One reason it is difficult to isolate and assess privacy costs is that the interests of privacy are served by sound information processing practices.

5. Establish procedures to implement notification and challenge rights. Authorization forms for consent of use or release of information may be required. Appeal routines need to be established. In many cases procedures can be automated, but in each organization at least one individual should be given responsibility for planning security and privacy measures, coordinating privacy policies with legal requirements, and overseeing privacy policy implementation.

6. Anticipate privacy legislation. Design new information systems to report on sensitive data, and log and monitor use of the data, for such controls will undoubtedly be requirements of the future. Such features can be added to a system under development at low marginal cost whereas adding them after a system is operational involves expensive redesign. By adding privacy features to systems when they are being changed anyway due to technological advances in hardware or software, companies will be spared the high cost and disruption of redesign when new privacy legislation is passed.

COST OF PRIVACY

There are two types of expenditures involved when implementing corporate privacy policies: one-time **development costs** and recurring **operational disbursements.**

Development costs include analysis and design of procedures for privacy protection and the acquisition of equipment and software dedicated to that purpose. The main component of operations is salaries, primarily for clerks handling notification, access, challenge, correction, and erasures. The cost of a manager's time in monitoring procedures as well as standards, and resolving disputes, should be added to this category, as should fees paid for legal advice. Other operational costs are for computer time, data storage, data transmission, rental or maintenance of security equipment, and supplies. Operational costs will peak after passage of privacy legislation when many people exercise new rights of access and challenge, then stabilize at a lower level.

How much do privacy policies cost? Implementation of the 1974 Privacy Act has been estimated at $36 million for development, with annual operations costing an estimated $37 million.[10] Robert Gold-

---

[10]Quoted in D. K. Hsiao et al., *Computer Security* (New York: Academic Press, 1979), p. 21.

stein has developed a model to simulate cost components and total costs, given different assumptions of privacy protection requirements and management strategies. According to this model, the 1974 Privacy Act costs between $.29 and $4.97 per data subject.[11] In the private sector operational costs are estimated between $1.50 and $3.93 per transaction.[12]

One problem in determining costs is that so many implementation strategies for privacy policies exist. Some companies may require written consent from each data subject for each application. Others may use a single release for all applications. Companies may discontinue (or not initiate) applications because of privacy considerations. Should operational costs include estimates for degraded service?

Another problem is that the value of many variables used in making estimates is unknown. When the Fair Credit Reporting Act was passed in 1971, one credit agency reported the number of access requests rose by a factor of 2,000. Would a similar increase occur were the 1974 Privacy Act extended to the private sector?

A further problem is deciding how to allocate costs when practices that affect privacy also serve other business interests. For example, security measures that protect personal data reduce the danger of lost records, guard trade secrets, and circumvent sabotage of facilities. How can the cost of privacy policies be isolated from security costs?

Goldstein's model is based on the premise that privacy costs do not arise "out of the blue" but rather are in response to various events. Each time one of these events occurs, certain actions are taken to comply with privacy regulations. These actions consume resources and hence generate costs. The model includes 22 events and 19 requirements (laws are represented as sets of requirements) and can calculate a potential of 7,500 different actions from the 18 most useful combinations of strategy variables. In spite of the complexity of this model, however, the costs produced will not be accurate figures for any given organization because of the many unproven assumptions on which the model is based. The model's usefulness is rather for comparing relative costs of various strategies and for identifying variable relationships and assumptions.

SECURITY

To ensure privacy of information, computer systems must be secure. That is, data must be protected against unauthorized modifica-

---

[11]Robert C. Goldstein, "The Costs of Privacy," *Datamation* 21, no. 10 (October 1975), p. 67.

[12]Robert C. Goldstein and R. L. Nolan, "Personal Privacy versus Corporate Computer," *Harvard Business Review* 53, no. 2 (March–April, 1975), p. 66.

tion, capture, destruction, or disclosure. Personal data are not the only vulnerable data. Confidential data on market strategies and product development must be kept from the hands of competitors. The large sums of money transferred daily by EFT must be protected against theft. The very volume of business information processed by computers today means the rewards for industrial espionage and fraud are of a much higher magnitude than in the past. Records must also be protected from accidents and natural disasters. For example, a breakdown in the air conditioning system may cause a computer to overheat, resulting in loss of computing capabilities. Fire, floods, hurricanes, even a heavy snowfall causing a roof to collapse can cause destruction of data and valuable equipment.

The **security measures** described in the following sections are designed to guard information systems from all of the above threats.[13] The measures can be envisioned as providing layers of protection, as shown in Figure 13.1 Access controls, for example, guard against in-

Figure 13.1   **Layers of protection**

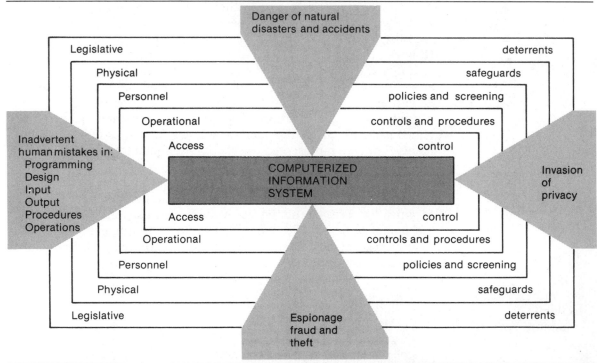

---

[13]For supplementary reading on security classifications, threats, and countermeasures, see Dorothy E. Denning and Peter J. Denning, "Security," *Computing Surveys* 11, no. 3 (September 1979), pp. 227–49, and Lance Hoffman, *Security and Privacy in Computer Systems* (Los Angeles: Melville Publishing, 1971), pp. 92–93.

filtration for purposes of data manipulation, alteration of computer programs, pillage, or unauthorized use of the computer itself. Other measures guard the physical plant, monitor operations and telecommunications, and regulate personnel. All of the layers of protection shown in Figure 13.1 will be discussed except for legislative deterrents, which are described in a separate chapter, Chapter 26. Since control of inadvertent errors was the subject of Chapter 12, this chapter will focus on protection against calamities and criminal acts.

Access control

Access control is one method of guarding a system from unauthorized use. When all terminals are located in the computer center, closing the center to unauthorized personnel will provide access control. Badge systems, locked doors, a buffer zone, or entry guards—procedures common to restricted areas in security-sensitive factories or research divisions—can be used. A librarian who checks out stored files and programs provides additional control.[14]

With online systems using telecommunications, security is a greater problem, for stringent access controls to terminals may not exist at remote sites. The computer itself must, therefore, determine the legitimacy of users. Access control should have three dimensions: **identification,** verifying the identity of the user requesting service; **authentication,** verifying the user's right to access a requested file or portion of the data base; and **authorization,** verifying the type of access permitted (i.e., read, write, update, or no access).

The user's identity may be checked by a machine-readable badge, a voice print, fingerprints, or handprints, though the latter equipment is expensive at the present time. More common is the use of **passwords.** The secrecy of passwords can be guarded by frequently changing the password, by using a system to generate passwords for each user, or by techniques for generating passwords for each session, called **session passwords.** The user can also be identified by a project or account number, and be constrained by time locks (system operational only during specified times), hardware locks (physical locks on machines), and the amount of computer time allocated per job.

A data directory security matrix stored in the computer can control authentication and authorization. For example, the computer may check the level of security code needed for access to specific data elements of files before processing a user's job—information that is stored in an access directory. In addition, the computer can reference a table which specifies the type of access permitted, or the time of day when access is permitted. The data elements accessible from each terminal can also be regulated. For example, the terminal in the data

---

[14]For details see Stephen S. Weston, "Program Library Control and Security," *EPACS* 7 (September 1979), pp. 1–9.

base administrator's office may be the only one permitted to access all files and programs, and the only terminal that has access to the security matrix itself.

A sample printout from an access directory, sorted by user identification number, is shown in Table 13.2.

Table 13.2   **Access directory**

User identification: 076–835–5623 Access limitation: 13 hours (of CPU time for current fiscal year) Account No.: AS5842				
Data elements	Type of access	Security level	Terminal number	Time lock
Customer No.	Read	10	04	08:00–17.00
Invoice No.	Read	10	04	08.00–17.00
Cash receipt	Read/Write	12	06	08.00–12.00

Limitations exist with all these methods of access control. The use of passwords may dissuade a casual intruder, but not someone determined to breach the system, for even passwords as complex as algebraic transformations of a random number generated by the computer have been broken with the assistance of readily available minicomputers. Password lists or their algorithms are vulnerable wherever they are stored as well. Badges can be counterfeited. Equipment to recognize physiological attributes (hand prints, voice prints, etc.), of special interest to defense industries and the FBI, has been under development for many years, but only recently have technological breakthroughs been made which enable successful discrimination of patterns.[15] The problem is one of pattern recognition under less than optimal conditions. A blister, inflammation, cut, even sweat on hands can affect fingerprints. Health or mood can change one's voice. A combination of devices (i.e., voice plus hand analyzers) might ensure positive identification but such equipment is too expensive at the present time to be cost-effective for most operations in business.

Assigning access levels is not a trivial problem either. Information is power, and the right to access it is a status symbol. Employees may vie for clearance even when they do not require it for their jobs. Access controls must take into consideration such human factors, for they are designed to recognize impostors, not to antagonize loyal employees. Too many controls may cause delays, inconvenience, and frustration to legitimate users, tempting them to circumvent the sys-

---

[15]For details, see D. J. Sykes, "Positive Personal Identification," *Datamation* 24, no. 11 (November 1978), pp. 179–86.

tem. Choice of controls must also be based on accurate recognition of authorized users. Denying access to entitled individuals may cause more ill will than a business can afford.

Operational security

Control points to protect information systems during processing were discussed at length in Chapter 12. What needs to be emphasized here are general administrative strategies to protect the system as a whole. For example, empirical evidence shows that systems are particularly vulnerable to intrusion during conversion, once the new system has passed acceptance tests and is being readied for operations. Employees inexperienced with the new system are not alert to possible security infringements, while technicians, exhausted by the rigors of conversion, are often less attentive than usual. As a result, changes in procedures, data, and programs may be introduced without notice. Experience has shown that it is advisable to intensify security during conversion.

During daily operations a careful check of logs, utilization reports, and irregular behavior should be the norm. Most companies schedule periodic audits as well. (For more on audits, see Chapter 14.) Private detectives to oversee security are hired by some firms, though this can have an adverse effect on employee morale.[16] There are even reported cases of companies hiring individuals on parole for programming fraud, on the premise that someone who knows how to break the system also knows how to prevent security violations.

But even the best security cannot prevent natural disasters, and determined malefactors have circumvented controls too often to guarantee a given system's immunity to attack. Insurance will compensate for monetary losses in some cases, but an essential part of operational security is planning for recovery of what is lost, be it data or programs, and planning to place the system speedily back in operation. This is a manager's responsibility. Many vendors supply customers with manuals, including checklists, to assist in reconstruction planning. For example, Table 13.3 is a sample from an IBM manual showing how to select material for a vital records program.[17]

In order to plan what procedures should be implemented following a disaster or system collapse, management must:

1. Determine the minimum resource configuration needed to resume operations.

---

[16]See Kenniston W. Lord, "Data Center Security: A Case for the Private Eye," *Infosystems* 23, no. 12 (December 1976), pp. 30–33.

[17]IBM manuals include: *Physical Security in a Computer Environment*, G520-2700-0, 1972; *Data Security Forum*, G 520-2965-0, 1974; *Suggestions for Improving Security in Data Processing Operation*, G520-2797-0, 1974; and *The Fire after The Fire*, G20-2741-0, 1973. See also Jack P. Curry, "Planning for Disaster Recovery," *Infosystems* 25, no. 3 (March 1978), pp. 64–69.

Table 13.3   **Guidelines to vital records planning**

In choosing the material that is to be maintained in a vital records program, the following questions can serve as a guide:
1. Which functions are to be reconstructed?
2. What assets of the corporation and evidence of stockholders' equity must be preserved?
3. Is recorded information necessary for (1) and (2)?
4. What information is needed?
5. What records contain this information?
6. How is each record created?
7. Can extra copies be made?
8. Are copies dispersed in the course of normal business?
9. Will this dispersal be satisfactory?
10. Are there other records being protected which also have this information?

Source: IBM, *The Considerations of Physical Recovery in a Computer Environment*, G520–2700, p. 20.

2. Identify what computer records are vital.
3. Establish job priorities. (Given reduced capacity, which jobs should be run? What turnaround times are crucial?)
4. Assign recovery responsibility. (Who has the authority to mobilize organizational resources and rule on conflicts of interest during recovery?)

An alternative processing site should also be planned should the computer facility be extensively damaged. Since a backup computer in the same building might also be destroyed in the same disaster, a distant secondary facility is advisable, though this adds communication difficulties to problems of recovery. Firms with distributed processing generally can function when one network link is broken. It is firms with centralized computing that require this secondary facility.

One solution is to seek a mutual assistance arrangement with another firm. Each firm agrees to carry an extra workload (a third shift, perhaps) when their partner is in need. In such cases, problems of system compatibility need to be resolved, and backup files for the alternative site must be maintained.

Some auditors recommend surprise tests at EDP installations to check the effectiveness of disaster planning as part of regular auditing procedures.[18] Certainly, planning for system breakdown should take place in all firms, and employees should be informed what actions to take in emergencies. A simple memo may suffice or detailed handbooks may be necessary, depending on the nature or complexity of the business.

Communications security

Computer processing is today closely linked with telecommunications, allowing the transference of computer data between remote

---

[18]For an auditor's view, see Arthur J. Hallinan, "Internal Audit of a Computer Disaster Plan," *The Internal Auditor* 1, no. 6 (November–December, 1970).

points. Protecting the confidentiality of this data at the terminal when transmission is initiated or received, or from intrusion during transmission itself, has required the development of sophisticated security techniques.

A **handshake,** a predetermined signal which the computer must recognize before initiating transmission, can control access to the system. This prevents individuals from **masquerading,** pretending to be a legitimate user of the system. Protocols, conventions, and procedures for user identification and dialogue termination help maintain the confidentiality of data.[19] These are generally specified by the manufacturer of the computer equipment.

During transmission, messages are vulnerable to **wiretapping,** the electromagnetic pickup of messages of communication lines. This may be **eavesdropping,** passive listening, or active wiretapping, involving alteration of data, such as **piggy-backing,** (the selective interception, modification, or substitution of messages). Another type of infiltration is **reading between the lines,** in which an illicit user taps the computer when a bona fide user is connected to the system and is paying for computer time but is "thinking," so the computer is idle. This and other uses of unauthorized time can be quite costly to a business firm. In 1979, for example, a 15-year-old was charged with felony grand theft and vandalism for unlawfully accessing computer time worth an estimated $10,000 from the University of California, Berkeley.

One method of preventing message interception is to encode or encrypt data in order to render it incomprehensible or useless if intercepted. (**Encryption** is from the Greek root "crypt," meaning to hide.) This can be done by either **transposition** or **substitution.**

In transposition, characters are exchanged by a set of rules. For example, the third and fourth characters might be switched so that 5289 becomes 5298. In substitution, characters are replaced. The number 1 may become a 3, so that 514 reads 534. Or the substitution may be more complex. A specified number might be added to a digit, such as a 2 added to the third digit, making 514 read 516. Decryption restores the data to its original value. This process is illustrated in Figure 13.2.

The **key** used in Figure 13.2 for coding the message is derived from a key base (base of keys). It could be a random number key, or a key based on a formula or algorithm. As in all codes, the key must be difficult to break. Frequent changing of the key adds to the security of data.

The U.S. government is as concerned as is business regarding security of telecommunications. The National Bureau of Standards, entrusted by the 1974 Privacy Act with the security of federal data, produced a **Data Encryption Standard (DES)** in 1977 which has been

---

[19]For more details, see P. E. Green, "An Introduction to Network Architectures and Protocols," *IBM System Journal* 18, no. 2 (1979), pp. 202–22.

Figure 13.2   **Encrypting and decrypting data in teleprocessing**

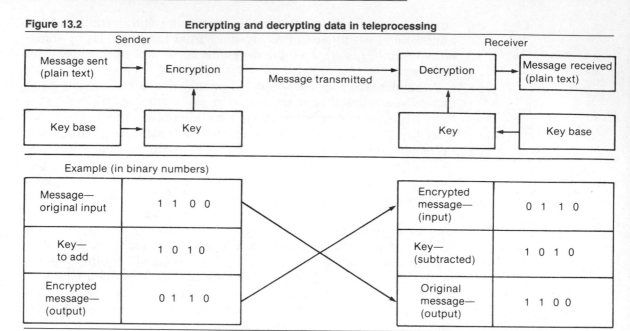

accepted by most manufacturers of teleprocessing equipment. The DES incorporates transposition and substitution repeatedly in each encryption.

In addition to DES, some computer manufacturers have developed encryption products that generate codes using cryptology.[20]

For example,

> . . . IBM encryption products feed back part of the immediately preceding, already transformed message and combine it with the plain text about to enter, and their sum is enciphered under control of the key. . . . Such is the security offered by that arrangement that its project work factor is considerable: the time needed to decipher the message encrypted by it would engage the most powerful of all present computers for many years, in which time the value of the information would have long faded and the key many times changed.[21]

Cryptography requires use of a key, a key which both sender and receiver possess. The transportation of this key to authorized users has proved an Achilles' heel to system security in the past. There may

[20]See A. G. Konheim, M. H. Mack, R. K. McNeill, B. Tuckerman, and G. Waldbaum, "The IPS Cryptographic Programs," *IBM Systems Journal* 19, no. 2 (1980), pp. 253–83. See also James Martin, *Security, Accuracy and Privacy in Computer Systems* (Englewood Cliffs, N.J.: Prentice Hall, 1973), pp. 451–59.

[21]L. Sandek, "Privacy, Security and Ciphers," *Data Processor* 21, no. 1 (January 1978), p.5.

also be insufficient time to pass the key to a legitimate receiver. The problem can be avoided by a multiple access cipher in a public key cryptosystem. This system has two keys, an E public encryption key used by the sender, and D secret decryption key used by the receiver. Each sender-receiver has a set of D-E keys. To code data to send to Firm X, for example, a business looks up Firm X's E key, published in a public directory, and then transmits a message in code over a public or insecure transmission line. Firm X alone has the secret D key for decryption. This system can be breached but not easily, for a tremendous number of computations would be needed to derive the secret of D. The security in codes lies as much in the time required to crack the algorithm as in the computational complexity of the cipher, for the value of much data resides in timeliness. Once a deal is made, the stock market closed, or a patent application filed, there is no longer need for secrecy.

Cryptography, in effect, serves three purposes: identification (helps identify bona fide senders and receivers); control (prevents alteration of a message); and privacy (impedes eavesdropping). With the increased reliance of businesses on teleprocessing, much research has been done on cyptographic systems. But there is disagreement among experts about how secure even the most complex codes are. Some claim that quadrillions of combinations in a well-conceived code will no longer be secure by the mid-1980s once computers are specially built for cryptoanalytic purposes. Others claim that the work factor required to decipher a doubly encrypted message would require a computer using 1,000 times the current U.S. energy reserves for power.

In spite of our knowledge of protocols, DES, and encryption devices, computer crime continues to plague U.S. business. In 1978, for example, a computer consultant to a bank intercepted the bank's telecommunications and transferred bank money to a Swiss account for the purchase of Russian diamonds. This case had an unexpected twist, for the bank actually profited from the theft. When the FBI caught the culprit the resale of the diamonds brought the bank a rate of return many time higher than could have been earned had the funds been legally invested in a savings account.

Few victims of computer crime, however, can report similar happy endings. Unfortunately, many firms are reluctant to publicize known security breaches lest their credibility suffer. This means that analysts designing security measures are not always aware of the tricks and techniques used by perpetrators of fraud to break system security. We know that in the future decryption will be faster, taking only days or hours instead of weeks. And certainly the ingenuity of thieves and the resources allocated to theft will increase once billions of dollars are transferred daily by EFT. Improvement in teleprocessing security is a major challenge to the computer and communications industries to-day.

Personnel safeguards

One might expect that external threats to security would be a firm's major concern, but Andrew Chambers' study shows that users and computer personnel within an organization are more likely to breach security than outsiders.[22]

The Stanford Research Institute study of 148 cases of computer fraud made public that occurred between 1964 and 1973 agrees with Chambers' conclusion. Culprits of internal theft were identified as terminal operators, programmers, computer operators, even vice presidents. (A summary of the findings of this SRI study appears in Table 13.4.) Managers should be cognizant of their vulnerability to internal security violations when screening applicants, assigning duties, and supervising operations.

Table 13.4   **Job position of perpetrator, scheme of fraud, method of manipulation**

Job position	Transactions Added	Altered	Deleted	File changes	Program changes	Improper operation	Miscellaneous (unknown)
Data entry/ terminal operator	9	4	0	1	0	0	1
Clerk/teller	9	6	0	1	0	0	0
Programmer	0	0	0	0	14	0	1
Officer/manager	8	4	3	1	3	1	1
Computer operator	1	4	0	1	0	3	0
Other staff	1	0	1	1	0	0	2
Outsider (nonemployee)	3	1	0	0	0	0	1
Unknown	0	1	0	3	0	0	0
Totals	31	20	4	8	17	4	6
Schemes of fraud used							
Payments to employee and other individuals	40	2	6	2	2	4	56
Accounting/inventory control/disbursements	44	3	3	7	1	11	69
Billings/deposits	17	2	1	5	0	2	27
Miscellaneous	0	0	2	0	0	2	4

*These totals are not mutually exclusive. Some cases are entered under more than one category.

Source: Adapted from: Brandt Allen, "The Biggest Computer Frauds: Lessons for CPAs," *The Journal of Accountancy* 143, no. 5 (May 1977), pp. 56 and 59. Copyright © 1977 by the American Institute of Certified Public Accountants, Inc.

One well-known organizational principle that serves security is **separation of responsibility**: no employee should perform all the steps

[22]Andrew D. Chambers, "Computer Abuse and Its Control," *EDPACS* 6 (December 1978), pp. 3–12.

in a single transaction. For example, record keeping should be separated from the physical custodianship of records. Computer systems can be divided into five basic functions: programming and system development; handling input media; operation of data processing equipment; documentation and file library; and distribution of output. It is advisable that the work assignment of no employee cross these functional lines. This is feasible in a large installation, but in many small firms employees may be required to perform more than one job since technical expertise is limited. In such cases, screening procedures during hiring[23] and access and processing controls should be stringent.

System security can also be promoted by rotating duties and responsibilities of employees, unannounced audits, adequate personnel training, encouraging a climate of honesty, and close observation of disgruntled employees. Publicizing security measures should also serve as a deterrent to attempted system intrusions.[24]

Physical security

Physical security includes protection of computer facilities from unlawful entry, sabotage, fire damage, or destructive acts of nature such as floods, earthquakes, windstorms, or lightning. Many protective measures can be incorporated in the construction or renovation of buildings, for example, earthquake-proof foundations, locks and window grills, alarms and panic buttons,[25] smoke detectors, and automatic fire extinguishers. (The fire extinguishers should be gas extinguishers, not water. Water can be almost as destructive as fire to electronic equipment, particularly to magnetic storage.) Access procedures discussed earlier should deter saboteurs. So should the presence of security guards. Employees should be trained in emergency procedures and drilled periodically to test the appropriateness, adequacy, and readiness of emergency planning. But nothing can prevent natural disasters. One can only reduce losses through insurance and minimize down time through effective recovery planning.

Many experts agree that the mechanization of security, such as alarms and detectors, is easy. What is difficult is motivating employees to be alert and sensitive to security issues.[26]

---

[23]See Louis Scoma, "Catch Dishonesty at the Hiring Step," *Data Management* 16, no. 10 (October 1978), pp. 26–29.

[24]For more on personnel security, see Charles F. Hemphill, Jr. and John M. Hemphill, *Security Procedures For Computer Systems* (Homewood, Ill.: Dow Jones-Irwin, 1973), pp. 144–54. For surveillance of personnel, see Peter Hamilton, *Computer Security* (London: Cassell Associated Business Programmes, 1973), pp. 63–81.

[25]For a discussion of several such warning systems, see James Martin, *Security, Privacy and Accuracy in Computer Systems* (Englewood Cliffs, N.J.: Prentice-Hall, 1973), chaps. 16–17.

[26]T. E. Diroff, "The Protection of Computer Facilities and Equipment: Physical Security," *Data Base* 10, no. 1 (Summer 1978), p. 24.

SECURITY RESPONSIBILITY OF MANAGEMENT

Figure 13.3 summarizes management's role in planning, implementing, monitoring, and evaluating security measures. A firm's survival may be at stake when losses must be absorbed due to sabotage or theft. Its reputation for quality service may be imperiled and years of accumulated goodwill endangered when security proves inade-

Figure 13.3   **Security overview and action process**

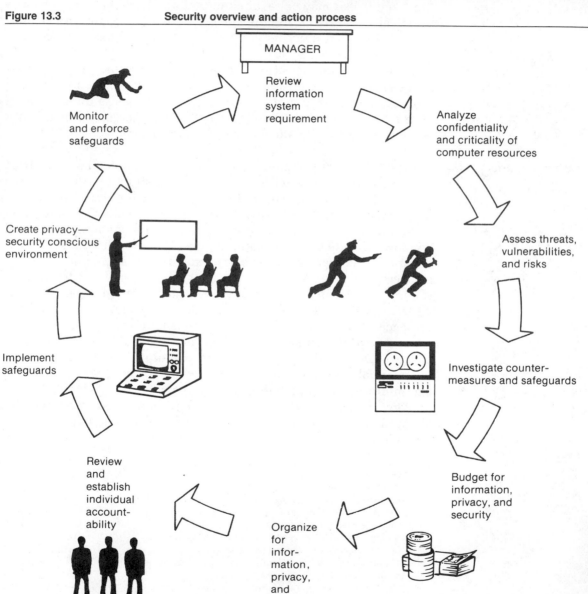

MANAGER

Review information system requirement

Analyze confidentiality and criticality of computer resources

Monitor and enforce safeguards

Create privacy— security conscious environment

Assess threats, vulnerabilities, and risks

Implement safeguards

Investigate counter- measures and safeguards

Review and establish individual account- ability

Organize for infor- mation, privacy, and security

Budget for information, privacy, and security

Source: Adapted from IBM Document G320-1372, 1974, pp. 35, 42–43.

quate. Though EDP personnel should participate in technical control decisions, corporate management must identify vital data, establish security points, outline security procedures, assign enforcement personnel, allocate needed resources, and take corrective action when security is violated. Management is also responsible for training programs that will make employees sensitive to privacy and security issues. All security measures adopted should be flexible, effective, and enforceable.

HOW MUCH SECURITY?

Security is costly. In addition to the expense of equipment and personnel to safeguard computing resources, there are other costs to be considered, such as employee dissatisfaction and loss of morale when security precautions delay or impede operations. In deciding how much security is needed, management must analyze **risk.** How exposed and vulnerable is the system? What threat scenarios are possible? Figure 13.4 shows factors that must be considered when assessing system risk.

Figure 13.4 **Factors in assessing expected losses from system intrusion**

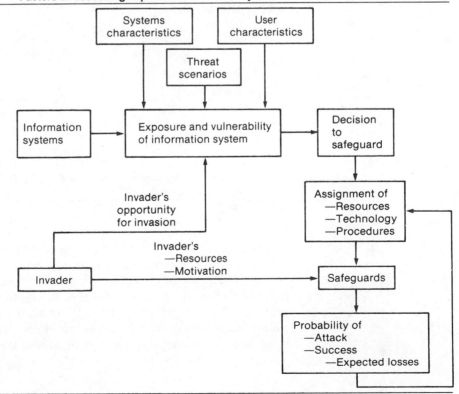

The amount of security that should be given to a system should be based, in part, on an evaluation of expected losses should the system be breached. One way to calculate losses to expect from intrusion is by application of the formula:

$$\text{Expected loss} = L \times P_A \times P_B$$

Where

$$
\begin{aligned}
L &= \text{Potential loss} \\
P_A &= \text{Probability of attack} \\
P_B &= \text{Probability of success}
\end{aligned}
$$

An insurance company or computer vendor can help management determine the value of L. Probability values are more difficult to obtain. Rather than attempting to assign a specific value to probabilities, especially to the value of P_B, relative risk should first be determined (high, medium, or low) and a numerical value assigned to each of these relative probabilities (e.g., 0.8, 0.5, and 0.2 respectively). The risk costs can now be calculated according to the formula, as shown in the example in Table 13.5. Loss is determined for each exposure. The sum of the expected losses is the total risk value to the system. In Table 13.5, if P_A and P_B are probabilities for the year, expected loss is $168,000 per year.

Table 13.5   **Calculations of risk**

Exposure	L (Potential $ loss of exposure)	P_A	P_B	Expected loss ($) ($L \times P_A \times P_B$)
1	500,000	1.0	0.2	100,000
2	200,000	0.6	0.5	60,000
3	50,000	0.2	0.8	8,000
Total expected loss				168,000

The application of this formula will help management determine whether adding security measures is worth the cost and where the greatest reduction of expected losses could occur by improving security, but it should be recognized that the figures derived from the formula are approximations at best. We simply do not have the data to calculate reliable probabilities. News of security invasions is seldom broadcast, impeding collection of data, and the computer industry is too new to have a long historical record on invasions on which to base probability assessments.[27]

SUMMARY

Computer technology poses a threat to personal privacy because of the speed of processing, the collection of vast data banks, instantaneous retrieval capabilities, and the worldwide network of data transmission through teleprocessing. The 1974 Privacy Act has imposed restrictions of use on personal data for U.S. federal agencies, but the debate continues over privacy requirements for the private sector.

Privacy is closely linked to system security. No one disputes that information systems must be guarded from unlawful intrusion, that human errors should be detected, and damage from natural disasters minimized. Management's dilemma is not whether security is needed but how much. Prior to 1974, there were 90 reported cases of computer fraud, with the firms involved suffering an average loss of $617,000.[28] Forecasts are equally gloomy. Computer crime is increasing at an estimated annual growth rate of 400 percent,[29] due, in part, to the temptation arising from the large sums being transferred by EFT and to the fact that more criminals are becoming knowledgeable about computer technology and are becoming equipped with minis to help them plan and execute their crimes. There are also individuals who are challenged simply to "beat the system." In Oregon, an 18-year-old used a remote terminal to gain access to the computer of Department of Motor Vehicles, then put the system into irreversible disarray just to illustrate its vulnerability.

According to commentators:

> . . . (Computer crime) figures are destined to rise unless effective countermeasures are taken against the more expert attacks of the second generation of computer criminals who are now learning their trade.[30]

All known protective mechanisms can be broken, given enough time, resources, and ingenuity.[31] Perhaps the major objective of secu-

[27]For more on risk analysis, see Lance Hoffman, *Modern Methods for Computer Security and Privacy* (Englewood Cliffs, N.J.: Prentice-Hall, 1977), pp. 17–73; National Computing Center, *Where Next for Computer Security* (Manchester, England: National Computing Center, 1974) pp. 89–96; and Peter Hamilton, *Computer Security*, (London: Cassell Associated Business Programmes, 1972), Chapters 2, 3 and 7.

[28]D. B. Parker, *Crime by Computer* (New York: Charles Scribner's Sons, 1976), p. 32.

[29]A. Pantages, "The Price of Protection," *Datamation* 22, no. 3 (March 1976), p. 144.

[30]Dorothy E. Denning and Peter J. Denning, "Security, Audit, and Control," *Data Processing Digest* 25, no. 11 (November 1979), p. 227.

[31]AFIPS. *Security: Systems Review Manual* (Montvale, N.J.: AFIPS Press, 1974).

rity systems should be to make intrusion too expensive (in equipment costs and risk) and too time-consuming (in planning effort and time needed to actually breach safeguards) to make attempted violations worthwhile.

Risk analysis is one method of helping management determine which security strategies are most cost-effective, given budgetary constraints. System security can be provided by access controls, physical safeguards, personnel screening and policies, and operational controls as discussed in this chapter and the one preceding. All of these measures of security are summarized in Table 13.6. Legal deterrents will be discussed in Chapter 26.

Table 13.6	Countermeasures to threats	
	Access control	*Physical controls*
	Authorization/authentication (e.g., passwords, cards)	Vaults
		Fire extinguishing equipment
	Hardware locks	Physical restrictions to:
	Logging access	Peripherals
	Time locks	Libraries
	Librarian control of:	CPU
	Data	
	Programs	*Organizational controls*
	Documentation	Separation of duties
		Rotation of duties
	Processing controls	Bond personnel
	Transformation of data	Identify disgruntled personnel
	Ciphering/deciphering	Train personnel
	Validity checking	Remove conflicts of interest
	Control totals	Disaster insurance
	Form control	Background check
	Procedure control	Appoint control and security officer
	Backup	
	Equipment	
	Personnel	

CASE STUDY: LACK OF DP CONTROLS AT EQUITY FUNDING*

In 1973, a scandal involving computer fraud at Equity Funding Life Insurance made headlines. The case was so complex that, when investigated, three volumes of the Trustees Bankruptcy Report were required. The company allegedly kept two sets of books, reporting $143

*Sources: Donn B. Parker, *Crime by Computer* (New York: Charles Scribner's Sons, 1976), pp. 118–24 and R. A. McLaughlin, "Equity Funding: Everyone Is Pointing at the Computer," *Datamation* 19, no. 6 (June 1973), pp. 88–91.

million for the sale of life insurance policies to fictious firms in the reinsurance business. Approximately 63,000 of its 97,000 policies were falsified records supported by fake policy applications. Apparently the alleged fraud, begun in 1964, originally involved only a few top officials who made false entries in the company's books in hopes of giving their firm the appearance of growth and prosperity. But additional conspirators were soon enlisted to help cover up the imbalances in the company's accounts which resulted. Eventually an entire office was devoted to the production of falsified policy files. Fraud participants gained from the sale of Equity's inflated stock.

How could the fraud remain undetected for so long? Where did data processing controls fail? When the fraud was uncovered, Bill Gootnick, vice president of the parent company, Equity Funding Corp., asserted that,

> The Equity data processing division had the same controls that most installations our size would have had, including programmer project control, file retention, and report balancing. We're no different than 90 percent of the shops around.[1]

However, a number of new controls were initiated following the scandal, from which one can infer which controls were lacking. All tapes of value were placed under armed guard in a confidential off-site storage place, tape access was tightened, programmers were required to sign in and out of their work areas, and write-protect rings were added to tapes. The fact that auditors had been duped is a clear indication that adequate controls were lacking. Controls, especially internal ones, may have been purposely avoided by management to hide the fraud.

Following the Equity scandal, many firms reevaluated their data processing procedures and controls. According to Warren White, a respected data processing consultant, "No one can protect against truly massive collusion, but you can design a system to make it necessary to involve large numbers of people."[2]

KEY WORDS

Access control	Cryptography
Authentication	Data Encryption Standard (DES)
Authorization	Development costs

[1] R. A. McLaughlin, "Equity Funding: Everyone Is Pointing at the Computer," *Datamation* 19, no. 6 (June 1973), p. 89.

[2] Ibid., p. 91.

Eavesdropping

Encryption

Handshake

Identification

Key

Masquerading

1971 Fair Credit Reporting Act

Operational disbursements

Passwords

Physical security

Piggy-backing

Privacy

Privacy abuse

Privacy Act of 1974

Privacy cost

Privacy Protection Study
   Commission

Reading between the lines

Recovery

Rights

Risk

Security measures

Separation of responsibility

Session passwords

Substitution

Transposition

Wiretapping

DISCUSSION QUESTIONS

1. Comment on the statement: A computer system adds significantly to the probability of errors, fraud, and destruction of data and information.

2. Describe types of crimes perpetrated against computerized systems.

3. Describe five situations in which personal identification might be required before access to a computer is granted. In each case, which of the following methods would you recommend:
   a. I.D. card?
   b. Password?
   c. Signature identification?
   d. Hand form identification?
   e. Voice identification?
   f. Handprint identification?

4. Why is privacy of data important to business clients and customers? What other segments in business are affected and why? How can each privacy problem be successfully approached?

5. How can the conflict between need for data privacy and need for data access be resolved? What trade-offs can be made?

6. What is a password?

7. Give two examples of unexpected results that might be produced because of:
   a. Malfunction.
   b. Mistakes.
   c. Fraud.
   d. Theft.
   e. Sabotage.

How might security be improved to prevent incorrect results caused by each of the above?

8. What are some common abuses of computerized information systems? How can these abuses be prevented?

9. Has your privacy been invaded by business computers? How can such invasion of privacy be prevented?

10. Can a computer system ever be completely secure? What are the trade-offs in costs? What are the social and nonmonetary costs?

11. Identify control points where measures should be taken to ensure security of data. Explain what measures you would require and why.

12. What should be management's role in planning system security?

13. What makes particular industries more vulnerable to security violations than the average? What makes a particular firm within an industry more vulnerable than others? How can this vulnerability be reduced, if not eliminated?

14. What would you do if you suspected a fellow employee of being a computer criminal? Should your action depend on your industry? Would your action differ if you were working in a:
    a. Bank?
    b. Retail store?
    c. Multinational firm?
    d. Insurance company?

15. Are laws in the United States adequate for detecting, discouraging, and punishing:
    a. Computer crime?
    b. Privacy violations?

16. Is the cost of privacy excessive? How can a firm decide what security precautions to ensure privacy are worth the cost?

SELECTED ANNOTATED BIBLIOGRAPHY

ACM Computing Surveys 11, no. 4 (December 1979), pp. 281–413.
    This is a special issue on cryptology. The common theme of the articles is concern for the privacy and security of electronically stored information and new methods for encryption to provide the desired protection.

Bushkin, Arthur L., and Samuel I. Schaen. *The Privacy Act of 1974: A Reference Manual for Companies*. McLean, Va.: System Development Corporation, 1978, 183 p.
    The subtitle is an apt description of the book. It discusses the coverage of the act, basic compliance requirements, technical considerations for implementation, and the establishment of appropriate safeguards.

Comer, Michael J. *Corporate Fraud*. London: McGraw-Hill, 1977, 393 p.
    A comprehensive book on the classification of fraud, its detection and prevention. Thirty cases of computer crime (pp. 153–88) are described and many cases analyzed.

Data Management 15, no. 5 (May 1977), pp. 7–30.

This special issue on security discusses EDP auditing, authentication methods, fire danger, and "meeting the ultimate disaster."

Diffie, Whitfield, and Martin E. Hellman. "New Directions in Cryptography." *IEEE Transactions on Information Theory* IT22, no. 6 (November 1978), pp. 644–54.

The authors have contributed to recent research in cryptography and are well equipped to write on this subject. They are very confident that we are now "beginning to provide tools to solve cryptographic problems of long standing . . . changing this ancient art into a science." The discussion is mathematical in part, as in the section on the PnP problem of computational complexity. This article is for the serious reader and may require supplementary reading.

Diroff, T. E. "The Protection of Computer Facilities and Equipment: Physical Security." *Data Base* 10, no. 1 (Summer 1978), pp. 15–24.

An excellent discussion of personnel, access, and physical security including problems arising from poor security, such as losses, and recovery from disasters.

Glaseman, S.; R. Turn; and R. S. Gaines. "Problem Areas in Computer Security Assessment." *Proceedings of the National Computer Conference* (1977), pp. 105–12.

The authors come from the RAND Corporation, an organization very active in research on security. The article provides an introduction to security assessment, surveys the field, and suggests promising directions of research in security assessment methodology.

Hoffman, Lance J., ed. *Computers and Privacy in the Next Decade*. New York: Academic Press, 1980, 250 p.

This book is a set of readings and commentary written by well-known experts in the field (e.g., W. H. Ware, Paul Armer, Rein Turn, Abbe Mowshowitz). The topics are balanced, and very provocative. Included are articles on privacy, the personal computer, EFT, transborder flow and non-uniform privacy laws. Problems and issues arising from the preservation of individual autonomy and the protection of public order in future decades are also addressed.

Hoffman, Lance J. *Modern Methods for Computer Security and Privacy*. Englewood Cliffs, N.J.: Prentice-Hall, 1977, 255 p.

This a continuation of a series of books and articles on this subject by Hoffman. It is a cram course in security threats and countermeasures. The legal aspects of privacy are discussed as well as the transformation of data to maintain privacy by traditional hardware and software methods. The book makes an excellent reference. It is technical but written in nontechnical language. Questions and sample answers are included for each chapter.

Hsiao, David K.; Douglas S. Kerr; and Stuart E. Madnick. *Computer Security*. New York: Academic Press, 1979, 299 p.

This book is a superb guide to the extensive literature on security. Each chapter has a postscript which reviews the literature relevant to the chapter, followed by references, including annotated bibliographies. A total of 720 references with 353 annotations are included in the text. The book is tutorial in approach. A good chapter on privacy is included. Throughout the book areas for future research are identified and discussed.

Martin, James. *Security, Accuracy and Privacy in Computer Systems.* Englewood Cliffs, N.J.: Prentice-Hall, 1973, 626 p.

One excellent section of this book is "Physical Security and Administrative Controls." There are also good sections on the design of computer systems, and the legal and social environment as it relates to security and privacy. The appendix includes an extensive 92 page section of summaries and checklists. The book is somewhat outdated but is still an excellent reference.

Pritchard, J. A. T. *Risk Management in Action.* Manchester, England: National Computing Center, 1978, 160 p.

An excellent discussion of the trade-offs in security management of a computing center. Discusses threats, countermeasures, auditing, contingency planning, and a risk control program.

Van Tassel, Dennis. *Computer Security Management.* Englewood Cliffs, N.J.: Prentice-Hall, 1972, 220 p.

In the mid-seventies this was considered one of the best books on the subject, but the subject has progressed greatly since then and numerous other excellent books now offer Van Tassel competition. Nevertheless, this text is worth your attention. It discusses all standard topics on security and has a checklist after each section to help readers evaluate the adequacy of their firm's security.

Ware, Willis H. "Handling Personal Data." *Datamation* 22, no. 10 (October 1977), p. 83.

Ware, the chairman of the 1973 HEW Report and an astute observer of the scene, traces the history of privacy legislation and discusses its implications to management, both corporate management and management of data processing.

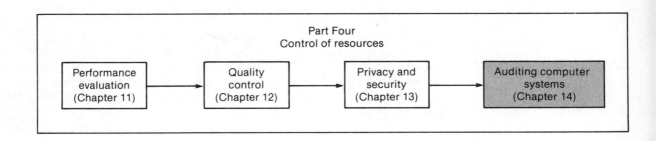

CHAPTER 14

Auditing computer systems

Here and elsewhere we shall not obtain the
best insight into things until we actually see them
growing from the beginning.

Aristotle

Every computer system should be monitored for performance and evaluated for efficiency and effectiveness. Control points should be established and control measures implemented to ensure protection of computing resources and to minimize error. Chapters 11–13 have dealt with these topics.

Auditing is yet another level of control. In this chapter the function of an auditor will be described and approaches to computer auditing considered. Since auditing requires professional training, no attempt is made to explain in detail how auditing is done, but the scope of an auditor's control over computing will be discussed at length. Sections are also devoted to auditing benefits, problems, and the role of auditors in the development of new information systems.

AUDITOR'S ROLE

The function of an **auditor** in a firm is twofold: (1) to ensure that controls to protect corporate resources are in place, and (2) to ensure that transactions are processed according to desired procedures and decision rules.

Traditionally, this has meant monitoring accounts and financial records under the jurisdiction of a firm's comptroller or financial officer. Today, however, sales, accounts receivable and payable, payroll, and inventory are processed by computers so auditors have an added area of concern: EDP centers. Auditors now require computing skills as well as accounting expertise to monitor all phases of record processing. And since error-free transactions depend on procedures, standards, decision rules, and security embodied in the design of systems, auditors now participate in the development of new systems to make sure adequate controls are formulated and incorporated in the design of systems they audit. Auditors must also make sure that proposed systems are auditable, that is, that the systems are so designed that audits during operations are feasible.

The auditor's responsibility in protecting corporate resources has also broadened by the introduction of computers. The auditor today must monitor the security of data, manuals, software, and even terminal access, in addition to traditional responsibilities.

In the two preceding chapters, strategies of control, control points, threats, and counter-measures were discussed. The computer center manager and EDP personnel are responsible for implementing these controls during daily processing. An internal auditor provides a second level of control, evaluating processing, the activities of the computer center, and the effectiveness of the controls themselves. To preserve the objectivity and independence of this audit, the auditor, an employee of the firm, should report directly to a senior executive, such as the firm's financial vice president, and should not be a member of the computer center staff. Many companies add yet a third level of control, an external auditor hired from outside the organization, to audit processing yet again and to audit the internal auditor's evaluation of EDP controls.

Figure 14.1 illustrates these three levels of control. It is management's responsibility in a given firm to evaluate a computer center's exposure, the potential magnitude of loss, and the probability of system intrusion when deciding whether all three levels of control are

Figure 14.1   **Layers of control**

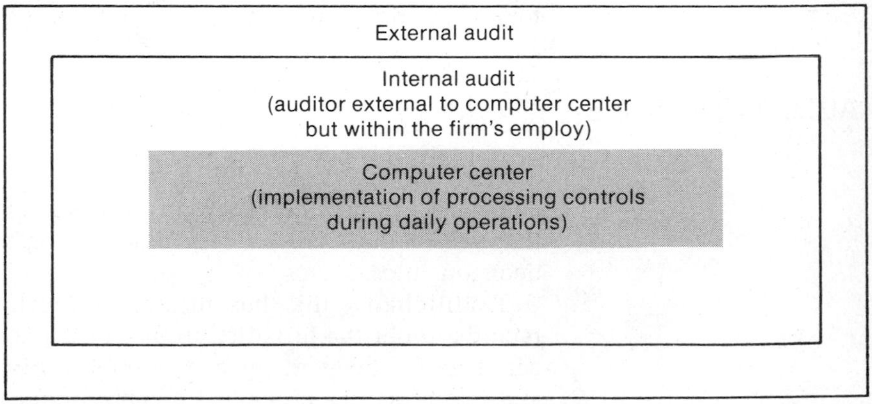

External audit

Internal audit
(auditor external to computer center
but within the firm's employ)

Computer center
(implementation of processing controls
during daily operations)

necessary. The depth of coverage and frequency of audits is also a management decision.

APPROACHES TO AUDITING

There are two main approaches to auditing computer-based applications: auditing around and auditing through the computer.

Auditing around the computer

When **auditing around the computer,** output is checked for a given input. It is assumed that if input is correct and reflected in the output, then the processing itself is also correct. Hence, the audit does not check computer processing directly. This type of audit uses traditional auditing methods and techniques, tracing who did what, when, and in what sequence.

The problem with this approach is that processing errors may exist even though no errors are apparent in output for this given set of input. Or there might be compensatory errors that do not show in output. Unfortunately, computer calculations provide few intermediate results for auditors to check processing accuracy by traditional trailing methods.

Auditing through the computer

To check both input and process, **audits through the computer** can be made. This auditing approach may use test data, auditor-prepared programs, auditor-software packages, or special-purpose audit programming languages.

Use of test data. In this technique, system response to a selected set of data is checked for reasonableness, validity, and consistency. Auditors search for extreme conditions, out-of-sequence data, out-of-balance batches, and so forth, the type of errors frequently found when testing applications programs. The accuracy of the computer program itself in performing calculations is examined and operation procedures used by the firm are scrutinized and checked for consistency with corporate policies.

Auditor-prepared programs. In this approach, specially written programs prepared by the auditors are used to check specific conditions and to identify situations that need further study and analysis.[1] The programs also spot check for unauthorized manipulations by programmers and operators, and provide listings of "before" and "after" changes which facilitate auditing.

---

[1]For a further discussion and examples, see W. T. Porter, *EDP Controls and Auditing* (Belmont, Calif.: Wadsworth, 1974), pp. 112–33.

Auditor-software packages. Standard auditing programs can be purchased. These are not as specialized as programs written by auditors for a specific information system, but they are less expensive and relatively easy to use.

Audit programming languages. Special programming languages can be used to generate output needed by auditors. System 2170, for example, developed by the accounting firm Peat, Marwick and Mitchell, is a language that can be learned in about one week, and has 21 audit commands.

Through-the-computer auditing approaches create problems when used on real-time systems, for sample data can get mixed with the live stream of data unless extreme care is taken and expensive precautions are adopted. One solution to this problem is to create a representative set of data for the company and use it for auditing independent of the live data system. This approach is referred to as the **mini-company approach,** since the test data base is a miniature representation of the company.

It is beyond the scope of this text to explain auditing techniques of computer systems in greater detail, for the subject is very complex and requires the skills of a professional accountant.[2] What needs to be stressed here is that auditors of today use computers when auditing information systems. Unfortunately, current computer audit techniques are not as advanced as the technology being audited and the computer profession shows no sign of slowing its pace to wait until auditors catch up.

THE PARTICIPATION OF AUDITORS IN THE DEVELOPMENT OF NEW SYSTEMS

Audit standards issued by the U.S. Government Accounting Office state:

> *The auditor shall actively participate in reviewing the design and development of new data processing systems or applications, and significant modifications, thereto, as a normal part of the audit function.*[3]

---

[2]For books on computers and auditing, see John G. Burch, Jr., and Joseph L. Sardinas, Jr., *Computer Control and Audit: A Total Systems Approach* (New York: John Wiley & Sons, 1978), 492 p.; William C. Mair et al., *Computer Control and Audit* (Institute of Internal Auditors, 1978), 489 p.; W. Thomas Porter, *EDP Controls and Auditing* (Belmont, Calif.: Wadsworth, 1974), 240 p; and Ron Weber, *EDP Auditing: Conceptual Foundations and Practice* (New York: McGraw Hill, 1982), 642 p.

[3]*Additional GAO Standards: Auditing Computer-Based Systems* (Washington, D.C.: U.S. Government Accounting Office, March 1979), p. 4.

This is to ensure that features that will facilitate auditing are incorporated in new or modified systems. Auditors are interested in documentation standards, testing samples, and recovery procedures. They want a voice in specifying programming decision rules, establishing logs, and determining backup. Table 14.1 lists the type of features that auditors assist analysts in designing. This is merely a sample, for lists will vary according to the firm, auditor, and type of application. One would expect greater auditor involvement during development of applications involving monetary transactions, funds, or assets than for a mailing list application, for example.

The auditor's participation in development activities may begin in the feasibility study if expensive audits are anticipated and they need to be included in cost estimates. Usually, however, the auditor's prime function in development is user specification and design, though the testing phase is also important to ensure that audit controls and security features work. When conflicts arise between auditors and project staff due to different points of view (EDP staff may

Table 14.1	Design features of interest to auditors
	Decision rules
	Rounding rules
	Consistency rules
	Validation rules
	Control points
	Control procedures for trace and trail features
	Access rules:
	Who?
	When?
	Why?
	What?
	Standards:
	Documentation
	Security
	Control
	Backup and recovery
	Special auditing reports:
	Reliability performance reports
	Cost indices
	Resource utilization reports
	Logs:
	Data access log
	System access log
	Invalid access log
	Sensitive file access log
	Secondary storage access log
	Program access log
	Data transmission log

favor operational ease and expediency over rigid controls and standards), the auditor usually has the authority to prevail.

Auditors have no assigned responsibility during conversion but should oversee the process to be sure only the tested and authorized version of the new system is implemented. Experience has shown that systems are vulnerable to malicious or fraudulent intrusions in this phase of development due to the euphoria of a job completed and the confusion of the transition period. This is one reason many firms require an auditor's sign-off approval after conversion is completed.

Whether auditors participate in project management depends on the industry and application. One would expect an auditor to assist in evaluation and review of the developmental activities for a complex accounting-oriented project, for instance. But practices differ among firms.

Figure 14.2 summarizes in graphic form which developmental activities fall within an auditor's purview. It should be mentioned that auditing features can be added to systems once they are operational, though this practice is costly in time and effort and very disruptive. However, it is done when the need for a feature is overlooked during

Figure 14.2   **Role of auditor in development**

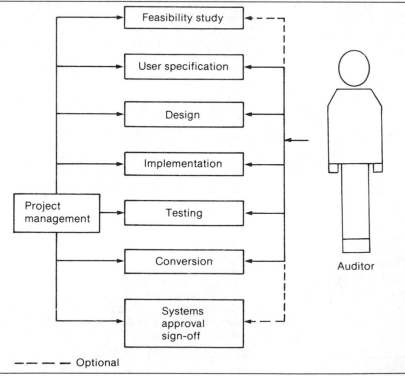

development or changed circumstances require added measures of control.

The auditor's role in the development of new systems is increasing in difficulty because data bases are expanding, data structures are becoming more complex, operating systems are growing in sophistication, and both computers and peripherals continue to add advanced features with each new model. But new technology has also contributed auditing aids. For example, data base management systems (DBMS) offer monitoring facilities, data element dictionary and directory information, utility programs, and special descriptive and manipulative languages. Table 14.2 lists still other auditing features of a DBMS. As research increases DBMS capabilities, auditors will undoubtedly be better able to perform their function of control.

Table 14.2	Auditing-related facilities in a DBMS
	Subtotals and final totals
	Testing footings and extension
	Record selection based on:
	Simple logical expression
	Complex logical expression
	Sorting
	Comparisons:
	Records
	Files
	Table look-up
	Account aging
	Statistical sampling
	Categorization
	Stratification
	Automatic preparation of notices

SCOPE OF AUDITING

What should be audited? Table 14.3 lists aspects of computer processing that concern auditors. Evaluation of performance has already been discussed in Chapter 11. An auditor uses many of the same criteria to evaluate efficiency and effectiveness, though the auditor's perspective may differ. For example, though concerned with error rates, an auditor may focus on the total dollar value of errors rather than the frequency of errors per se. Auditors are also much less worried about user satisfaction than ensuring that expenditures fall within allocated amounts. Whereas computer personnel correct problems as they occur, auditors search for weaknesses, test extreme values, and may attempt to break a system to test its limits. Indeed, a major responsibility of auditors is to evaluate the adequacy and sufficiency of systems

Table 14.3	Auditing concerns
	Acquisition of resources
	(above a certain level)
	Operations:
	Costs
	Financing methods
	Procedures
	Budget and finances:
	Development
	Operations
	Organizational structure
	Staffing:
	Performance
	Security
	Management of:
	Development
	Operations
	The computer executive
	Security
	Privacy
	Revenues
	Standards
	Scheduling
	Performance of resources
	User interface
	Workflow
	Cost effectiveness
	Reliability

not only for normal and peak workloads but for projected needs. In identifying points where demand will exceed capacity in the future, the auditor's report is a valuable tool in long-range planning.

Each of the auditing concerns listed in Table 14.3 consists of numerous subsets of activities. Let us look at just one detailed list: activities that are part of control of operations. Though firms may vary in their depth of audit coverage, an audit of operations generally consists of the activities listed in Table 14.4. Many of the statistics required can be provided by operating systems. Or in-house programs can be written to collect the needed data. But auditors also will have to examine logs and records to gather needed information.

For example, analysis of delays will include examination of statistics on average delay time, maximum delay time, average length of queue, maximum length of queue, etc.—data that can be collected by monitors. But to find reasons for delays the auditor will have to examine the workflow—from input submission, input preparation, preprocessing (e.g., validation of data), processing, and postprocessing (e.g., decolating and bursting) to distribution. Unless the cause is traced, be it faulty distribution procedures, poorly written manuals,

Table 14.4   **Factors to be considered in auditing operations of a computing center**

Scheduled jobs
  Jobs completed on deadline
  Jobs completed beyond deadline
    Reasons for delays
    Statistics on delays (e.g., queue length,
      mean and maximum waiting time)
Unscheduled jobs
  Response time turnaround by frequency distribution
  Reasons for delays beyond allowable threshold
  Statistics on delays
User assistance
  Input preparation
  Programming
  Online processing
User satisfaction
Resource availability
  Down time by frequency distribution
Reliability
  Down time
  Error rates
Scheduling
  Manpower leveling
  Resource leveling
Utilization of resources
Disaster planning and recovery
  Physical facilities
  Storage media
  Programs
  Supplies for crucial applications
Management and staffing
  Security clearance
  Separation of duties
Data
  Storage and retention
  Access and security
Input/output control
Access control

inadequate training of operating personnel, or understaffing, corrective action cannot be taken and the purpose of the audit will be defeated.

The computer center as a department or division of the firm should also be audited. Controls for security, backup, and recovery in particular need to Le examined. Expenditures also require close scrutiny because computer centers have become important cost units.

In addition, an auditor needs to look at job assignments to ensure that checks and balances exist. That is, duties should be separated so that no single individual participates in both system design and design approval, programming and program approval, or testing and test approval. In operations, duties should be separated by instituting distinctions between the following:

Source document preparation

Input preparation

File library

Output distribution

Systems programming

Hardware maintenance

Data base administration

Error corrections

Machine operation

The auditor should also be concerned with output of the computer center. It is possible that needed information is not being generated, that two reports might be more efficiently combined into one, or that certain reports have outlived their usefulness. A questionnaire, such as the one presented in Table 14.5, might be circulated to users to ascertain the value of given reports. The answers might lead to report alternatives not previously considered due to lack of information.

Though an auditor will not have the time to personally study the

Table 14.5   **User questionnaire on reports**

1. How useful do you consider this report?
2. How often do you use this report?
3. How many persons in your department use this report? How and why (briefly)?
4. How much of the data in this report do you use?
5. Can this report be:
   a. Subsumed in another report?
   b. Eliminated?
6. If this report were eliminated, would you easily find equivalent information elsewhere?
7. How do you store this report?
8. How long do you keep this report?
9. Is the report timely (available when needed)?
10. Is the report used for:
    a. Reference?
    b. Action and decision making?
    c. Exceptional reporting?
    d. Planning?
    e. Control?
    f. Operations?
    g. Analysis?
11. Do you consider the mode of processing satisfactory? Which mode would you prefer? Why?
12. Is the report likely to be useful to you in the future? For how long?

usefulness of each report, the following questions should be kept in mind when controlling output. Are reports economically justifiable? Relevant? Timely? Accurate? Complete? Are reports effective in their presentation and easy to use? Are they packaged logically? Used frequently to justify the cost? It may be that the cost of space, equipment, utilities, insurance, and security to store reports is more costly than the value of their retention. Or that the storage media might be changed to computer output on microfilm for more efficient storage and retrieval.

After one serious breakdown at a computer center which resulted in an entire week of processing being lost, one alert auditor questioned users and found that 34 percent missed a report and complained, 24 percent missed a report but did not complain, and 42 percent weren't even aware of reports not processed. This analysis led to canceling many superfluous reports. Another auditor determined that information included in a regularly scheduled report could be generated as efficiently at one third the cost if produced on a "need to know" basis on a terminal.

These examples illustrate that an auditor can help identify system weaknesses that may slip past users or computer center personnel who are too immersed in daily operations to recognize macro problems of control.

Project development budgets should be as tightly controlled by auditors as operational budgets, and similar controls over procedures, standards, documentation, privacy, and security are needed.

BENEFITS

Table 14.6 lists benefits of auditing according to data processing managers. It is surprising that 31 percent of the respondents in this

Table 14.6	Benefits of internal auditing as viewed by data processing managers
	Percent of data processing managers
Reduced operation errors and omissions	8%
Reduced fraud loss/exposure	17
Improved application systems control	23
Increased user confidence and satisfaction	15
Other benefits	6
No significant benefits	31
	100%

Source: William E. Perry, "Internal Auditing of DP," *Infosystems* 24, no. 8 (August 1977), p. 46.

survey stated that auditing has no significant benefit. Perhaps the survey is merely indicative of the desire of DP managers to be independent of corporate restraints. Certainly many executives depend on audits to control overruns and inefficiency, and would not consider managing a firm without them.

PROBLEMS

Auditing of computer systems is not limited to checking the accuracy of financial transactions these days. Many subjective judgments must be made which may be challenged by computer technicians or data processing managers. In the event of a dispute regarding an acceptable response time, level of utilization, or cost per unit of service, should the auditor's viewpoint prevail? Who should arbitrate controversy? Though management may intervene, most firms give auditors authority to both initiate and tighten controls when problem areas are identified.

Trade-offs are another area where differences of opinion between auditors and computer center personnel may surface. Sometimes one objective must be degraded in order to achieve a secondary objective. For example, higher accuracy may require increased response time. Here again, the auditor's recommendations may conflict with the viewpoint of computer technicians, creating friction in their working relationships. Auditors can also raise hackles when questioning the value of reports favored by users or recommending changes in procedures.

As a result of such conflicts of interest, auditors may not get the cooperation they need from EDP personnel during audits. Yet assistance in identifying problems and explaining discrepancies is needed. Since the purpose of an audit is better utilization of resources and improved efficiency and effectiveness, the image of the malevolent auditor is most unfortunate.

Another problem with audits is that they are expensive, and often disruptive. Audits require the preparation of special reports, the use of logs and other documents, and computer run time to collect and process audit data. Technicians and users are interrupted from their usual tasks for interviews, and the salary of professional auditors is not insignificant. Is it worth it? If so, how often should audits take place? The answer to these questions is the prerogative of corporate management. Though there is no rule of thumb regarding frequency of audits, regularly scheduled audits and surprise audits are indeed the norm, and they may be called for when problems arise that require thorough, objective analysis.

SUMMARY AND CONCLUSIONS

Daily operations in a computer center are the responsibility of the DP manager who supervises processing to ensure quality performance and system security. A second level of control is provided by an internal auditor who periodically reviews processing and the effectiveness of designed controls. To bring a measure of objectivity to the audit and to ensure the auditor's independence, the auditor should not be a member of the computer staff but should report directly to a corporation executive, such as the vice president of finance, whose authority parallels that of the vice president to whom the computer center director reports, as shown in Figure 14.3. An external auditor hired from outside the organization can provide a third level of control. It is in the interest of managers to see that these audits take place, if only for self-protection, since responsibility for system security and error-free computing is ultimately management's.

Auditors examine both micro and macro controls. They review and control components of the system, such as administrative procedures regarding input and output, and application controls, such as audit trails (micro controls). They also evaluate the system as a whole, looking into contingency and disaster planning, whether expenditures can be explained, and separation of duties (macro controls). A computer center can be characterized as a "high pay-off" audit area because of the concentration of records and activities to be audited and because

Figure 14.3　　　　　　　　　　**Audit structure**

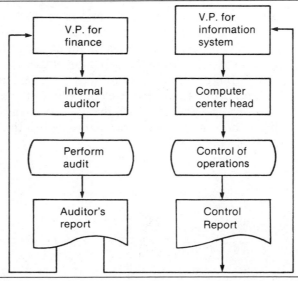

computer centers have a record of poor control with many past operational and developmental disasters.

It may seem to some readers that this chapter has been merely a restatement of Chapter 11 on system evaluation. True, auditors are concerned with the same processing controls that are scrutinized in performance evaluation. But the auditor's responsibility extends one step further, to control of controls: the review of the effectiveness of control measures and the establishment of new controls when existing controls prove insufficient.

Auditors of computerized information systems need more than accounting skills and auditing experience. They must be knowledgeable about computer systems, especially the implementation of data bases, documentation, data security, and recovery. In addition, programming skills are needed, not only to check the decision rules incorporated in a program but also because computer programs are used in the audits themselves. (COBOL is the language most commonly employed in business programs and audits.) Audit programs can control calculations, comparisons, and verifications; perform intermediary operations, such as sampling and extractions; and also perform the functions of monitors, collecting data on operations. Yet of 9,044 internal auditors surveyed by the EDP Auditors Association in 1977, only one out of eight were EDP qualified. The number of practicing and proclaimed EDP auditors is on the increase, but the shortage of auditors experienced in computing is still a major problem.

Unfortunately, auditing techniques have failed to keep pace with advances in computer technology. Computer input, for example, is the source of many inadvertent errors and the point where theft and fraud are often attempted. Computer scientists have spent many years analyzing the source and nature of errors and intrusions during input in order to design strategies of input control. Today, however, chips to receive voice input are being developed which will require controls quite different from those used for card or terminal input. In all probability, by the time adequate controls for the chips have been designed and implemented, the technology will have changed once again. This lag is one of the major problems facing the computer industry and auditors today.

CASE STUDY: INADEQUATE AUDITS AT EQUITY FUNDING*

Fraud at Equity Funding was described in a case study in the preceding chapter. The bankruptcy report by the trustees in this case dealt harshly with the parent company's auditors, charging that had they done their job, the fraud would have been caught years before the scandal broke. Many observers feel the blame is unjust, claiming accountants are watchdogs, not bloodhounds. No one disputes, however, that data processing controls were circumvented, indicating the need to reevaluate auditing procedures.

According to reports, the computer at Equity was programmed to skip over manufactured records during billing cycles. Fake records were unsupported by real paperwork unless an auditor asked for documentation, in which case the auditor was put off until phony records were generated. If an auditor requested written confirmation from a policyholder, "random" names and addresses were drawn from the files, the "random" names belonging to loyal employees. Extensive audits were conducted only every three years. Intervening audits were based primarily on the sworn statements of company officers. Frank Hyman, manager of Equity Funding's systems and programming, claims that no auditor ever asked that the master files be dumped to facilitate reference and checking. It appears auditors treated the computer system like a huge black box.

Lessons to be learned from the Equity Funding scandal are that auditing controls must be tightened and auditing tools upgraded. For example, Hyman recommends that certain audit files should be generated automatically, stored online, and accessible only to the audit team. Standards should be developed for master files, making it easier to read and maintain programs. Audit teams should include data processing professionals. An independent internal auditing staff responsible for developing controls and testing system software is also advisable. Audits of operating software matched against a copy of the program approved would reveal unauthorized rewrites or patches (changes or additions to programs).

In light of the Equity Funding fraud, the American Institute of Certified Public Accountants plans to form a special committee to review the need for change in existing auditing methods. Modern business

---

*Sources: Donn B. Parker, *Crime By Computer* (New York: Charles Scribner's Sons, 1976), pp. 118–24 and R. A. McLaughlin, "Equity Funding: Everyone Is Pointing at the Computer," *Datamation* 19, no. 6 (June 1973), pp. 88–91.

may require a new breed of accountants—watchhounds with the accounting skills to detect defalcation and training to investigate complex manipulative frauds.

KEY WORDS

Audit programming languages

Auditing around the computer

Auditor

Auditor prepared program

Auditor-software packages

Auditor's role in system development

Audits through the computer

External audit

Internal audit

Mini-company approach

Test data

User questionnaire

DISCUSSION QUESTIONS

1. Should computer operations be audited? If so, at what level or levels?
2. Consider a manufacturing plant with 1,200 employees and a computer system employing 30 people which processes 15 main applications.
   a. What level or levels should be audited?
   b. Would you recommend an internal auditor, an external auditor, or both?
   c. Would you also recommend internal control by the computer center itself?
3. When is an external auditor advisable?
4. In what ways do internal auditors, external auditors, and control personnel within a computing center complement or overlap one another?
5. Why should an auditor participate in the development of a computer application? What are the advantages and disadvantages of such participation?
6. What are the differences between auditing a computer application and a noncomputer application?
7. How is an EDP auditor different from other auditors? Why are they in scarce supply?
8. How can an auditor help prevent:
   a. Input errors?
   b. Design errors?
   c. Computer fraud through unauthorized modification of a program?
   d. Theft of computer time?
   e. Theft of a data tape?

   f. Unauthorized access to a data base through a terminal?
   g. Theft of manuals?
   h. Dishonest computer operation?
   i. Dishonest management?

9. How can an auditor help a firm recover from natural disasters or fire?

10. Do computers make internal controls easier or more difficult? How?

11. Do computers aid auditors or make their jobs more difficult? How?

12. List the steps in auditing:
   a. A computer application.
   b. Computer system development.
   c. A computer center.
   d. Computer personnel.
   e. A computer library.

13. How does one compensate for the fact that an audit trail is not available in a computer system?

14. Design procedures for auditing the effectiveness of a schedule for a computer center.

15. How could audit requirements be incorporated in the design of an accounting-oriented information subsystem?

16. How can an auditor defeat collusion among computer center staff? What types of clues might there be to such collusion?

17. Is it possible to over-audit? How could one detect an over-audit and prevent it from happening again?

SELECTED ANNOTATED BIBLIOGRAPHY

Cornick, Delroy L. *Auditing in the Electronic Environment.* Mt. Airy, Maryland: Lomond Books, 1981, 316 p.
 This book discusses the EDP environment and the auditor's trade, tools, techniques and role in EDP auditing. A chapter is also included on training and developing EDP auditing competence, an important topic in light of the shortage of EDP auditors. The second half of the book is devoted to an annotated bibliography and collection of auditing references.

Mair, William C.; Donald R. Wood; and Keagle W. Davis. *Computer Control and Audit.* Wellesley, Mass: Institute of Internal Auditors, 1978, 489 p.
 This book has extensive sections on auditing systems development and auditing an information processing facility.

Perry, William E., and Jerry FritzGerald. "Designing for Auditability." *Datamation* 28, no. 8 (August, 1977), pp. 46–50.
 This is an excellent discussion of the tools and techniques used by auditors at different stages of development. The article is based on the findings of a Stanford Research Institute study (sponsored by IBM) of 45 organizations in the United States, Canada, Europe, and Japan.

Sardinas, Joseph; John G. Burch; and Richard Asebrook. *EDP Auditing: A Primer.* New York: John Wiley & Sons, 1981, 209 p.

This is an introduction to EDP auditing. Discussed are tagging, tracing, computer-assisted audit techniques, audit software, Integrated Test Facility (ITF) and Parallel Test Facility (PTF). There are also good sections on controls for operations, administration, documentation, and security.

Wagner, Charles R. *The CPA and Computer Fraud.* Lexington, Mass.: Lexington Books, 1979, 150 p.

This book, written by an accounting professor, deals with the extent of computer fraud, its detection, and how an auditor can contribute to the eradication of fraud. Numerous tables of analysis on computer abuse are included.

Weber, Ron. *EDP Auditing: Conceptual Foundation and Practice.* New York: McGraw-Hill, 1982, 643 p.

The author focuses on control framework, the techniques of evidence collection, and how evidence itself should be evaluated. It is the author's premise that a good auditor must be better at business than clients. Many detailed and technical aspects of EDP control are discussed, such as concurrency, cryptography, kernel programs, data dictionary, and rollbook. This is a very impressive text.

PART FIVE

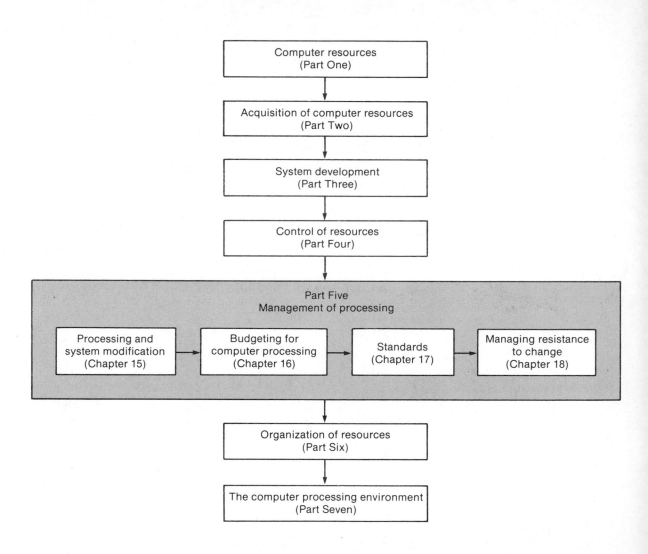

Computer resources
(Part One)

Acquisition of computer resources
(Part Two)

System development
(Part Three)

Control of resources
(Part Four)

Part Five
Management of processing

| Processing and system modification (Chapter 15) | Budgeting for computer processing (Chapter 16) | Standards (Chapter 17) | Managing resistance to change (Chapter 18) |

Organization of resources
(Part Six)

The computer processing environment
(Part Seven)

MANAGEMENT OF PROCESSING

Introduction to
Part Five

Part Five concerns the management of computer resources in daily operations. It focuses on the day-to-day responsibilities of a computer center head, and suggests ways to prepare employees in a firm for changes that occur when the role of computers is expanded.

Most of the issues raised in Part Five need to be considered during the development of an information system. However, subjects discussed in this part, such as scheduling and production controls, the supervision of maintenance and system modification, the preparation of computing budgets, the establishment and enforcement of standards, and the motivation of personnel, are matters that occupy management long after the development team is disbanded and conversion to the new information system has taken place. For this reason, a separate part has been devoted to management of processing, instead of adding the chapters to Part Three on system development.

Chapter 15 describes the flow of a job through computer processing, from scheduling to output control and distribution. When output proves unsatisfactory, system modification may be required, a process also examined in the chapter. Chapter 16 introduces budgetary approaches— examining elements and cost trends in computing budgets and alternative revenue schemes. This chapter also suggests methods of controlling budgets so that discrepancies between budgeted and actual expenditures are minimized.

The need for standards in computing is examined in Chapter 17 and the role of a standards committee in setting standards is explained. In addition, industry, professional, national, and international sources of standards are described.

The last chapter in this part, Chapter 18, deals with managing resistance to change. In this case, change means the introduction of computerized systems in a given firm. Strategies to foster positive employee attitudes toward computers are suggested.

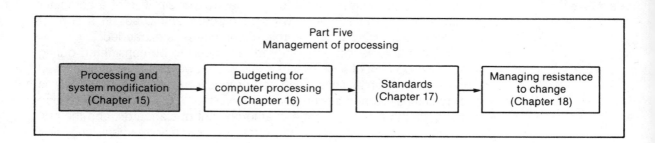

Part Five
Management of processing

| Processing and system modification (Chapter 15) | Budgeting for computer processing (Chapter 16) | Standards (Chapter 17) | Managing resistance to change (Chapter 18) |

CHAPTER 15

Processing and system modification

Leave room in the system for the feedback of experience to redesign the system itself.

Max Ways

Once an application has been developed and accepted by the user, the application is ready for processing and is sent to the department responsible for operations. This chapter describes processing activities, as shown in the flowchart in Figure 15.1. First the job needs to be scheduled, then run. Operational responsibility ends if the output is satisfactory once it has been delivered to the user. However, should output fail to meet required standards, corrections need to be made. Often operational personnel can identify the cause of the error, make the necessary adjustments, and schedule a rerun. For example, a peripheral device may have an incorrect setting, or the wrong output paper may have been used. But when the problem cannot be corrected by operators or they lack the authorization to make necessary changes, the job is sent to the group or department responsible for maintenance and redevelopment.

Throughout processing, jobs are controlled for performance, quality, privacy and security, and are subject to audits. These controls have been the subject of earlier chapters. Other production controls not mentioned heretofore (library and supplies) will be discussed with processing in this chapter (Boxes 2–15, Figure 15.1).

Figure 15.1   **Flow of a job through operations**

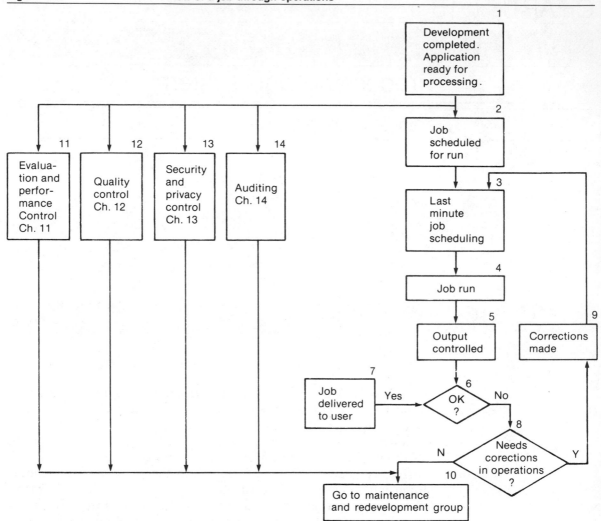

SCHEDULING

Ideally, there should be no constraints on processing. Run time should be available whenever needed. In practice, however, processing conflicts invariably arise. Curve A in Figure 15.2 is a typical demand curve, showing that capacity is exceeded at certain hours of the day. In such situations, jobs must be staggered to equalize the workload, to flatten Curve A to Curve B. (Curve C, with demand consis-

Figure 15.2 **Different patterns of processing demand**

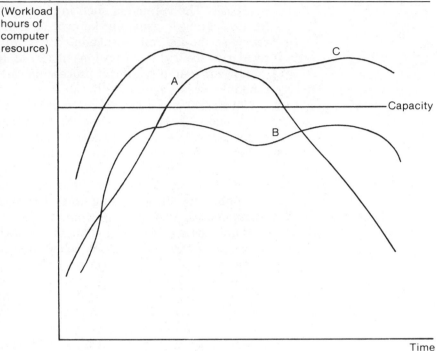

(Workload hours of computer resource)

Capacity

Time

tently higher than capacity, shows bad forecasting and poor capacity planning).

Systems that are exclusively batch require a **master schedule.** In systems that are mixed, the online real-time uses are controlled by internal computer scheduling mechanisms, while the batch processing is still regulated by a master schedule. Most firms form a **users committee** to establish scheduling procedures, guidelines, and priorities, though the actual scheduling will be delegated to someone in operations, such as a **schedule officer** or **production manager.**

Scheduling is not as easy is it may seem. When users are competing for limited resources, tension builds, and tempers may flare when priority conflicts arise. Sometimes computers are **peripheral-bound,** the speed of processing restrained by an input reader, printer, or other peripheral, so jobs backlog. More often, scheduling problems arise because processing demand is unpredictable or the availability of resources is difficult to forecast. Delivery of new equipment, for example, may fall behind schedule, or a breakdown wreak havoc with the master schedule.

The master schedule will include jobs that are processed on a regular basis. The volume of such input and the length of time required for processing is generally known, as is the time the job should be ready, so the job can be scheduled well in advance. When payroll is regularly received by operations at 12 P.M. the last working day of the month, for example, payroll processing can be blocked on the master schedule weeks, even months, ahead.

Not all batch jobs processed on a regular basis need to be as rigidly scheduled as payroll, however. Many weekly or monthly reports can be placed on the master schedule wherever there are open time blocks as long as they are scheduled within a given time period (within the last week of the month, for example). Other blocks of time can be allocated to regular users on the master schedule. Secretaries may be given one hour of processing time mornings and afternoons, and programmers assigned two hours daily.

Many jobs received by a computer center cannot be planned in advance, however, so **day-to-day scheduling** within the master schedule framework is also needed. During bargaining sessions with union representatives, for example, the need for a special report may arise, last minute information may be required to complete a sales bid, or a programmer may need extra run time to meet a deadline. A user may have forgotten to request computer time in advance, or the master schedule may be thrown out of kilter because a job scheduled months ahead is not ready for processing. A crisis atmosphere always seems to pervade computer centers.

To illustrate the dilemma of a schedule officer, let us consider the problem of deciding how to schedule four jobs competing for processing time (jobs listed in Table 15.1). One **scheduling algorithm** that could be applied is first come, first served, also called FIFO (first in, first out), an algorithm used in inventory control. Another option is least-processing-time-first. This is a very common decision rule when the amount of processing time required for some jobs is much less than for others. The rationale here is that users demanding only a second or fraction of a second of scarce processing time should be given priority over a single user wanting to "hog" the resource.

Table 15.1   **Data on four jobs competing for priority scheduling**

Job	Processing time required (units of time)	Arrival	Due date Target	Due date Deadline	Priority class (1 = urgent)
A	3	09.00	Mon.	Tues.	1
B	5	09.15	Mon.	Mon.	1
C	1	09.10	Tues.	Thurs.	4
D	4	09.20	Wed.	Fri.	3

Yet an●ther scheduling possibility is to give priority to the job that has the least slack time between target date and deadline. Or the job with the earliest target date (or earliest deadline date) might be processed first. Using still another decision rule, scheduling could be based on priority classifications, the numerical rating assigned to a job according to its urgency as assessed by the user. According to this rule, jobs classified as 1 in Table 15.1 (and approved by the scheduling committee) are run before the jobs with a 2 priority rating, 2s are run before jobs with a 3 classification, etc.

In Table 15.2 each of the jobs listed in Table 15.1 is scheduled according to the above algorithms. Note that processing order is not always clear cut, for some of the decision rules result in ties. In such cases, more than one rule would have to be applied.

Table 15.2   **Schedules for jobs in Table 15.1**

			Criteria used in scheduling		
First come, first served	*Least processing time first*	*Least slack time first*	*Earliest target date first*	*Earliest deadline date first*	*Highest priority classification first*
A	C	B	A or B	B	A or B
C	A	A		A	
B	D	C or D	C	C	D
D	B		D	D	C

Table 15.2 considers only four jobs competing for processing time. In reality, scheduling is far more complex. Hundreds of jobs need to be scheduled per day in large computer centers, and possible scheduling algorithms are not limited to the six used in the table. Jobs might be processed on a round-robin basis, or priority based on length of wait, elapsed time from request to deadline, processing cost, status of user, length of advance notice to computer center, or any number of factors deemed important by the users committee which establishes the scheduling algorithm(s) for a given computer center. Fortunately, a scheduler does not have to calculate the sequence permutations of all scheduling algorithms in daily operations though there are elaborate models in operations research that claim solutions. Software internal to the operating system of a computer usually does the scheduling, or software packages are purchased so that scheduling can take place automatically within parameters defined by the center.[1] Such software can be overridden manually, enabling an operator to inter-

---

[1]For a good discussion, see the index under scheduling in Per Bruich Hansen, *Operating Systems Principles* (Englewood Cliffs, N.J., Prentice-Hall, 1973). For another discussion, see Harold Lorin and Harvey M. Deitel, *Operating Systems* (Reading, Mass.: Addison-Wesley, 1981), chap. 15.

rupt and change priorities when special circumstances arise. Though the users committee mentioned earlier usually sets guidelines for scheduling, authority is generally delegated to the schedule officer to make on-the-spot decisions when conflicts or problems arise.

Scheduling algorithms can be categorized as either **user-oriented** or **data center–oriented.** That is, some stress service, while others minimize cost or optimize use of computing resources. When weighing the worth and effectiveness of possible algorithms, a users committee must decide what performance criteria are of primary interest and the relative importance of each criterion. Table 15.3 lists performance criteria that are commonly used to evaluate scheduling algorithms.

Table 15.3	Scheduling performance criteria
	User-oriented criteria
	Minimum mean job lateness (Lateness = completion time minus due time)
	Minimum mean job throughtime (Throughtime = job completion time minus job arrival time)
	Maximum mean earliness (Earliness = amount of time job completed before deadline)
	Data center–oriented criteria
	Maximum mean throughput (Throughput = number of jobs processed in a fixed time period)
	Minimum number of jobs waiting to be processed
	Maximum percentage of resource utilization
	Minimum total processing cost

Source: Howard Schaeffer, *Data Center Operations* (Englewood Cliffs, N. J.: Prentice-Hall, 1981), pp. 238–39.

Users should be informed of the decision rules a given computer center uses for scheduling and have access to processing schedules. Since the master schedule is prepared weeks or months in advance, it can be distributed in hard copy. The updated daily schedule should be available on a console or terminal at a convenient location on a need-to-know basis so that users can keep track of the status of their jobs. Many systems provide enhancements to this status output. For example, users may be able to interrogate the system for processing information, such as estimated time a given job run will start or reasons why a job is being delayed.

JOB RUN

Once scheduled, a job must be **run.** This should be straightforward if the operator's manual, written as part of system documentation, is

Figure 15.3   **Job run**

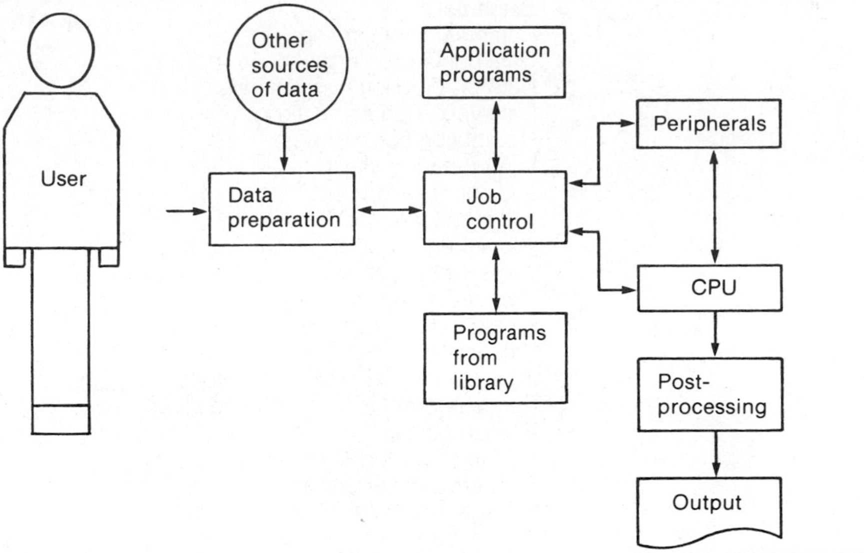

complete and the operations staff is well trained. Before processing, pertinent data and relevant programs must be assembled, and the computer and needed peripherals assigned to the job. Job control (operational parameters) can be automated, manual, or a combination of the two, depending on the sophistication of the computer center. The sequence of run activities is illustrated in Figure 15.3.

Most systems require operators to fill out a number of **forms** when jobs are run. Some are checklists describing what, how, and when steps must be performed. Others are control forms that help pinpoint errors. Table 15.4 is a list of forms commonly used during processing operations. These forms are studied by computer center staff when seeking the solution to problems, and used by performance evaluators and auditors.

The list in Table 15.4 is not all-inclusive. Many firms have supplemental forms to collect processing data for unique needs. Unfortunately, forms have a tendency to proliferate. Management should recognize the cost involved in designing and implementing forms and training personnel in their use. Storage of information and form inventories are also expensive. The need for new forms should be carefully reviewed by management, form design should be assigned to professionals, and strict control should be exercised by evaluators and auditors over each form used. Consolidation and elimination of forms without a loss of processing efficiency and effectiveness should be the goal.

Table 15.4	**Forms used in processing**
	Batch ticket
	Computer problem log
	Data conversion instructions
	Data preparation instructions
	Data validation instructions
	Distribution control sheet
	Input data log sheet
	Job control instructions
	Job monitoring log
	Job scheduling instructions
	Job setup sheet
	Output distribution log
	Problem statement log
	Production control log
	Program maintenance instructions
	Request form for computing services
	Routing tickets
	Shift turnover log sheet
	Software problem report
	Storage maintenance instructions
	Usage log sheet

Processing reports also assist in control of operations. Some can be generated by the operating system. Others are prepared by computer center staff. These should include information on scheduling, work-flow, job execution, down time, resource utilization, and the status of work stations. Like forms, reports have a tendency to multiply. They should be subject to the same stringent standards as forms, so that only data that are needed and used are collected.

OUTPUT CONTROL

In the batch mode, **output control** following a job run consists of checking to see that output specifications formulated during development and listed in system documentation are met. Some controls can be exercised by software, such as accuracy or completeness validation. The scrutiny of operators is also invaluable, for many errors can readily be spotted by eye, such as the wrong format or size of a report, incorrect number of copies, or faulty packaging.

An example of a costly error that could have been avoided by an attentive operator was the mailing of 14,000 duplicate grade reports to a single individual, Mr. L. C. Abel, the first name on a list of students at a university. A programming error caused the output to be a repetition of Mr. Abel's grade report instead of reports for the 14,000 students on the list, but a simple glance at the output by an operator or control clerk would have caught the mistake and saved the university embarrassment and the expense of materials, labor, and postage for the mailing. There are numerous anecdotes of a similar nature in computer literature which are humorous to the reader but not to those involved. These anecdotes serve a useful purpose by demonstrating the importance of output control in batch processing. Many computer centers assign the responsibility of checking all output to an internal control clerk.

Output for an online system is not reviewed by computer center personnel. It is controlled by the user with the assistance of software control checks.

DISTRIBUTION OF OUTPUT

Output for online systems goes directly to the user's terminal, but batch mode processing involves EDP personnel in an additional step: **output distribution.** Delay in a user's receipt of a run can often be traced to inefficient distribution rather than to an overloaded computer, so distribution requires careful planning. Since privacy of output is valued as highly as timeliness by many users, both security of output and speed should be priorities in delivery systems.

PRODUCTION CONTROL

From scheduling, through processing, to distribution to a satisfied customer, a job must be controlled. Computer centers assign the responsibility of job control to a **production manager** for batch processing. The manager also oversees most phases of online processing, though the user will control online input and output.

Activities under the production manager's jurisdiction include:

Input/output (batch)
Processing
Data
Privacy
Security
Costs
Documentation
Library
Supplies

These activities have been (or will be) discussed in other sections of this book, with the exception of library and supplies, which will be considered next.

Library control

A computer center **library** is the repository of data, programs, and documentation. Though security measures are the responsibility of management, a librarian should enforce these measures, so that stored materials are protected, and should control access to the resources to bona fide users only.

One of the librarian's primary duties is guarding resources from fraudulent use. Badges, logging, and check-out on a need-to-know basis can be used to keep resources from the hands of unauthorized users. An example of the latter, restricting individuals in the scope of resources they can access, would be permitting maintenance programmers or analysts to withdraw documentation and programs, but not the operator's manual. In theory, they would then lack the operational knowhow to run an illicit program. Restrictive policies may not be practical in small organizations where a single employee wears many hats, but in large firms, need-to-know is a useful control.

Table 15.5 summarizes the control responsibilities of a computer **librarian.**

Table 15.5	**Responsibilities of a computer librarian**
	To safekeep resources (data programs, and documentation) and backup.
	To ensure resources are updated.
	To control access to resources to authorized personnel.
	To maintain resources in usable condition.
	To record errors and malfunctions experienced by users of library resources.
	To charge, discharge, and log resource use.
	To keep statistics on library uses.

Supplies management

Control of supplies in a computer center is similar to inventory control of supplies in other departments. The computer, however, can resolve shortage of printed header forms if headers are in computer programs and a multifont printer is available for printing needed forms.

Security must be tight for many computer supplies, such as unprinted payroll checks or stock certificates. These must be counted upon receipt, tallied when printed, and a careful log kept of any damaged or destroyed during operations.

UNSATISFACTORY OUTPUT

Thus far in this chapter we have assumed that output meets specifications. Not all jobs pass output control successfully, however. Many need to be **rerun** because of hardware failure (CPU or peripheral breakdown), software problems (bugs, such as mistakes in programming logic), input errors, operator blunders, inadequate documentation, faulty procedures, or lack of controls. Sometimes the environment can be blamed, such as loss of electrical power. It is not always easy to trace what is the matter, why output fails to meet specifications, particularly when a combination of circumstances is responsible for errors.

Isolating the problem, making corrections, then repeating processing can be expensive. Should users be charged for reruns or assessed the cost of finding problem solutions?

Charging users the **cost of reprocessing** when they are at fault has advantages. Too often users are careless in their input preparation and shift the responsibility for finding errors to the computer center rather than controlling input before submitting a job for processing. For example, a receptionist in one user department was responsible for data preparation in free moments when the phone was not ringing or clients at the desk. The need for job reruns dropped significantly when a charge system was initiated, for the department hired a trained data entry clerk and took control measures to ensure that input was correct.

User responsibility for errors is not always so clear cut, however. Should users be charged for program errors due to inadequate user specifications or for poor documentation that has been approved by the user? It would certainly be unfair to charge users for equipment breakdown or operator mistakes.

Since computer centers usually absorb the cost of most reruns, it is in their interest to plan strategies that minimize the need for, and cost of, reprocessing. Stringent operating controls are advisable. The establishment of failure diagnosis and failure recovery procedures is useful. Preventive maintenance of equipment is a necessity. When hardware design or hardware manufacture causes a recurring problem, some firms complain to a higher level in the vendor's hierarchy each time the problem arises, believing this helps prod the vendor into corrective action. Careful analysis of rerun trends may help spot the reasons reruns are needed. One firm found that the rush during peak periods of demand reduced operator efficiency. By scheduling new jobs in off hours when personnel had more time for handling and troubleshooting unfamiliar reports, the number of reruns dropped.

Each firm has a unique environment, so control measures will vary from firm to firm. But all should make a determined effort to find ways to reduce the need for reruns.

In spite of control measures, unsatisfactory output will still occur on occasion. In such cases, if processing procedures are at fault, operators make the necessary corrections and schedule the rerun. If the problem is with the system, however, the job is sent to a committee or individual designated to decide whether program maintenance is the solution or whether system redevelopment is required. Modification will then follow one branch of the flowchart in Figure 15.4. **Maintenance** consists of design modification (Box 8), implementation (Box 9), and testing (Box 10). Satisfactory results lead to documentation (Box 12) and operations (Boxes 1 and 2) and the evaluation cycle (Boxes 3–6). Modification that is not minor (Exit No, Symbol 7) leads to **redevelopment** (Box 13). Redevelopment follows the development cycle outlined in Chapter 9, recycling to operations (Box 1).

SYSTEM MODIFICATION

System modification is needed when system output or results fail to meet user needs because of latent programming design errors, or when the specifications themselves change, requiring corresponding changes in programs and system design. A number of factors might be the cause of the latter, as summarized below.

Modifications imposed by external environment

New laws or changed government regulations are two reasons why systems must commonly be modified. Competitors may also so alter market conditions that system redesign must be initiated. Flexible programs can be written that make modification part of routine maintenance when regular changes in the external environment are anticipated, such as revision of tax rates, but sometimes unexpected modification is required.

Modifications initiated by user management

System modification is sometimes triggered by a change in the management and user environment. A different style of decision making may lead to the need for a different threshold of information (level of information detail). Or management may simply learn to use information systems more effectively. An increase in awareness of a system's potential often causes management to place increased demands on the system. Policies of an organization may change, requiring new methods for calculations, such as new depreciation methods. Or frequent errors and inconsistencies resulting from poor system specification, bad design, or hasty and incomplete testing may become apparent to users when the system is put into operation. A user may also have a wish list of features to be added to the system when finances permit.

Modifications initiated by EDP personnel

A system generally requires modification when new equipment is acquired. For example, more secondary storage would mean a larger data base and increased processing would be feasible. Technological advance in the computer industry is swift-paced. Organizations adopting new technology or merely expanding their systems with more so-

Figure 15.4   **Process of maintenance and redevelopment**

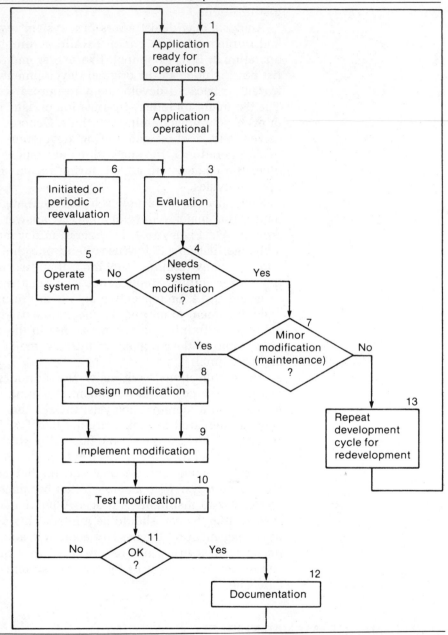

phisticated computers will find that their information systems need modification.

Analysts may detect errors in a system resulting from poor design and implementation or from invalid assumptions once the system is operational. EDP personnel, like management, may also have a wish list not included in the original development because the design was frozen or because development resources were lacking at the time. The list might include reorganization of data, new output form design, or even new programming solutions. Generally, these ideas were conceived and documented during development. Once the system is made operational, the suggestions are renewed and reevaluated, and often the changes are added during regular maintenance or redevelopment cycles.

Every firm needs a policy to differentiate between minor maintenance and major redevelopment, to answer the question posed in Symbol 7 of Figure 15.4. In general, minor modification is defined as a change that affects few users, and one that does not require much effort or many resources (not more than two weeks of a programmer's time, for example). Maintenance jobs can also be defined as routine or expected tasks, or preventive action to minimize errors. Some firms add adjustment to new equipment to the category of maintenance, including the training of user personnel in the new technology. On the other hand, redevelopment requires a major allocation of resources and personnel.

All modifications, both major and minor, should be economically justified. The cost of development is a sunk cost, so the justification is based on a marginal analysis: that is, the marginal cost of modifications compared to their marginal benefits. The same techniques of economic analysis used in the feasibility study apply.

It should be recognized that a system that has been repeatedly modified may become cumbersome and inefficient to operate. One might compare the system to an old car that becomes increasingly unreliable and costly to maintain with age. A point may be reached when the system, like the car, should be junked. This decision should be made by management on the basis of economic and effectiveness factors. In practice, most firms, like car owners, want the latest technology and choose redevelopment or totally new systems before such a juncture is reached.

MAINTENANCE MANAGEMENT

Once maintenance tasks are identified, maintenance responsibility must be assigned and resources allocated. Usually a committee composed of the data base administrator, an auditor, and users' representatives assigns priorities to maintenance requests and reconciles conflicts between user departments, settling jurisdictional problems of maintenance when they arise. The committee also establishes rules of maintenance control. This latter activity is exceedingly important, for statistics show that security violations often occur during maintenance procedures. There is also a tendency to cut corners in maintenance work to get to more exciting projects. Control procedures should ensure that one job is complete before the next is begun.

Even routine maintenance should not skip the steps outlined in the development cycle. Too often stages such as need specification or testing are omitted because of time pressures. This can lead to monumental blunders such as the error mentioned earlier: Mr. Able's receipt of 14,000 duplicate grade reports. This happened because a programmer changed statement numbers when patching a program. Figure 15.5

Figure 15.5   **Partial flowchart of a program carelessly maintained**

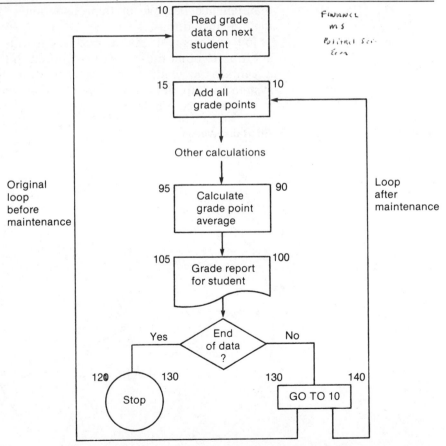

Notes: 1. Numbers to the left of each box are statement numbers before maintenance. Numbers to the right are statement numbers after maintenance.
2. The logic to check for last record and other parts of the program are not shown because it is not relevant.

shows the original statement numbers (to the left of each box) and modified numbers (to the right). Since the "Go To 10" statement was unaltered but the statement numbers had been changed, the program skipped "Read grade data on next student" and the same report was printed 14,000 times. In this case the maintenance programmer omitted an important step: testing. Maintenance procedures also proved inadequate since a supervisor should have caught the error. Errors of this nature can be expensive, disruptive, and ruin a firm's credibility.

One major problem in maintenance management is finding and retaining personnel with the skill and patience needed to trace errors and weaknesses of programs. Correcting, testing, and documenting changes is often less interesting work from an analyst's point of view than attacking a new project. The need for maintenance often results from inadequate documentation, bad design, and unrealistic procedures. Senior programmers and analysts who should be engaged in maintenance because of their experience and skill generally shun maintenance duties.

Job enlargement, giving analysts maintenance responsibilities in addition to other duties, is one solution to this problem. Rotation has advantages as well, for a pool of analysts for maintenance provides system backup and brings a variety of approaches and fresh solutions to maintenance problems.

Figure 15.6   **Effort distribution**

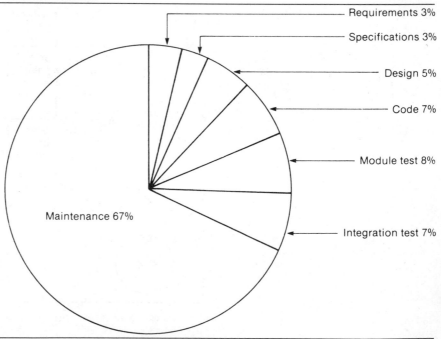

Source: M. V. Zelkowitz, "Perspectives on Software Engineering," *ACM Computing Surveys* (New York: Associations for Computing Machinery) 10, no. 2 (June 1978), p. 202.

Maintenance is very costly and takes a large share of effort when compared to the effort spent in the initial development of an information system, as shown in Figure 15.6. Managers should recognize that there is a strong correlation between high standards in the original development process and low maintenance. To reduce the need for maintenance, system developers should plan ahead for equipment and software compatibility, test thoroughly for system weakness, and maintain high standards of documentation so that the effort needed for future maintenance is minimized.

SUMMARY AND CONCLUSIONS

Processing begins with scheduling and input preparation. Jobs must be run, their output checked, and then delivered to users. Responsibility for these operations differs in a batch environment from responsibility in an interactive online environment, as shown in Table 15.6.

When output proves unsatisfactory, the problem must be identified. If an operational error, the correction can be made by operating personnel and the job rescheduled. If the system is at fault, maintenance

Table 15.6   **Responsibilities for operations in batch and an interactive environment**

Function	Responsibility	
	Batch environment	*Interactive online environment*
Determination of priorities	User committee	User committee
Scheduling algorithm and procedure determination	User committee	User committee
Schedule of jobs	Job scheduling software or production staff	Job scheduling software
Prepare input	User or data entry staff	User or data entry staff
Run jobs	Production staff	Computer (automatic)
Postprocessing	Production staff	User
Check output	User or control staff	User
Distribute output	Production staff	Job dispatch software

(minor changes to the system) or redevelopment (major modification) must be initiated.

Maintenance and redevelopment should follow the development cycle described in Chapter 9 and shown graphically in Figure 15.7. Though maintenance may skip some of the development stages, redevelopment should begin with a feasibility study and follow through to system evaluation, as in the figure. The cycle recommences whenever output or system evaluation is unsatisfactory calling for redevelopment.

Figure 15.7   **Development cycle**

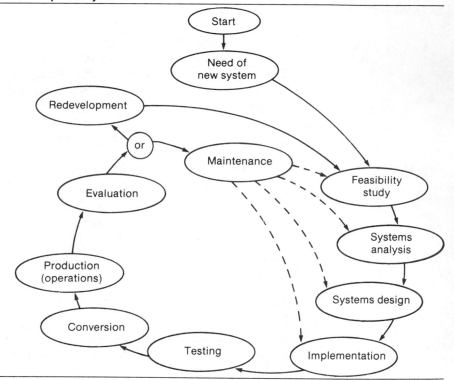

CASE STUDY: SCHEDULING AT TEXAS INSTRUMENTS INCORPORATED*

Texas Instruments manufactures electronic component equipment, including hand calculators. It has annual sales of more than $2.5 bil-

*For details, see Richard G. Canning, ed., "Managing the Computer Workload," *EDP Analyzer* 18, no. 1 (January 1980), pp. 11–13.

lion, employs some 7,800 people and has 38 manufacturing plants in 18 countries.

The bulk of the computer workload is batch, done at the Dallas headquarters on four IBM 3033s and two 370/168 APs which handle 7,000 jobs per day. 1,600 of them are scheduled in advance (up from 250 scheduled jobs in 1974). Over 4,000 unscheduled jobs are requested daily in Dallas between 7:00 A.M. and 7:00 P.M. Even though the work may be done on the firm's 87 remote computers, most of the work is scheduled and prepared in Dallas.

Scheduling is done by the Value Computing, Inc., scheduling system, which is supplemented by production control tools built inhouse. A subsystem of VCI tracks jobs' status and supports revision scheduling.

What are the results of all this automation? In a recent 52 week period, the system delivered 95 percent of all reports on schedule except for three weeks. In manufacturing control, approximately 50 jobs daily were considered late because they fell more than four hours behind schedule.

KEY WORDS

Cost of reprocessing

Data center–oriented algorithm

Day-to-day scheduling

Forms

Librarian

Library

Maintenance

Master schedule

Output control

Output distribution

Peripheral-bound

Processing reports

Production manager

Redevelopment

Rerun

Run

Schedule officer

Scheduling algorithm

System modification

User-oriented algorithm

Users committee

DISCUSSION QUESTIONS

1. A computer center is like a firm. It has to produce a product (information). It needs resources (hardware and software) and raw materials (data) for production. It requires specialized and professional labor. It must price and mark its product, and it must control costs. Comment.

2. Why is the scheduling at a computer center different from scheduling bus routes, policemen on patrol duty, or jobs on a factory lathe?

3. What are the differences in operations in batch mode compared to online processing?

4. Why is forecasting of demand and supply of computing resources different from the forecasting done by wholesalers or retailers?

5. How would you organize rerun problem analysis and correction activities?

6. Who should receive control reports on:
    a. Input?
    b. Output?
    c. Library?
    The production manager? Someone independent of the computer center?

7. What is system maintenance?

8. What is system redevelopment?

9. How are system maintenance and system redevelopment related?

10. How long can the life of an information system be extended by modification and redevelopment? How can the cost-effectiveness of these activities be determined?

11. What is the role and the importance of maintenance programmers? Why is maintenance often an unpopular assignment?

SELECTED ANNOTATED BIBLIOGRAPHY

Canning, Richard, ed. "That Maintenance Iceberg." *EDP Analyzer* 10, no. 12 (October, 1972), pp. 1–14.
This article has a very apt title. The author discusses why more than 50 percent of all programming costs are due to maintenance. Problems of maintenance are described. Two case studies are presented. Though this article is old by computer standards, it is still worth reading.

Lasden, Martin. "Squeeze More Out of Your Hardware Maintenance Dollar." *Computer Decisions* 11, no. 10 (October 1979), pp. 39–42 ff.
The content matches the title.

Leeson, Margorie. *Computer Operations Procedures and Management.* Chicago: Science Research Associates, 1982, 608 p.
This book describes operations of a computing center, with detailed discussions on hardware, peripherals, operating systems, microsystems, and time sharing. It is designed as a text, with each chapter ending with a summary followed by discussion questions, team and group projects, a glossary, and a study guide.

Lister, A. M. *Fundamentals of Operation Systems.* New York: MacMillan, 1975, chap. 8, pp. 91–113.
This text is a good introduction to allocation and scheduling of resources. Also presented are sections on allocation mechanisms, scheduling algorithms, deadlock, and process hierarchies.

Luit, Peter. "Why You Shouldn't Neglect Systems Maintenance." *Canadian Data Systems* 8, no. 2 (February 1976), pp. 37–38.

An excellent brief discussion on the importance of maintenance. Conditions that impair the effectiveness of a system are listed and ways in which companies can organize for maintenance are suggested.

Shaeffer, Howard. *Data Center Operations*. Englewood Cliffs, N.J.: Prentice-Hall, 1981, pp. 190–264.

This book has two chapters relevant to computer operations: Data Center Workflow and Job Scheduling, and Resource Allocation. Many samples of forms used in computer centers are included. The text is detailed, perhaps more appropriate for a professional computer center manager than for a corporate manager.

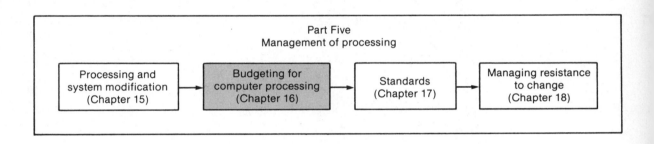

Part Five
Management of processing

| Processing and system modification (Chapter 15) | → | Budgeting for computer processing (Chapter 16) | → | Standards (Chapter 17) | → | Managing resistance to change (Chapter 18) |

CHAPTER 16

Budgeting for computer processing

*More people should learn to tell their
dollars where to go instead of asking them where
they went.*

Roger Babson

Although one-time costs of computing have been treated in earlier chapters, this is the first chapter to deal with budgeting of recurring and operational expenditures. Sections that follow will discuss approaches to budgeting, elements of an EDP budget, problems in costing and pricing computer services, and control measures to keep actual computing expenditures in line with budgeted figures.

APPROACHES TO BUDGETING

There are three possible approaches to computer budgeting. (1) An EDP manager can ask for needed resources, (2) be told the amount to be allocated, or (3) negotiate a budget based on changing demands and priorities from one year to the next.

In the early days of computing, an **asking budget** was common. Since corporate executives had neither background in computing nor experience managing computer centers, the EDP department would present a list of needs which would then be budgeted if the firm had the resources to pay for them. This approach was unsatisfactory since it denied top management the budgetary control exercised over other departments in the organization while it encouraged EDP managers to overstate basic requirements.

The other extreme, with top management making all decisions on spending for computer processing, results in a **telling budget.** This method may not provide sufficient resources for efficient computing, or, when funding is generous, result in panic spending to prevent budget cuts the following year.

Though a dialogue may take place between top management and technical personnel when both "asking" and "telling" budgets are being formulated, a **negotiated budget** based on periodic reevaluation of equipment requirements and operational costs is most responsive to EDP needs and managerial constraints. This latter method of budget preparation is better able to take into consideration the difficulty of making estimates and projections in the field of computing and allows for periodic reassessment of budgets. It also allows for fluctuation in computing expenses (e.g., a large budget one year for acquisitions, the next for development expenditures), and changes in priorities. A disadvantage is that top management and the EDP head must spend a great deal of time and effort in budget preparation, though the time is well spent if it contributes to efficient utilization of data processing resources.

ELEMENTS OF A BUDGET

Table 16.1, an example of **object class accounting,** lists elements to be found in EDP budgets, showing what percentage of the total EDP budget is allocated to each element based on 1980 U.S. industry figures. Some of the elements are fixed costs. Others are line items that vary according to load. (For instance, if the computer is fully saturated during normal hours, extra hours of work will involve overtime pay, a variable cost.) A breakdown of hardware and software costs appears in Table 16.2. Budget elements unique to EDP that need special explanation are discussed below.

Hardware expenditures are difficult to plan when constructing an EDP budget because equipment costs fluctuate from one year to the next. A model which incorporates new features may be considerably more costly than existing models on the market, or a dramatic drop in price may occur due to competitive pressures and savings resulting from innovative applications of technology. The final price will also depend on the type of financing decision reached (rent, purchase, lease) and negotiations over discounts, trade-ins, lease time, service contracts, etc. Flexibility in delivery dates must also be built into hardware budgets because manufacturers may be unsure when new models will be released or may fall behind in delivery schedules.

A measure of uncertainty is involved when budgeting for software as well. Software purchased with hardware may not fulfill needs. One firm, for example, spent $500,000 to develop a FORTRAN and COBOL compiler more appropriate to its command-and-control systems than

Table 16.1   **Elements of an EDP budget (% values are for industrial enterprises in United States in 1980)**

Hardware costs (35%)
  Computer and peripherals
    Purchase, lease, or rent costs
    Overtime charges
    Maintenance
    Insurance

Software costs (6.2%)
  Operating systems
  Teleprocessing monitors
  Packages

Salaries (43%)
  Wages and overtime
  Benefits (taxes, insurance, vacations,
    education, etc.)
  Education for personnel
  Hiring, firing, and moving expenses

Communications (1.2%)
  Equipment (modems, concentrators, voice)
  Maintenance, insurance, and taxes
  Line charges

Supplies (6.5%)
  Tapes, lists, microfilm
  Forms, cards, stock paper, binders
  Office supplies

Other (8%)
  Travel, convention, and conference costs
  Printing, postage
  Utilities
  Journals
  Consulting
  Outside services (time sharing,
    contract programming, etc.)

Source: Adapted from Louis C. Shaw, "Budgeting in 1980," *Datamation* 26, no. 1 (January 1980), p. 128.

the compiler that was supplied. There is also uncertainty whether supplementary packaged software will be available, or whether it will have to be developed in-house. Estimating costs of developing the latter is an inexact art at best. The time required is hard to predict and even salary costs are hard to estimate.[1] Should a programmer resign before project completion, for example, there are hiring costs to consider and a good replacement may demand more pay. Fortunately,

---

[1] For a more confident and optimistic view on software development, see Lawrence H. Putnam and Ann Fitz Simmons, "Estimating Software Costs," *Datamation* 25, no. 10 (September 1979), pp. 189–98. This is the first in a series of three articles which appear in consecutive issues.

Table 16.2   **Hardware and software budget breakdown**

Hardware:
Mainframes	23.5%
Peripherals	22
Minis	13
CPU memories	8
Micros	4.5
Word processing	5
Data communication	5
COM	3
Other	16
	100%

Software:
Operating systems	32%
Specialized packages	19
Compilers	10
Systems software	8
Data base management	8
Other	22
	99%

Source: Englebert Kirchner, "1982 Budget Survey,"
Datamation 28, no. 7 (July 1982), p. 64.

many companies are developing packaged software for the market, sparing individual firms the expense of designing, coding, testing, and debugging their own programs. A separate line item for software packages is common in computing budgets today.

An item not listed in Table 16.1, but one which will affect both hardware and software costs in the future, is word processing. Since the concept of the electronic office is still evolving, this represents still another uncertainty in budgeting. Other innovations and advances in computing present similar uncertainties.

Another problem in computing that is reflected in EDP budgets is that computer technicians are a scarce resource. It may cost more to hire analysts and programmers than other employees, and premium salaries may make EDP expenditures higher than in other departments. Education may also be an expensive EDP line item. Many firms sponsor in-house educational programs to train needed analysts, programmers, data specialists, and operators, or give employees subsidies to attend outside classes or to work toward a degree.

COST TRENDS

Though it is difficult to compare surveys based on diverse industry samples, different methods of offloading computing costs to the end user, or a variety of assumptions regarding cost categories, trends in the cost of components of EDP budgets are, nevertheless, apparent.[2] Unit costs of mainframe computers are dropping. But total equipment expenditures in many firms are on the rise since there is a demand for more and better equipment and sophisticated peripherals are available on the market. For example, intelligent terminals are demanded by clients today—terminals with color and graphic capabilities, voice synthesizers, attached printers, and connections to retrieval units with access to large data bases. Yet the slice of the budget allocated to equipment is still smaller than formerly because other cost components are making proportionately greater demands on budgetary resources. The fact that the total pie is getting larger every year, with EDP budgets growing an average of 10 percent to 20 percent annually,[3] means the increase in equipment expenditures can be absorbed without requiring a larger slice of the total budget.

With regard to personnel costs, it appears that the percentage of computer center budgets devoted to salaries is becoming smaller in spite of rising wages of data processing personnel and inflation. A close look at a firm's overall expenditures may reveal that this reduction can be attributed to a shifting of clerks and analysts to user departments responsible for data entry, operations, and analysis under distributed data processing, rather than to increased worker productivity. The increased reliance on software packages in many firms also reduces the need for analysts and programmers to develop new information systems.

Table 16.3, a comparison of computer processing budget components for 1972 and 1982, reflects these equipment and personnel trends. Note that software costs are on the rise. The budget percentage for software may actually be higher than shown, because software de-

Table 16.3	Computer processing budget breakdown, comparing 1972 and 1982		
	Budget items	1972	1982
	Personnel	47%	36%
	Hardware	39	31
	Software	1	10
	Communication services	5	2
	Media and supplies	6	11
	Outside services	2	5
	Miscellaneous		5
		100%	100%

Source: Englebert Kirchner, "1982 Budget Survey," *Datamation* 28 No. 7 (July 1982), p. 59.

[2]For an excellent analysis of EDP budgets see Englebert Kirchner, "1982 Budget Survey: Making Every Drop Count," *Datamation* 28, no. 7 (July 1982) pp. 57–66.

[3]Angeline Pantages, "1978: Some Budgets Climb, Other Stagnate As Economic Recovery Lags," *Datamation* 24, no. 3 (March 1978) p. 200B.

velopment costs are often buried in personnel costs. The budgets also fail to reflect the rising cost of teleprocessing (especially DDP and WP), software packages, minicomputers, small business systems, and educational services that are assumed by end users.

OPERATING AND DEVELOPMENT COSTS

Where do operating and development costs appear in Tables 16.1 and 16.3? In object class accounting, the salary of programmers, analysts, and technicians would appear under personnel expenses, and equipment or purchased software would be charged to the year the expenditure was incurred or amortized. Under this system of accounting, one cannot easily ascertain development costs of a project, nor isolate the expense of project implementation.

In **expenditure accounting,** an effort is made to assign a cost to each phase of development, such as design, testing, and conversion. This approach enables firms to keep a historical record of costs, and is useful in cost control and accountability, especially when different supervisors have responsibility for various stages of development. This method adds users' costs (time and resources) to those incurred by the EDP department. An effort is made to include the expense of collecting data used during development, since this is a real cost as well. Figure 16.1 shows what percentage of an EDP budget goes to applications development and maintenance compared with other EDP costs.

One limitation of expenditure accounting is that feasibility studies completed before implementation are usually charged as part of EDP overhead, as are programs or subsystems shared by many users or projects. Indirect or hidden costs in project development are also difficult to identify, such as the cost of data management or statistical packages ostensibly provided free by manufacturers when equipment is acquired, but actually included in the rental, lease, or purchase price.

In addition, it is difficult to determine personnel costs, since development effort is not spent in discrete units nor is effort distributed evenly throughout the period of development. Figure 16.2 shows how the need for analysts and programmers changes as development progresses. Of course, there may be variations to this pattern depending on the nature of specific projects, but the figure does illustrate that it would be incorrect to charge a project for full-time services of programmers or analysts throughout development. Most companies plan projects so that technicians can work on more than one project simultaneously, scheduling development so the peak demand for a programmer's services in one project coincides with troughs of demand in others. There are also maintenance, documentation, and redevelopment tasks that can be assigned during lulls of development.

Figure 16.1   **Costs of applications development and maintenance compared to other EDP costs**

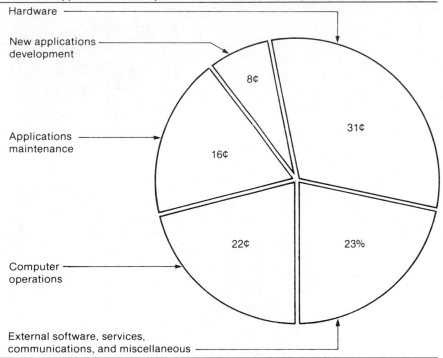

Hardware

New applications development

Applications maintenance

Computer operations

External software, services, communications, and miscellaneous

8¢

31¢

16¢

22¢

23%

Source: David C. Mollen and Van Bakshi, "How to Support Company End Users," *Data Processor* 24, no. 2 (May/June 1981), p. 7.

COSTING

One purpose of accounting is to obtain a measure of control over expenditures. **Costing** provides managers with data for analyzing expenses and for comparing actual versus target costs, while it establishes historical records which can be used as standards or for identifying cost trends. Cost figures can be collected by project (development discussed earlier is an example of a project), by line items (as in Table 16.1), by cost centers (computer room, computer library), or by product (reports, subsystems). There is a cost to costing that should be recognized, such as the cost of data collection and the cost of time for data analysis. Resource requirements for many reports can be generated by computer software, such as reports on terminal and peripheral use, paper consumed, or storage required. But other data collection is labor intensive, such as activity analysis of personnel. There is even a cost factor in planning for costing. However, as a tool for cost control and an aid in making future cost projections, costing is invaluable, and most firms engage in costing activities of one type or another.

Figure 16.2   **Effort distribution of analyst and programmer during system development**

Effort

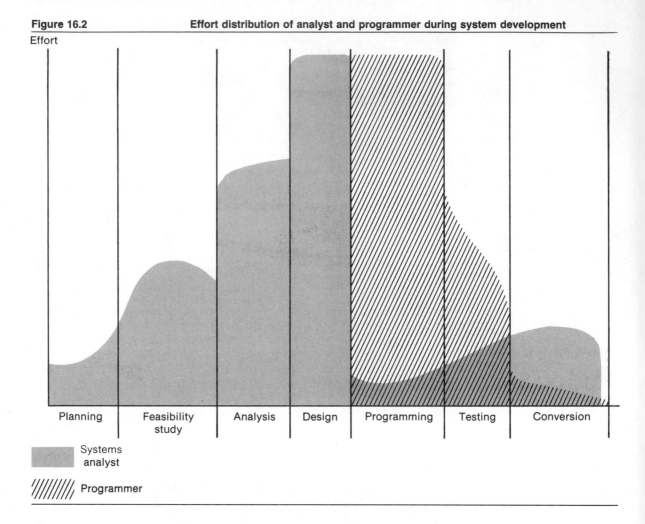

| Planning | Feasibility study | Analysis | Design | Programming | Testing | Conversion |

Systems analyst

Programmer

REVENUES

Thus far we have discussed costs, but these costs must be funded. **Funding** is a very controversial aspect of computer management. Many firms assign computing costs to overhead and do not charge internal user departments. Others develop formulas so departments can be charged for computing services. These two approaches will be discussed below.

Service overhead

Managing a computer center as a free service to departments is a good approach in the early life of a computer installation when skeptical potential users need an incentive to try computing as an alternative to traditional manual processing. Offering computer services as a free good helps reduce employee resistance to the new facility. In this case, the expense of computing is charged to overhead. This approach is appealing because of its organizational and accounting simplicity, though many such **free service** centers do keep records by cost center or user. If the latter, departments may be periodically notified of the cost of their computer time though no actual charges will be made. This has the salutary effect of reducing wastage of computer time, since users generally try to use the computer efficiently once aware of the cost of computer service.

The problem with this approach is that demand soon outstrips available overhead resources. In order to generate income to expand facilities, EDP management or the relevant committee usually starts charging users at this point. Departments are generally willing to pay their share of costs once they recognize the benefits of computing.

Charge systems

When fees are charged for computing services, users must weigh whether the speed and capabilities of computer processing justify the cost, or whether traditional processing methods should be continued. It is argued that this leads to a more rational use of computing resources, reducing waste of computer time which occurs when computing is free. But not all departments in need can afford to pay for computer services. Should selected users be subsidized? On what basis should charges be made?

These questions are not easily resolved but **partial costing** is one solution. For example, development costs might be assigned to computer overhead with users charged only operational costs. This breakdown still does not solve all problems, however. Many firms have integrated applications. How does one estimate a user's operational share? Maintenance poses another dilemma. Some firms assign it to the computer department. Others, to discourage unnecessary maintenance, charge users. Then there is the problem of input data collected by one department for use by others. Practices vary but many firms compensate the data collector to ensure quality collection and input preparation on schedule.

Figure 16.3 is an example of one firm's charge-out structure, though many other schemes are also feasible. Few companies have computing charge formulas that generate profit. It is common for computer departments to bear a portion of computing costs or to draw from the firm's reserve funds when computing costs do not balance revenues.

RATES

An easy method of rate setting is to charge a fixed flat fee per department per month or quarter for computing services, or simply to offer computer access free to users.

Figure 16.3   **Who pays for what?**

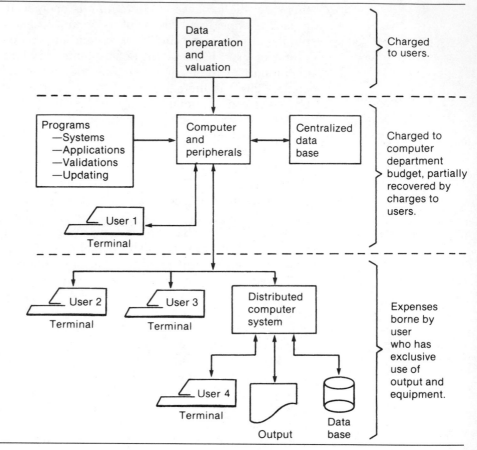

An alternative is to charge operational costs based on formulas for milliseconds of computer time, input read, lines printed, units of data stored, or other such services. Manufacturers and software houses provide users with software including such formulas, though the actual rates charged will have to be adjusted from one firm to another to make computing revenues meet expenses, since firms differ in their equipment configurations, stages of growth, levels of sophistication, and intensity of computer use. And each firm must decide how to charge for EDP overhead as mentioned earlier. Some firms run simulation programs to see how different rates affect revenues when determining rate structures. Others engage in a long period of trial and error before management is satisfied with pricing.

Rate structures can do more than simply provide revenues. They can encourage efficient utilization of resources (e.g., by charging low rates for night processing, surcharges for rush jobs) and be used to support corporate policy. An example of the latter would be setting teleprocessing charges artificially low to encourage the switch from centralized to decentralized processing.

The problem in pricing computer services is that there is often no market mechanism to help corporate management assess the value of information, no competitive structure to regulate charges. In the manufacture of an automobile, costs must be kept low so models will sell. Information is a product too, but the market doesn't provide cost guidelines as for manufactured goods. Indeed, since computing rate structures may be set to reflect corporate policy, pricing of services can be totally unrealistic from a strictly economic viewpoint.

One strategy that pressures computer departments to be competitive in service and price is to allow user departments the option of going outside the firm to a computer service bureau for their computing. This forces the firm's own computer center to root out inefficiency and keep rates low. Many firms also allow computer departments to take on external jobs when they have excess capacity, to sell their services on the open market like a utility. Both practices introduce market mechanisms in rate setting.

A great deal of controversy surrounds rate setting in the field of computing. Philosophical differences exist over questions such as whether computing should be a service or a profit maker, whether computer departments should have a monopoly or users be given free choice, or whether rates should be set to foster centralization or decentralization. Whatever rate structure is chosen, it should be periodically reviewed, since a firm's environment and needs will change in time, as will, perhaps, management's viewpoint.

CONTROL OF OPERATIONAL BUDGETS

Once a project is implemented, **control** of the operational budget of the project is the responsibility of the EDP manager. The first step of control is comparing the planned and authorized budget with actual expenditures for specific categories of costs. An example of such a comparison is shown in Figure 16.4 in which salaries, budgeted and actual, are plotted. This figure is in absolute values, but percentage values or variances might also be graphed. After studying the figures, the EDP manager will try to ascertain reasons why actual expenditures deviate from the budget. A delay in a planned subsystem from August to October might explain why expenditures were lower than expected in August in Figure 16.4, and higher than anticipated in October. November may have been a month with high overtime.

Similar graphs might be prepared for other expenditures, such as

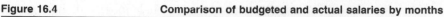

Figure 16.4   **Comparison of budgeted and actual salaries by months**

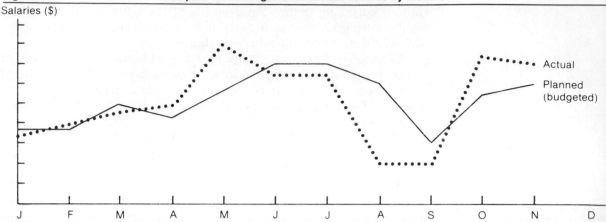

teleprocessing or software, or for costs by function, such as data entry or maintenance. Sometimes reasons for variances can be determined from control software provided by manufacturers at the time of equipment purchase or from programs bought from software houses or developed in-house. Finance and accounting staff can often help explain reasons for discrepancies. Auditors and consultants can also provide insights.

When variances pinpoint a problem, the EDP manager must take corrective action. Examples of such actions are consolidation of files, simplifying procedures, or revamping rate structures to give users incentives to save. Collecting and analyzing control data, then planning changes in operations involve a cost in staff time (and possibly computer time as well) that should be recognized. But most large installations, and those that find that planned budgets deviate greatly from actual expenditures, justify this expense by the savings generated when problems are identified and measures taken to improve operating efficiency.

Control data should also be used to identify mistakes made in planning the budget. When **feedback data** are sent to the development team and project manager, the team can analyze whether faulty procedures were used in formulation of the budget, or whether incorrect assumptions were made. The team can then make recommendations to future development teams that may help avoid a repetition of errors. This feedback cycle is illustrated in Figure 16.5.

Overruns are a frequent problem. These are unavoidable when budget planners lack precise data and must estimate line items (as for salaries when the length of the development period for a new infor-

Figure 16.5 **Control feedback for operations budget**

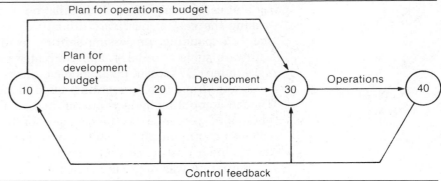

mation system is uncertain), but teams should analyze the cause of each overrun and explore approaches to minimize similar overruns in the future. For example, one firm found changes in user specifications during development were the main cause of cost overruns. By setting a freeze date after which no respecifications would be permitted, overruns were controlled. An improved salary structure to attract and retrain competent personnel proved the solution to time overruns attributed to high programmer turnover.

In both the above examples, the corrective action was a policy decision requiring intervention by top management. But many problems can be resolved by changing the assumptions and priorities of budget planners or by measures that fall within the jurisdiction of computing departments.

SUMMARY

In 1980 it was estimated that the production and use of information provided by computer departments involved 30 percent of the individuals within business organizations. By the late 1980s this figure may jump to 70 percent. Of our GNP, 8.3 percent (or $164 billion) will be spent on data processing by the middle of this decade, according to another recent projection.[4] These figures may well underestimate the full impact of the computer revolution in U.S. business and industry. We do know that EDP is taking an increasingly large share of organizational resources and that the formulation of EDP budgets

---

[4]T. A. Dolotta et al., *Data Processing in 1980–1985* (New York: John Wiley & Sons, 1976), p. 173.

presents many headaches for corporate managers due to the many uncertainties in computing. With inflation and technological advances making the cost of hardware difficult to estimate, applications constantly expanding, processing shifting to the user, delivery dates of hardware subject to delay, and computer personnel in short supply, no wonder EDP budget planners have ulcers.

Certain trends in computing budgets are discernible, however. Though computing budgets are on the rise, the cost of hardware, supplies, and personnel as percentages of the budget have dropped, whereas communications, software packages, conferences, and training are today costing proportionately more.

Computing was originally conceived as a service, charged to overhead at no cost to user departments. This helped reduce employee resistance to computer use and fostered centralization of computing resources. Once demand started to outstrip resources and users were willing to pay for services rendered, charging structures developed. This has encouraged more efficient use of resources and helped finance the expansion of computing facilities. However, other problems have arisen, such as how to set equitable rates for all users. And who should pay for integrated application costs?

Both development and operational expenditure should be periodically reviewed and deviations from the budget analyzed. The budget itself may prove unrealistic, in which case the assumptions and priorities of the budget planners should be studied, the errors identified, and recommendations made to future budget planners so that mistakes won't be repeated. In other cases, corrective action, such as new budgetary controls, may bring expenditures in line.

Budgets should be viewed as guidelines to management preferences and constraints, not as something to "beat." EDP budgeting is conceptually similar to budgeting in other departments within a firm, though line items, forecasting, and control differ.

CASE STUDY: DP BUDGETS FOR 1982*

In spite of the fact that 1982 was a year of recession, a 7.3 percent rise in the average data processing budget over 1981 was reported by respondents to *Datamation's* annual budget survey. Though this represents no real growth when inflation is taken into account, the surprise is that DP has remained relatively unscathed by recession com-

*Source: Englebert Kirchner, "1982 Budget Survey: Making Every Drop Count," *Datamation* 28, no. 7 (July 1982), pp. 57–66.

pared to other basic organizational functions. Drastic fiscal cutbacks did not occur though DP managers might give the opposite impression when asked about spending.

In personnel planning, for example, the average organization expected a 15 percent increase in DP staffing, according to the survey, while total employment was projected to rise only 2 percent. To be more specific, manufacturing companies and government agencies were reported holding the line, but financial institutions reported a DP personnel increase of 24 percent and retailers and distributors an average increase of 13 percent.

When the average DP budget was divided into categories (hardware, software, communications services, outside services, personnel, media, and supplies), no single 1982 category showed more than a 1 percent difference in its total budget share from 1981 figures. There was some variation in spending within these categories but the overall picture showed no change. For example, mainframe spending was down in educational institutions, but more of their budgets was allocated to minis and micros. Operating systems were down from 35 percent to 29 percent of the software budget for small manufacturing and financial businesses, but large users were spending more on such systems. There was no distinct change in software buying patterns either.

The statistics reflect that the novelty of data processing has worn off and that it has become routinized, so entrenched in business operations that data processing is not a candidate for the "last-in, first-out syndrome," not even in the worst financial year since the Depression.

KEY WORDS

Asking budget	Funding
Charge systems	Negotiated budget
Control	Object class accounting
Costing	Partial costing
Expenditure accounting	Rate structures
Feedback data	Service overhead
Free service	Telling budget

DISCUSSION QUESTIONS

1. How does the preparation of a budget for a computing center differ from budget preparation for other departments in a firm?

2. What elements of a computer center budget are unstable and unpredictable? How can the uncertainty be eliminated or reduced?

3. Is budget preparation in a distributed environment easier and more responsive to needs than budget preparation in a centralized environment? Explain.

4. Should a computer center budget be developed bottom-up or top-down?

5. Why is the revenue of a computing center hard to estimate?

6. What is an equitable way to charge for computing services? What are the advantages and limitations of alternative charge systems?

7. Should a computer center budget be zero-based budgeting, or would you recommend some other approach, such as an incremental cost approach. Justify your choice.

8. Which computer center costs do you think should be charged to overhead? Why?

9. A computer center budget often has overruns. Why? How can overruns be controlled?

10. How can software costs be controlled?

11. What are the cost trends in computing? To what factors do you attribute these trends? Are the trends irreversible?

12. Why is it difficult to cost each application and each job in a computer center using standard costing methods?

13. How can the high personnel costs in computing be reduced?

14. How can developmental costs be reduced without affecting quality?

SELECTED ANNOTATED BIBLIOGRAPHY

Bernard, Don, and Richard Nolan. *Charging For Computer Services: Principles and Guidelines.* New York: PBI Books, 1977, 120 p.
This book discusses in detail different approaches to pricing computing services.

Brandon, Dick H. *Data Processing Cost Reduction and Control.* New York: Van Nostrand Reinhold, 1978.
Brandon has written extensively on data processing and is well-known in the field. Part 3 of this book is on budget analysis, including an expense model, ROI analysis, and a presentation of the impact on planning. Part 5 examines user relations, including the concept of standard costs and user charging systems.

Cortado, James N. *Finance, Budgets and Cost Control in Data Processing.* Englewood Cliffs, N.J.: Prentice-Hall, 1980, 287 p.
This book includes sections on planning, how to justify applications and hardware, DP contracts, dealing with vendors, service bureau facilities management, and the development and control of a DP budget. The text is well organized, amply illustrated, and has a pleasing format.

Cotton, Ira W. "Microeconomics and the Market for Computer Services." *ACM Computing Surveys* 7, no. 2 (June 1975), pp. 95–111.

This is an excellent overview and includes an extensive bibliography of 60 references. Discussed are demand (including elasticity and cyclic variations), supply (including economies of scale and integration), product differentiation and market structure, and pricing (including priority mechanisms and the dual role of price). The article is illustrated by the classic economic curves of demand and supply with all the mathematics reserved for the appendix. Highly recommended for serious readers who remember fondly their first course in microeconomics.

Phister, Montgomery, Jr. *Data Processing Technology and Economics.* Santa Monica, Calif,: Santa Monica Publishing, 1974, 573 p.

This book is packed with statistical information on costs, products, and the market of the data processing industry.

Shaw, Louise C. "Budgeting in 1980." *Datamation* 26, no. 1 (January 1980), pp. 126–30.

This article is representative of articles on data processing that appear annually in *Datamation*. All have pie charts and bar diagrams.

Thornley, Michael. "Budgeting, Planning and Control of Computer Activities," in *Handbook of Computer Management*, ed. Ronald Yearsley and Roger Graham. Epping, Essex, England: Gower Press, 1973, pp. 138–50.

This is a typical article on budgeting and includes information that can be found in most handbooks on EDP.

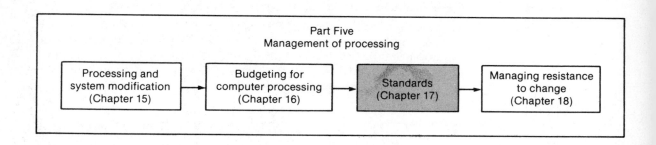

Part Five
Management of processing

| Processing and system modification (Chapter 15) | → | Budgeting for computer processing (Chapter 16) | → | Standards (Chapter 17) | → | Managing resistance to change (Chapter 18) |

CHAPTER 17

Standards

*If you think of "standardization" as the best
that you know today, but which is to be improved
tomorrow—you get somewhere.*

Henry Ford

When measuring weights, time, or distance, we adhere to standards, such as 16 ounces to a pound, 60 minutes to an hour, or 3 feet to a yard. We expect a dozen eggs to a carton, 8 hours to a work day, 100 yards in a football field, and 18 holes of golf. These are standards we all unconsciously accept. Businesses also have standards, such as the Uniform Product Code adopted by manufacturers and retailers. In the field of computer processing, most standards are concerned with work methods and procedures for controlling the productivity and performance of computer installations.

This chapter will discuss the evolution of computer processing standards as well as the organization needed for the creation, implementation, review, and enforcement of such standards. A section on documentation standards is included to illustrate problems in setting and implementing standards. The role of the industry, professional bodies, and both national and international organizations in establishing computing standards will also be reviewed.

EVOLUTION OF STANDARDS

When computers were first introduced, there were no generally accepted guidelines for writing programs, designing forms, or processing output. But in order to use software, one had to accept the premises of the programmer. As a result, according to Norman Sanders,

> Patterns of behavior arose which, with sanction of time . . . became standards accepted by the bulk of programmers.
>
> Eventually somebody discovered that we were de facto using standards, but that they weren't written down and given formal blessing. So the scribes got to work, created standards committees, and offered long careers to their members.[1]

Critics charge that much of the inefficiency, duplication, and incompatibility found in the computer industry can be traced to this slapdash approach to the development of standards in the early days of computing. Today's computer professionals are far more aware of the need for standards, and the computer industry is making a concerted effort to develop standards. The recent development of plug-compatible machines, for example, has helped spur standardization.

TYPES OF STANDARDS

Standards can be classified as **reactive,** a response to a problem or situation; **progressive,** providing a framework for operations; or **retrospective,** based on historical data and experience. Within a single installation, even within a single stage of processing, all three types of standards may coexist.

Figure 17.1 identifies areas of computing which require standards and illustrates the concept that standards should be interlocking. A three-dimensional figure would be an even better representation, since standards in all functional areas should mesh. That is, nonbordering activities in Figure 17.1, such as forms and data, should also interconnect.

Not all computer facilities will have identical sets of standards, because their needs will differ. Some centers may use cards as an input medium. Others may have terminal entry devices. Though most computer installations will have a common core of standards, each will have unique extensions or variations to fit local needs. A description of this core would require more pages than have been allotted to standards in this text[2] but two samples are given in Tables 17.1 and 17.2. The first is an example of a standard for file specification: the second, a standard for the findings of an analyst in the feasibility study. The discussion in the remaining sections of this chapter will be on how such standards are established and implemented.

---

[1]Norman Sanders, *A Manager's Guide to Profitable Computers* (Manchester, England: AMACOM, 1978), pp. 120–21.

[2]For details see Dick H. Brandon, *Management Standards for Data Processing* (Princeton N.J.: D. Van Nostrand Company, 1963), 404 p. For a survey of standards, see C. F. Tilstra, "Standards for Information Systems," *Journal of Systems Management* 29, no. 7 (July 1978), pp. 38–41.

Figure 17.1 **Sets of standards for computing**

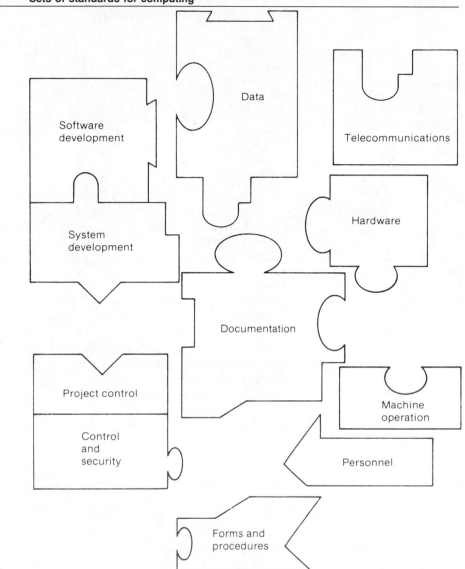

STANDARDS COMMITTEE

In firms with computer facilities, a committee is generally given responsibility for establishing computing standards. This **standards committee** should be a standing committee, not a special ad hoc assignment, because continual creation, revision, and updating of stan-

Table 17.1   **File specification standard**

Each file must have the following data:
   File name
   File label
   File number
   Summary file description
   Source of file
   Disposition data
   Blocking factor
   Record data for each:
      Record name
      Record code
      Record description
      Record size
      Record content for each:
         Element name
         Element number
         Element size (in 8-bit bytes)
   Prepared (initially) by
   Revised by

dards will be required as the firm expands, products change, or new technology is introduced. An additional responsibility of the committee should be assisting management in motivating employees to follow set standards. A work environment should be established in which standards are recognized as helpful discipline, not resented as leading to unnecessary conformity.

Membership in the standards committee should be drawn from upper levels of management in the functional areas served by the firm's computers, and include both users and technical personnel, with outside consultants added as needed.

Table 17.2   **Standard for analyst findings in feasibility study**

Timing: Part of feasibility study
Content: 1. Detailed and summary costs in work-hours and dollars for:
        Development of system
        Annual operation of system
     2. Nonmonetary cost of system for:
        Development
        Operations
     3. Listing of benefits of system:
        Tangible
        Intangible
     4. Estimated duration of project with probability associations
     5. Anticipated problems of development
     6. Evaluation of and comments on:
        Data on which estimates are based
        Any further investigation warranted
     7. Recommendations, if any
To be prepared by senior analyst assigned to project.

The first responsibility of the committee is to develop standards that govern the formulation of standards, i.e., standards for the structure, modularization, and contents of manuals; their physical form and format; standards for indexing and cross-referencing; and even the conventions for writing standards. Then computing standards should be set.

Generally, implementation, maintenance, and operational control of standards is delegated by the committee to a part or full-time **standards officer.** One rule of thumb states that one employee-week per year is required to create and maintain standards for each standard area. Some firms partially automate the control of standards. For example, a manufacturing firm may establish time/cost standards for given tasks, then monitor these tasks by computer through a badge or terminal check-in-check-out process. When operations consistently deviate from prescribed standards, the standard is automatically revised, or a computer report is sent to the standards officer, who then reviews the work. This review may lead to changed procedures, a reprimand to employees, or to recommendations to the committee for revisions of standards.

In firms with a standards committee and a standards officer, new standards will be set and evaluated according to the flowchart in Figure 17.2. But not all firms are so organized. In some firms, managers establish and implement standards in their areas of responsibility. Others have no formal modus operandi for adopting standards. More and more firms are forming standards committees, however, for experience has proven their value.

SETTING STANDARDS: PROCEDURES

Figure 17.3 is a network diagram showing the main activities in setting standards. First, the area where standards are wanting must be identified (activity 5–10). Then management should approve the purpose and potential scope of the new standards (10–20). Usually this approval is based on whether the proposal fits into a schedule of priorities that has been established by management, a plan helpful in controlling the number of new standards introduced and the availability of resources. Priority is generally given to standards that affect accuracy (e.g., data preparation), promote communication (e.g., documentation), or show immediate returns in terms of efficiency (e.g., programming). This screening also helps ensure that systems don't become overencumbered with needless standards.

At this stage, proposed standards may be circulated for comment to personnel who will use them. Since cooperation is essential if standards are to serve their purpose, employees should have a voice in standard formulation. There is no advantage to the introduction of

Figure 17.2   **Organization for setting and evaluating standards**

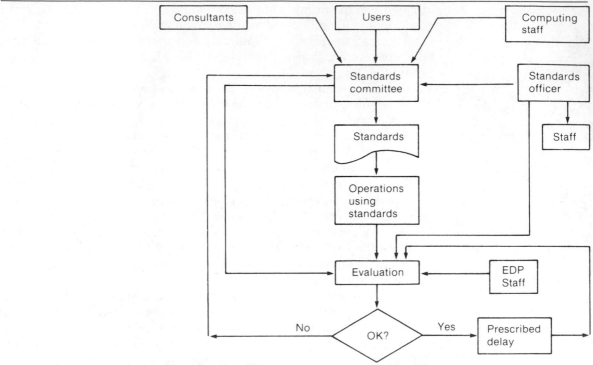

Figure 17.3   **Activities relating to standards**

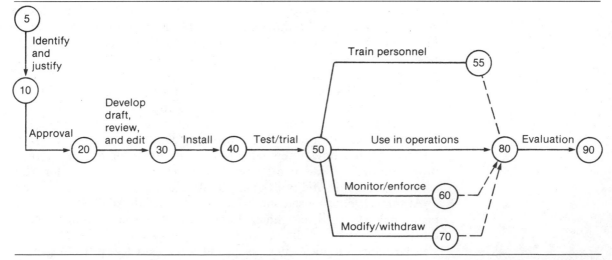

standards if employees are antagonized by them and spend time and effort circumventing them. Often the very process of assisting in the development of standards serves in raising employee awareness of the need for and value of standards, and helps motivate personnel to follow standards in their work.

The standards committee next drafts the new standards (20–30), which are then readied (30–40) and tested (40–50). If satisfactory, the standards are introduced (50–80), monitors are set in place for enforcement (50–60), and employees are trained in their use (50–55). If unsatisfactory, the standards are modified or withdrawn (50–70). Evaluation of operational standards (80–90) should take place periodically or when problems arise.

Detailed activities in the stages of development described by one source are listed in Table 17.3. Firms will vary in how they sequence the activities in this list.

Table 17.3

Activities in the development of standards

Step no.	Description
1.	Identify the area for standardization.
2.	Identify the nature of the proposed standard, within the area.
3.	Identify potential author and collaborators.
4.	Determine scope (i.e., who or what it applies to).
5.	Evaluate justification.
6.	Define purpose of the standard.
7.	Prepare specification, assess priority, and agree with proposed author.
8.	Check who will be affected.
9.	Check who should be consulted.
10.	Assemble material, with consultation.
11.	Check material for compatibility.
12.	Draft the standard.
13.	Check the draft for effectiveness.
14.	Discuss the draft with representative committee.
15.	Obtain formal approval.
16.	Check and agree with those who will be responsible for applying the standards, including agreeing the proving period.
17.	If required, "test run" the standard in one or more locations.
18.	Evaluate the test runs and, on advice from representative committee, decide on: *(a)* withdrawal, *(b)* return to author for modification, *(c)* plan the introduction.
19.	Introduce the standard.
20.	Monitor the justification, compatibility, and effectiveness of the standard during the proving period.
21.	At the end of the proving period, or earlier if experience of using the standard so requires, reevaluate the standard.
22.	From the reevaluation decide whether to *(a)* confirm or *(b)* modify (i.e., return to Step 10) or *(c)* withdraw the standard.
23.	Determine when the standard shall be reviewed again.
24.	At the review date carry out Steps 21, 22, 23, as appropriate.

Source: D. R. A. Coan, *Standards Management* (Manchester, England: National Computing Center Publications, 1977), p. 19.

EXAMPLE: DOCUMENTATION STANDARDS

What types of decisions are involved when setting standards? The first problem is to decide how standards should be structured, as a whole or in modules, and the level of detail to be standardized. In design, for example, should a single design methodology be specified for a given installation? A choice of this nature would be arbitrary, bound to antagonize analysts and programmers, for there is no "preferred" methodology for all situations. Instead, the committee might set guidelines for choice of methodology, specifying the environments most suitable for each choice.

Documentation is an activity that is generally unpopular at computer facilities, but one that is essential to communication and system continuation. There are many tales in the literature of systems having to be redeveloped because an analyst or programmer resigned without leaving adequate documentation for successors to maintain the existing system. Only by setting standards for documentation and enforcing them can such problems be avoided. In doing so the committee must address the problem of structure and level of detail, as stated above.

Modular documentation, easy to use and control, is generally favored by large- and medium-size installations. Operational documentation is typically set in four manuals: a **systems manual**—general information on the system and its objectives; a **programmer's manual**—description of programs; an **operator's manual**—directions for running programs; and a **user's manual**—procedures for use of the system, including data flow diagrams, decision tables, and program descriptions written in terms that users understand. This division allows simultaneous access to documentation information by groups with differing needs. The material to be contained in each manual may be prescribed by the standard's committee or responsibility may be delegated to the development team. Usually abstract, detailed, and summary documentation is required for each manual.

What level of detail should the standards committee set? Symbol shapes for flowcharts? (International shape conventions differ from the IBM template that is commonly used in the United States.) What about character shapes? The look-alikes 5 and S cause confusion, as do the letter I and numeral 1, or letter O and numeral 0. (The Department of Defense convention is to slash the letter O [Ø] whereas many analysts slash the zero. Abroad, the letter O is frequently underlined [O]). Because of the inaccuracies that can result in reading and interpreting alphameric data and codes, documentation standards for input preparation generally do include character shape specifications.

Another example of detail in documentation standards is paragraph structure. Some installations require that the main paragraphs be headed by sequential decimal codes that identify topics and subtopics. It is the view of other committees that such rigidity inhibits creativity, lowers morale, and causes problems in enforcement.

Timing standards must also be set by the standards committee. Completion of documentation might be required one month after a job is operational, or six weeks after acceptance testing, for example. Figure 17.4 shows a standard for documentation that prescribes progressive documentation after milestones in the development process. According to this standard, documentation prepared following the feasibility study is used in testing to ensure that the expectations of the system are fulfilled; design documentation is used during implementation; and the final documentation (operational and systems documentation) serves as the basis for operations and maintenance.

Few standards committees have the time to set standards for all functional areas of a large installation, so they delegate this responsibility to others. The problem is deciding who should set, evaluate, and implement standards. In documentation, should an analyst, programmer, user, or outside consultant prepare manuals? Should computer programs automate documentation, such as AUTOFLOW in flowcharting? Who should evaluate and test documentation, take custody of manuals, assign and control manual access, and be responsible for updating and revisions? The standards committee however, is generally the body responsible for deciding what control measures should be adopted to ensure documentation standards are followed, where manuals are stored, and who is authorized to use and modify documentation.

Programmers and systems analysts generally dislike documentation for it is a tedious and time-consuming task. They often argue that they

Figure 17.4   **Documentation at different stages of development**

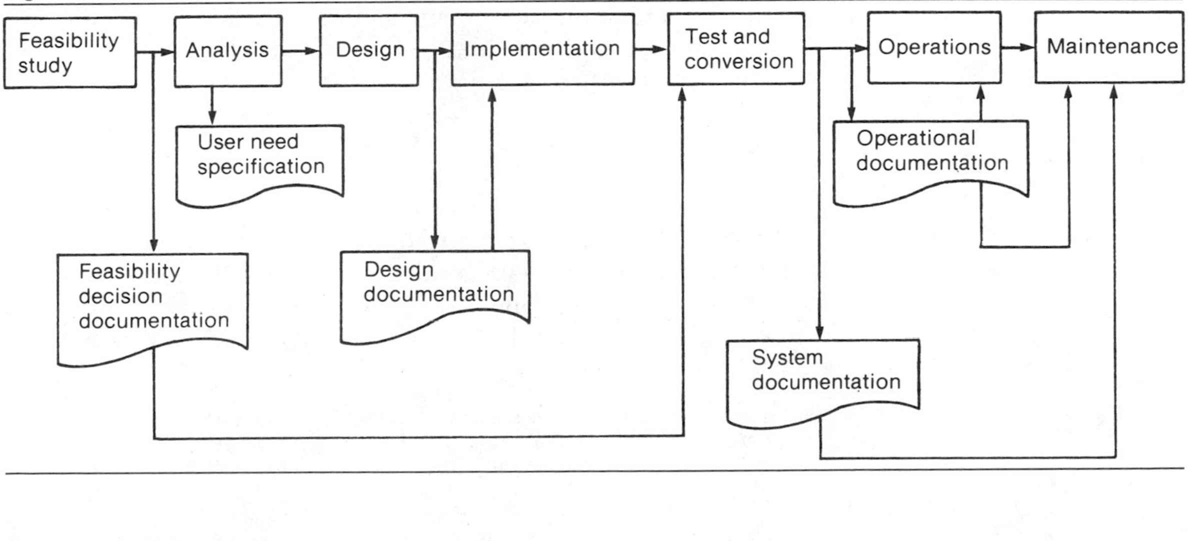

are too busy or that documentation should wait until the system stabilizes. Since systems are constantly redesigned, such stabilization
rarely occurs, so documentation tends to be indefinitely postponed.
Some companies will contract for system development at a 20 percent
reduction in cost if no documentation is required. Acceptance of such
a proposition is penny-wise and pound-foolish, for documentation is
too important to be compromised in this manner. A major responsibility of the standards committee is to educate both employees and
management as to the importance of documentation standards—indeed of all standards set by the committee. For example, in pointing
out the value of documentation standards, the committee should
stress that standards:[3]

1. Ensure that all commitments and expectations are on record.
2. Provide a package to help initiate and train newcomers to the sys-
    tem.
3. Provide a package that will provide information needed to change
    the system should the environment or management's needs alter.
4. Prevent system dislocation and cost that might otherwise occur if
    knowledge of the system were centered in a few individuals who
    resigned, relocated, or were subsequently reassigned to other du-
    ties.
5. Provide a package to facilitate routine evaluation, auditing, and
    control.

An equally strong case could be made regarding the importance of
standards for all of the components of an information system. It is
obvious that no firm can permit secretaries to organize unique filing
systems or programmers unique symbol sets. The problem is recognizing the fine line between standards that promote productivity and
those that stifle creativity. The objective should be a set of standards
that facilitate communication, control, and compatibility—standards
that employees recognize as useful in promoting efficiency and effectiveness in operations.

COST/BENEFITS

In assessing the **cost of standards,** the salary of the standards officer, committee time, and secretarial expenses in drafting, typing, editing, and reviewing/updating standards should be calculated. There
is also a cost to enforcement of standards and employee training, and

---

[3]For more on documentation, see J. Van Duyn, *Documentation Manual* (Philadelphia: Auerbach Publishers, 1972), 158 p., and Larry L. Long, *Data Processing Documentation and Procedures Manual* (Reston, Va.: Reston Publishing, 1979), 239 p.

a price to be paid for greater conformity and reduction of choices, though the latter, in particular, is difficult to quantify.

Benefits include:

Better communication.

Quicker training.

Improved utilization of computing resources.

Portability of data, procedures, equipment, software, personnel, sometimes even subsystems or entire systems.

Guidelines for training.

Ease, speed, and less expense in maintenance of programs and systems.

Improved planning, control, and security.

SOURCES OF STANDARDS

Thus far the discussion has related to standards developed inhouse. These need not be unique, for there are many books and manuals to assist Standards Committees and procedures can be copied from organizations with similar environments. In addition to in-house standards, many standards are set by industry, or originate in professional or national organizations. Figure 17.5 shows sources that have made major contributions to computing standards in the United States. Compliance with standards set externally is usually in a firm's interest, ensuring compatibility with other firms and often reducing costs. Examples of standards set externally will be given in the concluding sections of this chapter, with one standard, the Data Encryption Standard, discussed in detail to provide an insight into the controversy which often accompanies the development of industry-wide standards.

Industry standards

One example of an **industry standard** is the magnetic ink character (MIC) found on the base of checks, a standard adopted by the banking industry. Use of MIC speeds processing, because checks can pass through a machine which reads the data, then sorts and routes checks according to the preprinted magnetic ink codes.

Another industry standard familiar to most readers is the Universal Product Code (UPC) found in retailing. This standard was developed by the Symbol Standardization Subcommittee of the Uniform Grocery Product Code Council Inc. to speed grocery checkouts.[4] Scanning

---

[4]For more on the UPC and its development, see D. Savir and G. H. Laurer, "The Characteristics and Decodability of the Universal Product Code," *IBM Systems Journal* 14, no. 1 (1975), pp. 16–34.

Figure 17.5   **Sample sources for computing standards in the United States**

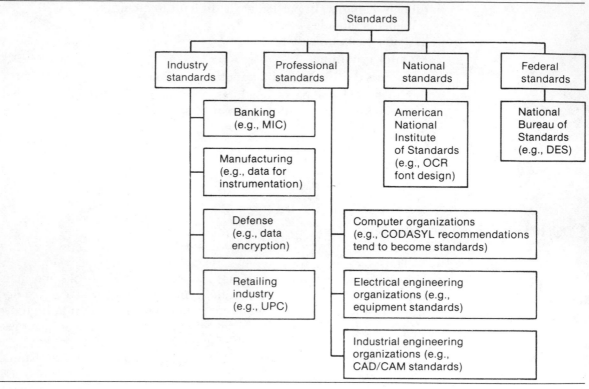

equipment reads the product identification code, which is fed to a computer to ascertain retail price and maintain other control information.

Yet another example is the agreement on common technical standards which precedes the launching of most electronic products. But agreements in electronics stick only when a major company leads the way, or when consumers demand compatible products. For example, the attempt by some small firms to get a standard accepted for the size of disk memories failed, but the introduction of the PC (personal computer) by IBM may well become the standard for personal computers for other manufacturers to follow.

Professional organizations

Among **professional organizations** concerned with standards in computing, CODASYL (Conference on Data Systems Languages) is perhaps best known. This group has contributed basic concepts to COBOL that have been widely accepted. CODASYL has also worked somewhat less successfully on the development of specifications for data base management systems.[5]

National institutes

The **American National Standards Institute (ANSI),** a nonprofit organization with 750 companies as dues-paying members, is a national organization that is concerned with standards in many scientific and technical fields. Though this organization was founded only in 1969, it had forerunners under different names: American Engineering Standards Committee founded in 1918; American Standards Association founded in 1928; and United States Standards Institute founded in 1966. Figure 17.6 shows the broad range of ANSI activities in developing standards for computers and information processing. Of special interest to business programmers is the subcommittee X3J4 on COBOL, which is working in close affiliation with CODASYL to revise COBOL. Table 17.4 is just a partial list of standards developed by ANSI affecting computer management in business.

Federal government

The federal government also plays a major role in formulating computer standards. For example, federal information processing standards include codes for states, countries, and calendar dates to facilitate information exchange between federal agencies, and these codes have become adopted in the private sector.

The **National Bureau of Standards (NBS)** is another body that has had significant impact on the computer industry. It is currently promoting DES, an encryption standard developed in 1974 for the Bureau by IBM, for coding unclassified government data.[6]

Controversy over DES illustrates the problem of gaining widespread acceptance of any new standard, for there is always disagreement in professional circles when new standards are promulgated. In this case, allegations were made when DES was first introduced that the code was too short, that pressure from the National Security Agency limited DES to a 56-bit code when a key size of 64 bits would have been more secure. Though a Senate select committee on intelligence investigated the allegations and found the code to be free from any statistical or mathematical weakness, critics were not silenced. The claim that the code, with 100,000 million combinations, would require 2,000 years to test all possible keys at one test per microsecond was challenged by opponents such as Martin Hellman and W. Diffie,

---

[5]See James P. Fry and Edgar Sibley, "Evolution of Data Base Management Systems," *Computing Surveys* 6, no. 1 (May 1978), pp. 25–33. This issue is devoted entirely to data base management systems and has many references to the CODASYL approach to DBMS.

[6]A technical summary of the encryption algorithm is available at Software Division, Code 193, Technology A265, National Bureau of Standards, Washington, D.C., 20234.

Figure 17.6   **Organization chart for ANSI (as of 1978)**

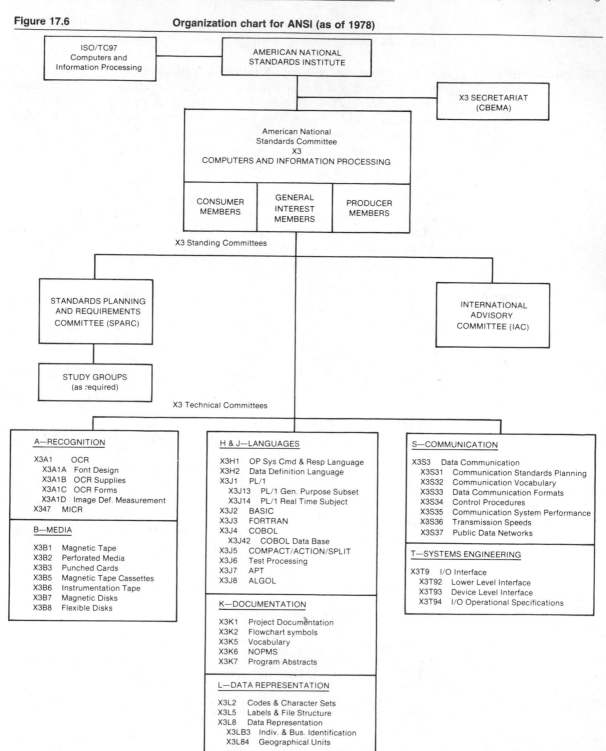

Table 17.4	**Partial list of ANSC–X3 standards (as of 1974) on computers and information processing**

X3.1–1969	Synchronous Signaling Rates for Data Transmission
X3.2–1970	Print Specifications for Magnetic Ink Character Recognition
X3.3–1970	Bank Check Specifications for Magnetic Ink Character Recognition
X3.4–1968	Code for Information Interchange
X3.5–1970	Flowchart Symbols and Their Usage in Information Processing
X3.6–1965	Perforated Tape Code for Information Interchange
X3.9–1966	FORTRAN
X3.10–1966	Basic FORTRAN
X3.11–1969	Specifications for General Purpose Paper Cards for Information Processing
X3.12–1970	Vocabulary for Information Processing
X3.14–1972	Recorded Magnetic Tape for Information Exchange
X3.15–1966	Code for Information Interchange in Serial-by-Bit Data Transmission
X3.16–1966	Character Structure and Character Parity Sense for Serial-by-Bit Data Communication in the American National Standard Code for Information Interchange
X3.17–1966	Character Set for Optical Character Recognition
X3.18–1967	One-Inch Perforated Paper Tape for Information Interchange
X3.19–1967	Eleven-Sixteenths Inch Perforated Paper Tape for Information Interchange
X3.20–1967	Take-Up Reels for One-Inch Perforated Tape for Information Interchange
X3.21–1967	Rectangular Holes in Twleve-Row Punched Cards
X3.22–1973	Recorded Magnetic Tape for Information Interchange (800 CPI, NRZI)
X3.23–1968	COBOL
X3.24–1968	Signal Quality at Interface between Data Processing Terminal Equipment and Synchronous Data Communication Equipment for Serial Data Transmission
X3.25–1968	Character Structure and Character Parity Sense for Parallel-by-Bit Communication in the American National Standard Code for Information Interchange
X3.26–1970	Hollerith Punched Card Code
X3.27–1969	Magnetic Tape Labels for Information Interchange
X3.28–1971	Procedures for the Use of the Communication Control Characters of American National Standard Code for Information Interchange in Specified Data Communication Links
X3.29–1971	Specification for Properties of Unpunched Paper Perforator Tape
X3.30–1971	Representation for Calendar Date and Ordinal Date for Information Interchange
X3.31–1973	Structure for the Identification of the Counties of the United States for Information Exchange
X3.32–1973	Graphic Representation of Control Characters of ASCII
X3.34–1972	Interchange Rolls of Perforated Tape for Information Interchange
X3.38–1972	Identification of States of the United States (including the District of Columbia) for Information Interchange
X3.39–1973	Recorded Magnetic Tape for Information Exchange
X3.40–1973	Unrecorded Magnetic Tape for Information Interchange
X2.34–1959	(To be redesignated as an X3 standard) Method of Charting Paperwork Procedures

who argued that with faster computers and parallel processing the code could be broken in 12 hours.

The NBS then convened a panel of experts to reevaluate the code. They concluded that a computer costing $50–70 million might break the code, but the likelihood of success would be only 10–20 percent.

In 1978, however, Hellman described to a national computer conference how a conventional computer costing $4 million could break DES in 24 hours.[7] He argued that a 128-bit code was needed to ensure code security. But according to IBM, two DES chips can simulate a 128-bit code so that the 56-bit key in the DES is not a weak link in the security chain.[8]

The debate over DES continues to rage with cryptographers proposing alternatives, such as Hellman's public key system being developed at Stanford. The argument has served a purpose, for the DES algorithm has been publicly validated, but the public interest may have been hurt in the long run because many firms have delayed adoption of a needed encryption standard due to the controversy. And no firm has been willing to finance development of an alternative to DES.[9]

International standards

ANSI represents the United States in TC97, the Technical Committee of the **International Standards Organization (ISO).** This is a private body affiliated with the United Nations, its membership drawn from most of the countries of the world. *TC97* has 130 specialized committees, many of which are related to computing, as shown in Figure 17.7. *X25*, a standard for teleprocessing (interconnections for a public data network) is one example of a standard being developed by the ISO that will have far-reaching repercussions. For example, EFT, electronic mail, and teleconferencing will all be affected by the standard.

The **Organization of Economic Cooperation and Development** is another body that is concerned with international standards. Studies on transborder flow and privacy of information are among the problems being addressed by this organization.[10]

Though many of the standards adopted in the United States have

---

[7]W. Diffie and Martin E. Hellman, "Exhaustive Cryptanalysis of the NBS Data Encryption Standard," *Computer* 10, no. 6 (June 1977), p. 74.

[8]D. E. Denning and P. J. Denning, *Computing Surveys* 11, no. 3 (September 1979), p. 244.

[9]For an excellent discussion and bibliography on data encryption, see "Data Encryption: Is it for You?" *EDP Analyzer* 16, no. 12 (December 1978), pp. 1–13.

[10]See D. Firnberg, "Security Standards for Transborder Data Flows," in OECD, *Transborder Data Flows and the Protection of Privacy* (Paris, France: Organization for Economic Cooperation and Development, 1979), pp. 65–68.

Figure 17.7   **Organization structure of the International Standards Organization, Technical Committee 97**

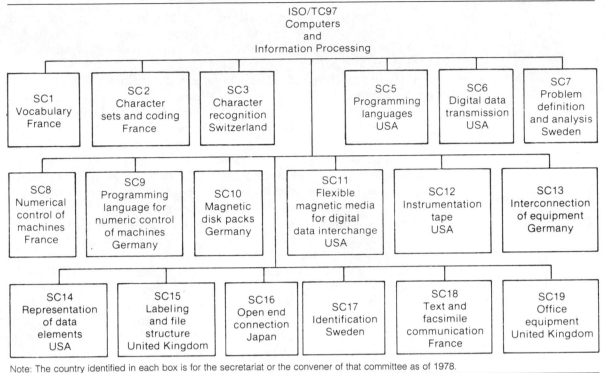

Note: The country identified in each box is for the secretariat or the convener of that committee as of 1978.

been embraced abroad, we have not always been successful in winning foreign converts. COBOL, for example, is not the standard for business processing in European countries.

Getting agreements on international standards is a difficult process because each delegate has a vested interest in promoting standards implemented at home. The speed of advance in computer technology accentuates the problem since the machinery for getting international agreements on standards is too cumbersome to keep pace.

SUMMARY

According to many experts, incompatibility of computer systems will be a major problem of the 80s. But James Martin, an authority on telecommunications, sees a solution.

In the long run, there is a way out of the maze, and that is standardization.[11]

Formulation of standards within a firm may be the responsibility of a standards committee or a standards officer or both. Industry, professional groups, and both national and international organizations also contribute to computing standards.

It should be recognized that the term *standard* has a slightly different meaning at each of these levels. Firms develop standard practices or guidelines for in-house operations, such as guidelines for documentation, which they refer to as standards. Industries, standard institutes, or governments develop standards of an entirely different nature, such as length of a second, or rules for FORTRAN 77. Professional organizations, such as CODASYL, propose computing specifications which they hope will become adopted as a FIPS (Federation of Information Processing Standards) or ANSI standard. A manufacturer may produce a product that becomes a de facto standard. Businesses may sign an agreement to adopt a common method of operations, creating standards such as UPC.

In each of these cases, the nature of the standard, the procedure for setting the standard, and the obligation of individuals to follow the standard differs. But all standards have a common purpose: to promote communication so that groups within and between firms can integrate operations and compare results, and to contribute to productivity by providing guidelines for products or operations. Most computer professionals recognize that standards are a prerequisite to orderly, efficient, and effective growth of data processing.

A major problem is motivating employees to follow set standards since conformity and discipline are not popular concepts. There is also a cost to standards: staffing, training, implementation, and updating. But:

> You have two choices with standards: either you pay for them or you pay later for not having them.[12]

CASE STUDY: UPC, A STANDARD IN RETAILING*

The Universal Product Code (UPC), a bar code used for optical scanning of products in grocery stores, is one example of a national

[11]"Interview: At Home with James Martin," *Computer World* 14, no. 38 (September 17, 1980), p. 118.

[12]Dick Brandon, quoted by D. R. A. Coan, *Standards Management* (Manchester, England: National Computing Center Publications, 1977), p. 1.

*Source: D. Savir and G. J. Laurer, "The Characteristics and Decodability of the Universal Product Code Symbol," *IBM Systems Journal* 14, no. 1 (December 1975), pp. 16–34.

standard. This standard was developed when grocers throughout the country recognized their common interest in designing a nationally accepted code for precise point-of-sale data capture. Increased grocery checkout productivity and inventory control were two of the benefits which grocery store managers hoped to derive from the standard. Reduced consumer waiting and service time were other advantages.

A subcommittee of the Uniform Grocery Product Code Council Inc., a council composed of representatives of grocery distributors and supermarket chains, was assigned responsibility for soliciting and reviewing code proposals. The subcommittee engaged McKinsey and Co., Inc. as consultants and prepared code specifications. These were:

```
Mode . . . . . . . . . . .    Online real time
Size of code  . . . . . . .    12 decimal characters
Area of symbol . . . . . .⩾1.5 square inch
Speed of scanning . . . . .⩾100 inch/second
Scanning reject rate  . . . .⩾0.01 percent
Undetected error rate  . . .⩾0.0001 percent
Normal conditions of abrasion and dirt allowed.
```

Samples of designs submitted and the code selected by the council are shown below. The UPC code is used extensively in the United States and Canada. Many countries abroad have been considering adoption of the UPC standard as well.

Sample proposals

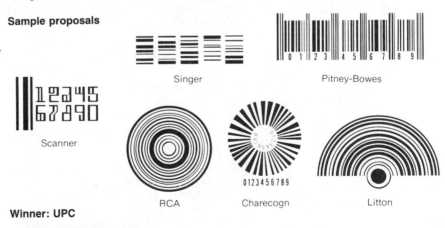

Singer

Pitney-Bowes

Scanner

RCA

Charecogn

Litton

Winner: UPC

IBM

KEY WORDS

American National Standards Institute (ANSI)

Cost/benefits of standards

Documentation

Industry standard

International Standards Organization (ISO)

National Bureau of Standards (NBS)

Operator's manual

Organization of Economic Cooperation and Development (OECD)

Professional organizations

Programmer's manual

Progressive standards

Reactive standards

Retrospective standards

Standards committee

Standards officer

Systems manual

User's manual

DISCUSSION QUESTIONS

1. Standards are expensive to institute, difficult to enforce, unpopular with users, and disruptive in implementation. Comment.

2. At what stage of the development of an information system should one start thinking of standards?

3. Who should initiate standards for a computer center? Someone within the computer center, someone within the organization but in another department, or an outside consultant? Explain.

4. Comment on the following statement: The benefits of standards are largely intangible. Does it matter that a cost/benefit ratio for standards cannot be calculated?

5. How can one determine whether expenses for a standards program are justifiable?

6. How do standards depend upon:
   a. Size of computing center?
   b. Complexity of applications portfolio?
   c. Number of users?
   d. Industry?
   e. Clients?
   f. Maturity of computing center?
   g. Computer executive?

7. Do we need standards for standards? Do we need to control standards? Explain.

8. Under what circumstances would a firm adopt local standards which differ from standards adopted by:

   a. The firm's own computer center?
   b. The industry the firm represents?
   c. National standards organizations?
   d. International standards organizations?

9. Under what circumstances should standards be mandated by:
   a. The industry of the firm?
   b. Computer professional organizations?
   c. National standards organizations?
   d. International standards organizations?

10. Who should be responsible for the enforcement of standards? Should this be an ongoing responsibility, should spot checks be the norm, or should controls wait until something goes wrong?

11. Explain how standards help:
    a. Avoid disasters.
    b. Improve performance.
    c. Control operations.
    d. Assist in employee training.
    e. Contribute to good working habits.

12. Should we have standards for:
    a. Performance?
    b. Procedures?
    c. Design?
    Are these areas too intangible and variable to be standardized?

SELECTED ANNOTATED BIBLIOGRAPHY

Brandon, Dick H. *Management Standards for Data* Processing. Princeton, N.J.: D. Van Nostrand Company, 1963. 404 p.
   In the late 1960s and early 1970s, this was a reference used by many computer center directors. It details standards for systems analysis, programming, operations, installation, equipment, personnel, performance, and punched card installations. This book, though old, is still a useful standards reference.

Card, Chuck, et al. "The World of Standards." *Byte* 8, no. 2 (February 1983), pp. 130–42.
   Excellent on the organization of national and international standards. The article helps the reader "better appreciate the importance of standards and the standard process to our technological world."

Coan, D. R. A. *Standards Management*. Manchester, England: NCC Publications, 1977. 199 p.
   This thin soft-covered book, sponsored by the British National Computing Center Ltd., discusses the need for standards and the planning, implementation, operation, control, and staffing of a standards program. Though examples from the United Kingdom are used, the material is applicable to U.S. businesses.

Long, Larry E. *Data Processing Documentation and Procedures Manual.* Reston, Va.: Reston Publishing, 1979. 239 p.

This book includes chapters on the documentation of a feasibility study, standards for systems analysis and design, programming, conversion, implementation, evaluation, hardware and software selection, structural organization, personnel, training, and career development. There is also a good discussion of documentation principles, practices, and uses.

Szweda, Ralph A. *Information Processing Management.* Princeton, N.J.: Auerbach Publishers, 1972, 612 p.

Chapter 4 is on management control through the use of standards. Discussed are benefits and enforcement of standards as well as guidelines and examples of standards for charting, programming. operations, and documentation. This chapter constitutes one sixth of the book, reflecting the importance Szweda places on standards.

Tebbs, David. "Control and Management Standards," in *Handbook of Computer Management*, ed. L. Yearsley and R. Graham. Epping, Essex, England: Gower Press, 1973, pp. 169–81.

The article is a good survey of standards including the standard program, its organization and maintenance, and the structure of manuals. Examples of standards for project control are given.

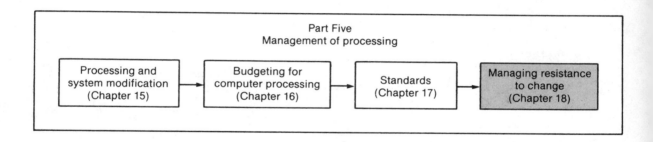

Part Five
Management of processing

| Processing and system modification (Chapter 15) | → | Budgeting for computer processing (Chapter 16) | → | Standards (Chapter 17) | → | Managing resistance to change (Chapter 18) |

CHAPTER 18

Managing resistance to change

More than machinery, we need humanity.
Charlie Chaplin, in the film *Modern Times.*

Over 400 years ago, Machiavelli observed:

> It must be considered that there is nothing more difficult to carry out, nor more doubtful of success, nor more dangerous to handle, than to initiate a new order of things. For the reformer has enemies in all those who profit by the old order, and only lukewarm defenders in all those who could profit by the new order. This lukewarmness arises partly from fear of their adversaries, who have the laws in their favor, and partly from the incredulity of mankind, who do not truly believe in anything new until they have had an actual experience of it.[1]

Resistance to a new order has not lessened in this century. Indeed, the pace of the technological revolution has heightened fears that humans are becoming subservient to machines, stiffening resistance to technology that threatens to disrupt the status quo. This threat is perceived in information systems which incorporate advances in process control, microtechnology, teleprocessing, robots, graphics, voice recognition, distributed processing, and word processing. Implementation of change in computing, as in other fields, does not require the guile of a Machiavelli, but one does need to identify and analyze why employees oppose innovations and one needs to develop strategies to promote acceptance of change. Figure 18.1 is an overview of the stages in the management of change. These stages will be discussed in the following sections of this chapter.

---

[1]Machiavelli, *The Prince*, translated by Luigi Rice, revised by E. R. P. Vincent (New York: New American Library, 1952), pp. 49–50.

Figure 18.1   **The management of change**

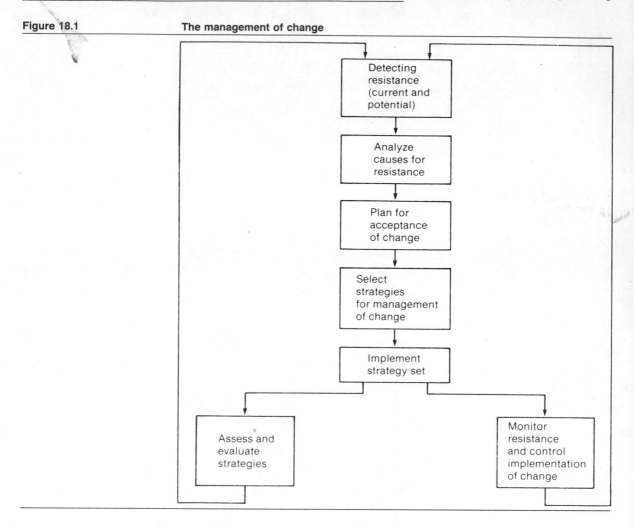

RESISTANCE IN A COMPUTER ENVIRONMENT

A drop in production, failure to meet deadlines, absenteeism, mounting employee turnover, complaints and low morale, and a reluctance to learn new job skills are all symptoms of employee resistance to change. What makes human resistance to computers different from the antagonism felt toward machines, an antagonism that has existed since the industrial revolution, is that software adds a new dimension to the conflict. Today, one must add human-software interface, machine-software interface, and human-machine-software inter-

Figure 18.2   **Relationship between human, machine, and software**

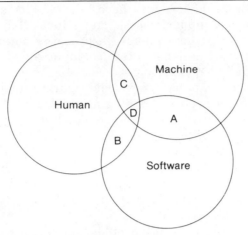

Area A = Machine-software interface.   Area C = Human-machine interface.
Area B = Human-software interface.   Area D = Human-machine-software interface.

face to the problem of human-machine interaction, as shown in Figure 18.2.[2]

Human factors, sometimes referred to as **human engineering** or **ergonomics,** is a field in which human-machine interrelationships are studied.[3] European research focuses on physiological considerations, such as fatigue, breathing rates, and pupil size when operating machines, whereas the American emphasis is more on psychological factors. On both sides of the Atlantic, recommended solutions to improve the computing environment can sometimes seem quite mundane though they are important considerations. For example, it is recommended that work stations be comfortable and pleasing, for the arrangement of furniture and work space around a terminal can affect user morale and an inconvenient layout may contribute to employee errors. The size of terminal keys, the angle of the screen, flicker, and the color of displays are all factors that may affect production.

When designing EDP equipment and developing software, many human engineering problems arise from the fact that users have a

---

[2]For more on this subject, read Gloria Grace in her preface to a special issue of *Human Factors* 12, no. 2 (March–April 1970), pp. 161–64.

[3]See Thomas Martin, "The User Interface in Interactive Systems," in *Annual Review of Information Science and Technology,* vol. 8, ed. Carlos A. Cuadra. (Washington, D.C.: American Society for Information Sciences, 1973), pp. 203; and K. D. Eason, L. Damodaran, and T. M. Stewart, "Interface Problems in Man-Computer Interaction," in *Human Choice and Computers,* ed. E. Mumford and H. Sackman. (Amsterdam, Netherlands: North-Holland Publishing, 1975), pp. 91–105.

wide range of background knowledge and experience.[4] The same hardware devices may have to serve clerks (who use terminals primarily as input devices), professionals (analysts and programmers), managers (whose interest in primarily output), and specialists (such as product designers using computer-aided design). It should be recognized that nonprofessionals often have difficulty communicating with a computer. They may require interactive and conversational modes,[5] or special training materials and documentation in order to take full advantage of the potential of computers in problem solving, features that technicians do not need. As David McCarn states, computer experts, who tend to be highly rational and mechanistic in their thinking, often tend to deny the existence of individuals who see broad patterns and total pictures rather than well bounded problems, so that they fail to incorporate features in a systems design appropriate to all classes of users.[6]

Growing recognition of the importance of human factors should help correct this shortcoming. The literature on human factors is, indeed, quite extensive (over 1,000 references as early as 1971). Management should follow research in this field because no computerized information system can achieve its full potential as a tool in management decision making when aspects of human engineering are ignored.

Figure 18.3 summarizes relationships in a computer environment. Human-machine relationships exist between the computer and management/clients, and human-human interchange takes place between management, computer personnel, and clients. Computer information systems should not be categorized as machine systems, or even machine-dominated systems, for humans play a major role: first, in specifying the need for information; second, in designing and implementing systems; third, in providing input; and finally, as users of the information. The very importance of the human role is what makes it vital to establish a climate receptive to the change which accompanies the introduction of information systems.

WHY RESISTANCE?

That employees resist change should come as no surprise to business managers since this phenomena has been well documented. For

---

[4]See Victor R. Bassili and Robert W. Reiter, Jr., "An Investigation of Human Factors in Software Development," *Computer* 12, no. 12 (December 1979), pp. 20–40. See also the editorial in the same issue by J. D. Gannon, pp. 6–8.

[5]See Ben Shneiderman, "Human Factors in Designing Interactive Systems," *Computer* 12, no. 12 (December 1979), pp. 9–20.

[6]David B. McCarn, "Getting Ready . . .," *Datamation* 16 no. 8 (August 1970), p. 26.

Figure 18.3   **Computer-human interaction**

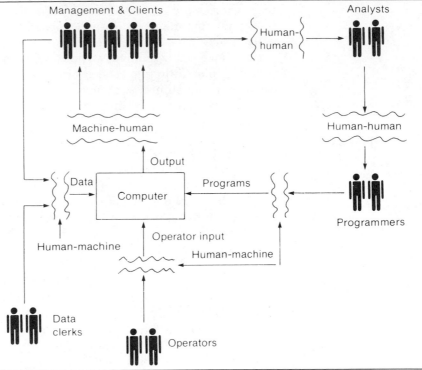

example, the Hawthorne Study at Western Electric in the late 1920s noted that factory conditions or salaries alone did not explain worker attitudes. Actions perceived as a threat to job security triggered a strong emotional response. When mathematical and statistical methods of decision making were first introduced, managers as a group also displayed a negative reaction, according to the literature of operations research and management science.

Resistance to computers can be found at all levels of an organization. Though an assembly line worker may have different reasons for fearing computers than secretaries or managers, the reaction is no less intense. All groups are disturbed by disruption of the status quo. Procedures are altered, jobs gain or lose status, and totally new relationships must be forged as departments are restructured in accordance with the expanded role of computers. Resistance can also be traced to job insecurity, the fear that computers will cause unemployment or lead to job displacement, requiring employees to acquire new work skills. Certainly, to learn that one's duties are to be reassigned to a computer in the interest of efficiency is hard on an employee's ego.

Managers themselves often feel hemmed in by computers, believing their choices are restricted, since information systems seem to centralize all important decisions. Some local managers resent having daily goals defined, the action to achieve these goals specified, and performance evaluated by a computer system in which personal relationships play little role. The system may also provide data that managers prefer to suppress, or may reveal staff incompetence.[7] For example, a report by one company comparing monthly sales showed a correlation between low performance and deer season. Foremen lax in controlling unexcused absences of hunters were easily identified.

But perhaps the main reason managers oppose information systems is that computers alter the decision making process. Decisions are no longer based on intuition but on data provided by the system supplemented by human judgment and experience. This type of decision making requires a different type of conceptual thinking. Many managers find their former style of decision making under attack, and are unable to adjust to the new technology.[8]

Company politics are another factor that often explain employee attitudes toward change. Employees who feel they will have an opportunity to attain privileged status because of their expertise in computers will naturally favor the introduction of information systems, but others, who see their power base eroding, will, in self-interest, scheme to defeat the new technology.

Reasons for resistance at each level of personnel are summarized in Table 18.1. Though resistance generally has adverse effects, it should be acknowledged that not all resistance is bad. If management examines the objections of employees and improves the proposed system by listening to constructive criticism, resistance can serve a useful purpose. Perhaps technicians have not paid enough attention to human needs in designing the work environment, perhaps the stress has been on technology, ignoring human-machine interface on which success of the new system depends. A careful assessment of employee objections may help avert a costly flop. Those who assume that all resistance is the grumbling of malcontents do their firm a disservice.

Tolerance to change is dependent on a number of variables. Some commentators suggest that resistance is greater among older employees who have a long record of service to a company than among younger workers, and is more likely among those with limited education and little background in computers, but not all observers agree. Resis-

[7]Chris Argyis, "Resistance to Rational Management Systems," *Innovation*, no. 10 (1970), pp. 28–35. Also reprinted in Gordon B. Davis and Gordon C. Davis, *Readings in Management Information Systems* (McGraw-Hill, 1976), pp. 245–51.

[8]For more on this problem, see John Paul Kotter and Leonard H. Schlesinger, "Choosing Strategies for Change," *Harvard Business Review* 57, no. 2 (March–April 1979), pp. 106–14.

Table 18.1 **Reasons for resistance and effects of new technology on employees**

Reason for resistance ↓ / Level primarily affected →	Operating personnel	Operating management	Middle management	Top management
Loss of status	X	X		
Economic insecurity	X			
Interpersonal relationships altered	X	X		
Change in job content	X	X	X	
Change in decision-making approach			X	X
Loss of power	X	X	X	
Uncertainty/ unfamiliarity/ misinformation	X	X	X	X
How affected by new computer technology	Unemployment or displacement	Job content changed	Job content changed	No change

tance is generally proportional to the number of persons involved in the change, and also increases as the rate of change increases. Rapid change has been known to produce dysfunctional behavior such as alienation, withdrawal, apathy, and depression, but even controlled change can lead to emotional stress and illness.

This phenomena has been studied by psychologists T. S. and T. H. Holmes, who devised a system of scoring events in a person's life according to the amount of trauma they produce.[9] A change in hours of work is given a stress rating of 20 points; a change in responsibilities, 29; trouble with the boss, 23; being fired, 47. Points are also given for divorce, birth of a child, vacations, death in the family, and other non-work-related events, but changes in employment represent 20 percent of the list and have high score values. A score of 200 at any

---

[9]T. S. Holmes and T. H. Holmes, "Short-term Intrusions into Life-Style Routines," *Journal of Psychosomatic Research* 14 (1970), pp. 121–32.

given time is so disruptive that an individual is susceptible to disease or illness, according to the Holmeses. Changed work conditions due to the introduction of an information system would score highly under this system, explaining the dysfunctional behavior of some individuals when their departments are computerized.

Once resistance is identified, plans need to be made to change employee attitudes, as discussed in the next section.

PLANNING AND IMPLEMENTING CHANGE

Planning for change should resemble the planning of a project. Once the need for change is identified, strategies to implement the change should be developed, responsibilities assigned, and a schedule for implementation adopted. Often a systems analyst is the change agent, but firms that have little experience in the management of change may hire a technical consultant to effect the change.[10] This individual should be technically competent and skilled in communication and procedural skills. Change agents should also have expertise in human-machine interaction[11] and have knowledge of human performance technology. In addition, they should be knowledgeable about the integration of human factors with instructional technology, and be schooled in industrial and organization psychology.[12] Their purpose is to recommend policies that will smooth transition to new technology and alter the behavior and attitude of employees resisting change.

Behavior alteration may be a **participative change,** which starts from within the individual, or be change in response to management initiatives, called a **directive change.**

A participative change starts with new knowledge (formal education, self-instruction, or observation), knowledge that kindles new attitudes which, in turn, affect behavior—first individual, then group behavior. Such change can be nurtured by the environment. For example, time off may be given employees for class attendance or a bonus given for joining educational programs.

A directive change is one that is imposed by management. Policies are formulated that require alteration of group behavior, which should modify the knowledge and attitude of individuals accordingly. For ex-

---

[10]For case studies in the use of consultants for managing change see, "How Companies Are Preparing for Change," *EDP Analyzer* 8, no. 2 (February 1980), pp. 7–10.

[11]For more on this, see Stephen R. Barkin, "The Nature of the Interface: Man and Machine," *Data Base* 9, no. 4 (Spring 1978), pp. 9–11.

[12]For an excellent discussion on this, see H. O. Holt, and F. L. Stevenson, "Human Performance Considerations in Complex Systems," *Journal of Systems Management* 29, no. 10 (October 1978), pp. 14–19.

ample, participation at orientation sessions may be compulsory or employees may be told their jobs are in jeopardy if new job skills are not learned. A change in attitude can also be fostered by involving employees in systems development projects. Resisters can be co-opted, given an active role in identifying problems and planning solutions. Generally when so involved, individuals begin to see computers as valuable business aids and their fears of a machine take-over fade.

Improved communication can also speed employee acceptance of change. When rumor runs rampant, resistance is intensified. Many firms have found that when the nature, extent, and anticipated implications of change are fully stated, with problems of displacement and unemployment openly discussed, resistance is assuaged. Given a period of adjustment, affected employees have time to learn new job skills or time to seek alternate employment. Firms can help smooth adjustment by providing in-house retraining, or offering the option of early retirement to affected personnel.

One firm that announced retrenchment due to the installation of a computerized information system but failed to identify which individuals would lose their jobs found that 40 percent of the work force resigned, even those in positions that would have been unaffected by the change. In this case, the firm lost some of its best workers just when conversion was beginning, a time when competent employees were sorely needed, leaving deadwood, persons with poor qualifications and hence little job mobility, on the job.

Which of the two approaches to change, participative or directive, works best in an EDP environment? Generally a participative change is most desirable. Self-motivated employees tend to imbue others with their enthusiasm, and their willingness to try new ideas often serves as a catalyst to a change in attitude of co-workers. The approach is also more appealing because it is open and democratic.

But when no employees voluntarily engage in activities that will transform behavior, management must implement strategies to encourage a positive attitude toward change even when these strategies smack of rigidity, formality, and bureaucratic authoritarianism.[13] Time may also be a factor mandating the directive approach, for participative change is generally a slower process.

Figure 18.4 shows that the impetus for change comes from opposite points in participative and directive change.[14]

---

[13]For a discussion on employee manipulation, see John P. Kotter, "Power, Dependence and Effective Management," *Harvard Business Review* 55, no. 4 (July–August 1977), p. 135.

[14]This conceptual framework originates with Elton Mayo and is discussed in Paul Hersey and Kenneth H. Blanchard, *Management: A Behavioral Approach* (Englewood Cliffs, N.J.: Prentice-Hall, 1977), pp. 280–84.

Figure 18.4   **Participative and directive changes**

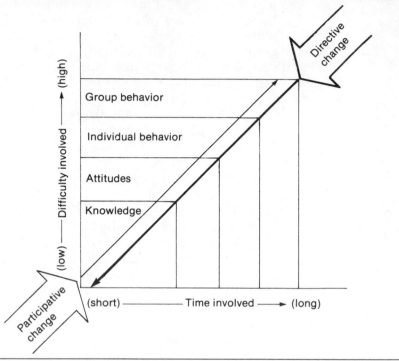

Source: Adapted from Paul Hersey and K. H. Blanchard, *Management of Organizational Behaviour: Utilizing Human Resources* (Englewood Cliffs, N.J.: Prentice-Hall, 1977), pp. 281–82.

CHANGE STRATEGIES

The objective of management of change is to gain employee receptivity to innovation and worker willingness to cooperate with the implementation of change. There is a cycle in one's attitude toward change, as depicted in Figure 18.5, that management hopes to influence. The cycle begins with one's background and education, which precondition an individual's emotional response to change as does experience with change in the past (Box 1). Emotional responses lead to attitudes (Box 3) that affect whether the impact of innovation at work will be perceived as beneficial or as a threat (Box 4). This perception, in turn, influences whether change will be accepted or opposed (Box 5), and the degree of willing participation in the implementation of the change (Box 6). This experience becomes part of the employee's background (Box 1), conditioning future reaction to change. If management can break into the cycle, interjecting new experience or knowledge, reinforcing positive responses to change by handing change in an equitable and humane manner (Box 2) so an

Figure 18.5   **Cycle in attitude toward change**

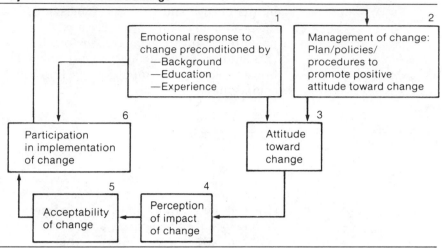

individual's attitude toward change is altered, then resistance will be diminished and change in the future will be less objectionable.

Table 18.2 is a list of **change strategies** that will help promote acceptance of change and ease the throes of conversion to a new system. The key to success of these strategies lies in management's ability to

Table 18.2   **Strategies to promote acceptance of change**

Involve employees in development of new systems.
Open lines of communication between employees and management.
Provide employees with information regarding system changes.
Incorporate recommendations of human factors research to improve work environment, i.e., machine design refinements.
Initiate morale-boosting activities, e.g., company parties and newsletters.
Pace conversion to allow readjustment period to new system.
Redevelop modularly.
Reward ideas that will improve throughput.
Document standards so new procedures are easy to learn and reference.
Clearly establish in advance the demarcations of authority that will exist following changeover.
Upgrade work environment following change, e.g., more space and design for comfort.
Conduct pilot study to examine impact of change.
Alter job titles to reflect increased responsibility.
Show sympathy and be receptive to complaints following conversion.
Conduct orientation sessions.
Arrange job transfers.
Give separation pay.
Call a hiring freeze until all displaced personnel are reassigned.
Give job counseling.
Organize group therapy.
Retrain employees.

demonstrate support and sympathy for employees adversely affected by the change and to show understanding when the disruption and dislocation of change produces anxiety and tension even among those not directly involved in conversion. It is largely management's skill in handling interpersonal relationships that determines whether a firm can keep pace and absorb technological advances in the field of computing.

SUMMARY

In computing, information systems are commonly redeveloped every 4–6 years. The new system may affect the firm's organizational structure and require the forging of new interpersonal relationships among technical personnel, users, data providers, and clients. To prevent escalation of costs, disrupted production schedules, and lowered morale, change must be carefully planned, implemented, and controlled.

Figure 18.6   **Responses to change**

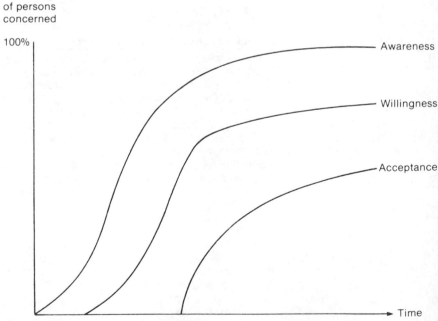

Percentage
of persons
concerned

Note: The shapes of the curves (the starting point, slope gradient, and time horizon) will vary with:
    a. The complexity of technological change being implemented.
    b. Education, training, and communication (will especially affect awareness curve).
    c. Strategies of change (will affect willingness and acceptance curves).

Management of change is more than merely supporting and sympathizing with workers adversely affected by new systems. It involves an active role in system development to ensure that human factors are incorporated in the design and implementation of systems. It is establishing a work environment receptive to change, ready to "change with change so that when change comes, there will be no change."[15]

Figure 18.6 illustrates that awareness of a projected change, willingness to implement the change, and acceptance—all have different curves over time. The starting point and gradient of these slopes can be altered by management by policies that create an atmosphere fostering change. The object of management of change is to shift the curve up and to the left, to increase acceptance and reduce the time for acceptance. Orientation sessions, retraining programs, and modular redevelopment are examples of strategies that predispose employees to acceptance of technological innovations in computing. Examples of other strategies are listed in Table 18.2. A major goal of such strategies is to humanize computer systems, to make them friendlier and easy to use, and to ensure that no employee perceives computers as an intolerable economic, psychic, or social threat.

CASE STUDY: PLANNING FOR CHANGE AT LINCOLN NATIONAL LIFE INSURANCE COMPANY*

In 1977, Lincoln National, the 11th largest life insurance company in the United States with $4.7 billion of assets and 8,300 employees, began planning for implementation of an office automation program. This program had three objectives:

1. To reduce paperwork by 90 percent.
2. To establish distributed processing, tying together all key processing locations in a computer network.
3. To provide computational capabilities at end user locations.

It was recognized that the introduction of computerization would have disruptive effects on the organization, and that achievement of the objectives by the target date, 1984, would require careful planning for change. It was decided to follow the Japanese "quality circle" (grass roots) style of management. That is, employees would participate with management in planning and implementing change.

---

[15]Advice given to the old patrician uncle in Giuseppe Lampedusa's novel *The Leopard* at a time when Garibaldi's armies are overthrowing the old Sicilian order.

*Richard G. Canning, ed. "The Coming Impact of New Technology," *EDP Analyzer* 19, no. 1 (January 1981), pp. 1–3.

Lincoln National's program has four main elements.

1. An automation committee, consisting of eight senior officers, meets monthly to formulate policy and plans, review project requests, and monitor project progress. This committee set the objectives listed above.
2. Executive responsibility for managing the company's information resources has been realigned. The senior executive responsible for data processing has been given responsibility for office services. The new department is responsible for keeping abreast with new technology for computerized offices and developing strategies for implementing the 1984 goals.
3. A quality commitment program has been instituted. Every employee is given an opportunity of meeting with a small group of peers once a week to discuss ways of improving productivity and making the work experience more rewarding.
4. Project committees have been established to implement computerized systems.

Lincoln National Life is pleased with the progress the company is making toward office computerization. The introduction of new technology has been accomplished by astute management of change: by realigning executive responsibility in order to meet automation objectives and by actively seeking employee participation in implementation of new systems.

KEY WORDS

Change strategies	Human factors
Directive change	Participative change
Ergonomics	Planning for change
Human engineering	Resistance

DISCUSSION QUESTIONS

1. Resistance to change resulting from the introduction of computer technology is not unusual and should be expected when implementing a new information system. Comment.
2. In a computing environment, resistance may occur not only when a

change is first introduced but throughout the life of a system. Comment and explain the reasons why.

3. Will the same types of resistance to computer applications be found in a bank, manufacturing plant, government office, warehouse, and retail outlet? Explain.

4. Will resistance differ in:
   a. Old and young employees?
   b. Skilled and unskilled workers?
   c. Management and workers?
   d. Top management and operational management?
   e. Small and large organizations?
   Explain.

5. Comment on the following. A project that will displace 30 employees is kept secret until it is ready to be implemented. What are the ethical implications of such a strategy?

6. How is the management of change in a computer environment different from change in another technological environment, such as factory automation? Will resistance be of a different nature and magnitude?

7. How should strategies of change differ in the following situations?
   a. Implementation of a functional application.
   b. Implementation of an integrated system.
   c. Implementation of computer-aided design.
   d. Implementation of computer-aided manufacturing.
   e. Implementation of a DBMS.
   f. Implementation of a network application.
   g. Implementation of a distributed processing environment.
   h. A change from decentralized to centralized computing.

8. Under what circumstances would you approach human resistance on an individual level rather than a group level?

9. Is the problem of management of change in computer systems going to become easier because of experience or harder because systems are becoming more complex? Explain.

10. In the future we may have:
    a. Automated offices.
    b. Home computers connected to offices with work done at home.
    c. Robot-driven factories.
    d. Cashless businesses and teleshopping.
    e. Telemail and telenewspapers.
    f. A wired city.
    g. Intelligent MIS with artificial intelligence capabilities.
    In each of these cases, what unique problems of resistance should be expected? How would you plan to minimize adverse human factor effects?

11. Where should responsibility for human factors lie? With the vendor, analyst, or users?

12. What variables are important in anticipating, measuring, and dealing with resistance to organizational change?

SELECTED ANNOTATED BIBLIOGRAPHY

Argyris, Chris. "Resistance to Rational Management Systems." *Innovation* 10 (1970), pp. 28-35.
This is a psychologist's perspective of resistance to computerized information systems. Argyris discusses the impact of computers on management, power structure, style, and behavior.

Elam, Phillip G. "Change: How Users React." *Computer World* 14, no. 51 (December 15, 1980), pp. 9–16 of "In Depth" section.
Computer World is a trade journal of computer news and advertisements. Frequently, it has an "IN DEPTH" section in which practitioners and, occasionally, scholars discuss topics in detail as Elam has done on the subject of change. Good summary tables are included.

Grindley, Kit, and John Humble. *The Effective Computer*. (London: McGraw-Hill, 1973), pp. 122–59.
This book has a chapter entitled, "A Plan for Managing Change" in which human conflict and a "strategy of learning" to handle change are discussed. Training and development are recommended as a means of overcoming resistance. Numerous examples are given of resistance in England which could also occur in the United States.

Kotter, John P., and Leonard A. Schlesinger. "Choosing Strategies for Change." *Harvard Business Review* 57, no. 2 (March/April 1979), pp. 106–14.
An excellent article on the causes of resistance and strategies for overcoming it.

Siegel, Paul. *Strategic Planning of Management* Information Systems. New York: Petrocelli Books, 1975, Chap. 12, pp. 229–67.
Chapter 12 on interaction between man and machine discusses the synergistic effect of man-man, man-machine, and machine-man interaction.

Tomeski, Edward A., and Harold Lazarus. "A Humanized Approach to Computers." *Computers and Automation* 22, no. 6 (June 1973), pp. 21–25.
The authors suggest that resistance is a function of rapid technological change and the limited capacity of humans to absorb change. They recommend that social as well as technical and economic factors should be taken into consideration when introducing and using computer technology.

Tomeski, Edward A., and Harold Lazarus. *People-Oriented Computer Systems*. New York: Van Nostrand Reinhold, 1975, 229 p.
The authors argue that computers have failed to serve people and organizations. This book is a plea to vendors and users to adopt policies and practices that will make computerized information systems sensitive and responsive to human and social needs.

Wadsworth, M. D. *The Human Side of Data Processing Management*. Englewood Cliffs, N.J.: Prentice-Hall, 1973, 244 p.
This book describes cases of resistance and suggests solutions to people

problems an EDP manager can expect to encounter in an EDP department. For example, the handling of nonconformists, gripers, malingerers or employees who require constant reassurance is described.

Zaltman, Gerald, and Robert Duncan. *Strategies for Planned Change*. New York: John Wiley & Sons, 1976, 404 p.
This book is based on extensive interviews with over 75 professional change agents. The change to computer systems as well as organizational change and innovation diffusion are discussed. Among the issues presented are planning change, issues of resistance to change, social problems, and ethical dilemmas resulting from change.

PART SIX

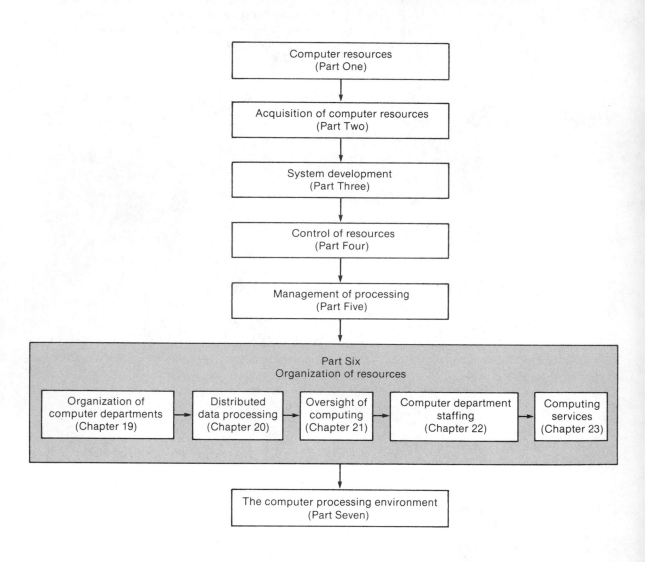

Computer resources
(Part One)

Acquisition of computer resources
(Part Two)

System development
(Part Three)

Control of resources
(Part Four)

Management of processing
(Part Five)

Part Six
Organization of resources

Organization of computer departments (Chapter 19)

Distributed data processing (Chapter 20)

Oversight of computing (Chapter 21)

Computer department staffing (Chapter 22)

Computing services (Chapter 23)

The computer processing environment
(Part Seven)

ORGANIZATION OF RESOURCES

**Introduction to
Part Six**

Part Six describes how a firm organizes its computing resources.

The location of computer departments within a firm's organizational hierarchy and problems of communication between computer departments, corporate management, and users is the topic of Chapter 19, the opening chapter in this part. Chapter 20, an extension of Chapter 19, discusses distributed data processing (DDP), a processing mode made feasible by recent technological advances in microelectronics and telecommunications that is growing in popularity. A separate chapter has been devoted to this topic to explain how DDP affects equipment, software, and personnel in information system management.

Chapter 21 describes the role of management and steering committees in the oversight of computing. Chapter 22 focuses on in-house computer staffing, job design, hiring, and turnover. Finally, Chapter 23 deals with service organizations that can supplement in-house resources. Considered are consultants, vendors, facilities management, service bureaus, remote processing, and utilities.

Note that Part Six includes a discussion of the organization of resources for both internal and external processing. The diagram which follows illustrates processing options and shows the chapter locations for information on the various types of processing.

Processing modes and their correspondence to Part Six

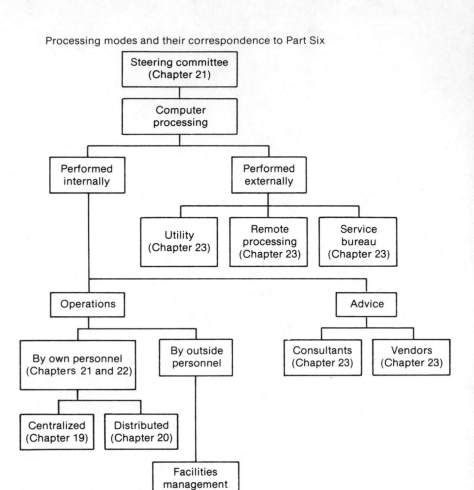

CHAPTER 19

Organization of computer
departments

*You can't sit on the lid of progress. If you do,
you will be blown to pieces.*

Henry Kaiser

This chapter traces the evolution of computer centers from their early beginnings as subdepartmental units to present day distributed data processing centers. How the internal organizational structure of computer departments[1] may differ from one organization to another is examined, and the horizontal integration of computing with users is discussed.

Problems of communication between data processing management and corporate executives are also considered in this chapter, as are sources of conflict between data processing technicians and users. Though it is noted that the changing nature of responsibility of computer departments over time has kept these relationships in a constant state of flux, a number of solutions are offered for improving harmony between computer personnel, users, and corporate management.

---

[1]Originally, data processing was the only responsibility of an EDP center. When text processing was added to data processing, many firms changed the name of their computing facility to computer department or computer processing center because the term EDP center was too restrictive. Information Processing Center, MIS Center, or Automation Management Office are also common names for a computer center today, particularly in firms which have added such functions as record-keeping and communications to their computer departments.

LOCATION OF COMPUTING IN ORGANIZATIONAL HIERARCHY

There are many possible locations for a computer department within the organizational structure of a firm. Six alternatives are shown in Figure 19.1.

When computing was in its infancy and computer applications were limited to basic data processing, EDP was commonly a subdepartmental unit, as in Case 1. Small centers were established in more than one division needing information, such centers being physically dispersed with no centralized authority to coordinate their activities. Data processed in this manner was slow to reach middle and top management, and frequently failed to provide the information needed for decision making. In addition, the scarcity of qualified personnel meant that such centers were often poorly run.

When more resources were devoted to computing and applications became diversified, EDP rose in the organizational hierarchy of most firms. This placed EDP personnel directly under a department head (Case 2) or division chief (Case 3).

Then, as the need for expensive data processing resources grew and applications extended to all functional areas, sharing of data and equipment across division lines was initiated to cut costs. This gave impetus to **centralized data processing,** the establishment of a single computer department reporting directly to top management (Case 4).

Figure 19.1   **Alternative locations of EDP within a firm's organizational structure**

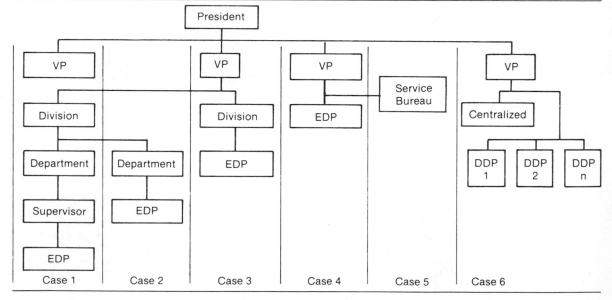

Common data bases were established to be shared by users, analysts, and programmers pooled in one location, and planning, computer operations, administration, and data base management were consolidated within a single department. It was expected that costs would drop (indeed, studies showed that a single large installation was less expensive to run than small dispersed centers),[2] that information processing would be more responsive to management needs than formerly, that the delivery speed of information would increase, that redundancy in processing and files would be eliminated, and that security and control of information would be tightened.

Unfortunately, these expectations have not all been realized. Lack of communication between users and analysts continues to exist under centralization. Users resent the hours required to justify and document requests for service and feel isolated from computing facilities, complaining that analysts are unresponsive to their needs. Analysts, in turn, chafe at criticism, believing that the length of time required for system development is simply not understood by users. The bureaucracy of centralization is often inept at mediating such conflicting interests.[3]

Nevertheless, centralization is a common organizational schema. The use of service bureaus (Case 5) to supplement a company's internal computing facilities or to handle all of its data processing is also prevalent.

A flip-flop back to **decentralization** has become an increasingly attractive alternative due to the dramatic drop in the cost of computers in recent years and the development of **distributed processing** which permits segmented, replicated, and distributed data bases under local control (Case 6). The claim formerly used to support centralization, that firms can better attract and retain competent personnel when equipment is easily accessible at a central location, has lost validity as new technology in telecommunications has made remote job entry practical. In addition, the argument is now advanced that users are better served and applications more easily implemented and maintained when distributed data processing (DDP) is combined with centralized processing. (DDP is the subject of the next chapter in this book, Chapter 20.)

Figure 19.2 is a closer look at one configuration for DDP. Personnel is still needed at the corporate center to administer overall control of data processing. For example, dispersed sites are counseled and coordinated from the center to ensure equipment compatibility and to minimize duplication of effort. Control over budgets and auditing procedures is also still centralized, with headquarters responsible for de-

---

[2]Martin Solomon, "Economics of Scale and Computer Personnel," *Datamation* 16, no. 3 (March 1970), pp. 107–10.

[3]See Peter Berman, "A Vote against Centralized Staff," *Datamation* 16, no. 5 (May 1976), pp. 289–90.

Figure19.2   **Sample DDP configuration**

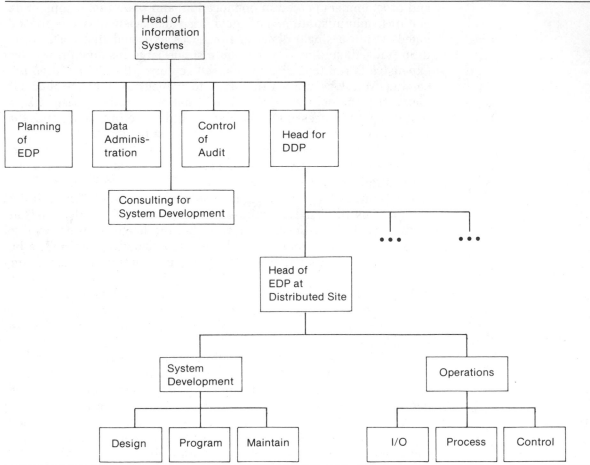

veloping and enforcing performance standards for equipment, software, and personnel at all DDP locations. But under DDP, local systems development and operations are the responsibility of managers at remote sites. These managers also make minor acquisition decisions, establish development priorities, and manage the local data base. Firms are learning that one advantage to the distribution of data files is that access control is easier to administer at small processing sites. In addition, the potential loss from fire or sabotage is minimized when data files are not all stored in one place. However, DDP is vulnerable to wiretapping and other transmission penetrations so security remains an issue.

Centralization–decentralization is not an either/or proposition. As shown in Table 19.1, a variety of centralization–decentralization com-

Table 19.1 **Some alternative centralization–decentralization combinations**

Alternative	Development personnel	Equipment and operation	Development activities	Data base	Planning
1	C	C	C	C	C
2	D	C	C	C	C
3	D	D	C	C	C
4	D	D	D	C	C

C = Centralized.
D = Decentralized.

binations are possible. Alternative 4 has become increasingly popular in recent years for it allows decentralization of operations and developmental activities with local control over personnel, but centralizes planning and data base control.

INTERNAL ORGANIZATION OF COMPUTING CENTERS

The **internal organization** of a computing facility will vary from firm to firm. Some companies structure computer development along **project lines.** Others organize development activities by **function,** with personnel assigned to specialized tasks such as systems design, programming, or maintenance, as shown in Figure 19.3. The problem with this latter organization is that personnel are too compartmentalized. Integration of phases of development is impeded and development responsibility split, which often delays projects and leads to cost escalations.

An alternative organization is to structure development along the same functional lines as divisions within the firm, as illustrated in Figure 19.4. This configuration achieves coordination of applications

Figure 19.3 **Functional organization for systems development**

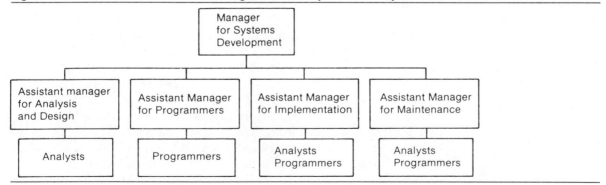

Figure 19.4   **Systems development organization by functional departments under centralized EDP**

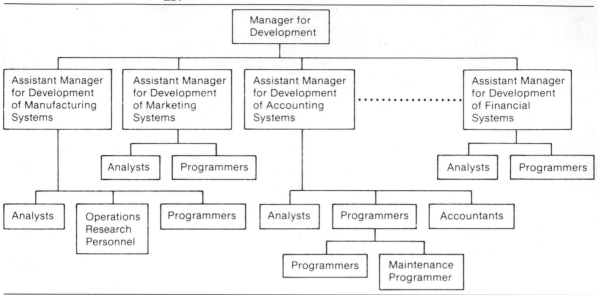

development and creates a close working relationship between analysts and clients, thus helping to ensure that the center is sensitive to users' needs. Problems with interface and split responsibility arise, however, when an integrated system is under development which crosses functional lines. Another disadvantage is that personnel become too specialized. For example, analysts and programmers assigned to the development of financial systems may find that they cannot assist marketing or manufacturing programmers because their expertise is too narrow.

HORIZONTAL INTEGRATION

The **horizontal integration** of computer departments with other departments in a firm is a third type of organization that must be considered. One possible schema with a broad span of control is shown in Figure 19.5. In this schema, note that the EDP department is only one of many information processing departments that fall under the jurisdiction of a vice president for information services. The exact title of this position may vary from firm to firm (vice president for information resource management is also common), but the role of the office remains the same: to coordinate users who must share computing facilities. This type of structure is becoming increasingly common due

Figure 19.5   **Horizontal integration under Vice President for Information Services**

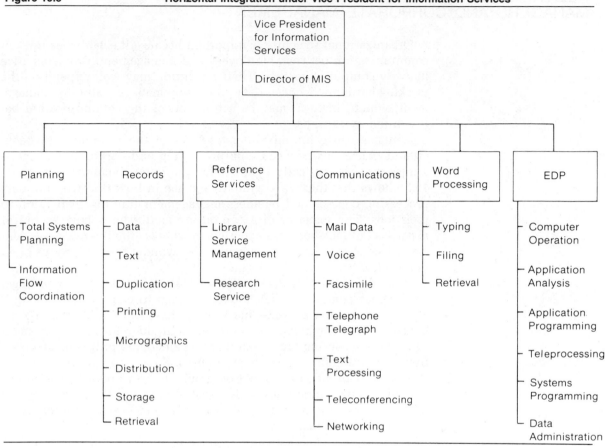

to the growth of computer applications and the increased reliance of businesses on information processing today.

Figure 19.5 is only one example of horizontal integration. Some firms will combine record-keeping with EDP. Others will join word processing with reference services. It should be recognized that whatever organization is chosen will be temporary at best, for rapid advances in computer technology will require management to integrate new MIS applications in the future which may mean restructuring departments. For example, there is much controversy today over the electronic office. Should it be integrated with data processing or remain organizationally decentralized? This may well prove a major issue of the 1980s.[4]

---

[4]See Lawrence K. Williams and Thomas M. Lodahl, "Comparing WP and Computers," *Journal of Systems Management* 29, no. 2 (February 1978), pp. 9–11.

RELATIONSHIP BETWEEN DATA PROCESSING
MANAGERS AND CORPORATE MANAGEMENT

Organizational structure is important because it establishes lines of communication between employees and management. Problems arise in every computing facility. Their resolution may well depend on the working harmony between data processing managers and top management, which, in turn, may be a function of the communication between the two groups.

A major cause for misunderstandings is the difference in background that exists between data processing and corporate managers. The former are basically technicians: the latter, businessmen. Table 19.2 shows that there is a wide divergence in how the two rank data processing courses and business management training in relation to their jobs. The manager of a computing facility may have technical expertise but lack business experience, whereas the the reverse is generally true of the corporate executive. No wonder the two groups often fail to view problems in the same light.

It is advocated that it is easier and faster to train senior management about computers than for technicians to acquire the prerequisites for managing a firm. This is why most companies provide in-house training programs on computer technology for high level management, sponsoring group seminars or videotape programs acquired from consulting firms or software houses. Some firms release time for managers to attend educational programs in their home communities. Others organize pilot studies, demonstrations, and briefings. Another method of keeping management technically up to date is to circulate journals and pertinent literature.[5]

The purpose of all of these educational approaches is to smooth communication between upper management and computing management. When the two groups use the same vocabulary and corporate managers have enough background to understand computing problems, relations between the groups generally improve. Improved relations, in turn, can raise employee morale and lead to higher productivity.

Another factor which affects the relationship between upper-level and computer managers is that the two groups differ in their attitude toward change. Corporate managers seek stability whereas computer personnel are committed to change. Indeed, change and motion are viewed as constants in the field of computing. From an EDP manager's point of view, stability within change is a viable concept and not a contradiction of terms.

A divergence also exists in attitude toward the dissemination of

---

[5]See "Educating Executives on New Technology," *EDP Analyzer* 18, no. 8 (November 1980), pp. 1–13.

Table 19.2 Courses needed by senior corporate executives and data processing executives in their jobs, ranked by order of importance

BUSINESS MANAGEMENT COURSES (Ranked in order of importance)		DATA PROCESSING COURSES (Ranked in order of importance for senior-level executives)	
By corporate presidents	*By data processing managers*	*By corporate executives*	*By data processing executives*
Economics	Decision Making	Computer concepts	Computer concepts
Financial accounting	Problem solving	Using models	Data Base concepts
Decision making	Business information systems	Data base concepts	Using models
Finance	Writing	Project planning	Project planning
Writing	Financial accounting	Estimating techniques	Systems analysis
Management psychology	Management psychology	Introduction to teleprocessing	Introduction to teleprocessing
Problem solving	Public speaking	Systems analysis	Estimating techniques
Marketing	Business policies	Systems design	Systems design
Public speaking	Managerial accounting	Programming concepts	Computer organization
Mangerial accounting	Management theory	Data communications	Data communications
Management theory	Finance	Real-time systems	Real-time systems
Business information systems	Statistics	Computer organization	Programming concepts
Business policies	Economics	Operating systems	Hardware configurations
Business cycles and forecasting	Business cycles and forecasting	Hardware configurations	System simulation
Statistics	Marketing	System simulation	Operating systems
Operations research techniques	Principles of auditing	Algorithmic processes	Algorithmic processes
Theory of the firm	Operations research techniques	Computer systems architecture	Computer systems architecture
Principles of auditing	Theory of the firm	FORTRAN	FORTRAN
		COBOL	COBOL
		Assembler language	Assembler language

Source: Robert S. Hoberman, "The Billion-Dollar Chasm," *Computer World* 14, no. 17 (April 28, 1980) p. 11.

information. Generally, computer managers are committed to the concept of free and wide distribution of information whereas corporate executives favor restrictions, lest information be misused. (The charge is often made that the real reason management wants information controlled is to keep unfavorable reports quiet.)

A further source of discord is that computer managers feel corporate managers unfairly judge them on quantitative measures (budget variances, for example) and general efficiency measures, measures which poorly reflect important performance characteristics of an EDP administration.[6] The computer manager also claims to be the scapegoat when embarrassing mistakes are made but never credited with managerial ability when the computer center functions well. EDP managers complain that they are considered merely computer technicians so that the road to other executive positions is blocked, creating a dead end to a career path which should lead to the top managerial echelons of the firm. This is resented by computer management, souring relationships with corporate executives.

RELATIONS BETWEEN USERS AND COMPUTER PERSONNEL

Another relationship that should be examined when considering how a computer department functions within the organizational structure of a firm is relations between users and computer personnel. Unfortunately, most users, be they clerks or management, have a negative view of computer technicians, especially system analysts and programmers. Users see such individuals as overzealous in changing existing procedures, disdainful of others (even employees with years of experience in the firm), long on theory but short on common sense, and lacking both humility and company loyalty. Stories abound to the discredit of EDP personnel, such as the quoted response of one programming applicant who, when asked to explain having three jobs in three years, responded, "I feel I'm loyal. I'm loyal to the computer. All these jobs were with computers."[7]

Computer personnel are also criticized for the impersonality of their reports, their inability to relate to clientele, their nonresponsiveness to inquiries, their insensitivity to user desires, their lack of functional involvement, and their occasional dishonesty, such as the unauthorized sale of address lists or other information.[8]

[6]Richard G. Nolan, "The Plight of the EDP Manager," *Harvard Business Review* 51, no. 3 (May–June 1973), pp. 145–147, and 152.

[7]Kit Grindley and John Humble, *The Effective Computer* (London: McGraw-Hill, 1973), p. 130.

[8]For ways to improve relations with clientele, see Thomas D. Sterling and Kenneth Laudon, "Humanizing Information Systems," *Datamation* 16, no. 3 (December 1976), pp. 53–59.

Criticism of computer personnel comes from within the profession as well. According to Dick Brandon, author and computer consultant,

> The average programmer is excessively independent—sometimes to the point of mild paranoia. He is often eccentric, slightly neurotic, and he borders upon a limited schizophrenia.[9]

Brandon's description is perhaps unjust, but it reflects an antagonism to computer specialists that is, unfortunately, very common.[10] Perhaps one factor contributing to this widespread view is that programmers and analysts have high job mobility. The rate with which they change jobs prevents them from forming deep interpersonal relationships with other employees and gives them little time to improve their image.[11]

On the other side of the coin, computer personnel complain that users often do not know what they want, fail to articulate their needs even when they do know, and keep changing their minds throughout system development and implementation. Analysts argue that if a manager asked for a two-story building, then an additional story after the first two were built, that manager would be fired. Yet the equivalent is asked during system development, with the analyst getting blame for subsequent time/cost overruns.

One way of reducing friction between users and computer technicians is through educational programs which teach users computer technology and analysts business management so that each group understands the other's vocabulary, viewpoint, and function.

Another approach is establishing an ombudsman position to resolve or arbitrate complaints. For example, the concept of an ombudsman is used in Canada where a Computer Ombudsman Service was established in 1974 with the cooperation of the Consumer Association of Canada and the Law Reform Commission in an effort to humanize information systems.[12]

A third approach to lessen friction during development is to set sign-off (or kill-off) points which protect the analyst while giving the user an opportunity to monitor development progress. A sample sign-

---

[9]Quoted in Jac Fitz-enz, "Who Is the DP Professional?" *Datamation* 24, no. 9 (September 1978), p. 125.

[10]Ibid., pp. 124–28. In a profile of computer personnel, Fitz-enz examines the DP professional in terms of Herzog's five motivators: achievement, recognition, work, responsibility, and advancement. See also D. Couger, J. Daniel, and R. A. Zwacki, "What Motivates DP Professionals?" *Datamation* 24, no. 9 (September 1978), pp. 116–23.

[11]R. A. McLaughlin, "That Old Bugaboo, Turnover," *Datamation* 25, no. 11 (October 1978), pp. 97 ff.

[12]For details, see Sterling and Laudon, "Humanizing Information Systems," pp. 53–59. This article also has a list of criteria for humanizing management information systems, p. 54. See also Theodore D. Sterling, "Computer Ombudsman," *Society* 17, no. 2 (January/February 1980), pp. 31–35.

off/kill-off schema is shown in Figure 19.6. Such points add to bureaucracy and delays, but reduce misunderstandings.

Development committees, such as a feasibility study group or data administration group, can also mediate conflicts and provide interface between technicians and users. Still another technique is to appoint individuals who participated in development to serve as liaison between EDP personnel and users throughout subsequent operation, evaluation, and maintenance. Such individuals may be able to trace the cause of problems quickly because of their familiarity with the system and be able to take prompt corrective action that will prevent a recurrence of problems.

The trend toward distributed processing which shifts responsibility for development of information systems from centralized computer personnel to users is mitigating some of the friction between users and EDP personnel described in this section. Hardware selection, acquisitions, installation, operations, and maintenance are also being transferred to users, reducing the need for interaction between computer personnel and users and hence reducing potential areas of discord. One reason users can take over responsibilities formerly assigned to analysts is that today's minis, micros, and packaged systems are easy to use and administer. Technical knowledge is not needed to manage many modern systems.

The history of computing has been one of constant shifts of this nature, as reflected in Figure 19.7. For example, responsibility for the data base has switched back and forth between computer personnel and users. Originally local data was kept by users (1950–60). With the centralization of EDP and the advent of common data bases, data processing departments assumed jurisdiction over data (1960–75). Today's minis enable local sites to manage local data, and distributed data processing technology permits users to control replicated or segmented parts of the common data base as well, so again responsibility for data is reverting back to the user (after 1975). In the 1980s, EDP at the corporate level may include systems planning, and coordination and maintenance of the common data base, with users responsible for hardware, software, and the development of their own information systems. In such cases, users will inherit problems of human factor engineering which, heretofore, have fallen to EDP management.

Whenever changes in responsibility occur, such as those cited above, they trigger reorganization of computer departments. This constant reorganization has kept relationships between users and computer personnel in a continual state of flux. Technological advances will certainly bring still other organizational changes to computer departments in the future, outdating this chapter, so one can expect that interaction between users and computer personnel will always be volatile.

Figure 19.6   **Sign-off or kill-off points**

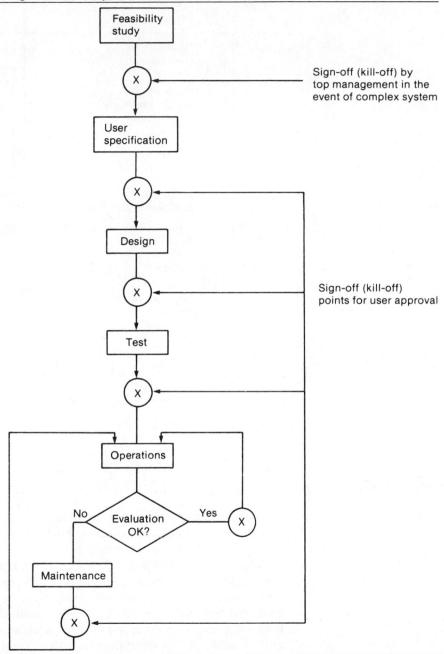

Figure 19.7   **Changing responsibilities of user and computer departments**

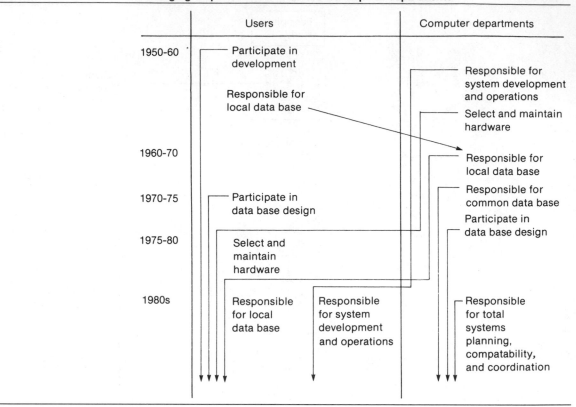

SUMMARY

It is no simple task to describe where computer departments fit into a firm's organizational schema, for technological advances have changed the nature of EDP responsibilities over time and altered the location of computer centers within the hierarchy of firms as a consequence. In the 1950s, computers were generally found in subdepartmental units wherever data processing was needed. As more resources were allocated to computing, centralization was favored to take advantage of economies of scale and to ensure better integration and management of computer facilities. Today, distributed data processing is becoming popular, with local autonomy over development activities and operations, and centralization for planning, standards, and management of common systems. Each of these shifts has altered the relationship of EDP personnel with corporate management and users.

The organizational position of computer departments is still evolving. Unfortunately, employee frustration and anger over the expanding role of computers is commonly vented on EDP personnel who have demonstrated little sympathy for the non-technician in the past, thereby exacerbating the problem. This chapter identifies many sources of misunderstandings and suggests ways to improve relations between computer personnel and management/users. For example, educational programs help both groups learn one another's vocabulary, viewpoint, and function. Sign-off points foster user-analyst agreement at specific stages of development. Interface committees and ombudsmen provide a forum for airing problems and reaching collective decisions.

Crises in computing need not embitter relationships among employees of a firm. It has been noted that the Chinese expression for "crisis" has two characters. The first character represents danger, the other opportunity.

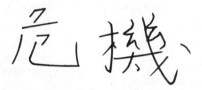

CASE STUDY: ORGANIZATION OF INFORMATION PROCESSING AT MARS, INC.

In 1979, Mars, Inc., known for its chocolate candy, consolidated its information processing in a new division, the Information Services Group (ISG). The purpose of this reorganization was to improve the handling of the company's information resources and to make processing more responsive to end users' needs. The new division has been given responsibility for information flow for all products, from the arrival of raw materials to the shipment of finished products to customers. It is also to plan the use of information technology throughout the company in areas such as data processing, office automation, telecommunications, and factory automation.

The organization chart on next page shows the six units of the new ISG. The division, located near Dover, New Jersey, is a full-absorption cost center, with its own administrative and financial functions.

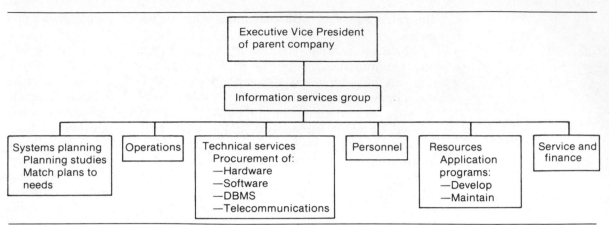

Source: Richard G. Canning, ed., "The Coming Impact of New Technology," *EDP Analyzer* 19, no. 1, pp. 4–5.

KEY WORDS

Centralized data processing

Decentralization

Distributed processing

Horizontal integration

Internal organization

Organization along project lines

Organization by function

Relations between corporate managers, computer personnel, and users

DISCUSSION QUESTIONS

1. What are the central issues in the controversy between centralization and decentralization?

2. Does the decision to centralize or decentralize depend on:
   a. Firm size?
   b. Whether the firm is multinational?
   c. Whether the firm has branch offices?

3. What are the merits of locating a computer department under:
   a. Vice president of finance?
   b. Department of accounting?
   c. Executive vice president?

4. Should the location of the computer department in an organization be a function of:
   a. Size of the computer department and its maturity?
   b. Size of the organization?
   c. Power politics of the organization?
   d. The industry?
   e. Personality of the computer executive?

5. Should the computer department be a staff or a line department? What

conflicts arise in each case? What organizational structure would avoid or minimize these conflicts?

6. Would you recommend horizontal integration of all departments using computers? Explain.

7. Would you favor internal organization of a computer department along functional or project lines? Justify your choice.

8. What measures should be taken to foster a smooth working relationship between computer personnel and users?

9. How can understanding between corporate management and computer personnel be promoted?

10. Do you agree with the concept of an ombudsman as an arbitrator and facilitator between the frustrated user and the computing center? If so, what qualifications should the ombudsman have?

11. Do you believe that computer technology will soon make users independent of computer departments? Explain.

12. Are conflicts between corporate management and computer personnel based on differences in educational background? Or do differing attitudes and biases contribute to dissension? Explain.

SELECTED ANNOTATED BIBLIOGRAPHY

Barnett, Arnold. "Securing User Involvement." *Data Management* 15, no. 1 (January 1978), pp. 52–57.
This article is written by a CPA who shares his experiences as a user.

Gildersleeve, Thomas R. "Organizing the Data Processing Function." *Datamation* 20, no. 11 (November 1974), pp. 46–50.
This is an excellent discussion of alternative structures of organization for development, flow of data, and computer center operations. Good diagrams and lists are included.

Glaser, George. "The Centralization vs Decentralization Issue: Arguments, Alternatives and Guidelines." *Data Base* 2, no. 3 (Fall/Winter 1970), pp. 28–35.
This is an excellent survey of the issues of centralization and decentralization.

Head, Robert V. "Systems Organization and the Technology of the Future." *Journal of Systems Management* 30, no. 8 (August 1979), pp. 6–11.
The author makes projections regarding future organizational structures of computer centers. This article compliments Gildersleeve's article, cited above, which discusses concepts and fundamentals but is otherwise outdated.

Kroeber, Donald W., and Hugh J. Watson. "Is There a Best MIS Department Location?" *Information and Management* 2 (1979), pp. 165–73.
Kroeber discusses the options of central MIS, distributed MIS, and dispersed MIS. Criteria for selection are information needs, extent of homogeneity in applications, and the technological and managerial investment the organization is willing to make.

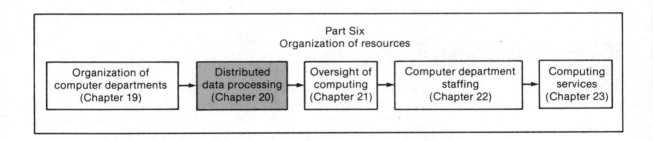

Part Six
Organization of resources

| Organization of computer departments (Chapter 19) | → | Distributed data processing (Chapter 20) | → | Oversight of computing (Chapter 21) | → | Computer department staffing (Chapter 22) | → | Computing services (Chapter 23) |

CHAPTER 20

Distributed data processing

Decentralization evokes deep-seated reactions.
Simon Nora and A. Minc

Distributed data processing (DDP), the decentralization of processing to dispersed locations of an organization, such as branch offices, regional warehouses, or plants distant from corporate headquarters, is one way of organizing equipment and personnel to implement a management information system. A network of computers connects the processing centers with one another and corporate management. This network permits coordination and control of operations even though processing takes place at a number of locations. Ideally, a decision to utilize this processing structure is made during the development stages of a new information system, but sometimes an ongoing system is converted to DDP.

This chapter describes the evolution of DDP, DDP equipment configurations and systems architecture, and how data bases can be distributed. Sections on DDP planning, implementation, and management are also included. The material is an extension of Chapter 19, but merits a separate chapter because of the newness and growing popularity of this mode of operations. The purpose of the chapter is to explain how DDP affects the management of equipment, software, and personnel.

EVOLUTION OF DDP

As described in the preceding chapter, the first EDP centers were physically dispersed and had no centralized authority coordinating their activities. The centers were small, established within departments or divisions wherever information was needed.

It soon became apparent that such centers were inefficient. There was redundancy in data collection, files, and processing, the centers were unresponsive to corporate management needs, and processed information was slow to reach decision makers. As a result, a move toward centralization of computing facilities took place. It was hoped that costs would drop, that duplication of effort would be eliminated, and that tighter control of processing would produce more timely, more relevant information for management.

However, not all of these expectations were realized when centralization took place. Users still complained that their needs were not being met and communication problems between technical personnel and users were not resolved.

Dissatisfaction with centralized processing led to reconsideration of dispersed processing. Technological developments in the meantime made distributed data processing practical and economically feasible. Micro and minicomputers with capabilities exceeding many former large computers were now on the market at low cost. Chip technology had increased CPU and memory capacity while reducing computer size and cost. Strides in telecommunications meant processing networks could be established, linking dispersed processing sites. In addition, experience with data processing had given users confidence that they could manage and operate their own processing systems. By the late 1970s, many firms were committed to DDP and the popularity of this mode of operations was growing.

WHAT IS DDP?

Among computer scientists the definition of DDP is still evolving. For the purposes of this text we shall define distributed data processing as the linking of two or more processing centers (**nodes**) within a single organization, each center having facilities for program execution and data storage. Note that this definition excludes computer networks like ARPA (Advanced Research Projects Agency) and EFT (Electronic Fund Transfer) because they serve many clients in business, industry, and government.

Network linkage of processing nodes under DDP permits centralized control over policies and processing yet the system retains the flexibility of decentralization. For example, integration of sites minimizes duplication of effort, though each site is under operational control of local management and each site may have unique equipment configurations according to local processing needs.

Distributed systems differ from one another in architecture, software, protocols, controls, and data transmission capabilities. A number of equipment configurations will now be discussed.

EQUIPMENT CONFIGURATIONS

The difference between DDP and earlier dispersed processing is the linkage between processing nodes. In the early days of computing, decentralized centers processed information on stand-alone computers. DDP involves a network of processors. Figure 20.1 shows sample DDP configurations. In a **star network,** failure of the central computer impairs the entire system. The **ring** structure overcomes this problem, for rerouting is possible should one processing center or its link fail. The ring allows interaction and **offloading** (the transference of processing from one site to another) without dependence on a central host.

Both star and ring configurations are essentially **horizontal systems.** That is, each node processor is equal. The hardware may be unique at

Figure 20.1   **Sample DDP configurations**

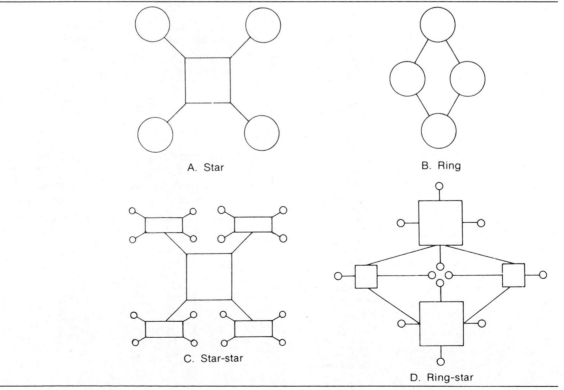

A. Star

B. Ring

C. Star-star

D. Ring-star

each node, which means that equipment may be purchased from any number of vendors, an advantage when the market responds to technological advances by introducing new hardware. But this flexibility has a negative aspect: it increases problems of linkage and compatibility between nodes. Many variations of ring-star networks are possible, such as the star-star and ring-star configurations shown in Figure 20.1.

Hierarchical distribution is the configuration that many firms prefer since it requires the least reorganization, corresponding to the hierarchical structure that is already in existence within many corporations. This system, illustrated in Figure 20.2, has a central host computer and common data base with minis and micros at dispersed sites. Generally, all equipment and software are supplied by the same vendor, minimizing problems of compatibility between nodes. Because many computers have either a **fail-safe capability** (ability to continue operations, in spite of breakdown, due to the existence of backup) or a **fail-soft capability** (the ability to continue with a degraded level of operations), a breakdown in the hierarchy should not

Figure 20.2   **Hierarchical distributed data processing**

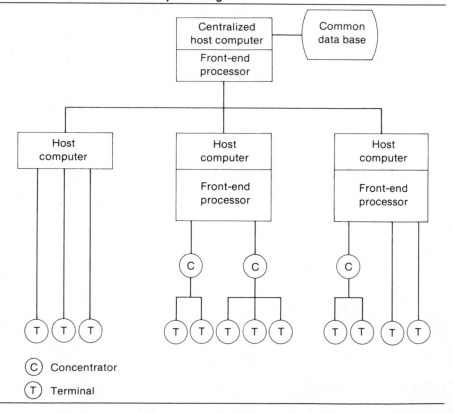

incapacitate the entire system. Even minis and micros have independent processing capabilities to some extent. Of course, Figure 20.2 is merely a model. Firms will design hierarchical configurations according to their needs.

SYSTEMS ARCHITECTURE

DDP, regardless of configuration, requires a system for data control, for resource sharing, and for coordination of dispersed processing. Procedures, software, hardware, and personnel are all needed to support DDP. How these resources are combined is part of the **systems architecture.** Systems architecture is not merely a design. It includes protocols for running DDP as well. Many computer vendors market architecture systems. In 1977, 16 different systems were in use in the United States alone;[1] others were available abroad.

However, choice of systems architecture is more limited than these figures imply. Vendors design software for specific equipment to encourage purchase of that hardware. Furthermore, lack of industry standards and rapid changes of technology add to problems of equipment interface within network systems. Users often find that only one network architecture can be adapted to their equipment configurations.

The most widely used architecture is **SNA (Systems Network Architecture).** IBM first introduced SNA in 1974 for hierarchical distributed processing.[2] In 1978, the IBM 8100 was placed on the market, a computer specifically designed for DDP using SNA. Because of IBM's dominance in the computer industry, its promotion of SNA and the 8100 gave impetus and legitimacy to DDP as a concept. And with the 8100, DDP became a commercial reality. An important feature of the 8100 is that it is a stand-alone computer designed for online processing and need not be linked to a host computer. Furthermore, installation does not require technical expertise. As an IBM press release notes, ". . . portions of the new system can be installed by users—with a set of easy to follow directions—in much the same way as a basic household stereo system might be set up."[3] By 1983, SNA had between 60,000 and 80,000 users and an estimated $30 billion invested in user code.

---

[1]For a detailed comparison, see Anthony Durniak, "Special Report: New Networks Tie Down Distributed Data Processing Concept," *Electronics* 51, no. 25 (December 7, 1978), pp. 101–22. For another editorial comparison, see Ralph G. Berglund, "Comparing Network Architectures," *Datamation* 24, no. 2 (February 1978). Both discuss American network architectures, but Durniak also discusses architectures commonly used in Europe and Japan.

[2]For a detailed study of SNA, read R. J. Cypsen, *Communications Architecture for Distributed Systems* (Reading, Mass.: Addison-Wesley Publishing, 1978), 711 p.

[3]Larry Woods, "IBM's 8100, First Impressions," *Datamation* 25, no. 3 (March 1979), p. 142.

DDP DATA BASES

There are many ways to organize DDP data bases.[4] All data can be centralized, or processing centers can keep **segments** of the data base. Sometimes dispersed centers keep data needed for local processing that **replicates** data stored in the central repository. A **hybrid approach** to data organization is also possible, in which dispersed processors keep both segmented and replicated data. The advantages of each type of organization are outlined below.

Centralized data base

Centralization of data is possible under DDP, but costs are high when all data must be transmitted to distributed nodes for processing. A centralized data base is appropriate when infrequent access to that data is needed or when updating needs to be strictly controlled.

Segmented distributed data base

Under **segmented distributed data base** organization, parts of the data base are stored at dispersed sites. The segments might be data from a function or data pertaining to a geographic area. The data is segmented according to local processing needs so that each site is basically independent, though other sites may draw on the distributed data base as a shared resource.

Replicated distributed data base

When more than one dispersed processor needs the same data, a common approach to data base organization is to store the data base at a central repository with duplicate segments needed for local processing stored at decentralized computers. This is called a **replicated distributed data base.** The local bases used for processing, including online real-time operations, are then periodically used to update the centralized data base. From the updated centralized base, the replicated data bases at distributed sites are updated in turn.

Large regional banks frequently adopt this system. Central processing takes place after banking hours and replicated distributed data bases are then created for branch offices. These latter bases are essentially working files used for local transactions such as deposits and withdrawals. At the end of each working day, the central data base is again updated by incorporating data on transactions conducted at the branches during the day, and the cycle begins once again with the creation of updated distributed data bases for the branch offices.

In general, the centralized data base includes all control and summary data, whereas transactional data and local data is in the replicated distributed data bases. Branch offices might still have to access the centralized data during the course of the day. This would occur

---

[4]For a further discussion of this subject, see a set of articles on distributed data bases in Burt H. Leibowitz and John H. Carson, *Distributed Processing* (Long Beach, Calif.: IEEE Computer Society, 1978), pp. 381–444.

when a customer of the bank wished to cash a check at a branch that did not have a record of his or her account. In this case, the transaction would have to be routed through the central data base.

One advantage of replicated data bases is that they provide backup, so the system is less vulnerable should failure occur at the central location. An additional advantage is that systems are more responsive to local needs when data is managed locally. (An advantage that applies to segmented data bases as well.) In particular, maintenance and updating of large and complex data bases are more effective when sections of the bases are under local control. Certain types of processing are also more efficient. For example, retrieval by indexes requires careful cross-indexing. Personnel on location with a need for the retrieved data will be more highly motivated in updating and maintaining indexes and retrieval software, and more knowledgeable about user needs than programmers at a centralized data base.

A major problem with replicated distributed data bases is minimizing redundancy. For efficient processing, no more data than absolutely necessary should be stored at remote sites. Unfortunately, the exact need of distributed centers for data is not easily determined.

Hybrid Approach

Some firms both segment and replicate their data bases. This is the **hybrid approach** to data base organization. For example, a large national business may segment its data base geographically, giving regional headquarters segments relevant to their operations. Replicated data from these headquarters is then distributed to branch offices within each region. Warehouse inventories are often controlled in this manner.

In a DBMS environment, both distributed DBMSs and a central DBMS are possible. Though the distributed systems would satisfy local needs, the central DBMS would have the overall schema of the entire logical data base, and be concerned with problems of security, integrity, and recovery for data, including selected data at distributed centers.[5]

WHEN TO IMPLEMENT DDP

Distributed data processing is not applicable to all organizations. How does a firm decide whether DDP is appropriate? Unfortunately, there is no formula or precise decision rule to guide management in reaching a DDP implementation decision. However, firms with geo-

[5]See James Martin, *Security, Accuracy and Privacy in Computer Systems* (Englewood Cliffs, N.J.:Prentice-Hall, 1973), and Jan Palmer, *Data Base System: A Practical Reference* (Wellesley, Mass.: QED Information Sciences, 1977), chap. 2, sections 2.26– 2.41.

Table 20.1   **Illustration of grid analysis**

Needs / Informational Sites	A	B	C	D
Process 1	X	X	X	X
2	X			
3		X	X	
Files 1	X			
2	X	X	X	X
3			X	X

graphically dispersed outlets, firms with a matrix structure rather than functional organization, multinationals, project-based companies (such as construction firms), and conglomerates have organizational structures that lead naturally to decentralization and the distributed mode.

In less obvious cases, a grid analysis may help determine the appropriateness of DDP. A sample is shown in Table 20.1. Here a hypothetical firm with sites A, B, C, and D (X axis) has informational needs satisfied by Processes 1–3 and Files 1–3 (Y axis). The informational requirements of each site are marked on the grid. Since Process 1 and File 2 are required by all sites, centralization of their processing is indicated. Since Process 2 and File 1 are needed by only a single site, they are clear candidates for the distributed mode while Process 3 and File 3 are possible candidates.[6]

However, management must assess the impact of DDP on the firm before DDP is implemented. How will DDP affect corporate decision making? Is DDP economically feasible? Usually, consideration of DDP as an alternative to centralized processing in use is triggered by dissatisfaction with current operations. Management must decide whether dissatisfaction will be remedied, in fact, by DDP and whether the benefits of DDP will be worth the cost and disruption which reorganization entails. Implementation considerations which go into a DDP decision are discussed below.

Costs

One component of cost is CPU hardware. Today's micros and small computers are dropping in price while increasing in computing power due to recent technological advances. This means DDP is economically feasible for many businesses that formerly could not afford dispersed processors. For example, a computer equalling the PDP-1 that

---

[6]See P. J. Down and F. E. Taylor, *Why Distributed Computing?* (Oxford, England: The National Computing Center, 1976), p. 41.

sold for $150,000 in 1965 could be purchased in 1979 for $700. And a computer such as the Amigo 300, a $32,000 (1979 figure) small business model with a megabyte memory has a computing capacity that exceeds the capacity of all 1965 models.

Terminal hardware is also dropping in cost, but as users demand more sophisticated units, such as intelligent terminals with local processing capabilities, actual terminal expenditures may rise. Figure 20.3 shows a relative cost curve for various types of terminals.

At the present time, transmission costs are not dropping as dramatically as the cost of hardware, so it is tempting to install additional processors in the distributed mode rather than transmit data to a centralized computer. High transmission costs are due, in part, to the monopolistic character of the transmission industry. However, changes in federal regulations may alter this situation in the future, so that firms implementing DDP should periodically make a financial reassessment of their equipment configurations.

Cost elements other than hardware and data communication facilities are software, processing staff requirements, end user staffing, and training. It should be recognized that 0.5 to 3.0 percent of a firm's budget is allocated to data processing as a norm in largely centralized

Figure 20.3   **Cost of terminals for varying degrees of distribution**

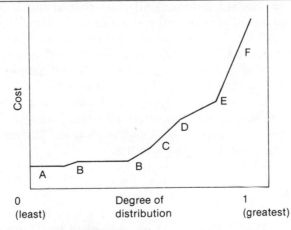

A = Unintelligent terminal
B = Introduction of some limited intelligence
C = Provision of more software to use local processing capability
D = Conversion of the intelligent terminal to a full blown mini-
     computer system with peripherals
E = More software to process more applications locally
F = Tending towards complete independence from the central site

Source: P. J. Down and T. E. Taylor, *Why Distributed Computing?* (Oxford, England: The National Computing Center, 1976), p. 78.

organizations. When a firm chooses DDP, processing costs may increase to as much as 5.0 percent.[7]

In general, DDP proves economically feasible when:

1. A high remote transaction rate exists.
2. Remote sites have a total mass data storage capability of approximately 40 megabytes.
3. A distributed local data base will handle most local needs. (No more than 20-30 percent of data base access requirements from other locations.)
4. Data transmitted is much smaller than local data use.
5. Distribution would improve overall organizational efficiency.

At present, small, high-powered, dedicated computers are proving cost-efficient when the central computer is overloaded, but, of course, every situation must be examined on an individual basis.

EDP reorganization

Distributed data processing requires that EDP personnel be shifted to dispersed centers for operations. Responsibility for systems development, security, and acquisitions may also be transferred to local managers. The EDP staff at the corporate center will be dismantled, managers will loose "empires," and new sets of interpersonal relationships will have to be forged. How far to go with decentralization may often depend on human factors rather than economic and technological considerations. Will managers accept a redefinition of their responsibilities or will jealousies undermine DDP service? Is competent staff available to manage and operate local computing sites? Will employees agree to transfer to distributed centers? Will distributed processing promote greater efficiency and happier staff relationships once the trauma of reorganization is over?

Conversion to DDP is much easier in a receptive environment, but the key to DDP success in all firms is careful DDP planning and competent management of DDP networks. The next sections of this chapter will discuss these topics.

PLANNING FOR DDP

The planning process, described in Chapter 8, applies to planning for distributed data processing as well as planning for a centralized processing system. Once in operation, both types of processing centers engage in planning, using the same guidelines, such as planning for the development of new systems, planning for expansions of facilities,

---

[7]George A. Champine et al., *Distributed Computer Systems: Impact on Management, Design and Analysis* (New York: North-Holland Publishing, 1980), p. 307.

or planning for new procedures or protocols. This section focuses on planning issues that are unique to DDP—how to decide the jurisdiction of local nodes, and how to coordinate operations and management in a firm with semiautonomous processing centers.

A cardinal rule in establishing a DDP center is to include users in a **planning task force.** This task force should develop a series of master plans which describe the flow of information within the organization under DDP and how responsibility for this flow is to be divided. These should include:

1. A master plan which outlines goals, functions, schedules, performance levels, and expenditures for each node and the center.
2. A master system design which details the structural relationship of nodes to center, the communications subsystems to be used, standards for hardware and software, and protocols for synchronization and security.
3. A master management plan which describes the degree of autonomy granted node managers, training plans, career development paths, possible job rotations, and control procedures.[8]

Planning for DDP structure is largely dependent on the technology available and forecasts on equipment to be expected in both the short- and long-term future. The nature of the business, top management's organizational philosophy, stage of growth of the firm, existing organizational structure, and management style also have a bearing.

There are three organizational variables in distributed processing which must be planned: degree of centralized control, hardware configurations, and data base distribution. At one extreme, a firm might choose to distribute only limited functions; at the other, total distribution and decentralization of processing with complete profit and loss responsibility assigned to local managers. In most cases, a firm will choose a position somewhere in between.[9]

The hypothetical firm described in Table 20.2 is one example of DDP. Here, the central staff has global responsibilities. That is, central management sets standards for planning and controls, is responsible for system maintenance and network design, prepares budgets, and assigns staff. This results in uniform standards throughout the organization, flexibility in personnel placement and utilization (small processing centers do not need nor can they afford the full-time services of on-site hiring and maintenance personnel), system backup, and centralization of major financial decisions. Managers on site have con-

---

[8]For more on this subject, see Champine et al., *Distributed Computer Systems*, pp. 318–19.

[9]For a good discussion of alternatives, see Grayce M. Booth, *The Distributed System Environment: Some Practical Approaches* (New York: McGraw-Hill, 1981).

Table 20.2   **Sample DDP structure: distribution of activities between center and nodes**

Center	Distributed node
Overall planning of:	Local planning for processing
Corporate systems	
Policy determination	
Resource needs	
Compatibility	
Planning and control of:	Planning and control of:
Major software	Local software
Global security	Local security
Global standards	Local standards
Common data base	Local data base
Management and control of:	Management and control of:
Central resources	Local resources
Network management of:	
Design	
Operations and control	
Maintenance	
Budgeting of central and	Budgeting of local spending
network expenditures	
Systems quality control	Local quality control
Systems audit	Local audit
Hiring/coordinating	Local personnel management
systems personnel	

trol over local planning, local resources, and local processing. Figure 19.2 in the preceding chapter is basically this DDP configuration.

Another approach is to assign specific functions to individual nodes. For example, the New York office of a firm might be responsible for policy and resource planning, the Chicago office responsible for the common data base and quality control, San Francisco for standards and network management, and so on. Table 20.3 shows this concept. Under this structure, some duties assigned to the center in Table 20.2 are distributed among the nodes.

These two examples are oversimplifications, for in practice, many firms have mixed processing modes, combining features of centralized, decentralized,[10] and distributed processing. For example, Hewlett-Packard manufactured 4,000 products in 38 plants in 1978, and had 172 sales offices around the world. The company's 1,400 computers served 4,500 employees, mixing all processing modes. For example, materials, services, legal reporting, and employee benefits were centralized; customer service, inventories, payroll, and personnel decentralized; with production information, orders, and accounts receivable handled by the distributed mode.[11]

---

[10]Decentralized processing refers to physically separated, stand-alone processing entities.

[11]See Cort Van Renssalear, "Centralize? Decentralize? Distribute?" *Datamation* 25, no. 9 (April 1979), p. 90.

Table 20.3   **Sample DDP structure (distributed functions)**

Function \ Site	New York	Chicago	San Francisco	London
Planning Need assessment Policy determination	X X			
Resource Compatibility Acquisitions Major spending	X X X			
Common data base		X		
Standards			X	
Major software development				X
Network management			X	
Quality control		X		
Auditing	X			

MANAGEMENT OF DDP

The management of distributed processing can be divided into the areas of static and dynamic control. Because firms may differ in network configurations, the location of managers responsible for these controls may vary from one firm to another, but both types of control are necessary in DDP systems. **Static control** deals with equipment, data base structure, and applications whereas **dynamic control** concerns monitoring, testing, interfacing, and security.

With regard to static control, compatibility is the key issue. Equipment guidelines and language standards are essential. For example, management might decide that all equipment should support an ANSI standard version of COBOL or that all hardware used for scientific processing provide a standard FORTRAN compiler. Data bases for applications must be designed for integration and interface protocols established for information exchange. Above all, management must check to see that duplication of effort is avoided.

Dynamic control involves monitoring the network so that problems or failures at each node can be detected and corrected. Each component of a DDP system should have self-test facilities to assist in isolating the source of problems. A veritable arsenal of security measures is needed in managing the transmission of data over long distances because the possibility of wiretapping and electrical interference must be added to conventional security issues, such as access, integrity of data, privacy, threat monitoring, and auditing. In addition, statistics should be collected on the system and use patterns analyzed to help identify potential network weakness.

Because of the complexity of distributed data processing, many firms today assign one person from top management with the specific responsibility of **network administration.** Obviously, a person in this position would need managerial and technical skills of the highest order since issues such as compatibility of hardware, language choice, division of the data base, and system security (issues that affect the entire operation of the firm) would be within the manager's jurisdiction. The duties assigned to this position also include error detection and correction, equipment monitoring, and traffic monitoring.

RISKS AND REWARDS OF DDP

The initiation of DDP involves a multiplicity of risks. Among the more common are poor system design resulting from inexperience, redundancy among nodes, problems with interface, costs that are hidden or that escalate, and employee resistance to change. Companies may have technical, personnel, and organizational problems coordinating multiple vendors and models of equipment. They may lack sufficient personnel to staff the different nodes, and have problems attracting professionals and training employees in DDP. Privacy, security, and standardization become major managerial headaches.

The rewards, however, are many. Harry Katzan cites increased system responsiveness, planned growth, resource sharing, a data base customized to organizational patterns, and improved reliability.[12] Information sharing, the ability to incorporate new services and technologies with ease, longer system life expectancy based on increased adaptability, and possible integration of multiple systems into networks are other advantages. Certainly, increased motivation among distributed staff should be included in this list of benefits. Travel expenses should be reduced and the importance of geographical location of facilities diminished. In addition, distributing responsibility among departments will reduce pressures on top management.

---

[12]Harry Katzan, An *Introduction to Distributed Data Processing* (New York: Petrocelli Books, 1978), 242 p.

FUTURE OF DDP

The future of DDP is clouded due to uncertainty in two major areas: federal regulations and standards. Though recent court decisions enable both AT&T and IBM to enter the field of data communications (of benefit to DDP users since competition between these corporate giants should lower communication costs), the FCC's stance on DDP is unclear. Lack of agreement over network standards is also an impediment to DDP research and development. The Europeans utilize X.25 standards: the Americans, SNA and SDLC (Synchronous Data Link Control).[13] DDP will not be widely implemented until universal standards are adopted and DDP equipment and software of competing manufacturers can be integrated into a single DDP system.

Once DDP is cost-effective and hardware, systems architecture, and communications are integrated into reliable and robust systems, DDP will become more viable. Advances are being made in distributed data base technology and software so that data can be accessed with ease no matter where it is stored in the distributed network. Solutions to problems of deadlock and optimal routing of queries are presently being researched. Future systems must be less vulnerable to failure and more easily restructured in response to growth or changed informational needs. DDP applications will undoubtedly broaden from current use for data entry and validation to full office automation and shop floor control.

DDP should give computing power to large segments of the population heretofore lacking efficient and speedy access to information processing. Indeed, DDP's greatest impact may be democratization of the computer. Already personal computers are in the price range of many households and their widespread use means computers are no longer the prerogative of corporate boardrooms and the business elite. When the computing power of personal computers is extended through low cost networks, the mysticism of computers should disappear entirely.

SUMMARY AND CONCLUSIONS

DDP takes computing power from one large centralized computer and disperses this power to sites where processing demand is generated. The equipment used is a mix of terminals, minis, and small-business computers integrated by appropriate system architecture.

---

[13]See F. P. Corr and D. H. Neal, "SNA and Emerging International Standards," *IBM Systems Journal* 18, no. 2 (1979), pp. 244–62.

Some computers are being specially designed for DDP applications. The computers themselves can be linked in a variety of configurations, such as star, ring, or hybrid configurations, though the hierarchical structure with fail-soft capability is more common.

Distributed processing offers firms an increasingly wide range of organizational alternatives as opposed to the former black and white choice of centralization or decentralization. The willingness and ability of EDP personnel to manage local computer centers, and advances in chip technology and telecommunications have made DDP feasible.

Deciding when to distribute depends on how much processed data is needed by the corporate center and how much is utilized at branches. One rule of thumb states that distributed processing is indicated when 20 percent of the processed information is needed by the center and 80 percent at local sites. Other factors indicating the need for DDP are decentralization of responsibility, distributed functions, and limited information flow to headquarters.

A major advantage of DDP is that systems can begin simply and grow modularly. DDP can also be adapted to various organization structures and modified when necessary to adapt to changing patterns in the flow of information. These and other advantages are listed in Table 20.4. Limitations appear in Table 20.5. Most of the technological limitations will be overcome in time. The computer industry is already researching systems architecture, equipment, software, and data base management systems in response to users' needs and technological needs of an EDP environment. Resistance to change will slow the spread of DDP, but once a firm restructures its data process-

Table 20.4	Advantages of distributed data processing
	1. Offers decentralized processing and satisfies desire for local autonomy and local application development. Facilitates user accessibility to computer centers.
	2. Local control over needed segments of the data base is retained at the distributed centers.
	3. Quality of input and processing is improved because of greater sensitivity to local conditions.
	4. Users feel analysts at dispersed sites are more responsive to their needs.
	5. Enables modular growth with little disruption at central site.
	6. Enables use of different equipment at sites, provided interface problems are resolved.
	7. Provides stand-alone operations with fail-soft capability for hierarchical structures and alternative routes for ring structures.
	8. Provides middle management at distributed level with unique, relevant, and timely information, and consequently a measure of independence from top management.
	9. Enables use of heterogeneous equipment and resource sharing, including dynamic load balancing (by moving around and distributing load) to maximize throughput.

Table 20.5	**Limitations of DDP**
	1. Can be more expensive than centralized processing in spite of low-cost minis, largely because of the cost of transmission, software necessary for DDP, and the overlapping of equipment (especially disks in cases of replicated data bases).
	2. The interface of expensive equipment from different vendors at dispersed nodes is a problem, for equipment may differ in instruction sets and operating systems.
	3. Most existing software packages are designed for stand-alone computers and need to be adapted for DDP.
	4. Communication systems of DDP are vulnerable to security violations.
	5. National and international standards for network communication do not exist, causing problems of interfacing and implementing DDP.
	6. With autonomous distributed sites, corporate standards of development, integration, and data base are more difficult to enforce.

ing and new relationships and power structures are forged, DDP will prove its value to users as well as to technical personnel.

One final word. DDP requires the total commitment of top management. Special staffing and new positions, such as data base administrator and network administrator, should ease systems implementation and operations, but the involvement of management in planning for DDP and setting standards and controls is essential to ensure that the system meets the firm's needs. Though many of the planning decisions are technical, they should not be delegated exclusively to technicians. Coordination, integration, and control are keystones to DDP success and these are the responsibility of corporate management.

CASE STUDY: DISTRIBUTED PROCESSING AT TEXAS INSTRUMENTS INCORPORATED*

Texas Instruments, the 15th largest U.S. company in the computing industry, with revenues of $666.7 million in 1981, sells primarily minis and peripherals. It has 48 plants in 18 countries, 5,100 terminals, and 190 remote job entry stations, with expectations of expanding to 25,000 terminals and 10,000 minicomputers by the mid-1980s. Distributed processing was adopted in the 70s to handle the multifaceted needs of this multisite company.

The central host system handles 6,000 batch jobs, 320,000 transactions, and 1,250 TSO log-ons per day. It also processes inquiry, mi-

---

*Source: Ron Person, "How TI Distributes Its Processing," *Datamation* 25, no. 4 (April 1979), pp. 98–103.

crofiche and copy services, data preparation, Xerox 1200 printing, and plotting. The applications portfolio includes automated design of printed circuit boards using interactive graphics, work in progress, a schedule and control system for production, controls for processing, a worldwide inventory system, customer service management in the field, in-factory use of distributed processing, as well as real-time visibility of job status, dynamic work queue sequencing, and shop load analysis.

The main data base is maintained in 300 megabytes at the host in Houston. Remote CRTs and printers are connected to the company's 11 dispatch sites (each having 9.2 megabyte disks), and the entire network is tied together by two 4800 baud data lines.

KEY WORDS

Distributed data base	Offloading
Distributed data processing (DDP)	Planning task force
	Replicated distributed data base
Dynamic control	Ring network
Fail-safe capability	Segmented distributed data base
Fail-soft capability	SNA (Systems Network Architecture)
Hierarchical distribution	
Horizontal systems	Star network
Hybrid approach	Static control
Network administration	Systems architecture
Node	

DISCUSSION QUESTIONS

1. Describe the essential elements of a distributed processing system.
2. What are the characteristics of DDP? Which activities should be distributed? Which centralized? Would this distribution change with:
   a.   Size of organization?
   b.   Organizational structure of firm?
   c.   Geographical distribution of branches?
3. Would you select a star computer configuration in preference to a ring or hierarchical configuration? Why? Give examples of each in business and industry.
4. What configuration of computer equipment in a DDP environment would you select for the following situations:

    a. A bank with many branches?

    b. A wholesaler with many warehouses?

    c. A factory with distributed plants each manufacturing a different component?

5. What problems arising out of personnel conflicts and power struggles should be expected in the transition from centralized EDP to DDP? What can be done to minimize the harmful effects of such conflicts?

6. What are the problems of control, security, and privacy to be expected in a DDP environment? How can one overcome such problems?

7. What is the role of telecommunications and teleprocessing in a DDP environment? How will costs and regulation of telecommunications affect DDP?

8. What type of business or industrial environment lends itself to DDP?

9. What factors should be taken into consideration in deciding whether to implement DDP?

10. In planning for DDP, what types of master plans should be formulated?

11. Describe the difference between dynamic and static control in DDP. Does the type and degree of control vary among businesses and among different firms within an industry?

12. What is the role of a network administrator? When is a network administrator needed?

13. List disadvantages and risks in DDP.

14. List the benefits of DDP.

SELECTED ANNOTATED BIBLIOGRAPHY

Becker, Hal B. "Let's Put Information and Networks into Perspective." *Datamation* 24, no. 3 (March 1978), pp. 81–86.

    Becker identifies the pitfalls and unresolved problems of distributed data processing. The author is optimistic that all the problems will be resolved.

Booth, Grayce M. *The Distributed System Environment: Some Practical Approaches.* New York: McGraw-Hill, 1981, 286 p.

    This book, written by a practitioner from Honeywell, does not have an IBM bias nor the theoretical bias of an academician. Good sections on distributed network architectures, distributed systems structures, and design considerations are included.

Champine, George A. *Distributed Computer Systems: Impact on Management, Design, and Analysis.* Amsterdam: North-Holland Publishing, 1980, 380 p.

    Comprehensive coverage of distributed processing, including excellent chapters on human interface in distributed systems (Chapter 6) and the management of distributed systems (Chapter 15).

Champine, George A. "Six Approaches to Distributed Data Bases." *Datamation* 23, no. 5 (May 1977), pp. 69–72.

This is a good discussion of centralized versus distibuted data processing (and distributed data bases) with a description and evaluation of six actual approaches used: ARPANET (a national nonbusiness-oriented system), SITA, Celanese, Bank of America, Aeroquip, and Loews Companies, Inc.

Down, P. J., and F. F. Taylor. *Why Distributed* Computing? Manchester, England: National Computing Center, 1976, 168 p.
This book is the result of a project to investigate the alternatives and implications of DDP for the corporate planner in the business environment in England. The concepts discussed and even some of the cost data are applicable to this country. It is an excellent overview of the subject of DDP, including operational and design considerations.

Durniak, Anthony. "Special Report: New Networks Tie Down Distributed Processing Concepts." *Electronics* 51, no. 3 (December 1978), pp. 107–20.
An excellent article on network architecture, including both American and foreign approaches. Somewhat technical but not difficult reading.

Katzan, Jr., Harry. *An Introduction to Distributed* Data Processing. New York: Petrocelli Books, 1978, 242 p.
This book is in three parts: Management Overiew of the Distributed Concept; Data Communications Concept; and Distributed Systems Concepts. In other words, the communications link is emphasized. A well-written, easy-to-read, nonmathematical text that is generously illustrated.

Kaufmann, Felix. "Distributed Processing: A Discussion for Executives Travelling over Difficult EDP Terrain." *Data Base* 10, no. 1 (Summer 1978), pp. 9–13.
A pleasure to read. Many terms are defined and concepts are well stated.

Liebowitz, Burt H., and John H. Carson. *Distributed Processing Tutorial,* 2d ed. Long Beach, Calif: IEEE Computer Society, 1978.
This book is not a tutorial nor is the text limited to a discussion of DDP. It is a set of over 50 articles on topics such as communications, networks, intelligent terminals, multiprocessors, and distributed data bases. As with most sets of readings, it is a mix of excellent and mediocre articles. But overall, it is a good collection, including both survey-type and technical articles.

Lorin, H. "Distributed Processing; An Assessment." *IBM Systems Journal* 18, no. 4 (1979), pp. 582–603.
This article discusses the potential benefits and pitfalls of DDP: centralized management, historical relationship of DDP with online systems, the reliability and growth of fail-soft systems, and adjusting DDP to the organization structure of the firm. Lorin concludes, "We do not know, in general, whether complexity will increase or decrease distributed processing systems, or how operational costs will evolve. We are just discovering an art."

McLaughlin, Michael J., and Michael S. Katz. "Distributed Processing—The Second Generation." *Infosystems* 26, no. 2 (February 1979), pp. 38 ff.
The author analyzes the first generation of DDP and concludes that it was

difficult to implement, operate, and maintain. The author then discusses the second generation and the continuing need for distributed data base management software, applications programs, operating systems, and user acceptance.

Patrick, Robert L. "A Checklist for System Design." *Datamation* 26, no. 2 (January 1980) pp. 147–53.

This article is an excerpted verion of the author's *Design Handbook for Distributed Systems*, discussing 15 ideas on systems design (out of 186 ideas in the book). He describes how each idea has been successfully implemented in practice. The article is especially good on the human factors of designing and implementing a distributed system.

Scherr, A. L. "Distributed Data Processing." *IBM Systems Journal* 17, no. 4 (1978) pp. 324–43.

This article discusses different configuration choices of distributed data processing and evaluates them in terms of price–performance ratio, organizational needs, communications, and software. This is a scholarly but nontechnical article.

Thierauf, Robert J. *Distributed Data Processing*. Englewood Cliffs, N.J.: Prentice-Hall, 1978, 305 p.

The fact that a textbook is published on this new and controversial topic is an indication of the importance of this subject as early as 1978 and its approaching maturity. This book includes some material from the author's previous work, *Systems Analysis and Design of Real-time Management Information Systems*. Both books are packed with lists, tables, and diagrams and are very tightly written.

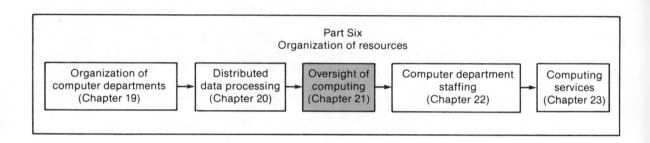

Part Six
Organization of resources

| Organization of computer departments (Chapter 19) | → | Distributed data processing (Chapter 20) | → | Oversight of computing (Chapter 21) | → | Computer department staffing (Chapter 22) | → | Computing services (Chapter 23) |

CHAPTER 21

Oversight of computing

All the time the Guard was looking for her, first through a telescope, then through a microscope, and then through an opera-glass. At last he said, "You are travelling the wrong way..."

Lewis Carroll, *Through the Looking-Glass*

Though computer centers have often been called "a business within a business," for reasons described in this chapter, they are tied to corporation management and user departments through a committee structure which involves management/users in development projects and control of computing. The sections which follow will describe both the responsibilities and interaction of steering committees, the computer director, top management, and users in the oversight of computing.

It should be recognized that roles in computing are not static but continually evolving. Distributed processing—the trend of the 80s—requires corporate managers to integrate diverse systems into cohesive information infrastructures. New skills are required for the management of high-speed communication networks. Changes in the computer environment affect users as well. For example, DDP has shifted the responsibility for local data bases and processing to users. In time, the committee structure outlined in this chapter may be replaced by a totally new concept of how computer centers should be organized. For the moment, however, this chapter represents how many firms attempt to integrate their computing facilities with management and users.

COMPUTING CENTER: A BUSINESS WITHIN A BUSINESS

In the organizational framework of a firm, a computer center is merely one of many departments. In structure, however, computer departments resemble independent businesses. Indeed, they can be compared to manufacturing concerns, for they operate as a job shop (in batch mode) or a continuous production shop (real-time processing) to provide a product (information). There is a correlation in specific activities as well, as shown in Table 21.1. For example, facilities planning in manufacturing could be compared to computer configuration and network planning, tooling to programming, and a product line to the center's applications portfolio. The primary difference is product disposal, because computer centers do not have to rely on market mechanisms for pricing or selling. Their product is often for a captured market when sold to other departments in the company, or considered a service when provided to user departments without charge.

Nevertheless, computer centers seek to provide a product that is competitive with outside information processing centers. To do so they must be managed with efficiency and effectiveness. Usually a

Table 21.1   **The computer center compared to a manufacturing business**

Manufacturing business	Information processing center
Product planning	Information systems planning
Facilities planning	Computer configuration and network planning
Market research	Computing demand forecasting
Product research	Keeping abreast with computer technology
Market development	User education
Design	System design
Analyze problem	System analysis
Tooling	Programming
Production scheduling	Job scheduling
Production	Computing and operations
Production control	Production/operations control
Inventory control	Supplies inventory
Quality control	I/O control
	Information quality control
Consumer survey	User satisfaction survey
Consumer services liaison	User liaison
Personnel management	Personnel management
Administration	Administration
Product for sale	Information (sold, or as a service)
Product line	Applications portfolio
Product line strategy	Applications development strategy
Product cost analysis	Applications project estimation
Pricing policy	Charge policy

steering committee acts like a board of directors to oversee the center, with an appointed head or director given responsibility for daily operations. Some officers are shared with the corporate body, such as a general counsel, auditors, or purchasing officers. Planning, development, and operations are generally controlled by a committee structure described below.

STEERING COMMITTEE AND SUBCOMMITTEES

In most firms, planning for a computer center is the prerogative of a **steering committee** once a charter is received from top management outlining the services the center is to deliver. The steering committee usually establishes corporate policy toward information systems, makes long- and short-range plans for the computer center, and allocates computing resources. It may also set standards and performance levels, schedule, monitor and control operations, and resolve conflicts. See Table 21.2 for a summary of the responsibilities of a typical steering committee.

Some steering committees are more successful than others. Many computer center directors consider them bureaucratic nonsense, rubber-stamp committees of little value. Those that function effectively do so because of the following reasons:

1. They involve senior management (as committee members) in setting goals, in allocating information resources, and in project selection.

2. They promote increased senior management awareness of the in-

Table 21.2	Functions of a typical steering committee
	Establishes corporate policy for information systems.
	Assures coordination of information systems policy with corporate goals, objectives, and policies.
	Approves strategic, tactical, long- and short-range plans.
	Recommends to top management the allocation of resources (budgetary decisions).
	Evaluates and approves proposals for resource acquisition and development of projects.
	Reviews and monitors milestones of major development projects.
	Establishes criteria and levels of performance for computing operations.
	Establishes evaluation procedures.
	Monitors and controls operations and schedules.
	Resolves and arbitrates conflicts on priorities and schedules.
	Formulates standards, guidelines, and constraints for both development and operations.
	Allocates scarce resources.
	Exercises funding discipline over major expenditures.
	Provides communication link between computer center and corporate management.
	Provides forum for feedback from users.

formation management function in an organization, and enlist top management's support of project and manpower plans.

3. They make long-range plans instead of approving projects singly.
4. They involve users in project development and require them to justify needs and defend claims of benefits.

In organizations with a small computing facility, a single steering committee may suffice. Control of large centers offering complex services will necessitate a steering subcommittee structure. For example, a project review committee may be given responsibility for project development; a tactical steering committee, responsibility for operations. Other common subcommittees and their possible reporting units are listed in Table 21.3. The function of **standing committees** differs from **ad hoc committees** insofar as the latter are created to solve an immediate problem, then dissolved after a solution is reached, whereas the former have ongoing responsibilities.

Top management should be represented in the steering committee as should management representatives from user groups. Sometimes consultants will be added to the committee to ensure a balance between technically oriented members and those knowledgeable about the goals, objectives, and policies of the organization. A balance between line and staff representatives is also advisable, as is a balance between planners, production personnel, and individuals from accounting and finance. The committee then becomes a forum for com-

Table 21.3   **List of committees and their reporting units**

Committee	Responsible to
Standing committees:	
Steering committee	Top management
Tactical steering committee	
Operating committee	
Users' committee for operations	
Project priority committee (for development, maintenance, and redevelopment)	Steering committee
Resource planning committee	
Data base committee	Steering committee or director of systems
Ad hoc committees:	
Resource selection committee	
Hardware committee	
Software committee	
Resource acquisition and implementation committee	Steering committee
Security advisory committee	
Privacy advisory committee	
Control advisory committee	
Project team	Project manager and project review committee

puter management and user departments to express their views, air their problems, and reconcile their differences with regard to information systems. The committee also helps establish lines of communication between management, EDP staff, and users, facilitating the absorption of computer technology within the framework of organizational goals.

At times, the steering committee may act as a crisis center. However, problems should be brought to the committee before reaching crisis proportions through feedback and control of the subcommittee structure, through standard and exceptional reporting, or by the computer director who reports to the committee on performance of the computing center, user satisfaction, and project development progress.

ROLE OF TOP MANAGEMENT

Top management oversees and controls computing by chartering the steering committee and serving on the committee and subcommittees as members. It also makes budgetary decisions for computer center funding. Management's role is not strictly supervisory, however, for management users participate in developing new systems and are directly affected by quality of computing output and services.

To be more specific, management, through the steering committee, will screen computer projects proposed for development, then monitor, review, and control development of selected projects. Management representatives will also participate in feasibility studies and user specifications when new applications are being developed for management, and help evaluate testing to see that systems developed do, in fact, meet managerial needs. Thus, top management both supervises development (on steering committee) and has representatives serving as working members on development teams, as shown in Figure 21.1. In addition, corporate management has budgetary control over development activities, making GO/NO GO decisions following feasibility studies, selecting methods of financing projects, and ap-

Figure 21.1 **Relationship of management to development**

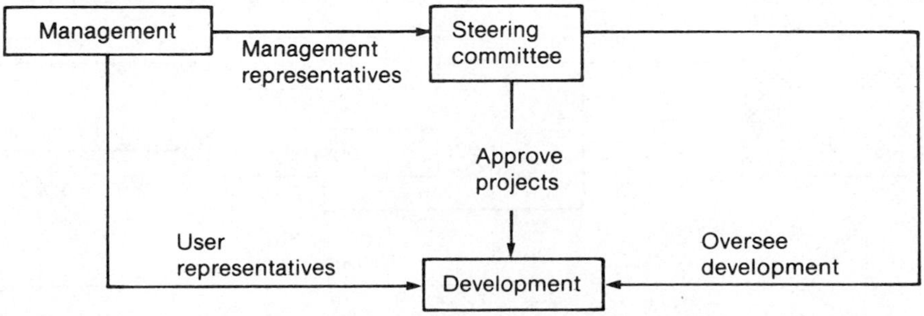

proving major resource acquisitions as can be seen in Figure 21.2. This latter figure also clarifies the relationship of management and computer center staff to each stage of development.

With regard to operations, management again has a dual role: as user and as controller through the steering committee and subcommittees. Management users will request scheduling of jobs, provide data for processing, and utilize output, exercising a measure of control by refusing to accept output that fails to adhere to system specifications. Through membership in the steering committee, management will appoint auditors to evaluate efficiency and effectiveness of daily operations. Approval of maintenance or redevelopment and the setting of priorities is also a responsibility of the steering committee which gives management control over operations. Figure 21.3 shows the user/controller facets of management's role in operations.

Figure 21.2   **Role of management in the development process**

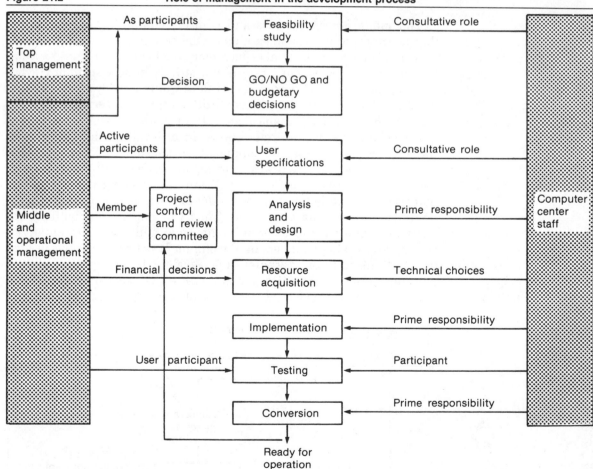

USERS

This chapter has already discussed management as **users** (management's role as a user in development teams, in requesting processing service, and controlling output). Users are found in nonmanagerial levels of an organization as well. They may be terminal operators, coders, schedule clerks, programmers, engineers using CAD/CAM, or secretaries in an electronic office. Whatever their level, users do have some responsibility in the oversight of computing. For example, user

Figure 21.3   **Corporate management's role in operations**

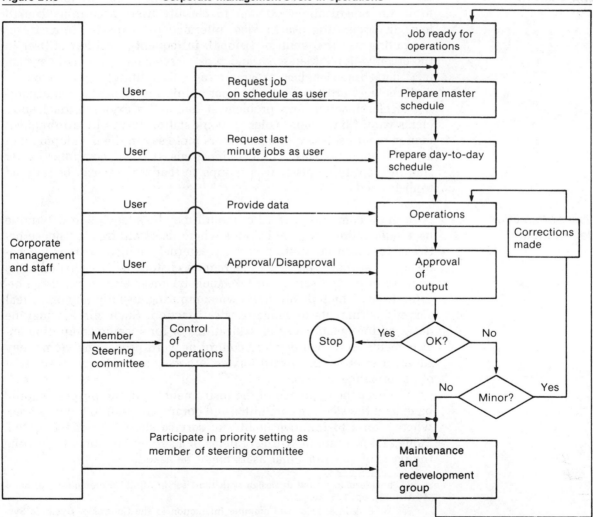

representatives serve as members of the steering committee and participate in the development of new systems just as management representatives do. What makes users of special value in oversight is that they have daily experience with the effectiveness of computing and can provide feedback to the steering committee and computer director regarding system weaknesses. To collect and act on user feedback requires (1) mechanisms for identifying and classifying users, (2) instruments for determining user satisfaction, and (3) procedures for evaluating user criticisms and improving service.

User identification and classification

Opinion regarding effectiveness of operations is sought from all users, regardless of their level in the organizational hierarchy of a firm. But organizations attempt to **classify** users according to skill level in computing use (novice, intermediate, expert),[1] intensity of computing use (frequent, occasional, infrequent), position of user in the organization's hierarchy, and type of systems used: static system (e.g., data base searches, programming, text editing) versus dynamic systems (e.g., process control).[2] User opinion is then weighed according to classification and problem at hand. For example, data entry clerks would have more voice in work station layout than infrequent management users; experienced users more say in the development of a DBMS than novices. The classifications also aid computer center staff in identifying major user groups so that services can be tailored to their needs.

User satisfaction determination

In small companies, word of mouth may be adequate to determine **user satisfaction.** In organizations where users are free to choose between in-house computing and an external facility, market mechanisms are at play. Satisfied users remain customers. Dissatisfied users demand improved service or take their business elsewhere. Large organizations, which do all their own computing, usually rely on formal survey instruments to gauge user satisfaction. Such surveys may be designed for specific user classifications or for specific computing environments, such as inventory control or word processing. Some may survey user attitudes toward service, others concentrate on evaluation of performance criteria.

Whatever the approach of the instrument used, the purpose should be to help the steering committee and computing staff to identify areas where efforts to improve quality of service should be concentrated. Table 21.4 is a sample listing of items in a survey instrument, showing the types of questions that users might be asked.

---

[1]B. Shneiderman, "How to Design with the User in Mind," *Datamation* 28, no. 4 (April 1982), pp. 125–26.

[2]See W. B. Rouse, "Human-Computer Interaction in the Control of Dynamic Systems," *Computing Surveys* 13, no. 1 (March 1981), pp. 71–99.

Corrective action   Usually an individual (or committee) from the computing center staff will be assigned to analyze responses to user surveys. Problems that can be quickly solved are sorted from those requiring long-term solutions, the former sent to the appropriate staff member for action, the latter to the steering committee or relevant project team for study.

Surveys may indicate a demand for an added peripheral, such as a faster printer or plotter, identify problems with program maintenance, or show the need for development of a new application. A common

Table 21.4	Sample user satisfaction questionnaire

A. *User inventory*
   Name:
   Department:
   Position:
   Relationship to computer center:
   Participation in computer center organization (committees):
   Computer center resources used:

Resource	*Frequency and degree of usage*

   Knowledge of computing:
   Interest in computing:

B. *Satisfaction Survey* (You may wish to answer some of the questions below for each output you use.)
   Development:
   Was your project developed on time?
   Was your project adequately tested?
   Did your project meet your initial needs? Changing needs?
   Is your application using the most recent technology available?
   Is your application satisfactorily integrated with other applications?

   Operations:
   Is your report:
   a. Timely?
   b. Accurate?
   c. Well packaged?
   d. Corrected promptly when errors occur?
   e. Available in mode desired?
   f. Easy to use/understand/verify for accuracy?
   Are computer center personnel helpful and cooperative?
   How can your existing reports be improved?
   How can the service to you be improved?
   How can the computer center be more responsive to your needs?
   How can the structure of the computer center be changed
   to improve:
   a. Performance?
   b. Responsiveness?
   Is user orientation and training:
   a. Adequate?
   b. Timely?

complaint is lengthy turnaround time. In response, many centers, especially those with a DBMS environment, institute a quick response service (QRS), the equivalent of the express lane in a grocery store, for users needing fast service for short simple reports. Some centers will negotiate a user contract which is easy to monitor and control. This might include a response time guarantee (e.g., no more than five seconds 95 percent of the time). Many complaints can be resolved at small incremental cost yet yield a high payoff in user good will. The computing center can then count on the support and cooperation of users when tackling problems that have long-term solutions.

An emerging phenomenon is that of an information center which is a walk-in office that offers information and help to users on everything related to computers. This may include software debugging, advice on resource acquisition, assistance with solving computing-related organizational problems, etc.

In summary, user opinion helps the steering committee and the computer director determine how computer service might be improved. User representatives on the steering committee are in a position to see that user concerns, once identified, are followed by corrective action. So users exercise control in two ways: by reporting problems and by overseeing computer center operations through representation in the steering committee structure.

ROLE OF COMPUTER DIRECTOR

The computer director is responsible for daily operations of the computer center. This responsibility is delegated by the steering committee in many firms. In such cases, the computer director can be hired/fired by the committee and approach top management only through the committee.

Like other departmental managers in a firm, the computer director must prepare and control budgets, and select, hire, train, and evaluate personnel. The personnel roster includes individuals with a wide range of skills, from clerks engaged in repetitive tasks such as data preparation who have hourly deadlines and a short-term outlook, to highly trained professionals engaged in experimental system design whose vision is long-term. Such diversity complicates management. Management of such a department requires both theories of leadership advocated by Douglas McGregor.[3] For clerks, machine operators and maintenance programmers, **Theory X** is useful, a theory which assumes that people must be coerced, controlled, directed, and even threatened with punishment. **Theory Y,** which assumes people are self-motivated, self-controlled, and have no conflict between self-ac-

---

[3]Douglas McGregor, *The Human Side of Enterprise* (New York: McGraw-Hill, 1960), 246 p.

tualization and effective organizational performance, is appropriate for analysts and professionals like the DBA.

Whatever mode of leadership is chosen, a degree of tension will exist between the center director and computer personnel, a tension that is inherent in boss–employee relationships. The computer director, however, must also contend with the hostility of users. Computer technology tends to upset traditional organizational and operational patterns, sending disruptive reverberations throughout the firm. It is the computing head who is responsible for orchestrating the introduction of new computer applications, for setting up interface committees to interpret technology to users, and smoothing conversion to new systems. The role of change agent requires knowledge of human factors and a thick skin since the director must often work with those who resent the intrusion of computers in their work spheres.

The computer director cannot seek solace with other department heads, however, for they, too, often harbor resentment against the computer department. They are piqued that computing is given favored status yet produces no tangible product or benefit that has an ascertainable market value.[4] And they are embittered that the failure rate accepted in computer projects would lose them their jobs.

There is also a strain in the relationship between corporate management and the computer director. (The computer director may interact with management through the steering committee or be directly responsible to management, reporting to a vice president of information services or some similar officer.) This strain is based in part on differences in their backgrounds, technical orientation, and objectives, but can also be traced to problems in communication, for technical jargon and computer acronyms are not always understood by persons outside the computing field. "Talking down" to management is also inappropriate for management is becoming increasingly knowledgeable about computer capabilities. A genuine dialogue should be sought: corporate management sharing its vision of the firm's future, the computer director explaining in nontechnical terms how computer advances, such as microtechnology, telecommunications, networking, office automation, CAD/CAM, and robots, can further corporate goals.

In view of all the tense relationships a computer director faces on the job, no wonder there is a high turnover in the position: 35 percent in 1975 compared to 10–15 percent in other senior executive positions.[5]

---

[4]See John N. Petroff, "Why Are DP Managers So Unpopular?" *Datamation* 19, no. 2 (February 1973), pp. 77–79.

[5]These statistics come from a study by Richard L. Nolan reported in "Business Needs a New Breed of EDP Manager," *Harvard Business Review* 54, no. 2 (March–April 1976), p. 34b. The 1980 turnover for computer executives was estimated between 30 and 40 percent in Richard L. Nolan and Frederic E. Finch, "Towards a Theory in Data Processing Leadership," in *Managing the Data Processing Function*, ed. Richard L. Nolan. (St. Paul, Minn.: West Publishing, 1982), p. 363.

Risk is also an important element in a computer director's job. Technical risks are run when trying to incorporate the latest computer advances in new systems. Financial risks are high due to the probability of time and cost overruns in system development. Security of computer resources and privacy of data are vulnerable to assault while reputation and credibility depend on user satisfaction. These risks, however, should be shared by the steering committee which is responsible for planning and control. Top management can help moderate job stress by being accessible for counsel, and by establishing a fair approach to evaluation of the director's performance.

The role of a computer director is determined to some degree by the size of the applications portfolio a computer director must oversee. When the portfolio is limited (which would mean a small budget and few computer employees), the director's job is more technical and less managerial. As the size and complexity of applications increase, however, technical tasks will be delegated to analysts and specialists, freeing the executive for managerial concerns associated with an enlarged staff and budget. Figure 21.4 shows that the skill requirement of a director's job is a function of portfolio size and complexity.

New roles for computer center directors have brought about changes in their style of management. Today, computer directors need business skills in addition to technical qualifications since more of their time is spent responding to management information needs than formerly when data processing was strictly a back shop operation. Planning has also gained in importance because of the large funds involved and long lead time required for equipment delivery and systems development. Directors are now concerned with coalescence planning, deciding what activities should be part of an information

Figure 21.4   **Computer director skills required as a function of application portfolio size**

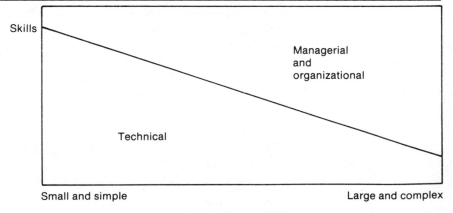

function. Indeed, many firms have added their computer director to the corporate planning team in recognition of the increasingly important role of information systems in management decision making.

Associated with the role of **planner** is that of **change agent,** the director's responsibility to "sell" technology and smooth conversion to new systems. Traditionally computer directors asked users, "What can we do for you?" The approach is much more aggressive today, with directors in a **proactive role** saying, "Here is what we can do for you."

Richard Nolan lists still other roles for the "new breed of EDP manager" that inevitably affect management style. He states that computer directors today must be **politicians** (able to recognize power bases and win converts) and **integrators** (able to merge computers, communications, and data bases into effective delivery systems), as well as **controllers** and **strategists.**[6] Technical knowledge must be kept up-to-date to maintain respect and credibility with professional staff, but management skill must extend beyond technology to people, equipment resources, systems projects, user relations, management interfaces, budgets, and capital expenditures.[7]

Nolan has observed that computer directors today can be categorized as either architects or insiders. **Architects** concentrate on allocation of resources and prefer decentralization of computing profit centers, letting users determine what services are offered by their willingness to pay. **Insiders** favor centralization and are not as concerned with generating departmental profits as with developing systems to improve corporation profits. They assign analysts to user departments to help determine user needs and to study how the computer center might better integrate subsystems. They hope that closer working relationships between computer center and user will result, that an atmosphere of trust and cooperation will be fostered.

Which style is better? That depends on the philosophy of top management. Perhaps the ideal would be a combination of the profit-conscious architect and the service-oriented insider.

SUMMARY AND CONCLUSIONS

Computing consists of a web of relationships between corporate management, computing personnel, and users. This chapter has focused on committees that provide the formal structure for interaction between these groups in the oversight of computing. In Figure 21.5, a

---

[6]Nolan, "Business Needs a New Brand of EDP Manager," p. 123–33.

[7]William Synnott and William Gruber, *Information Resources Management* (New York: John Wiley & Sons, 1981), pp. 45–52.

Figure 21.5   Sample configuration of a steering committee and subcommittees in relation to corporate management and the computer director

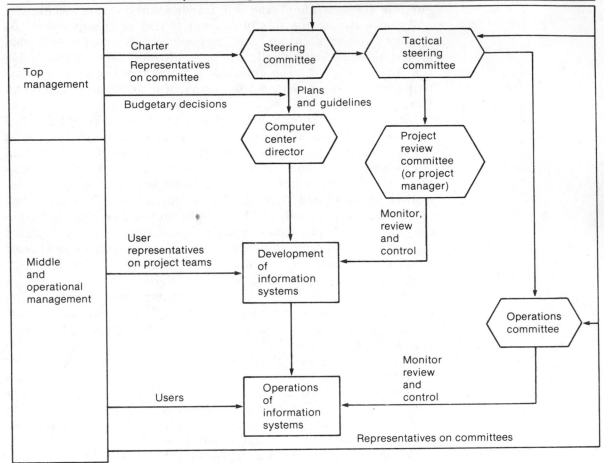

Note: To simplify this figure, only a few steering subcommittees have been included. See Table 21.3 for a listing of other possible subcommittees.

sample committee configuration, the computer center director reports directly to a steering committee. The steering committee also receives reports on performance from subcommittees that oversee development activities and operations. Some steering committees require that all computing be done in-house. Others allow users within the firm to request bids for jobs, placing in-house computing facilities in competition with outside service centers.

Top management controls computing by chartering the steering committee, making budgetary decisions, and serving with other users as members of the steering committee and subcommittees. Management is also a receiver of computing services and so participates in development projects as a team member and criticizes output just as other users do.

Users are found at all levels of an organization, from data clerks to company presidents. The steering committee and computer director need a method of determining whether the services offered meet users' needs. Many firms conduct user surveys for this purpose.

New responsibilities are continually being added to the job of computer center director. The expansion of applications, the addition of word processing to traditional data processing, and the movement toward distributed processing centers requires technical expertise and business skills that former EDP heads did not need when computing was a mere back shop operation. The computer director of the future will be an information manager who takes the initiative in business information planning, one who discovers opportunities for improving the effectiveness of information utilization, and "sells" these options when appropriate and beneficial to the company.

Computer directors with demonstrated proficiency in managing modern computing centers have administrative talent that should not be wasted. Director of computing should not be a dead-end job, but should lead to a career path in corporate management.

CASE STUDY: OVERSIGHT OF COMPUTER PROCESSING*

In a regional bank in the United States, management was dissatisfied with the bank's data processing as were departmental users within the bank. The bank officers were concerned about the data processing budget. User departments felt that data processing should be of greater service but weren't sure how. Computing management worried about staff turnover and how best to allocate computing resources. There was general consensus that the bank needed an organizational body to provide direction and control to computing.

The first step in setting up a guiding body was to establish objectives for such a group. It was agreed that the group would be responsible for setting data processing directions and services, and for the establishment of priorities for data processing activities and development.

An Executive Steering Committee (ESC) was then chartered which asked a consulting firm to assist bank personnel in evaluating the bank's data processing. It was found that systems maintenance and

*Source: Richard L. Nolan, ed., *Managing the Data Resource Function*, 2d ed. (St. Paul: West Publishing, 1982), pp. 381–83.

enhancement were inadequate and that efficiency pressures had gone too far, resulting in damage to many systems and technical resources. The ESC then formulated a data processing funding evaluation strategy and established new funding directions for the bank's data processing. In time, the ESC broadened its scope to include more technical oversight of data processing.

The ESC has proved effective in its oversight role. One key to the committee's success is that the ESC members have developed a working relationship and analysis procedures which lead to consensus of opinion regarding the current status of data processing, issues, and resolution of problems. They are also able to communicate this consensus in business language and business structure to bank officers.

This case illustrates that management can provide oversight of data processing if it establishes an effective instrument to investigate, evaluate, and act on data processing issues.

KEY WORDS

Ad hoc committees	Proactive role
Architect	Risk
Business within a business	Standing committees
Change agent	Steering committee
Computer director, role in oversight	Strategist
	Theory X
Controller	Theory Y
Insider	Top management, role in oversight
Integrator	
Management style	User classification
Planner	User satisfaction
Politician	Users, role in oversight

DISCUSSION QUESTIONS

1. How does corporate management oversee computer center operations?
2. How can the following be controlled in a computer center?
   a. Spending.
   b. Standards.
   c. Scheduling.
   d. Integration of systems.
   e. Honesty and integrity of staff.

      f.   Priorities for maintenance jobs.

      g.   Computing center director.

3.   In what ways do computing centers differ from a:

      a.   Contracting business?

      b.   Wholesale business?

      c.   University?

      d.   Government office?

      e.   Public library?

4.   What mechanisms should be implemented to achieve a satisfactory interface with users in:

      a.   Conversion?

      b.   Debugging user programs?

      c.   Meeting user hardware needs?

5.   Can the same user interface mechanisms be used in centralized and decentralized processing?

6.   When managing a computer center, is the element of risk the same for both:

      a.   Small and large computing systems?

      b.   Centralized and distributed systems?

      c.   Functional and integrated systems?

      d.   Batch and online systems?

      e.   A large computer and network of minis?

7.   At what point and under what circumstances should a steering committee delegate its authority and responsibility to other committees?

8.   What is the purpose of classifying users? How best can this be done?

9.   What qualities and qualifications are desirable in a computer director?

10.   Should computer directors have technical or business management backgrounds? Explain.

11.   What qualifications would you recommend for appointees to a steering committee?

12.   What are the main risks faced by computer directors and steering committees? How can they be minimized or eliminated?

13.   What role (if any) should the computer director play in corporate policy decision making?

14.   How should user satisfaction be determined?

SELECTED ANNOTATED BIBLIOGRAPHY

Crane, Jane. "The Changing Role of the DP Manager." *Datamation* 28, no. 1 (June 1982), pp. 96–108.

    Opinion on the changing role of DP managers collected in interviews with DP consultants and managers.

Fried, Louis. *Practical Data Processing Management.* Reston, Va.: Reston Publishing, 1979, pp. 61–69.

A full chapter is devoted to steering committees in this book. Only a few texts include a formal discussion of such committees.

McCartney, Laton. "The New Info Centers." *Datamation* 29, no. 7 (July 1983), pp. 30–46.
An excellent discussion of the new emerging organizational structure designed to help users of computing help themselves. There are numerous cases described and a list of "dos and don'ts" for establishing and running such centers.

Nolan, Richard L. "The Plight of an EDP Manager." *Harvard Business Review* 51, no. 3 (May–June 1973), pp. 143–52.
This article, written over ten years ago, is still a relevant presentation of the problems and risks faced by EDP managers. Suggestions are also given for minimizing management problems.

Rogan, Winnie R. and Herbert W. Perkins III. "Steering Committees," in *Managing the Data Resource Function*, ed. Richard L. Nolan. St. Paul, Minn.: West Publishing, 1982, 417 p.
This book has several chapters of interest. "Steering Committees," pp. 370–83, describes the role of the committee in direction setting, in budgeting, in bridging the user–provider gap, and in providing management controls. Another recommended chapter is "Towards a Theory of Data Processing Leadership," pp. 361–69.

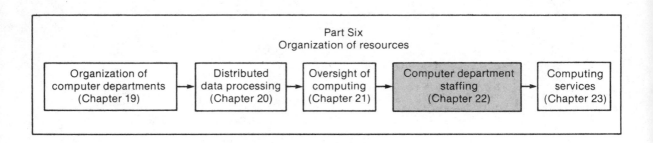

Part Six
Organization of resources

| Organization of computer departments (Chapter 19) | → | Distributed data processing (Chapter 20) | → | Oversight of computing (Chapter 21) | → | Computer department staffing (Chapter 22) | → | Computing services (Chapter 23) |

CHAPTER 22

Computer department staffing

*The extension of man's intellect by machine,
and the partnership of man and machine in handling
information may well be the technological advance
dominating this century.*

Simon Ramo

Though computerized societies are often pictured as machine-dominated with humans subservient to technology, computers exist to serve people, to aid managers in reaching decisions. And they cannot execute given tasks without the assistance of a large number of professionals and support personnel.

For example, input, be it data, operating instructions, or applications programs, is initiated by humans. It takes analysts to assess the needs of users and skilled programmers to convert these needs into bits, the only medium understood by machine. Collection and updating of data are an iterative human activity. Programmers are needed for the preparation of computer instructions, and many technicians are required for operating and servicing the computer itself. Without analysts, programmers, operators, managers, clerks, librarians, schedulers, and other support personnel, computers are unable to produce the information users request.

This chapter focuses on computer department staffing. First, the duties and responsibilities of computer personnel will be described. Job design, hiring, and turnover will next be discussed. Since studies have shown that computer people place a high value on professional growth, both career development and training are also addressed in the chapter.

COMPUTER PERSONNEL

Who are the professionals and support personnel needed to run a computing facility? Data processing is usually subdivided into three functional areas: **systems development, operations,** and **support,** as shown in Figure 22.1. Programmers and analysts fall in the first category, operational and production personnel in the second, with librarians, standards officers, schedulers, supply clerks, training coordinators, and others providing technical support in the third.

Figure 22.1   **Organizational structure of a computer processing department**

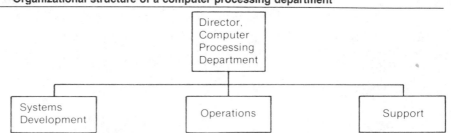

The schema in Figure 22.2 serves as an example of how a computer center can be organized and lists positions within these three functional areas. Figure 22.3 shows the typical mix of personnel in each area in percentages. Of course, the mix will have to be adapted to the environment of each computer department. For example, a distributed processing configuration would require more operational and fewer support personnel at each node. A centralized computer installation would have the opposite mix: more support and fewer operational personnel. Indeed, departmental organization, job titles, and job descriptions will vary from firm to firm.

Even within a given facility, positions are not static, for needs are constantly changing. A salary survey by *Datamation* in the early 1950s listed 27 computer positions. A similar survey in 1980 listed 55. This increase can be attributed to the growth of computing facilities and the complexity of computer operations today. Not all computer centers have 55 positions, however. Small companies may have far fewer positions, a single individual filling several jobs.

In the sections that follow, the work of analysts, programmers, operators, and data base administrators will be described. For an explanation of the duties of other employees, check the index for many are described in other chapters of the text.

System analyst

A **system analyst** is a technician who participates in the development, implementation, and maintenance of systems. The analyst stud-

Figure 22.2   **Organization structure for a computer department**

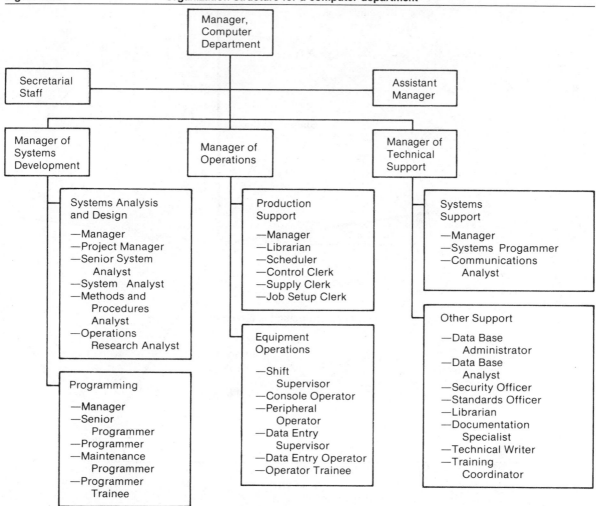

ies a problem and decides what procedures, methods, or techniques are required for the problem solution using computers. Analysts must be skillful in human relations as well, for they serve as the link between users and the computing staff. It is the analyst who must interpret client needs and formulate user specifications. Analysts must also be able to communicate the capabilities and limitations of computing to users with no technical background, must be able to resolve complaints, and to serve as mediator in user–EDP staff disputes.

Figure 22.4 outlines the responsibilities of analysts during each phase of MIS development. During the feasibility study, analysts provide cost/benefit estimates and advise the committee on the technolog-

Figure 22.3   **Percentage mix of computer personnel**

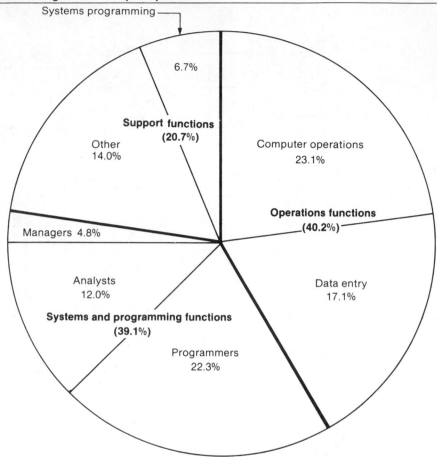

Source: Bruce Hoard, "Division of 250 Employees Found in Typical MIS Profile," *Computer World* 14, no. 34 (August 25, 1980), p. 4.

ical feasibility of proposals. During the user specification phase, analysts take an active role in structuring the problem, in helping to synthesize and crystallize user desires so that system specifications can be prepared. When conflicting user interests arise, analysts must find a compromise.

When the design phase is reached, analysts have technical concerns: design specifications for output, input, files, forms, and procedures. In implementation, analysts become users' advocates, working with programmers for solutions that consider human factors. During conversion, analysts may seem to switch sides, for they prod reluctant users who want to procrastinate conversion, and refuse user requests

Figure 22.4   **Roles of system analysts**

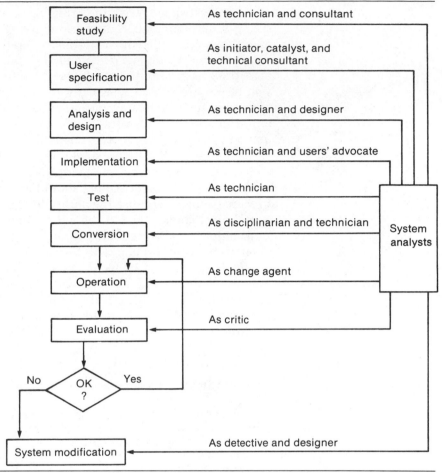

for late specification changes, working on behalf of the computer center to resolve technical problems and speed conversion.

Although most analysts are assigned other projects when a system
is finally operational, some may assist management in planning and
implementing strategies to reduce employee resistance to the new system. An analyst can advise management how the new technology will
affect daily operations and may be astute in gauging the amount of
change an organization can comfortably absorb. Analysts may also assist in orientation and training programs, acting, in effect, as change
agents to promote favorable attitudes toward computing. Once the system is operational, analysts often participate in system evaluation,
helping detect errors and recommending system modifications.

All of the above are potential roles. In a given project, however, no single analyst should have the prime responsibility in a project for all stages of development. That would violate the principle of separation of duties, a principle which stipulates that those who plan and design a system should not take part in testing and approval decisions. Since most projects require the expertise of a number of analysts, this division of responsibility can usually be enforced. It is over the life of a number of projects that an individual analyst may be required to perform the spectrum of roles shown in Figure 22.4. Small firms with limited personnel may require a single analyst to perform many or all of the above functions for a single project, however.

The ideal system analyst should have the characteristics listed in Table 22.1. One look at the list should explain why good analysts are in scarce supply. Because the ability to handle people is as important as technical competence in the job, and because knowledge of an organization, its power structure, policies, and procedures is essential to analysts, many firms like to hire analysts from within the firm, individuals who may lack technical skills but have demonstrated aptitude for the job and have the right temperament. These persons are then given in-house technical training. It is thought by some that analysts hired and trained in this fashion are more quickly of value to the firm than analysts hired from outside who have technical qualifi-

Table 22.1	Desirable characteristics of system analysts
	A system analyst should:
	Have technical expertise in systems analysis and systems design.
	Have a working knowledge of hardware, software, data bases, operating systems, and telecommunications.
	Have a detailed knowledge of a programming language, preferably COBOL.
	Have a creative mind.
	Have the ability to think in the abstract, to work with symbols and problem logic.
	Be receptive to different approaches to problem solving, analysis, and design.
	Have the ability and patience to teach and train both professionals and nontechnical users.
	Be a good listener.
	Have project management skills.
	Enjoy working with people.
	Have a sensitivity to people and be knowledgeable about human factors.
	Have knowledge about clients, their business, and industry.
	Be sensitive to the company's power structure.
	Be able to work in nonstructured, ill-defined and conflict-prone environments.
	Have the ability to function well under pressure, resolve conflicts, and balance trade-offs.
	Be able to work in a team.
	Have a halo—if possible.

cations but lack familiarity with key personalities and how the company is run. Not all managers agree with this viewpoint, however.

Programmers

The job of a **programmer** is to write and test the instructions that tell the computer what to do. Whereas the analyst deals with the marriage between people and machines and must often deal with unpredictable human emotions, programmers solve problems of logic in a more predictable environment—a machine environment. They work with analysts to decide how to solve a problem, then prepare a logic chart, code instructions in a language the computer can understand, establish input/output formats, allocate storage, follow testing procedures, and prepare documentation. Though some of a programmer's duties overlap with those of analysts, programmers do not require the social skills of analysts in their jobs. Indeed, the typical programmer is characterized as:

> A loner, an individual who wants to avoid confrontation, avoid being directed, is willing to do without much social interaction on his job, does not have an interest in social science—has no apparent desire to enter into the aggressive, competitive, confront-laden situation that is associated with true managership. He is a "staff man"—but a staff man working very much in isolation.[1]

Small firms that cannot afford a large staff often merge the responsibilities of analysts and programmers in one position. Even large firms like the combination of analyst-programmer for it helps reduce the misunderstandings that often arise between the two professional groups, and eliminates finger pointing and blame shifting when things go wrong. The problem is finding qualified personnel. The development of special-purpose high level languages which makes programming easier has contributed to the number of analysts doing their own programming, so the analyst-programmer may become more common in the future.

With regard to programming skills, there is great diversity among programmers. Some specialize in COBOL, FORTRAN, or other high level languages. Others specialize in packages for decision support systems (DSS) or languages for DSS. Still others, schooled in operations research, focus on simulation and languages like GPSS and SIMSCRIPT. Systems programmers with expertise in hardware deal with low level languages (assembler or machine language). These programmers work more closely with operations than applications development.

In development projects, programmers work under the supervision of system analysts.

---

[1]Analysis of Edward M. Cross who has studied programmer characteristics, as quoted in Milt Stone, "The Quality of Life," *Datamation* 18, no. 2 (February 1972), p. 42.

Operators

The job of **operator** has changed greatly since the early days of computing for both peripheral and computer operators. Formerly, operators loaded machines with tapes, disks, or cards, and monitored relatively simple machine consoles. Vocational or junior college training was adequate for the job. Today's operators must be knowledgeable about hardware, software, and data bases for they operate sophisticated systems.[2] An estimated 80–90 percent of an operator's time is in software-related activities, where knowledge of the system's job control language is required to optimize the system's resources. Operators have responsibility for the security and privacy of data and hardware as well. Operating errors can lead to damage of expensive equipment, necessitate reconstruction of the data base, require costly reruns, or result in lost business due to delay or inconvenience to users.

Data base administrator (DBA)

The position **data base administrator** has emerged in recent years due to the growth in size and complexity of data bases. The primary duties of this administrator include upkeep of data, meaning completeness of files; data maintenance, which may entail moving data from one storage media to another for quick and efficient access; maintenance of historical data, including modification of files when definitions of data elements and classifications change; and purging of useless data. Any changes to the data base, directories, or dictionaries must also be approved and supervised by the DBA.

In addition, the DBA resolves conflicts (when users dispute data classifications or who should create data), establishes policies for segmented or replicated data bases, and determines the distribution of data. Table 22.2 lists still other activities of the DBA. Because of the scope of the DBA's responsibilities, most large organizations provide the DBA with a staff, including data specialists and analysts experienced in public relations and liaison with users. Usually the DBA reports to the computing department head, but some firms give the position independent status, with the DBA reporting directly to a user's committee.

JOB DESIGN

Though there is general agreement regarding the duties of computer personnel, as outlined in the preceding sections, the exact responsibilities of employees will vary from firm to firm. A manager will define these responsibilities in **job descriptions** which are prepared for

---

[2]For an excellent article on this subject, see William A. Hansen, "The Operator's Changing Status," *Datamation* 25, no. 1 (January 1979), pp. 189–91.

Table 22.2   **Functions of a data base administrator**

<table>
<tr><td>

Data base design
  Content
    Creation
    Reconciling differences
  Dictionary/Directory
    Create
    Maintain
  Data compression
  Data classification/coding
  Data integrity
    Backup
    Restart/recovery

Data base operation
  DED custodian/authority
    Maintain
      Add
      Purge
  Data base maintenance
    Integrity
      Detect losses
      Repair losses
    Recovery
    Access for testing
    Dumping
  Software for DED/DD
    Utility programs
    Tables/indexes, etc., for
      end user
  Storage
    Physical record structure
    Logical-physical mapping
    Physical storage device
      assignments
  Security/access
    Assign passwords
    Assign lock/key
    Modifying passwords/keys
    Logging
    Cryptography
    Modification

</td><td>

Retrieval
  Search strategies
Statistics
  Access
  Frequency of processing
  Space use
  User utilization
  Response time
Design operational
  procedures
  Access to data base
  Access for testing
  Interfaces
  Testing system

Monitoring
  Quality of data
    validity
  Performance
  Efficiency
  Cost
  Use/utilization
  Security/privacy
  Audit
  Compliance
    Standards
    Procedures

Other functions
  Liason/communications with:
    End users
    Analysts/programmers
  Training on data base
  Consultant on file design
  Design operational
    procedures
    Access to data base
    Access for testing
    Interfaces

</td></tr>
</table>

each position when organizing a department and will use these descriptions when hiring and evaluating personnel. A sample job description, that of a maintenance programmer, appears in Table 22.3.

How does a manager decide what duties to assign a given job? One technique is to first draw up a list of all responsibilities of computer center staff, then to distribute the workload among the positions funded. A sample from such a **task list** appears in Table 22.4.

Table 22.3   **Sample job description**

Data Processing Job Description–Page 1	Classification No. 222

Job Title: Maintenance Programmer	Grade

Reports To: Manager of Programming

Job Titles Supervised Directly:	Approximate No. of Positions
None	

Narrative Description

Performs maintenance and modification of programs currently in production to keep them responsive to user needs and to assure efficient operation in the production environment. Modifies or expands coding to accomplish specified processing changes. Tests modified programs to ensure that changes operate correctly and that changes have no adverse impact on program or system operation. Updates program historical and procedural documentation to reflect modifications. Creates special reports and file extracts from existing data bases, using generalized routines.

Responsibilities

1. Analyzing existing program logic to determine best method of accomplishing required changes or causes of program malfunction.
2. Designing change modules and adjustments to existing coding to accomplish correction or modifications.
3. Testing modified programs.
4. Maintaining installation test data base. _____

Duties

1. Analyze production programs to isolate problems or to determine more efficient methods.
2. Design program logic to eliminate problems, accomplish needed changes, or increase operational efficiency.
3. Expand test data to perform more thorough validation and to reflect requirements of program modifications.
4. Update program documentation to include changes.
5. Fulfill user requests for data extracts and special reports.
6. Fulfill administrative reporting requirements.

External Job Contacts

1. Systems designers and analysts.
2. EDP operations personnel.
3. Applications programmers.

Qualifying Experience

1. High school diploma and two to four years of college.
2. Programming fundamentals.
3. Six to twelve months as a programmer trainee.
4. Proficient in at least one of the programming and job control languages used in the department.

Achievement Criteria

Source: IBM, *Organizing the Data Processing Installations,* White Plains, N. Y.: IBM, C20-1622-2.

Table 22.4 **Sample from task list**

Sample task no.

1. To act as coordinating point for all data processing plans in the organization.
14. To be responsible for achieving the agreed annual data processing revenue.
44. To agree and maintain data processing priorities.
58. To maintain staff records.
117. To direct and control systems feasibility studies.
145. To prepare user procedure manuals for new systems.
223. To document written programs in accordance with departmental standards.
237. To prepare, agree on, and maintain the department's five-year hardware plan.
262. To control the process of hardware selection.
283. To direct induction training for recruits engaged on the systems function.
288. To ensure that computer run job streams are scheduled to obtain maximum utilization of equipment.
320. To conduct routine purges of files in order to release redundant files.
333. To record data preparation work done, and maintain appropriate logs.

Source: Drawn from task list of Anthony Chandor, *Choosing and Keeping Computer Staff* (London: George Allen & Unwin, 1976), pp. 165–200.

Many managers like to customize assignments to individuals in their employ, matching aptitude, skill, and preference, while rotating unpopular duties. They prefer general job descriptions so that a change in a given employee's duties will not require a corresponding change in title and job. Figure 22.5 shows how such flexible assignments might be made. Note that though both Adams and Hawk are junior programmers, Hawk is not responsible for Task 223. This could be for any number of reasons. Perhaps Hawk is poor at documentation, or is a trainee so is still learning the firm's documentation standards. Maybe Hawk has just served as a maintenance programmer and is now being rotated to other duties, or strongly dislikes documentation.[3]

Making job assignments from a task list has many advantages. The task list serves as a checklist to ensure that all tasks are allocated and that backup for crucial tasks is assigned. In computing, where continual adjustment must be made to new hardware, software, and changed environmental conditions, new tasks are constantly being identified. The list helps a manager restructure jobs to incorporate the new tasks or plan changes to allow for job enlargement and job enrichment. In addition, the list can serve as a basis for evaluation when using the MBO (management by objective) approach to evaluation.

---

[3]For a case study of a programmer released from maintenance because of dissatisfaction with the task, see *EDP Analyzer* 19, no. 4 (April 1981), pp. 3–4.

Figure 22.5   **Sample task assignments for system development personnel**

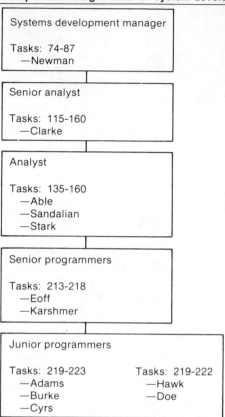

Another useful managerial tool when designing jobs is a **job diagnostic survey (JDS).** Such surveys give employees an opportunity to express views on their own jobs and recommend changes. Suggestions should be adopted for humanizing jobs, for making them more enjoyable as well as more challenging and efficient. A follow-up attitude survey will help managers evaluate the effectiveness of changes made. In computing, job redesign should be an ongoing process, for jobs cannot remain static when computer technology is moving at such a fast pace.

HIRING COMPUTER PERSONNEL

Computer personnel, especially those in professional classifications, are in demand. As observed by R. A. McLaughlin in a 1979 study,

The shortage of computer personnel runs across all job functions, through all sizes of computer installations, over all geographic areas. The lack is creating delays in implementation applications, large financial rewards for professionals who are willing to job hop, and high rates of employee turnover.[4]

Because there are seldom enough qualified job applicants in computing, firms may have to hire inexperienced programmers and analysts, or train people to fill openings. Unfortunately, it's difficult to predict aptitude or potential for many computing positions. A few multiple choice tests for programmers have been developed, but those existent are used so often that applicants in the job market will probably be given the same test over and over. Many try to gain experience with the test before applying to firms of their choice by first interviewing with companies low in their preference list. To make testing effective, a battery of tests is needed, or a large data base of questions should be prepared from which a test can be generated at random.

Because of the demand for qualified personnel and the shortage of suitable candidates, salaries for computer personnel, already high, are constantly rising.[5] Personnel officers must guard against hiring new inexperienced employees at a higher rate than the salary received by employees on the same job hired earlier. **Compression,** the reduction of salary differentials because of inflation, can also be the source of employee dissatisfaction if new employees are hired at high pay. Salaries should synchronize so that employees who change to other occupational ladders (switching from operator to programmer, for example) do not experience loss of pay.

Sometimes a fringe benefit package is negotiated that will attract applicants, or an appealing career path or promotion schedule is offered. Competition for applicants is sometimes so keen that companies may even give bounties ($2,000–4,000) to employees who succeed in enticing (raiding) experienced computer personnel from competitors or other firms, though most managers consider this practice unethical.

TURNOVER

Lack of qualified personnel is not the only staffing problem of computer departments. High **turnover** is also a major concern. According to McLaughlin,

---

[4]R. A. McLaughlin, "That Old Bugaboo, Turnover," *Datamation* 25, no. 11 (October 1979), p. 97.

[5]Since 1974, *Datamation* has published an annual salary survey of computer personnel. This usually appears in the January or February issue.

DP employee turnover is now running at 28 percent per year. That's a big number; at that rate, half the employees at an average dp site won't be there two years from now. The odds are that every chair will have a new occupant within four years—and that in a profession where it may take 12 to 18 months for a new hire to become productive. . .[6]

Statistics from McLaughlin's study of jobs unfilled and annual personnel loss appear in Table 22.5. Unless the supply of job applicants increases, the percentages in the first column are bound to rise in the years ahead, for the competition among firms for qualified personnel is increasing due to the spread of computing and proliferation of new applications. Percentages in the second column (turnover) can be lowered if firms institute policies that encourage employees to remain on the job. This requires the identification of positive and negative work motivational factors. Though there have been many studies on employee motivation in the past, only recently has the question been addressed whether factors motivating computer personnel are different from those for other employees in the work force. In 1978, Jac Fitzenz questioned 1,500 computer personnel[7] on how they ranked a list of job satisfiers and dissatisfiers, criteria drawn from a previous study by Fred Herzberg[8] whose work is still widely referenced in industrial training. A comparison of the responses in the two studies is shown in Table 22.6. Note that the rankings for three criteria (achievement, work itself, and advancement) are identical in the two surveys. However, significant divergence is apparent in other rankings. Computer personnel list recognition and salary as much less important than

Table 22.5	Jobs waiting to be filled and annual turnover for computer personnel		
	Occupation	Jobs waiting to be filled	Annual personnel loss
	Applications programming . . .	17%	34%
	Data base administration	10	8
	Data communications	27	21
	Data entry	9	30
	Operations	7	29
	Production control	6	20
	Systems analysis	17	20
	Systems programming	17	22
	Other functions	8	18
	Total staff	10	28

Source: Adapted from R. A. McLaughlin, "That Old Bugaboo, Turnover," *Datamation* 25, no. 11 (October 1979), p. 99.

---

[6]McLaughlin, "That Old Bugaboo, Turnover," p. 97.

[7]Jac Fitz-enz, "Who Is the DP Professional?" *Datamation* 14, no. 9 (September 1978), p. 126. The sample was from a dozen companies in the western United States and taken in the latter part of 1977. Fitz-enz's study also did rankings by job level and sex.

[8]Fred Herzberg, Fred B. Mausner and B. S. Snyderman, *The Motivation to Work*, 2d ed. (New York: John Wiley & Sons, 1959), p. 65.

Table 22.6   Rankings by Herzberg and Fitz-enz on satisfiers and dissatisfiers

Herzberg's satisfiers and dissatisfiers	Herzberg's ranking	Fitz-enz's ranking
Achievement	1	1
Recognition	2	4
Work itself	3	3
Responsibility	4	7
Advancement	5	5
Salary	6	10
Possibility of growth	7	2
Interpersonal relations, subordinate	8	9
Status	9	14
Interpersonal relations, supervisors	10	12
Interpersonal relations, peers	11	8
Supervision, technical	12	6
Company policy and administration	13	15
Working conditions	14	16
Personal life	15	11
Job security	16	13

Source: Adapted from Jac Fitz-enz, "Who is the DP Professional," *Datamation*, 24, no. 9 (September 1978), p. 126.

Herzberg's respondents, whereas possibility of growth and certain other criteria are valued more highly.

In another study, J. Daniel Couger and R. A. Zwacki[9] compared the attitudes of 2,500 computer employees with the findings in a survey done by J. R. Hackman and Greg Oldman using the same diagnostic survey instrument (JDS).[10] The two main findings of Couger and Zwacki are: that analysts and programmers express a greater need for personal growth and development than the 500 other occupational groups surveyed, and express a lower social need strength (desire to interact with others) than any other job category analyzed. However, Couger hastens to add:

> Programmers and analysts are not anti-social; they will participate actively in meetings that are meaningful to them. But their high growth

---

[9]J. Daniel Couger and R. A. Zwacki, *Motivating and Managing Computer Personnel* (New York: John Wiley & Sons, 1980). For a summary, see their "What Motivates the DP Professional," *Datamation* 24, no. 9 (September 1978), p. 123, or J. D. Couger, "What Motivates MIS Managers," *Computer World* 14, no. 1 (March 10, 1980), "In Depth" section, pp. 9–16. The sample used by Couger and Zwacki consisted of approximately 1,000 programmers and analysts and 1,500 data processing managers and staff from over 34 companies and 16 governmental organizations, each organization having a staff size ranging from 25 to 300 persons.

[10]The JDS was developed in the mid 70s and was validated by testing over 6,000 individuals in over 50 organizations performing over 500 different jobs.

need also causes intolerance for group activities that are not well organized and conducted efficiently.[11]

These findings should alert management to the need for training
and career development programs to keep computer personnel content with their jobs. Instituting such programs should help reduce
turnover. Of course, good personnel administration is also needed, the
features of which are found in general business texts and will not be
repeated here. What will be stressed in the remaining sections of this
chapter are aspects of personnel management unique to a computer
environment.

PERFORMANCE EVALUATION

Performance evaluation, an essential of personnel administration,
is difficult in the field of computing because the profession lacks standards for measuring performance, in part because of the newness of
the field, but primarily because of inherent measurement problems. In
evaluating the annual performance of system analysts, for example,
what criteria of evaluation should be used? Should evaluation be
based on user satisfaction? A user may be happy with an inefficient
system, not realizing that improvements could reduce costs or produce more information. Is it enough that the product works and the
user has the perception of being well served? Another problem is that
errors or flaws in the work of analysts or programmers may not be
exposed until months or years after the work is completed. In the
meantime, the employee will have received promotions or may have
left the firm.

Lines of code (LOC) is a common measure of a programmer's productivity,[12] but there is no universally accepted way to measure optimal program design and logic or even the correctness of a program.
Metrics, defined as measures that are quantified numerically and have
useful accuracy and reliability, have been developed by Tom Gilb and
others for evaluating programmers in an attempt to remedy this problem. A sample appears in Table 22.7. But even metrics do not eliminate subjectivity, since evaluators have to assign values to criteria that
are difficult to measure, such as readability of documentation or maintainability of programs. The concept of metrics is appealing, but in
the business world there is little time or inclination to apply such
numerical evaluation techniques at the present time.

---

[11]Quoted in *EDP Analyzer* 19, no. 4 (April 1981), p. 10.

[12]For an article favoring LOC as a method of evaluating performance, see James R.
Johnson, "A Working Measure of Productivity," *Datamation* 23, no. 2 (February 1977),
pp. 106–10.

Table 22.7   **Productivity metrics for a programmer**

Criteria	Measure
Quantity of work	Lines of code
Quality of work	Errors found in:
	Testing
	Operations
	Time of compiling
	Time of execution
Core storage used	K bytes used
Documentation	Completeness
	Readability
Maintainability	Easy to maintain/modify
Requirements of program met . . .	Budget constraints met
	Time constraints met

CAREER DEVELOPMENT

As mentioned earlier, computer personnel place a high value on professional development. To attract and retain competence, a computing facility should offer employees career paths that progress in responsibility, authority, and compensation. These paths should allow employees to move laterally or upward in the hierarchy of the department from any position.

Figure 22.6 illustrates how such **career paths** work. The example shows that an applicant's education and previous experience determine level and salary when hiring a data preparation clerk. The different entries also mean that employees who transfer to the position from other jobs can be placed at a level with equal responsibility and authority, and receive a salary commensurate with, or better than, their former pay. Data preparation clerks can exit laterally to other computer jobs as they gain experience and learn new skills or they can work up to a supervisory position, then switch to other departments as a management trainee.

Career ladders should be developed for all computing positions with entries and exits[13] and lists should be available to employees showing the body of knowledge and skills that belong to each professional position. These lists would help employees select career paths and guide them in planning the training they need. Table 22.8 is an example of such lists. It ranks in order of importance occupational prerequisites for system analysts and programmers according to a survey of 32 information systems managers in the nation's largest organizations. Note that once introductory computer and information sys-

---

[13]See Anthony Chandor, *Choosing and Keeping Computer Staff* (London: Allen & Unwin, 1976), pp. 139–47.

Figure 22.6   Career paths for punch operators

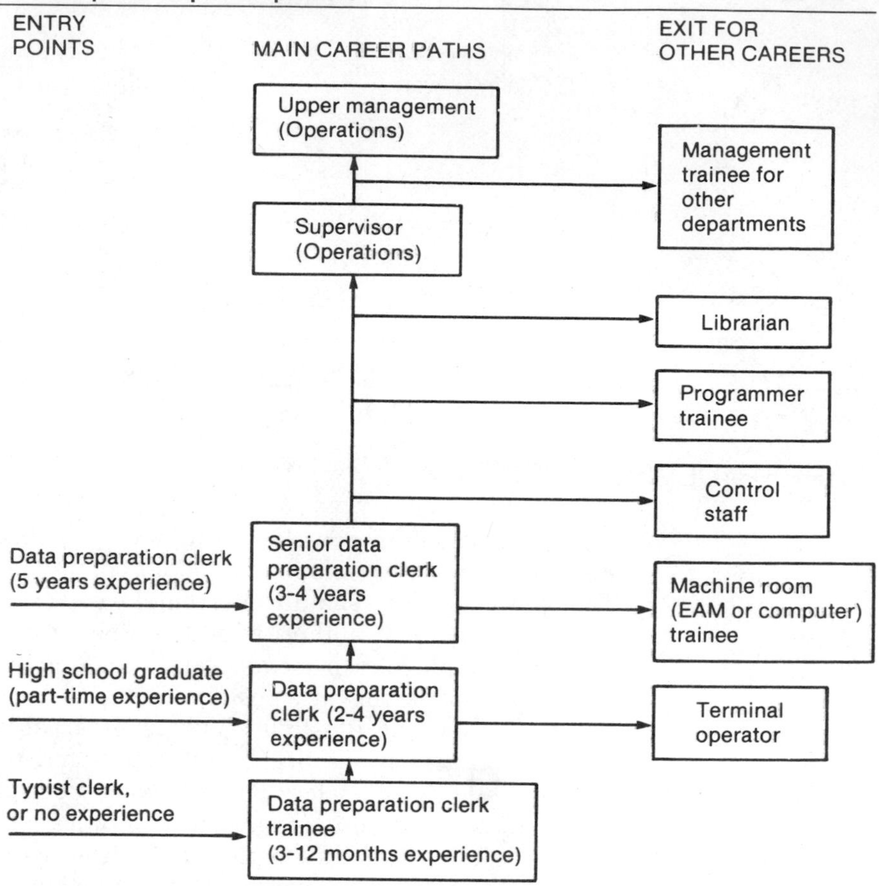

tems concepts are mastered, each job has different priorities of required knowledge.

Each job in a career ladder should also be associated with a set of required skills so an employee knows what training or experience is necessary to move up the ladder. These requirements are subject to frequent change, for computer technology is not static. For example, analysts of the future will have to know about personal computers, graphics, and voice synthesizers—subjects not part of their jobs 10 years ago. In addition, since there are optimal times for switching from one job ladder to another, employees should be cognizant of how jobs mesh. For example, Figure 22.7 shows that an operator wishing to become a programmer trainee should make the switch no later than senior or lead operator, for an operations or production manager

Table 22.8 **Knowledge required for job as system analyst or programmer according to priority rankings**

	System analyst	Programmer
Introductory computer and information systems concepts	1	1
Computer security controls and auditing	13	13
Planning and controlling of systems development projects	9	14
Improving computer center productivity	18	18
Human relations in systems development . . .	4	9
Software package analysis	15	17
Computer scheduling	16	16
Legal aspects of computing	19	19
Human factors in equipment design and layout	7	13
Telecommunications concepts	8	7
Hardware characteristics	10	8
Database management systems	6	5
Operating systems characterization	11	4
Information gathering techniques	2	11
Minicomputer characteristics and uses	14	2
Systems design topics	12	6
Applications programming languages	5	3
Computer simulation	17	19
File design	3	2
Job control languages	12	3
Introductory statistics	20	20
Statistical decision theory	23	21
Regression analysis and sampling theory . . .	24	22
List processing	21	15
Sorting	22	10

Source: Adapted from Paul H. Cherney and Norman R. Lyons, "Information Systems Skill Requirements: A Survey," *MIS Quarterly*, 4, no. 1 (March 1980), p. 42.

would take a great loss of pay in becoming a programmer trainee, the only level where an inexperienced programmer can enter the programming ladder in this schema.

Sometimes courses or a college degree are prerequisites for advancement along a career path. Firms differ in their policies regarding released time or financial support for studies, but all should offer advice and encouragement to employees willing to make an educational commitment in order to advance their careers. Indeed, management should encourage job mobility since it is in the interest of a firm to have an experienced core of employees who know the organization and can provide backup for a number of jobs. And since career development is a key to job satisfaction, advancement within the firm should help foster company loyalty and reduce job hopping to other companies.

Figure 22.7   **Two career paths shown with salaries**

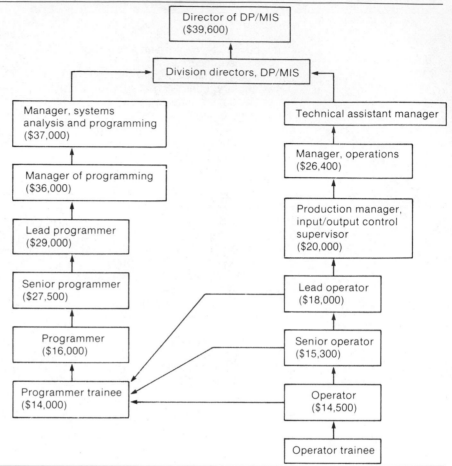

Source: Salary data from Stephen B. Gray, "1982 DP Salary Survey," *Datamation* 28, no. 11 (October 1982), p. 121. Values have been rounded.

Though theoretically an employee should be able to cross over and move up career ladders to reach any desired position in computing by gaining qualifications and experience, openings must be available and management willing to promote or transfer the employee. Often, however, managers turn down requests for promotion or transfer. For example, programmers who wish to switch to the more prestigious career ladder of system analyst may lack the requisite temperament though they may have the required technical competence. Programmers tend to be loners who shun interpersonnel relationships whereas analysts need to be at ease when dealing with people and perceptive of group dynamics. This example illustrates that though jobs may be designed to allow for vertical or lateral movement, an individual may find blocked a career path of choice.

TRAINING

Many computer departments sponsor training programs to provide employees with the background knowledge, skills, and up-to-date information needed to support the firm's hardware and software. The programs may also be designed to promote career development of personnel. The justification for the expense of the career programs is that they help reduce turnover, improve productivity, instill cooperation and loyalty to the firm, attract applicants, and also help retrain at less cost than firing/hiring when new computer applications upset the job structure of the firm.

The training approaches used in computer departments are much the same as those used in other departments of a firm.[14] Programs range from on-the-job training, briefings, and seminars, to course work that rivals degree programs at universities. Unique to computing, however, are training materials provided by software houses and manufacturers of hardware, such as programmed instructions that come in manuals or a package for a terminal.

Some firms organize training by setting up an educational matrix that identifies groups of employees and courses needed by those groups, scheduling courses on the basis of the matrix. Other firms build courses around jobs, scheduling courses needed for becoming a programmer or manager, for example. Still others provide counseling to employees, customizing the training for individual career development. Table 22.9 shows a sample training status report of one em-

Table 22.9	Sample training status report
Name:	Karen Dallenbach
Social security number:	327-40-3216
Current title:	Programmer
Manager's name:	Marion Latch
Interests:	Working with people
Personal dislikes:	Documentation
Future job:	System analyst
Training needs:	
(Internal)	Courses on systems analysis
	Basic course in accounting
	Needs assignment to development projects, especially accounting-oriented projects
(External)	Computer auditing
Other recommendations:	Courses on DBMS
Target date of achievement:	1986
Last date of update:	5/2/84
Date of run:	12/6/84

---

[14]For a good discussion on training, see Mitchell S. Novit, *Essentials of Personnel Management* (Englewood Cliffs, N.J.: Prentice-Hall, 1979) pp. 109–24.

ployee under such a program. The company then draws up a list of training needs prepared from the status reports and plans and schedules courses accordingly.

Though training based on individual needs is expensive, it may prove the solution to firms otherwise unable to fill openings due to the low supply and high demand for qualified computer personnel. And such training may be the only way to get needed specialists, such as employees trained in computer-aided design or in languages such as APT used in numerical control.

SUMMARY AND CONCLUSIONS

In the 1950s, when firms first introduced computing, a single employee may have acted as programmer, analyst, and operator. As computing grew, more positions were added to computing departments. This is graphically portrayed in Figure 22.8. Note that the temporal evolution of computing corresponds with growth of firm size, and that some jobs in the 70s and 80s are completely new. These include the data base administrator, security officer, word processing specialists, problem analysts (who might be compared to earlier time-and-motion experts tracing back to Taylor), and policy analysts (who evaluate EDP input and output for policy implications). Yet companies today with limited EDP may still retain the computing structure of the 1950s, consolidating operations, programming, and analysis.

Computer personnel can be grouped in three categories: systems development, operations, and support. The systems development group, consisting of analysts and programmers, is concerned with medium-and long-term projects. Operations concerns daily activities. Maintenance programmers, production personnel, and operators of peripherals fall into this category. Support includes systems programmers, the DBA, security and standards officers, the librarian, and training personnel. This chapter has outlined the duties and responsibilities of some of these employees and described how their jobs are designed.

Hiring, motivation, evaluation, and training of computer department personnel should be consistent with traditional theories of personnel management, such as Fred Herzberg's theories on work,[15] Abraham Maslow's on motivation,[16] and E. Schein on organizational psychology.[17] Special attention, however, should be paid to the em-

---

[15]Herzberg, *The Motivation to Work.*

[16]Abraham Maslow, *Motivation and Personality* (New York: Harper & Row, 1954), 369 p.

[17]E. Schein, *Organizational Psychology,* 3d ed. (Englewood Cliffs, N.J.: Prentice-Hall, 1970), 274 p.

Figure 22.8   **EDP personnel configurations**

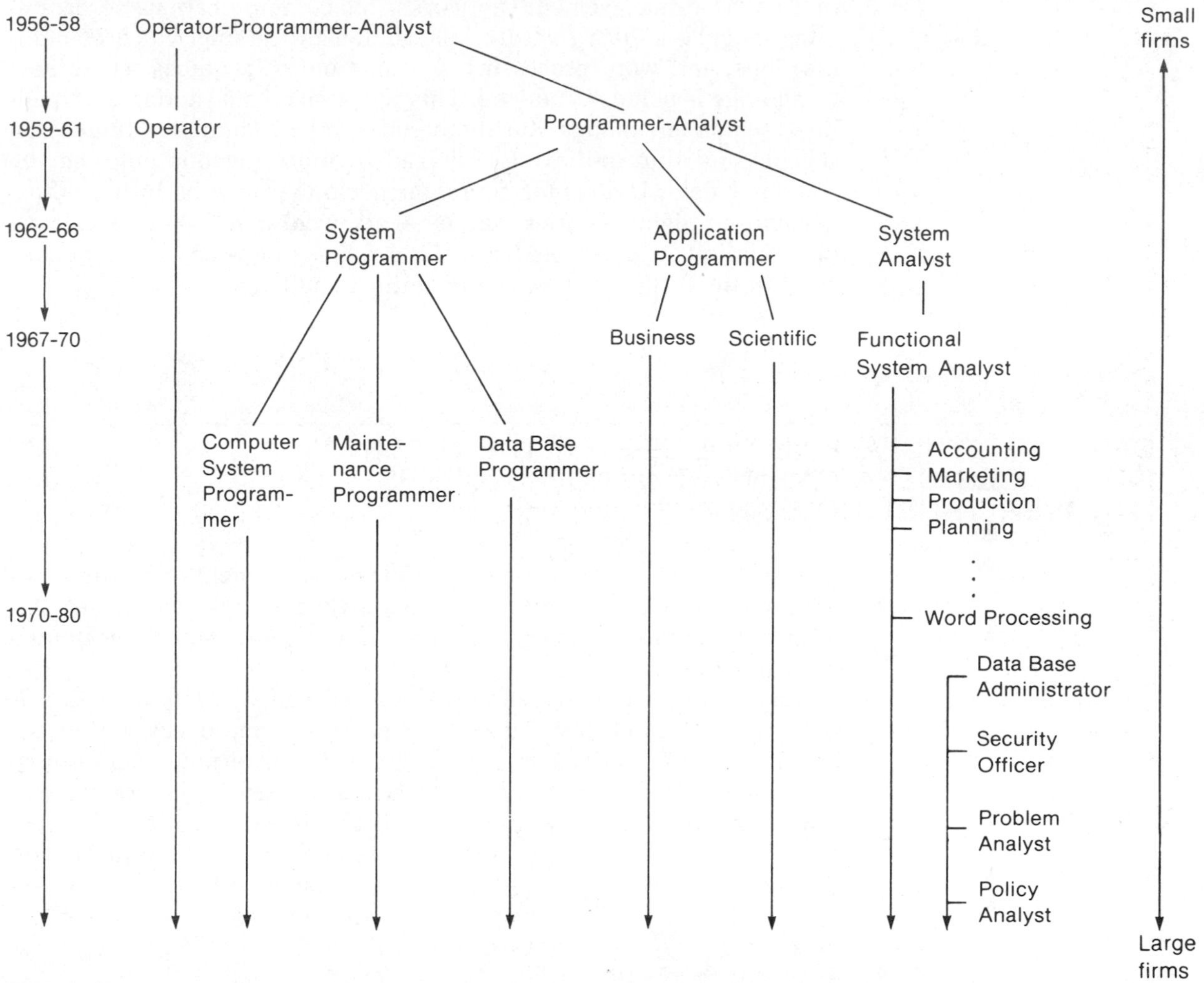

phasis computer personnel place on career development. Enid Mumford suggests that computer employees should also be made more aware of the social implications of their work.[18] Mumford wants computer people to be better trained in catering to human needs when designing computer systems, and feels that integrating mechanisms should be introduced in organizations faced with change so that user groups can develop a close association and common set of values.

---

[18]Enid Mumford, *Job Satisfaction: A Study of Computer Specialists* (London: Longman, 1972) p. 155.

Computer personnel in the 1980s will need skills and knowledge in data base management, networks, telecommunications, programming languages, data security, distributed processing, voice communications, and word processing, to name but a few areas where new technology is being introduced. This will exacerbate shortages of qualified personnel, though the increased level of computer literacy in schools and universities should lead to more persons entering the computer field. Unions for computer personnel may be in the offing, demanding higher salaries, shorter work weeks, and more employee participation in job-related decisions. Managing a computer department in the future promises to be quite a challenge.

CASE STUDY: STAFFING POLICIES OF THE HUMAN RESOURCES DEPARTMENT AT MANUFACTURERS HANOVER TRUST COMPANY*

The functions of the Human Resources Department of Manufacturers Hanover Trust include hiring, mobility, career development, performance appraisal, contract programming, education, and personnel administration.

The department prefers internal to external hiring where this is possible. A "search firm" seeks out potential employees within the organization and proposes a "draft" to managers of potential employees. A manager has one refusal right which is exercised when the employee is on a critical assignment. But this refusal right lasts for only six months as it is assumed that management can find a replacement during that period, that no employee is indispensable. Once the manager has accepted the transfer, the potential employee is offered the position. If the employee turns down the job, it is offered to the next employee on the list.

Each employee in the department sets a long-term goal for career development in the company. A job description is written for the desired job and the skills and level of proficiency needed for the job are determined. An education plan is prepared by the department for acquiring the job prerequisites and this plan is regularly monitored by a status report. The report lists skill matrices, identifies the skills of each employee, and shows how individuals are progressing on their chosen career ladders. One purpose of this program is to reduce employee turnover.

---

*Source: Charles D. LaBelle, Kimball Shaw, and Leslie J. Hellenack, "Solving the Turnover Problem," *Datamation* 26, no. 4 (April 1980), pp. 144–52.

Personnel are also hired from the labor market. Their applications are evaluated by peers and they are offered training and salaries appropriate to the position they will assume. This is part of the organization's planning, accounting, and management system for human resources.

KEY WORDS

Career paths	Performance evaluation
Compression	Programmer
Data base administrator (DBA)	Support
Job descriptions	Systems analyst
Job diagnostic survey (JDS)	Systems development
Metrics	Task list
Operations	Training
Operator	Turnover

DISCUSSION QUESTIONS

1. Are personnel concerns in a computer department different from personnel concerns in other departments of a firm?

2. Should authority over computing personnel reside within the computer department or should the personnel office of a firm handle personnel matters for all departments of the firm?

3. Are computer staff given privileges or special treatment? Explain. Does this create tension and dissatisfaction among other employees? How can a firm minimize or eliminate dissatisfaction arising from unequal treatment?

4. Once development, input preparation, and output generation are shifted to the user, the nature of personnel problems in computer departments will change. Comment.

5. Is it true that computer personnel do not mix well with other employees in a firm? Explain.

6. Is the danger of becoming professionally obsolete any different for a computer technician than for an engineer? How can computer professionals keep abreast with new technology?

7. Is the current shortage of computer personnel a temporary problem? How can this problem be solved?

8. Are personnel policies for motivating employees that are studied in personnel administration applicable to computer personnel? Explain.

9. Many employees believe evaluation procedures for computer jobs are irrelevant and unfair. Comment. What evaluation procedures and criteria
   would you use to evaluate the work of programmers, analysts, computer
   managers, and other computer department personnel?

10. Why is there high turnover among computer personnel? How can turn-
    over be reduced?

11. Is a user-friendly computer environment just a matter of improving per-
    sonal relations between user and computer technicians or does it also
    require the special design of hardware, software, and data systems to
    bridge the gulf between the user and the computer personnel? Explain.

SELECTED ANNOTATED BIBLIOGRAPHY

Chandor, Anthony. *Choosing and Keeping* Computer Staff. London: Allen &
   Unwin, 1976, 203 p.
   This is an excellent book on recruitment, selection, and development of
   computer personnel. Though the background is England, most of the
   principles apply to the United States as well. The book has especially
   good sections on task definitions, recruitment, turnover, and career development.

Gilb, Tom. *Software Metrics.* Sweden: Studentliterature, 1977, 282 p.
   Gilb identifies and discusses metrics for reliability, flexibility, structure,
   performance, resources, data, stability, and other areas. The book is quantitative and uses subscript notation, but should not deter the serious
   reader.

Grindley, Kit, and John Humble. *The Effective Computer.* London: McGraw-
   Hill, 1973.
   Recommended are pages 62–121 regarding an efficient computer department (including five case studies) and the section on training, pp. 143–
   57.

La Belle, Charles D.; Kimball Shaw; and Leslie Hellenack. "Solving the Turnover Problem." *Datamation* 26, no. 4 (April 1980), pp. 144–52.
   This is a case study on the approach of Manufacturers Hanover Trust to
   career development for 1,000 persons in their data center. Many good
   supporting diagrams are included.

Lucas, Henry C., Jr. *The Analysis, Design and* Implementation of Information
   Systems. 2d ed. New York: McGraw-Hill, 1981, 419 p.
   Chapter 17 discusses the organization and staffing of a computer department, its relationship with users, security, control of processing, management of computer operations and the computer room, and charging for
   services.

Mumford, Enid. *Job Satisfaction—A Study of Computer Specialists.* London:
   Longman, 1972, 240 p.
   Mumford uses Parson's framework of contracts to discuss contractual

areas between computer personnel and the firm, including the efficiency contract, the ethical contract, and the task structure contract. The statistics in the text are based on English sources.

Tomeski, Edward A., and Harold Lazarus. *People-Oriented Computer Systems.* New York: Van Nostrand Reinhold, 1975, 300 p.
The entire book is recommended reading, though Chapter 12 on organizing and staffing a computer department is particularly relevant to the preceding chapter.

Wadsworth, M. D. *The Human Side of Data Processing* Management. Englewood Cliffs, N.J.: Prentice-Hall, 1973, 244 p.
This book on the management of a computer department emphasizes the human aspects of management. It has separate chapters on minimizing salary and benefit problems, achieving an effective maintenance group, increasing productivity of operations, attaining cooperation of users, and gaining support from top management.

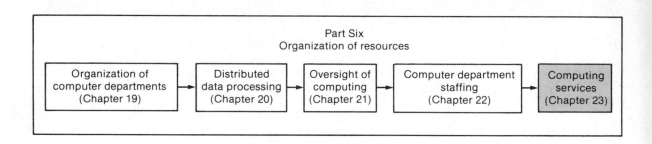

Part Six
Organization of resources

| Organization of computer departments (Chapter 19) | → | Distributed data processing (Chapter 20) | → | Oversight of computing (Chapter 21) | → | Computer department staffing (Chapter 22) | → | Computing services (Chapter 23) |

CHAPTER 23

Computing services

If you want to make a long trip through a far wilderness, find a guide who has made the journey before.

Old proverb

When computer departments need assistance with internal processing, consultants may be hired to give managerial or operational counsel. The department may also turn to vendors for advice. When the problem is lack of personnel to manage and run the computing facility, a facilities management company (FM) can be contracted on a short or long-term basis to operate the center.

Firms with no computer of their own may turn to a service bureau, remote processing, or a utility for data processing. Such external processing services are also used by firms that want access to more computing power to supplement in-house capability and by firms needing specialized services.

This chapter will discuss the advantages and disadvantages of each of the above computing services. It should be understood that these alternatives are not mutually exclusive. A variety of mixes is possible. For example, a firm with an in-house computer center may contract certain jobs to a service bureau. A firm with FM may use remote processing to access a utility's specialized data base. Following the discussion of services, this chapter examines the future of the service industry as a whole.

CONSULTANTS

Since few firms can afford to staff their computer departments with experts in all technical fields, most firms find problems arise that no one within the firm is qualified or competent to handle. A **consultant** is then hired to assist in decision making. Jerome Fuchs, President of the Society of Professional Management Consultants, asserts that consultants are in the forefront of the state-of-the-art within their areas of expertise and have made substantial contributions to business.

> They (consultants) have been instrumental in creating a need for, and accelerated growth in, applications such as organization planning and manpower forecasting, management development, executive compensation, profit planning, cost and budgetary control, materials management, and strategic business planning. Consultants have been at the cutting edge of innovative and advanced techniques, such as operations research, PERT and critical path analysis, management information systems, and manufacturing automation.[1]

The expertise of consultants helps firms stay up-to-date and competitive in computing when they cannot afford to hire full-time specialists. Even large firms with a wide range of specialists in their employ often contract for consultants. They may do so for a variety of reasons. The technicians they want to hire may be unavailable in the marketplace or the broad view of consultants may be needed. For example, in user specification and design, it is advantageous to have a team member with practical experience solving similar problems for other firms. Sometimes a consultant rather than a full-time specialist is hired because the latter's wage demands would distort the organization's wage and salary plan and create conspicuous wage inequities. Sometimes a large firm finds all its personnel already committed to ongoing projects, and so hires consultants when new projects are undertaken. The hiring of consultants is common in government to provide needed expertise, especially when a hiring freeze is in effect.

A primary advantage of consultants is that they are not a party to the internal power struggles within a firm and so can be more objective when seeking problem solutions. Their job and future promotions are not jeopardized by any recommendations they make. And they are not bound to firm traditions or precedents, so should be able to evaluate vendors and systems without bias.

However, objectivity is not always an advantage. The outside consultant may have no acquaintance with the personalities in the firm, no understanding of how departments interact or how the firm functions. Recommendations made without time to gain familiarity with

---

[1]Jerome H. Fuchs, "Management Consulting Services Reduce Costs," *The Office* 89, no. 1 (January 1978), p. 30.

the firm's unique environment may prove inappropriate. There is also the question whether sensitive data should be exposed to consultants who have not demonstrated loyalty to a firm. Since security will depend on the integrity of the consultant, care in selection is essential.

The need for an outside opinion can arise in all phases of development and operations. For example, consultants often participate in feasibility studies, in decisions of resource acquisition, system specifications, and the design of new systems. They may be hired to set standards, to establish privacy and security procedures, to help select personnel, or to run training programs. They have even been known to function as project managers for short-term highly technical development projects. Managerial consultants may also help organize departments, assist in planning, or devise strategies to reduce resistance to change. The very range and critical nature of these activities is why consultants must be selected with care, their qualifications and reputations carefully screened.

Selection of consultants

When searching for consultants, the advice of firms which have used consultants successfully in the past is a good starting point. Often contacts at conferences or among user groups will make recommendations. In addition, many professional organizations compile consulting lists. In England, for example, the British Institute of Management distributes a list of 1,400 consulting firms and practitioners. In the United States 693 consultants are listed in the *Consultants and Consulting Organizations Directory*. Many consultants are drawn from academia.

Consultants may be hired by the hour or by the job. Rates are high (though without fringe benefits), but most firms feel the money is well spent. Surprisingly, consulting firms find their clients mainly among successful companies rather than companies which are in trouble. As stated by Ira Gottfried, President of Gottfried Consultants,

> The growing, profitable corporation recognizes its limitations and is able to spend the money to gain additional assistance from outside the company.[2]

VENDORS

Vendors are an underutilized source of technical expertise. Unlike consultants, vendors have a bias in favor of their own products but this bias does not necessarily preclude sound advice on equipment and systems, though a company would be wise to check the literature and other users for corroborative opinion.

---

[2]Quoted in Louis Fried, *Practical Data Processing Management* (Reston, Va.: Reston Publishing, 1979) p. 285.

Vendors can often provide technical information on controls, security, and even installation of equipment. For example, when a computer center is being planned, vendors frequently furnish an installation expert to help design the layout. The expert may supply tables and charts on clearances and power needs, and even provide templates and sample layout diagrams.

A classic example of vendor assistance with system design was IBM's contribution to the first commercial airline reservation system for American Airlines. Vendors commonly provide documentation and training on systems they supply. Indeed, many clients require these services. One vendor specializes in training programs featuring management games played at a country club, with golf interspersed between training sessions. This is good publicity for the vendor, while informative and fun for the trainee. Vendors often keep clients informed regarding industry scuttlebutt as well, such as who is in the job market and what new products are being launched.

Of course, not all vendors perform such roles, but many do offer valuable counsel. Establishing good rapport with vendors can also speed up delivery dates of equipment, ensure adequate documentation, result in frequent calls, and even result in visits by the vendor's analysts and engineers. There is no doubt that most vendor representatives are knowledgeable in their respective fields, well supported by their companies, carefully trained, and well rehearsed. That they can be smooth talkers and high pressure salesmen should come as no surprise. It is up to computer departments to be as well prepared, to know what questions to ask, and to review responses critically, compensating for bias.

Sometimes a vendor representative responsible for equipment maintenance is assigned to a given firm and is on site daily. Such individuals become well acquainted with the staff and problems of the computer department and often act as informal consultants. On occasion, they take sides in disputes, have even been known to appeal to corporate management to reverse computer department decisions and have won. It should be recognized that some vendors have clout and sometimes use it.

FACILITIES MANAGEMENT

Facilities management (FM) is the use of an independent service organization to operate and manage the contracting firm's own data processing installation. Firms which contract some or all of their computing to FM corporations do so for a variety of reasons. Some companies lack the technical personnel needed to run their data processing center. Others do not want responsibility for operating computing equipment. Still others utilize facilities management because the firm's computer department has been so badly mismanaged (users dissatisfied, deadlines missed, equipment poorly utilized, time and cost overruns frequent) that it must be reorganized, rebuilt, and restaffed. In the interim, the FM company handles the firm's computing needs. Some firms never intend to take back management control from the FM firm. They prefer to contract indefinitely for facilities management, paying for the service as they might contract for management of the firm's cafeteria.

Advantages and disadvantages

FM companies are able to attract highly qualified personnel, for they offer good salaries and challenging work. Computer professionals are drawn by the range of experience that they can gain when employed by an FM firm, experience which helps them move quickly along their chosen career paths. Specialists in fields such as teleprocessing, numerical control, and planning using linear programming or simulation are also attracted to FM because they are able to concentrate on their specialities full-time in an FM job, whereas employment in a regular firm might mean other assignments due to lack of work in their speciality. Few firms can match an FM corporation in the quality of its computing staff—one reason companies turn to FM for computing assistance.

FM can also operate more economically than computer departments in many business firms. This is partly because FM firms buy in lots and get better discounts from vendors than other firms, but also because their highly trained professionals get better efficiency, reliability, and utilization from computer resources than the average employee in a data processing center. Standards are high in most FM corporations, and analysts can redesign systems, reorganize, and eliminate redundancies to achieve better performance in client firms without being encumbered by obligations to individuals or power blocks within that firm. Such an overhaul would be difficult, at best, for the client firm's internal computing staff.

With FM, however, interface problems are compounded—because computing is no longer organizationally in-house. The user must now interact with computer personnel whose primary loyalty lies with the FM company. New liaison procedures must be established, and new boundaries of authority and responsibility defined between user and EDP personnel. Though obligations of the FM corporation should be detailed in the contract[3] (see Table 23.1 for a list of subjects to be included in FM contracts), it takes time to develop smooth working relationships when a FM firm takes over management of a firm's com-

---

[3]For an excellent discussion of some of the legal problems and contract pitfalls, see William A. Fenwick, "Facilities Management," *Data Management* 16, no. 1 (January 1978), pp. 28–34.

Table 23.1	Subjects for inclusion in facilities management contracts
	Duration of contract
	Availability of personnel
	Availability of expertise
	Lines of reporting for personnel
	Liaison
	Ownership of equipment
	Ownership of software
	Security
	Privacy of data
	Property interests
	Applications portfolio
	Extension of applications
	Standards
	Input requirements
	Documentation scope
	Output portfolio and schedule
	Priorities
	Changes
	Payments
	Limitations and liabilities
	Right to audit FM firm's operations
	Contract termination procedures
	Scope and level of effort of FM personnel and contracting firm

puter center. There may be considerable disagreement between users and FM staff regarding performance under FM as well, for evaluation of performance can be a highly subjective judgment. In such cases, relations are bound to be strained.

Another disadvantage of FM is that users lose control over their data and worry about privacy and security under FM, particularly when the FM company is also servicing a competitor. (FM companies must guard against legal violations in such cases.) User flexibility is lost as well. And how can clients ensure that FM employees are motivated to act in the client's best interest?[4] Designing contract incentives can challenge a user's lawyer.

When negotiating for FM services, the length of the contract period will depend on what type of service is required. Activities that have

---

[4]Steve Stibbens, "A Difficult Business to Manage," *Infosystems* 16, no. 1 (January 1979), p. 54. This is an excellent discussion of the rather volatile FM industry.

a long period of gestation, such as development of integrated systems or training programs, cannot be undertaken when the FM contract is short-term. (An FM company may prefer to omit training since lack of training may extend the company's need for FM and hence create a dependency on FM.) A long contract period, however, may so entrench FM that it is hard for the client to take back management responsibility for processing. Most users do plan to eventually manage their computer departments and try to estimate the length of time needed to develop the technical expertise to do so, signing an FM contract for this interim period only. Indeed, many client firms find reliance on FM insulting to corporate management and believe their own personnel will be more responsive to internal processing needs than will FM staff. A compromise strategy is to take a short-term contract with an option to renew.

Cost of FM

Cost of FM will depend on the size of the data processing configuration to be managed, scope of processing activities of the client firm, level of performance to be achieved, and ownership conditions. Contract length is also a factor. (Most contracts run two to six years.) The contract awarded Bunker Ramo by the National Association of Security Dealers to run the nationwide stock market quotations and trading for over-the-counter securities is one example of what facilities management costs: $10.5 million for a three-year contract. Though this figure may seem high, many firms find that FM is less expensive than the cost of developing equivalent in-house expertise and capability.

Cost-plus contracts are sometimes negotiated for facilities management. The problem is defining the "plus" component.

FM variations

FM contracts are based on user needs. Although most facilities management means processing is on the client's hardware, some FM firms will also contract for services on their own equipment. (A third of a major FM corporation's 90 client firms use the FM company's hardware, for example.) Advantages to the client include freeing equipment and personnel for other activities, and the creation of backup. Security and transportation are major problems in this arrangement.

Another variation is a contractual agreement whereby the FM company selects equipment, installs it, and makes it operational, providing the client with a **turnkey system.** The client takes possession and manages processing once all problems associated with system development, implementation of the data base, programming, testing, and conversion have been resolved. This concept is popular in the Middle East where technical expertise is in short supply but companies don't want outsiders, particularly Americans, responsible for operations.

SERVICE BUREAUS

Service bureaus can provide equipment, software, or personnel to clients according to their needs. For example, the contracting firm may have its own computer department but lack hardware or programs for computations such as linear programming. Special compilers (like SIMSCRIPT) required for a simulation run may be lacking or more data storage capacity may be needed for a prediction model. Some bureaus provide access to specialized data bases, such as the full text of state and federal court decisions or updated daily lists of stock market transactions. One service bureau has a data base of extracts from SEC filings from over 12,000 publicly held companies; another has data on the Japanese economy, including a macro model and forecasts. Service bureaus can also prepare data, assist in data collection, consult, and even contract facilities management. A list of service bureau offerings is summarized in Table 23.2.

Why service bureaus?   Many of the advantages of facilities management apply to service bureaus as well. Service bureaus can attract highly qualified personnel and specialists, and can therefore operate at a higher level of efficiency and professionalism than the average firm. They can also operate at lower cost, taking advantage of economies of scale. For example, program development is less costly when shared by a large base of users. Because of this base, service bureaus can also maintain large computer installations, develop extensive data bases, and offer all modes of processing (batch, interactive batch, online, real time, and online–real time). Firms which utilize service bureaus may not have the capability in-house of performing needed activities, or may find it more economical to use a service bureau than to gear up for the activity. Even well-known large firms, including Boeing, Chase Manhattan, Control Data, GE, GTE, Lockheed, The New York Times, Time Inc., and Xerox Corporation, are service bureau customers.[5] In some cases (e.g.: Boeing and Control Data), these same firms sell services to others and buy services concurrently.

Though service bureaus do offer a variety of services, most clients today contract for routine accounting and bookkeeping services. However, this may change in the future.

Selection   A firm considering the option of a service bureau should first examine the economic feasibility of handling the activity in-house, then contact a number of service bureaus and compare their offerings, for service bureaus differ in their fee structures. Some charge a flat rate.

---

[5]For details, see Walter Kiechel, "Everything You Always Wanted to Know May Soon Be On-Line," *Fortune* 10, no. 9 (May 5, 1980), pp. 226–40.

Table 23.2	Services offered by a service bureau

Contribute to one or more stages of development
Provide specialized data base
Prepare firm's data base or assist in data conversion
Prepare data for ongoing data base
Provide programs
    Standard functional programs, e.g., accounting
    Programs for decision support systems
    Industry specialized programs
    Customized programs
Process data in a variety of modes
    Batch
    Interactive-batch
    Online
    Online real time
Provide storage capacity
Provide facilities management
Provide capacity for excess workload
    Unexpected
    Seasonal
    Growth
Handle processing when firm lacks:
    Capital for hardware acquisition
    Space
    Personnel
    Time
    Processing capacity
Miscellaneous
    Data collection
    Output delivery
    Consulting

Others base fees on the amount of resources used, how they are used, and for what applications. Costs should also be compared with other alternatives before a service bureau contract is signed (for example, facilities management or acquisition of minis and software packages).

According to a 1972 survey of service bureau clients, surprisingly few users make such a comparative cost analysis.

> Most service bureau clients failed to investigate the feasibility of edp; in fact, many may not need automated systems. Their pre-service bureau systems may have been as efficient as the current service bureau system and may have cost less.[6]

---

[6]Michael J. Cerullo, "Service Bureaus: User Appraisal," *Datamation* 18, no. 3 (May 1972), p. 87.

The survey showed, for example, that 60 percent of the respondents did not know if they were saving money by using a service bureau, and only 12 percent claimed to be receiving financial benefits.

But cost of service should not be the only criterion for selection of a service bureau. Table 23.3 lists other factors which should be considered.

The service bureau industry

In 1967, service bureau revenue was $600 million. By 1977, 2,000 companies were in the field, with revenues over $4 billion. This fast-growing industry is today threatened by minis which can provide users with turnkey systems at less cost than a secretary's annual pay. Minis are robust, do not require highly trained technicians to run, and are supported by packages in direct competition with processing services of service bureaus. Recognizing this threat, many service bureaus are developing software packages for minis themselves, and selling or leasing minis to customers.[7]

Table 23.3

Factors in selecting a service bureau

Services offered
Reputation of service bureau
  Years of operation
  Experience with firm's industry
  Competence of personnel
  References
  Financial stability
  Promptness record
  Quality of service
    Errors
    Reruns
  Integrity
Security and privacy record
Hardware configuration
Software portfolio
  Compatibility
Arrangements for data transfer
  Time involved
  Convenience
  Frequency
Availability for access
Benchmark results
Backup facilities
Pricing algorithms
  Normal load
  Offload
  Reruns
Liability and damage conditions
Discontinuation conditions

---

[7]For one view, see Leslie Ball and Kent McLean, "Will the Service Bureau Service the Mini/Micro Boom?" *Journal of Systems Management* 28, no. 11 (November 1977), pp. 20–23.

Boeing, McDonnell Douglas, GE, and Control Data Corporation (which acquired IBM's service bureau subsidiary as part of a legal settlement) are examples of large manufacturing firms with service bureaus. In 1978, for example, GE had a service bureau network which included 600 cities in 21 countries. The field also includes many independent service bureaus, and bureaus which are offshoots of consulting firms. Because of the lack of availability of technically qualified personnel, many service bureaus are merging to acquire the personnel they need. (In 1977, 40 percent of the service bureau ADP's top managers were merger acquisitions.) It is estimated that mergers will eventually weld the 200 existing service bureaus into a few dozen companies, each with over $250 million in annual revenues.

REMOTE PROCESSING

Remote processing is defined as the processing of computer programs through an input/output device that is remotely connected to a computer system. That is, jobs are submitted online to a computer from a terminal that is physically distant from the CPU.

There are two types of remote processing: (1) access to the firm's in-house computer using a terminal not in the computer department but on another floor or in another building of the firm's complex, and (2) access to computer time at an external source, such as a service bureau. In the first case, the terminal will probably be connected by in-house cable to the CPU. In the second, telecommunications, such as telephone or microwave, are the norm.

The mode of processing may be either **continuous** or **batch** with both types of remote processing. Data can be transmitted online as it is generated for instantaneous processing (**active online processing**) or can be stored upon receipt by the computer for later batch processing (**passive online processing**). Passive online access to computing is used by an Arizona car dealer who daily sends data by remote job entry on cars and parts received and sold to a company-wide center in Detroit—data which is stored and processed along with data from other dealers for overnight processing. Reports based on this data are then transmitted back to the dealers online to aid in management decision making.

Active online processing may be subdivided into two parts: processing that does not require any updating of the data base (**nonmodifying**) and processing that does (**modifying**). A query to an existing data base or processing of scientific input data are examples of nonmodifying processing. Functional online real-time systems (OLRT) dedicated to process control, or transaction processing in banking or reservations, are examples of processing that modifies the data base. Modification is also required in some general-purpose online computing, such as when a manager or production engineer wants to know the effect of a certain parameter change. **Time-sharing** (sharing a computer with other users, though the speed of response may give one the illusion of being the sole user), is becoming an increasingly popular mode of remote processing in the business sector.

Figure 23.1 classifies the modes of remote processing discussed in this section.

Why remote processing?

In-house remote processing is a time-saver. Employees no longer have to go to the location of the computer to do their computing. Remote processing to an external source saves space, equipment, and personnel since the firm does not have to manage its own computer department. In addition, remote processing may provide access to

Figure 23.1   **Classification of modes of remote processing**

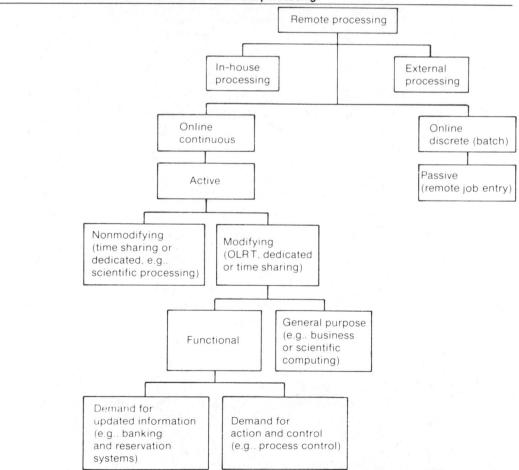

more storage capacity, specialized data bases, and many of the services offered by service bureaus (see Table 23.2). Some firms utilize remote processing to an external source as an interim solution to their processing needs while developing an in-house facility. Others combine remote (external processing) with in-house processing to cushion surges in processing demand. Professional personnel and corporate management may want the computational power of a large computer but need it only intermittently. Remote processing is particularly attractive to them.

Selecting external remote processing service

Factors which should be considered when deciding whether **external remote processing** is advisable are listed in Table 23.4. Many of the factors apply to a service bureau choice as well, though some factors bear more weight in remote processing. Turnaround time, for example, may be critical, so benchmarks should test the response time of prospective suppliers during peak periods (peak periods of both supplier and user) as well as during hours with normal workloads. Teleprocessing costs may also be decisive. Pricing is usually based on transmission costs plus computing costs (per unit of connect time or per unit of computing time). Most supplier firms have elaborate pricing algorithms[8] which vary as much as 200 percent[9] based on type of

Table 23.4	Factors to be considered in deciding on external remote processing
	Type of assistance needed:
	Hardware
	Software
	Operating systems, DBMS, etc.
	Applications packages
	Support
	Financial payoff
	Remote processing performance:
	Turnaround and response time
	Error rates and accuracy
	Effect on credibility and public relations when work is not done in-house
	In-house knowledge and experience with remote processing
	Experience to be gained by contact with outside firm
	Telecommunications problems
	Loss of control over data?
	Need to submit to outside standards?
	Adds to vendor contacts and hassles?
	Human factor considerations
	Organizational impact

[8] See Lynn J. McKell, James V. Hansen, and Lester E. Heitger, "Charging for Computing Resources," *Computing Surveys* 11, no. 2 (June 1979), p. 107.

[9] Sherman, J. Richard, and Abott Ezrilov, "How to Get into Remote Computing Sources (And How Not To)," *Datamation* 24, no. 4 (April 1978), p. 98.

use and length of job with adjustments made for guaranteed minimum usage, and discounts given according to number of terminals and numerous other special considerations. Charges may drop 20 percent by simply mentioning a competitor. To help users understand their pricing algorithms, many suppliers provide users with accounting reports so that expensive jobs can be identified and possibly redesigned or rescheduled to cut costs.

Studies show, however, that firms are not as cost conscious with regard to remote processing as one would expect. H. A. Seidman's study[10] found that a financial analysis was the determining factor in selecting a remote processing supplier less than 20 percent of the time. In fact, a financial analysis was not even performed in 50 percent of the firms surveyed. Instead the decision was often based on the personal preference of the computer head for nonfinancial reasons—such as top management's desire to improve the status and corporate image of the firm. Frequently, a feasibility committee was convened after the fact to give legitimacy to the decision, and financial justifications sought from the supplier.

This type of decision making is, unfortunately, common in selection of service bureaus as well. A careful financial analysis is recommended before deciding on either remote processing or service bureaus and before selecting a supplier. A financial review should be conducted periodically thereafter, since increases in transmission costs and change in volume of service may reduce the economic viability of remote processing (or service bureau contracts) over time.

Remote processing industry

In 1975, 50,000 companies were using remote processing to external sources, paying $1.8 million to 140 suppliers.[11] In 1981, the growth rate of the remote processing industry was pegged at 22.5 percent. This rate, however, is threatened by minis which are becoming increasingly popular. (The 1981 growth rate of minis was 35 percent.)[12] Utilities, discussed in the following section, also offer formidable competition. In all probability, however, remote processing will continue to grow though it may lose its separate identity as an industry. This will occur as suppliers expand to offer other services and large firms offer remote processing as one of many client options. This will make it hard to separate the profits of remote processing for measurement. Another prognosis is that remote processing will become more specialized in the future, both by industry and function,

---

[10]Herbert A. Seidman, "Remote Computing Service or In-House Computer?" *Datamation* 4, no. 4 (April 1978), p. 93.

[11]Sherman and Ezrilov, "How To Get into Remote Computing Sources," p. 96.

[12]Seidman, "Remote Computing Service," p. 94.

such as word processing. Also, local and area networks may offer an alternative.

COMPUTER UTILITIES

A **computer utility** is a source of remote processing, selling computer time and services. Utilities offer unique processing features that distinguish them from service bureaus and other remote processing suppliers. Instead of contracting with a client for a specific service, time-sharing is available at any time to any user who can pay for it for as long as the user requests. The computer utility resembles an electric utility insofar as computing power, like electric power, must be continuously offered and able to handle fluctuations of demand. This requires a grid or network so that computing power can be accessed from a distant site if regional facilities are overloaded.

Figure 23.2 shows a sample utility configuration. Individual customers at home or business may be serviced by a utility node supported by a variety of resources (software, data bases, and computers) as illustrated. The node may draw on computing power from other nodes for special services or during peak periods of demand. Compatibility of hardware, software, and interfaces is therefore needed. Telecommunications and protocols to link utility nodes are also required.

A computer utility is an old concept[13] but because of regulation and networking problems, utilities offering comprehensive services have still to be developed in this country. However, recent court decisions in relation to AT&T and IBM may well spur growth of this industry and foster fierce competition for customers. It is conceivable that computer networks of the future may connect thousands of computers and service millions of users. They will undoubtedly carry both voice and video traffic, be fail-soft, and have sharing protocols for both terminal and file transfers.[14] The X-25, a standard in communications, is a start is this direction.[15] Technologically, large utilities may soon be feasible but public fears over data security and privacy issues may slow public acceptance of such systems. Will linked data bases infringe upon individual privacy rights? How utilities should be regulated is also an unanswered question. The social implications of computer networks should be addressed by computer spe-

---

[13]See Richard D. Sprague, *Information Utilities* (Englewood Cliffs: Prentice-Hall, 1969), 200 p.

[14]See John D. Day, "Resource Sharing Protocols," *Computer* 12, no. 9 (September 1979), pp. 47–56.

[15]David Gilbert and James Perry, "The Significance of X-25," *Mini-Micro Systems* 12, no. 9 (September 1979), pp. 61–70.

Figure 23.2   **One configuration of a utility**

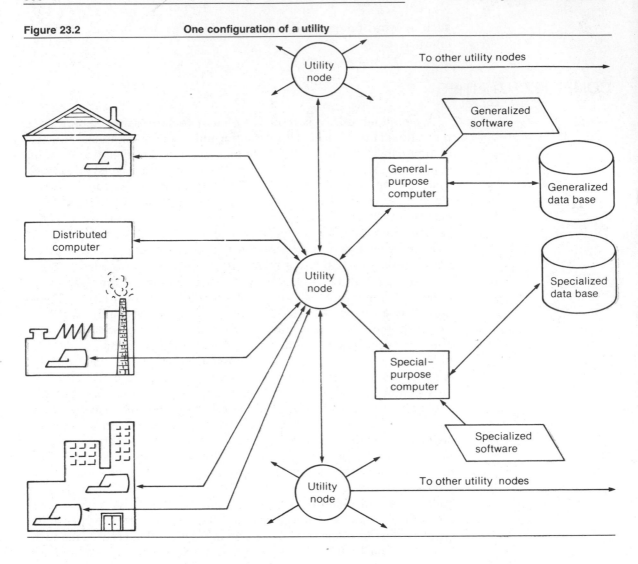

cialists, political theorists, and social scientists now, for the regulation and control of utilities will be an issue in the near future.

SERVICE INDUSTRY AS A WHOLE

The **service industry** can be divided into three sectors. **Remote processing** is the fastest growing sector (21 percent), **professional services** the slowest (13 percent), with **software services** somewhere between. Data base management systems account for the major share of growth in the latter sector. Figure 23.3 shows annual revenues of each of these segments for U.S. suppliers.

In 1980, the service industry as a whole, consisting of over 3,000 firms, had annual revenues of $8 billion, a 19 percent increase over the preceding year.[16] IBM service revenues accounted for $2 billion of this figure, a 35 percent rise from 1970. Control Data Corporation, the fourth largest company in data processing (in 1980), earned $69.7 million in services, up 19 percent from 1979.[17] Though the demand for processing, professional, and software services is projected to grow in coming years, the service industry as a separate entity may cease to exist. Service companies are beginning to offer integrated hardware, communications networks, support services, software, and consulting, while manufacturers are expanding in much the same direction, making it difficult to distinguish between the two. Both will be service

Figure 23.3   **Share of segments for service industry**

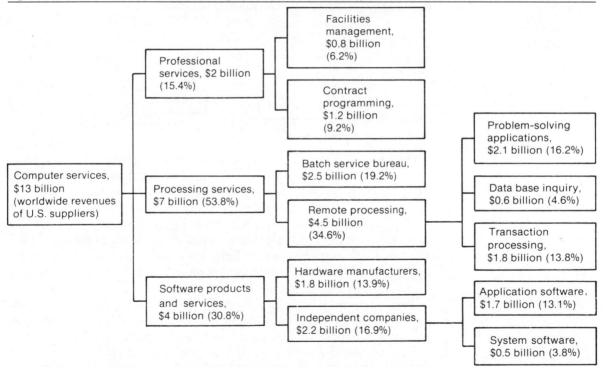

Source: Automatic Data Processing Inc., 1981.

[16]Peter A. Cunningham and Walter P. Smith, "Computer Services: A Menu of Options," *Datamation* 25, no. 5 (May 1979), p. 89.

[17]"The Datamation 50," *Datamation* 25, no. 6 (May 25, 1979), pp. 21–22.

vendors and provide information products in the future. The primary difference may be approaches to marketing.[18]

SUMMARY AND CONCLUSIONS

This chapter describes segments of the computing service industry. Both consultants and vendors offer professional services based on their technical knowledge and experience. Consultants will be more objective, have a broader base of experience and wider range of knowledge, but the services of vendors are usually free, and within narrow parameters, equally professional. Another difference between the two is that consultants may be hired to give advice to corporate management or the computer department, whereas vendors counsel mainly the latter, a difference illustrated in Figure 23.4

Figure 23.4   **Relationship of consultants and vendors to the client**

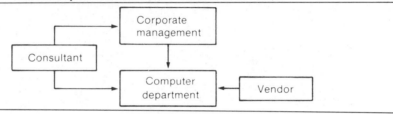

Facilities management (FM) is useful when a firm owns equipment but does not wish to operate it. This may be because the firm has had a bad experience with ineffectual internal management of computing in the past, or because the shortage of qualified candidates means personnel capable of managing high technology cannot be hired. FM can be a short- or long-term solution to computing problems for small- and medium-size companies. Large firms are usually able to attract or generate the management necessary for their computing operations and so seldom use FM.

Two other sources of professional assistance not discussed in the chapter deserve mention. One is auditors whose functions are described in Chapter 14. The other: software houses. Software houses—sellers of standard packages—can also be contracted to develop customized software, and will provide (if paid) programmers and analysts to assist in software implementations, including documentation.

Table 23.5 summarizes professional services available to computer departments by source.

---

[18]Cunningham, "Computer Services," p. 91.

Table 23.5   **Professional services available to computing departments by source**

	Management consultant	Computer consultant	Auditors	Vendors	Facilities management	Software houses
Planning for computing	X	X		X		
Organization of computer depártment	X	X				
Phases of development		X	X		X	
Standards		X	X		X	
Program implementation				X	X	X
Control systems design		X	X	X	X	
Audit of efficiency and performance		X	X			
Hiring of computer personnel		X		X		
Training		X		X	X	X
Planning for change	X	X		X	X	
Selection of computing resources		X				
Operations					X	

Service bureaus, remote processing, and utilities may be contracted for external processing. Many small- and medium-size firms that want a full range of computer services are attracted to service bureaus. Remote processing is more appropriate for firms which want access to special processing or data bases not available in-house, or have occasional demand for a powerful computer. Remote job entry is also an alternative for firms that want to gain experience in computer processing before setting up an in-house processing facility.

In selecting a supplier for computing services, cost/benefit studies should be conducted and bids from more than one vendor received because pricing and services vary considerably. Alternatives should also be periodically reevaluated since costs and benefits may change in time. Utilities, for example, will undoubtedly be formidable service competitors in the future, and minis may enable firms to handle their processing without outside assistance in the years ahead.

CASE STUDY: SCHAEFER VERSUS EDS: A FACILITIES MANAGEMENT CASE*

The first round in a case between F & M Schaefer Corporation, a beer manufacturer, and EDS, a facilities management corporation, took place in 1977. Schaefer originally sued EDS for $114 million, claiming the system EDS had been putting together for Schaefer didn't work and was responsible for errors that had caused Schaefer enormous damage. For example, the system, which had cost Schaefer over $12.5 million, had made erroneous tax computations and had proved inaccurate in short-range forecasting, according to Schaefer executives. In addition, accounts receivable had mistakenly reported a number of Schaefer's dealers delinquent in payments, and reports to this effect had been sent to the New York State Alcohol Control Board which prohibited the dealers from operating until their accounts were settled. This so angered the dealers that they subsequently refused to push a new Schaefer product, costing the firm an estimated $7.6 million in lost business.

EDS countered that Schaefer had canceled its facilities management contract in 1976, a year before the contract was due to expire, and still owed EDS $1.3 million in deferred payments. EDS filed a motion for either repossession of the system or the $1.3 million.

The repossession motion hearing took place before the original Schaefer suit went to trial. At the hearing, Judge Motley ruled in favor of EDS. Schaefer's argument that software is a body of intangible ideas and concepts and so can't be repossessed was not accepted by the judge. The judge also rejected Schaefer's claim that the system EDS turned over to it in 1976 was the same system Schaefer had developed on its own prior to the contract. (EDS claimed to have spent more than $4 million and several hundred thousand man-hours developing the system for the brewer.) Finally, the judge found that Schaefer had no

---

*Source: Laton McCartney, "EDS Wins First Round," *Datamation* 25, no. 4 (April 1977), pp. 54–56.

performance clause in its contract, so performance was not a condition for payment.

The ruling was hailed by facilities management, software, and systems development organizations, for it set a precedent, establishing system ownership, offering protection to software that can't be patented. The ruling also warned FM clients that a performance clause should be included in contracts. Such a clause will have to define performance criteria and establish how performance is to be measured.

KEY WORDS

Active online processing	**Passive online processing**
Batch processing	**Professional services**
Computer utility	**Remote processing**
Consultant	**Service bureaus**
Continuous processing	**Service industry**
External remote processing	**Software services**
Facilities management (FM)	**Time-sharing**
Modifying	**Turnkey system**
Nonmodifying	**Vendors**

DISCUSSION QUESTIONS

1. How can consultants be used by:
   a. Computer executives?
   b. Steering committees?
   c. Top management?
   d. User managers?
   e. Project managers?
   f. Planning personnel?
2. What are the problems and limitations of engaging a consultant? How can these be minimized?
3. What are the advantages of using a computer consultant? What environmental conditions must be created to maximize these advantages?
4. If you were top management, would you hire a computer consultant if you had a computer executive with equivalent experience and knowledge or your staff? Why?
5. A consultant is a highly paid outsider and is therefore respected. An in-house expert is relatively underpaid and much less respected. Do you agree? Comment.

6. What are the advantages of contracting software development to a consultant or software house as opposed to developing the software in-house? Would there be a difference in:
    a. Documentation?
    b. Run efficiency?
    c. Maintainability?
    d. Reliability?

7. Would you use vendors as sources of information, to help with recruiting, training, design, or as a sounding board on future developments?

8. Comment on the statement: In dealing with FM, a lawyer is needed to protect the contracting firm's interests.

9. Do you believe that FM does not help, in fact hinders, in building in-house processing capability? Comment.

10. List arguments for and against FM for a:
    a. Department store in a middle-size town.
    b. Warehouse of shoes.
    c. Drugstore chain of 20 stores.
    d. Hospital with 450 beds.
    e. University with 7,000 full-time students.
    f. Race track.
    g. Broker.
    h. Restaurant.
    i. Grocery chain of 25 stores.

11. Time-sharing is most appropriate for firms or departments that have specialized tasks using special programming languages or data bases. Comment.

12. Time-sharing is most appropriate to supplement centralized processing for intermittent and one-shot jobs. Comment.

13. Compare the difference between online real time and time-sharing service for a manufacturing business.

14. How does the interactive capability of time sharing affect a user in business? Which type of use will be most affected?

15. Compare the advantages and disadvantages of time sharing from a commercial outside source with time-sharing in-house?

16. Can remote processing be used profitably for testing programs remotely? What limitations exist?

17. What are the advantages and pitfalls of using a service bureau? Under what circumstances would you recommend it?

18. Why might management choose an external computing service instead of developing an in-house processing capability?

19. Under what conditions would a firm decide to use:
    a. A service bureau.
    b. Remote processing.
    c. A computer utility.
    d. In-house computing.
    Identify the problems and pitfalls with each.

20. What future do you foresee for remote processing, utilities, and service bureaus?

21. Should the sale of computer services be regulated by federal law like the sale of electricity? Explain.

22. "The problem of privacy and security is much more difficult to control with time-sharing, a service bureau, or a utility, and the problems will get worse in the future, not better." Comment.

23. The service industry has matured and is growing into a stable, important, and well-defined sector of the computer industry. Comment.

SELECTED ANNOTATED BIBLIOGRAPHY

Bice, Fred, and E. William Withrow. "Facilities Management," in *Information Systems Administration*, ed. F. W. McFarlan et al. New York: Holt, Rinehart & Winston, 1973, pp. 240–45.
This reference provides a delightful insight into the early years of facilities management. There are numerous quotes from managers and users of FM describing their problems.

Bull, G. M., and S. F. G. Packham. *Time-sharing Systems*. London: McGraw-Hill, 1971, 140 p.
This book has chapters on user facilities (editors, filing systems, debugging aids and terminal sources), and approaches to time-sharing (RJE, roll-in/roll out, multiprogramming and swapping, paging and communications). Chapters on design features and systems management are technical but somewhat outdated.

Cortado, James W. *Finance, Budgets and Cost Control in Data Processing*. Englewood Cliffs, N.J.: Prentice-Hall, 1980.
This is an unexpected source to find information on personnel services. Chapter 6, "Source Bureaus and Facilities Management" and Chapter 8, "Dealing with Vendors and Consultants" are useful.

Holland, Geoffrey. "Service Bureau and Time-Shar ing," in *Handbook of Computer Management*, ed. R. B. Yearsley, and G. M. R. Graham. Epping, U.K.: Gower Press, 1973, pp. 117–34.
This excellent coverage of service bureaus and time-sharing includes checklists, objective specification, applications, selections, contract preparation, and control of implementation.

Laver, F. J. M. "Facilities Management," in *Handbook of Computer Management*, ed. R. B. Yearsley and G. M. R. Graham. Epping, U.K.: Gower Press 1973, pp. 95–106.
A good overview of the concept of FM, applications, problems, and costs.

Moore, D. W. "Computer Consultants" in *Handbook of Computer Management*, ed. R. B. Yearsley and G. M. R. Graham. Epping, U.K.: Gower Press, 1973 pp. 73–92.
Services, cost, choice, and evaluation of consultants are discussed.

Negus, Ron. *Guide to Computer Bureau Services*. London: Pitman Publishing, 1972, 158 p.

This text is a little outdated but is otherwise a good discussion of services including time-hire, interactive systems, remote batch, turnkey operations, and education and training services. Problems arise for the American reader because the author uses English definitions of terms, which differ from American usage.

Radley, George W. *Managing the Computer*. London: International Textbook Company, 1973, pp. 187–90.

Chapter 11 discusses consulting services in Great Britain.

Regan, Fonnie. "Choosing a Remote Computing Service." *Computer Decisions* 10, no. 4 (April 1978), pp. 39–41.

This article, extracted from a DATAPRO report, "All about Time-Sharing and Remote Processing," is good on user benefits, caveats, and selection of a vendor.

Seidman, Herbert A. "Remote Computing Service or In-house Computer?" Datamation 24, no. 4, pp. 93–95.

This is the first of a series of three articles discussing the benefits and disadvantages of remote computing services. The three articles cover most of the ground between thinking about using remote services and actually doing it, with case histories to illustrate the right and the wrong paths.

Sprague, Richard E. *Information Utilities*. Englewood Cliffs: N.J. Prentice-Hall, 1969, 199 p.

This book is one of the early books on utilities. Though somewhat outdated with regard to technology and equipment, it is still of interest and conceptually valid.

Varnum, MacVernon, and Stephanie Kress. "A Survey of Remote Computing Services." *Datamation* 25, no. 9 (August 1979), pp. 101–16.

This comparison of 100 services provides addresses and information on applications, geographical coverage, facilities offered, prices, and year of introduction.

PART SEVEN

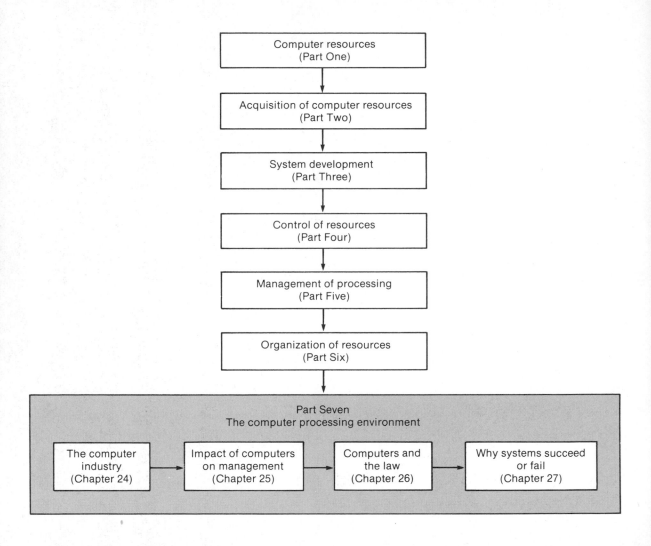

Computer resources
(Part One)

Acquisition of computer resources
(Part Two)

System development
(Part Three)

Control of resources
(Part Four)

Management of processing
(Part Five)

Organization of resources
(Part Six)

Part Seven
The computer processing environment

The computer industry
(Chapter 24)

Impact of computers on management
(Chapter 25)

Computers and the law
(Chapter 26)

Why systems succeed or fail
(Chapter 27)

THE COMPUTER PROCESSING ENVIRONMENT

Introduction to Part Seven

The chapters in this final part do not fit together under a topic heading as nicely as chapters in preceding sections, yet they are all important to business managers. They address issues of concern regarding the data processing environment.

Chapter 24 is an overview of the computer industry, discussing growth sectors of the industry, competition among equipment manufacturers, and pricing strategies of vendors. It is suggested that social issues and the merging of communications with computing will have more impact on the direction of computing in the near future than technological advances.

Chapter 25 is on the impact of computers on management and organization. How computers have changed management decision making, job responsibility, and span of control are subjects addressed. The chapter also explores whether jobs at the managerial level are jeopardized by computer.

Computers and the law is the subject of Chapter 26. Firms engaged in computing must be cognizant of antitrust statutes, copyright provisions, and laws regulating contracts, patents, trade secrets, tort, and computer crime. This chapter discusses statutes and common law relevant to computing in each of these areas. It also reviews cases that set guidelines for computer operations and helped create new sectors of the computer industry.

The book closes with Chapter 27, "Why Systems Succeed or Fail." Factors critical to system success (factors identified in earlier chapters) are reviewed and summarized. The importance of focusing on human needs in creating information systems rather than concentrating solely on technological considerations is stressed.

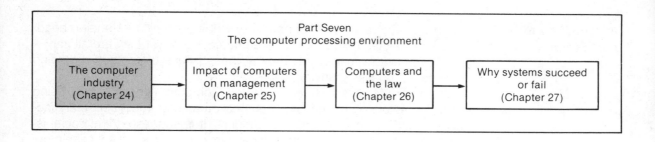

Part Seven
The computer processing environment

| The computer industry (Chapter 24) | → | Impact of computers on management (Chapter 25) | → | Computers and the law (Chapter 26) | → | Why systems succeed or fail (Chapter 27) |

CHAPTER 24

The computer industry

Wherever we are, it is but a stage on the way to somewhere else, and whatever we do, however well we do it, it is only a preparation to do something else that shall be different.

Robert Louis Stevenson

Is there free entry in the computer industry? Is the industry overregulated? Should IBM be constrained or should its dominance in computing be encouraged because it contributes to U.S. world leadership? These are questions addressed whenever the computer industry is discussed, whenever legislation regulating the industry is proposed, or antitrust action is contemplated. How these questions are answered will depend, in part, on the political orientation of each speaker, but knowledge of the status of the industry is a prerequisite to informed opinion.

This chapter will provide the reader with background to enter into the debate. Managers will also find the chapter useful because it first presents an overview of the computer industry, then describes several sectors of the industry in detail (mainframes, semiconductors, peripherals) in relation to the end user and consumer. The effect of plug-compatible manufacturers on the mainframe and peripheral markets will also be described. In addition, pricing strategies within the industry will be examined, constraints on innovation discussed, and future directions in computing explored.

OVERVIEW OF THE COMPUTER INDUSTRY

The computer industry is big business. In 1980, the top 100 U.S.-based firms in computing had total annual revenues of $55.6 billion and a growth rate of 20.4 percent.[1] U.S. computer processing expenditures as a percent of the GNP are on the upswing: 2.1 percent in 1970, 5.2 percent in 1980, and an estimated 8.3 percent in 1985.[2] In the last 25 years, the industry has grown 35 times faster than the rest of the economy. Its 1980 profits, 12.43 percent, compared favorably to profits in steel, chemicals, food, and oils (5.19 percent, 8.82 percent, 10.5 percent and 14.14 percent, respectively.)[3] The industry weathers recessions well in spite of the fact that the fortunes of customers fluctuate with business cycles. In the three years following the recession of 1974–75, for example, the computer industry grew 17.6 percent as compared with the growth rate of 11.3 percent for other segments of the economy.[4]

When speaking of the computer industry, one is talking about companies with diversified computer products. There are firms offering computer systems, personal computers, micros, minis, software, EDP services, peripherals, subsystems, supplies, and accessories. Table 24.1 shows a listing of firms in the industry trading stock in 1982. Though the list is long, a few large firms dominate the industry in the United States. For example, the top 12 in the industry, listed in Table 24.2, generate 73 percent of the revenue of the top 100. Note that IBM is the industry leader, exceeding others in revenue, employment, and capital expenditures. Its revenue in 1981 was approximately 7.3 times greater than the next ranked company, Digital Equipment Corporation. This figure is significant, since a measure economists frequently use to identify a monopoly is whether an industry leader exceeds its nearest rival by twice its revenue. IBM is frequently accused of monopolistic practices but does not have exclusive control of market. Twelve of its competitors in the world market had data processing annual revenues greater than $1 billion in 1978 (see Table 24.3). These companies are leviathans in their own right. Most earn considerably more than $1 billion, drawing revenue from other products and services. Hitachi and Toshiba, for example, earn less than one fourth of their revenues from data processing.

---

[1]Peter Wright, "The Datamation 100," *Datamation* 27, no. 6 (June 1981), p. 91.

[2]Jack Nussbaum, "Computers and Cyclicality," *Datamation* 26, no. 2 (February 1980), p. 161.

Figures determined from an AFIPS study.

[3]Statistics for the first eight months of 1980 as reported in *Business Week*, no. 267 (January 12, 1981), p. 49.

[4]For more on the subject of the computer industry and its sensitivity to the business cycle, see Nussbaum, "Computers and Cyclicality," p. 161.

Table 24.1 — Diversified structure of computing industry

Exchange	Computer systems	Exchange	Software and EDP services	Exchange	Peripherals and subsystems
A	AMDAHL CORP	O	ADVANCED COMP TECH	P	AM INTERNATIONAL
N	BURROUGHS CORP	O	ADVANCED SYSTEMS INC	A	ANDERSON JACOBSON
O	COMPUTER AUTOMATION	O	AGS COMPUTERS INC	O	AUTO-TROL TECHNOLOGY
A	COMPUTER CONSOLES	O	AMERICAN SOFTWARE	O	BANCTEC INC
N	CONTROL DATA CORP	N	ANACOMP INC	A	BEEHIVE INT'L
N	CRAY RESEARCH INC	O	ANALYSTS INTL CORP	A	BOLT, BERANEK & NEW
N	DATA GENERAL CORP	A	APPLIED DATA RES.	O	CAMBEX CORP
N	DATAPOINT CORP	O	ASK COMPUTER SYSTEMS	N	CENTRONICS DATA COMP
N	DIGITAL EQUIPMENT	B	ASTRADYNE COMP IND	A	CETEC CORP
A	EECO INC	N	AUTOMATIC DATA PROC	O	COGNITRONICS
N	ELECTRONIC ASSOC.	O	CGA COMPUTER ASSOC	O	COMPUTER COMMUN.
N	FLOATING POINT SYST	O	COMPUTER ASSOC INT'L	O	COMPUTER DEVICES INC
N	FOXBORO	O	COMPUTER HORIZONS	O	COMPUTER TRANSCEIVER
O	FULCRUM COMP GRP	O	COMPUTER NETWORK	N	COMPUTERVISION CORP
O	GENERAL AUTOMATION	N	COMPUTER SCIENCES	N	CONRAC CORP
N	HARRIS CORP	●	COMPUTER TASK GROUP	A	DATA ACCESS SYSTEMS
N	HEWLETT-PACKARD CO	O	COMPUTER USAGE	A	DATAPRODUCTS CORP
N	HONEYWELL INC	●	COMPUTONE SYSTEMS	A	DATARAM CORP
N	IBM	O	COMSERV CORP	O	DATUM INC
O	IPL SYSTEMS INC	●	COMSHARE	O	DAVID JAMISON CARLYL
				O	DECISION DATA COMPUT
O	MAGNUSON COMP SYSTS	N	CULLINET SOFTWARE	O	DELTA DATA SYSTEMS
N	MANAGEMENT ASSIST	O	CYCARE SYSTEMS INC	N	ELECTRONIC M & M
O	MINI-COMPUTER SYST	O	DATA DIMENSIONS INC	O	EVANS & SUTHERLAND
N	MODULAR COMPUTER SYS	O	DATATAB	O	GANDALF TECHNOLOGIES
N	MOHAWK DATA SCI	O	DYATRON CORP	N	GEN'L DATA COMM IND
N	NCR	N	ELECTRONIC DATA SYST	O	GENERAL TERMINAL CP
N	PERKIN-ELMER	N	INFORMATICS INC	O	GREAT SOUTHWEST IND
N	PRIME COMPUTER INC	O	INSYTE CORP	N	HAZELTINE CORP
N	SPERRY CORP	O	IPS COMPUTER MARKET.	O	ICOT CORP
O	TANDEM COMPUTERS INC	O	KEANE ASSOCIATES		
N	TEXAS INSTRUMENTS	A	LOGICON	O	INFORMATION INTL INC
A	WANG LABS "B"	O	MNGT SCI AMER INC	O	INTEL CORP
A	WANG LABS "C"	O	MATHEMATICA INC	O	IPL SYSTEMS INC
		O	MATHEMATICAL APP GRP	A	LUNDY ELECTRONICS
		O	NATIONAL DATA CORP	A	MSI DATA CORP
	Leasing companies	O	PANSOPHIC SYSTEMS	O	NETWORK SYSTEMS CORP
O	BOOTHE FINANCIAL CP	N	PLANNING RESEARCH	O	OMEX
N	COMDISCO INC	O	POLICY MGMT SYSTS CP	N	PARADYNE CORP
B	COMMERCE GROUP CORP	O	PROGRAMMING & SYS	A	PENRIL CORP
O	COMPUTER INVSTRS GRP	O	REYNOLDS & REYNOLD	O	RAMTEK CORP
O	CONTINENTAL INFOR SYS			N	RECOGNITION EQUIP
N	DPF, INC	O	SEI CORP	O	SCAN DATA
O	INTEL	O	SHARED MEDICAL SYST	N	STORAGE TECHNOLOGY
O	LEASPAC CORP	O	SCIENTIFIC COMPUTERS	O	SYKES DATATRONICS
N	U.S. LEASING	O	SOFTWARE AG	A	T BAR INC
		N	TYMSHARE INC	A	TAB PRODUCTS CO
	Supplies and accessories	A	URS CORP	A	TEC INC
N	AMERICAN BUS PRODS	N	WYLY CORP	N	TEKTRONIX INC
O	BALTIMORE BUS FORMS			N	TELEX
N	BARRY WRIGHT			O	TESDATA SYSTEMS CP
O	CYBERMATICS INC				
A	DUPLEX PRODUCTS INC			N	TIMEPLEX INC
N	ENNIS BUS. FORMS			O	VISUAL TECHNOLOGY
N	3M COMPANY			O	WILTEX INC
N	MOORE CORP LTD				
N	NASHUA CORP				
O	STANDARD REGISTER				
N	WALLACE BUS FORMS				

Exchanges: N = NEW YORK; A = AMERICAN; P = PACIFIC; B = BOSTON; L = NATIONAL; M = MIDWEST; O = OVER-THE-COUNTER. O-T-C PRICES ARE BID PRICES AS OF 3 P.M. OR LAST BID (1) TO NEAREST DOLLAR.

Table 24.2 **Selected statistics on the top 12 U.S. data processing firms**

	Revenue rankings							Employment	Revenue ($ millions)	Return equity (percent)	Growth rate (percent)	DP revenue as percent of total
	1975	1976	1977	1978	1979	1980	1981					
International Business Machines	1	1	1	1	1	1	1	278,200	26,340	19.1	16.7	90.6
Digital Equipment Corporation	7	7	6	6	6	4	2	60,000	3,586.6	12.7	30.7	89.5
Control Data Corporation	5	5	4	4	4	3	3	49,000	3,103	10.4	12.2	74.6
NCR Corporation	6	6	3	3	3	2	4	65,500	3,071	11.7	4.1	100.0
Burroughs	2	2	2	2	2	6	5	57,300	2,934	6.8	24.6	86.1
Sperry Univac Corp.	4	3	5	5	5	5	6	47,435	2,781	14.1	8.9	50.2
Hewlett-Packard	9	8	9	8	8	8	7	28,000	1,875	16.3	18.4	50.7
Honeywell	3	4	7	7	7	7	8	29,000	1,773.7	13.2	8.5	33.5
Xerox	19	22	15	19	12	9	9	†	1,106	18.0	15.7	12.8
Memorex	8	9	8	9	9	10	*	10,700	—	—	—	—
Wang Labs	45	32	28	25	23	11	10	14,000	1,008.3	16.7	47.9	100.0
Data General	22	17	12	12	10	12	13	14,370	764.4	18.1	13.6	100.0

Note: The fiscal year does not end at the same time for all of the above firms but normalizing would not appreciably affect the ranking.

*Acquired by Burroughs.
†Not available.

Source: *Datamation* 28, no. 6 (June 1982), pp. 124–25. The information is also drawn from the annual issues of *Datamation*, "The Datamation Top 100 (or 50)," 1976–82.

Table 24.3   **Companies with DP revenues of more than $1 billion for 1978**

	Country	Revenues ($ millions)	DP as percent of total revenue
International Business Machines . . .	United States	17,072	81%
Burroughs	United States	2,101	87
NCR Corporation	United States	1,932	76
Control Data Corporation	United States	1,867	68
Hitachi Ltd.	Japan	1,832	17
Sperry Rand Corp.	United States	1,807	48
Toshiba	Japan	1,683	22
Digital Equipment Corp.	United States	1,437	100
Honeywell	United States	1,294	37
Fujitsu Ltd	Japan	1,248	71
Cu–H.B.	France	1,061	100
ICL	Britain	1,019	100

Source: *Datamation* 25, no. 6 (May 1979) pp. 18 and 79.

IBM does dominate the industry worldwide. Its data processing sales exceed those of other firms in all countries except the United Kingdom and Japan. It tolerates competition, critics charge, only to keep the Justice Department at bay. (Chapter 26 discusses antitrust court actions against IBM at length.) IBM combines technological know-how with management foresight and aggressive marketing. The company also has powerful friends in Washington where many decisions governing the industry are made. During Carter's administration, for example, the secretaries of state, defense, and housing were drawn from IBM's board of directors. No overview of the industry would be complete without acknowledging IBM's dominance, its leadership in setting both standards and directions in computing.

This chapter will now discuss the different sectors of the computer industry, starting with mainframe manufacturers.

MAINFRAME MANUFACTURERS

The top six U.S. **mainframe manufacturers** are IBM, Burroughs, Honeywell, Sperry, NCR, and Control Data Corporation. The six are called the giant and five dwarfs by insiders, but the dwarfs are small only when measured against the giant, IBM. In absolute terms, their revenues are considerable (see Table 24.2) and each has a tradition of service in business with a loyal cadre of customers. Burroughs, for example, has roots in adding and bookkeeping machines; NCR, long associated with cash registers, has a speciality in banking and retail markets; and Control Data, which debuted in large computers, draws clients through its service bureaus and its focus on energy applications like PLATO.

Nevertheless, IBM's leadership in mainframe manufacture is undisputed. In the 60s, when IBM introduced the 360 with a revolutionary single architecture for a family of computers (leading to the 370), the company set a standard for computer architecture which all other mainframe manufacturers soon followed. With each new IBM model introduced, competitors scrambled to market enhanced versions of their own computers with matching computing capability.

IBM's leadership extended to pricing as well, in the 60s. Competitors operated under IBM's price umbrella, keeping their mainframe users captive by slightly undercutting IBM in price.

Though some jockeying for position did occur in the early 70s (CDC made changes in its high-end computers and both Burroughs and NCR introduced new series), IBM's dominance in mainframes was uncontested throughout the 70s. This was even though IBM's 370/168 was becoming technologically outdated as demand for high-end computers increased. Gene **Amdahl,** an IBM designer of high-end processors, had forecast this as early as the 60s. He had recommended that IBM develop a new mainframe family with increased computing capacity and an improved price/performance ratio, but IBM, committed to the price/performance ratio of the 370s and not seeing enough demand for the new series to make development profitable, did not heed Amdahl's advice. So Amdahl decided to leave IBM in 1970 to become a mainframe manufacturer on his own.

Amdahl planned to manufacture a mainframe that would be plug-compatible with software and peripherals developed for IBM computers. Though plug-compatible peripherals were common on the market, Amdahl was proposing the reversal, a **plug-compatible mainframe.** Intel was already at work on this concept, developing the Intel AS/5 which reached the market in 1978. But the technology Amdahl proposed was different. His problem was lack of funding, the estimated $33–44 million needed for development.[5] The stock market decline of 1972 made the prospect of a public offering unfavorable. Businesses and investors lacked faith that Amdahl could challenge IBM, a company with cash reserves of $5 billion and a formidable marketing organization as well. How could Amdahl expect to succeed where GE, RCA, and Xerox had failed? Amdahl did succeed in raising $7.8 million in the U.S. but the crucial funding came from Fujitsu of Japan. The Amdahl mainframe was put on the market in 1976 and today is prospering as a high-end computer as is Intel's machine.

Amdahl's success was a surprise both to industry observers and to economists because they had not believed that demand for high-end

---

[5]"Taking on the Giant: An Interview with Gene M. Amdahl," *Harvard Business Review* 58, no. 2 (March/April 1980), p. 86.

computers was elastic. Amdahl's success proved such elasticity did exist. It also demonstrated:

> . . . that it was possible to build compatible computers . . . to obtain customer acceptance, to provide the hardware and software support adequate to synergize this acceptance, and to grow rapidly while doing it. Perhaps the most sincere recognition of this success was the sudden appearance of other companies emulating our (Amdahl's) activities.[6]

Companies which followed Amdahl's lead in marketing a plug-compatible mainframe include Magnuson, Nanodata, Cambridge Memories, Citel, and NCSS.[7]

IBM's immediate response to Amdahl's plug-compatible mainframe was to booster its 370/168. Then in 1977, IBM introduced a new series of its own (the 3033, followed by the 3032 and 3021) with a better price/performance ratio. By this time, however, Amdahl has sold 40 of his mainframes, totaling $170 billion in market value.

Other IBM countermeasures included the reduction of prices on IBM equipment, "bundling" of some software and peripherals with IBM mainframes, and charging separately for systems software.[8] The company's marketing strategy had to change because the strength of applications and support would no longer sell mainframes. The introduction of compatible mainframes meant that all system components, including hardware, would now face competition.

As mainframe competition has quickened from **PCMs (plug-compatible manufacturers)** and other mainframe manufacturers (such as Siemens which has sold Fujitsu computers in the United States through a joint subsidiary with TRW), IBM has been forced to reduce the life cycle of its models and has tried to operate under a lower price umbrella while still retaining its lease base. Other manufacturers have followed suit. Users and buyers have been the primary beneficiaries. IBM has been a beneficiary from the competition to some extent as well, at least in antitrust legal battles with the Justice Department, for Amdahl has demonstrated that entry barriers in the mainframe market are not insurmountable, helping refute the charges that IBM has a monopoly in mainframes.

What share of the mainframe market have plug-compatible main-

---

[6]Gene M. Amdahl, "The Early Chapters of the PCM Story," *Datamation* 25, no. 2 (February 1979), pp. 113–16.

[7]For detailed comparisons of these PCMs with the Amdahl and 1979 Intel machines (since bought out by NAS), see Mary Bartholomew and Elinor Gebremedhin, "The PCM Vendors," *Datamation* 25, no. 2 (February 1979), pp. 104–11. The article also discusses possible Amdahl/Fujitsu and Siemens/Fujitsu systems.

[8]For a good discussion on this subject, see Lawrence Solomon, "IBM versus the PCMs," *Datamation* 25, no. 2 (February 1979), pp. 101–3, and Stephen J. Ippolito, "Measure for Counter Measure," in the same issue, pp. 120–26.

frames captured? Table 24.4 shows that the share is small, but growing.[9] Compatibility with IBM saves companies software development time since IBM's applications programs are immediately accessible, and plug-compatibles are spared the cost of program development as well. IBM has made enormous investments in software research and development from which competitors now benefit at no cost to themselves. How will IBM try to retain its dominance in mainframes? According to Stephen Ippolito:

> [IBM] will time price cuts and new machine announcements carefully. It will time delivery schedules to cause maximum damage to its competitors. It will foster confusion and doubt in the market through its tactical moves. It will announce new features and spread new rumors of others to come. It will dispatch its thousands of salesmen to convince customers that any move away from IBM will be foolhardy.[10]

Yet despite these actions, Ippolito predicts that IBM will lose a significant portion of the system 370 mainframe market to PCMs. Indeed, IBM's mainframe market share has been dropping steadily—from 82 percent during the 60s and early 70s,[11] to 64.2 percent in 1978, to a forecasted 60 percent in 1983. (See Table 24.4.)

Amdahl is still the leader of mainframe PCMs. In 1981, Amdahl had an annual revenue of $442.7 million, a growth rate of 12.2 percent, and ranked 22d in the mainframe industry. The company's original price/performance ratio was 70 percent of IBM's. By 1980, that ratio had improved to 40 percent of Amdahl's starting ratio.[12]

Table 24.4   **Worldwide percent share of general-purpose mainframe market for 1978 and projected for 1983**

	1973	1978	1983*
IBM	65.8%	64.2%	60.0%
PCM	0	1.3	8.2
Total IBM and IBM-compatible	65.8%	65.5%	68.2%
Honeywell	12.6%	11.0%	9.3%
Burroughs	6.6	7.6	6.8
Sperry Univac	7.1	7.1	6.0
NCR	3.8	3.9	3.4
Control Data	3.0	2.4	1.7
Others	1.1	2.5	4.5
Total non-IBM compatible	34.2%	34.5%	31.8%

*Projected market.

Source: *Datamation* 25, no. 6 (May 25, 1979), p. 94. Figures compiled by Paine, Webber, Mitchell, and Hutchins.

---

[9]See J. Garrett Sanford, "The PCMs: So Far, So Good," *Datamation* 25, no. 6 (May 25, 1979), pp. 92–96.

[10]Ippolito, "Measure for Counter Measure," p. 126.

[11]F. M. Scherer, *Industrial Market Structure and Market Performance* (Chicago: Rand McNally College Publishing, 1980), p. 67.

[12] "Taking on the Giant," p. 91.

Gene Amdahl is lauded and envied for his success but also criticized for taking capital from Fujitsu because this may lead to leakage of U.S. computer technology into Japan. In 1980, Fujitsu did hold 34 percent of Amdahl stock and produced many components for Amdahl mainframes, including LSI chips. Amdahl's response to this criticism is that:

> Before we ever negotiated with Fujitsu, we tried to get semiconductor companies in the United States to work with us, and they did not want to because we were not big enough.[13]

Amdahl also asserts that Fujitsu has no licensing rights for the product of Amdahl's technology in the United States and Canada, so does not constitute a threat to mainframe firms in the North American market. However, Fujitsu has sold large machines in Spain, Korea, and Australia and has been negotiating joint relationships with Siemens in Germany and TRW in the United States.

Amdahl does recognize that the Japanese are a threat to U.S. firms producing semiconductors needed for mainframes. The Japanese willingness to invest in research and development in chips even when a relatively small volume of sales is anticipated gives them a competitive advantage. American firms invest only when there are expectations for enormous volume, a short-sighted view, according to Amdahl.

> In Japan, the government has convinced industry to take the long-range view. The Japanese look at the technologies necessary to make the products that most probably will be successful, and they put their money in those. Japanese managers believe that developing those capabilities is absolutely essential to their future, while in this country, each company is asking, "Can I get my return in two years?"[14]

The following section will look more closely at the crucial semiconductor industry.

SEMICONDUCTORS

The **semiconductor industry** is important not only to mainframes, but to minis, micros, and word processors as well. 40 percent of the semiconductors produced are for memory devices, which had global sales of $13 billion in 1980.[15]

The Japanese got a strong foothold in the chip market in 1977–79 when U.S. manufacturers failed to expand to meet the increase in demand for 16K memory chips. At that time, U.S. manufacturers thought

---

[13]Ibid., p. 89.
[14]Ibid.
[15] Gene Bylinsky, "The Japanese Chip Challenge," *Fortune* 103, no. 6 (March 23, 1981), p. 116.

the increase was merely the upswing in a boom-and-bust cycle, underestimating potential semiconductor sales. The high cost of money at that time also contributed to their reluctance to expand. Even Intel, which held 40 percent of the 16K market, did not produce enough 16K chips to satisfy its customers, having diverted production to other products for which Intel was the sole supplier.

But Japanese manufacturers, notably Hitachi, Fujitsu, and NEC, having a more limited range of products, were able to shift their output to 16K chips and quickly fill the gap. By 1980, the Japanese share of the semiconductor industry had boomed to $370 million, up from $62 million in 1977.

The semiconductor industry has advanced since 1977. The earlier 16K chips have been replaced by 64K dynamic RAM (random access memory) chips. A 256K chip is projected for the mid-80s, and greater intensity of LSI and VLSI will produce minicomputers on a chip.[16] Semiconductors today are produced in many major countries—replacing steel, airlines, and satellites as a status symbol. An annual production of $50–100 million is the critical mass needed. In Japan, this critical mass is absorbed by internal demand which is greater than demand for semiconductors in all European countries combined. Japan is the only country outside the United States where a major share of the semiconductor market is held by a domestic manufacturer (69 percent on value basis as far back as 1976).

Yet despite the increased demand for chips, the number of manufacturers producing semiconductors for sale to industrial companies is actually dropping. This is because user firms are increasing their own in-house chip production capacity. For example, IBM, Burroughs, Data General, Delco, Digital Equipment, Hewlett-Packard, Honeywell, and Tektronik all make their own chips. This ensures the company of a supply of chips and enables the company to have proprietary circuits. But even these firms commonly supplement in-house production with chips purchased from merchant suppliers. Many U.S. firms choose Japanese suppliers because of their cooperative approach toward the development of hardware and software, and because they are "highly reliable" and "quite innovative."

In testimony before the House Ways and Means Committee, Charles Sprock, President of National Semiconductors Corporation, explained

---

[16]It is forecast that the 30,000 transistors on a chip of the late 70s will increase to a half million by 1985, to 10 million by 1990. The following articles provide a good tutorial on projected advances. Edward K. Yasaki, "Buying into $100 Billion," *Datamation*, special issue, circa 1980, p. 10, and Hollis L. Caswell et al., "Basic Technology," *Computer* 11, no. 9 (September 1978), pp. 10–17. See also an article by Bob Noyce on the future of the semiconductor industry in the same issue; Jean-Michel Gabet, "VLSI: The Impact Grows," *Datamation* 25, no. 7 (June 1979), pp. 108–22; and John W. Bremer, "Hardware Technology in the Year 2001," *Computer* 9, no. 12 (December 1976), p. 36.

that the Japanese are resolute competitors because, "Japanese semiconductor companies are able to employ high debt-to-equity ratios because of their affiliation with large industrial groups, Japanese lending practices, and a supportive government policy."[17] Their debt to equity ratio was cited by Sprock as between 150 and 230 percent compared to an average of less than 25% for U.S. companies. Sprock's figures were drawn from a Chase Manhattan Bank study which observed that, ". . . leverage of this magnitude would not be available from conventional banking or (other) capital market sources in the United States."[18] With regard to government support, Japanese firms receive as much as $2 billion annually in the form of accelerated depreciation, investment reserves, and special treatment for R&D expenses. The cost of capital to Japanese companies? 9.3 percent compared to the prevalent U.S. rate of 17.5 percent at the time of the Chase Manhattan study.

Some observers fear that the American semiconductor industry will respond to Japanese competition as did U.S. TV manufacturers who just went to sleep and stopped fighting. But as long as U.S.-based companies continue to battle for their share of the market, semiconductor manufacture should be an exciting competitive business.

PERIPHERALS

The **peripheral market** represented nearly 20 percent of the revenues of the computer industry in 1980. Plug-compatible peripherals accounted for a large share of this market. They were first introduced in the 1960s by companies such as Memorex and Ampex to compete with IBM tape and disk drives, memories, and printers. In response to the competition, IBM improved its performance/price ratio and offered customers a wider range of choice in equipment.

Withdrawals, mergers, and new entrants realigned the peripheral market in the 1970s. It was also a decade of litigation challenging IBM's supremacy.[19] For example, Calcomp, Hudson General Corp., Marshall Industries, and TransAmerican Computer Corporation asked for injunctions against IBM market practices and sued for divestiture of the company. They also sought $642 million in damages for unfair competition. DPF and Farro Precision filed for another $81 million in

---

[17]Yasaki, "Buying into $100 Billion," p. 13.

[18]Ibid.

[19] For an excellent discussion how litigation affects competitive action, see Gerald W. Brock, *The U.S. Computer Industry* (Cambridge, Mass: Ballinger Publishing, 1975), pp. 163–82. For an anti-IBM view, read Rex Malik, *And Tomorrow the World: Inside IBM,* (Londen: Millington, 1975), pp. 336–427.

damages. Most cases were settled out of court. But one case with far-reaching ramifications that went to trial was a suit by Telex charging IBM with monopoly. IBM countersued. The decision went against Telex insofar as the company was found guilty of infringing on IBM copyrighted manuals and inducing former IBM employees to reveal IBM secrets. But IBM was required to publicly disclose the interface of its products at the time of announcement, and to separate pricing of the CPU, memory, and functionally different products, such as tape drives and their control units. This decision benefited competitors of IBM for a time. However, the new rash of suits against IBM which followed the Telex suit destroyed investor confidence and dried up some venture capital for plug-compatible peripherals.

The struggle among peripheral manufacturers has served consumer interests. Competition has led to enhanced peripherals and lower peripheral prices.

OTHER MARKET SEGMENTS

Mainframes and peripherals make less than half of the revenues in the computer industry, as shown in Table 24.5. Other segments of the industry include minis, micros, word processors, data communica-

Table 24.5	Percent of revenues per sector of the computer industry for 1980		
	Systems		
	Mainframe	27.2%	
	Minicomputers	15.9	
	Microcomputers	1.4	
	Word processing	1.6	46.1%
	Peripherals		
	OEMs*	7.1	
	End users	12.4	19.5
	Data communication . . .	2.1	
	Software products	3.1	
	Maintenance	16.0	
	Service	11.6	
	All other	1.6	34.4
			100.0%

Note: The revenue of the top 100 companies in 1980 was $55.6 billion.

*OEM stands for original equipment manufacturers. These peripherals are bought by systems vendors to include in their hardware systems packages which they then sell to the end user.

Source: Peter Wright, "The Datamation 100," Datamation 27, no. 7 (June 1981), p. 96.

tions, software, maintenance, and service. Microtechnology is responsible for the phenomenal growth in many of these market segments. For example, the popularity of home and small business computers, the manufacture of smart consumer products (products with embedded micros such as programmable microwave ovens), and the growing use of robots in industry can be attributed to the micro revolution. The mainframe may become the dinosaur of computing, replaced by supercomputers at one extreme, and minis or micros at the other.

Though IBM dominates mainframes, there is lively competition in all other segments of the computer industry. Indeed, IBM is not even among the top three competitors in most segments, as shown in Table 24.6. IBM is a full-line company, producing the hardware and software necessary to support its own mainframes, whereas many firms specialize in one market only and, as a result, outsell IBM.

Table 24.6   **Top three leaders in different segments of the computer industry**

	1981 revenue ($ millions)	Percent change in revenue 1980–1981	Average growth for sample (percent)
Mainframes			9.4
IBM	12,000	9.0	
Burroughs	1,254.8	23.6	
Honeywell	1,108.6	4.3	
Peripherals			24.0
IBM	5,000	11.1	
Control Data (CDC)	1,116.4	16.3	
Sperry Corp.	1,112.4	8.9	
Mini manufacturers			30.6
Digital Equipment Corp.	2,068.1	19.6	
Data General Corp.	573.2	13.5	
Hewlett-Packard Corp.	435.0	16.0	
Word processing producers			32.3
IBM	1,600.0	33.3	
Wang Lab., Inc.	605.1	28.6	
Lanier Business	228.0	18.4	
Computer processing services			26.0
Computer Science Corp.	624.7	11.4	
Automatic Data Processing	613.0	20.9	
General Electric	550.0	80.3	
Micro manufacturer.			52.7
Apple Computer Corp.	401.1	147.7	
Tandy Corp.	293.0	95.8	
Hewlett-Packard	235.0	17.5	
Data communications equipment manufacturers			33.6
Rolm Corp.	271.7	37.6	
Racal Corp.	240.0	13.2	
Motorola Inc.	180.0	42.8	

Source: Pamela Archold, "The Datamation Top 100," *Datamation* 23, no. 6 (June 1982), pp. 116–18.

Any listing of leaders in computing, such as that in Table 24.6, is quickly outdated since the industry has had a volatile record of entries and exits. The growing popularity of minis, word processors, and personal computers, for example, has enabled newcomers, such as Apple, Radio Shack, and Wang, to capture substantial market shares. Mergers have also brought new firms into computing (e.g., GTE and Telenet, NCR and Comten, ITT and Qume), whereas acquisitions have strengthened certain competitors (e.g., Siliconix bought by Westinghouse, Intersil by General Electric, Mostek by United Technology, and Synertek by Honeywell). Future marriages forecast across international boundaries will cause further dislocation in the marketplace (e.g., Burroughs with ICL of the United Kingdom, Sperry Univac with Phillips of Holland, Control Data with Hitachi of Japan). In addition, new technology in telecommunications has brought firms such as SBS into computing. So have court decisions, such as the recent decision which allows AT&T to compete in the computer industry. Some firms already in one area of computing are diversifying (e.g.: Honeywell, Incotern, Varian). Exits from mainframe manufacture include such giants as GE, RCA and Xerox. Intel has dropped from the peripheral market and Singer has left the field of computing altogether, its computing division absorbed by TRW and ICL.

All of the above entries and exits affect competition. In antitrust litigation, the volatile nature of the industry has been cited by both prosecutors and defendants in support of their cases. IBM has been under fire by the Justice Department for its alleged monopolistic practices since the 50s (see Chapter 26). The exits of competitors, such as GE and Xerox, are cited as evidence of IBM's stranglehold on the market. IBM counters that its dominance is in one segment of the computing industry only and that the industry as a whole should be considered in monopoly litigation, not just mainframes. IBM argues that it has no monopoly when software, peripherals, maintenance, services, minis, micros, programmable hand calculators, military computers, and special purpose computers (such as those used in process control) are taken into consideration. According to IBM, the number of new firms entering computing proves market entry is without barrier, the sine qua non of monopoly.[20]

Another aspect of monopoly is pricing. If, in fact, the market is free, pricing should be relevant and competitive. Is it? The next section will examine pricing practices in the computer industry.

---

[20]According to IBM's definition of the boundaries of computing, it held only 32 percent of the market in 1972. This figure encompassed a 72 percent share of the general-purpose digital computing market, a percentage the government defined as monopolistic.

PRICING

Amdahl proved the high elasticity of demand at the high-end of the CPU. Similar elasticity could exist all along the CPU spectrum and should affect price, but IBM's mainframe competitors operate under IBM's price umbrella which allows for profit-making and a payoff period of only 4–5 years. It has been estimated that the cost of IBM mainframes is only 15 percent of their selling price.[21] The mainframe market might be categorized as an oligopoly with price leadership.

The peripheral market is much more competitive in price. IBM tolerates competition within bounds, out of fear of the Justice Department, but reacts sharply when its market share is in jeopardy, using pricing strategies as one competitive tool. The problem is that there is a fine line between pricing in pursuance of profit maximization, a legitimate goal, and **predatory pricing** intended to restrict competition, a violation of the Sherman Act. Unfortunately, no legal definition of predatory pricing exists for the computer industry. (If predatory pricing is pricing below cost, should cost be defined as average total cost, short-run average, short-run marginal, or long-run marginal cost?)[22] In the absence of such a definition, IBM and IBM's competitors adopt pricing strategies in accordance with what they perceive as the boundaries of the law.

Price tying

IBM originally combined hardware, software, education, documentation, and consulting in a single price package. To counter critics and antitrust action, IBM "unbundled" its prices in 1970. Though this helped some competitors, particularly software houses, IBM still had the advantage of economies of scale in software development. Other mainframe vendors, following IBM's lead, also separated software from mainframes, charging for what they traditionally gave away.

Despite unbundling, **price tying** is a strategy still commonly used when products can technically be justified as one unit. Critics charge that, too often, IBM uses the strategy in the face of fierce peripheral competition—tying vulnerable peripherals with a CPU (which has a high market entry barrier) and supportive software.

---

[21]Gerald Brock calculated this figure by using an econometric model by Darius Gaskins. See Brock, *The U.S. Computer Industry*, p. 79. Mainframe profit margins are kept high to absorb development costs. Formerly, development costs were shared by all system components. With unbundling and the introduction of plug-compatible peripherals, IBM's competitors, spared mainframe development, could offer peripherals at cutthroat prices. To be competitive, IBM had to match the price of competitor's peripherals and make mainframe sales pay for mainframe development.

[22]Phillip Arreada and Donald F. Turner, "Predatory Pricing and Related Prices under Section 2 in the Sherman Act," *Harvard Law Review* 28, no. 2 (February 1975), pp. 697–733.

Price cutting   Just before introducing a new product, firms often cut the price of
the product being replaced. Competitors must respond with cuts of
their own. Prices of IBM's 370/158 and 168 were slashed 30 percent
before the introduction of the 3031 and 3032, for example. The new
machines had only modest enhancements but cost even less than the
reduced rates for the 158 and 168. (IBM refrained from more than a
30 percent reduction of the old models to prevent undercutting the
rental of installed equipment.)

Price cutting also occurs in peripherals. For example, a repackaged
IBM disk pack was offered at a 26 percent discount. Knowing that old
customers are often unwilling to make an equipment change or are
oblivious of price differentials, IBM did not lower the price of the
original disk pack. Disguising a price cut as a model change in this
manner puts competitors on the defensive. They must be able to con-
vince customers that their models match the new equipment in performance, or respond with modified models of their own.

An alternative price-cutting strategy is to reduce the price of products facing competition, while raising the price of products with no
competition.

Value pricing   **Value pricing** is charging a high price for an indispensable product
to cover low profit margins for other products in a company's line. An
inflated price for a disk drive is an example of value pricing, since
customers do not have the ability to change disk drives and are
"locked in" to their purchase.

Profit pricing   Sometimes companies will alter their profit margins in response to
competition, the market, or environmental conditions. It was expected
that IBM might lower its profits while being tried for antitrust violations during the 70s, for example. But IBM continued to price aggres-
sively, not linking its defense with **profit pricing.**

Price differentiation   **Price differentiation** is pricing a product in order to help favored
customers or damage specific competitors. It is alleged that IBM used
this strategy in pricing the 360 mod. 44 and mod. 90, taking an estimated loss of $100 million.[23]

Pricing over a fixed   **Pricing over a fixed term** was a strategy used by IBM when it of-
term   fered customers a 16 percent discount for peripherals leased for a
fixed term of two years without the usual option of a month's cancel-
lation notice. This strategy was directed against plug-compatible manufacturers who have to wait until new IBM mainframes are on the

---

[23]Scherer, *Industrial Market Structure,* p. 536.

market before they can start development of plug-compatible peripherals. Since peripherals have a limited life span due to the pace of technological change in computing, PCMs have only a limited time to recoup their investments. With potential customers locked into two year IBM leases, IBM hoped the PCMs would decide it was not worth their while to risk developing plug-compatible peripherals in competition with IBM's own peripherals.

Are the above pricing strategies predatory and hence illegal? Charges of unfair competition in computing abound, and the courts are burdened with deciding questions such as whether IBM purposely sets lease/purchase prices to drive out third party lessors. Most firms see pricing as just another card in the game of competition and employ pricing strategies to increase their share of the market within what they perceive as the boundaries of the law. IBM considers itself as entitled as other firms to use pricing as a competitive tool.

It should be recognized that pricing is only one element of sales policy. A unique product, application sales emphasis, stable charges for service, technological excellence of product, and good management may be as important as pricing strategies in making sales.

INNOVATION IN COMPUTING

Innovation in business is closely linked to capital expenditures and outlays in research and development. This is particularly true in the computer industry where technology quickly becomes obsolete and products have a short life span. As might be expected, IBM towers over competitors in such expenditures (see Table 24.7). Innovation at IBM is part of the company's broad marketing strategy. According to observers of the industry, IBM evaluates whether customers are ready to accept innovation, determines whether maximum profit from old technology has been milked, and decides where the benefits of research would most effectively throw competitors off stride.

Lack of capital is a major restraint to technological innovation in computing.[24] Even large corporations, such as RCA, GE, and Xerox, have not had the success or the capital needed to be competitive and have consequently left the field. Government regulation is also a factor constraining the industry, particularly growth in the area of telecommunications. It is charged that FCC constraints are the reason why the United States lagged behind France, Germany, and Japan in wired

---

[24]See Hesh Wiener, "Funding the Computer Industry," *Datamation* 27, no. 6 (June 1981) pp. 198–205. See also Becky Barnes, "Business Ready to Up R&D," *Datamation*, special issue, circa 1979, pp. 27–28.

Table 24.7   **Top 10 in R&D and capital expenditures for 1980 ($ millions)**

	R&D	Capital expenditures
IBM	1,277	1,985
Digital Equipment Corp.	217	321
Sperry	216	117
NCR	201	156
Control Data	183	296
Burroughs	175	147
Honeywell	150°	*
Hewlett-Packard	139	148
Data General	68	†
Amdahl	63	†
Wang Labs	†	96
Storage Technology	†	76
Automated Data Processing . . .	†	70
Total for top 10	2,689	3,412
Percentage of total revenues . .	4.8%	6.1%

*Not in top 10.
†Data not available.

Source: Adapted from Peter Wright, "The Datamation 100," *Datamation* 27, no. 7 (June 1981), p. 94.

cities and applications such as CEEFAX and PRESTEL found in the United Kingdom.

FUTURE DIRECTIONS IN COMPUTING

Most industry observers agree that few revolutionary concepts will be introduced in the near future that will change basic computer technology.[25] Work on Josephson junctions, bubble memory, and telecommunications will continue; intensification of VLSI will occur; and improvement in input/output devices, such as speech processing, OCR stations, graphics and displays, and "smart" terminals, are to be expected; but all represent refinements of existing technology.

Though one can predict the technological direction of computing for the near future, governmental regulation and economic strictures that will be placed on computing firms in coming years are far harder to forecast. What confrontations between the nation-state and computer, telecommunications, and semiconductor firms lie ahead? How will multinationals fare? According to Erwin Tomash, we will be liv-

---

[25]See John W. Bremer, "Hardware Technology in the Year 2001," *Computer* 9, no. 12 (December 1976), pp. 31–36; Caswell, "Basic Technology," *Computer* 11, no. 9 (September 1978), pp. 10–17; Robert M. Englund, "The Coming Decade of Innovation," *Computer* 14, no. 4 (April 1981), pp. 77–80; *The Waves of Change* (New York: Advanced Computer Technologies Corp. 1977), pp. 133–64 on software technologies and pp. 165–85 on hardware technologies; and Frederick G. Withington, "Beyond 1984: A Technology Forecast," *Datamation* 21, no. 1 (January 1975), pp. 54–73.

ing in a world far more socialistic than capitalistic by the year 2007. It will be a world:

> where political considerations will decide economic matters; where os-
> cillation between periods of inflation and unemployment will be the
> rule; where industrial development will vie with economic considera-
> tion; where the majority of mankind will be occupied with the provi-
> sion of products; and, where risk capital for innovative enterprise will
> be scarce. Will innovative high-risk, high-technology in industry be able
> to thrive in such an environment? To whom does the economy belong?
> And who is to control it?[26]

The future direction of computing will depend, in part, on whether Tomash's prophecies are fulfilled, and how his questions are answered.

Another uncertainty is whether IBM will continue its dominance in computing. In January 1982 the Justice Department announced an out-of-court agreement that will allow AT&T to merge its communications with data services. The agreement also broke AT&T's monopoly in communications so that IBM and such multibillion dollar firms as ITT, Exxon, RCA, and General Telephone and Electronics may compete in data communications and offer integrated office systems connected by communication networks. The AT&T agreement was announced the same month that IBM's position in the industry was strengthened by the dismissal of the Justice Department's 1969 antitrust suit against the company. AT&T and IBM are now both freer from governmental constraints and have joined in battle since computers have become essential to modern communications, and communication facilities are essential to information processing. The collision between these two giants will shape the computing industry in the years ahead.

AT&T is a formidable antagonist. Since homes and offices are all wired for telephones, AT&T equipment is already on the premises of most potential customers for data services and its UNIX operating system is used by many small systems. IBM will have to displace the company from this entrenched position to gain control over data communications. AT&T's universal market presence is supported by an eminent research division, the Bell Laboratories, and a production arm, Western Electric, which rivals IBM in size and product quality. Indeed, the company's total resources are superior to IBM's. AT&T has also demonstrated that it can raise vast sums of investment capital. If this capital should be focused on new products where IBM is weak, such as home terminals in local networks, AT&T could threaten IBM's dominance in computing.

The struggle between IBM and AT&T will not be a case of winner-

---

[26]Erwin Tomash, "SOS: The Next 11111 Years," *Computer* 9, no. 12 (December 1976), p. 11.

take-all because AT&T may continue to provide communication services while IBM will concentrate on data processing products. The competition in data transmission, however, will affect new markets and the relative growth rates of the companies. Will AT&T, with its experience in telephone communications, develop transmission of voiced messages between computers and terminals? Will the yellow pages be converted into electronic yellow pages, then expanded into an information bank to include daily news? The American Newspaper Publishers Association, alert to this possibility, objects that this would put American Bell in the position of both carrier and controller of information.

IBM's strength lies in the fact that the company has welded its software and hardware sales, manufacturing, distribution, and services into an integrated whole, giving the company worldwide marketing muscle. The company has a wide range of products and a record of applying its research and development to innovative product lines. IBM's data processing standards are another weapon in its arsenal. Customers that have invested in IBM equipment and software cannot readily switch vendors. Yet to wrest the lead from IBM would require wooing such customers from IBM. Unless AT&T can find markets where IBM's presence is negligible or where no de facto standards exist, AT&T's challenge may well be limited to developing plug-compatible information appliances.

Table 24.8 summarizes the areas of confrontation between AT&T and IBM at the present time. Competition between these corporations should ultimately benefit the user because it will foster a wider spectrum of cost-effective products and services than offered previously. The potential for wired offices, wired shopping, wired newspapers, even wired cites should leave markets for other competitors as well. GTE and the U.S. Postal Service, for example, are interested in long distance data communications. Ethernet by Xerox is concentrating on short distances, Waynet has three separate channels, and Rolm Corp. connects small desktop terminals to existing phone lines. Advances are being made abroad as well. France, the United Kingdom, and Japan, with backing from their respective governments, have data transmission applications in use, such as CEEFAX and electronic phone books, that private enterprise here in the United States has thus far been unable to match. It is possible that leadership in data communications may come from overseas.

The future of computing will also be affected if IBM splits into two or three parts, each offering a full range of products and becoming direct competitors.[27] The original intent of the Justice Department's

---

[27]See Fred Lamond, "IBM versus IBM," *Datamation* 25, no. 2 (February 1979), pp. 143–47. This article has an excellent diagram and discussion of IBM's organization structure at the top. See also *State of the Art Report: IBM* 1 (Maidenhead, England: Infotech International, 1978), pp. 161.

Table 24.8 **Areas of confrontation/competition between AT&T and IBM**

Home, office, and factory	Comunications Interface	Transmission	Communications Interface	Home, office, and factory
Telephone Television Terminal —Typewriter —Visual display unit —Voice unit Electronic office —Word processor —Copiers —Printers —Info retrieval Computers —Minis —Micros Peripherals —Input readers —Printers	PBX Smart swtiches Equipment —Modem —Multiplexer —Concentrator Networks —Protocols Earth stations —Local —National	Telephone or telegraph line Low and intermediate speed Cable Microwave transmission High speed	PBX Smart switches Equipment —Modem —Multiplexer —Concentrator Networks —Protocols Earth stations —Local —National	Telephone Television Terminal —Typewriter —Visual display unit —Voice unit Electronic office —Word processor —Copiers —Printers —Info retrieval Computers —Minis —Micros Peripherals —Input readers —Printers
Weak	Strong	Strong		Weak
AT&T				
Strong	Weak	Weak		Strong
IBM				

1969 antitrust suit was to break IBM's alleged monopolistic control of the industry and force such a split. Though the 1969 suit has been dropped, another suit demanding **divestiture** might be filed in the future. But many experts believe IBM may initiate divestiture on its own. This is not as farfetched as the reader might first surmise. The company's General Services Division has already seperated from the Products Division, creating internal competition within the firm. Should IBM management decide that the firm has become too large to control, that the company's self-interest would be served by breaking into smaller, more manageable units, the company might choose to subdivide. Many competitors, who have complained about IBM's size and dominance in the past, view the possibility of divestiture with alarm.[28] From their standpoint, they believe it is better to have one IBM facing antitrust litigation acting on the defensive than two or three IBMs on the offensive, operating without restraint.

In summary, one might state that confrontations between nation-

---

[28]A. Pantages found user groups unwilling to make formal comment on this subject. See A. Pantages, "User Unprepared and Unwilling to Comment," *Datamation* 21, no. 6 (August 1975), pp. 74–77.

state and the industry, and IBM versus its competitors, will have more impact on the future direction of computing than will technology. As Erwin Tomash states, the future of information processing is assured, but the future of information processing enterprise is not. The debate over what is best for society will become heated as companies grow in their dependence on computers. Challenging and exciting years lie ahead for the computer industry.

SUMMARY AND CONCLUSIONS

In 1970, revenues from the computer industry represented 2.1 percent of the GNP of the United States. This figure is projected to reach 8.3 percent in 1985.[29] The growth of the computing sectors of the economy is also reflected in employment statistics, the number of firms offering data processing products, and in percentages of corporation budgets allocated to data processing.

The industry itself is fragmented into segments: mainframes, small systems (minis, micros, and word processors), peripherals, terminals, software, and service. Each segment is highly competitive with many players, with the exception of mainframes where IBM controls over 60 percent of the market, though IBM's presence is felt in all segments of the industry.

IBM's total share of the data processing market is dropping, however—down from 80 percent in the 70s to an estimated 60 percent in 1985. This is due to the emergence of competitors such as Amdahl in mainframes and plug-compatible manufacturers. IBM has reacted to competition with product enhancements and pricing strategies, such as tying and bundling prices, price cutting, value pricing, profit pricing, and pricing over a fixed term. Nevertheless, IBM's market share has continued to slip.

The profile of the industry will change in the 80s. Mainframes are no longer a major growth sector of the industry, for example. In 1981, the growth rate of micros was 52.7 percent, telecommunication equipment was 33.6 percent, office systems 32.3 percent, minis 30.6 percent, processing services 26.0 percent, with mainframes only 9.4 percent. Peripherals are also gaining at the expense of mainframes in relation to the total data processing market. Acquisitions and mergers, not only within the United States but between domestic and foreign companies, are realigning competition. Revision of governmental policy will also change the nature of competition. It is already apparent that a merging of data processing and data transmission will take place, bringing AT&T and IBM, two industrial giants, into direct con-

---

[29]For statistics on the computing industry, see T. A. Dolotta et al., *Data Processing in 1980–1985* (New York: John Wiley & Sons, 1976), p. 173.

frontation. U.S. computer companies will also be challenged by companies from abroad, particularly the Japanese. Many computing experts in this country believe foreign competition can be countered only if the American government removes the threat of antitrust action against U.S. computer firms, at least until the domestic industry stabilizes, matures, and regains international dominance.

Whatever direction the industry takes in the future, it seems certain IBM will be in the forefront, even if the company splits. Most experts agree that no revolutionary technological developments in computing are in the offing. The future is uncertain mainly because of social and political unknowns. The future also depends on the ability of the industry to find solutions to these problems:

1. Paperwork pollution generated by prolific computer printouts.
2. Unacceptable usages of computer information.
3. Dehumanization of business transactions with computing.
4. Over-concentration on technical aspects of computing to the detriment of systems designed to benefit people and society.
5. Loss of computing credibility because cost savings and improved efficiency have not been realized by users.

Many critics charge that the euphoria of unparalleled growth has blinded the industry to basic problems of this nature. They claim that the industry has lost sight of its primary objective: to serve users. It is time that the industry shift its focus from technological concerns to people who feel "bent, stapled, and mutilated" by computer systems. Unless such a shift takes place, a groundswell of public reaction against the industry may occur.

CASE STUDY: GROWTH AT ATARI*

Atari is perhaps best known for its video games such as Pac-Man and Yar's Revenge, but the company has captured 10 percent of all desktop computer sales and as much as 40 percent of home computer sales, according to market estimates. The company's phenomenal growth since 1971, when it was founded by Nolan Bushnell and two associates with $500 in borrowed capital, is astounding even by computer industry standards where success stories are not uncommon. The firm, which has grown by a factor of 22 in the last four years, is currently doubling in size every eight months. Purchased only six years ago by Warner's for $28 million, it is estimated that 1982 revenues will be in the neighborhood of $2 billion.

*Source: Laton McCartney, "Atari: Playing with House Money, *Datamation* 28, no. 13 (December 1982), pp. 89–92.

What factors have contributed to Atari's success? Though video games have been around since 1962, Bushnell's first games, such as Pong, were coin-operated, placed in arcades to compete with pinball machines. By the time competitors succeeded is gaining a lion's share of that gold mine, Atari was ready with home video games that would hook into the family TV.

The company was sold to Warner Communications Inc. in 1976. Though idea-man Bushnell continued at Atari's helm after acquisition, he was subsequently replaced with a business executive, Raymond Kassar, who has had experience running Burlington Industries, an $800-million-a-year concern. Under Kassar, Warner's has made marketing of Atari products a high-spending priority. It is estimated that a major share of the $159 million spent by Warner's for advertising in 1981 was for promoting the Atari line. R&D is also heavily supported, with a budget estimated between $60 and $100 million. The future, according to company scientists, will include promotion of fantasies with voice synthesis, interactive graphics, animation, and 3-D.

Today, video games are just one product in the Atari arsenal. The company hopes to battle with giants such as IBM and Texas Instruments for home computer sales, counting on its marketing and distribution capabilities for a competitive edge. It already has two formidable assets: a brand identity and a large base of consumers. With 5 million video games in American households, competitors in the home computer field have reason for concern.

Video games may be a passing fad, as was citizen's band radio and the Rubik's cube. However, they have served Atari, providing the company with entry into the computer industry, and they may be given historical credit as the door through which computers entered the American home.

Since writing this case study in 1982, Atari has suffered financial reverses. In an attempt to regain competitiveness, it has moved its production to Southeast Asia to reduce production costs. The company's plight is a good example of the rapidly changing fortunes of firms in the computer industry.

KEY WORDS

Amdahl

Divestiture

Mainframe manufacturers

Mainframes

PCM (Plug-compatible manufacturer)

Peripheral market

Plug-compatible mainframe

Predatory pricing   Pricing over a fixed term
Price cutting   Profit pricing
Price differentiation   Semiconductor industry
Price tying   Value pricing

DISCUSSION QUESTIONS

1. Is there free entry into the computer industry? Does this vary with the segment of the industry? Why is there variation? Does it serve the consumer and industry to have free entry in all segments? Explain.

2. How has the manufacture of minis and micros affected the manufacture of mainframes?

3. How has the computer industry been affected by:
   a. Unbundling?
   b. Antitrust litigation?

4. Should the computer industry be regulated by the government?

5. Does the computer industry in the United States face a serious challenge from abroad? If so, in what sectors? What should be done to retain U.S. dominance in computing?

6. Must the computer industry be an oligopoly in the United States in order to provide strength to compete with nationalized computer industries abroad and at the same time provide consumers at home with both innovative and cheap products?

7. What does the computer industry need most: entrepreneurs, capital, government protection, researchers and scientists, more R&D investment, or growth in computer applications? Justify your position.

8. What are the future prospects of the computer industry? Which segments will grow and which will decline?

9. It is said that the computer industry spends too much effort developing new technology, not enough effort developing user interface or applications for the technology? Do you agree? How should the industry change?

10. Should the computer industry in the United States be protected by quotas and tariffs against competition from abroad? Comment.

11. Should the transfer of computer technology to friends and foes in the world be controlled? If so, by whom and how?

12. Would it be in the best interest of the consumer to have an unrestricted computer industry?

13. Do you believe that a confrontation between IBM and AT&T will serve the interests of the end user? What can be done to maximize the benefits of such confrontation and minimize the negative effects?

14. Should the computer industry be provided financial incentives and legal protection by the government to make U.S. computer firms competitive

with foreign firms receiving such support? What incentives and protection do you recommend?

15. Is unbundling good for the consumer?

16. Should the Justice Department take a more active role in controlling pricing strategies and collusion in the computer industry, or leave regulation of the industry to economic and competitive forces?

SELECTED ANNOTATED BIBLIOGRAPHY

Brock, Gerald W. *The U.S. Computer Industry*. Cambridge, Mass.: Ballinger Publishing, 1975, 251 p.
This is an excellent economic analysis of the computer industry. Though written by an economist, you do not have to be one to understand the text. Includes useful discussions on the capital requirements for market entry, economies of scale, and performance in the computer industry. Appropriate for graduate students.

Infotech. *IBM*. Vol. 1. Maidenhead, England: Infotech International, 1978, 202 p.
In this book, 29 experts from both sides of the Atlantic, representing diverse views and experiences, comment on past IBM actions and suggest possible IBM strategies for the future. An excellent bibliography is included, updated through 1978. 127 entries are related to the computing industry, with 15 books and reports and 45 articles on the subject of IBM.

Infotech. *IBM*. Vol. 2. Maidenhead, England: Infotech, 1978, 293 p.
This second Infotech volume includes 20 invited papers on a range of topics such as PCMs, antitrust laws, unbundling, marketing, technological change, IBM's plans for data bases, network architecture, and the "future system."

Lecht, Charles. P. *The Waves of Change*. New York: Advanced Computer Techniques Corp., 1977, 186 p.
Chapter 1 is a good overview of the computer industry with many growth curves on computing size, speed, capacity, and costs (programming, design, and storage).

Malik, Rex. *And Tomorrow . . . The World?* London: Millington, 1975, 496 p.
The author has great animosity toward IBM, a bias apparent throughout the text. Malik has culled damaging statistics and details from trial documents that others more sympathetic to IBM have missed.

Osborne, Adam. *Running Wild: The Next Industrial Revolution*. Berkeley, Calif.: Osborne/McGraw Hill, 1979, 182 p.
Chapters 1 and 2 recount the history of the microelectronic industry, including tales of rags-to-riches. Interesting facts and analogies are cited, such as the following: If transportation technology had developed at the same rate as microtechnology, the Concorde would have carried a million passengers at 20 million miles/hour for a ticket costing less than a penny.

Tomash, Erwin. "SOS: The Next 11111 Years," *Computer* 9, no. 12 (December 1976), pp. 11–21.
The author speculates on the future of the computing industry. The title, the binary equivalent of the decimal number 31, is as provocative as the article itself.

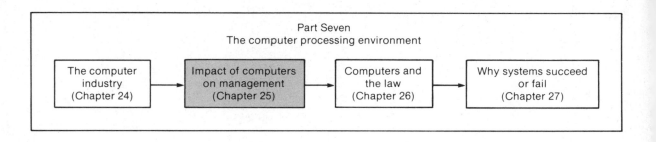

Part Seven
The computer processing environment

| The computer industry (Chapter 24) | → | Impact of computers on management (Chapter 25) | → | Computers and the law (Chapter 26) | → | Why systems succeed or fail (Chapter 27) |

CHAPTER 25

Impact of computers on

management

The purpose of computing is insight, not numbers.
Richard Hamming

There is virtually no American business untouched by the computer revolution. Payroll and accounting computer applications are common. Office work is being transformed by word processing, instantaneous data retrieval, and the storage of information and correspondence on disk and tape. Robots and process control affect many workers in the factory. Even firms which hand process data undoubtedly deal with automated suppliers and clients. Certainly no one escapes from the clutches of the computerized Internal Revenue Service.

As the popular press and unions frequently call to our attention, the widespread use of computers is changing the nature of work for employees in the United States. The impact of computers on business management receives less notice. Are computers dictating the organizational structure of companies? Are they replacing humans in decision making? Are computer specialists indispensable to top management or a dangerous elite? This chapter will attempt to answer these questions. It will begin by examining whether computer technology determines the location of a computer center and how computers have changed decision making at operational, middle, and top management levels. The chapter will also discuss how computers have altered management style, job responsibility, and the problems managers must solve. In addition, the vulnerability of management to displacement by computer and the role of information specialists will be addressed.

CENTRALIZATION–DECENTRALIZATION
OF COMPUTING

In 1958, H. J. Leavitt and T. L. Whistler made a number of predictions regarding how computers would affect business management in the 1980s.[1] At that time, computers were usually found in subdepartmental units wherever data processing was needed. Leavitt and Whistler forecasted the need for centralized computer centers. They believed managers would be unable to cope with the large amount of information that computers would make available by the l980s, and that control over decision making in large organizations would necessitate centralization of computing.

Leavitt and Whistler were correct, in part, for centralization of computing was the organizational structure favored by most firms during the 60s and 70s. But Leavitt and Whistler failed to envisage the technological breakthroughs in microtechnology and telecommunications that have led in recent years to distributed data processing. Computers of the 80s enable top management to view operations as an entity, to integrate, process, and communicate data and information rapidly even when the firm's computing is at dispersed locations. Technology enables management to choose centralization of computing, decentralization, or a mix of the two, as described in Chapters 19 and 20, without loss of control. Corporate philosophy and preferred management style are factors that today decide the location of a computer center. No longer does computer technology dictate the organizational structure of computing.

EFFECT ON MANAGEMENT

Another prediction by Leavitt, Whistler, and other early commentators was that computers would be the managers of the future.[2] This has not happened. Managers continue to be indispensable. However, computers have altered management style in modern business. Solutions to many problems can now be programmed. This requires a different conceptual approach to problem solving. Computers also provide more timely information than was formerly available and the information is better in quality and wider in coverage. Managers are expected to utilize this information in making decisions instead of relying entirely on intuition.

Though the actual percentage of **programmed** versus **nonpro-**

---

[1]H. J. Leavitt and T. L. Whistler, "Management in the 1980s," *Harvard Business Review* 36, no. 6 (November/December 1958), pp. 35–43, ff.

[2]Herbert Simon, *The Shape of Automation for Man and Management* (New York: Harper & Row, 1965).

grammed decision making varies from one industry to another, somewhere between 50 and 80 percent of all managerial decisions are programmable or semiprogrammable, given the current state of the art, especially in areas such as accounting, finance, and manufacturing. In actual practice, however, a much lower percentage of decision making is actually computerized. Figure 25.1 approximates current computer problem-solving effort in relation to decisions that could be programmed. Though managers do not maximize the potential of computers, without question computer technology has affected management style.

In many automated factories, computers have also altered managerial **span of control** by changing the number and level of employees a manager supervises, and transformed the **content** of a manager's work. For example, drilling machines were formerly operated by workers following blueprints; the shop floor was managed by a supervisor. In many firms today, instruction tape (the blueprint) is fed into numerically controlled machines, machines which do the drilling without worker intervention. The semiskilled or skilled workers who formerly operated the drilling machines have been replaced by professional designers who prepare the instruction tape. The supervisor has been replaced by a worker who monitors production on a machine console. Figure 25.2 illustrates how such changes have affected the production manager.

Computer-aided design automates the production process one step further, changing managerial responsibilities. In 1981, Lockheed trained 3,000 engineers in CAD at a cost of $3,000 per person.[3] One wonders how much structural unemployment will result (such as how

Figure 25.1   **Current problem-solving effort by computer (relative to programmable solutions possible, given current technology)**

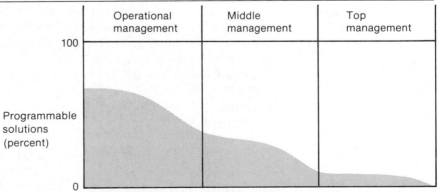

Note: The shaded area approximates current computerized problem-solving effort.

[3]*Business Week*, no. 2699 (August 3, 1981), p. 55.

Figure 25.2   **Traditional and computerized approaches to operating a drilling machine**

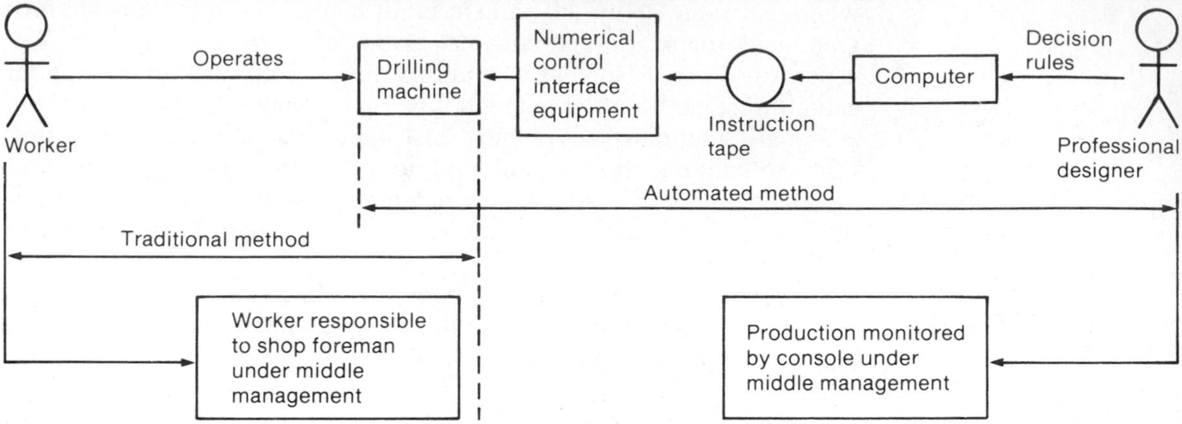

many machine operators will be displaced), and how many operational and middle managers will find the scope of their jobs and content of work altered. For example, should computer-aided design result in displacement of workers while keeping constant the number of managers, managerial span of control will narrow. Should the company choose to eliminate some managerial jobs and redistribute control responsibilities among the managers who remain, the job scope of the latter may broaden.

The emergence of the electronic office is another example of how computers are changing the job content and scope of control of managers. Word processing is replacing conventional office procedures for the creation of correspondence, documents, reports, and memos. Electronic processing is speeding computations and retrieval of data. Traditional office communication patterns are being altered by electronic mail. The need for business travel is being reduced by teleconferencing. These and other activities which have been affected by the introduction of computers in the office are listed in Table 25.1. These changes have altered the duties of clerks, secretaries, and administrative assistants, and as a consequence, the responsibilities of office managers.

It is predicted that the jobs of 45 million people, roughly 45 percent of the current working population, will be affected by automation by the year 2000. (See Table 25.2.) Nine million of these will be managers. These figures are an indication of the profound impact computers will have on management in the years ahead.

Top management is less affected than **operational** and **middle management** with regard to computer technology, for many decisions in the higher echelons of a firm are what Herbert Simon calls "nonprogrammable" decisions. These are ill-structured problems

Table 25.1

Computer-induced changes in office work

Without a computer	With a computer
Typing	Word processing
Human memory	Auxiliary memory of computer
Manual filing	Computerized record-keeping
Manual search and human recall	Information retrieval
Keeping calendar manually	Automated calendar with prompts
Postal service	Teleprocessing
Estimation from experience	Estimation through quantitative models
Manual supervision and control	Exceptional reporting
Specialization of tasks	Functional and integrated system
Judgment, intuition, and experience	Testing alternatives, simulation, and planning models
Manual drawing	Graphic display Interactive displays
Use of old or current data	Use of real-time data
Conference attendance (in person)	Teleconferences

("wicked" problems), complex in nature, with variables that can't easily be quantified. For example, personnel decisions (hiring and firing) fall into this category. So do decisions regarding goals and policies. Top management's business acumen in promoting innovation, motivating the work force, and resolving disputes cannot be programmed. Indeed, there are many areas of business decision making that may

Table 25.2

Employees who will be affected by automation by the year 2000

In factories		
Assemblers	1,289,000	
Checkers, examiners, inspectors, testers	746,000	
Production painters	185,000	
Welders and flame cutters	713,000	
Packagers	626,000	
Machine operatives	2,385,000	
Other skilled workers	1,043,000	
Total in factories		6,987,000
In offices		
Secretaries and support workers	5,000,000	
Clerks	10,000,000	
Total in offices		15,000,000
Professionals		14,000,000
Managers		9,000,000
Total employees affected		44,987,000

Source: "The Impact of Robots on the Workforce and Work Place," *Business Week*, no. 2699 (August 3, 1981), p. 55. Figures by Carnegie Mellon University and Booz, Allen & Hamilton Inc.

never be automated. A list of management functions where computers have thus far had relatively little impact appears in Table 25.3.

Table 25.3   **Impact of computers on functions of management**

	Top management	Middle management	Operational management
Identify areas of improvement . . .	Seldom	Scant	Some
Analyze these areas	None	Scant	Some
Develop alternate solutions	Scant	Moderate	Moderate
Evaluate alternate solutions	Scant	Moderate	Moderate
Implement decision	*	Moderate	Heavy
Job content	Scant	Moderate	Major
Job numbers	None	Scant	Moderate

*Not applicable.

Source: Adapted from Jerome Kanter, *Management-Oriented Management Information System*, (Englewood Cliffs, N.J.: Prentice-Hall, 1972), pp. 180, 182.

Top management does receive reports based on operational and control information generated by computer, and the utilization of planning and control models is becoming more common. Computer **decision support systems (DSS)** are of particular value to top management in finding solutions to semistructured problems. In such problems, managerial judgment alone is not:

> . . . adequate, because of the size of the problem or the computation complexity and precision needed to solve it. On the other hand, the model or data alone are also inadequate because the solution involves judgment and subjective analysis. Under these conditions the manager plus the system can provide a more effective solution than either alone.[4]

But top management should guard against total reliance on heavily processed data, data that filters out emotion, feeling, sentiment, mood, and all of the irrational nuances of human situations. According to John Gardner, effective management and decision making often depends on judgments based on the very elements which have been filtered out. The manager who makes intuitive decisions that are just below the level of consciousness often has a clearer vision of reality than managers who base decisions solely on data that has been sampled, screened, compiled, coded, and expressed in statistical form, for that process omits or seriously distorts all "information that cannot readily be expressed in words or numbers or cannot be rationally condensed into lists categories, formulae, or compact generalizations."[5] The corporate executive glued to the computer console who ignores

---

[4]Peter G. W. Keene and Michael S. Scott Morton, *Decision Support Systems: An Organizational Perspective* (Reading, Mass.: Addison-Wesley, 1978), p. 86.

[5]John Gardner, *Self Renewal: The Individual and the Innovative Society* (New York: Harper & Row, 1965), pp. 78–79.

the subtleties of human interaction is indeed an Orwellian parody of what effective management should be.

COMPUTER IMPACT ON MANAGEMENT QUANTIFIED

The preceding section discusses the impact of computers on management in general terms. Can this impact be quantified? Jerome Kanter has attempted to do so. He divides management into **five functions, planning, organizing, staffing, direction,** and **control,** and has given each a number indicating susceptibility to computerization. He has also assessed the percent of time spent in each function by operational, middle, and top management. A weighted value for each function is then determined and a computerized coefficient derived for each level of management. (See Table 25.4.) According to Kanter's calculations, 29 percent of top management's functions, 43 percent of middle management's functions, and 61 percent of operational management's functions can be computerized.[6]

This analysis is simplistic insofar as it does not allow for industry differences or variations over time. Kanter's conclusions are also based on highly subjective weight assignments. Nevertheless, many commentators would argue that Kanter's percentages of susceptibility are reasonable approximations of the actual contribution made by computers to decision making at the three levels of management at the present time. The analysis is also useful because it stresses that not all managerial functions can be computerized and that the mix of functions at a given level is what determines the limits of computer assistance.

In coming years, as more operations research models are put into use and as progress is made in artificial intelligence, many functions not currently susceptible to computerization may become so, and Kanter's percentages will have to be changed. But we are not yet close to Herbert Simon's prediction that,

> we shall . . . (acquire) an extensive and empirically tested theory of human cognitive processes and their interaction with human emotions, attitudes and values."[7]

Nor is Norbert Weiner's prediction—that whatever man can do, a computer will also do[8]—in the foreseeable future. Managers are still needed to recognize and infer patterns from nonquantifiable variables,

[6]Jerome Kanter, *Management-Oriented Management Information System* (Englewood Cliffs, N.J.: Prentice-Hall, 1972), p. 196.

[7]Quoted by J. M. Bergey and R. C. Slover, "Administration in the 1980s," *S.A.M. Advanced Management Journal* 14, no. 2 (April 1969), p. 31.

[8]Ibid., p. 26.

Table 25.4 **Calculation of the computerization coefficient for different levels of management**

	Percent susceptible to computerization	Top management		Middle management		Operating management	
		Percent of job devoted to	Weighted value	Percent of job devoted to	Weighted value	Percent of job devoted to	Weighted value
Plan	30%	70%	21%	20%	6%	5%	1.5%
Organize	15	10	1.5	10	1.5	5	1.0
Staff	25	10	2.5	10	2.5	5	1.5
Direct	5	5	—	20	1.0	20	1.0
Control	80	5	4	40	32.0	70	56.0
Computerization quotient			29%		43%		61%

Source: Jerome Kanter, *Management-Oriented Management Information System* (Englewood Cliffs, N.J.: Prentice-Hall, 1972), p. 196.

especially human variables, to interpret information, to evaluate divergences between planned and actual performance, and to determine corrective actions. Even programmed decision making requires managers to initially think through problems and establish decision rules for problem solutions. As Peter Drucker states:

> We are beginning to realize that the computer makes no decisions; it only carries out orders. It's a total moron, and herein has its strength. It forces us to think, to set the criteria. The stupider the tool, the brighter the master has to be—and this is the dumbest tool we have . . . It shows us—in fact, it compels us—to think through what we are doing.[9]

INFORMATION SPECIALISTS

The impact of computers on management would be even greater today if the full potential of existing computer technology were exploited. Though resistance to computers, described in earlier chapters of the book, is found at all managerial levels, failure to maximize computer potential is due primarily to lack of know-how. More and more business managers recognize that they do not know how to effectively utilize computing resources at their disposal and are turning to **information specialists** for help.

Information specialists are either computer scientists knowledgeable about business and management, or individuals drawn from operations research who have acquired an expertise in computers and data bases. The role of an information specialist is analogous to the role of secretary in a traditional business organization insofar as both secretaries and information specialists channel information to management. Secretaries control access to management: information specialists control the flow (and sometimes content) of computerized information to management.

Like secretaries, information specialists wield far more power than is apparent from a firm's organizational chart. They decide how information is presented (flashed on a terminal screen or buried in a printed report), how data should be correlated, what processing mode to use, the form of output, and which models are appropriate. Such decisions may subsequently limit the range of choices open to management. Though officially only technical advisors, information specialists are actually decision makers of considerable importance. Unless management learns about computers and their limitations, and takes an active role in defining variables and constraints in problem solving, management may lose decision-making prerogatives by default to information specialists without awareness of the fact.

---

[9]Peter Drucker, *Technology, Management and Society* (London: Heineman, 1970), pp. 147–48.

The authors do not intend to denigrate information specialists or suggest that top management should dispense with their services. On the contrary, information specialists are a valuable resource. But management should both understand and authorize delegated decision making, and should carefully define, monitor, and control the work of information specialists.

MANAGEMENT PROBLEMS ARISING FROM COMPUTERIZATION

Thus far the chapter has focused on how computers have changed management methods of decision making. Before closing the chapter, a few comments are in order on **problems** arising from computerization.

For example, a firm's power base is altered as a result of computerization. P. J. Hickson et al. have identified four **variables associated with corporate power**: links to others, irreplaceability, dependency, and uncertainty.[10] In all four, computer departments score highly. They are **linked** to many functional departments through functional applications, applications such as payroll or accounting, which are **irreplaceable.** Other departments **depend** on computing, particularly when integrated systems have been implemented. Computer planning models and programs for control and decision making also reduce **uncertainty** among users. No wonder computer departments and personnel have gained so much power.

Shifts in power, however, are accompanied by bruised egos, jealousy, and conflict as traditional power bases erode. Management skill in reducing tension and restoring harmonious interpersonal/interdepartmental relationships is taxed to the limit following computerization.

Resentment against computer personnel also stems from the fact that computer departments often win in competition for scarce corporate resources. Computers require major capital investments and large operating budgets. Few departments will admit being less deserving. Should hostility to computer personnel become overt, the computer center may assign low priority to job requests from opponents which, in turn, reinforces and sustains their resentment.

Unrealistic expectations of users, poorly drawn system specifications, or projects which have fallen behind schedule may also be the cause of hostility directed toward computer personnel. Often computer professionals working in a crisis atmosphere fail to take the time

[10]P. J. Hickson, C. R. Henings, C. A. Lees, R. E. Schneck, and J. M. Pennings, "Strategic Contingency Theory of Interorganizational Power," *Administrative Science Quarterly* 16, no. 2 (June 1971), pp. 216–729.

to develop positive relationships with users. Unions may exacerbate existing tensions. The *London Times* first ceased publication, then was sold because of industrial strife over computerization. Modern management that proves inept in coping with the social and psychological tensions which accompany computerization may find the very survival of their firms at stake.

SUMMARY AND CONCLUSIONS

Computers are changing the nature of a manager's work and altering methods of decision making. Managers are also being displaced by computers, though the threat of unemployment is less acute at top levels of management than at operational levels, and far fewer managerial jobs are jeopardized by computers than are workers' jobs. (See Figure 25.3.) There are still too many "wicked" problems for management to resolve, problems which defy programmed solutions because their variables cannot easily be quantified. However, research in artificial intelligence, data management, linguistics, and psychology will undoubtedly expand the role of computers in decision making in the future and lead to further managerial displacement.

The immediate concern of corporate management is to learn how

Figure 25.3　　　　　　　　　**Displacement caused by computerization**

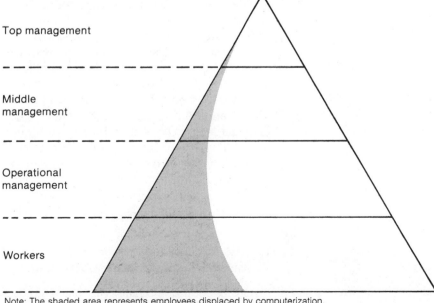

Top management

Middle management

Operational management

Workers

Note: The shaded area represents employees displaced by computerization.

to utilize computers to best advantage. This may be as simple as phrasing questions differently or as complex as adopting a whole new mind set, a whole new approach to problem solving. More and more managers are turning to information specialists for assistance in maximizing the use of computing resources. At the same time, the widespread use of minis and personal computers allows managers to access information and even do simple programming without the intercession of programmers and analysts, giving management a measure of independence from computer professionals.

Computer departments and computer personnel are today becoming power centers indispensable to normal operations. This has upset the traditional power structure in most firms and has led to conflicts, rivalries, and corporate dissension. While computers have contributed to the problem-solving ability of management, it should be recognized that they have created management headaches as well.

CASE STUDY: DSS AT INTERNATIONAL HARVESTER*

International Harvester is a manufacturer of trucks, agricultural and construction equipment, and parts. The company employs over 87,000 people, had sales of $6.3 billion in 1980, and was ranked by *Fortune* as the 49th among U.S. corporations in that year.

To serve its worldwide operations, IH has two data centers, in Wisconsin and Illinois. These are operated by the company's ISS group (Information Systems and Services) which develops multigroup applications, such as accounting and payroll. Headquarters also has several specialist data processing groups, including one within the planning department for decision support systems (DSS).

The DSS group, formed in 1978, applies management science techniques and computers to "large payoff" corporate problems, assisting management by providing information and analysis for problem solutions. The group first studied areas where computerized systems would have the greatest financial impact on the company, identifying fleet sales bidding, corporate financial management, production scheduling, and materials management as potential project areas. Projects in a number of these areas have since been implemented, including:

1. The development of financial models addressing cash flow under varying loan agreements and economic conditions.

*Source: Richard G. Canning, ed., "Interesting Decision Support Systems," *EDP Analyzer* 20, no. 3 (March 1982), pp. 2–4.

2. Development of models simulating financing requirements and costs for day-to-day operations.
3. Development of a production scheduling system to include forecasting, scheduling, physical distribution, and financial analysis. One component of this system is an inventory allocation model which takes into account such factors as seasonal and geographic demand.

The DSS group uses FCS-EPS, a financial analysis and modeling package; RAMIS, a data management system; SAS, a statistical analysis package; and TELL-A-GRAF, for business graphics. These packages fit the emphasis at International Harvester: involvement of end users. Participation helps users see the value of computer assistance in problem solving, and increases their acceptance of the DSS group's services.

KEY WORDS

Centralization-decentralization	**Operational management**
Content of work	**Power variables**
Decision support systems (DSS)	**Problems**
Functions of management (5)	**Programmed decision making**
Information specialists	**Span of control**
Middle management	**Top management**
Nonprogrammed decision making	**Variables, corporate power (4)**

DISCUSSION QUESTIONS

1. How have computers benefited management?
2. What negative impact on management have computers had?
3. How can the adverse effects of computers on decision making be minimized? How can benefits be enhanced?
4. How have computers altered decision making at the following management levels?
   a. Top.
   b. Middle.
   c. Operational level.
5. Would the impact of computers on management vary with:
   a. Size of firm?
   b. Style of management?

     c. Content of management?

     d. Qualifications of managers?

6. What problems do managers have to face when implementing a computerized information system? How can these problems be minimized?

7. It is said that the computer industry has now switched from an applications generation to a user generation. That is, the emphasis is now on making computers easier to use whereas formally firms concentrated on expanding applications. Do you agree that this change has taken place? If not, should it? What user needs should be met?

8. Do computers turn managers into conformists? Do managers lose their:

     a. Individuality?

     b. Creativity and innovativeness?

     c. Self-confidence and self-assurance?

     d. Independence in thinking?

9. Computers may solve technical problems for managers but they create more problems than they solve (including human and social problems). Comment on this statement.

10. How are managers affected by the addition of a:

     a. DBMS?

     b. Online real-time system?

     c. Query language and interactive processing?

     d. Simulation language?

     e. Word processing work station for secretary?

     f. Teleprocessing?

     g. Artificial intelligence?

11. How has computer technology affected the quality of decision making? The quality of management?

12. How can a manager's knowledge of computing contribute to:

     a. Decision making?

     b. Control of the negative impact of computers?

     c. Improved efficiency and effectiveness of computer usage?

13. Why do managers feel threatened by computer technology? What can be done to alleviate management fears?

14. How has computer technology affected the way managers view and use business information?

15. Why are young managers more favorably oriented to computer systems than their seniors?

16. Which levels of management have been most and least affected by computer technology? Why? Do you expect this to change in the near future? Why?

SELECTED ANNOTATED BIBLIOGRAPHY

"A New Era for Management." *Business Week*, no. 2787 (April 25, 1983), pp. 50–86.

This is a special report including articles on the shrinking of middle management (pp. 54–61), how computers remake the manager's job (pp. 68–70), and who will retain the obsolete manager (pp. 76–80).

Drucker, Peter. *Technology, Management and Society.* London: Heineman, 1969, 209 p.

This well-known author refers to the impact of computers on business in many of his books. Chapter 10, "The Manager and the Moron," in the above text, is a sample reference. In *Age of Discontinuity,* approximately 100 pages are devoted to computers and the knowledge industry. Drucker frequently writes for journals on computers as well. See *Fortune* (November 1980), *Harvard Business Review* (May 1971), and *Foreign Affairs* (August 1978).

House, William. *The Impact of Information Technology on Management Operations.* Princeton, N.J.: Auerbach Publishers, 1971, 436 p.

Although most of the articles in this book of readings were written in the 60s, the book is, nevertheless, still relevant. The articles are primarily on development, planning, and control.

Kanter, J. *Management-Oriented Management Information* System. Englewood Cliffs, N.J.: Prentice-Hall, 1972, chap. 6.

This is a good reference on how computing affects different levels of management.

Lucas, Henry C., Jr. *The Analysis, Design, and Implementation of Information Systems.* New York: McGraw-Hill, 1981, 419 p.

Chapter 4 is recommended. It discusses the impact of computers on organizations and individuals, and also discusses changes in the distribution of power which arise as a result of computerization.

Simon, Herbert. *The Shape of Automation for Men and* Management. New York: Harper & Row, 1965, 111 p.

Simon is an organization theorist who has contributed greatly to heuristic programming. He has written numerous books on computers such as the above title. *New Science of Management Decision* is another useful reference. Look for his work in magazines as well (e.g., *Science,* March 1977).

Ward, Tom. *Computer Organization, Personnel and* Control. London: Longman, 1973, 134 p.

This book gives the British view of the effects of computerization. Chapter 6, "The Impact of Computers on the Company," is recommended.

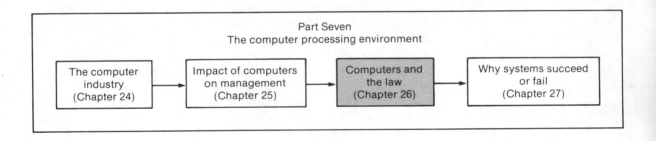

Part Seven
The computer processing environment

| The computer industry (Chapter 24) | → | Impact of computers on management (Chapter 25) | → | Computers and the law (Chapter 26) | → | Why systems succeed or fail (Chapter 27) |

CHAPTER 26

Computers and the law

*In a computer battle, lawyers fight with Latin
phrases and DP persons retaliate with jargon.*
Thomas K. Christo

The body of law governing the computer industry is complex. Managers must be cognizant of antitrust statutes, copyright provisions, and laws regulating contracts, patents, trade secrets, tort, privacy, theft, freedom of information, communications, and fair employment. But knowledge of written statutes is not enough because the courts, in interpreting these laws when resolving disputes, have established precedents which have given shape to the industry.

This chapter discusses the application of general business laws to computing and reviews cases that have had an impact in creating new sectors to the industry or set guidelines for computer operations. Both common law and statutes which relate to computer law are considered. **Common law** derives from custom, usage, and the decisions and opinions of the courts, whereas **statute law** is enacted by a legislative body. The two are complementary. When common law proves deficient or incomplete due to changed social conditions or the development of advanced technology, the need for statutes to establish new rules or principles of behavior arises. Unfortunately the legislative process is slow. In a field as dynamic as computer science, the law simply can't keep pace with technological advances. As a result, the computer industry today lacks an adequate legal framework for operations.

The laws discussed in this chapter are listed in Figure 26.1 with connecting lines to show the statutory counterparts of common law. Several of the preceding chapters have already touched on legal considerations. For example, Chapters 12 and 13 dealt with system secu-

Figure 26.1   **Constituent parts of computer law**

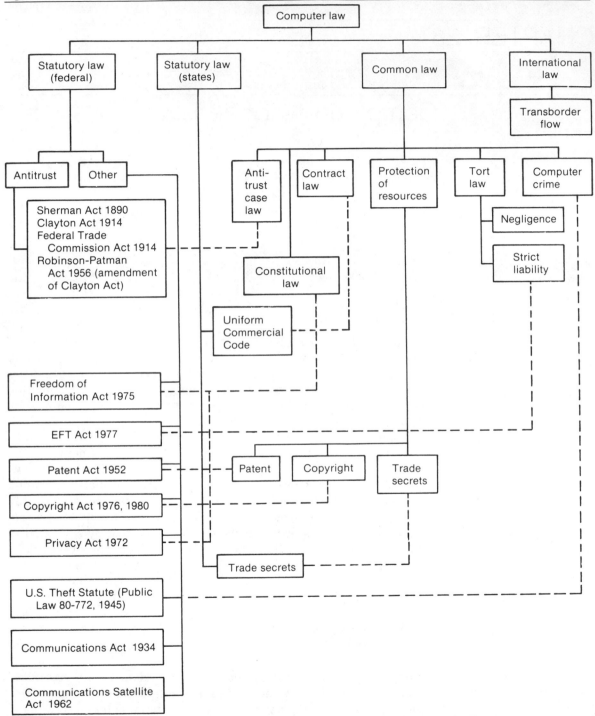

NOTE: The dashed lines indicate the complementary relationship between branches of common law and specific statutes.

rity and computer crime. The emphasis in this chapter is on laws protecting computing resources and laws regulating the operational environment of the industry. Sections appear on antitrust laws, communications, transborder flow, contracts, patents, trade secrets, copyrights, tort, and computer crime.

ANTITRUST LAWS

The basic framework of **antitrust laws** governing U.S. corporations is shown in Figure 26.1. Disputes over interpretation of these laws have resulted in much litigation, particularly in technological fields. Since 1932, IBM has been a defendant in most of the antitrust suits directed against firms producing computers and software. The company's size and leadership in pricing makes it a natural target for the application of antitrust principles to computer manufacture and sales. Table 26.1 lists major suits to which IBM has been a party. The number of suits and the time elapsed before settlement are evidence of the massive effort and commitment of the corporation in fighting antitrust actions. The number of cases dropped, dismissed, or settled out of court shows IBM is a formidable opponent. Cases against IBM which have influenced the basic structure of the computer industry are described below.

The first landmark case was in the 1930s when the federal government charged IBM and Remington Rand with restraint of trade for monopolizing the market for punched cards. (IBM dominated 85 percent of the market, Remington Rand 15 percent.) At that time both firms required that their own cards be used in their tabulating units and card machines, both tying card purchase with equipment purchase. A 1936 Supreme Court decision ruled against this practice. But the judgment proved academic, for IBM subsequently drew up such rigid card specifications for IBM machines that only their own rotary presses could manufacture the cards.

This led, in part, to a second suit in 1952 in which IBM was again charged by the government with restraint of trade for its restrictive leasing agreements and price discrimination, and accused of violating the spirit, if not the letter, of the 1936 decision. An out-of-court settlement was reached (the **1956 IBM Consent Decree,**)[1] avoiding a court battle. Though a consent decree means that neither innocence nor guilt are determined, IBM agreed to offer customers the option of buying or leasing equipment. This provided an opening for smaller companies in computer leasing, for they could now purchase computers

---

[1]*United States* v. *IBM*, Civil No. 72-334 (S.D.N.Y., 1952). For details see Bruce Gilchrist and Milton R. Wessel, *Government Regulation of the Computer Industry* (Montvale, N.J.: AFIPS Press, 1972), pp. 177–99.

and compete successfully with IBM leasing by depreciating equipment over a longer lifetime than IBM and accepting a lower unit profit margin. IBM also agreed to establish a separate service subsidiary and to release technical information on machine maintenance. These latter provisions led to the establishment of the independent services segment of the computer industry, a segment which today consists of over a thousand companies, many of which have become substantial enterprises.

IBM was also required to reduce its share of the punched card market and sell some of its rotary presses. (By 1956 IBM controlled 90 percent of a greatly expanded card market.) This spurred the growth

Table 26.1   **Antitrust litigation against IBM**

Case and date initiated		Action taken	
1932	*U.S.* v. *IBM and Remington*	1936	Court decision
1952	*U.S.* v. *IBM*	1956	Consent decree
1969	*U.S.* v. *IBM*	1971	Judge Edelstein assigned
		1975	Trial starts
		1977	IBM defense starts
		1982	Case dropped/withdrawn by U.S.
1971	*Greyhound* v. *IBM*	1972	Case dismissed
		1972	Greyhound appealed
		1981	Greyhound upheld
1971	*Memorex* v. *IBM*	1972	Cases dropped
	IBM v. *Memorex*		
1971	*Symbolic* v. *IBM*	1975	Case dismissed
1971	*Advanced Memory* v. *IBM*	1972	Case settled out of court
1972	*Telex* v. *IBM*	1973	Court decision totally favoring neither
		1974	Telex appeals settlement
		1975	Partial decision on appeal
		1978	Case settled out of court
1972	*Marshall* v. *IBM*	1975	Case settled out of court
1973	*Calcomp* v. *IBM*	1977	Court decision favoring IBM
		1977	Calcomp appeals
		1979	Appeal dismissed
1973	*Memorex* v. *IBM*	1979	Case dismissed
		1980	Case appealed but dismissed
1973	*Transamerica* v. *IBM*	1979	Case dismissed
		1983	Case appealed but dismissed
1974	*Memory Tech.* v. *IBM*	1976	Case settled
1975	*Sanders* v. *IBM*	1977	Case dismissed
		1979	Case appealed by Sanders
		1979	Sanders drops appeal

of independent card producers. Other provisions required IBM to sell equipment discounted for age, and to make both current and future patents available on an unrestricted nonexclusive basis, though reasonable royalties on new patents could be charged. A 1963 revision of the decree limited IBM still further, requiring the company to divest itself of 50 percent of the punched card market.

Antitrust suits have been filed against IBM by competitors as well as by the government. A suit of this nature was filed in 1968 by Control Data Corporation (CDC) charging IBM with violation of the Sherman Act.[2] Charges are summarized in Table 26.2. CDC hoped that its suit would force IBM to divest itself of its Scientific Research Association, Service Bureau Corporation, and Office Products Division, and force the company out of terminal manufacture, education, and training.

Table 26.2	*CDC* v. *IBM*, primary charges summarized, Civil Action No.: 3-68-312

IBM:
  Monopolizes and attempts to monopolise markets and submarkets.
  Exploits size, profits, and pricing power, impeding competition.
  Engages in discriminatory and exclusionary pricing practices, including leasing at a loss.
  Misrepresents status of design, development, production and performance software.
  Coerces employees and improperly influences customer procurements.
  Falsely disparages plaintiffs' computers, software, maintenance policies, personnel, financial position, and overall capabilities.
  Engages in "bait and switch methods" to deceive customers and deprive plaintiff of sales.
  Violates the 1956 Consent Decree with its time-sharing service business.
  Uses its patent position to entrench its monopoly.

Again, a settlement was reached out of court. IBM paid CDC $51 million and sold its service bureau far below its true value. But in return, CDC destroyed a computerized index of 80–100,000 discovered documents in support of its case, a data base compiled at an estimated cost of $3 million and gathered from over a million documents researched. Plaintiffs in other cases against IBM, the Justice Department in particular, were enraged, because the documentation could have been used by other litigants lacking the financial resources or staying power to duplicate CDC's effort. One can surmise from the price IBM paid for its destruction that the data base did indeed contain damaging evidence. But the information was the property of CDC and could be disposed of at will. Incidentally, CDC's use of a data

---

[2]A copy of this civil action can be found in Gilchrist and Wessel, *Government Regulation*, pp.211–28.

base for evidence is a computer application one might expect from a computer manufacturer.[3]

In January 1969, on the last business day of the Johnson administration, the Department of Justice again filed an antitrust action against IBM, again for violation of the 1890 Sherman Act and later Clayton and Robinson-Patman Acts.[4] The government alleged that IBM had "pursued a manufacturing and marketing policy that has prevented competing manufacturers of general purpose digital computers from having an adequate opportunity effectively to compete."[5] The complaint echoed familiar charges ("monopolized, restrained, dominated, improperly deprived") and called for divestiture, divorcement, and reorganization of IBM as remedies. (See Table 26.3 for a list of formal charges.)

Table 26.3	Extract, *U.S.* v. *IBM* antitrust suit, 1969
	IBM
	a. Maintained a pricing policy whereby it quotes a single price for hardware, software and related support, and, thereunder, *(i)* discriminated among customers by providing certain customers with extensive software and related support in a manner that unreasonably inhibited the entry or growth of competitors; and *(ii)* limited the development and scope of activities of an independent software and computer support industry as a result of which the ability of its competitors to compete effectively was unreasonably impaired;
	b. Used its accumulated software and related support to preclude its competitors from effectively competing for various customer accounts;
	c. Restrained and attempted to restrain competitors from entering or remaining in the general-purpose digital computer market by introducing selected computers, with unusually low profit expectations, in those segments of the market where competitors had or appeared likely to have unusual competitive success, and by announcing future production of new models for such markets when it knew that it was unlikely to be able to complete production within the announced time; and
	d. Dominated the educational market for general-purpose digital computers, which was of unusual importance to the growth of competitors both by reason of this market's substantiality and by reason of its ultimate impact on the purchasing decisions in the commercial market, by granting exceptional discriminatory allowances in favor of universities and other educational institutions.

Source: *U.S.* v. *IBM*, Civil No. 69–200, (S.D.N.Y., 1969).

---

[3]IBM has AQUARIUS (A Query and Retrieval Interactive Utility System), a data base online used by its own lawyers. Included are documents connected with major suits in which IBM has had an interest or been a party including dispositions, exhibits, and legal documents presented in court by plaintiffs and defendants. Needless to say, this data base is elaborately indexed.

[4]*United States* v. *IBM*, Civil Action No. 62-200 (S.D.N.Y. 1969). See Gilchrist and Wessel, *Government Regulations*, pp. 201–6.

[5]Gilchrist and Wessel, *Government Regulations*, p. 169.

In a 1972 Justice Department affidavit filed in connection with the pending suit, the government claimed IBM's share of the general-purpose digital computer market was in excess of 70 percent, leaving competitors "patently vulnerable." IBM, in defense, asserted that the data processing industry consisted of more than 600 companies, the corporation's own share of the market being only 32 percent.[6] An excess of 20 million pages of evidence had been amassed by IBM for governmental review by 1972, several hundred depositions by the plaintiff were foreseen, and at least a year of additional discovery and preparation were anticipated before the case could come to trial. Efforts by Judge Edelstein to "speed things up" proved futile. Indeed, IBM's interest was delay, to allow free entry into the market by new competitors, such as Amdahl and Intel, which would refute the charges, and to allow time for the election of a more friendly administration in Washington.[7]

The case dragged through the 70s at enormous cost to both IBM and the taxpayer. (IBM's defense in the shorter, less complex CDC suit cost an estimated $60 million.) Senator Gary Hart, Chairman of the Senate Antitrust and Monopoly Subcommittee in 1974, calling the computer industry the "nervous system of our economy," pressed for early resolution of the case, concerned that:

> Most people seem to argue that IBM has about 70 percent of the central processing unit or mainframe market. If so, that is the greatest concentration of economic power in an unregulated industry today.[8]

By 1978, 80,000 pages of transcript had been recorded, yet the suit was still far from settlement. Senator Ted Kennedy expressed public frustration with the interminable delays, stating that the trial's protraction represented:

> too much time for a law enforcement tool to operate effectively. We want to know why . . . Is the problem with the statutes, with trial procedures, or with limited resources?[9]

Others were not surprised at the endless litigation, citing the government at fault for lack of aggressive prosecution of the case. According to William Rodgers, author of THINK: A Biography of the Watsons, "The government has for years been so intertwined with

---

[6]Laton McCartney, "IBM on the Defense," Datamation 25, no. 1 (January 1979), p. 107.

[7]Cravath Swaine, attorney for IBM, has been quoted as saying that he could "take the simplest antitrust case . . . and protract it for the defense to almost infinity." W. David Gardner, "From Here to Eternity," Datamation 22, no. 1 (July 1979), p. 53.

[8]Linda Flato, "Washington's Concern with Antitrust Stalemates," Datamation 25, no. 7 (July 1979), p. 88.

[9]Ibid., p. 88.

corporate power that effective antitrust enforcement would constitute a radical departure from ingrained habit."[10]

Attorney General Griffin Bell in 1977 suggested an alternative to action through the courts: resolving major antitrust issues through the legislative process.

> The process would necessarily be more political but the questions at hand in a sense are political. They involve the basic restructuring of American Industry and the shape of the American Economy.[11]

In **January 1982** after 13 years of litigation, the 1969 antitrust suit against IBM was dismissed. IBM declared itself "totally vindicated." During the course of the suit the corporation had become bigger than ever, its annual revenues tripling and its share of the market undiminished. Most observers of the trial agreed that the suit had long outlived its relevance. Mainframe computers are no longer the issue: small computers, communications, computing services, and software are markets where competition now centers. There is less agreement about implications of the dismissal. Some experts predict that IBM, unshackled by legal and political restraints, will expand into new markets, moving relentlessly against competitors. Others suggest that IBM, because of its size, will restructure, split of its own accord, the very action the government was trying to force.[12]

Dismissal does not affect an ongoing antitrust dispute between IBM and the European Commission. Europe has had a long tradition of market sharing. Its definition of monopoly is also narrower. In Britain, for example, a share of 25 percent or more of the market is sufficient to render a firm liable for investigation by the Monopolies and Mergers Commission. IBM's overall share of the European computer market is currently estimated at 60–75 percent.[13] However, there is no European precedent for determining monopoly for the computer industry. Indeed, many European observers think that the dismissal of the U.S. suit will strengthen IBM's position in international trade.

COMMUNICATIONS AND THE LAW

Another branch of computer law deals with communications. At the time the **Communications Act of 1934** was enacted establishing the **Federal Communications Commission (FCC),** the linkage of tele-

---

[10]William Rodgers, *Think: A Biography of the Watsons and IBM* (London: Weidenfeld and Nicholson, 1979), p. 320.

[11]Flato, "Washington's Concern," p. 89.

[12]"IBM Wins Again," *Datamation* 28, no. 2 (February 1982), pp. 46–48.

[13]See J. Bornet, "IBM, Antitrust and Europe," in IBM, vol. 2 (Maidenhead, England: Infotech International, Limited, 1978), pp. 67–71.

communications with computers was not envisioned. The FCC's mandate, to control all "interstate and foreign communications by wire or radio and all interstate and foreign transmission of energy by radio" has today given it jurisdiction over EFT (electronic fund transfer), the electronic office, teleconferencing, and home shopping, to name but a few computer applications which require a communications network. The very importance of computer telecommunications for transmission of business data has given the FCC immense power. Some critics charge that this independent agency has become, in effect, the fourth branch of government.

One of the first suits relating to telecommunications was the one filed by the government against AT&T, a firm which has dominated communications from the start. This suit was resolved by a consent decree in 1956 in which AT&T agreed to limit its offering to the regulated common communications carriers.

Growth in the number of computer systems involving communications led the FCC to initiate an inquiry in 1966 into the question of the interdependence of communications and computers. Responses to the inquiry by individuals, associations, and government agencies were evaluated by Stanford Research Institute which submitted a seven-volume report to the Commission in 1969. In its response, the Department of Justice stated that unless restrained, the communications industry might dominate or restrict competition in the computer industry. The department also stated its view that basic antitrust policy should regulate companies holding exclusive government franchises.

A **Final Order,** issued by the FCC in 1971 at the conclusion of the inquiry, established three main points.

1. The FCC would retain jurisdiction over those aspects of the computer field related to communications.
2. **Maximum separation,** the principle that the generation of information must be separate from its flow, was established as a doctrine central to FCC regulatory schemas.
3. The requirement was confirmed that common carriers must not give preferential treatment to their data processing affiliates.

Unfortunately, the Final Order left many questions unanswered. It was unclear whether the order nullified the 1956 Consent Decree or preempted state regulations. Could AT&T and other common carriers offer "enhanced services?" How were intelligent terminals or microcomputers, when part of a communications network, to be classified? Were they to be regulated, like telephones, as customer premise equipment?

The lack of precise rulings by the FCC in this highly technical field has hampered the development of a telecommunications infrastructure needed to maximize the potential of computers. More statutes, such as the Communications Satellite Act of 1962, need to be written.[14] The judicial process can be used to resolve disputes but litigation is too slow and too expensive to be an effective avenue for establishing the needed legal framework.

A landmark case, however, may revolutionize the telecommunications industry. In January 1982, the U.S. government settled a seven-year-old antitrust suit against AT&T, freeing it from restrictive federal regulation and allowing it to compete in whatever business it chooses, thereby repudiating the principle of maximum separation.[15] AT&T is now expected to enter the fields of electronic information, office information, home banking, and perhaps even computer mainframe manufacture. IBM, ITT, RCA, and General Telephone and Electronics overnight have gained a formidable new competitor. Will these firms now move to challenge AT&T's dominance in the field of data communications? Will the public interest be served if the computer and communications industries merge? How computer firms will restructure as a result of the AT&T settlement is the subject for much speculation, but certainly a new relationship between computing operations and communications will evolve. FCC rulings, the courts, and legislation will define this relationship in time. This is a good example of how computer law is in a continual state of flux.

TRANSBORDER DATA FLOW

A third branch of computer law deals with the flow of data across national borders. Much political controversy has centered on this topic. As stated by Louis Jorvet while Magistrate of Justice in France:

> Information is power, and economic information is economic power. Information has an economic value and the ability to store and process certain types of data may well give one country political and technological advantage over other countries. This, in turn, may lead to a loss of national sovereignty through supernational data flows.[16]

Many Third World countries believe cultural and institutional bias accompanies data flow, and are fearful that their traditions and national identity will be lost if their nationals are exposed to unrestricted foreign information. Other countries are fearful that multinational integration will lead to unemployment. For example, an

---

[14]Internationally, one independent agency, INTELSAL (International Telecommunications Satellite Consortium), regulates satellite transmissions. INTELSAL has 60 national members, with COMSAT representing the U.S.

[15]"Stalking New Markets," *Time* 119, no. 4 (January 25, 1982), pp. 54–57.

[16]Quoted by John Eger, "Transborder Flow," *Datamation* 24, no. 12 (November 15, 1978), p. 50.

estimated 23,000 Canadian jobs worth $1.5 billion will be lost by 1984 due to system integration of U.S. firms with Canadian outlets.[17]

To control transborder flow of data, many countries have passed restrictive legislation. In France, for example, a fine of $400,000 and five years of prison is the penalty for **transborder data flow** of information that is defined as "sensitive." In England, the post office has the right to read all transmitted messages, a right that implies that firms must share their cryptographic codes. In Italy, a proposal has been made that transmission costs be proportional to the volume of messages, which could increase transmission costs tenfold.

Some countries require that all transborder data flow be handled by public carriers. This results in loss of control by the user and often means degraded service. A 1973 data act in Sweden empowers a Data Inspection Board to approve all transmissions of personal data crossing its borders. There are over 20 countries with data privacy acts, many using the acts as a way to monitor data for their own economic and political objectives.

U.S. firms want the unrestricted flow of information but recognize that freedom of economic opportunity must be balanced against information privacy rights. At the present time, efforts are being made to establish international conventions on transborder data flow at the United Nations and through the OECD (Organization of Economic Cooperation and Development).[18] Just how such conventions will impede or promote growth and integration of information systems of U.S. firms remains to be seen.[19]

COMPUTER CONTRACTS

Contract law is also an essential component of computer law. The importance of well written contracts and warranties governing the sale/lease of computers and delivery of software cannot be overstressed. More than monetary losses are at stake: disruption of operations can damage a firm's reputation and cause loss of customers, while time-consuming litigation can tie up personnel and resources needed for other projects.

A contract case of significant interest to the computer industry is

[17]Rein Turn, "Transborder Data Flow," *Computer World* 14, no. 9 (March 3, 1980), p. 62.

[18]Peter Safirstein, "How to Best Control the Flow of Electronic Information across Sovereign Borders," *AFIPS Conference Proceedings, 1979* (New York: AFIPS Press, 1979), pp. 279–82.

[19]For an excellent discussion of this whole subject, see the articles by August Bequai, Rein Turn, and Dick Sizer in *Information Privacy* 3, no. 1 (January 1981), pp. 6–25.

Carl Beasley Ford, Inc. v. *Burroughs Corp.*, which reached a Pennsylvania federal court in 1973. Beasley had contracted for a Burroughs accounting machine valued at $35,000. During negotiations for the sale, the Burroughs' salesman took verbal responsibility for 13 programs and recommended that record processing, then handled by an outside service bureau, be canceled. The equipment arrived on schedule, with Burroughs assuring Beasley that the programming would be completed in two months. Fourteen months later the software for critical accounting reports had still not been delivered, so Beasley rejected the entire Burroughs system.

At the trial, Burroughs contested that Beasley had not rejected the system within a reasonable amount of time. But the court ruled that there was sufficient communication and enumeration of deficiencies during the 14 months to make the rejection valid. This decision sets the precedent that failure to advise a seller of system inadequacies may constitute legal acceptance of the system.

The jury award to Beasley of $56,012.32 is also of significance, since Beasley was granted consequential damages for breach of contract in addition to recovering the original purchase price and interest on the loan for purchase. These damages were allowed in spite of express warranty disclaimers written into the contract disavowing all delay in installation, training, or programming, and a written disclaimer for all incidental and consequential damages. Though Burrourghs contended that the written agreement constituted the entire contract, the court accepted evidence on the oral agreement for programming services. Since there was no mention in the written contract about contracted programming services, and since Burroughs salesmen were specifically instructed not to make a programming commitment in writing, it was the court's decision that there were, in effect, two agreements: a written hardware contract and an oral agreement for software. Therefore, the waiver on consequential damages in the written contract did not apply to the oral programming agreement.

This case should make clear the importance of carefully worded written contracts with effective disclaimers for all portions of a system. In entering any contractual arrangement, particularly when a long-term commitment is being made, the advice of a corporation lawyer with a high level of computer literacy is recommended. Users today are, fortunately, gaining experience in structuring contracts, reducing the advantage vendors have traditionally had in preparing such documents.

Also of interest in the Beasley case is the fact that the decision was based on the **Uniform Commercial Code (UCC).** The UCC governs the sale of goods (hardware) but does not apply to services such as computer programming. However, since the Beasley software agreement was linked to the sale of hardware, the court viewed it as one transaction, and turned to the UCC for guidance in determining the amount of consequential damages to award.

In another case against Burroughs, the Kahl Bottling Company was awarded $401,690 when their Burroughs system consistently made errors.[20] *Univac* v. *Teamster Security Fund* was also a contract dispute which reached the courts. Univac was found guilty of failing to deliver an operational system to process insurance claims.[21] Litigation in such cases might be avoided if agreements included built-in checkpoints to alert both user and vendor at an early stage of problems. Users can also use periodic payments based on progress as leverage to ensure fulfillment of contractual obligations. Definitions of terms such as "satisfactory performance" remain a problem. Until the profession agrees on meanings or court decisions establish definitions for such terms, contracts must define terms included within their text.

PROTECTION OF COMPUTING RESOURCES

Protection of computing resources, another branch of computer law, can be by patents, copyrights, or trade secret laws.

Patents

The **Patent Act of 1952,** a statutory law, gives inventors a legal monopoly over their inventions for a period of 17 years. This act applies to computer hardware only. To date, the courts have not deemed programs patentable. In *Dann* v. *Johnson*, the Supreme Court sidestepped the issue of program patents. In *Gottschalk* v. *Benson*,[22] a 1972 case involving a method of converting binary-coded decimal notation to pure binary, the Supreme Court struck down the patent application. The reason for the patent denials? Programs are ideas expressed in mathematical algorithms, and one may not patent an idea. However, in *Bernhart* v. *Fetter*[23] and the Knowton decision,[24] it has been ruled that programs as part of a "machine-system" may be patented.[25]

Certainly the computer industry recognizes the need to protect software propriety. But are programs literary or artistic creations? Should they be protected by copyrights? Or is software an invention, hence

---

[20]Ann Dooley, "User Wins $401,690 from Burroughs Corp.," *Computer World* 13, no. 20 (May 14, 1979), p. 12.

[21]Molly Upton, "Univac Found Guilty in Breach of Contract Suit," *Computer World* 12, no. 8 (February 20, 1978), pp. 7–8.

[22]*Gottschalk* v. *Benson*, US 409 US 63.3, CLSR 256.

[23]2 CLSR 359 417 F 2d 1395.

[24]4 CLSR 799 481 F 2d 1357.

[25]See Martin A. Goetz, "Software Protection: You Bet Your Company," *Infosystems* 24, no. 7 (July 1977), p. 60.

patentable? In *Parder* v. *Flook,* the court seems to be awaiting a statutory directive from Congress on the problem of software **patents.**[26] Some suggest that the issue should be resolved by an international convention, such as the Berne convention on copyrights.

Copyrights

Although most programs are not patentable, they do receive some protection under both common and statutory **copyright laws.** Under common law, an author has the right to control the distribution of unpublished writing. The Copyright Office extended this common law protection by starting to accept computer programs for copyrights in 1964, provided the subject matter was patentable, and the programs were original, novel, utilitarian, and nonobvious.[27] By 1977, however, only 1,200 programs were registered, over 75 percent of these being IBM or Burroughs programs, although approximately one million programs had been written and were in circulation.[28]

The 1976 Copyright Act classified programs and data bases as nondramatic literature works under Class TX, giving further statutory protection to the computer industry. According to the provisions of this act, a copy of the protected material has to be in a form visible to human beings without the use of a computer. The author's controlling rights are extended to death or 50 years, with the copier liable for actual damages or an award of $250 to $10,000 in statutory damages if the exact amount of the damage cannot be proven.[29]

Copyright statutes still do not protect ideas or programming concepts, not even in the updated 1980 Copyright Act. Shouldn't programmers be given equal protection to inventors, whose ideas can be patented?[30] Users can identify copyrighted programs by a copyright notice. The symbol © or word *copyright*, the name of the copyright owner, and year of first copyright must appear on documentation, including listings and printout, as well as on the physical embodiment of the copyright (disk or tape).

What constitutes a program has been defined by the National Commission of New Technological Uses of Copyrighted Works (CONTU) as follows:

> A "computer program" is a fixation of a series of statements or instructions to be used in conjunction with a computer to bring about a certain result.[31]

[26]Charles R. Franz, Susan J. Wilkins, and Jonathan C. Bower, "A Critical Review of Software Protection," *Information and Management* 4 (1981).

[27]Robert P. Bigelow and Susan H. Nycum, *Your Computer and the Law* (Englewood Cliffs, N.J.: Prentice-Hall, 1975), p. 75.

[28]National CONTU, *Software Subcommittee Report,* undated, p. 16.

[29]Harold F. Lusk et al., *Business Law: Principles and Cases* (Homewood, Ill.: Richard D. Irwin, Inc., 1978), p. 1056.

[30]Paul Hirsch, "The Patent Office Examines Software," *Datamation* 12, no. 11 (November 1966), pp. 79–81.

[31]National CONTU, *Software Subcommittee Report and Additional Views,* p. 16.

But the legal definition of "copying" remains cloudy. For example, in *Data Cash Systems, Inc.* v. *JS&A Group, Inc.*,[32] the court held that duplication of an object code was not a copyright infringement, whereas the ruling in a similar case, *Tandy Corporation* v. *Personal Micro Computers, Inc.*[33] was that a similarly stored object code was a "copy" under the Copyright Act.

U.S. copyrights are not honored in many foreign countries so programs have little protection from international pirating.

Trade Secrets

Common law is the basis of **trade secret laws,** though states differ in the protection they have codified. Most, however, define intentional unauthorized use as a criminal offense though the firm which sues must prove that the violation was of a trade secret, protected and treated by the firm as such.

The term *trade secret*, defined by the courts "as any formulae, pattern, device or compilation of information which is used in one's business, and which gives him an opportunity to obtain an advantage over competitors who do not know or use it,"[34] is often applied to programs. To protect the secrecy of their programs, vendors may incorporate restrictions of use in written contracts or prepare licensing agreements specifying conditions relating to enhancement and maintenance of programs.

Protecting a secret program from a firm's own employees is also a difficult task. With programmers constantly changing jobs (the current shortage of programmers means employers compete with lucrative job offers), program secrets leak with frequency. Guilt is difficult to establish. Does taking a flowchart to a new job constitute violation of a trade secret? How about remembered flowcharts, or experience gained in solving particular programming problems? Students learn in their first programming class that plagiarism in programming is hard to prove. Changes in variable names, statement numbers, and comment cards make programs look quite different though the programming logic may be "borrowed." Pirating companies gain not only new ideas, but are spared program development costs and long lead times which are crucial in a competitive situation.

Contracts for programmers and system designers that disallow employment by a competitor for a given period after leaving the firm might prevent programming secrets from leaking. However, apart from legal problems in enforcing such contractual provisions, this has proven impractical since many programmers refuse to sign. Demand for their services is great enough that jobs without such restrictions are readily available.

---

[32]480 F Supp. 1063. N.D. Ill 1979.

[33]*CCH Copyright Law Reports*, 303, D.D. Cal. Aug. 1981, p. 25.

[34]*Keewanee Oil Co.* v. *Bicron Corp.*, 416 U.S. 470 1974. See Bigelow and Nycum, *Your Computer and the Law*, p. 67, and also Lusk, *Business Law*, p. 1054.

Employees can carry hardware secrets to new jobs as well. In a 1971 suit, IBM charged that Memorex, in an attempt to develop a competitive replacement for the IBM 3330 disk drive, hired IBM former employees (18 months after they had left their IBM jobs), assigned them to the replacement project, and induced them to violate their permanent nondisclosure contracts. It asked the court for a 30-month injunction against the Memorex replacement. Memorex responded with a countersuit, claiming that IBM so monopolized the industry that it had no right to trade secrets. In an out-of-court settlement in 1972 both suits were dropped. Neither party admitted guilt and no compensation was paid, but IBM did win an agreement from Memorex not to enter the disk market for six months. It has been claimed that Memorex capitulated because it did not have the resources for a full-scale legal battle, having lost $13.4 million in the course of business operations in 1971.[35] Certainly the high cost of litigation encourages disputing firms to reach out-of-court settlements.

COMPUTERS AND TORT

Tort law deals with a wrongful act, injury, or damage (but not involving breach of contract) for which a civil action can be brought. Tort can be intentional or unintentional (such as negligence resulting from a careless act). A surge of lightning or loss of electric power which causes a computer to malfunction, producing erroneous bank balances or credit ratings, might be judged unintentional tort if the malfunction led to personal injury. In such a case, liability without fault would be assigned.

Ford Motor Credit Co. v. *Swareus* is an example of a tort case involving computers that reached trial. Swareus's car had been repossessed by the credit company for nonpayment although Swareus had twice presented canceled checks to the company proving that money owed had been paid. Ford Credit admitted its error in court, saying its computer was at fault. Swareus won both punitive and compensatory damages in a judgment which stated, in part:

> Men feed data to a computer and men interpret the answer the computer spews forth. In this computerized age, the law must require that men in the use of computerized data regard those with whom they are dealing as more important than a perforation on a card. Trust in the infallibility of a computer is hardly a defense, when the opportunity to avoid the error is apparent and repeated as was here presented.[36]

---

[35]Gerald W. Brock, *The U.S. Computer Industry* (Cambridge, Mass: Ballinger Publishing, 1975), p. 173.

[36]*Ford Motor Co.* v. *Swareus*, 447 SW 2d, (Ky. 1967).

Even if the error is not "apparent and repeated," management is responsible for human–computer error. In *Ward v. Superior Court,*[37] for example, a business was found liable for unfair competition because one of its employees had wrongfully gained remote access to the file of the plaintiff from a service bureau. Since the firm gained from the criminal offense, the employer's liability is understandable, but what if mistakes are the malice of disgruntled or maladjusted workers intent on damaging the company's reputation? Would the employer still be held responsible for tort? Most managers would prefer careful supervision of employees and prompt rectification of errors rather than a suit in court to test such questions.

The law in computer cases is sketchy at best. The death of Kenji Urada, killed by a robot at Kawasaki Heavy Industries in Japan in July 1981, has made the industry aware that legal responsibility in such accidents is unclear. Is the company which manufactured the robot liable for Urada's death, or does fault lie with the programmer who wrote the robot's software? Can the manager who approved funds for the robot's design and purchase be held responsible? In the United States there is no statute or legal precedent for such a case. The law simply hasn't kept pace with computer technological developments, leaving the industry in legal limbo in part of its operation.

COMPUTER CRIME

Unlike tort, where the injured party sues for compensation, victims of **computer crimes** are not granted awards or damages. Rather sanctions, such as fine or imprisonment, are imposed on the perpetrator of the crime. Computer crimes may involve fraud or theft, or be physical actions, such as sabotage directed against a computer system. Elsewhere in print there are many examples of such crimes and recommendations for system security measures.[38] A major problem in dealing with computer theft is that the crime is not always apparent: when information is stolen, nothing detectable is missing.

Laws applicable to computer crime depend on the exact nature of the case and vary from state to state. Generally, computer-related cases are prosecuted under laws written for other purposes. For example, a programmer who takes stolen software to a new job may be charged with violation of the Trade Secrets Act or copyright infringement. In Texas, a program is tangible property with an ascertainable value so that stealing a program may be prosecuted as theft, but not

[37]*Ward v. Superior Court,* 3CLSR 206 (1972).

[38]For other cases, see Donn Parker, *Crime by Computer* (New York: Charles Scribner's Sons, 1976), 308 p. See also M. Gemignani, "Computer Crime: The Law in '80," *Indiana Law Review* 13 (April 1981) pp. 681–723.

many states provide this program protection. U.S. theft statutes cover programs but only if the thief crosses a state boundary.[39] They also cover theft of computer time. More than 40 sections of the United States Code can be cited to provide sanctions for computer-related criminal conduct.

As the number of computers increases, applications expand, and data bases grow, preventing and detecting computer crime will become an even greater problem. Comprehensive laws need to be written that will help deter potential felons by the penalties they impose. One attempt to streamline and update the law dealing with computer fraud and abuse was the proposed Federal Computer Systems Protection Act of 1979,[40] a bill that defined four broad categories of criminal activity.

1. The introduction of false data into a computer.
2. The use of computer facilities for unauthorized or illegal purposes.
3. The alteration or destruction of a computer, its information or files.
4. Electronic burglary of money, financial instruments, property, services, or valuable data.

Though this bill died in the Senate Judiciary Committee at the close of the 96th session of Congress, similar legislation will undoubtedly be introduced in Congress again. Such legislation would be an important mechanism for the prosecution of computer-related crimes.[41]

SUMMARY AND CONCLUSIONS

The law has had a profound impact on the structure of the computer industry. For example, antitrust legislation led to the 1956 IBM Consent Decree, which in turn helped give birth to the service and leasing sectors of the industry. Antitrust pressure is also cited as instrumental in IBM's 1969 **unbundling** decision to no longer price hardware offerings to include software and services. This decision gave impetus to firms specializing in software, education, and maintenance. The recent settlement of the government suit against AT&T which has repudiated the principle of maximum separation, long the basis of FCC regulatory schemas, may lead in the future to the merger of the computer industry with the communications industry.

[39]*Hancock v. State*, 402 SW 2d 906 (1966).

[40]For details and a good discussion of the subject, see J. L. Bookholdt and Jerome S. Horvitz, "Prosecution of Computer Crime," *Journal of Systems Management* 29, no. 12 (December 1978), pp. 11–12.

[41]Linda M. Marquis and Virginia M. Moore, "Proposed Federal Computer Systems Protection Act," *DPA Journal* 50, no. 12 (December 1980), pp. 29–32.

The protection of computer resources is by patent, copyright, and trade secret laws. Table 26.4 compares the features of these laws.

Both common law and statutes form the basis of computer law. But the legal framework for the computer industry has not kept pace with technological developments in the field. More statutes, such as the Privacy Act of 1974,[42] the Information Act of 1975, and the EFT Act of 1977, need to be written to supplement existing laws, particularly

Table 26.4   **Comparison: Patent, copyright, and trade secret laws**

Characteristics of law	Patents	Copyrights	Trade secrets
Basic source of law	Statutory	Statutory and common law	Common and state law
Administered	U.S. government patent	Copyright office	Management of the firm
Eligibility criteria	Original idea, useful, involving skill	Novelty, utility, originality of ideas	Gives firm competitive edge
Protection provided against	Making, selling, or using the embodiment of an inventive idea	Unauthorized use or copying of physical expression, not the concept or algorithm or approach	Unauthorized copy or use
Remedy	If successful court action, 50 percent of proven loss	Actual damages Statutory damages Injunctions Attorneys' fees	Damages, if proven in civil or criminal action
Period of protection	17 years	50 years or until author's death	Unlimited
Appropriate for	Hardware	Software (object and source programs)	Software, data base, design of system, procedures, mailing list
Implementation	Registration with Patent Office	Copyright notice; registration required for certain remedies	Controlled access and security
Initial cost	$1000–$2500	$100/registration	Can be significant
Maintenance cost	$500	Nil	Can be significant
Most applicable	For algorithms or inventions of high value, or when long period of protection is required	For large volume multiple-copied products	For algorithms Important to businesses with high value, even with low dissemination

---

[42]For details of this act and its historical evaluation, see O. E. Dial and E. M. Goldberg, *Privacy, Security and Computers* (New York: Praeger Publishers, 1975), pp. 24–26.

in the areas of protection of computer resources, tort, and computer crime. The amount of regulatory legislation commentators recommend is often based on political orientation rather than legal or technological grounds.

KEY WORDS

Antitrust laws

Common law

Communications Act of 1934

Computer crime

Contract law

Copyright laws

Federal Communications Commission (FCC)

Final Order

January 1982

Maximum separation

1956 IBM Consent Decree

Patent Act of 1952

Patents

Statute law

Tort law

Trade secret laws

Transborder data flow

Unbundling

Uniform Commercial Code (UCC)

DISCUSSION QUESTIONS

1. Has the law in the United States inhibited or protected the computer industry?
2. Would the growth of IBM have been different without the constant threat of antitrust suits? Explain.
3. Has the overpowering size and power of IBM inhibited the growth of small firms in the computer industry? Should the law protect the small firm, or should the competitive market determine survival? Explain.
4. Should the U.S. government assist the computer industry in view of the fact that many other nations directly or indirectly subsidize their computer industries? What steps would you recommend?
5. Firms will vary as to the type of legal support they have. Would you recommend full-time legal staff, lawyers on retainer, lawyers engaged on cases as they arise, or no lawyers at all in the cases below?
   a. Drawing up a contract for the acquisition of a large CPU.
   b. Acquisition of a computer peripheral with the purchase price of $6,000.
   c. Suing IBM for breach of contract.
   d. Defending a charge of breach of warranty.
   e. Subcontracting development work to a software company at the cost of $500,000.

   f. Acquiring a maintenance contract for a peripheral.

   g. Suing another company for an antitrust violation.

   h. Suing a foreign company for violating a patent.

   i. Claiming damages from another company for violating a copyright.

   j. Getting a restraining order against a former employee for stealing trade secrets.

6. What type of protection would you seek in each of the following:

  a. Invention of a unique fast disk device.

  b. The writing of a computer program for portfolio management.

  c. Invention of a new compiler.

  d. Development of a computer programming language.

  e. Development of an algorithm for automatic navigation in a data base.

  f. Development of a sorting algorithm.

  g. Development of a technique of systems analysis.

  h. Development of a form to determine users' requirements.

  i. Development of a method for computing the benefits of a computer system.

  j. Development of a standard for computer costing.

  k. Development of a new approach to charging for computer services.

  l. Development of a standards manual.

7. Common law is irrelevant to the computing industry because it is based on decades of tradition which the computer industry does not have. Comment.

8. Law, especially legislative law, is too slow to be responsive to the fast-moving and dynamic computer industry. Comment.

9. The computing industry in the United States needs to be protected by the government if it is to be competitive with the Japanese computer industry. Comment. If you agree with the statement, what protective measures do you recommend?

10. Can law prevent or reduce computer crime? If so, how?

11. How would you protect software?

12. Do you favor laws restricting transborder flow of information? Justify your position.

13. Have antitrust proceedings initiated by the Department of Justice served a useful purpose in restraining monopolistic tendencies of giant computer companies? Have the proceedings allowed small firms free entry into computer markets? Explain.

14. Is the computer industry overregulated or not adequately regulated? Give examples in one sector of the computer industry.

SELECTED ANNOTATED BIBLIOGRAPHY

Bigelow, Robert P., and Susan H. Nycum. *Your Computer and the Law.* Englewood Cliffs N.J.: Prentice-Hall, 1975, 283 p.

  This book is a guide to the legal ramifications of computer operations for purchase, sale, lease and rental of hardware and software (including an extensive checklist for making contracts), taxation, data communications, security, privacy, personnel, and insurance. The chapters and sections are self-contained units for easy reference and study. Especially interesting is Part VI that addresses the legal aspects of the daily activities of a computer installation manager.

Burton, Robert P. "Transnational Data Flows: International Status, Impact and Accomodation." *Data Management* 18 (June l980), pp. 27–34.
This is a report on guidelines for the protection of privacy and transborder flow of personal data by the Organization of Economic Cooperation and Development, of which the United States is a member.

Gilchrist, Bruce, and Milton R. Wessel. *Government Regulation of the Computer Industry.* Montvale, N.J.: AFIPS Press, 1972, 247 pp.
Included are the documents of the 1956 Consent Decree, the CDC complaint against IBM, and the 1969 U.S. antitrust complaint against IBM. The book has chapters on regulation by government of acquisitions and marketing activities as well as on regulation of exports, imports, communications, and banking.

Mooers, Calvin A. "Computer Software and Copyright." *Computing Surveys* 7, no. 1 (March 1975), pp. 45–72.
An excellent survey on copyright laws as they relate to software protection.

Sanders, Norman. *A Manager's Guide to Profitable Computers.* London: MA-COM, 1978, chaps. 18 and 19, pp. 145–61.
Norman Sanders has a delightful way of writing lightly but meaningfully on a difficult and serious subject. His discussion of computers and law will give you no deep insights into the body of law but you will get a chuckle, especially from the chapter on a hypothetical case in court.

Seipel, Peter. *Computing Law.* Stockholm: Liber Forlag, 1977. 375 p.
The author, who teaches law at the Stockholm Law Faculty in Sweden, has based this book on his 20 years experience in law. The book is addressed to both the newcomer in the field and the experienced reader. It is concerned more with the principles of law than with case law. There is an extensive bibliography (24 pages) including foreign references, some written in French and German.

Smith, Larry W. "A Survey of Current Legal Issues from Contracts of Computer Goods and Services." *Computer/Law Journal* 1, no. 3 (Winter 1979), pp. 475–699.
This article focuses on hardware (CPU and peripherals), software, and design effort, and addresses the problems of liability arising out of contract disagreements. Many citations and examples of cases are given. Detailed and elaborate footnotes help the non-lawyer reader.

Tapper, Colin. *Computer Law.* London: Longman, 1978, 190 p.
This is a successor to the author's book *Computers and the Law* written for the series *Law in Context.* It follows the case study approach, being grounded throughout on decided cases and on legislation, enacted and proposed. Though the author is English, there is no neglect of American

law (205 U.S. cases are cited). The bibliography is extensive, listing 32 books and reports. The book is tightly written. Unfortunately, small print makes the book difficult to read.

Washington University Law Quarterly 63, no 3 (Summer 1977), pp. 372–540.
An excellent special issue from a symposium on "Computers in Law and Society." The journal has numerous articles on government regulations, the impact of technology on prevailing legal principles, and law as it relates to computer abuse, communications, and EFT.

Willenberg, Wayne. "Protection of Computer Software By Copyrights, Patents, and Trade Secrets." Paper presented at the 15th Hawaii International Conference on Systems Sciences, 1982, 23 p.
An excellent review of the subject by a lawyer with a knowledge of computer software.

Journals

Because of the changing nature of computer law, journals are the best source of recent information. Some relevant journals are listed below:

Computer Law and Tax Report
Specialized for tax considerations.

Computer Law Journal
Has broad coverage.

Datanverarbeitung in Recht
Articles written in German have an English summary.

Law and Computer Technology
More concerned with technological considerations.

Rutgers Journal of Computers and Law
Wide coverage of topics. Includes bibliographies.

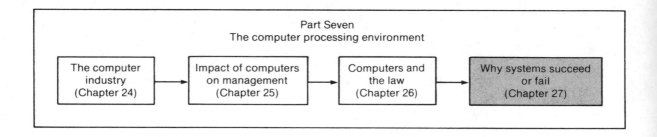

Part Seven
The computer processing environment

| The computer industry (Chapter 24) | Impact of computers on management (Chapter 25) | Computers and the law (Chapter 26) | Why systems succeed or fail (Chapter 27) |

CHAPTER 27

Why systems succeed or fail

To live effectively is to live with adequate information.

Norbert Weiner

The effectiveness of an information system can be measured by the ability of the system to meet design and operational demands within prescribed tolerance limitations in a given environment. The system should satisfy users' needs during normal and peak periods of demand, prove easy to modify should environmental conditions change, and have maintenance, backup, and recovery procedures that minimize down time.

Effective systems may vary widely in performance. Indeed, a system deemed a success in one firm might be considered a failure in another because the objectives and specifications of a successful system might be appropriate in only a very specific environment. There is no single formula for successful information systems, no checklist of specifications guaranteeing system success.

However, factors contributing to successful systems can be identified. Most of these factors have been discussed in earlier chapters of this book. In this concluding chapter, these success factors will be reviewed and summarized. The chapter will also discuss ways to humanize information systems since technological efficiency must be balanced with attention to human factors in order for systems to succeed.

FACTORS AFFECTING SUCCESS OF INFORMATION SYSTEM DEVELOPMENT

User attitude is perhaps the most important factor affecting successful system development. After all, the system is being designed to assist users in their jobs. Analysts can formalize system specifications, but users must contribute by expressing needs and outlining on-the-job problems that analysts may not know about. Unless users are persuaded that the computer, as a resource, can help them perform their duties, they will not be receptive to computer solutions to problems, nor be willing to consider innovative problem-solving methods proposed by the development team. In all likelihood, they will not even use the information system once it is implemented. It is essential, therefore, that positive user attitudes toward information systems be promoted by management. Strategies to this effect will be outlined later in this chapter.

Managers must also have a positive attitude toward computerized information systems for system development to be successful. Management sets the tone in an organization. A half-hearted commitment to the development of an information system will be signaled to others and buttress resistance to change. The development team needs the support of top management in order to gain access to corporate records when gathering data on existing operations. **Management support** is also required to gain the cooperation of personnel when the development team solicits user opinion regarding system specifications. When top management publicizes potential benefits of a proposed information system, participates in system planning, and directs middle and operational management to actively assist the development team, a receptive environment is created that helps the team perform its functions. The attention and support of management is of particular value at the outset of a project.

Management should also ensure that EDP personnel have the technical expertise to undertake systems development. This may mean recruiting additional qualified computer specialists or hiring consultants to add to the development team. Since complex information systems require a data base management system, the team should include members with DBMS knowledge and experience.

In the planning phase of development, long-range plans, not merely stop-gap solutions to problems, should be considered. Applications showing the best benefit/cost ratio should be given priority. It is recognized that some benefits are intangible, difficult to give a monetary value, but projects should be weighted so that their relative merits can be compared.

When system failure is traced to poor system design, the cause is usually one or more of the following:

1. Users did not participate in formulating system specifications.
2. The flow of data, documents, and information was not adequately considered.
3. The development team failed to recognize the multiple uses of data, allowing the proliferation of files instead of formulating an integrated data base.
4. System flexibility is lacking so that additions or changes prove difficult to make. Usually modular systems developed according to a long-range plan do not have this problem.
5. Documentation is lacking. To keep a system on track regardless of changes in personnel, documentation should include a system description, charts, program descriptions, data base description, a list of hardware, policy, and procedural requirements, input/output descriptions, and detailed implementation descriptions.
6. Human factors were not given sufficient attention. The system evokes anger, frustration, or fear instead of being friendly and easy to use.
7. Lack of an adequate overall system development plan.

Sometimes systems fail because the design does not allow efficient processing of various types of data. Sometimes the mix of resources committed to the system is far from optimal. Sometimes users require more prompts or explanations. For example, prompts should assist users in correcting errors caught by the system, and users should never be at a total loss as to how to proceed in resolving problems.

The reasons for design failure may be multiple and complex, or as simple as poor screen acuity resulting in user eyestrain and headaches. Given the technical competence of the development team, however, lack of sensitivity to human factors is most often the cause of design failures. A section will be devoted to humanizing information systems later in this chapter.

FACTORS IN OPERATIONS LEADING TO INFORMATION SYSTEM SUCCESS

The key to information system success in operations is **control.** Unfortunately, the term *control* has an oppressive connotation, and indeed, too many controls can deter users from effective system use. For example, access controls may become so restrictive that potential users bypass the system entirely. Yet controls are necessary to ensure the privacy and integrity of data, to guarantee system security, and to ensure efficiency in processing. In addition, data must be collected so that system performance can be evaluated and the need for modification or redevelopment can be documented. The challenge is to establish meaningful, unobtrusive controls to monitor system performance and protect the system from abuse. Most users will support the implementation of controls as long as their need can be demonstrated and efforts are made by EDP personnel to minimize the adverse effect of such controls on system use.

As in development, human factors must be given consideration during operations. Is the system easy to access? Is adequate user interface provided? Some systems include a hot line for custom quick jobs; others, a hot line for reporting service breakdown. Are special services of this nature needed? Since users' needs may change over time, do procedures exist to ensure routine evaluation of performance and system relevancy?

Successful operation requires capacity planning so that there is no break in service during peak loads. The budget should allow for modification and redevelopment of outdated systems, and permit purchase of new equipment as technology advances. To help management oversee operations, some firms schedule weekly task force meetings to evaluate reports of auditors and function representatives so that operating problems do not escape management attention. This helps ensure that corrective action is quickly taken.

The failure of systems to operate at designed or expected levels may be attributed to one or more of the following.

1. Poor systems planning.
2. Inadequate operating procedures.
3. Faulty scheduling.
4. Lack of evaluation and feedback mechanisms.
5. Poor maintenance facilities or procedures.
6. Design restricts system expansion when service demands increase.
7. Inappropriate organizational structure for computer processing unit within the corporate structure.
8. Inappropriate procedures for assigning computer resources and priorities.
9. Strategies to reduce resistance to change lacking.
10. Training of users and EDP personnel insufficient.
11. Poor budgeting.
12. Failure to keep up-to-date on technological developments in the computer industry.
13. Failure of corporate management to establish work environment receptive to computerized systems. This may be due to lack of understanding about computers and their potential, or underestimating the impact of computing on management and the organization.

During conversion, systems are particularly vulnerable to failure. Competent managers who truly understand the systems approach should be responsible for conversion and managers who can't adjust to change or show inability to develop new skills should be transferred or replaced. Acceptance attitudes of all personnel should be monitored with no "footdragging" allowed. Indeed, high performance standards of all personnel should be demanded so the traditional "let down" period during conversion is avoided. Preplanning conversion—making sure that staff is well trained to accept new responsibilities, that the computer center is scheduled to allow for the additional loads during conversion, and that a backup computer is available in case of emergencies—should help prevent disruption of service during conversion. While testing the new system for inaccuracies and redundancies, staff must also maintain prior programs and be given adequate resources to do so.

ROLE OF MANAGEMENT

Corporate managers are responsible for both system and human performance. Success of an information system may depend on management's ability to oversee development and operations so that needed output is provided efficiently and on management's ability to promote human productivity in a computer environment.

With regard to system performance, managers are responsible for seeing that both **objectives and technical specifications** are met by the system. The following questions are guidelines in evaluating whether performance is satisfactory.

1. Time: Is the system working as fast as expected?
2. Cost: Is system performance up to financial expectations in terms of labor, facilities, materials, maintenance, expansion, modification, training, data entry, data output, data storage, programming, software, carrier charges, and backup equipment?
3. Hardware: Does hardware meet the standards set for speed, reliability, service, maintenance, operating costs, power requirements, and necessary training?
4. Software: Does software meet the standards set for processing speed, amount and quality of output, accuracy, reliability, amount of maintenance and updating, and training requirements?
5. Productivity: Is the relationship of input cost to output level satisfactory?
6. Accuracy: Does the system have tolerable frequency of error and magnitude of error?
7. Integrity: Does the system provide sufficient security and control in relationship to cost?
8. Security: Does the system protect computing resources from misuse and abuse?

9.   User satisfaction: Given the resources and other constraints, is the user satisfied?

When the need for system maintenance or redevelopment is indicated, resources must be allocated and personnel assigned to the project by management. Though technical problems will be solved by computer professionals on the staff, management is ultimately responsible for system performance.

System performance may be satisfactory yet information systems fail if **human performance** is below standard. Astute management of employees and human–computer interaction is as important as machine efficiency. As stated by Col. Joseph Warren, in a study of Department of Defense data processing activities:

> I would like to offer the following speculations: As computer applications come to have a more direct impact on the activities of every organization, management attention must be focused on the people involved in computer systems as designers, programmers, users, and recipients of the computer-provided services or there will arise a misplaced reaction against continued application of computers to the solutions of problems.[1]

It is management's responsibility to establish a work environment receptive to computerization. This may require the organization of orientation programs so employees become familiar with potential benefits of information systems. It may be necessary to establish training programs to keep personnel technologically up-to-date. Policies should be initiated to minimize turnover, such as the establishment of career ladders, for the marketplace is chronically short of qualified EDP personnel. Most important in information system success is management's role in overseeing the incorporation of human factors in system design and the humanization of systems.

HUMANIZING INFORMATION SYSTEMS

To humanize an information system means giving priority to human needs rather than to technological considerations. That is, the emphasis is placed on how the computer can best serve the user, rather than focusing on machine efficiency at the expense of the user. For example, assembly language is the most efficient in processing time, but with high level languages, persons with little technical background can input data and utilize output in their jobs. High level languages, in effect, make the system more "friendly" and of greater ser-

---

[1]Quoted in Leon K. Albrecht, *Organization and Management of Information Processing Systems* (New York: The Macmillan, 1973), p. vi.

vice as well. The development of interactive dialogue languages is another step in the direction of humanizing software.

Other guidelines for humanizing information systems, especially terminal-oriented systems, include:

1. Easy-to-follow instructions in the use of systems. This includes self-explanatory prompts and messages, and use of menus or fill-in techniques to assist in inputting data.
2. User-friendly hardware, such as touch-sensitive screens, voice output, or devices such as a joystick, "mouse," or light pens to facilitate user interaction with the computer.
3. Tolerant systems that allow simple "errors" and assist users in identifying and correcting mistakes.
4. Quick system response to user demands for service.
5. Simple procedures for exceptions or overriding defaults.
6. Coding that is easy to master and easy to remember.
7. User options, such as whether terminals will be intelligent, able to process graphics, have voice output, etc.
8. Physical compactness of system. User work stations should also be comfortable, convenient, and a pleasing environment in which to work (e.g., low noise level).

The system should be designed so that minimum effort on the part of users is required. That is, repetitive tasks should be done by the computer, coding should be programmed, file recovery should be automatic, and input monitored so only essential data is collected by the system. The system should be easy to master, with little learning or memorization of operational steps required. Help should be built into the system but not overdone. That is, users should be able to bypass help menus if they are not needed.

The system should be based on patterns familiar to users, and be both logical and consistent. Familiar formats and a standard type-writer keyboard in word processing, for example, facilitate system use. So does use of common abbreviations and symbols for information recovery.

Visual or video signals to call the attention of users to problems are helpful. For example, syntax or spelling errors should be signaled, changes in processing mode clearly indicated, and warning given when file capacity reaches 80–90 percent. Maximum worker control should be built into the design, giving users flexibility in sequencing and defaults. The system should also provide maximum task support, such as documentation and indexing.

Ideally, systems should be easy to access and use; intelligent but not intimidating; honest with no intent to trick or deceive; and considerate of individuals, not manipulative. There should be provisions for evaluating information stored in the system, procedures for correcting this information, and user knowledge regarding how stored information will be put to use. Systems should be adaptable, able to service individuals with different backgrounds and levels of proficiency. The system should allow for differences in age, experience, education, professional orientation, and organizational level of users.

Throughout the literature on information systems, one finds that the major cause for unsatisfactory system performance is attributed to **human factors.** For example, a survey of conference attendees at national APICS meetings in the early 1970s showed that 80 percent of the respondents considered communications, understanding, and human problems the most significant determinants in systems progress, not system or technical expertise.

Table 27.1 presents a list of human factors which affect performance, and suggests strategies management might implement to minimize dysfunctional behavior. Many computer technicians dismiss human factors. This is where management's role becomes so important because the success or failure of an information system very often depends on recognition of the importance of these factors. It is management's responsibility to see that the lessons of ergonomics[2] are understood by system developers and that features are incorporated in the systems' design that minimize human shortcomings.

Table 27.1   **Human factors affecting information system success and strategies to minimize dysfunctional behavior**

Work group	Human factors	Motivation and information systems strategy
Operating employees	Resistance to new systems	*Extrinsic motivational factors*
	Tendency to believe rumor versus fact	Set achievable goals/standards
	Need for reassurance as to job security	Pay, as a major incentive
	Need for group motivation	Organize into small work groups
	Dislike for more rigid work pace	System of rewards
	Instinct for self protection from blame	System of punishments
	Faith in company promises	System of promotions
	Tendency to short-range goals	
	Fear of machines	*Intrinsic motivational factors*
	Desire for affection, recognition, attention	Do not suppress informal organization
	Desire to know reasons for change	*Other strategies*
	Influence of key workers	Prepare and distribute brochures describing the new system
		Intra-company training programs

---

[2]For Europeans, ergonomics is the study of workers and their physical environment, how to adapt machines to the convenience of operators in order to maximize machine efficiency. The American equivalent of ergonomics, called human factors, has its roots in human psychology.

Table 27.1   *(concluded)*

Operating management and middle management	Fear of replacement by young workers
	Tendency to concentrate on technical aspects of jobs
	Need for visable evidence of production
	Lack of job mobility
	Desire to air views and participate
	Worry about ability to learn and supervise new procedures
	Pride in status symbols of position
	Fear of becoming mere machine monitors
	Fatigue and pressure during system change
	Fear of loss of promotional opportunity
		Extrinsic motivational factors
		   Set achievable goals
		   Participation in systems change
		   System of promotions
		   Pay incentive systems
		   Bonuses
		Intrinsic motivational factors
		   Praise from supervisors
		   Interesting work
		   Tenure
		   Status symbols
		Other strategies
		   Tailor system to meet manager needs
		   Provide only needed information
		   Intracompany training programs
		   Distribute brochures describing new systems
		   Simplify reporting structure
		   Avoid information overload
		   Standardize report formats, headings
		   Provide accurate, objective, timely, understandable information

Top management	Status symbols as motives for change
	Courage to carry through change
	Isolation to top people
	Tendency toward secrecy
	Ability to adjust and learn
	Impatience with rate of progress
	Promptness in making decisions
	Concern for human relations
	Willingness to use new tools and skills
		Extrinsic motivational factors
		   Bonuses
		   Stock options
		Intrinsic motivational factors
		   Status symbols
		Other strategies
		   (See operating and middle management work group for list.)

Source: Michael J. Cerullo, "Information System Success Factors," *Journal of Systems Management* 31, no. 12 (December 1980), p. 12.

SUMMARY AND CONCLUSIONS

To be deemed a success, an information system should be profitably applied to at least one area of major concern within a company, the system should be widely used, and it should improve the quality of decision making and operations. Note that success depends on both system performance and user interaction with the system. The two cannot easily be separated since technical components inevitably have an impact on human effectiveness and satisfaction.

In the past, technical components of system design have been the focus of most system developers. It is now recognized that more effort must be devoted to humanizing systems if they are to succeed. Though management is theoretically responsible for both the technical components and human aspects of system development and implementation, in practice, professional computer personnel are delegated responsibility for technical matters. Since technicians have a poor track record regarding their sensitivity to user concerns, needs, foibles, and limitations, it would be a mistake to likewise delegate responsibility for humanizing the system to technical personnel.

Successful information systems require active corporate and EDP management support and involvement. This includes planning for systems, participating in the development process, being involved in systems design to ensure human factors are not ignored, and implementing programs and policies to create a work environment receptive to computerization.

CASE STUDY: INFORMATION SYSTEMS MANAGEMENT

At a 1980 meeting of the Society of Management Information Systems, a panelist reported on the recent appointment of a friend as computer executive for a company with the following resources:

IBM 370/168 with 500 remote terminals.

100 other terminals.

8 operation programmers.

1 system analyst.

60 percent personnel turnover.

700 programs, including 15 major programs and one assembly language program with 50 pages of code (most programs poorly documented).

208 change requests (in 1979).

The panel then discussed the problems of this company and agreed that the firm's many undocumented outdated systems, its shortage of personnel, and numerous change requests are quite typical. Inadequate computer maintenance—in fact, underestimating the very need for maintenance—is also a common problem. According to panel members, lack of management understanding of the growing complexity of computer environments contributes to many of these problems.

There was consensus that the continuing shortage of the "Three E" (expert, experienced, and eager analysts and programmers) exacerbates the problem of computer resource management, and indeed, may be largely responsible for the failure of many information systems.

KEY WORDS

Control

Human factors

Human performance

Management support

Objectives and technical specifications

System performance

User attitude

DISCUSSION QUESTIONS

1. Who should be given responsibility for compiling a list of factors influencing success or failure of an information system in a given department, firm, or industry? How should data be collected?

2. As manager of a computer department, what strategies would you implement to ensure success of information systems under your jurisdiction?

3. What level of management is most responsible for success or failure of an information system?

4. Is experience the best or only way to learn about success and failure factors in a given environment? Is there a faster, less painful method of gaining the knowledge one accrues through experience?

5. What sources of information should be used to identify how success and failure factors are altered by changing technology?

6. What personnel in an organization are crucial to the success of information systems?

7. List factors that contribute to the success of information system development.

8. Discuss principles of design that help humanize information systems.

9. Where do you feel the emphasis on future research for management information systems should be focused? On technology or human factors? Justify your answer.

SELECTED ANNOTATED BIBLIOGRAPHY

Cerullo, Michael J. "Information System Success Factors." *Journal of Systems Management* 31, no. 12 (December 1980), pp. 10–19.

Results of a survey of 280 U.S. corporations listed in the Fortune 1000 regarding critical success factors in MIS development.

Ginzberg, Michael J. "Steps toward More Effective Implementation of MS and MIS." *Interfaces* 8, no. 3 (May 1978), pp. 57–63.
The emphasis in this article is on management science models and their integration in management information systems. Problems and factors leading to successful implementation are reviewed.

Putnam, Arnold O. *Management Information Systems: Planning, Developing, Managing.* Boston, Mass.: Herman Publishing, 1977, 240 p.
Many insights are given throughout this text regarding factors leading to success and failure of information systems, such as ways to promote receptivity to change. A formal discussion of success factors in MIS design appears in pages 70–84.

Senn, James A. "A Management View of Systems Analysts: Failures and Shortcomings." *Management Information Systems Quarterly* 2, no. 3 (September 1978), pp. 25–32.
Senn discusses relationships between users and analysts which he believes are crucial to MIS success. Assumptions and perceptions that lead to system dissatisfaction are examined and ways to improve satisfaction suggested.

Silver, Gerald A., and Joan B. Silver. *Introduction to Systems Analysis.* Englewood Cliffs, N.J.: Prentice-Hall, chap. 11, pp. 197–207.
This chapter, "Evaluating The System," includes a list of criteria commonly used to measure whether system performance is satisfactory.

Smith, Ronald B. *How to Plan, Design, and Implement a Bad System.* New York: Petrocelli Books, 1981, 157 p.
The author proposes ways to eliminate negative factors affecting system development and suggests approaches and techniques to assist in successful application development.

Zmud, Robert W. *Information Systems in Organizations.* Dallas: Scott, Foresman, 1983, chap. 13, pp. 353–70.
This chapter discussess success and failure factors in information systems. A list of discussion questions, brief cases, and a bibliography are also included.

Glossary in prose

This glossary will introduce information systems terminology in a meaningful context. The definitions are informal, designed to give the reader an intuitive appreciation and understanding of computers and computer resource management. An index at the end of this glossary will enable quick reference to the line on which each term is used or defined. A conventional glossary in alphabetical sequence follows this glossary in prose.

EQUIPMENT

One of the earliest examples of mass processing of data was the use of a **punched card** by Herman Hollerith in 1880 to process census data. The card was redesigned in 1889 and has since been produced in very large quantities by IBM. It is referred to as an **IBM card** or **Hollerith card**. The card has 80 **columns**. Holes are punched in each column according to a code to represent a character of data. The cards are then fed into special equipment, passing one at a time between **photo cells** carrying electric current. Wherever the punched holes appear, the current passes through the card. The characters represented by the holes are then read by machine in the form of electrical impulses and interpreted as the characters the holes represent, be they data or instruction on how to process data. Machines predating the computer (e.g., calculators, sorters, and collators) followed the instructions for simple processing, such as adding, subtracting, or classifying the data. Such processing is known as **data processing**.

Handling cards requires much special equipment. A **keypunch**, used like a typewriter, punches holes in a **data card** to represent data

	1
	2
	3
	4
	5
	6
	7
	8
	9
	10
	11
	12
	13
	14
	15
	16
	17
	18

or processing instructions; a **verifier** identifies errors in keypunching; 19
a **reproducer** generates duplicate cards and has the added capability 20
of moving columns of data to another position on a card; a **sorter** 21
classifies cards according to coded data classifications; and a **collator** 22
merges data cards, combining two similarly sequenced sets of cards 23
into one set. 24

The use of cards for **input** is rapidly being replaced by **voice input** 25
devices, scanners that read typed or printed characters of different 26
sizes and styles (called **fonts**), or **keying devices**, such as **terminals** 27
with keyboards that resemble typewriters. All these devices, called 28
input equipment or **peripherals**, transfer data directly to a computer 29
or to a **storage device** for later processing. Peripherals may also dis- 30
play results or **output**, in which case they are called **output equip-** 31
ment. Examples of output peripherals are **printers**, which print re- 32
sults in single or multiple copies; **decollators**, which separate the 33
carbon sheets from the multiple sheets of output paper, called a mul- 34
tiple **ply** paper; and **bursters**, which break the perforation in the 35
sheets, creating pages from the long continuous sheets of paper. **Plot-** 36
ters, which plot output graphically, **card readers**, and **magnetic ink** 37
character recognition readers (MICR), used in bank accounting to 38
read the coded symbols that appear on bank checks, are also exam- 39
ples of peripherals. 40

Originally, data processing equipment was used primarily for ac- 41
counting purposes. Because the machines used electrical impulses, 42
they became known as **electric accounting machines (EAM)**. An- 43
other term applied to such equipment was **unit record equipment** 44
since each input card processed usually represented one record of 45
data. Because EAM equipment was for the purpose of automating 46
office processing, use of the equipment was called **automatic data** 47
processing (ADP). 48

Much of equipment described in preceding paragraphs is no 49
longer used to perform the functions of data processing because such 50
equipment has been replaced by **computers**, electronic machines ca- 51
pable of complex operations with data at fantastic speeds. The early 52
computers in the 1950s performed arithmetic operations that were 53
measured in **milliseconds** (thousandths of a second). As computers 54
developed, the time for operations was reduced to **microseconds** 55
(millionths of a second), then to **nanoseconds** (billionths of a sec- 56
ond), and will soon be measured in **picoseconds** (a thousandth of a 57
nanosecond). Some computers still use cards for input and output, 58
so supplementary unit record machines may be used as well. Supple- 59
mentary machines are called **offline devices** when they are not under 60
direct control of the **central processing unit (CPU)** of the computer. 61

The CPU has three parts: the **arithmetic and logic unit**, to perform 62
arithmetic calculations (such as add and subtract) and make choices 63

(Yes and No); the **internal memory unit**, to store information tempo-   64
rarily; and the **control unit**, to select the order of operations and co-   65
ordinate the other units.   66

The computer is **electronic** because the processing of data is done   67
by the movement of electrons rather than electrical or mechanical   68
means as in ADP or EAM. Therefore, computer processing of data is   69
called **electronic data processing (EDP)**. In recent years, equipment   70
to process text and words (**word processing or WP**) has been devel-   71
oped to supplement data processing. **Information processing** is the   72
term commonly used when both data and text are processed.   73

One type of electronic computer is a **minicomputer**, also known   74
as the **mini**. It performs simple applications economically, requires   75
no special environment in order to operate (e.g., doesn't need leveled   76
floors and room air conditioners required for large computers), and   77
is small enough to be placed on a desk. When within the budget   78
range of families, a minicomputer may be purchased as a **home com-**   79
puter or a **personal computer** to keep track of household inventories,   80
bank accounts, monthly menus, or other home uses.   81

Microprocessors perform a special task, such as controlling a car   82
carburetor or controlling factory operations, instead of doing general   83
purpose computing. Such machines are extremely small, smaller   84
than the size of a fingertip, and require very little energy to operate.   85
They consist of one or more **semiconductor chips** made of **silicon**   86
with etched circuitry. This chip performs computations like a com-   87
puter. When assembled and related together, the chips form an **inte-**   88
grated circuit (IC). Large-scale integration of circuits may consist of   89
10,000 to 20,000 **transistors** on one or several chips, each transistor   90
performing the function of the earlier **vacuum tube**, a small elec-   91
tronic device capable of processing data coded in **binary values**   92
(values of 0 or 1).   93

Microprocessors can also be built into configurations that have in-   94
put/output capability as well as memory capacity. They then consti-   95
tute a **microcomputer**. Microcomputers are generally designed for   96
specific applications, such as use in microwave ovens or gas station   97
pumps. With the expanded capabilities of microcomputers of today,   98
one tends to speak of minis and microcomputers as if there were   99
little difference between the two.   100

Online equipment are devices that are under direct control of the   101
CPU. Examples are printers that produce output and **terminals** that   102
both receive input and produce output directly from the CPU.   103
Terminals may be **typewriter terminals** or **cathode ray tubes**   104
(CRT). A **CRT terminal** looks much like a television set sitting on top   105
of a typewriter. The terminal may be physically part of the computer   106
(in which case it is called a **console**) or it can be located apart, con-   107
nected to the computer by direct cable or by telephone (in which case   108

the terminal is said to have **remote access)**. **Intelligent terminals** are   109
terminals that can be programmed to perform limited functions, such   110
as storage of data or checking the accuracy of input data.   111

The equipment discussed in this section may be grouped in many   112
combinations or **configurations**. All computer-related equipment is   113
termed **hardware**.   114

SOFTWARE

In contrast to hardware, physical objects that can be touched,   115
there is software written as **programs** stored on an input medium,   116
such as cards, tapes, or disks. A program instructs the computer on   117
the **algorithm** to be used; that is, the specific computer procedure to   118
be followed in order to achieve the desired results and the sequence   119
in which the operations are to be performed. Computational opera-   120
tions, such as adding, subtacting, finding logs and square roots, and   121
rearrangements of data are done quickly and accurately by computer   122
without further manual intervention. Programs can also be written to   123
sort, match, update, and **search** data, functions that are commonly   124
used in business data processing. These are called **utility programs**   125
because they are part of the repertoire of most business-oriented com-   126
puters.   127

Programmers are individuals who write programs instructing the   128
computer what to do. The computer only recognizes electronic   129
pulses so programs must be written in a manner to generate these   130
pulses. **Machine language**, a programming language in which in-   131
structions are written as numbers, is a **low level language** used by   132
many programmers. This language contrasts to **natural languages**,   133
such as English, which are **high level languages**. There is a wide   134
spectrum of programming languages in between. The closer the pro-   135
gramming language is to a natural language, the higher it is in the   136
computer language hierarchy, and the easier it is for programmers to   137
write. Low level languages are more difficult to write but are more   138
efficiently run by the computer.   139

High level programming languages have to be interpreted and   140
translated into machine language to be understood by a computer.   141
This is done by special programs that convert high level language   142
into machine language. These conversion programs are called **com-**   143
pilers, assemblers, translators, and **interpreters**. Other computer   144
programs govern the scheduling of programming **jobs** and automate   145
the relationship of the computer to its peripheral devices. These pro-   146
grams are called **monitors** or **supervisors**. Still other computer pro-   147
grams perform "household" duties, frequently performed operations   148
of a computer, such as label checking and **listing** an information file.   149

Compilers, assemblers, translators, interpreters, monitors, super- 150
visors, and utility programs are collectively referred to as **system** 151
programs and are frequently provided with computer equipment by 152
the manufacturer. These programs are distinct from **application pro-** 153
grams that are typically written by the user firm. **Software** is a col- 154
lective term that includes both system and application programs. 155

System programs constitute the **operating system** of a computer. 156
The operating system plus the hardware configuration may be unique 157
for each computer model. This is why programs run on one computer 158
system cannot always be run on another. Two computer systems that 159
run the same set of computer programs are considered **compatible** 160
with one another. One system can then serve as a **backup** for the 161
other in the event of a breakdown. Another type of backup is dupli- 162
cate data files and programs. Duplicates are needed in case the orig- 163
inals are stolen or either accidentally or maliciously altered or de- 164
stroyed. 165

Many computer programs are written by users or programmers in 166
the user's employ. Others may be purchased from **software houses**. 167
Whereas each computer model may have its specific machine lan- 168
guage, standard programming languages can be used for writing pro- 169
grams for many types of computers. There are tens of high level pro- 170
gramming languages. **COBOL** and **RPG** are most commonly used for 171
information systems and business data processing. Many languages 172
are used in scientific programming though **FORTRAN, Pascal**, and 173
Ada are popular in the United States and **ALGOL** favored by many 174
Europeans. Some languages serve dual purposes, being used for both 175
scientific and business data processing. Examples are **PL/1** and 176
BASIC. Languages like **APL** are **conversational** or **interactive lan-** 177
guages, enabling fast terminal response. Of interest to business man- 178
agement are **simulation languages** like **GPSS** and **SIMSCRIPT** that 179
are designed specially for business problems in planning and control. 180
Some languages are appropriate for nonnumerical processing, such 181
as text processing. **SNOBOL** and **LISP** are examples. Other program- 182
ming languages are used in production, such as **APT**. 183

DATA

As mentioned, programs are sets of instructions for processing 184
data. This data must be organized and managed so that it can be 185
efficiently and effectively processed. This is known as **data manage-** 186
ment or **file management**. Organized data is a **data base**, also called 187
a **data bank**, consisting of a set of **integrated files**. A **file** is a set of 188
records; a **record**, a set of data elements; and a **data element**, a fact 189
or an observation with a value that the user needs to record. Data 190

elements are formed by **characters** of data. A set of characters can be   191
alphabetic (A to Z), **numeric** (0–9), **alphanumeric** or **alphameric** (the 192
license plate AEJ472), special symbols ($ * +), or a combination of   193
all these types.   194

A character must be machine-readable to be understood by the   195
computer. That is, the character must be represented by a set of **bits**   196
(**binary** digits of 0 or 1). A set of electric currents can be made to   197
represent these digits by being off (0) or on (1). Bits are represented   198
by changing these states and bits combined to represent unique char-   199
acters. For example, the number 9 can be represented in binary digits   200
as 1001 (on-off-off-on). Similarly, letters and symbols can be repre-   201
sented by a unique permutation of 0 and 1 bits. In this way, bits can   202
be made to represent the entire **hierarchy** of data from data elements,   203
records, and files, to the entire data base itself.   204

A data element is usually the lowest level of data a manager uses.   205
Each data element is defined in a **data element dictionary (DED)** pre-   206
pared specially in each business according to its data element needs.   207
In large information systems, data elements have to be classified, in-   208
dexed, and organized so as to facilitate access and use. This function   209
is performed by a **data directory**. The data directory and the DED are   210
then used by a set of computer programs to structure, access, and   211
manage the data base. This is known as a **data base management**   212
system. There are many such systems sold by computer manufactur-   213
ers and software companies. These include **TDMS, MARK IV, TOTAL,**   214
ADABAS, IMS, and **SYSTEM 2000**.   215

Data and programs to be processed are stored on a **storage** or   216
memory device. There are many types of such devices. One is called   217
core. It is part of the CPU equipment and is referred to as **internal**   218
storage (internal to the CPU) or as **primary storage.** Such storage   219
may be supplemented by additional storage on an **external memory**   220
device. An example is a **magnetic tape** similar to that used in tape   221
recorders. Tape is especially suitable for recording data that must be   222
processed and retrieved **sequentially**, such as a payroll. Some pro-   223
cessing and retrieval is done in **random** order, allowing any word in   224
the memory to be accessed. The memory device appropriate for such   225
random processing is a **disk**, which is similar to a phonograph rec-   226
ord. On small computers, a smaller and less rigid disk called a **floppy**   227
disk or **floppy** is used. The tape (**magnetic** or **paper tape**) and the   228
disk are referred to as **auxiliary, secondary,** or **external storage.**   229

Data are stored on tapes or disks as **bits** when representing one   230
character, or stored as **bytes**, sets of bits. The size of a byte for many   231
computers is eight bits. Data are also stored as **words** which vary   232
with computer manufacturers between 8 and 64 bits. Large data bases   233
are measured in tons of data, where a **ton** is 40 billion bits of data.   234
Many businesses have tens of tons of data.   235

Some data is kept in a **common data base.** This data is collected   236
and validated only once, then stored to be shared by all authorized   237
users in the organization for many purposes. Such a system is an   238
integrated set of files.   239

Management information systems may be integrated in several   240
ways. **Vertical integration** is sharing of data by all levels of manage- 241
ment even though this may be confined to one function only, such as   242
marketing or production. Other systems are integrated at one level of   243
management but integrated for all functions at that level. Such inte-   244
gration is called **horizontal integration.** There is also integration over 245
time, called **longitudinal integration**. In making sales projections   246
based on the past five years of data, such longitudinal integration is   247
necessary. When an information system has all three types of integra-   248
tion, it is then called a **total system** or a **management information** 249
system (MIS).   250

INFORMATION SYSTEMS

Thus far, computer technology, hardware, software, and data bases   251
have been discussed. If these components are organized as a whole   252
to produce desired information, an **information system** is created. A   253
management information system (MIS) can be used to produce in-   254
formation needed by managers for planning, control, and opera-   255
tions.* However, information systems are not a panacea to all of a   256
manager's information needs for there are many "**wicked problems**"   257
that defy computer solutions. These are ill-defined and ill-structured   258
problems that have nonquantifiable data variables. An example   259
would be personnel problems since human variables are not easily   260
quantified.   261

Information systems are developed in **stages**, each consisting of a   262
set of jobs called **activities.** The first group of activities (first stage) of 263
the development process is a **feasibility study.** During the study, al- 264
ternative approaches to producing information within constraints of   265
the organization are considered. A **constraint** is a factor that places a 266
limit on what is possible.   267

Once an alternative is chosen by management, the next stage in   268
the developmental process is for the manager to define information   269
needs specifically in order for the system to be designed to meet   270

---

*Readers will note that the term MIS has been defined in two ways in this glossary.
There are still other definitions. Many terms used in this book have more than one
definition. This is because computer science is a relatively new field. It will take many
years to develop universal standardization of terms. **The American National Standards
Institute (ANSI)** is one organization presently working on the problem of formulating
standards.

these needs. This stage is one of **analysis** and is referred to as the   271
user specification stage. The **design** starts with the specification of   272
the user's need of **output**; that is, determining what information the   273
system should generate. From the output needs, the **input** (resources   274
put into the system) can be deduced. This includes a determination   275
of equipment, data, computer programs, and procedures needed to   276
produce the output. The **procedures** are sets of instructions and   277
rules governing the human-machine (user-computer) relationship.   278

The designed system is then **implemented.** This includes writing   279
programs to manipulate data in order to generate the desired output.   280
The system is then **tested** with actual performance compared with   281
desired performance. Further **debugging**, locating and correcting er-   282
rors, may be necessary. Once the system performs as expected, it is   283
documented, a process of stating all relevant facts about the system.   284
This documentation includes **decision tables**, which specify the   285
logic as decision rules, and **flowcharts**, which show the logic and the   286
flow of data. The documentation is stored in **manuals** and deposited   287
in a **library** where it is handled and controlled by a **librarian**. The   288
librarian also has jurisdiction over stored programs.   289

The system, when satisfactorily tested and documented, is then   290
converted, the old system **phased out** and the new system made   291
operational.   292

INFORMATION PROCESSING

Computer operations have many **modes** of operation. One is   293
batch processing in which jobs are collected into a **batch** before   294
they are processed. Another is **time sharing** where users take turns   295
being serviced. The very fast processing speeds of modern computers   296
means that users are serviced almost instantly, giving each user the   297
illusion of being the only individual **online**, of having the machine   298
dedicated solely to one's own use. Time-sharing systems are used   299
largely by programmers and users for scientific computations. Some   300
businesses require a **real-time system**. This system searches the data   301
base, updates it, and gives results in time to affect the operating en-   302
vironment. **Remote processing**, processing through an input/output   303
device that is physically distant from the CPU, can be combined with   304
the above mentioned processing modes.   305

Sometimes a firm hires a **facilities management** vendor to operate   306
their computer center instead of assigning responsibility to in-house   307
personnel. Others contract their processing to **service bureaus**. A   308
computer utility is another processing option. Instead of contracting   309
with a client for a specific service, the utility provides service on   310
request, offering continuous service in somewhat the same manner   311
as an electric utility. In order to be able to meet fluctuation of de-   312

mand, a utility needs a **telecommunications network** so that com- 313
puting power can be accessed from a distant **node** if regional facili- 314
ties are overloaded. 315

Information systems require the services of a number of profes- 316
sionals and support personnel. A **system analyst** is a technician who 317
studies processing problems and decides what procedures, methods, 318
or techniques are required for the problem solution using computers. 319
Programmers write and test the instructions that tell the computer 320
what to do. Processing itself is done by **operators**. Large and com- 321
plex data bases require a **data base administrator** to keep files up- 322
dated and to monitor and control data use. Examples of other support 323
personnel are **data entry clerks, security officers, communication** 324
analysts, and **technical writers**. It is management's responsibility to 325
decide what tasks are needed in a given computing facility, to write 326
job descriptions for each position to be used in hiring and evalua- 327
tion of personnel, and to establish **career ladders** so employees can 328
advance within the computer center. 329

During operations, the system is **controlled** for quality of infor- 330
mation. Controls are also designed to protect the system from inten- 331
tional data tampering and theft. However, **security** is not always 332
completely successful. Part of the problem is that design procedures 333
and training for control do not keep up with advances in technology, 334
especially hardware developments and needs for **privacy.** 335

All information systems should be regularly evaluated. This **eval-** 336
uation should be based on both efficiency and effectiveness. **Effi-** 337
ciency refers to the relationship between input and output, while 338
effectiveness refers to the successful achievement of critical factors 339
of performance set by the user. Examples of critical factors are **ac-** 340
curacy, a specified percentage of freedom from error; **timeliness**, the 341
availability of information when needed; and **completeness**, the 342
availability of all relevant data. 343

Auditing is yet another level of control. An **internal auditor**, an 344
employee of the firm, or an **external auditor**, hired from outside the 345
organization, is concerned with the same processing controls that 346
may be scrutinized in performance evaluation conducted by the com- 347
puter center itself. However, the auditor's responsibility extends one 348
step further, to control of controls: the review of the effectiveness of 349
control measures and the establishment of new controls when exist- 350
ing controls prove inadequate. 351

THE COMPUTER ENVIRONMENT

Within the computer industry, IBM dominates **mainframe** manu- 352
facture. However, Gene **Amdahl** has demonstrated that the main- 353
frame market can still be breached with his successful introduction 354

of a mainframe that is **plug-compatible** with software and peripher-   355
als developed for IBM computers. The Japanese have a strong foot-   356
hold in the American market for **semiconductors**, an essential com-   357
ponent of minis, micros, word processors, and mainframes. Other   358
segments of the market are **peripherals, data communications, soft-**   359
ware, maintenance, and the **service sector**, which includes **educa-** 360
tion and **training**.   361

With advances in technology, applications have expanded. Many   362
managers today use **decision support systems (DSS)** to assist in   363
planning and control. Such systems have altered methods of decision   364
making. Computers have also changed the job of corporate managers.   365
They must be familiar with computer terminology and understand   366
how information systems are developed and implemented to effec-   367
tively use computers in their work, and they must know how to man-   368
age computing resources. Many managers employ **information spe-**   369
cialists to help them effectively utilize computing resources at their   370
disposal.   371

Managers must also be knowledgeable about the law in relation to   372
computing. That is, they must know how **antitrust statutes, patents,** 373
copyrights, trade secrets, and **tort** affect their computerized opera- 374
tions. Managers should also be aware of **human factors** or **ergon-** 375
omics that are unique to computer environments. These two terms   376
have similar meanings, though ergonomics emphasizes the physio-   377
logical aspects of computing, whereas human factors focuses on the   378
psychological aspects of human-machine relationships. The success   379
of an information system may well depend on the manager's sensitiv-   380
ity to employee concerns and the establishment of a climate receptive   381
to **change**, for computerization inevitably alters organizational struc-   382
ture and interpersonal relationships within a firm.   383

The degree of **computer literacy** within a firm will determine to   384
some degree the ability of the firm to absorb computer technology   385
and the firm's receptivity to computerization. The efficiency and ef-   386
fectiveness of operations will depend on management's knowledge   387
and experience regarding computer resources and their management.   388
It is hoped that this book will provide readers with background that   389
they need to be effective managers in a computer environment.   390

APPENDIX B

Index to glossary in prose

APPENDIX C

Glossary

This glossary includes operational definitions of terms that are needed for the management of computing resources. Since precise technical definitions too often obscure meaning, the definitions in this list have been written in simple terms in order to facilitate understanding. Readers wishing a complete technical glossary of computer terms should consult dictionaries such as the *American Standard Vocabulary of Information Processing* published by the American National Standards Institute. Dictionaries of computer terms can be found in most libraries.

Access: the manner in which files or data sets are referred to by the computer. See *direct access, random access, remote access,* and *serial access*.

Access time: the period of time between a request for information and the availability of that data.

Address: name given to a specific memory location, either within the computer (memory address) or on the storage media (disk address), where information is stored.

Algorithm: a step-by-step process for the solution of a problem in a finite number of steps. Usually developed in an outline or by a tool of analysis before coding begins.

Alphanumeric: alphabetic, numeric, and punctuation characters (but not special symbols like $).

American National Standards Institute (ANSI): an organization sponsored by the Business Equipment Manufacturers Association (BEMA) for the purpose of establishing voluntary industry standards.

Analog computer: (1) a computer in which analog representation of data is mainly used; (2) a computer that operates on *analog data* by performing physical processes on these data. Contrast with *digital computer*.

Analog data: data represented in a continuous form, as contrasted with *digital data* represented in a discrete (discontinuous) form. Analog data are usually represented by means of physical variables, such as voltage, resistance, and rotation.

Analog signal: a continuous electrical signal representing a condition (such as temperature or the position of game control paddles). Unlike a *digital signal,* which is discrete, an analog signal can be any frequency or strength.

Analyst: see *system analyst.*

Application program: a program written for or by a user that applies to the user's own work.

Application software: software programs that perform a specific user-oriented task, such as line balancing or payroll. Application software can be either purchased as a package or custom designed by a programmer.

Architecture: the structure of a system. Computer architecture often refers specifically to the CPU.

Arithmetic and logic unit (ALU): the element in a computer which can perform the basic data manipulations (arithmetic, logic, and control functions) in the central processor.

Artificial intelligence (AI): the ability of a computer to imitate certain human actions or skills, such as problem solving, decision making, perception, and learning.

Assembler: a computer program that converts (or translates) assembly language programs into a form (machine language) that the computer can understand. The assembler translates mnemonic instruction codes into binary numbers, replaces names with their binary equivalents, and assigns memory locations to data and instructions.

Assembly language: a programming language in which the programmer can use mnemonic instruction codes, labels, and names to refer directly to their binary equivalents. The assembler is a low level language since each assembly language instruction translates directly into a specific machine language instruction.

Attribute: a characteristic. For example, attributes of data include record length, record format, data set name, associated device type and volume identification, use, and creation data.

Audit trail: the procedure of tracing the steps in processing data to ensure that results are within either expected or standardized limits.

Auditing around the computer: checking output for a given input.

Auditing through the computer: checking both input and computer processing. May use test data, auditor-prepared programs, auditor-software packages, or audit programming languages.

Auditor: person authorized to make a formal periodic examination and check of accounts or financial records to verify their correctness. A computer auditor may also be assigned to verify the correctness of computer information processing to ensure that processing conforms to the firm's goals, policies, and procedures (such as policies with regard to security and privacy.)

Authentication: verifying the user's right to access a requested file or portion of the data base.

Authorization: verifying the type of access permitted such as read, write, update, or no access.

Automatic data processing (ADP):   (1) data processing largely performed by automatic means; (2) by extension, the discipline which deals with methods and techniques related to data processing performed by automatic means; (3) pertaining to data processing equipment, such as electrical accounting machines and electronic data processing equipment.

Auxiliary storage: (1) data storage other than main storage. For example, storage on magnetic tape or direct access devices. Synonymous with *external storage and secondary storage*; (2) a storage that supplements another storage. Contrast with *main storage*.

Backup: (1) copying of one or more files onto a storage medium for safekeeping should the original get damaged or lost; (2) redundant equipment or procedures used in the event of failure of a component or storage medium.

Bandwidth: the difference between the lower and upper limits of the wave frequencies that can be transmitted over a communications channel. A high bandwidth means more data can be transferred in a given time interval.

Bar code recognition: a form of machine-readable encodation formed by vertical bars and spaces. A scanner measures the presence or absence of a reflection over time to determine bit patterns of characters. See *optical character recognition*.

BASIC (Beginner's All-purpose Symbolic Instruction Code):   a relatively easy-to-use programming language that is available in many small computer systems.

Batch processing: a traditional method of data processing in which transactions are collected and prepared for processing as a single unit.

Baud: a measurement of communication speeds between devices. Generally means bits transferred per second. Divide the number by 10 to translate to characters per second.

Benchmark: a point of reference from which measurements can be made.

Binary: the basis for calculations in all computers. This two-digit number system consists of digits 0 and 1 which are represented in the computer as the presence or absence of small electrical pulses.

Bit: the contraction of "binary digit," the smallest unit of information that the computer recognizes. A bit is equivalent to the presence or absence of an electrical pulse (0 or 1). Bits are usually grouped in *nibbles* (4), *bytes* (8), or larger units.

Boolean: (1) pertaining to the processes used in the algebra formulated by George Boole; (2) pertaining to the operations of formal logic.

Broadband: a communication channel having a bandwidth greater than a voice grade. Allows higher speed data transmission.

Buffer: a storage area in memory or in a peripheral which is used for temporary storage of data awaiting further processing.

Bug: a mistake in a program or in an electrical circuit. Eliminating the mistakes is known as *debugging*.

Byte: a group of bits (usually 8). A byte can be used to represent one character (number or letter) of information, all or part of binary numbers, and machine language instructions.

Canned program: a software package developed and made available (sold by software houses or provided free by vendors) to multiple users who have similar needs and problems.

Card reader: a device that senses and translates into machine code the holes in punched cards.

Cassette tape storage: storage of data on a serial device that records magnetically on a removable tape cassette.

Cathode ray tube (CRT): an electronic vacuum tube, such as a television picture tube, that can be used to display graphic images, text, or numerical data on visual display terminals.

Central processing unit (CPU): the part of the computer that controls the execution and interpretation of the machine language processing instructions.

Channel: (1) a path for electrical data transmission between two or more stations; (2) a hardware device that connects the central processing unit and main storage with the I/O control units; (3) synonymous with circuit, line, link, path, facility. See also *voice-grade channel*.

Character: any letter, number, symbol, or punctuation mark.

Check: a process for determining accuracy.

Check digit: a digit added to a set of digits that is used for the purpose of checking the accuracy of input data.

Checkpoint: (1) a place in a routine where a check, or a recording of data for restart purposes, is performed; (2) a point at which information about the status of a job and the system can be recorded so that the job step can be later restarted.

Chip: a thin semiconductor wafer on which electronic components are deposited in the form of integrated circuits.

Circuit: a means of communication between two or more points. Normally, the telephone linkage is a two-wire or four-wire circuit.

COBOL: an acronym for *C*ommon *B*usiness-*O*riented *L*anguage. A high level programming language designed for business data processing on large computers.

Code: (1) in data processing, the representation of data or a computer program in symbolic form according to a set of rules; (2) in telecommunications, a system of rules and conventions according to which the signals representing data can be formed, transmitted, received, and processed; (3) to write a routine.

Collate: to combine items from two or more ordered sets into one set having a specified order not necessarily the same as any of the original sets. Contrast with *merge*.

Command: an order to the computer in the form of words and numbers typed on a keyboard, words spoken into a microphone, positions of a game paddle or joystick, etc.

Common data base: pooled data integrated for common use as a shared resource.

Common carrier: a government-regulated private company that furnishes the general public with telecommunications service facilities. For example, a telephone or telegraph company.

Common law: derives from custom and the decisions and opinions of courts.

Communication: transmission of intelligence between points of origin and reception without alteration of sequence or structure of the information content.

Communication line: any medium, such as a wire or telephone circuit, that connects a remote station with a computer.

Communication link: the physical means of connecting one location to another for the purpose of transmitting and receiving data.

Compatibility: (1) the ability of an instruction, program, or component to be used on more than one computer; (2) the ability of computers to work with other computers that are not necessarily similar in design or capabilities.

Compile: to prepare a machine language program from a computer program written in another programming language by making use of the overall logic structure of the program, or generating more than one machine instruction for each symbolic statement, or both.

Compiler: a translation program which converts high level instructions into a set of binary instructions (object code) for execution. Each high level language requires a compiler or an interpreter. A compiler translates the complete program which is then executed. Every change in the program requires a complete recompilation. Contrast with *interpreter*.

Computer: A system designed for the manipulation of information, incorporating a central processing unit (CPU), memory, input/output (I/O) facilities, power supply and cabinet.

Computer code: a machine code for a specific computer.

Computer instruction: a machine instruction for a specific computer.

Computer network: a computer system consisting of two or more interconnected computing units.

Computer utility: a service facility that provides computational capability that is generally accessed by means of data communication.

Computer-assisted instruction (CAI): the direct use of a computer for the facilitation and certification of learning—that is, using the computer to make learning easier and more likely to occur (facilitation), as well as using the computer to create a record proving that learning has occurred (certification).

Computing system: a central processing unit, with main storage, input/output channels, control units, direct access storage devices, and input/output devices connected to it.

Concentrator: a communications device that provides communications capability between many low-speed channels. Usually different speeds, codes, and protocols can be accommodated on the low-speed side. The concentrator may have the ability to be polled by a computer and may in turn poll terminals.

Configuration: the group of devices that make up a computer or data processing system.

Console: that part of a computer used for communication between the operator or maintenance engineer and the computer.

Constraint: a restriction.

Control program: a program that is designed to schedule and supervise the performance of data processing work by a computing system.

Control unit: (1) the part of the central processing unit that directs the sequence of operations, interprets coded instructions, and sends the proper signals instructing other computer circuits to carry out the instructions; (2) a device that controls the reading, writing, or display of data at one or more input/output devices.

Controller: a device used to manage a peripheral device such as a CRT, printer, or disk drive.

Conversational: pertaining to a program or a system that carries on a dialog with a terminal user, alternately accepting input and then responding to the input quickly enough for the user to maintain his train of thought. See also *interactive*.

Conversion: (1) the process of changing from one method of data processing to another or from one data processing system to another; (2) the process of changing from one form of representation to another; e.g., to change from decimal representation to binary representation.

Core storage: a form of high-speed storage using magnetic cores.

CRT display device: a display device on which images are produced on a cathode ray tube.

Cryptography: the art of writing or deciphering messages in code.

Cursor: an electronically generated symbol that appears on the display screen to tell the operator where the next character will appear.

Custom software: tailor-made computer programs prepared for a specific purpose. Contrast with *packaged software*, in which the programs are written for general purposes.

Cycle: (1) an interval of space or time in which one set of events or phenomena is completed; (2) any set of operations that is repeated regularly in the same sequence. The operations may be subject to variations on each repetition.

Data: facts, numbers, letters, and symbols that become usable information when processed.

Data acquisition: the process of identifying, isolating, and gathering source data to be centrally processed in a usable form.

Data bank: a comprehensive collection of libraries of data. For example, one part of an invoice may form an *item*, a complete invoice may form a *record*, a complete set of such records may form a *file*, the collection of inventory control files may form a *library*, and the libraries used by an organization are known as its *data bank*.

Data base: a collection of interrelated data *files* or *libraries* organized for ease of access, update, and retrieval.

Data base administrator (DBA): person delegated authority to coordinate, monitor, and control the data base and related resources, including the *DED* and *DD* system.

Data base management system (DBMS): a generalized set of computer programs which control the creation, maintenance, and utilization of the data bases and data files of an organization.

Data collection: (1) a telecommunications application in which data from several locations is accumulated at one location (in a queue or on a file) before processing; (2) accumulation of data in a form usable by computer.

Data definition language (DDL): a computer program used to describe data at a sufficiently high level in order to make use of a common programming language to access data in a data base management system.

Data directory (DD): lists or tables that facilitate quick reference to pertinent information regarding an information system using a DED.

Data element: a fact or observation collected and recorded as data.

Data element dictionary (DED): defines data elements by use of descriptors which describe characteristics, attributes, and other related information concerning the data element.

Data layout sheet: used in planning the physical space of data (field width) in data records.

Data management: a major function of operating systems that involves organizing, cataloging, locating, storing, retrieving, and maintaining data.

Data manager: software which describes the logical and physical organization of the data base and enables manipulation of the base by programmers.

Data manipulation language (DML): a computer program for accessing and modifying the data base.

Data network: telecommunications network designed specifically for data transmission.

Data organization: the arrangement of information in a data set. For example, sequential organization or partitioned organization.

Data processing (DP): the manipulation of data by following a sequence of instructions to achieve a desired result.

Data processing system: a network of machine components capable of accepting information, processing it according to a plan, and producing the desired results.

Data security: protection of computerized information by various means, including cryptography, locks, identification cards and badges, restricted access to the computer, passwords, physical and electronic backup copies of the data, and so on.

Data structure: the manner in which data are represented and stored in computer system or program.

Data transmission: the sending of data from one part of a system to another part.

Debug: to find and eliminate mistakes or problems with software or hardware and eliminate them.

Decision support systems (DSS): Computerized applications used by management for decision making. These applications often use mathematical and statistical models, such as linear programming, CPM or PERT models included in operations research and management science.

Decision table: a table of all conditions that are to be considered in the description of a problem, together with the actions to be taken. Decision tables are sometimes used in place of flowcharts for problem description and documentation.

Decollate: to separate the plies of a multipart form or paper stock.

DED/DD committee: committee that takes responsibility for the content and control of data in an information system.

Dedicated: if a computer or piece of hardware is assigned exclusively to one task, it is said to be a dedicated system.

Derived data: data obtained by manipulating or processing other data, especially raw data. For example, age may be derived from date of birth and current date.

Descriptor: a word or phrase used to identify, categorize, or index information or data.

Device: in computers, a piece of hardware that performs a specific function. Input devices (e.g., keyboard) are used to get data into the central processing unit. Output devices (e.g., printer or display monitor) are used to take data out of a computer in some usable form. Input/output devices (e.g., terminal or disk drive) are able to perform both input and output of data.

Digital: the representation of data using a discrete medium, such as sticks, markers, bits, or anything that is counted to determine its value.

Digital computer: a computer that operates on digital data by performing arithmetic and logical operations on the data. Contrast with *analog computer*.

Digital to analog converter: device that transforms a computer's digital electrical pulses into a continuous analog signal in order to relay information to or power some nondigital device outside of the computer.

Direct access: (1) retrieval or storage of data by a reference to its location on a volume, rather than relative to the previously retrieved or stored data; (2) pertaining to the process of obtaining data from, or placing data into, storage where the time required for such access is independent of the location of the data most recently obtained or placed in storage; (3) pertaining to a storage device, such as magnetic disk or drum, in which the access time is effectively independent of the location of the data. Synonymous with *random access*. Contrast with *serial access*.

Direct access storage device: a device in which the access time is effectively independent of the location of the data.

Disk: a circular plate with magnetic material on both sides. This plate rotates for the storage and retrieval of data by one or more "heads" which transfer the information to and from the computer. The computer-readable information may be placed on a floppy or a rigid (hard) disk, and may have information on one or both sides. Also known as *diskette* or *disc*.

Disk storage: storage on direct access devices that record data magnetically on rotating disks.

Display unit: a terminal device that presents data visually, usually be means of a cathode ray tube.

Distributed data base: a data base needed for local processing kept by the processing center at a distributed node.

Distributed data processing (DDP): the arrangement of computers within an organization in which the organization's computer complex has many separate computing facilities all working in a cooperative manner, rather than the conventional single computer at a single location. Frequently an organization's central files are stored at the central computing facility, with the geographically dispersed smaller computers calling on the central files when they need them.

Distributed network: a network in which all node pairs are connected, either directly or through redundant paths through intermediate nodes.

Divestiture: the act of becoming disencumbered or rid of something.

Documentation: (1) the creating, collecting, organizing, storing, citing, and disseminating of documents or the information recorded in documents; (2) a collection of documents or information on a given phase of development or all development documentation of an information system.

Down time: the period during which a computer is not operating.

Dumb terminal: a terminal that lacks computing and storage capabilities of its own.

Dummy: pertaining to the characteristic of having the appearance of a specified thing but not having the capacity to function as such. For example, a dummy character, dummy plug, or a dummy activity.

Dump: to copy or print out certain contents in memory or to transfer information from memory to an external storage device.

Duplex: a method of operating a communications channel between two devices. *Full duplex* allows both units to send and receive simultaneously. *Half duplex* allows only one unit to send information at one time.

Eavesdropping: unauthorized listening in a telecommunications system.

Economic feasibility: a check to see whether expected benefits equal or exceed expected costs.

Edit: to modify the form or format of data. For example, to insert or delete characters such as page numbers or decimal points.

Effectiveness: system readiness and design adequacy. Effectiveness is expressed as the probability that the system can successfully meet an operational demand within a given time when operated under specified conditions.

Efficiency: the ratio of useful work performed to the total energy expended. A system is efficient if it fulfills its purpose without waste of resources.

Electronic data processing (EDP): processing of data largely performed by electronic devices.

Encrypt: to encipher or encode.

Ergonomics: the science of human engineering which combines the study of human body mechanics and physical limitations with industrial psychology.

External storage: same as *auxiliary storage.*

Facilities management (FM): the use of an independent service organization to operate and manage a data processing installation.

Fail-safe: ability to continue operations in spite of breakdown because backup processing exists.

Fail-soft: ability to continue operations in spite of breakdown but with a degraded level of operations.

Feasibility study: an analysis to determine whether or not desired objectives of a proposed (information) system can be achieved within specific constraints.

Feedback: the return of part of the output of a machine, process, or system to the computer as input for another phase, especially for self-correcting or control purposes.

Field: in a record, a specified area used for a particular category of data.

File: a logical collection of data, designated by name, and considered as a unit by a user. A file consists of related *records.* For example, a payroll file (one record for each employee showing rate of pay, deductions, etc.) or an inventory file (one record for each inventory item showing the cost, selling price, number in stock, etc.).

File layout: the arrangement and structure of data in a file, including the sequence and size of its components.

File maintenance: updating the file to reflect changes in information. Data might be added, altered, or deleted. File maintenance also refers to reorganizing files, deleting records that are no longer in use, etc.

Financial feasibility: a check to see whether funds are available to meet expected costs.

Floppy disk: a record of data on a flexible disk.

Flowchart: a graphical representation of a procedure or computer program.

Font: a family or assortment of characters of a given size and style. For example, large print for preparing transparencies, italicized print for emphasis, etc.

Format: a specific arrangement of data.

FORTRAN: *FOR*mula *TRAN*slating system. A language primarily used to express arithmetic formulas in computer programs.

Front-end processor: processing equipment in a telecommunications environment that can relieve the CPU of certain processing tasks.

Full duplex: See *duplex.*

General purpose computer: a computer that is designed to handle a wide variety of problems.

Half duplex: see *duplex.*

Handshaking: the electronic process when communicating units query one another to ensure each is ready for transmission and information will not be lost.

Hard copy: information generated by a computer and normally printed on paper.

Hardware: the electronic circuits, memory, and input/output components of a computer system. Components made of steel or metal that one can see and touch. Contrast with *software*.

Hash total: a summation for checking purposes of one or more corresponding fields of a file that may be in different units.

Header label: a file or data set label that precedes the data records on a unit of recording media.

Heuristic: pertaining to exploratory methods of problem solving in which solutions are discovered by evaluation of the progress made toward the final result. Contrast with *algorithm*.

Hierarchical computer network: a computer network in which processing and control functions are performed at several levels by computers specially suited for the functions performed; e.g., in factory or laboratory automation.

Hierarchy of data: a data structure consisting of sets and subsets such that every subset of a set is of lower rank than the data of the set.

High level language: a programming language in which the statements represent procedures rather than single machine instructions. FORTRAN, COBOL, and BASIC are three common high level languages. A high level language requires a compiler or interpreter.

Horizontal integration: the integration of functional information subsystems (e.g., production, marketing, and finance) at one level of an organization (e.g., operations, control, or planning).

Host computer: a computer and associated software which, although run as a separate entity, can be accessed via a network.

Housekeeping: in a program, the taking care of details and repetitive functions.

Human factors: physiological, psychological, and training factors to be considered in the design of hardware and software and the development of procedures to ensure that humans can interface with machines efficiently and effectively.

Index: (1) an ordered reference list of the contents of a file or document, together with keys or reference notations for identification or location of those contents; (2) to prepare a list as in (1); (3) a table used to locate the records of an indexed sequential data set.

Information: data that is processed and transformed into a meaningful and useful form.

Information retrieval system: a computing system application designed to recover specific information from a mass of data.

In-house: a system for use only within a particular company or organization, where the computing is independent of any external service.

Input: (1) the data that is entered into programs; (2) the act of entering data into a computer; (3) data used by programs and subroutines to produce output.

Input device: any machine that allows entry of commands or information into the computer. An input device could be a keyboard, tape drive, disk drive, microphone, light pen, digitizer, or electronic sensor.

Input/output (I/O): that part or procedure of a computer system that handles communications with external devices.

Inquiry: a request for information from storage. For example, a request for the number of available items or a machine statement to initiate a search of library documents.

Installation: process of installing and testing either hardware or software or both until they are accepted.

Integrated circuit (IC): complete module of components manufactured as single, solid units made by either a film deposition or a diffusion process. Used as logic circuitry or for storage of information. Integrated circuits are contrasted to discrete components, such as transistors, diodes, capacitors, and resistors which can be assembled into circuits.

Intelligent terminal: a terminal that is programmable and can process its messages. For example, checking validity of input data.

Interactive: commonly used to describe a software program that provides give and take between the operator and the machine. The program may ask a question to elicit a response from the operator or present a series of choices from which the operator can select. Also referred to as *conversational mode.*

Interface: the juncture at which two computer components (hardware and/ or software) meet and interact with each other. Also applies to human-machine interaction.

Interpreter: a translation program used to execute statements expressed in a high level language. An interpreter translates each such statement and executes it immediately. Instructions can be freely added or modified in the user program, and execution may be resumed without delay. Compare with *compiler.*

Inter-record gap: an area on a data medium used to indicate the end of a bloc or record.

Iterate: to repeatedly execute a loop or series of steps. For example, a loop in a routine.

Job: a specified group of tasks prescribed as a unit of work for a computer. By extension, a job usually includes all necessary computer programs, linkages, files, and instructions to the operating system.

Joystick: an input device consisting of a normally vertical stick which can be tilted in any direction to indicate direction of movement.

K: computer shorthand for the quantity 1,024 which is 2^{10}. The term is usually used to measure computer storage capacity. It is approximated as 1,000.

Key: a field of data in a record which is used for accessing the record.

Key data element: data element used to link files.

Keyboard: the panel of keys which is connected to a computer and used to enter data. It looks similar to the keys of a typewriter.

Keypunch: a keyboard actuated device that punches holes in a card to represent data.

Language: see *programming language.*

Large scale integration (LSI): the combining of about 1,000 to 10,000 circuits on a single chip. Typical examples of LSI circuits are memory chips, microprocessors, calculator chips, and watch chips.

Lease: a contract by which one party gives another the use of hardware for a specified time for a payment.

Leased line: a line reserved for sole use of a single leasing customer.

Librarian: person in charge of data, programs, and documentation in the computer library.

Light pen: an input device for a CRT. It records the emission of light at the point of contact with the screen.

Linkage: in programming, coding that connects two separately coded routines.

Listing: a printout, usually prepared by a language translator, that lists the source of language statements and contents of a program. A listing of a file is a printout of the contents of the file.

Location: a physical place in the computer's memory, reached by an address, where an item of information is stored.

Logging: recording of data about events that occur in time sequence.

Logical file: a collection of one or more logical records.

Logical record: (1) a collection of items independent of their physical environment. Portions of the same logical record may be located in different physical records; (2) a record from the standpoint of its content, function, and use rather than its physical attributes; that is, one that is defined in terms of the information it contains.

Low level language: a language which is easily understood by the computer. In a low level language, programs are hard to write (by programmers) but quickly executed by machine. Examples are machine or assembler language.

Machine language: set of codes representing the instructions which can be directly executed by a computer processor.

Machine-independent: pertaining to procedures or programs created without regard for the actual devices that will be used to process them.

Magnetic ink: an ink that contains particles of a magnetic substance whose presence can be detected by magnetic sensors.

Magnetic ink character recognition (MICR): the machine recognition of characters printed with magnetic ink. Contrast with *optical character recognition.*

Magnetic tape: a tape with a magnetic surface on which data can be stored by selective polarization of portions of the surface.

Main memory: the internal memory of the computer contained in its circuitry, as opposed to peripheral memory (tapes, disks).

Main storage: (1) the general purpose storage of a computer. Contrast with *auxiliary storage;* (2) all program-addressable storage from which instructions may be executed and from which data can be loaded directly into registers.

Mainframe: the main part of the computer, generally referring to the CPU.

Maintenance: any activity intended to eliminate faults or to keep hardware or programs in satisfactory working condition, including tests, measurements, replacements, adjustments, and repairs.

Malfunction: the effect of a fault or unexpected functioning.

Management information system (MIS): a computerized information system that processes data to produce information to aid in the performance of management functions.

Mark-sense: to mark a position with an electrically conductive pencil for later conversion to machine-readable form.

Masquerading: pretending to be a legitimate user to access a system.

Master file: a file that is either relatively permanent or that is treated as an authority in a particular job.

Master schedule: used to schedule batch processing.

Match: to check for identity between two or more items of data.

Matrix: a commonly used method of storing and manipulating data. A matrix format consists of rows and columns of information.

Matrix organization: borrows staff from functional divisions—staff that is responsible to the project manager for the life of a project.

Maximum separation: principle that the generation of information must be separate from its flow.

Medium: the material, or configuration thereof, on which data are recorded. For example, paper tape, cards, magnetic tape.

Memory: the section of the computer where instructions and data are stored. Each item in memory has a unique address that the central processing unit can use to retrieve information.

Menu: a list of alternative actions displayed on the terminal for selection by the user.

Merge: a computerized process whereby two or more files are brought together by a common attribute.

Message switching: a telecommunications application in which a message received by a central system from one terminal is sent to one or more other terminals.

Metrics: measures that are quantified numerically and claim useful accuracy and reliability that are used in performance evaluation.

Microcomputer: a small but complete microprocessor-based computer system, including CPU, memory, input/output (I/O) interfaces, and power supply.

Microfiche: a sheet of microfilm on which it is possible to record a number of pages of microcopy.

Microfilm: film on which documents are photographed in a reduced size.

Microprocessor: an integrated circuitry implementation of a complete processor (arithmetic logic unit, internal storage, and control unit) on a single chip.

Millisecond: one thousandth of a second.

Mini-company approach: use of a representative set of data to represent a company when auditing. Allows audit independent of live data stream.

Minicomputer: a small (for example, desk-top size) electronic, digital, stored-program, general purpose computer.

Mnemonic: a short, easy-to-remember name or abbreviation. Many commands in programming languages are mnemonics.

Mnemonic symbol: a symbol chosen to assist the human memory. For example, an abbreviation such as mpy for multiply.

Mode: a method of operation. For example, the binary mode or the interpretive mode.

Model: a computer reproduction or simulation of a real or imaginary person, process, place, or thing. Models can be simple or complex; artistic, educational, or entertaining; serious, part of a game, or a mathematical representation.

Modem (modulator-demodulator): a device that transforms a computer's electrical pulses into audible tones for transmission over the phone line to another computer. A modem also receives incoming tones and transforms them into electrical signals that can be processed and stored by the computer.

Modify: to alter a part of an instruction or routine.

Module: (1) a program unit that is discrete and identifiable with respect to compiling, combining with other units, and loading. For example, the input to, or output from, an assembler, compiler, linkage editor, or executive routine; (2) a packaged functional hardware unit designed for use with other components.

Monitor: (1) a microcomputer program that directs operations of the hardware; (2) may also refer to a video display.

Multiplexer: a hardware device that allows handling of multiple signals over a single channel.

Nanosecond: a billionth of a second. Most computers have a cycle time of hundreds of nanoseconds. High-speed computers have a cycle time of around 50 nanoseconds.

Natural language: a spoken, human language such as English, Spanish, Arabic, or Chinese. Compare to *programming language*.

Network: an interconnection of computer systems, terminals, and communications facilities.

Node: (1) an end point of any branch of a network or a junction common to two or more branches of a network; (2) any station, terminal, terminal installation, communications computer, or communications computer installation in a computer network.

Object program (object code):   the output from an assembler or compiler.

Offline: used to describe equipment which is neither connected to, or under the control of, the central processing unit.

Offloading: the transference of processing from one system to another.

Online: directly connected to the computer and in operational condition.

Online processing: processing of input data in random order without preliminary sorting or batching. Contrast with *batch processing.*

Online system: in teleprocessing, a system in which the input data enters the computer directly from the point of origin or in which output data is transmitted directly to where it is used.

Operand: (1) that which is operated upon. An operand is usually identified by an address part of an instruction; (2) information entered with a command name to define the data on which a command processor operates and to control the execution of the command processor.

Operating system: a collection of programs for operating the computer. Operating systems perform housekeeping tasks, such as input/output between the computer and peripherals and accepting and interpreting information from the keyboard.

Operator's manual: directions for running programs and operating equipment.

Optical character recognition (OCR):   the machine identification of printed characters through use of light-sensitive devices. Contrast with *magnetic ink character recognition.*

Optical reader: a device that reads handwritten or machine-printed symbols into a computing system.

Optical scanner: (1) a device that scans optically and usually generates an analog or digital signal; (2) a device that optically scans printed or written data and generates their digital representations.

Original equipment manufacturer (OEM):   a term commonly used to refer to a computer sales organization that has an arrangement to package and sell a manufacturer's product.

Output: (1) any processed information coming out of a computer via any medium (print, CRT, etc.); (2) the act of transferring information to these media.

Output device: a machine that transfers programs or information from the computer to some other medium. Examples of output devices include tape, disk, and bubble memory drives; computer printers, typewriters, and plotters; the computer picture screen (video display); robots; and sound synthesis devices that enable the computer to talk and/or play music.

Packaged software: a program designed to be marketed for general use that may need to be adapted to particular installation.

Packet switching: the transmission of data by means of addressed packets whereby a transmission channel is occupied for the duration of transmission of the packet only. The channel is then available for use by packets being transferred between different data terminal equipment. Note: the data may be formatted into a packet or divided and then formatted into a number of packets for transmission and multiplexing purposes.

Packet switching network: a network designed to carry data in the form of packets. The packet and its format is internal to that network. The external interfaces may handle data in different formats, and conversion is done by an interface computer.

Paper tape: continuous strips of paper on which data is stored by way of punched holes.

Parallel conversion: operating a new system in a test mode before the old system is fully phased out.

Parity: a 1-bit code that makes the total number of bits in the word, including the parity bit, odd (odd parity) or even (even parity). Used for error detection during data transmission.

Password: a secret identification code keyed by the user and checked by the system before permitting access. Each user or group of users has a unique password.

Peripheral: any unit of equipment distinct from the central processing unit, which may provide the system with outside communication.

Peripheral-bound: a system which backlogs because of the slowness of peripheral equipment.

Physical record: a record from the standpoint of the manner or form in which it is stored, retrieved, and moved; that is, one that is defined in terms of physical qualities. A physical record may contain all or part of one or more logical records.

Piggy-backing: interception and switching of messages.

Plotter: a mechanical device for drawing lines under computer control.

Plug-compatible: the ability to interface a peripheral or CPU produced by one manufacturer with hardware or software produced by another.

Polling: a technique by which each of the terminals sharing a communications line is periodically interrogated to determine whether it requires servicing.

Port: a channel of communication between the central processing unit and a peripheral.

Portability: properties of software which permit its use in another computer environment.

Price differentiation: pricing a product to help favored customers or damage specific competitors: a strategy to enter or/and capture a desired market share.

Price tying: combining two or more products or services (hardware, software, education, documentation, and consulting) in a single price package.

Primitive data: synonymous with raw data.

Printer: a computer output device that produces computer output on paper.

Priority: a rank assigned to a task that determines its precedence in receiving system resources.

Private line service: a communication service used exclusively by one particular customer. Also, the whole process of providing private line circuits.

Process chart: a document used to collect information on each step of a process. Used in systems development to analyze procedures to be computerized.

Processor: in hardware, a data processor.

Program: a sequence of instructions directing a computer to perform a particular function; a statement of an algorithm in a programming language.

Program error: any mistakes or problems in a computer program that keep the computer from performing the proper computations.

Program library: a collection of debugged and documented programs.

Programmer: person who writes programs.

Programmer's manual: descriptions of programs.

Programming language: a set of symbols and rules that can be used to specify an algorithm in a computer-executable form.

Project management: in information system development, the planning, coordination, and control of activities during the development from the feasibility study through conversion.

Project organization: the creation of a separate organizational unit for the sole purpose of completing a project.

Protocol: the rules governing how two pieces of equipment communicate with one another.

Random access: an access method whereby each record of a file or location in memory can be accessed directly by its address.

Raw data: data that has not been processed.

Read: to read is to accept data from a disk, card, etc. for storage and/or processing.

Reading between the lines: engaging a system illicitly when a user is connected to the computer but the computer is idle.

Real time: in synchronization with the actual occurrence of events.

Record: a collection of data items stored on a disk or other medium which may be recalled as a unit. Records may be fixed or variable in length. One or more records usually make up a data *file*.

Recovery: to reestablish operations following breakdown of CPU or I/O devices.

Redevelopment: recycling the development cycle for major modification of an information system.

Refresh: the process of restoring the contents of a dynamic memory before they are lost. Also, the process of redrawing (many times per second) the image on a CRT before it can fade from sight.

Remote access: pertaining to communication with a data processing facility by one or more stations that are distant from that facility.

Remote job entry: submission of job control statements and data from a remote terminal, causing the jobs described to be scheduled and executed as though encountered in the input stream.

Replicated distributed data base: a duplicate segment of a data base which is needed for local processing that is stored at the local site.

Report program generator (RPG): a computer programming language that can be used to generate object programs that produce reports from existing sets of data.

Resistance: in the context of information systems, the act of opposing change which is brought about by the use of computers.

Response time: the time required for the system to respond to a user's request or to accept a user's inputs.

Run: the execution of a program by a computer on a given set of data.

Secondary storage: same as *auxiliary storage.*

Security: prevention of access to or use of data, documentation, or programs without authorization.

Semiconductor: a substance whose conductivity is poor at low temperatures but is improved by the application of heat, light, or voltage.

Sensor: any device that monitors the external environment for a computer. Types of sensors include photoelectric sensors that are sensitive to light; image sensor cameras that can record visual images and transform them into digital signals; pressure sensors that are sensitive to any kind of pressure; sensors that record infrared information; and ultrasonic transducers that produce a high frequency sound wave that bounces off objects and lets the computer calculate the distance between itself and those objects.

Separation of responsibility: a management control technique that can be applied to management of information systems. The information system is divided into functions, and employees are assigned duties and responsibilities that do not cross functional lines.

Sequence: (1) an arrangement of items according to a specified set of rules; (2) in sorting, a group of records whose control fields are in ascending or descending order according to the collating sequence.

Sequential access: a storage method (such as on a magnetic tape) by which data can only be reached or retrieved by passing through all intermediate locations between the current one and the desired one.

Serial: the handling of data one item after another. In communications, a serial transmission breaks each character into its component bits and sends these bits one at a time to a receiving device where they are a reassembled.

Service bureau: provides computing services to customers.

Simplex channel: a channel that is capable of transmitting data in only one direction.

Simulation: a computerized reproduction, image, or replica of a situation or set of conditions.

Smart terminal: see *intelligent terminal.*

Software: a general term for computer programs involved in the operation of the computer.

Software maintenance: the adjustment of an existing program to allow acceptance of new tasks or conditions (e.g., a new category of payroll deduction) or to correct previously undiscovered errors detected by users.

Sort: (1) a procedure to reorder data sequentially, usually in alphabetic or numeric order; (2) the action of sorting.

Stand-alone system: a computer system that does not require a connection to another computer.

Statute: law enacted by a legislative body.

Storage: the general term for any device that is capable of holding data which will be retrieved later.

Subsystem: a secondary or subordinate system, usually capable of operating independently.

Supervisor: a control routine or routines through which the use of resources is coordinated and the flow of operations through the central processing unit is maintained.

System: usually refers to a group of related hardware and/or software designed to meet a specific need.

System analysis: the analysis of an activity to determine precisely what must be accomplished and how to accomplish it.

System analyst: an individual who performs system analysis, design, and many related functions in the development and maintenance of an information system.

Systems manual: general information on a system and its objectives (an overview, not details.)

Tape: inexpensive mass storage medium. Must be accessed sequentially.

Tape drive: a device that moves tape past a head.

Tape unit: a device containing a tape drive together with reading and writing heads and associated controls.

Task: a program in execution.

Telecommunications: (1) pertaining to the transmission of signals over long distances, such as by telegraph, radio, or television; (2) data transmission between a computing system and remotely located devices via a unit that performs the necessary format conversion and controls the rate of transmission.

Teleconferencing: two-way communications between two or more groups (or three or more persons) remote from one another, using electronic means.

Teleprocessing: the processing of data that is received from or sent to remote locations by way of telecommunication lines.

Terminal: a keyboard plus a CRT and/or printer that can be connected to a computer.

Throughput: a measure of the amount of work that can be accomplished by the computer during a given period of time.

Tie line: a private-line communications channel of the type provided by communications common carriers for linking two or more points together.

Time sharing: a method of sharing the resources of the computer among several users so that several people can appear to be running different computer tasks simultaneously.

Top-down development: downward from the skeletal outline of program design to detailed levels, continuously exercising the actual interfaces between program modules. The opposite from developing bottom-level modules first and working up, finally integrating and testing the entire system.

Tort law: law dealing with a wrongful act, injury, or damage (not involving breach of contract) for which a civil action can be brought.

Transaction file: a data file containing relatively transient data to be processed in combination with a master file.

Transmission: (1) the sending of data from one location and the receiving of data in another location, leaving the source data unchanged; (2) the sending of data.

Transposition: the interchange of position. May be an exchange of data positions; e.g., 15 instead of 51.

Turnaround documents: document produced as output which becomes input when user supplies additional data on the document.

Turnaround time: the measure of time between the initiation of a job and its completion by the computer.

Turnkey vendor: one who provides a complete system including the computer, software, training, installation, and support.

Update: to modify a master file with current information according to a specified procedure.

User friendly: descriptive of both hardware and software which are designed to assist the user by being scaled to human dimensions, self-instructing, error-proof, etc.

User's manual: procedures for use of an information system written in terms that users understand.

Utility program: a program used to assist in the operation of the computer; e.g., a sort routine, a printout program, a file conversion program, etc. Generally, these programs perform housekeeping functions and have little relationship to the specific processing of the data.

Validation: process of checking compliance of data with preset standards and verifying data correctness.

Value pricing: charging a high markup for an indispensable product to cover low profit margins for other products in the company's line.

Variable: a quantity that can assume any of a given set of values.

Vendor: a supplier or company that sells computers, peripherals, or computer services.

Very large scale integration (VLSI): in practice, the compression of more than 10,000 transistors on a single chip.

Voice-grade channel: a channel suitable for transmission of speech, digital or analog data, or facsimile, generally with a frequency range of about 300 to 3,000 cycles per second.

Wand: a portable scanning device often used in stores and factories to read data for computer processing..

Width of field: the amount of space allowed for data in a data record.

Wiretapping: electromagnetic pickup of messages off communication lines.

Word: a unit of data or the set of characters which occupies one storage location. In microcomputing, a character, a word, and a byte are interchangeable. In most minicomputers, a word is equal to two bytes.

Word processor: a text editor system for electronically writing, formatting, and storing letters, reports, and books prior to printing.

SELECTED LIST OF TECHNICAL ABBREVIATIONS AND ACRONYMS

ADP	Automatic Data Processing
ADS	Accurately Defined System
ALGOL	ALGOrithmic Language
ALU	Arithmetic and Logic Unit
ANSI	American National Standards Institute
APL	A Programming Language
ARPA	Advanced Research Projects Agency
AT&T	American Telephone and Telegraph
BASIC	Beginner's All-purpose Symbolic Instruction Code
CAD/CAM	Computer-Aided Design/Computer-Aided Manufacturing
CASE	Computer-Aided System Evaluation
COBOL	COmmon Business-Oriented Language
CODASYL	Conference On DAta SYstems Languages
COM	Computer Output on Microfilm or Microfiche
CPE	Computer Performance Evaluation
CPM	Critical Path Method
CPU	Central Processing Unit
CRT	Cathode Ray Tube
DBA	Data Base Administrator
DBMS	Data Base Management System
DDL	Data Definition Language
DDP	Distributed Data Processing
DED	Data Element Dictionary
DED/D	Data Element Dictionary/Directory
DED/DD	Data Element Dictionary/Data Directory
DES	Data Encryption Standard
DML	Data Manipulation Language
DSS	Decision Support System
EAM	Electrical Accounting Machines
EDM	Event-Driven Monitor

EDP	Electronic Data Processing
EFT	Electronic Fund Transfer
ENIAC	Electronic Numerical Integrator And Calculator
FCC	Federal Communications Commission
FIPS	Federation of Information Processing Standards
FM	Facilities Management
FOCUS	FOrecasting Control and Updating Schedule
FORTRAN	FORmulae TRANslator
GE	General Electric
GERT	Graphic Evaluation Review Technique
HEMT	High Electron Mobility Transistor technology
IBM	International Business Machines Corp.
I/O	Input/Output
IQF	Interactive Query Facility
IRG	Inter-Record Gap
IRS	Internal Revenue Service
IS	Information System
ISBN	International Standard Book Number
ISO	International Standards Organization
JDS	Job Diagnostic Survey
KOPS	Thousands (K) of Operations Per Second
KWIC	Key Word In Context
KWOC	Key Word Out of Context
LISP	LISt Processing
LOC	Lines Of Code
LSI	Large-Scale Integration
MBO	Management By Objective
MCT	Microelectronics and Computer Technology corporation
MIC	Magnetic Ink Character recognition
MIPS	Millions of Instructions Per Second
MIS	Management Information System
NBS	National Bureau of Standards
NCR	National Cash Register
OECD	Organization of Economic Cooperation and Development
OEM	Original Equipment Manufacturers
OLRT	OnLine Real Time
PCM	Plug-Compatible Manufacturer
PERT	Program Evaluation Review Technique
PL/1	Programming Language 1
PV	Present Value
QRS	Quick Response Service
RAM	Random Access Memory
RAMIS	Rapid Access Management Information System
R&D	Research and Development

RFI	Request For Information
RFP	Request For Proposals
RPG	Remote Program Generator
SAM	System Accuracy Model
SCERT	System and Computer Evaluation and Review Technique
SDLC	Synchronous Data Link Control
SEC	Securities and Exchange Commission
SEQUEL	Structured English QUEry Language
SNA	Systems Network Architecture
SOP	Study Organization Plan
SQUARE	Specifying QUeries As Relational Expressions
TCM	Thermal Conduction Modules
TDM	Time-Driven Monitor
UCC	Uniform Commercial Code
UPC	Universal Product Code
VP	Vice President
WP	Word Processing
4GL	Fourth (4) Generation Language

INDEX

A

Access
  control, 279–81
  directory, 280
Accuracy, evaluation, 231–32
Accurately Defined System (ADS), 176
Acquisition of resources, 97–142
Active online, 503
Address, 36, 81
Airborne Freight Corp., case study, 218
Amdahl, Gene, 526–29, 535
American Airlines, case study, 191–92
American Express Company, case study, 161
American National Standards Insitute (ANSI), 373–74
Analog signal, 62–63
Analyst; see System analyst
Antitrust litigation, 567–72
Application generator, 41
Application software, 44
Arithmetic and logic unit, 18–20
Assembler, 37,43
Assembly language, 37–38
Atari, case study, 543–44
AT&T
  competition with IBM, 539–42
  antitrust litigation, 573
Auditing around the computer, 301
Auditing through the computer, 301–2
Auditor, role, 299–305
Audits, 299–316
Australia, Social Security Department, case study, 116–17

Authentication, of user, 279
Authorization, of user, 279
Availability, 231

B

Backup, 254
Band, 60
Bandwidth, 60
Batch procesing, 17–18
Baud, 60
Beasley, Carl, Ford, Inc., 576
Bell, Griffin, 572
Benchmark, 105–7, 109
Binary digits, 17
Bite-size fraud, 257
Bits, 17, 34, 81
Blumenthal, Sherman, 148
Boole, George, 17
Bottom-up, 149, 179
Brandon, Dick, 415
Brooks, Fred, 205
Budgeting, 343–59
Buffer, 63
Burroughs, contract litigation, 576
Byte, 81

C

Canned programs, 43
Capacity planning, 153
Card, 52, 81–82
Career
  development, 481–84
  paths, 481–84
Cathode ray tube terminal, 54–55, 64
Central processor, 18–19
Centralized
  data base, 428
  data processing, 406–9, 550

Chambers, Andrew, 286
Change
  case study: Lincoln National Life, 397–98
  resistance to, 385–98
  strategies, 394–96
Channels, teleprocessing, 60
Character, 34, 81
Check digit, 260–62
  case study: ISBN, 265–66
CODASYL, 372–73
Collection, data elements, 73–76
Common data base, 71, 84–85
Communication services, modes, 61
Communications
  law, 572–74
  programs, 43
  security, 282–86
Communications Act of 1934, 572–73
Compiler, 38, 43
Completeness, 258
Component testing, 185
Computer
  crime, 581–82
  department staffing, 465–89
  director, 454–59
  growth, 5–10
  industry, 521–46
  law, 565–87
  output on mocrofilm, 56, 58–59
  performance evaluation (CPE), 225–45
  processing, 16–27
  services, 493–516
Concentrator, 62
Consistency, 259
Consultant, 494–95
Contracts, 134–36, 575–77
  case study, 139–40

This book has been set Linotron 202, in 10 and 9 point Melior, leaded 2 points. Part numbers and titles are 20 point Helvetica Light. Chapter numbers and titles are 20 point Helvetica Light. The overall size of the type page is 37 by 47½ picas.